Second Metropolis

By exploring and comparing North America's, Russia's, and Japan's "second cities"—Chicago, Moscow, and Osaka—*Second Metropolis* discloses the extent to which social fragmentation, frequently viewed as an obstacle to democratic development, actually fostered a "pragmatic pluralism" that nurtured pluralistic public policies. Such policies are explored through six case studies—the politics of street railways and charter reform in Chicago, adult education and housing in Moscow, and harbor revitalization and poverty alleviation in Osaka—that illustrate how even those with massive political and economic power were stymied by the complexity of their communities. Chicago, Moscow, and Osaka, although the products of very different nations and cultures, nonetheless shared an important experience of inclusive politics during an era of extraordinary growth and social diversity. The success of all three cities, which went well beyond mere survival, rested on a distinctive political resource: pragmatic pluralism.

Blair A. Ruble is the director of the Kennan Institute for Advanced Russian Studies, a program of the Woodrow Wilson International Center for Scholars, where he is also codirector of the Comparative Urban Studies project. Ruble is the author of *Leningrad: Shaping a Soviet City* and *Money Sings: The Changing Politics of Urban Space in Post-Soviet Yaroslavl.*

WOODROW WILSON
CENTER SERIES

Continued on page following index

Second Metropolis

Pragmatic Pluralism in Gilded Age Chicago,
Silver Age Moscow, and Meiji Osaka

BLAIR A. RUBLE

WOODROW WILSON CENTER PRESS

AND

CAMBRIDGE
UNIVERSITY PRESS

PUBLISHED BY THE PRESS SYNDICATE OF THE UNIVERSITY OF CAMBRIDGE
The Pitt Building, Trumpington Street, Cambridge, United Kingdom

CAMBRIDGE UNIVERSITY PRESS
The Edinburgh Building, Cambridge CB2 2RU, UK
40 West 20th Street, New York, NY 10011-4211, USA
10 Stamford Road, Oakleigh, VIC 3166, Australia
Ruiz de Alarcón 13, 28014 Madrid, Spain
Dock House, The Waterfront, Cape Town 8001, South Africa

http://www.cambridge.org

First published 2001

Printed in the United States of America

Typeface Sabon 10/13 pt.   *System* QuarkXPress [BTS]

A catalog record for this book is available from the British Library.

Library of Congress Cataloging in Publication Data
Ruble, Blair A., 1949–
Second metropolis : pragmatic pluralism in Gilded Age Chicago,
Silver Age Moscow, and Meiji Osaka / Blair A. Ruble.
p.   cm. – (Woodrow Wilson Center series)
Includes bibliographical references.
ISBN 0-521-80179-6 (hardback)
1. City planning – Russia (Federation) – Moscow.   2. City planning – Illinois –
Chicago.   3. City planning – Japan – Osaka.   4. Moscow (Russia) – Politics and
government.   5. Chicago (Ill.) – Politics and government.   6. Osaka (Japan) –
Politics and government.   I. Title.   II. Series.
HT169.R82 M655   2001
307.1′2–dc21   00-063096

ISBN   0 521 80179 6   hardback

For Katya, Galya, and Ira

A City is like a person: if we don't establish a genuine relationship with it, it remains a name, an external form that soon fades from our minds. To create this relationship, we must be able to observe the city and understand its peculiar personality, its "I," its spirit, its identity, the circumstances of its life as they evolved through space and time.

Ivan Klima
"The Spirit of Prague"

Contents

List of Illustrations

Preface

This is the third of three volumes examining the fate of Russian provincial cities during the twentieth century. The first—*Leningrad: Shaping a Soviet City* (1990)—traced that city's decline following World War II from former imperial capital and co-leading city to mere regional center by the end of the Soviet regime. The second—*Money Sings: The Changing Politics of Urban Space in Post-Soviet Yaroslavl* (1995)—captured the confusion and optimism widely felt at the time of the collapse of the Soviet Union. This third volume represents an effort to place Russia's great heartland metropolis—Moscow—into a comparative perspective just as it was about to become the Soviet capital. Taken together, these studies turn up a tiny corner of the curtain behind which so much of Russian urban life has been experienced during the troubles of the past century, far away from the raw ambition, stilted ceremony, and pervasive anxiety of the political capital.

The chapters that follow constitute a rather unwieldy study that has depended on the support and good cheer of colleagues and friends from whom far too much patience has been expected on my part. I would like to express my sincerest gratitude to Allison Abrams, Akizuki Kengo, Boris Ananich, Harley Balzer, Pinar Batur-Vander Lippe, Theodore C. Bestor, Susan Bronson, Geoffrey Dabelko, Tony French, Cathleen M. Giustino, Helena Goscilo, Jeffrey W. Hahn, David Hoffman, Peter Holquist, Robert Huber, Pavel Ilyn, Grigorii Kaganov, Nina Khrushcheva, Steve Lagerfeld, Susan Goodrich Lehmann, Robert Litwak, Ruth O'Brien Miller, David W. Plath, Nancy Popson, Susan Gross Solomon, Peter Stavrakis, Stefan Tanaka, Robert Thurston, Ronald Toby, Joseph Tulchin, Galina Ulianova, Douglas Weiner, Elizabeth Wood, Igor Zevelev, and several anonymous reviewers for their thoughtful comments on previous versions of these chapters. Seki Hajime biographer Jeffrey Hanes has been more generous and supportive than, I suspect, my work deserves. Jeffrey Brooks, William Chase, Timothy J. Gilfoyle, and William Gleason have been truly heroic supporters and, when required, cogent critics.

I will never be able to repay the especially warm backing of Muramatsu Michio, of Kyoto University, and Tanami Tatsuya, initially of the International House of Japan and subsequently of the Nippon Foundation in Tokyo. Akizuki Kengo of Kyoto University has become an intellectual soul mate and a genuine friend during this project. Kamo Toshio of Osaka City University and Shibamura Atsuki of Momoyama-gakuin University have given me tremendous help and encouragement. Other Kansai historians—especially Matsushita Takao, Mizuguchi Nori-hito, and Inatsugu Hiroaki—have offered much appreciated and needed help along the way. American Japan specialists Theodore C. Bestor, Stefan Tanaka, and Ron Toby have urged me at various times and in myriad ways to continue my forays into Osaka. Many thanks are due as well to Alexei Kral and Kaori Hanamura Kral for helping me under-stand a few of the Japanese language's many mysteries. The generous encouragement, gracious hospitality, and tolerant curiosity of Japanese scholars and American Japan specialists toward a non-Japanese-speaking, Russian-specialist interloper have made this project personally rewarding beyond any reasonable expectation. I owe these splendid col-leagues in Japan and the United States more than I can ever express or fully acknowledge.

I realize that not speaking or reading Japanese is a profound handi-cap in a comparative study of this ambition. The materials that follow on Osaka are necessarily more limited and less textured than the dis-cussions of Chicago and Moscow. I have knowingly taken the risk of appearing to be even more foolish than usual because the contrasts and insights to be gained by adding this particular third city to my com-parison of Moscow and Chicago are so exciting. I hope that readers will find the relevance of Osaka to this study to be no less compelling than I have. I also hope that readers will be open to the observations of a researcher who can never know Osaka—or the native-language materi-als about that city—as well as he should. In the end, my writing about Osaka will be a success if it can serve as a bright thread woven against the more textured backdrop of observations about Moscow and Chicago.

The intellectual journey that culminates in this volume began with a friendly suggestion by Pavel Ilyn that I write an article comparing turn-of-the-century New York and Moscow. That article, which appeared in *Moskovskii zhurnal* in 1992, raised so many questions in my own mind that I became a captive of that era's Moscow. I must thank Pavel and his wife, Ella Kagan, for their moment of genuine inspiration.

I have learned more from Vyacheslav Glazychev, Grigorii Kaganov, and Josep Subiros about how to think about cities, see cities, and feel their pulse than from any other human beings. Slava and Grisha may well be among the last true *intelligenty*. Barcelona-based Pep, despite an absence of Russian-ness, may be considered so as well. I have been blessed by their friendship. I hope that this volume approaches their scholarly standards and reflects a modicum of the profound insight of their own work.

I would like to take this opportunity to thank Kennan Institute for Advanced Russian Studies interns Collin Brink, Alina Entin, Anthony S. Lauren, Timothy J. Louzonis, Kelly Elizabeth Massicotte, Cynthia Neil, David Russell, Joseph Schill, Lajos F. Szaszdi, Matt Warshaw, and Monique Wilson, as well as Kyoto University's Kitamura Wataru, for their assistance with the research on which this study has been based. Cynthia Neil was especially helpful during the final preparation of the manuscript for publication. I also would like to acknowledge the material support and incorporeal encouragement of the Woodrow Wilson International Center for Scholars, the Faculty of Law at Kyoto University, and the Suntory Foundation (Osaka). Copy editor Traci Nagle has improved the manuscript immeasurably.

Like so many researchers, I would have been lost without the assistance of librarians and staff at the Library of Congress—perhaps the single best library in the world for researching this particular project—and the Chicago Historical Society. The staff of the Woodrow Wilson Center Library has been valiant in managing my interlibrary loan requests. Hotta Akio of the Osaka City History Editorial Office has been particularly thoughtful and helpful, as have his colleagues at the Osaka Prefectural Library. Edward Kasinec of the New York Public Library has demonstrated time and again why he and the NYPL are so important to our field.

Readers should note that I have used the Library of Congress transliteration system for Russian words and names, except in those few instances when there is an alternative, commonly accepted English spelling, such as "Leo Tolstoy" instead of "Lev Tol'stoi." The names of individual Japanese appear in their traditional Japanese order, with family names preceding personal names.

The brief historical overviews of each city found in Part I are intended to highlight elements of the past that are relevant to the subsequent case studies rather than being comprehensive reviews of each city's history. The arguments that follow are complex and ambiguous. I have tried not to force all of my empirical evidence into a single narrative or argument. The careful reader will detect internal contradictions, instances when my evidence points in a direction opposite that of my general argument.

I similarly fear that some outright mistakes of fact may have crept onto a page or two, although I certainly have tried to keep such lapses to an absolute minimum. Specialists on each of the cities and societies under examination will find much to criticize, much to dispute, and much to argue against. I hope that in the end, like the pragmatic pluralists about whom I have written, readers will conclude that the gains from tolerance and perseverance outweigh the debits of confronting an author who is likely to be outside their own disciplinary and regional special-izations. The act of reading this volume may require the very metropol-itan tolerance about which it was written.

Finally, I have had the good fortune of working with three remark-able Muscovites throughout the writing and researching of this book. Ekaterina Alekseeva, Galina Levina, and Ira Petrova have represented the Kennan Institute well in Moscow since the early 1990s. Their imag-ination, compassion, integrity, and good cheer have set high standards for all of us working with them from Washington. Katya, Galya, and Ira personify the values about which I have tried to write in this book. They represent all that is right about Moscow, and it is to them that I dedi-cate this book.

ACKNOWLEDGMENTS

Preliminary versions of this work appeared in the following articles: "St. Petersburg's Courtyards and Washington's Alleys: Officialdom's Neglected Neighbors," in Pep Subiros, ed., *Debat de Barcelona III: Ciutat real, ciutat ideal* (Barcelona: Centre de Cultura Contemporania de Barcelona, 1998), pp. 11–27; "Daikibo Shogyo Toshi no Hatten: 1870–1920 nen no Chicago, Moscow, Osaka" [Governing the private metropolis: 1870–1920 in Chicago, Moscow, Osaka], trans. Muramatsu Michio, in Norihito Mizuguchi, ed., *Ima Naze Toshika* [Why the city now?], Osaka Institute of Urban Studies Series (Tokyo: Keibundo, 1997), pp. 269–94; "Failures of Centralized Metropolitanism: Inter-war Moscow and New York," *Planning Perspective* (U.K.) 9 (1994), pp.

353–76 [published in Russian translation by Grigorii Kaganov as "Provaly 'tsentralizovannoi stolichnosti': Moskva i N'iu-Iork mezhdu mirovymi voinami," *Chelovek* (Moscow) 1996, no. 1, pp. 52–67]; "Moskva–N'iu-Iork: Arkhitekturnye tendentsii v razvitii gorodov na rubezhe stoletii," *Moskovskii zhurnal* 1992, no. 2, pp. 12–15; "Vasil'evskii ostrov i Betteri-Park-Siti," trans. N. A. Khomenko, *SShA. Ekonomika, Politika, Ideologiia* 1990, no. 4, pp. 68–76; [with Joseph Tulchin] "Sel'skii megalopolis: Novyi predmet issledovaniia," *Arkhitekton* (Ekaterinburg) 1993, no. 1, p. 45; and "Ethnicity and Soviet Cities," *Soviet Studies* 41, no. 3 (1989), pp. 401–14.

1

Introduction: From Hegemony to Pragmatic Pluralism

Moscow of any period is not commonly thought of as an example of urban pluralism. Moscow's past century has been viewed until recently through the lens of the revolutions and civil wars of the early twentieth century (1905–7, February 1917, October 1917, 1917–21, 1928–32).[1] Late-imperial Russian history is being re-examined now that the meaning of this authoritarian revolutionary heritage has become more ambiguous. Placing Russia's urban experience in comparative perspective may help to clarify a number of issues in the emerging postcommunist debates over Russia's pre-Soviet past.

The difficulty in coming to terms with Russia at the beginning of the twentieth century—as at the beginning of the twenty-first—is that there was—and is—no single Russian reality. Numerous Russias coexisted: rich Russias and poor Russias, cosmopolitan Russias and provincial Russias, market-oriented Russias and feudal Russias. . . . The majority of the Russian population lived in peasant villages, yet a few million Russians inhabited two of the world's largest cities. Many more Russians lived in small cities and towns, each with its own peculiarities.[2] No single explanation can convey what happened to all of these Russias. Such past multiple Russias have often been captured better by the great literature

---

[1] This observation was forcefully set out by Ronald Grigor Suny in a seminal article. "Historians have understandably had difficulty," Suny wrote, "separating their political preferences for or abhorrence of the Soviet Union from their treatment of the complexities of the revolutionary years. Frequently, history has been written backwards, beginning with the knowledge of the single-party dictatorship, Stalin, collectivization, and the Great Purges and retreating in time toward the heady days of 1917 [and before] to find what went wrong." Ronald Grigor Suny, "Toward a Social History of the October Revolution," *American Historical Review* 88, no. 1, pp. 31–52: 31.

[2] Such communities are the subject of Daniel R. Brower's important monograph, *The Russian City between Tradition and Modernity, 1850–1900* (Berkeley: University of California Press, 1990).

1

of the period than by subsequent social science. Russia, to borrow from
Aleksandr Solzhenitsyn, had become a series of archipelagos. How can
one make sense of all of these inherent contradictions a century later,
especially in the light of several overlapping and, at times, seemingly
incompatible story lines?

One strategy, employed here, is to relate distinct Russian realities to
a broader comparative context. Many observers of the Russian scene
have greeted such approaches with skepticism. Russia, after all, is a very
particular place. It has long been caught between European-oriented
modernizing visions on the one hand and traditional attitudes and aspirations on the other. Russian cities of the era reflected both sides of a
national identity torn "between tradition and modernity."[3]

This volume does not challenge Russia's many peculiarities, for every
society and culture is unique to some degree. Rather, it seeks to extend
understanding of what made Russia exceptional by coming to terms with
the ways in which Russia was not so very different from the world
beyond its borders. It does so by comparing Moscow during the half-
century prior to the Bolshevik Revolution of 1917 to two other cities
that, in many respects (though not in every detail), were similar: Chicago
in the United States and Osaka in Japan.

This study is a response to the many historians who have begun to
call for a post-Soviet renewal of the study of the Russian city. One such
historian, Louise McReynolds, notes that "[s]tudies written from the
hindsight of 1917 have given a disproportionate amount of space, especially when compared to non-Russian urban history, to impending class
conflict and/or the inability of local leaders to effect meaningful civic
reforms. . . . How effectively did civic consciousness challenge the class
consciousness about which we already know much?"[4]

McReynolds and other historians of a similar mind are not posing a
binary, "either-or" question when inquiring whether or not civic consciousness was able to challenge class consciousness in the late-imperial

---

[3] This duality is the subject of Brower's powerful study. Ibid.
[4] Louise McReynolds, "Urbanism as a Way of Russian Life," *Journal of Urban History*
20, no. 2 (February 1994), pp. 240–51: 250. Interestingly, McReynolds's observations
about the extent to which local historiography on Russia emphasized labor issues and
class conflict were prefigured a decade and a half earlier by Kathleen Neils Conzen in a
review of U.S. local historiography. See Kathleen Neils Conzen, "Community Studies,
Urban History, and American Local History," in Michael Kammen, ed., *The Past Before
Us: Contemporary Historical Writing in the United States* (Ithaca: Cornell University
Press, 1980), pp. 270–91. Conzen argued that the best such work "represents a creative
blending of urban history with a labor history tradition" (p. 283). The study of Russian
local history has only sporadically produced such "a creative blending."

Russian city. These historians instead delve deeper into the social dynamics of the era for more textured explorations of what was taking place in the years leading up to 1917. The result is a historical approach that highlights process more than—but not to the exclusion of—classification.

As these historians have demonstrated, civic and class consciousness competed not only within urban society but also within each and every urban resident. Russian townspeople carried multiple identities, defining themselves by a variety of characteristics such as class, region, gender, religion, ethnicity, and hometown or neighborhood, depending on the circumstances at a given moment.

A number of historians thoughtfully explored various aspects of Russia's urban history long before McReynolds's essay.[5] Their studies have shed considerable light on how late-imperial Russia functioned on a daily basis. Their debates and discussions over the role of representative institutions and a nascent public sector have expanded understanding of precisely how governance in the Russian empire simultaneously succeeded and failed. Their collective message is ambiguous; they have identified points of friction and irremovable conflict between representative institutions and governmental officials on the one hand, and moments when participatory politics were becoming institutionalized on the other, and have sought ways in which local city politics succeeded or failed in shaping national policies.[6]

The case studies presented here would have been unimaginable were it not for the noteworthy work of these esteemed colleagues. Their scholarship deserves renewed attention, especially as their impact on general perceptions of Russian history has been far less than their accumulated wisdom. This study will be a success if it directs greater attention to the excellent work on which it is based.

---

[5] James Bater, Joseph Bradley, Jeffrey Brooks, Daniel Brower, William Chase, Katerina Clark, Timothy Colton, Barbara Alpern Engel, William Gleason, Michael Hamm, Patricia Herlihy, Robert E. Johnson, Diane Koenker, Stephen Kotkin, Joan Neuberger, Thomas Owen, Alfred J. Reiber, Robert W. Thurston, James L. West, and David Wolff, as well as McReynolds herself, are but a few of the more prominent American and Canadian scholars who have pursued urban themes in their research on Russia. The Bibliography provides basic information about these scholars' works.

[6] These observations are also put forward by Mary Schaeffer Conroy in her introduction to a volume on emerging democratic institutions during the late tsarist period. See Mary Schaeffer Conroy, "Introduction," in Mary Schaeffer Conroy, ed., *Emerging Democracy in Late Imperial Russia: Case Studies on Local Self-Government (the Zemstvos), State Duma Elections, the Tsarist Government, and the State Council Before and During World War One* (Niwot: University of Colorado Press, 1998), pp. 1–29.

THE IMPORTANCE OF COMPARATIVE PERSPECTIVES

Russia of a century ago is widely held to have been different from the societies of Europe and North America. Russia, it is said, was a society without a middle class, without "authentic" cities, without an autonomous private sector. Such assertions of difference do not, in and of themselves, produce understanding. Comparison becomes necessary for a more fulsome appreciation of precisely those peculiarities so often seen as lying at the core of Russian being.

Comparative examinations of Russian development have looked first and foremost to Europe. "Despite frequent claims of detachment and objectivity," Ronald Suny complained nearly two decades ago, "scholars often make their judgments about the revolution [of 1917] and the Soviet Union against the standard of quite different European and American experiences."[7] As Suny's comments imply, analogies with Europe might not constitute the most agreeable framework for analysis. Other societies caught between modernity and tradition, such as Meiji and Taisho Japan, may offer more informative similarities and contrasts. A study of a single Russian city cannot resolve grand methodological concerns. Yet an attempt to place the life of one major Russian city such as Moscow within a comparative context facilitates meaningful discussion of Russia at large in relation to the world outside.

Chicago, Moscow, and Osaka are ideal sites for the sorts of explorations of continuity and difference required to bring fresh perspectives to the study of Russia. The 1860s were a decade of wrenching political reform and social change in the United States, Russia, and Japan. The Civil War and the accompanying economic boom and constitutional revisions in the United States, the Great Reforms in Russia, and the Meiji Reforms in Japan set all three societies on new social, economic, and political paths. Wars—victories and defeats—reshaped the national economies in all three cities' host societies, bringing wealth—and, in the Russian case, eventual ruin—to local manufacturers and financiers.

Despite being embedded in distinctly anti-urban national cultures, all three cities influenced national politics and policies. All three were among the fastest-growing in the world as the new century dawned.[8]

---

[7] Suny, "Toward a Social History," p. 32.

[8] This point is developed further in Joseph Bradley, *Muzhik and Muscovite: Urbanization in Late Imperial Russia* (Berkeley: University of California Press, 1985), pp. 3–5; as well as in Henry D. Smith II, "Tokyo as an Idea: An Exploration of Japanese Urban Thought until 1945," *Journal of Japanese Studies* 4, no. 1 (Winter 1978), pp. 45–80.

Metropolitan Chicago's population leapt from 493,531 in 1870 to 3,394,996 in 1920.[9] Moscow's population grew by some 300 percent, from just over 600,000 in 1871 to just under 2 million in September 1917.[10] Osaka similarly blossomed from a town of some 350,000 residents to a city of approximately 2.2 million residents during roughly the same period.[11] Driven by industrial, commercial, transportation, and technological revolutions that would transform the world economy in the decades to come, all three cities absorbed new arrivals by the tens of thousands.[12]

Chicago, Moscow, and Osaka stood at the top of the era's global urban hierarchy. According to contemporary estimates, Chicago was the fifth-largest city in the world when World War I broke out in August 1914, while Moscow was the ninth.[13] Osaka was left out of such lists at the time, but probably ranked among the world's top dozen cities based on population size.

All three metropolitan centers were, in today's concepts, points of connection between national and global economies. Their tethers to an emerging international capitalist economy; their reliance on the latest technologies in electrical engineering, transportation, communication, and construction; their combination of age-old greed and enormously diverse local economies driven by private interest—all of these factors made them twentieth-century cities before the twentieth century. They dominated their North American, Central Eurasian, and Kansai

---

[9] Irving Cutler, *Chicago: Metropolis of the Mid-Continent*, 3d ed. (Dubuque, Iowa: Kendall/Hunt, 1982), Appendix A.

[10] Robert W. Thurston, *Liberal City, Conservative State: Moscow and Russia's Urban Crisis, 1906–1914* (New York: Oxford University Press, 1987), pp. 197–98; Adol'f Grigor'evich Rashin, *Naselenie Rossii za 100 let (1811–1933gg). Statisticheskie ocherki* (Moscow: Gosstatizdat, 1956), p. 115.

[11] Anthony Sutcliffe, "Introduction: Urbanization, Planning, and the Giant City," in Anthony Sutcliffe, ed., *Metropolis, 1890–1940* (Chicago: University of Chicago Press, 1984), pp. 1–18: 7.

[12] The importance of a number of simultaneous revolutions in transportation technology cannot be underestimated in the cases of Chicago, Moscow, and Osaka. Transportation appears in several of the chapters that follow, often confirming William H. McNeill's arguments about the significance of transportation for the emergence of modern economies. See William H. McNeill, "The Eccentricity of Wheels, or Eurasian Transportation in Historical Perspective," *American Historical Review* 92, no. 5 (December 1987), pp. 1111–26; and William H. McNeill, "The Changing Shape of World History," in Philip Pomper, Richard H. Elphick, and Richard T. Vann, eds., *World Historians and Their Critics* (Middletown, Conn.: Wesleyan University, 1995), pp. 8–26.

[13] A. Mikhailovskii, "Munitsipal'naia Moskva," in N. A. Geinike, N. S. Elagin, E. A. Efimova, and I. I. Shitts, eds., *Po Moskvie. Progulki po Moskvie i eia khudozhestvennym" i prosvietitel'nym" uchrezhdeniiam"* (Moscow: Izdanie M. i S. Sabashnikovykh", 1917), pp. 121–58: 121.

hinterlands even as political power resided elsewhere in their nations' political capitals—Washington, St. Petersburg, and Tokyo. They represented what was distinctive and particular about their societies even as they were sufficiently similar to one another to make comparison possible.[14]

By exploring these three cities a century or so ago in relation to one another, this study seeks reinterpretation of each community in order to expand general understanding of the Russian urban experience and to urge more comparative urban scholarship. This volume highlights the considerable extent to which social fragmentation—frequently viewed as an obstacle to democratic development—actively fostered what might be called "pragmatic pluralism" by denying any single group access to unlimited power. It argues that fragmentation—combined with a modicum of accumulated wealth, the absence of de jure or de facto central control, the upheaval of a social and economic transition, and a pragmatic leadership style among key local elites—can establish the necessary conditions for pluralistic public policy.

Pragmatic pluralism may be seen within Moscow even though the broader pattern of Russian autocracy was arguably to enforce social isolation and fragmentation as a means for denying access to power to anyone not already in the tsar's circle of counselors, advisers, and ministers. What would today be labeled a "civil society" was emerging in Moscow by the early years of the twentieth century.[15] As will become apparent in the discussion to follow, the tsar's governance strategies ultimately thwarted the maturation of autonomous social groups, frequently leading to gridlock, polarization, and eventual systemic collapse. As Christine Ruane perceptively observes, one of the many paradoxes of the late-imperial period in Russian history is that "the government's reforms undermined the very social system they were intended to perpetuate. What could have been a sustained cooperative effort between state and society to create a modern industrialized nation became a continual struggle of the government and old privileged elite against the newer elites."[16] Moscow was one of several arenas for

---

[14] This combination of exceptionality and representativeness is forcefully explored in relation to Chicago in Karen Sawislak, *Smoldering City: Chicagoans and the Great Fire, 1871–1874* (Chicago: University of Chicago Press, 1995), pp. 9–11.

[15] The case in support of an emerging civil society at the time of the outbreak of World War I has been forcefully argued most recently in relation to the Russian art scene in Aaron Joseph Cohen, "Making Modern Art National: Mass Mobilization, Public Culture, and Art in Russia during the First World War" (Ph.D. diss., Johns Hopkins University, 1998).

[16] Christine Ruane, *Gender, Class, and the Professionalization of Russian City Teachers, 1860–1914* (Pittsburgh: University of Pittsburgh Press, 1994), p. 4.

Ruane's sustained battle between new and old in turn-of-the-century Russia.

The complexities of urban life in Moscow nonetheless forged pragmatic coalitions and inclusive municipal management strategies. At times social fragmentation promoted cooperation among diverse elements within the Moscow social and political scene. Again, to draw on Ruane's work, the notion of a public sphere was so new in Russia at the time that the shape of that public domain constantly changed and evolved in the face of persistent challenges from many directions within Russian society.[17] This book purposefully highlights instances when Moscow functioned more like many other metropolitan communities around the world than might be commonly thought.[18]

The chapters to follow do not pretend to examine the distribution of power per se. Nor, for that matter, do they speak to the issue of internalized values, thoughts, or feelings. This volume focuses on external behavior. The formation of a coalition is sufficient for the argument here, even if such an alliance did not change what was taking place in the participants' hearts and minds. This study merely seeks to illustrate how even those with massive political and economic resources at their disposal were stymied in the exercise of their power by the complexity of the communities in which they lived. Simply put, the most powerful Muscovite—like the most powerful Chicagoan and Osakan—could not always force others to do that which they otherwise would not have chosen to do. Power was divided, dispersed, and contested. Moscow, when viewed from this vantage point, becomes a much less particular urban phenomenon.

The first approach for coming to terms with Moscow within a comparative context that extends to both Chicago and Osaka is to consider all three cities through writings in urban theory and history. They were, after all, cities, among the largest in the world, in fact. The literature on comparative urban development establishes some initial terms for intellectual engagement.

THE SIGNIFICANCE OF URBAN SIZE

About a century ago, a seemingly new urban form—the giant industrial city—came into being. Very large cities had been around for some time,

---

[17] Ibid., p. 195.
[18] This study thereby builds on the research of Robert W. Thurston, who initially explored commonality between Moscow public administration and that of other cities of the era in such works as *Liberal City, Conservative State*.

of course. The giant city, as Anthony Sutcliffe has reminded us, "has been a component of human civilisation for several thousand years."[19] But these new "metropolises" horrified many observers. The speed of their growth, the ease of their communications, the mobility of their populations, and the "tense standoff between bourgeois and proletarian values"[20] appeared to be unprecedented. Traditional social, political, and cultural institutions collapsed under the weight of uncommon challenges.

The openness and accelerated pace of urban expansion differed from the slower and more organic growth of medieval and early-modern towns.[21] Metropolitan expansion often placed burgeoning industrial towns at odds with the surrounding countryside and national governments. A constant back-and-forth between metropolis and national government was evident even in the relatively young United States, where a restive business class sought unrestrained political and cultural power against previously entrenched local and vernacular interests.[22] Metropolitan society everywhere was not only germinal, but was also becoming increasingly diverse—and fragmented.[23]

The city of the nineteenth century remade the urban form. Industrial machinery drastically altered the physical layout of the nineteenth-century city within just a generation or two.[24] Factories, commercial avenues, rail yards, and tenement blocks produced an urban environment that was disorientingly mutable. As a number of observers then and since have noted, impermanence became the trademark of the

---

[19] Anthony Sutcliffe, "Introduction: The Giant City as a Historical Phenomenon," in Theo Barker and Anthony Sutcliffe, eds., *Megalopolis: The Giant City in History* (London: St. Martin's, 1993), pp. 1–13: 1. This volume is a collection of essays developed from panels at the International Historical Congress convened in Madrid in 1990, at which the theme of the giant city over time was a major focal point for research.

[20] A turn of phrase used by Henry Francis Mallgrave in his introduction to a new edition of Otto Wagner, *Modern Architecture. A Guidebook for his students to this Field of Art,* intr. and trans. Henry Francis Mallgrave (Santa Monica, Calif.: Getty Center for the History of Art and Humanities, 1988), pp. 1–55: 11.

[21] A point made by Peter Hanek in his essay, "Urbanization and Civilization: Vienna and Budapest in the Nineteenth Century," in Peter Hanek, ed., *The Garden and the Workshop: Essays on the Cultural History of Vienna and Budapest* (Princeton: Princeton University Press, 1998), pp. 3–43: 3.

[22] As argued by John Bodnar in *Remaking America: Public Memory, Commemoration, and Patriotism in the Twentieth Century* (Princeton: Princeton University Press, 1992), p. 35.

[23] For a concise and perceptive examination of the reception of industrial metropolises, see Peter Hall, "Metropolis, 1890–1940: Challenges and Responses," in Sutcliffe, ed., *Metropolis,* pp. 19–66.

[24] Peter Fritzsche, *Reading Berlin, 1900* (Cambridge: Harvard University Press, 1996), pp. 28–29.

"modern" city.[25] Sustaining a civic consciousness beyond group identity in an age preoccupied with speed and velocity was no humble task.

The new metropolis was so large and differentiated that no single social, political, economic, or ethnic group could dominate local politics for long. The giant city was not "a discrete historical actor." Rather, "its great aggregate wealth [was] divided into multiple ownerships. The result [was] *diversity*."[26] As Peter Hall has noted in his monumental history of urban civilization, *Cities in Civilization*, the issue is not merely that great cities are large. Rather, bigness implies complexity. Big cities, according to Hall, not only have more people living in them, but also "contain so many different kinds of people, different in birthplace and race and social class and wealth, different, indeed, in every respect that differentiates people at all."[27] For the more decorous elements of society, the late-nineteenth-century large industrial town, as Elizabeth Wilson reminds us, became a "cesspool city" marked by "the promiscuous mingling of classes in close proximity on the street."[28]

Social groups in these new giant cities were forced to choose their ground carefully, moving to protect interests only in those areas that really mattered for their survival or well-being. A new era of metropolitan pluralism began to take shape, disrupting previous understandings of power and political efficacy both locally and nationally. Municipal politics became at times a forced accommodation of competing private interests precisely because the metropolis had become so contentious.[29] Politics required a spectrum of accommodation as policy choices could no longer be reduced to simple either-or choices. The cost of not accommodating others was too frightful to bear, as would become painfully apparent for many in Russia following the collapse of the imperial regime in 1917.

Chicago photographer Sigmund Krausz left a document that both suggests the medley of late-nineteenth-century metropolitan life and captures the prejudice of the era's bourgeoisie.[30] Krausz's "character studies"

---

[25] See, for example, such works as Christopher Prendergast, *Paris and the Nineteenth Century* (Cambridge, Mass.: Blackwell, 1992); and Marshall Berman, *All That Is Solid Melts into Air: The Experience of Modernity* (New York: Simon and Schuster, 1985).

[26] Sutcliffe, "Introduction," p. 3.

[27] Peter Hall, *Cities in Civilization* (New York: Pantheon, 1998), p. 612.

[28] Elizabeth Wilson, *The Sphinx in the City: Urban Life, the Control of Disorder, and Women* (Berkeley: University of California Press, 1991), p. 29.

[29] Carl Abbott, "Thinking About Cities: The Central Tradition in U.S. Urban History," *Journal of Urban History* 22, no. 6 (1996), pp. 687–701: 698.

[30] Sigmund Krausz, *Street Types of Chicago: Character Studies* (Chicago: Max Stern and Co., 1892).

1. A peddler selling feather dusters, Chicago, 1891. From "Street Types of Chicago," Sigmund Krausz, 1891. Courtesy Chicago Historical Society, ICHi-09274.

of three dozen carefully posed "street types" reflect every stereotype that the photographer and his literary contributors could muster. Krausz evidently compiled this photo album, a local example of a popular genre of the era, in 1892 to cash in on the much-anticipated World's Fair tourist trade. The photographer managed to capture a hint of the variety of 1890s Chicago.

Scanning this collection of African-American, Chinese, Irish, Italian, Russian, Jewish, and Syrian peddlers and urchins, one imagines the visual expression of the discomfort of the propertied classes with industrial-age cities so articulately discussed by Elizabeth Wilson. Office workers and organ grinders, letter carriers and street children, weathered Civil War veterans and blind panhandlers, "tennis girls" and rag pickers, ice men and beer men and produce hawkers all contended for the same urban space in the American heartland metropolis. Krausz's work reflects this wealth of difference even if his subjects demand far more dignity than he was willing or able to offer them in his studio.

The urban giants that appeared during the turn of the last century defined a great deal of human experience over the course of subsequent decades, with even larger "megalopolises" and "global cities" to follow.[31] Volumes have been written about the form and function of these titans, their successes and failures. Yet, their significance for political life has not always held center stage in the writing on modern urbanism.

In addition to being a book about Moscow, this study also seeks to explore the significance of metropolitan government for local and national political life by clarifying the relationship between metropolitan growth and the pluralism of municipal politics. It does so through a comparison of Chicago, Moscow, and Osaka during the half-century beginning around 1870. The chapters that follow attempt to go beyond explaining the peculiarities of Moscow by pursuing issues of social diversity, tolerance, and pluralism. The case studies presented here also try to answer from an international comparative perspective one of what Carl Abbott has identified as the two central issues of a century and a half of American urban historiography: "How have the members of these aggregations [the mushrooming cities of the mid-nineteenth century] managed to coalesce, interact, and function as civic entities [or metropolitan

---

[31] For a discussion of the "giant city" phenomenon at the end of the twentieth century, see Mattei Dogan and John D. Kasarda, eds., *The Metropolis Era*, 2 vols. (Beverly Hills: Sage, 1988); Anthony D. King, *Global Cities: Post-Imperialism and the Internationalization of London* (New York: Routledge, 1990); Saskia Sassen, *The Global City: New York, London, Tokyo* (Princeton: Princeton University Press, 1991); and Deyan Sudjic, *The 100-Mile City* (New York: Harcourt Brace, 1992).

communities, to use twentieth-century language]?"[32] In other words, how did the era's new metropolitan centers mediate the political, social, economic, cultural, ethnic, and religious diversity that made them appear at the time to be so unprecedented and threatening?

METROPOLITAN GROWTH AND THE MEDIATION OF DIFFERENCE

Drawing on the work of David C. Hammack, Sally Ann Hastings has argued that, from the point of view of the distribution of power in an urban community, one's vantage point determines what one sees. Observers focusing attention on formal structures and senior political leaders tend to discern the concentration of community power within a limited circle of participants.[33] Those, such as Hastings herself, who focus on a wide variety of neighborhood and social, formal and informal organizations tend to discover the dispersion of power, whether such investigation focuses on New York, New Haven, Tokyo, or Dar es Salaam.[34] Hammack poses the issue by writing, "Although most historians who have focused on elites have stressed the concentration of power, those who have written detailed studies of entrepreneurship, social policy, lower status groups, or local politics . . . have more frequently insisted that power was dispersed."[35] The point is an important one and may help to explain why this study will highlight points of diversity even in such a nominally centralized municipal administration as that of late-imperial Moscow or Meiji Osaka.

As Hastings's own work on Tokyo demonstrates, the matter is greater than merely acknowledging that what one sees depends on where one stands. The critical issue is the dynamic relationship between often highly exclusionary formal structures of power and the actual arrangements of daily life. The greater the potential for conflict and disparity, this study will argue, the greater the capacity for pluralistic mediation of difference.

---

[32] Carl Abbott, "Thinking about Cities," p. 688. The second central question identified by Abbott is "Why and how have all of these people come together in large cities?"

[33] Sally Ann Hastings, *Neighborhood and Nation in Tokyo, 1905–1937* (Pittsburgh: University of Pittsburgh Press, 1995), p. 196.

[34] The work of Mohamed Halfani on his native Dar es Salaam illustrates this same point in a contemporary context. See, for example, Mohamed Halfani, "Marginality and Dynamism: Prospects for the Sub-Saharan African City," in Michael A. Cohen, Blair A. Ruble, Joseph S. Tulchin, and Allison M. Garland, eds., *Preparing for the Urban Future: Global Pressures and Local Forces* (Washington, D.C.: Woodrow Wilson Center Press, 1996), pp. 83–107.

[35] David Hammack, "Problems of Power in the Historical Study of Cities, 1800–1960," *American Historical Review* 83, no. 2 (April 1978), pp. 323–49: 333.

This is so even if many groups are formally excluded from direct access to power. Rather than clear-cut choices, the challenge of politics becomes the management of competing interests in order to meet shared social needs and move forward.[36]

Like Hastings's book, this work seeks to build explicitly on Hammack's contributions to the study of urban community power by placing his work in a comparative context.[37] Hammack's research emphasizes the seeming disparity between the high concentration of wealth and power in a limited circle of New Yorkers at the turn of the last century, and the sense of those same wealthy and powerful that they could not always have their way in a system that granted suffrage universally to male citizens.[38] Many prominent New Yorkers withdrew from municipal politics in any formal sense. They nonetheless continued to protect their interests whenever necessary by less direct means.

Some observers have argued that political bosses ruled the town, while others asserted that rich individuals or wealthy corporations dominated the city.[39] More intricate accounts—such as those by a perceptive Russian visitor to America of a century ago, Moisei Ostrogorski—portrayed political bosses as mediating between capitalists and voters.[40] The political machine, by bringing together mass-based social groups with economic elites, determined who would control the local state in a period of rapid change.[41] It succeeded by providing an effective middle ground among some of the most volatile elements of the late-nineteenth- and early-twentieth-century American city.

Hammack forcefully makes the case why such mediation was so necessary. "The wealthy and well-informed," he writes, "usually assumed that wealth and status conferred power. But their persistent concern about the power of the electorate, the roles of the political parties, the attitudes of the immigrants, and the virtue of the various economic elites all suggest, at least, that the wealthy could not simply dominate without exerting themselves."[42]

---

[36] Lawrence W. Kennedy, *Planning the City upon a Hill: Boston since 1630* (Amherst: University of Massachusetts Press, 1992), p. 253.

[37] See, for example, Hammack, "Problems of Power"; and David C. Hammack, *Power and Society: Greater New York at the Turn of the Century* (New York: Russell Sage Foundation, 1982).

[38] Hammack, *Power and Society*, p. 7.   [39] Ibid., pp. 7–19.

[40] Moisei Ostrogorski, *Democracy and the Organization of Political Parties* (New York: Macmillan, 1902).

[41] Harvey Boulay and Alan DiGaetano, "Why Did Political Machines Disappear?" *Journal of Urban History* 12, no. 1 (November 1985), pp. 25–50: 26.

[42] Hammack, *Power and Society*, p. 19.

Hammack's work examines the urban experience of the United States at the turn of the last century. The issues he examines transcend American politics and its highly open and participatory customs and traditions. Hastings's work demonstrates that similar contradictions between the concentration of power and the impotence of the powerful may be found in a number of divergent historical, cultural, and political settings. Neil L. Waters's stunning exploration of local politics in the superficially tranquil Kawasaki region during Japan's Meiji transition similarly demonstrates the potentially soothing capacity of fragmented social and political institutions at a time of intense change.[43]

Waters describes Kawasaki's late-Edo and early-Meiji administration as "a three-colored checkerboard on which some squares change from one color to another, while a few actually take on several hues."[44] Such complexity, rather than eroding regional identity and coherence, ensured that each single local unit could be insulated from capricious or arbitrary action from above. "No single local lord could act alone," Waters continued, "without running afoul of the interests of other *ryoshu*."[45]

Although Waters is writing about a fundamentally rural area during a period prior to full-scale industrialization, his observations remain pertinent to the sprawling metropolitan regions about which this study speaks. "Administrative complexity not only insulated the villages in the Kawasaki region from unusual or arbitrary exploitation, but also assured that horizontal organizations between villages would have considerable power. Despite the intricate nature of vertical control within the area, the region as a whole was economically interdependent."[46] No single group of lords or elites could assert its will, thereby ensuring Kawasaki's sedate transition to the industrial age.

The stories told here underscore the importance of administrative complexity and individual political action evident in the works of Hammack, Hastings, and Waters, standing somewhat at odds with many group and elitist approaches to governance.[47] Power will be presented here as having become tied to specific issues that were often fleeting, provoking a variety of temporary and more permanent coalitions among

---

[43] Neil L. Waters, *Japan's Local Pragmatists: The Transition from Bakumatsu to Meiji in the Kawasaki Region* (Cambridge, Mass.: Harvard University Press, 1983).
[44] Ibid., p. 41.   [45] Ibid., pp. 41–42.
[46] Ibid., p. 41.
[47] For further discussion of the extent to which group approaches to politics devalue the importance of individual leaders, see Raymond E. Wolfinger, *The Politics of Progress* (Englewood Cliffs, N.J.: Prentice-Hall, 1974), p. 11.

interested groups and citizens.[48] Those alliances, in turn, are rooted in the private nature of the modern metropolis.

THE PRIVATE METROPOLIS

Chicago, Moscow, and Osaka were not merely large cities. They were also the product of private economic development rather than assertions of state power. All three were, first and foremost, commercial cities predicated on exchange among diverse traders of all sizes and scales.

The complexity of these three great cities created an abundant yet deeply fractured social, economic, and political landscape. Similar tendencies can be seen both then and later in other metropolises that were not political capitals, such as Barcelona, Bombay, Glasgow, Manchester, Milan, and São Paulo. Manchester, the world's first industrial city, was a prototype in many ways for the sorts of industrial "second cities" under consideration here.[49]

Removed from the national political arena, successful metropolitan politicians in such "second metropolises" often sought compromise and accommodation rather than command and political dominion. Local governance in Chicago, Moscow, and Osaka a century ago generated a politics of pragmatic pluralism. The experiences of Moscow and Osaka with political tolerance could not be sustained in hostile national political environments, thereby establishing interesting contrasts with Chicago.

Chicago's industrialists, Moscow's merchants, and Osaka's financiers nurtured a metropolitanism unique to the past century or so, one dominated by private capital. Some of history's previous "giant cities" benefited immensely from private economic activity. London, Amsterdam, and Antwerp were major metropolises in which government expenditure constituted a much lower proportion of gross urban product than was the case in other pre-industrial global cities.[50] Yet the large city prior to the nineteenth century remained largely an artifact of the residence of a monarch or potentate.

Tudor London offers perhaps the most interesting prior example of trade-driven metropolitan development. Pre-industrial London

---

[48] A point made in Nelson W. Polsby, *Community Power and Political Theory: A Further Look at Problems of Evidence and Inference*, 2d ed. (New Haven: Yale University Press, 1980), p. 115.

[49] For further discussion of Manchester's emergence, see Hall, *Cities in Civilization*, pp. 310–454.

[50] Sutcliffe, "Introduction," pp. 1–13: 8.

accumulated wealth by producing goods and adding value to goods produced elsewhere.[51] Given the separation of court life in Whitehall from
the commerce of the City, one might argue that London developed during
these years remarkably free from state direction and political interference.

London was a bustling, bursting city, home to a commercial elite that
enriched itself alongside the swelling ranks of migrants of a distinctly
"meaner" sort.[52] Pre-industrial London remained a commercial giant
standing at the center of a growing economy while nearby Westminster
remained the stately seat of royal power.[53]

Karl Polanyi observed in his 1944 study *The Great Transformation*
that "nineteenth century civilization"—which was dominated by a later
London in so many ways—was distinctive because "it chose to base itself
on a motive only rarely acknowledged as valid in the history of human
societies, and certainly never before raised to the level of a justification
of action and behavior in everyday life, namely gain."[54] Chicago,
Moscow, and Osaka were among the leading centers of this singular
approach to social organization.

Finance-driven (as opposed to state-sponsored) metropolitan dominance is nonlinear.[55] Unemployment threatened the worker and office
clerk while bankruptcy haunted the factory owner and shopkeeper.[56]
Fortunes were won and lost overnight.[57] Economic uncertainty sparked
intense conflicts among speculators large and small, as competition,
fraud, ill luck, and incompetence could easily result in sensational loss.[58]

[51] Theo Barker, "London: A Unique Megalopolis?" in Barker and Sutcliffe, eds., *Mega-lopolis*, pp. 43–60: 49.
[52] Roy Porter, *London. A Social History* (Cambridge: Harvard University Press, 1995), p. 49.
[53] A point made by Anthony Sutcliffe in "Introduction," p. 8.
[54] Karl Polanyi, *The Great Transformation* (New York: Farrar and Rinehart, 1944), p. 30.
[55] This point can be illustrated by the volatility of the Moscow banking community during this period in contrast to the relative stability of banks in St. Petersburg. Moscow stock associations, banks, and trading houses came and went with good times and bad. St. Petersburg's commercial banks tended to remain in place, taking advantage of their dependence on state deposits to dominate imperial Russian capital markets through-out the late-imperial period. For further discussion of this contrast, see I. F. Gindin, *Russkie kommercheskie banki. Iz istorii finansovogo kapitala v Rossii* (Moscow: Gosfinizdat, 1948).
[56] William L. O'Neill, *The Progressive Years: America Comes of Age* (New York: Dodd, Mead, 1975), p. 2.
[57] Rima Lunin Schultz demonstrates this in a study of four hundred businesses in pre–Great Fire (1871) Chicago. Rima Lunin Schultz, "The Businessman's Role in Western Settle-ment: The Entrepreneurial Frontier, Chicago, 1833–1872," (Ph.D. diss., Boston Uni-versity, 1985), esp. the discussion on pp. 358–81.
[58] Frederic Cople Jaher, *The Urban Establishment: Upper Strata in Boston, New York, Charleston, Chicago, and Los Angeles* (Urbana: University of Illinois Press, 1982), p. 476.

2. State Street and Marshall Field's department store, Chicago, between 1907 and 1910. Detroit Publishing Co. Library of Congress, Prints and Photographs Division, LC-D4-500190.

Many Chicagoans, Muscovites, and Osakans lurched between prosperity and bankruptcy throughout the period.

The private metropolis battled with competing cities for money and people, much as individual enterprises and companies fought for profit. Its citizens were subject to the vagaries of regional, national, and international economic realities over which they often had scant control. The stability rooted in the bedrock of a royal court or a seated parliament simply did not exist in the private metropolis. Commercial cities such as Chicago, to borrow from Garry Wills in an observation equally apposite for Moscow and Osaka, simply made themselves up as they went along, forever overexposed to the boom-and-bust cycles of unregulated capitalism.[59]

The organizational complexity of noncapital metropolises—which are often subordinate simultaneously to national, regional, and local authorities as well as to a host of private and corporate interests—denies extensive power to any single group. The relative absence of direct state intervention into local life creates the room required for the individual compromises and inclusive leadership strategies so necessary for the emergence of the pragmatic pluralism described here.

State hegemony is never total in an urban environment. In some instances—such as London and perhaps Edo-Tokyo—the state's capacity to shape a capital city remained limited.[60] It is important to recognize that state power can never be totally absent in a city that is "the seat of power." The state was less evident in Chicago, Moscow, and Osaka at the turn of the last century. Such second cities, for this reason, may provide more distilled examples of metropolitan pluralism than preeminent cities.

INDUSTRIAL CAPITALISM AND PRAGMATIC PLURALISM

If metropolitan urbanity represents one base of comparison among Chicago, Moscow, and Osaka, capitalism represents a second. Capitalism, while concentrating power, wealth, and resources in a few hands, also undermines the capacity of any single group to establish durable

[59] Garry Wills, "Chicago Underground," *New York Review of Books*, October 21, 1993, pp. 15–22: 16.
[60] For further discussion of London and Edo-Tokyo, see Roy Porter, *London: A Social History* (Cambridge, Mass.: Harvard University Press, 1995); and the essays contained in James L. McClain, John M. Merriam, and Kaoru Ugawa, eds., *Edo and Paris: Urban Life and the State in the Early Modern Era* (Ithaca: Cornell University Press, 1994).

dominance over others. This is especially so at those moments when capitalist modes of production come into being.

Later observers of nineteenth-century capitalist cities could easily identify concise three-class systems "with men of great wealth and power at the top, lesser businessmen, professionals and white collar workers in the middle, and the mass of wage earners below."[61] Such schemes vaporize at closer range.

David Hammack convincingly argues that power is increasingly dispersed as communities become larger, and as their economies become more specialized and dependent on expertise and coordination.[62] Bargains must be made, accommodations offered, concessions fulfilled for contending groups and individuals to cooperate with one another.[63] And cooperate they must in a rapidly changing and increasingly complex urban environment. The social fragmentation and upheaval produced by capitalism in formation—like metropolitan urbanity—nurtures a pragmatic pluralism that may eventually ripen into more fully fledged democratic social, political, cultural, and economic customs and patterns of behavior. As Dietrich Rueschemeyer, Evelyne Huber Stephens, and John D. Stephens have argued, "[i]t was not the capitalist market nor capitalists as the new dominant force, but rather, the contradictions of capitalism that advanced the cause of democracy."[64]

The social contradictions and tensions of capitalism were never more visible than in the emerging metropolises of the industrial age. More than mere gestures were required before a transition to pluralistic politics could be completed. "Finally," Rueschemeyer, Huber Stephens, and Stephens add, "the installation of democracy requires complex class compromises that become embodied in new institutional arrangements."[65] This is so even if such arrangements reflect political and social compromises that participants in the political process neither desire nor want.[66] Social and political accord rests not so much

---

[61] Robert H. Wiebe, *The Search for Order, 1877–1920* (New York: Hill and Wang, 1967), p. 13.

[62] Hammack, "Problems of Power."

[63] Edward C. Banfield and James Q. Wilson, *City Politics* (Cambridge, Mass.: Harvard University Press, 1967), p. 47.

[64] Dietrich Rueschemeyer, Evelyne Huber Stephens, and John D. Stephens, *Capitalist Development and Democracy* (Chicago: University of Chicago Press, 1992), p. 7.

[65] Ibid., p. 78.

[66] A point emphasized by Amy Bridges in her study of the rise of machine politics in pre–Civil War New York. See Amy Bridges, *A City in the Republic: Antebellum New York and the Origins of Machine Politics* (Cambridge, U.K.: Cambridge University Press, 1984).

on the aspiration to accommodate as on the persistence of enduring conflict.

The essence of pragmatic pluralism, then, is the capacity to derive benefit from contact with individuals or groups who are otherwise considered to be personally loathsome. Pragmatic pluralism is not about "community," which by its very nature is an exclusive form of social organization. Communities are notoriously intolerant of those not already among the embraced. The wellspring of pluralism is the need to survive within what Lewis Mumford perceptively labeled the "purposive social complexity" of urban life.[67] Pragmatic pluralism emerges from a willingness to tolerate behavior that is in some degree offensive.[68] Such forced tolerance is a product of a diverse urban environment that tosses those in competition with one another, and of an emerging capitalist system dependent on cooperation as well as competition.

In 1975, Milton Rakove wrote an engaging account of his experiences "inside the Daley Machine." Rakove, who entered local political life at the lowest level while a graduate student in political science, notes in his introduction to *Don't Make No Waves, Don't Back No Losers* that "the awful truth is that there is no such thing as the public interest" in Chicago politics. Rather, there is "a wide divergence of conflicting private interests, all supported under the rubric of the public good."[69] Pragmatic pluralism is not so much the process of defining the public good as it is the process by which sufficient space is found under "the rubric of the public good" for a variety of conflicting private interests to coexist.

Both metropolitan urbanism and industrial capitalism account for much of the economic dynamism and fluid pluralism of Chicago, Moscow, and Osaka. A variety of Marxists and non-Marxists have written about the hegemonic power of the industrial bourgeoisie in the capitalist societies of a century ago. Yet, as is probably already obvious, the argument here runs somewhat counter to such ruminations. Beyond enforcing hegemonic power, capitalism unleashes Schumpeterian destructive forces that drive apart long-standing social, economic and political relationships.[70] The consequent fragmentation ensures that no

[67] Lewis Mumford, "What Is a City?" in Donald L. Miller, ed., *The Lewis Mumford Reader* (New York: Pantheon, 1986), pp. 104–7: 107.

[68] Edward C. Banfield, "Introduction," in Edward C. Banfield, ed., *Civility and Citizenship in Liberal Democratic Societies* (New York: Paragon House, 1992), p. xii.

[69] Milton L. Rakove, *Don't Make No Waves, Don't Back No Losers: An Insider's Analysis of the Daley Machine* (Bloomington: Indiana University Press, 1975), p. 9.

[70] For Schumpeter's classic 1942 discussion of capitalism's capacity for "creative destruction," see Joseph A. Schumpeter, *Capitalism, Socialism, and Democracy* (New York: Harper Torchbooks, 1975).

single class or social group will be able to hold sway on all issues. To be successful, participants in the metropolitan political game are forced to move beyond a zero-sum game toward an engagement with others in which they choose their ground carefully and to pursue inclusive strategies that reach out to possible allies on any given issue. Such compromises become the basis for the practice of pragmatic pluralism.

CAPITALIST CITIES IN TRANSITION

Chicago, Moscow, and Osaka were all capitalist cities in transition. Chicago was literally brand new. Moscow and Osaka were just emerging from pre-capitalist—or, perhaps more precisely, "proto-industrial"— social and economic systems.[71] Osaka—long a center of money-and-market functions—was already well along the road to a capitalist and

---

[71] Serfdom was abolished in Russia in 1861; Japan's modernization drive began in 1868 with the fall of the Tokugawa shogunate and the start of the Meiji Restoration. Ron Toby and others, for example, have highlighted an expanding network of interbank wholesale credit linking primary agricultural and more heavily industrial subregions throughout Japan with a money-and-market orientation that progressively altered the Japanese economic and social structures. Wealth was being transferred from the military caste to merchants and rural entrepreneurs.

Concerning the concept of "proto-industrialization," see Franklin Mendels's initial articulation of economies that were experiencing rapid growth in "traditionally organized, but market-oriented, primarily rural industry." Franklin Mendels, " 'Proto-Industrialization': The First Phase of the Industrialization Process," *Journal of Economic History* 32, no. 1 (1972), pp. 241–61. Readers may also wish to consult the work of Mendels's sometime collaborator Hans Medick. See, for example, Hans Medick, "The Proto-Industrial Family Economy," in Peter Kriedte et al., eds., *Industrialization before Industrialization: Rural Industry in the Genesis of Capitalism* (Cambridge, U.K.: Cambridge University Press, 1981).

Specialists on Japanese economic development have engaged in the proto-industrialization discussion, explicitly applying Mendels's model at times, as in the work of Ron Toby, and implicitly describing the process before Mendels had coined the term, as in the work of Thomas C. Smith. See, for example, Ronald P. Toby, "Both a Borrower and a Lender Be: From Village Moneylender to Rural Banker in the Tempo Era," *Monumenta Nipponica* 46, no. 4 (Winter 1991), pp. 483–512; Ronald P. Toby, "Changing Credit: From Village Moneylender to Rural Banker in Protoindustrial Japan," in Gareth Austin and Kaoru Sugihara, eds., *Local Suppliers of Credit in the Third World, 1750–1960* (New York: St. Martin's, 1993), pp. 55–90; Thomas C. Smith, "Japan's Aristocratic Revolution," *Yale Review* 50 (Spring 1961), pp. 370–83; Thomas C. Smith, *The Agrarian Origins of Modern Japan* (New York: Atheneum, 1966); Thomas C. Smith, "Premodern Economic Growth: Japan and the West," *Past & Present* 60 (1973), pp. 127–60; Thomas C. Smith, *Political Change and Industrial Development in Japan: Government Enterprise, 1868–1880* (Stanford: Stanford University Press, 1955); and Thomas C. Smith, *Native Sources of Japanese Industrialization, 1750–1920* (Berkeley: University of California Press, 1988). Smith's profound contributions to the study of Japanese economic history are reviewed in Osamu Saito, "Bringing the Covert Structure of the Past to Light," *Journal of Economic History* 49, no. 4 (1989), pp. 992–99. Saito underscores Smith's description of the "proto-industrialization" process prior to Mendels's and Medick's work.

an industrial orientation prior to the Meiji Restoration.[72] The city nonetheless experienced a qualitative change in economic structure and orientation over the half-century following 1868, which brought dramatic social and political transformations. Moscow and the Russian economy, for their part, were experiencing arguably greater dislocations in organization, orientation, and overall structure following Alexander II's Great Reforms of 1861.[73]

Chicago, Moscow, and Osaka were all growing with mind-bending speed; they were great commercial centers poised on the entrance to a new era. They were not traditional centers with firmly entrenched high-minded cultural elites (even though Moscow and Osaka were already

Subsequent research has explored these themes in relation to particular Meiji-era industries and firms. See, for example, W. Mark Fruin, *Kikkoman: Company, Clan, and Community* (Cambridge, Mass.: Harvard University Press, 1983); and David L. Howell, *Capitalism from Within: Economy, Society, and the State in a Japanese Fishery* (Berkeley: University of California Press, 1995).

Arcadius Kahan's writings on Jewish and Russian economic history similarly point to certain "proto-industrial" tendencies in Russian imperial economic development, although, like Smith, Kahan does not refer explicitly to the concept of "proto-industrialization." See Arcadius Kahan, "Notes on Jewish Entrepreneurship in Tsarist Russia," in Greg Guroff and F. V. Carstensen, eds., *Entrepreneurship in Imperial Russia and the Soviet Union* (Princeton: Princeton University Press, 1983), pp., 104–24; as well as various essays contained in Arcadius Kahan, *Essays in Jewish Social and Economic History*, Roger Weiss, ed. (Chicago: University of Chicago Press, 1986); Arcadius Kahan, *Studies and Essays on the Soviet and East European Economies*, Peter B. Brown, ed., 2 vols. (Newtonville, Mass.: Oriental Research Partners, 1992 and 1994); and Arcadius Kahan, *The Plow, the Hammer, and the Knout: An Economic History of Eighteenth-Century Russia*, with the editorial assistance of Richard Hellie (Chicago: University of Chicago Press, 1985). The state was more directly involved in every stage of the Russian industrialization process much earlier than was the case in Japan, with the role of indigenous, rural, market-oriented industrial activity appearing to be considerably more limited (though not non-existent) than the processes in Japan identified by Smith, Toby, and others.

[72] Nobutaka Ike, *The Beginnings of Political Democracy in Japan* (Baltimore: Johns Hopkins University Press, 1950), p. 12. Concerning Tokugawa economic development in Japan and Osaka, see E. Sydney Crawcour, "The Tokugawa Heritage," in William W. Lockwood, ed., *The State and Economic Enterprise in Japan: Essays in the Political Economy of Growth* (Princeton: Princeton University Press, 1965), pp. 17–44; and Kazushi Ohkawa and Henry Rosovsky, "A Century of Japanese Economic Growth," in Ibid., pp. 47–92.

[73] As Jeffrey Burds writes in an important post-Soviet reinterpretation of the Russian peasant experience, villages throughout the central industrial region surrounding Moscow had long "maintained a hybrid economy that blurred the now-familiar distinctions between subsistence and capitalist forms. Because they lived in an area of poor soil and a short, irregular growing season, peasants in this region had by the nineteenth century become habituated to meeting individual, household, and village subsistence requirements by supplementing village agriculture with a wide variety of predominantly non-agricultural jobs that augmented their typically meager agricultural earnings on village allotments." Jeffrey Burds, *Peasant Dreams and Market Politics: Labor Migration and the Russian Village, 1861–1905* (Pittsburgh: University of Pittsburgh Press, 1998), p. 17.

3. The market in Kitai Gorod, Moscow, 1898. Underwood and Underwood. Library of Congress, Prints and Photographs Division, LC-USZ62-073769.

centuries old). They drew on upstart talent from every direction. The contradictions posed by rapid social and economic change confronted people of talent, whether native or migrant, creating pools of innovation. They were cities that fundamentally confirm Peter Hall's hypothesis that innovation and transition go hand in hand. Chicago, Moscow, and Osaka were wide-open towns embedded in transitional economies.

Rapid social and economic change necessitated new and different skills to succeed. Quick wits and an acute appreciation of early capital formation mattered far more in determining winners and losers than any equivalent of "old-school ties." All three cities displayed many of the qualities that Hall argues are prerequisites for innovation: they were relatively free of older traditions, were full of "a nervous energy," and fostered a belief among new arrivals that there were no limits to the possible.

Chicago, Moscow, and Osaka became the sorts of "unstuffy, un-class bound, non-hierarchical places" to which Hall attaches so much importance in explaining how particular cities at particular times become immensely creative and exceptionally innovative.[74] Their relative openness was especially visible in relation to national political and financial centers in New York, Washington, St. Petersburg, Kyoto, and Tokyo. Some East Coast blue bloods managed to succeed in Chicago, to be sure, as did former samurai in Osaka and noblemen in Moscow. They did so out of a mastery of their cities' new realities rather than their personal or familial inheritances.

Hall has argued, for instance, that American society at the end of the nineteenth century was predicated on the mass reception of immigrants as well as on the acceptance of new ideas and concepts. Elites were unable to merely assert their status by right.[75] Tokugawa elites similarly had to demonstrate their worth under a Meiji emperor consumed by the need to make his country "modern." As will become evident in the chapters to follow, long-standing Russian patterns of social differentiation often broke down in Moscow.

Those once-privileged Chicagoans, Muscovites, and Osakans who acquired the survival skills required by burgeoning industrial capitalism managed to thrive.[76] Samurai often possessed knowledge well suited for the Meiji era.[77] Members of the Tokugawa samurai class were administrators, soldiers, educators, clerks, financial agents, artists, physicians, and writers in Meiji Japan.[78] Many former elites, of course, failed to master the skills and mind-set of the new era.[79]

What remains most remarkable about all three cities during this transitional period is that many of the figures who dominate the chapters

---

[74] Hall, *Cities in Civilization*, pp. 3, 493.   [75] Ibid., p. 305.

[76] E. Patricia Tsurumi, *Factory Girls: Women in the Thread Mills of Meiji Japan* (Princeton: Princeton University Press, 1990), p. 41.

[77] Gary D. Allinson, *Japanese Urbanism: Industry and Politics in Kariya, 1872–1972* (Berkeley: University of California Press, 1975), pp. 28–29; Bernard S. Silberman, *Ministers of Modernization: Elite Mobility in the Meiji Restoration, 1868–1873* (Tucson: University of Arizona Press, 1964), pp. 11–19, 32–33; and Smith, *Political Change*, pp. 31–34, 101–3.

[78] Allinson, *Japanese Urbanism*, pp. 28–29.

[79] R. Portal, "Industriels moscovites: le secteur cotonnier (1861–1914)," *Cahiers du Monde Russe et Sovietique* 4, nos. 1–2 (January–June 1963), pp. 5–46: 9.

to follow emerged from backgrounds of no special note prior to the 1860s.[80] Nearly half of Moscow's families whose heads were in the top merchant guilds in 1873, for example, had attained such status since 1861, whereas only one-sixth had been incorporated into that guild level prior to 1800.[81] Few, if any, of the early Armours, Fields, Swifts, Morozovs, Tretiakovs, Shchukins, Shibusawas, Nomuras, or Fujitas would have made it past the screening committees of the most tony New York, Kyoto, or St. Petersburg social clubs. They were all beneficiaries of capitalism in formation.

ESTABLISHED ELITES AND SOCIAL FRAGMENTATION

Chicago, Moscow, and Osaka share their metropolitan scale and transitional capitalist economies as bases for comparison. They were societies undergoing profound transition driven by industrial, commercial, and technological revolutions that would eventually transform how people everywhere would live their lives. Established elites who appear to have dominated their communities often failed to adjust to the dramatic changes taking place all around them.

Julia Wrigley notes in an authoritative study of public education in Chicago that many scholars who assume upper-class domination have viewed working-class resistance as little more than sporadic atavistic outbursts.[82] Such approaches fail to consider the extent to which class-based struggles actually transformed local reality, counterpoising alternative values to those of the dominant group.

In school reform, the specific object of Wrigley's work, laborers and their trade-union representatives "generated an ideology that was in significant respects counter to that held by the dominant elements in society."[83] Working-class parents and unionized teachers found temporary alliances with middle reformers and even business groups on specific issues. The result was not movement "toward a more perfect society," as writers in the pluralist tradition might have perceived. Educational policy in Chicago down to the level of the individual

---

[80] A point underscored in the case of Meiji Japan by Bernard S. Silberman's pioneering work on elite mobility. See, for example, Silberman, *Ministers of Modernization*.

[81] A. S. Nifontov, *Moskva vo vtoroi polovine XIX stoletiia. Stenogramma publichnoi lektsii, prochitannoi 26 Marta 1947 goda v Lektsionnom zale v Moskve* (Moscow: Izdatel'stvo "Pravda," 1947), p. 7.

[82] Julia Wrigley, *Class Politics and Public Schools: Chicago, 1900–1950* (New Brunswick, N.J.: Rutgers University Press, 1982), pp. 9–15.

[83] Ibid., p. 262.

public-school classroom was often the product of "a continuing, sometimes open, sometimes submerged, political struggle where gains can
often be important but are also only partial and subject to revocation."[84]

In an era of relatively weak political organization and disorganized
municipal governance such as in Chicago at the turn of the last century,
these battles were "fought out quite directly rather than being mediated
through a powerful and unified political party. Business, labor, and
liberal 'reform' elements developed strong organizations as they promoted their political programs in the disordered context of the city."[85]
Such a fragmented environment is especially conducive for the sort of
pragmatic alliance-building that occurs when established elites are challenged at every turn.

More important, space existed for numerous groups to contend for
influence in public life, even as business and financial interests surpassed
all others in economic resources and in the respect they commanded from
government officials.[86] Various social strata pursued different political
strategies.[87] Native white males enjoyed access to the ballot box.[88] Other
groups were forced to pursue their agendas by extra-electoral means.
Immigrant workers increasingly turned to labor unions; middle-class
women to a remarkable network of clubs, associations, and philanthropic organizations.[89] Such extra-electoral activities suggest that the
absence of suffrage rights in and of itself did not foreclose the possibility for individual and collective action. Voting may have represented an
ultimately necessary condition for the establishment of political institutions based on openness and tolerance. The presence of a relatively independent judiciary, discussed in the Chicago case studies to follow, may

[84] Ibid., p. 270. This local Chicago pattern of social hierarchy based on wealth—which
points back to David Hammack's observations about New York—is consistent with
what historians of the Progressive era have argued about American life and politics more
generally. The U.S. gross national product (GNP), when calculated in current prices,
rose from about $11 billion in the mid-1880s to $84 billion in 1919. Taking into account
the more than doubling of the country's population, per capita GNP increased from
$208 in the mid-1880s to $804 in 1919. However, by 1890, the wealthiest 1 percent of
the families in the United States owned 51 percent of the country's real and personal
property, whereas the 44 percent of families at the bottom of the economic scale owned
only 1.2 percent of all property. Nell Irvin Painter, *Standing at Armageddon: The United
States, 1877–1919* (New York: Norton, 1987), pp. xix–xx.

[85] Wrigley, *Class Politics*, p. 22.

[86] This observation is drawn from Richard L. McCormick's 1990 review of then-recent
historiography on the Progressive era (1877–1917). See Richard L. McCormick, "Public
Life in Industrial America, 1877–1917," in Eric Foner, ed., *The New American History*
(Philadelphia: Temple University Press, 1990), pp. 93–177: 99.

[87] Peter G. Filene, "An Obituary for 'The Progressive Movement,'" *American Quarterly*
22 (Spring 1970), pp. 20–34: 23.

[88] McCormick, "Public Life," p. 96.   [89] Ibid., p. 101.

have been of equal importance as competitive elections to the peaceful resolution of disputes.

Industrialization, the rise of corporations, the integration of women into public life, class-based violence, massive immigration from southern and eastern Europe, and deep economic depression during the years 1893–97 transformed how Americans lived their lives.[90] Every segment of American society was affected, and each group tried to protect itself from the harshest realities of the era. Yet it was in the industrial city that many of these forces came clashing together with greatest furor.[91]

Power within the worlds of capitalist Chicago and America was fragmenting simultaneously. The era of the robber baron was also the era of emergent corporate bureaucracy. A quarter of a century ago, social and business historians began to add welcome depth to descriptions of corporate life.[92] They challenged the assumptions of older debates between those observers who viewed the corporate reorganization of American society as inimical to American values and ethnical standards,[93] and others who portrayed a new salaried class as shaping the workplace in their own image.[94] Either way, the appearance of a

[90] For explication of such issues, see Paula Baker, "The Domestication of Politics: Women and American Political Society, 1780–1920," *American Historical Review* 89, no. 3 (1984), pp. 610–47; Alan M. Kraut, *The Huddled Masses: The Immigrant in American Society, 1880–1921* (Arlington Heights, Ill.: Harlan Davidson, 1982); Richard Oestreicher, "Urban Working-Class Political Behavior and Theories of American Electoral Politics, 1870–1940," *Journal of American History* 74, no. 4 (1988), pp. 1257–86; Glen Porter, *The Rise of Big Business, 1860–1920*, 2d ed. (Arlington Heights, Ill.: Harlan Davidson, 1992); and Stephen Skowronek, *Building a New American State: The Expansion of National Administrative Capacities, 1877–1920* (Cambridge, U.K.: Cambridge University Press, 1982).

[91] A point noted by Jane Addams in 1909 with considerable sorrow. See Jane Addams, *The Spirit of Youth and the City Streets* (New York: Macmillan, 1909), p. 141.

[92] See, for example, Alfred Dupont Chandler, Jr., *The Visible Hand: The Managerial Revolution in American Business* (Cambridge, Mass.: Harvard University Press, 1977); and Olivier Zunz, *Making America Corporate, 1870–1920* (Chicago: University of Chicago Press, 1990), esp. pp. 1–7.

[93] See, for example, Thorstein Veblen, *The Theory of the Leisure Class* (1899; reprint, New York: Viking, 1967); Thorstein Veblen, *The Instinct of Workmanship and the State of the Industrial Arts* (New York: B. W. Huebusch, 1918); Thorstein Veblen, *Higher Learning in America: A Memorandum on the Conduct of Universities by Business Men* (New York: B. W. Huebusch, 1918); Robert and Helen Lynd, *Middletown in Transition: A Study in Cultural Conflicts* (New York: Harcourt, Brace, 1937); C. Wright Mills, *The Power Elite* (New York: Oxford University Press, 1956); and C. Wright Mills, *White Collar: The American Middle Classes* (New York: Oxford University Press, 1951).

[94] See, for example, Richard Hofstadter, *The Structure of American History* (Englewood Cliffs, N.J.: Prentice-Hall, 1964); Richard Hofstadter, *The Progressive Movement* (Englewood Cliffs, N.J.: Prentice-Hall, 1963); Richard Hofstadter, *The Age of Reform: From Bryan to F.D.R.* (New York: Knopf, 1955); and Richard Hofstadter, *The Progressive Historians: Turner, Beard, Parrington* (Chicago: University of Chicago Press, 1979).

middle-level executive strata that was neither rich nor poor transformed American life.

The relationship between the corporation and society at large became the source of profound ambiguity. The rise of a corporate middle class simultaneously created the conditions for both social fragmentation and social consolidation, producing a disjointed hegemony in which even those who controlled a society's commanding political and economic heights were forced to tolerate and accommodate others. In an era in which politics were "fragmented, fluid, and issue-focused," in which intellectual coherence and ideological comprehensiveness were lacking, no single group could consistently dominate the political maelstrom even if white, Protestant, educated males entered from a position of distinct advantage.[95]

Class and ethnic dominance was consequential in Gilded Age America, lending credence to advocates of class approaches to urban history. As Karen Sawislak observes, the fact "that native-born businessmen were the bearers of a substantial amount of power will come as no surprise to students of urban history."[96] The diverse realities of Chicago nonetheless caution that a more complex and textured portrait of Chicago and American life emerges once one is "not interested simply in identifying incidents of 'dominance.'"[97]

DISJOINTED HEGEMONY AND URBAN FORCED TOLERANCE

The issue of dominance in Chicago and elsewhere is a complex one— especially so in an urban society whose political institutions are predicated on the ballot box. Sawislak's study of the intensely difficult months between the Great Fire of 1871 and the Panic of 1873 demonstrates that a majority of Chicagoans accepted the fundamental tenet of the "Yankee" elite that "merit and 'public good' [are to be] widely ascribed to the figure of the independent American individual" while all the time ensuring that "an array of voices were heard."[98] The city's "sharply accented lines" did not disappear. Fundamental issues of social organization were hotly contested, as Sawislak's own work demonstrates. A native-born elite frequently carried political debate, but, as will become apparent in the discussion of charter reform in Chapter 8, this was not

[95] Daniel T. Rodgers, "In Search of Progressivism," *Reviews in American History* 10, no. 4 (December 1982), pp. 113–32.
[96] Sawislak, *Chicagoans and the Great Fire*, p. 16.
[97] Ibid.   [98] Ibid., p. 279.

always so. Contestation rather than either reconciliation or accession was the rule of the day.

Few will be surprised by class hegemony and dominance; it is contestation that needs to be explained. The intense urbanity of Chicago, Moscow, and Osaka must come into play once again at this point, for although it would be impossible to ignore the impact of capitalism, industrialization, and technological change in any examination of these cities during the period under review, this volume seeks to modify the terms of discourse first and foremost by examining all three cities as very large urban centers in transition. Such cities stand at the juncture between larger national, as well as international, forces and the realities of daily life.[99]

Metropolitan life—at the height of capitalism, under Soviet-style socialism, or in various pre- and post-modern incarnations—by its very nature produces societies so complex and spatially dense that people of difference are forced by physical proximity to interact with neighbors quite unlike themselves. Existence is hardly always "pleasant." Single groups, no matter how powerful, rarely win every battle for power, wealth, and resources. Choices must be made—hard choices; but these rarely need to be limited to a menu of binary options. Large cities produce choices. They nurture the space within which difficult concessions and compromises become possible by their very density and diversity. Such is the essence from which springs what is identified here as "pragmatic pluralism."

This study, then, is about a tolerance of necessity rather than "democracy" in any classical sense.[100] Political arrangements in Moscow and Osaka were hardly "democratic" as that term is understood in late-twentieth-century North America.[101] For their part, some citizens of

---

[99] Sharon Zukin, *The Culture of Cities* (Cambridge, Mass.: Blackwell, 1995), p. 46.

[100] The processes under review are often closer to what Guillermo O'Donnell and Philippe C. Schmitter have labeled "liberalization" (i.e., "the process of redefining and extending rights") rather than what they call "democratization," which "involves both the *right* to be treated by fellow human beings as equal with respect to the making of collective choices and the *obligation* of those implementing such choices to be equally accountable and accessible to all members of the polity." Guillermo O'Donnell and Philippe C. Schmitter, "Defining Some Concepts (and Exposing Some Assumptions)," in Guillermo O'Donnell, Philippe C. Schmitter, and Laurence Whitehead, eds., *Transitions from Authoritarian Rule: Prospects for Democracy* (Baltimore: Johns Hopkins University Press, 1986), Part IV ("Tentative Conclusions about Uncertain Democracies"), pp. 6–15: 7.

[101] For a characteristic statement of late-twentieth-century criteria for defining and evaluating "democracy," see Juan J. Linz, "Crisis, Breakdown, and Reequilibration," in Juan J. Linz and Alfred Stepan, eds., *The Breakdown of Democratic Regimes* (Baltimore: Johns Hopkins University Press, 1978), pp. 3–124: 5–9.

Chicago had greater opportunity to participate in the local political arena than either Muscovites or Osakans had. Chicago's competitive elections—a feature of local political life that clearly distinguishes municipal politics in the United States from that of either imperial Russia or Meiji Japan—were limited nonetheless to a minority of the city's residents. Women and non-citizen immigrants were disenfranchised and often unempowered.[102]

Moderation and tolerance in these great "second cities" were the consequences of social dislocation associated with rapid urban growth and capitalism in formation. Difference and complexity proved to be positive, a finding that accords with the findings of Peter Hall's portentous volume, *Cities in Civilization*. Some urban residents past and present have come to view the serendipitous exposure to difference generated by complexity as "one of the main attractions of city life."[103] This study will explore some of the conditions under which this was so.

CULTURAL AND ECONOMIC PARTICULARITY

The metropolitan scale, capitalist formation, tolerance out of necessity, and pragmatic pluralism of Chicago, Moscow, and Osaka provide sufficient ground for meaningful comparison.[104] The dynamic commercialism and unbridled capitalist expansionism of all three cities would have been recognizable to residents of each of the other municipalities.

Many significant differences remain, as well. Divergence in the level of industrialization and economic development in the United States, Meiji Japan, and imperial Russia distinguished these cities from each other. The average American of the period consumed 500 kilowatt-hours of electricity in 1912, as compared to the just 16 kilowatt-hours used by an average Russian a year later.[105]

---

[102] For further discussion, see Michael Wallace Homel, "Negroes in the Chicago Public Schools, 1910–1941" (Ph.D. diss., University of Chicago, 1971).

[103] Larry Bennett, *Fragments of Cities: The New American Downtowns and the Neighborhoods* (Columbus: Ohio State University Press, 1990), p. 9.

[104] Moscow's modernization was not all that far behind western Europe's. For example, Moscow's telephone usage, as measured by the number of Bell telephones per thousand residents, was roughly equivalent to that found in Germany, the Netherlands, and Great Britain at the outbreak of World War I. P. V. Sytin, *Kommunal'noe khoziaistvo. Blagoustroistvo Moskvy v sravnenii s blagoustroistvom drugikh bol'shikh gorodov* (Moscow: Novaia Moskva, 1926), p. 162.

[105] Jonathan Coopersmith, *The Electrification of Russia, 1880–1926* (Ithaca: Cornell University Press, 1992), p. 47.

A culture of social and political confrontation that dominated imperial Russian life, but not necessarily Moscow, must be contrasted with a more absorptive American political culture that adapted with greater ease to the realities of social pluralism. The broad—although hardly universal—suffrage of the United States and its highly developed judicial system emerge as especially important factors in this context.[106] The American penchant for public accountability and more open institutional arrangements remained profoundly alien to Russians. Meiji political arrangements combined varying aspects of both.

The differences among the municipal regimes of Chicago, Moscow, and Osaka were also those of timing as well as fundamental substance. Chicago transformed itself into a "modern" metropolis between the Great Fire of 1871 and the 1893 World's Columbian Exposition (World's Fair). The city's first professional politician mayor—Carter Henry Harrison, Sr.—was initially elected in 1879. A fundamentally new political regime would be in place by the time of his son's first term in that same office in 1897.

Moscow's industrial political regime began in the 1890s with the appearance of merchant-mayor Nikolai Alekseev's "modernizing" administration. Alekseev is a complex figure who both won the French Legion of Honor for his effective municipal management and justifiably gained the eternal enmity of Russian Jewry for his role in prompting and implementing the imperial government's expulsion of Jewish merchants from his city.[107]

---

[106] Even though turn-of-the-century Chicago fell short of an ideal democracy, a not-unusual situation in American cities. This was the case even in Robert Dahl's New Haven, the model for discussions of urban pluralism in American cities. See Robert A. Dahl, *Who Governs? Democracy and Power in an American City* (New Haven: Yale University Press, 1961).

[107] Walter S. Hanchett, "Moscow in the Late Nineteenth Century: A Study in Municipal Self-Government" (Ph.D. diss., University of Chicago, 1964), p. 141. The city's 1897 census revealed that Jews constituted but 0.5 percent of Moscow's population, less than a third of the number and percentage found in 1882, when St. Petersburg authorities forced some ten thousand Jews to resettle in the Pale of Settlement to the west. Timothy J. Colton, *Moscow: Governing the Socialist Metropolis* (Cambridge, Mass.: Harvard University Press, 1995), p. 35. Further expulsions of leading Jewish business families followed in 1891 while Alekseev was mayor. Jo Ann Ruckman, *The Moscow Business Elite: A Social and Cultural Portrait of Two Generations, 1840–1905* (DeKalb: Northern Illinois University Press, 1984), pp. 23–24. Alekseev, however, would also join Finance Minister Sergei Witte during this same period in successful opposition to decrees restricting the commercial activities of Jews in Bukhara—an action that threatened the well-being of Alekseev's fellow textile manufacturers Thomas C. Owen, *Capitalism and Politics in Russia: A Social History of the Moscow Merchants, 1855–1905* (Cambridge, U.K.: Cambridge University Press, 1981), p. 103.

Constant interference from St. Petersburg undercut political reform, while an assassin's bullet brought Alekseev's own time in office to an abrupt conclusion in 1893. A halting evolution of municipal adminis- tration continued, only to be interrupted yet again by the 1905 Revolu- tion—an upheaval that left several deep social wounds festering until the imperial collapse in 1917.

Osaka's regime transformation began with Japan's victory over Russia in 1905 and was completed with the introduction of universal male suf- frage in local elections in 1926. Seki Hajime, arguably the first profes- sional urbanist to serve as the Osaka chief executive, took power in 1923. Osakans successfully completed and institutionalized a new local regime structure just as Muscovites were failing to do the same.

Finally, one can not escape the violence of Russia's revolutions and civil wars in 1905–7, 1917–21, and 1928–32.[108] The interpretation pre- sented here is based on the view that, prior to 1907, post-1861 Russia was more or less on a trajectory of reform that led toward the emergence of a "modern" European state.

The material to follow concerning Moscow's incipient civil society demonstrates that the path toward reform was never apiculate. Russian social, economic, and political reforms experienced more than their share of zigs and zags along the way. The tsar's final concessions required nothing less than a humiliating military defeat by the Japanese and nearly two years of societal breakdown at home. Nevertheless, Russia emerged from the 1905 Revolution as a Chekhovian world embracing an elected parliament, local governmental institutions, an emergent middle class, a growing privately financed industrial sector, and expanding agriculture and small farms.

Nicholas II stepped off the path of "modern" European state- building on June 3, 1907, when his prime minister, Petr Stolypin, suc- cessfully engineered a conservative coup against the Duma and sent Russian parliamentarians packing.[109] The reconstituted Third Duma,

---

[108] As numerous social historians have now demonstrated, these upheavals were but the most visible manifestations of social and political violence throughout the first years of the twentieth century. See, for example, Joan Neuberger, *Hooliganism: Crime, Culture, and Power in St. Petersburg, 1900–1914* (Berkeley: University of California Press, 1993).

[109] For an in-depth analysis of the events leading up to the Stolypin "coup" of June 3, 1907, see the second volume of Abraham Ascher's authoritative history of the 1905 Revolution: Abraham Ascher, *The Revolution of 1905*, Vol. 2: *Authority Restored* (Stanford: Stanford University Press, 1992). Christine Ruane provocatively explores the relationship between the 1905–7 events and the emergence of a public sphere in Russia in her study of Russian urban teachers: Ruane, *Gender, Class*, pp. 128–63.

EXTREMELY CROWDED AT THE POINT OF KITAHAMA,
THE CENTRE OF COMMERCE, OSAKA.

点又交済北の中心商界の (阪 大)

4. Postcard of the Point of Kitahama, Osaka. Photographer unknown, n.d.

elected under more restrictive election laws, effectively brought Russia's early democratic transition to an end. The revolutions of 1917 were not inevitable after June 1907, but they arguably could not have occurred had the Stolypin coup not taken place a decade before. Moscow grew increasingly different from Chicago and Osaka beginning at about this time.

Such contrasts among imperial Japan and tsarist Russia do not suggest that the United States was totally successful or consistent at pursuing the politics of social accommodation.[110] They nonetheless point toward greater understanding of the diverse fates of Chicago, Moscow, and Osaka during much of the twentieth century. More important, such distinctions among American, Japanese, and Russian political experiences do not invalidate comparisons among these three "second cities" for much of the period under review.

This study does not deny that the United States, Russia, and Japan—to say nothing of Chicago, Moscow, and Osaka—were and remain unlike one another in many of the essential realities of daily life. Local idiosyncrasies provide nuance and texture that energize and provoke. As Czech novelist Ivan Klima observes, "a city is like a person" with its own "peculiar personality, its 'I', its spirit, its identity, the circumstances of its life as they evolved through space and time."[111]

Social analysis contributes to an understanding of the world through the identification of shared characteristics among individuals who nonetheless remain distinct from one another in important ways. The argument to follow contends that more will be revealed about all three cities by approaching them as a shared social form—burgeoning capitalist "second" cities in transition—than by dwelling on communal particularity. This volume explicitly rejects the notion that Chicago, Moscow, and Osaka were incommensurable, unique, or singular.

SIX CASE STUDIES

This book will explore the meaning of the politics of pragmatic pluralism in Chicago, Moscow, and Osaka by comparing policy disputes. These controversies will include those in which groups either succeeded

---

[110] For an interesting discussion of the limits of American ethnic accommodation, for example, see Edgar Litt, *Beyond Pluralism: Ethnic Politics in America* (Glenview, Ill.: Scott, Foresman, 1970).

[111] Ivan Klima, "The Spirit of Prague," *The Spirit of Prague and Other Essays*, trans. Paul Wilson (New York: Granta, 1994), p. 39.

in carrying the day by reaching out to others in pursuit of a common cause, or failed by ignoring social and economic competitors.

Each of the disputes examined in the chapters to follow meets David C. Hammack's measure of major importance for case studies of this genre.[112] All affected "a relatively and absolutely large number of people" by changing the distribution of valued resources, the manner in which policies were established and administered, and "the values, beliefs, and information that constitute[d] the climate of opinion" in these three metropolitan giants. Such policy issues were "viewed as unusually important by contemporary and later experts, by reputedly powerful groups in the community, or by large segments of the community's population. Moreover, each took several years to resolve."[113]

It is important to remember that definitive claims of victory or defeat in the policy world proved illusory in all six instances under examination here. Furthermore, as the discussions to follow will reveal, the degree to which outcomes may be considered to have been "successful" or "failed" remains open to question. The three more positive examples—the traction fight in Chicago, adult education policies in Moscow, and port revitalization in Osaka—represent moments when the pragmatic politics of compromise produced policy outcomes that, though far from perfect, advanced the quality of life of city inhabitants in some meaningful way. The three negative examples—charter reform in Chicago, housing and sanitation reform in Moscow, and social welfare policies in Osaka—fell prey to deep-seated conflicts and contradictions that could not be subdued by a pragmatic search for compromise.

Following overviews of each city in Part I and the policy case studies in Parts II and III, the two chapters constituting the volume's concluding section will highlight the careers of four politicians who personified the vitality of pluralist politics in all three "second metropolises"— Carter Henry Harrison, Sr., Carter Henry Harrison, Jr., Nikolai Alekseev, and Seki Hajime—before returning the reader to the questions raised at the outset of this introduction. Dissimilar as they were in personality and national culture, in training and social status, the Harrisons, Alekseev, and Seki successfully wrestled with the practical problems of governing enormous, deeply divided, and rapidly changing industrial cities during the height of their capitalist explosion. At their best, they

---

[112] These criteria are set forth in Hammack, "Problems of Power," pp. 323–49: 345–46; and Hammack, *Power and Society*, p. 22.
[113] Hammack, *Power and Society*, p. 22.

pursued an inclusive politics that neutralized many of their cities' most profound conflicts (at his worst, Alekseev embraced policies that affirmed his own anti-Semitism). Their attention to pragmatic solutions to pressing problems often converted harsh ideological disputes into smaller tactical concerns that no longer demanded total victory by one side or another.

The examination of the careers of these four municipal leaders brings the reader back to the fundamental questions about late-nineteenth-century urbanism raised at the outset: How did civic leaders manage the social diversity, tolerance, and pluralism of unrestrained capitalist indus-trial development? How effectively did civic consciousness in late-imperial Russian cities challenge the consciousness of class?

Chicago, Moscow, and Osaka were—and remain—the products of very different nations and cultures. They nonetheless shared an impor-tant experience with the inclusionary politics of pragmatic pluralism just as they simultaneously entered an era of extraordinary growth and social diversity. Constantly shifting multipolar political games created surpris-ing coalitions, as no single group could dominate their rapidly shifting worlds. Successful politicians and civic leaders accepted complexity, viewing urban management as a process rather than a series of finite policy results. The insights gained from their achievements transcend time and place.

Chicago, Moscow, and Osaka were not easily governed communities. Edward Kantowicz's admonition about Chicago politics of the period also holds for Moscow and Osaka. "The politics of balance," Kanto-wicz wrote, "may sound boring, the stuff of safe-and-sane conservatism; but nothing could be further from the truth. In fact, maintaining a polit-ical balance in a rapidly growing, fractionalized city is a highly dynamic, even daring act."[114] Authority depended on an ability "to accommodate, with amazing dexterity and flexibility, the explosive growth and bewil-dering diversity" of such volcanic urban centers. Success beyond mere survival rested on a distinctive political resource shared by Chicago, Moscow, and Osaka alike: pragmatic pluralism.

---

[114] Edward R. Kantowicz, "Carter H. Harrison II: The Politics of Balance," in Paul M. Green and Melvin G. Holli, eds., *The Mayors: The Chicago Political Tradition* (Carbondale: Southern Illinois University Press, 1987), p. 16.

Part I

Three Industrial Giants

2

Porkopolis

Chicago at the turn of the last century was the magical city of Oz. Chicagoan L. Frank Baum's 1900 tale—and subsequent American film classic—about innocent Midwestern farm folk being drawn to a "wonder city" of danger and delight was inspired by his hometown, a city overflowing with wonderful wizards, scared men of straw, and wicked neighbors.[1]

Chicago's remarkable growth over less than a century from a wild onion field to North America's "second city" was remarkable by any standard.[2] The period framed by the signing away under duress of the last aboriginal claims of Native Americans in 1833 to the city's emergence as the continent's great transportation linchpin required but a human lifetime.[3]

Chicago's dynamism and diversity overwhelmed the city's infrastructure and governance structures alike. Successful politicians in this

[1] A point explored in Kenan Heise, *A Sampling of Chicago in the Twentieth Century: Chaos, Creativity, and Culture* (Salt Lake City: Gibbs-Smith, 1998), pp. 13–14.

[2] The origin of the city's name is generally assumed to be derived from the Native American appellation for the area, Che-cau-gou, which most accounts claim relates to the strong wild onions that grew along the banks of the small river now known as the Chicago. Accordingly, the name would be roughly translated as "wild onion field" or, perhaps, "stinking onion field." See, for example, Lois Willie, *Forever Open, Clear, and Free: The Historic Struggle for Chicago's Lakefront* (Chicago: Henry Regnery, 1972), p. 5. In a search for a more magisterial definition, Alfred Theodore Andreas, in his monumental three-volume history of the city published between 1884 and 1886, argued that the actual meaning depends on the aboriginal language chosen as the name's origin. It may have meant, in an argument seemingly unique to his work, "divine river." Alfred Theodore Andreas, *History of Chicago*, Vol. 1 (Chicago: A. T. Andreas, 1885–86), pp. 33–37.

[3] A point underscored by William Cronon in *Nature's Metropolis: Chicago and the Great West* (New York: Norton, 1991), pp. 25–30; and by Andreas, *History of Chicago*. Also see Michael P. Conzen, "A Transport Interpretation of the Growth of Urban Regions: An American Example," *Journal of Historical Geography* 1, no. 4 (1975), pp. 361–82.

hurly-burly world were forced to serve as brokers among highly fractured and decentralized social, business, and political institutions. The
city's most successful bosses of the era did not rule by fiat so much as
they headed to cigar-smoke-filled back rooms to cut deals among contending groups. Their considerable successes rested on Oz-like illusion
every bit as much as on hard, empirical realities.

If, as Priscilla Parkhurst Ferguson asserts, "[t]he modernity commonly
ascribed to nineteenth-century Paris is rooted in [its] sense of movement,
the perpetually unfinished, always provisional nature of the present and
the imminence of change," there could be no more "modern" a nineteenth-century city than Chicago.[4] Nor could there be a more "modern"
collection of rapscallion power brokers than those who lorded over this
"windy city." As this brief overview of the city's development seeks to
demonstrate, late-nineteenth-century Chicago was perpetually unfinished
and provisional by nature precisely because it had not existed when the
century began. Russian visitor Aleksandr Lakier complained as early as
1857 that it was impossible to purchase an accurate city plan or a valid
guidebook because new streets were being put down so quickly that
maps were dated before they could appear in print.[5] At more than a few
moments those responsible for the city's custodianship were every bit as
confused about the robust metropolis surrounding them as were visitors
from afar.

THE FOREORDAINED METROPOLIS

A sense of predestination surrounds Chicago's rise as a consequence of
the actions of Ice Age glaciers and alluvial deposits. Located astride
the lowest of North America's continental divides—a mere ten-foot-high
ridge separating two principal water systems (one extending through
the Great Lakes and St. Lawrence River to the Atlantic, the other running down the Mississippi to the Gulf of Mexico)—Chicago has several
incomparable natural advantages.[6] Its success was rooted in the explo-

---

[4] Priscilla Parkhurst Ferguson, *Paris as Revolution: Writing the Nineteenth-Century City*
(Berkeley: University of California Press, 1994), p. 35.
[5] Aleksandr Borisovich Lakier, *A Russian Looks at America: The Journey of Aleksandr
Borisovich Lakier in 1857*, trans. and ed. Arnold Schrier and Joyce Story (Chicago: University of Chicago Press, 1979), p. 174.
[6] The significance of Chicago's natural attributes—and the role of glaciers in creating the
city's physical surroundings—is described in Donald L. Miller, *City of the Century: The
Epic of Chicago and the Making of America* (New York: Simon and Schuster, 1996),
pp. 42–47.

sive interaction of human beings with nature.[7] The launching of the massive Chicago Sanitary and Ship Canal project began a process that converted a small, primitive, frontier settlement into North America's premier transportation center.[8]

Chicago traces its origins to the arrival of the region's first non-native resident, Baptiste Point Du Saible. Du Saible had been born in Haiti in 1745, the son of a Frenchman and a free black woman.[9] Highly successful, Du Saible and his Potawatomi wife, Kitthawa, built a trading compound on the lakefront that would eventually encompass nine buildings, including the city's first elegant lakefront mansion. Du Saible retired to St. Charles, Missouri, following his wife's death in 1809, where he lived until his own passing in 1818.

Migrants from upper New York State and New England joined immigrants from Europe to reinvent Chicago with such rapidity that there was seldom an opportunity for any single elite to gain total dominance.[10] It was "a divided city comprising gold coast and slum, semiurban retreat and teeming immigrant ghetto, slaughterhouses and counting houses, red lights and blue noses."[11]

The city's volatile mobility unleashed an intense search for the distinctly American in commerce, industry, and the arts. It drew on the wealth of the American Midwest to revolutionize the grain, meat, and lumber industries.[12] Chicago invented the twentieth-century capitalist metropolis while serving as political capital of nothing larger than its own county.[13]

---

[7] This interaction is the subject of William Cronon's magisterial environmental history of Chicago and the Midwest, *Nature's Metropolis*.

[8] For further discussion of the canal's role in promoting the rise of Chicago as a metropolitan center, see Louis P. Cain, *Sanitation Strategy for a Lakefront Metropolis: The Case of Chicago* (DeKalb: Northern Illinois University Press, 1978). For discussion of the canal's role in making early Chicagoans wealthy, see Isaac N. Arnold and J. Young Scammon, *William B. Ogden and Early Days in Chicago* (Chicago: Fergus Printing Co., 1882), pp. 10–31.

[9] Willie, *Forever Open*, pp. 7–10; Andreas, *History of Chicago*, Vol. 1, p. 70.

[10] Eighty-eight percent of the city's initial business class had been born in New England and the Mid-Atlantic states. The role of migrants from these regions is discussed in Rima Lunin Schultz, "The Businessman's Role in Western Settlement: The Entrepreneurial Frontier: Chicago, 1833–1872" (Ph.D. diss., Boston University, 1985), pp. 65–97, 403. Also see discussion in James Gilbert, *Perfect Cities: Chicago's Utopias of 1893* (Chicago: University of Chicago Press, 1991), pp. 5, 28.

[11] Edward R. Kantowicz, "Carter H. Harrison II: The Politics of Balance," in Paul M. Green and Melvin G. Holli, eds., *The Mayors. The Chicago Political Tradition* (Carbondale and Edwardsville: Southern Illinois University Press, 1987), p. 17.

[12] Cronon, *Nature's Metropolis*, pp. 97–259.

[13] Chicago's importance as the quintessential twentieth-century city has been commented on by many observers, including Witold Rybczynski, *City Life: Urban Expectations in a New World* (New York: Scribner, 1995), p. 116. Such a viewpoint became firmly fixed

Such ingenuity was the hallmark of American cities.[14] Chicago's success nonetheless drew on an uncommon audacity and "sporting spirit" that, according to polemicist Lincoln Steffens, nurtured an exceptional willingness to take risk even by American standards. "No matter who you are, where you come from or what you set out to do," Steffens wrote, "Chicago will give you a chance."[15]

Collective impudence enabled young, raw, upstart Chicago to confront more-established cities that were similarly seeking economic domination over the vast and extraordinarily wealthy United States Midwest.[16] Chicago grew into a prosperous city populated by industrious residents who were always looking forward to greater achievement.

Chicago's opportunists took the moral high ground of abolition while viewing the slavery conflict as an enormous business opportunity.[17] The Civil War made Chicago the nation's leading livestock market, meat-packing center, and railroad hub. Members of Chicago's local elite immediately linked up with East Coast—primarily New York—capital to launch a massive rail web focused on their city. New Yorkers, now dependent on their Midwest partners' control over Western trade, poured the necessary capital into Chicago to rebuild the city as quickly as possible following the Great Fire of 1871.[18] Within a decade, Chicago would be competing with New York itself for command over the entire North American economy.[19]

with the appearance in 1941 of Sigfried Giedion's *Space, Time, and Architecture* (Cambridge, Mass.: Harvard University Press, 1962), pp. 333–424. For an insightful discussion of Giedion's role in establishing the city's place in the history of the modern age, see David Van Zanten, "Chicago in Architectural History," in Elisabeth Blair Mac-Dougall, ed., *The Architectural Historian in America*, Studies in the History of Art 35 (Washington, D.C.: Center for Advanced Study in the Visual Arts, National Gallery of Art, 1990), pp. 91–99. Giedion explored the Chicago theme during his appointment as Charles Eliot Norton Professor of Poetry at Harvard University during the 1938–39 academic year. See Eduard F. Sekler, "Sigfried Giedion at Harvard University," in Mac-Dougall, ed., *The Architectural Historian in America*, pp. 265–73. More recently, these ideas have been examined by William Cronon in *Nature's Metropolis*.

[14] Robert Higgs, "Cities and Yankee Ingenuity, 1870–1920," in Kenneth T. Jackson and Stanley K. Schultz, eds., *Cities in American History* (New York: Knopf, 1972), pp. 16–22.

[15] Lincoln Steffens, *The Autobiography of Lincoln Steffens* (New York: Harcourt, Brace, and World, 1931), Vol. 2, p. 428.

[16] For an overview of such competition, see Carl Abbott, *Boosters and Businessmen: Popular Economic Thought and Urban Growth in the Antebellum Middle West* (Westport, Conn.: Greenwood, 1981).

[17] By contrast, St. Louis's leaders and their Southern supporters sustained a quaint faith in the advantage of riverboat transport while dividing their affiliations during the Civil War between those who sided with traditional partners in the breakaway Southern states and those who opposed slavery. Wyatt Winton Belcher, "The Economic Rivalry between St. Louis and Chicago, 1850–1880" (Ph.D. diss., Columbia University, 1947).

[18] Ibid., p. 185.   [19] Ibid., pp. 201–6.

Chicago's greatest economic achievements brought together commodities and finance, as local financiers invented unprecedented means for turning physical products into mobile monetary credits. As with Moscow and Osaka, Chicago drew on its role as a transportation axis to expand its economic power.[20] The city led the way in the use of such technological innovations as balloon-frame—and later, steel-skeleton—construction, mass electrification, grain storage and transport, as well as industrial food-processing technologies.[21] Chicago's magnates were more resourceful and more willing to pursue new industries than many of their East Coast counterparts.[22]

THE PEOPLING OF CHICAGO

Like many other American cities of the period, Chicago strove to become a home to the new urban middle class.[23] The city had gotten off to a good start in achieving this goal by initially attracting settlers with a higher literacy rate than did other Western cities.[24]

Chicagoland quickly embraced a hodgepodge of large worker and immigrant communities.[25] Chicago justly earned its reputation for brutal

[20] Chicago had surpassed Philadelphia to move into second place on population tables by the 1890 census. Gilbert, *Perfect Cities*, p. 16.

[21] Concerning the balloon-frame revolution in home construction, see Giedion, *Space, Time, and Architecture*, pp. 345–53; Miller, *City of the Century*, pp. 81–87; and Clay Lancaster, *The American Bungalow, 1880–1930* (New York: Abbeville, 1985), pp. 97–108. On skyscraper and steel-frame construction, see Frank A. Randall, *History of the Development of Building Construction in Chicago* (Urbana: University of Illinois Press, 1949); and Miller, *City of the Century*, pp. 300–377. On mass electrification, see Harold L. Platt, *The Electric City: Energy and the Growth of the Chicago Area, 1880–1930* (Chicago: University of Chicago Press, 1991). On food processing, see Louise Carroll Wade, *Chicago's Pride: The Stockyards, Packingtown, and Environs in the Nineteenth Century* (Urbana: University of Illinois Press, 1987); as well as Miller's discussions of both the introduction of grain elevators and the establishment of fully automated stockyards, in *City of the Century*, pp. 106–9, 198–224.

[22] Frederic Cople Jaher, *The Urban Establishment: Upper Strata in Boston, New York, Charleston, Chicago, and Los Angeles* (Urbana: University of Illinois Press, 1982), p. 491. More personal portraits of leading Chicago entrepreneurs may be found in Miller, *City of the Century*. See, for example, his brief biographical sketches of commercial modernizers William Butler Ogden (pp. 73–76), Cyrus Hall McCormick (pp. 103–6); Gustavus Franklin Swift (pp. 205–11); Philip Danforth Armour (pp. 211–16); and Potter Palmer (pp. 137–41).

[23] Chicago was particularly attractive to the offspring of merchants and professionals. See Schultz, "The Businessman's Role," pp. 1–15.

[24] Jaher, *The Urban Establishment*, p. 466.

[25] A point explored in Bessie Louise Pierce, *A History of Chicago*, Vol. 3: *The Rise of a Modern City, 1871–1893* (Chicago: University of Chicago Press, 1957), pp. 20–63. More recent historiography has tended to challenge the linkage of ethnicity and ecology in that all pre-automotive neighborhoods were less impenetrable than sometimes assumed, a point made in Kathleen Neils Conzen, "Immigrants, Immigrant Neighborhoods, and Ethnic Identity: Historical Issues," *Journal of American History* 66, no. 3

labor relations.[26] The city was the site of heated strikes during the 1870s, the well-publicized anarchist bombing of the 1886 Haymarket affair, the infamous Pullman strike of 1894, and a dramatic peaceful work stoppage in the stockyards throughout the summer of 1905.[27] As elsewhere in America, the politics of class frequently became subsumed by the politics of urban space and community, with the quest for social segregation simultaneously deconcentrating and suburbanizing the city.[28] Segregation increasingly involved questions of race as well as class.

Chicago's vigorous African-American community began to take shape during these same years. Race relations had remained relatively tranquil

(1979), pp. 603–15. Chicago's ethnic variety was nonetheless real, as may be attested to by any number of ethnic and neighborhood studies of the city during this era. See, for example, Florian Znaniecki and William I. Thomas, *The Polish Peasant in Europe and America*, ed. and abridged Eli Zaretsky (Urbana: University of Illinois Press, 1984); Humbert S. Nelli, *Italians in Chicago, 1880–1930: A Study in Ethnic Mobility* (Oxford, U.K.: Oxford University Press, 1970); or Glen E. Holt and Dominic A. Pacyga, *Chicago: A Historical Guide to the Neighborhoods: The Loop and South Side* (Chicago: Chicago Historical Society, 1979).

[26] As Carl Smith argues persuasively, Chicago's labor strife of the period, together with the catastrophic Great Fire, helped define an American view of the city—a creation of "civilization and progress"—as being under constant threat from disruption and disaster. Chicago's stormy labor relations were thus national as well as local phenomena. The image of a Chicago seething with social unrest and apocalyptic danger combined with American rural nostalgia to strengthen a pronounced anti-urban strain in the national culture. For a discussion of this process, see Carl Smith, *Urban Disorder and the Shape of Belief: The Great Chicago Fire, the Haymarket Bomb, and the Model Town of Pullman* (Chicago: University of Chicago Press, 1995).

[27] Concerning the general significance of labor conflict for Chicago's political culture, see Maureen A. Flanagan, *Charter Reform in Chicago* (Carbondale: Southern Illinois University Press, 1987), pp. 29–33. On the great railroad strikes of the 1870s, see Richard Schneirov, "Chicago's Great Upheaval of 1877," *Chicago History* 9, no. 1 (Spring 1980), pp. 2–17; and Shelton Stromquist, *A Generation of Boomers: The Pattern of Railroad Labor Conflict in Nineteenth-Century America* (Urbana: University of Illinois Press, 1987). Concerning the Haymarket affair, see Paul Avrich's definitive *The Haymarket Tragedy* (Princeton: Princeton University Press, 1984); as well as Miller, *City of the Century*, pp. 468–82; Henry David, *The History of the Haymarket Affair* (New York: Farrar and Rinehart, 1936); Bruce C. Nelson, *Beyond the Martyrs: A Social History of Chicago's Anarchists, 1870–1900* (New Brunswick, N.J.: Rutgers University Press, 1988), pp. 175–223; and Smith, *Urban Disorder*, pp. 99–174. On the Pullman strike, see Smith, *Urban Disorder*, pp. 175–270; Stanley Buder, *Pullman: An Experiment in Industrial Order and Community Planning, 1880–1930* (Oxford, U.K.: Oxford University Press, 1967), pp. 147–204; and Almont Lindsey, *The Pullman Strike: The Story of a Unique Experiment and of a Great Labor Upheaval* (Chicago: University of Chicago, 1942). On the stockyard strike, see Jane Addams, *Twenty Years at Hull-House* (1910; reprint, New York: New American Library, 1961), p. 164. Concerning a major stockyard work stoppage the previous summer, see Jane Addams, "Problems of Municipal Administration," *American Journal of Sociology* 10, no. 4 (January 1905), pp. 425–555: 433–36; and Robert A. Slayton, *Back of the Yards: The Making of a Local Democracy* (Chicago: University of Chicago Press, 1986), pp. 92–94.

[28] Ira Katznelson, *City Trenches: Urban Politics and the Patterning of Class in the United States* (New York: Pantheon, 1981). For further discussion of singularly American notions of urban space, see Rybczynski, *City Life*.

throughout the late nineteenth century.[29] This relative calm would change with the onset of the Great Migration of black Southerners to the industrial North during the 1910s and 1920s.

James R. Grossman's magisterial *Land of Hope* chronicles the experiences of Chicago's African-American migrants, who had ridden the Illinois Central railroad up from the Mississippi Delta states "to secure a foothold in the Northern industrial economy."[30] In the words of Paul Louis Street, "obtaining even one of the worst jobs in the 'Hellish' stockyards could seem a profoundly liberating experience for the black migrant."[31]

Chicago's African-American community more than doubled in size during in the years 1910–19.[32] African-American migrants arriving from Louisiana, Mississippi, Alabama, Arkansas, and Texas brought a new vitality to Chicago that transformed the local culture.[33] The first African-American Chicago City Council alderman—Oscar de Priest—was elected from the Second Ward in 1917.[34] The "robust, gregarious, flamboyant, and tempestuous" de Priest would go on to serve in the U.S. House of Representatives.[35]

De Priest's constituents were becoming steadily more segregated by race. Arriving Southern blacks poured into a three-mile-long, quarter-mile-wide corridor, surrounded by rail lines, known as the "Black Belt."[36] Enforced by white violence and connivance, Chicago's racial divide poisoned every aspect of local life. Race would replace ethnicity and class

[29] Michael Wallace Homel, "Negroes in the Chicago Public Schools, 1910–1941" (Ph.D. diss., University of Chicago, 1971).

[30] James R. Grossman, *Land of Hope: Chicago, Black Southerners, and the Great Migration* (Chicago: University of Chicago Press, 1989), p. 5.

[31] Paul Louis Street, "Working in the Yards: A History of Class Relations in Chicago's Meatpacking Industry, 1886–1943" (Ph.D. diss., State University of New York at Binghamton, 1993), p. 280.

[32] The number of the city's residents of African heritage grew from 44,103 to 109,458 during the decade 1910–19. Charles Russell Branham, "The Transformation of Black Political Leadership in Chicago, 1864–1942" (Ph.D. diss., University of Chicago, 1981), p. 16. The percentage of blacks in the overall Chicago population jumped from 1.2 percent in 1890 to 2.0 percent in 1910, to 4.1 percent in 1920. Paul Kleppner, *Chicago Divided: The Making of a Black Mayor* (DeKalb: Northern Illinois University Press, 1985), p. 17.

[33] For a discussion of the cultural impact of African Americans in Chicago during this period, see William Howland Kenney, *Chicago Jazz: A Cultural History, 1904–1930* (Oxford, U.K.: Oxford University Press, 1993).

[34] Branham, "The Transformation of Black Political Leadership," p. 64.

[35] Ibid., p. 94. Concerning de Priest's subsequent career, see ibid., pp. 94–140 and 240–92.

[36] By late in the decade 1910–19, more than nine out of ten black Chicagoans lived in areas that were more than 80 percent African American. Thomas Lee Philpott, *The Slum and the Ghetto: Neighborhood Deterioration and Middle-Class Reform, Chicago, 1880–1930* (Oxford, U.K.: Oxford University Press, 1978), pp. 141–47.

as Chicago's defining social and political issue following an especially ugly race riot during the summer of 1919, an event that provides a natural closing date for this particular study.[37]

Foreign-born immigrants constituted perhaps the most visible component of the local scene during the period under consideration.[38] Chicago remained a fundamentally German and Irish town throughout much of the period.[39] The city was home to more Poles, Swedes, Czechs, Dutch, Danes, Norwegians, Croats, Slovaks, Lithuanians, and Greeks than any other American city.[40]

Gilded Age Chicago was thus very much the sort of technologically innovative city described by Peter Hall as he sought to establish why particular places at particular moments in time emerge as exceptionally creative. Writing in his landmark study, *Cities in Civilization*, Hall sets down a set of conditions that precisely describe Chicago of this era. Inventive entrepreneurs, he writes,

may be found everywhere, but they are much more likely to make their break-throughs in certain kinds of regions. These regions are characterized ... by a set of developed social and cultural structures favorable to conceptual advances. They may be old-established, cosmopolitan, liberal metropolitan cities, but are often emerging city regions which serve as entrepôts between the already-developed world and a frontier region beyond it. Their economies are expanding rapidly through imports of goods from that developed world; and they have a high rate of immigration predominantly of young people, who are highly experimental and untraditional in their outlook. They have strong but often very informal structures for the exchange of technical knowledge and conceptual ideas. Barriers to the diffusion of innovation are so low as to be almost non-existent; there is a constant search for the novel. Levels of synergy, not only between like-minded individuals but also between quite disparate socio-economic-cultural groups are very high; this is the archetype of an open society.[41]

---

[37] For further discussion of the 1919 riots, see ibid., pp. 170–80, as well as the important works by William M. Tuttle, Jr., such as *Race Riot: Chicago in the Red Summer of 1919* (New York: Atheneum, 1970); and "Contested Neighborhoods and Racial Violence: Chicago in 1919: A Case Study," in Jackson and Schultz, eds., *Cities in American History*, pp. 232–48.

[38] By 1893, almost 41 percent of the city's population had been born abroad, while nearly as many residents were the offspring of parents who themselves had been born outside the United States. Flanagan, *Charter Reform*, p. 28. Chicago during this period was more diverse than were 39 states in 1960. Kleppner, *Chicago Divided*, pp. 17–18.

[39] Chicagoans of German heritage, for example, accounted for 20 percent of the city's population in 1860 and 15 percent in 1890, before dropping below 5 percent by 1910. Andrew Jacke Townsend, "The Germans of Chicago" (Ph.D. diss., University of Chicago, 1927), p. 6.

[40] For a discussion of the importance of ethnic communities in Chicago electoral politics of the period, see Claudius O. Johnson, *Carter Henry Harrison I: Political Leader* (Chicago: University of Chicago Press, 1928), pp. 189–96, 292–93.

[41] Peter Hall, *Cities in Civilization* (New York: Pantheon, 1998), p. 302.

NEIGHBORHOODS AND HOMES

Discussions of Chicago's evolution during the period under review must begin on October 8, 1871, with the conflagration that destroyed more than two thousand acres of densely built urban land in a swath four miles long and an average of three-quarters of a mile wide.[42] In the sort of tally that seems always to define such disasters, around 300 Chicagoans died in the fire and its aftermath; almost 100,000 were left homeless; and nearly 18,000 buildings were destroyed, with property damage approaching $200,000,000 (a third of the city's total valuation at the time).[43] Much of this destruction occurred north of the Chicago River, where neighborhoods suffered virtually complete destruction.[44] Subsequent ordinances prohibiting wooden-frame structures within certain areas of the city dramatically altered how the growing metropolis looked and felt to inhabitants and visitors alike.[45]

The Great Fire became Chicago's defining moment.[46] The city about which this study speaks bore the indelible psychological, political, social, and physical imprint of the conflagration.[47] It made possible many of the city's greatest achievements—especially in architecture and urban design—while underscoring the impermanence of human endeavor for more than a generation of Chicagoans.

The city's various ethnic groups lived in tightly knit, highly congested clusters around neighborhood centers spread along major transportation routes.[48] Individuals were far from immobile, even as their neighborhoods tended to remain home to largely one ethnic community over time.[49] At the center of neighborhood life stood the appropriate church,

[42] Smith, *Urban Disorder*, pp. 19–22. For a description of the actual fire, see Robert Comie, *The Great Fire* (New York: McGraw-Hill, 1958); as well as Miller, *City of the Century*, pp. 143–71.

[43] Smith, *Urban Disorder*, p. 22.

[44] Karen Sawislak, *Smoldering City: Chicagoans and the Great Fire, 1871–1874* (Chicago: University of Chicago Press, 1995), p. 29.

[45] Of the 13,800 prefire structures in the North Division—an area of expensive lakeside homes and a great mass of worker cottages, storefronts, small factories, churches, schools, and saloons—only 500 remained intact. An astonishing 74,450 people, one-fourth of the city's population, were left without shelter on the North Side alone. Perry R. Duis, *Chicago: Creating New Traditions* (Chicago: Chicago Historical Society, 1976), p. 14.

[46] A point explored in depth in Ross Miller, *American Apocalypse: The Great Fire and the Myth of Chicago* (Chicago: University of Chicago Press, 1990); and Sawislak, *Smoldering City*.

[47] Smith, *Urban Disorder*, pp. 19–98.

[48] Edith Abbott, *The Tenements of Chicago, 1908–1935* (Chicago: University of Chicago Press, 1936), pp. 20–22.

[49] Odd S. Lovoll, *A Century of Urban Life: The Norwegians in Chicago before 1930* (Northfield, Minn.: Norwegian-American Historical Association, 1988), p. 149.

5. Chicago, 1872, one year after the Great Fire. Joshua Smith for the Librarian of Congress. Library of Congress, Prints and Photographs Division, LC-USZ62-12313.

a school, and—much to the delight of 1893 Russian visitor Nikolai Pliskii—several saloons and beer halls.[50]

Long rows of old frame houses—rather than the aesthetic accomplishments of Chicago School architects—defined the streetscape and daily reality of a preponderance of city residents.[51] Edith Abbott, a pioneering figure with the University of Chicago's estimable School of Social Service Administration, would report in 1936 that "Chicago remains a city of one-family houses and small tenement buildings."[52] This city of one-, two-, and three-story tenements was dominated by narrow (25-foot-wide) wooden-frame buildings, each containing a couple of apartments—rarely more than three—and owned by an absentee landlord.[53]

Robert Hunter had sounded such themes in the report of a blue-ribbon commission's survey of tenement conditions during the summer of 1900. Hunter and five other prominent Chicagoans—Anita McCormick Blaine, Jane Addams, Caroline McCormick, L. V. LeMoyne, and Ernest P. Bicknell—convened by the City Homes Association oversaw one of the first major reviews of the city's slum conditions that made use of social science methodology. Hunter and his colleagues' *Tenement Conditions in Chicago* set the tone for much of social research to follow, including that of Abbott and her co-workers.[54] Hunter argued that controlling the evils of overcrowding, defective plumbing, and absentee slumlords would help the city curb social pathology and disease.[55]

---

[50] Pliskii evidently became an aficionado of Chicago's saloon culture, urging his fellow countrymen to drop by a neighborhood pub after a hard day at the World's Fair. Nikolai Pliskii, *Podrobnyi putevoditel' na Vsemirnuiu Kolumbovu vystavku v Chikago 1893ogo goda* (St. Petersburg: Stefanov i Kachka, 1893), p. 75.

[51] Abbott, *The Tenements of Chicago*, pp. 20–22.

[52] Ibid., p. 183.

[53] Abbott reports on the findings of a twenty-five-year study of tenement conditions covering 151 city blocks in widely separated neighborhoods canvassed on a house-to-house basis, including 18,225 apartments and single-family dwellings in all (ibid., p. x). Of these buildings, 59.7 percent were wood-frame, and another 8.7 percent were a combination of brick and frame (pp. 184–89); 22.8 percent were single-story "cottage type" structures, 58.9 percent were two-story buildings, and another 16.1 percent contained three floors (p. 199); 25.3 percent contained a single apartment or dwelling unit, 33.1 percent two units, and 16.1 percent three apartments (p. 202); nearly half of the apartments contained four rooms (48.1 percent), as opposed to 16.2 percent with three rooms, and another 13.3 percent with five rooms (p. 244). Homeownership for Chicago as a whole—including both the tenements surveyed by Abbott and her colleagues and more upscale dwellings—was 28.7 percent in 1890, 25.1 percent in 1900, 26.2 percent in 1910, and 27.0 percent in 1920 (p. 363).

[54] Robert Hunter, *Tenement Conditions in Chicago: Report of the Investigating Committee of the City Homes Association* (Chicago: City Homes Association, 1901).

[55] Ibid., pp. 1–20.

Hunter asserted the primacy of economic considerations in having produced Chicago's horrific housing conditions. Reviewing materials gathered in three discrete immigrant neighborhoods—one predominantly Polish, a second Jewish, and the third Italian—the City Homes Association group defined the housing question as one of profit maximization.[56] Landlords sought the highest possible return from their building lots, while the overcrowding of each room and unit became a means for residents to reduce the rent paid by each. This latter strategy had the perverse effect, Hunter feared, of encouraging the "thrifty and industrious of the working class"—the very hope for Chicago's future—to double up in substandard housing.[57]

Built on "shoe-string" lots typically 100 or 125 feet deep, Chicago's tenements left little room for yards and access to outside light or fresh air.[58] As Hunter and his colleagues observed, the "rear tenement" presented a particularly pernicious problem.[59] In order to maximize return on a building lot, landlords frequently moved older wooden homes to the back of their property and constructed a larger, sometimes brick tenement to the front.[60] Hygiene problems were exacerbated, as most housing for the poor of the period had no indoor toilet facilities, and the rear tenements almost never had facilities. "Cleanliness," Hunter and his colleagues concluded, "is almost a luxury in Chicago and a high price is paid for it."[61]

By World War I, a vast majority of Chicago's tenements were serviced by electricity, while more than half had shared bath and toilet facilities, the latter frequently being in outbuildings.[62] Shoddy construction, poor maintenance, overcrowding, and severely limited light and fresh air aroused frequent demands for regulation, with major city laws coming into existence in 1879–81. The city's first housing inspections began at that time. More regulation followed in 1902 with the passage of the city's first comprehensive housing ordinance.[63] Yet tenement housing would

---

[56] Ibid., pp. 21–24.   [57] Ibid., p. 51.

[58] Abbott, *The Tenements of Chicago*, pp. 171–74. Despite legislation passed in 1910 which decreed that no existing house could be altered, or new home built, that occupied more than 75 percent of a lot, or 90 percent of a corner lot, 26.3 percent of the buildings included in the University of Chicago survey covered 70 percent or more of the land available on their lot, while another 30.1 percent covered between 50 percent and 70 percent of their building area. Ibid., pp. 173–74.

[59] Hunter, *Tenement Conditions*, pp. 36–41.

[60] Ibid., p. 75.   [61] Ibid., p. 111.

[62] Abbott, *The Tenements of Chicago*, p. 206.

[63] These laws were frequently ignored. Several different departments regulated the enforcement of those laws that did exist, with each office being burdened with more duties than resources permitted it to fulfill. See Hunter, *Tenement Conditions*, pp. 161–63.

remain "a seemingly permanent problem despite years of effort to improve it."[64]

A LABORATORY OF DIFFERENT CULTURES

Housing was but one issue on the local reform agenda. Chicago's socio-economic and ethnic diversity led to a very fragmented political system in which desperate groups were forced to cooperate with one another in order to secure control of valuable patronage networks.[65] F. Herbert Stead captured this diversity in an 1893 article for the popular *Review of Reviews* when he wrote, "Chicago is one vast crucible, wherein is being poured ingredients from all races, and one looks with wonder to see what strange amalgam promises to result."[66]

Chicago during this era became the scene of endless factional struggles within parties embedded in a highly decentralized political system in which no single group held a firm grip on power.[67] Its volatile pluralism made the city, in the words of Garry Wills nearly a century later, "a perfect laboratory of different cultures crammed into narrow confines. Extreme wealth daintily picked its way through poverty and filth."[68] As Wills points out, it is more than understandable that the city's great university would become a world-recognized innovator in the social study of the city.[69]

Many American cities of the period were marked by "head-on collisions of different life-styles" among immigrants from southern and eastern Europe and earlier arrivals.[70] Brutal partisan conflict took place

---

[64] Abbott, *The Tenements of Chicago*, p. ix.
[65] Donald S. Bradley and Mayer N. Zald, "From Commercial Elite to Political Administrator: The Recruitment of the Mayors of Chicago," *American Journal of Sociology* 71: 2 (September 1965) pp. 153–67; and Kleppner, *Chicago Divided*, p. 22.
[66] F. Herbert Stead, "The Civic Life of Chicago," *Review of Reviews* 8 (1893), pp. 93–96.
[67] Steven J. Diner, *A City and Its Universities: Public Policy in Chicago, 1892–1919* (Chapel Hill: University of North Carolina Press, 1980), p. 54.
[68] Garry Wills, "Sons and Daughters of Chicago," *New York Review of Books,* June 9, 1994, pp. 52–59: 52.
[69] Ibid. Although, as Jane Addams would observe, settlement houses rather than universities led the way in sponsoring fact-finding surveys in many American cities. Jane Addams, *The Second Twenty Years at Hull-House: September 1909 to September 1929, with a Record of a Growing World Consciousness* (New York: Macmillan, 1930), p. 405. For further discussion of the emergence of urban social science in Chicago see John D. Fairfield, *The Mysteries of the Great City: The Politics of Urban Design, 1877–1937* (Columbus: Ohio State University Press, 1993), pp. 158–224; and Carla Cappetti, *Writing Chicago: Modernism, Ethnography, and the Novel* (New York: Columbia University Press, 1993), pp. 20–72.
[70] Gunthar Paul Barth, *City People: The Rise of Modern City Culture in Nineteenth-Century America* (Oxford, U.K.: Oxford University Press, 1980), p. 15; and Kleppner, *Chicago Divided*, pp. 17–18.

throughout the early years of the twentieth century, as ethnic groups lined up behind political parties largely in accord with religious affiliation. Chicago's various Roman Catholic immigrant groups emerged as the Democratic Party's mainstays in a pattern that would survive for decades.[71]

Chicago's particular laboratory of cultures was supported by an economy that expanded and diversified with unprecedented rapidity. The city's leaders won intense battles to place themselves at the focal point of a continental transportation system merging rail and water transportation routes. That primacy endowed Chicago with unrivaled advantages for trading the grain, lumber, and livestock that created the American Midwest's swelling wealth.[72] Local entrepreneurs quickly adopted new technologies—including grain elevators, harvesting combines, and the most efficient slaughtering facilities ever known—to speed produce along. Chicago had no peer as a transfer market for agricultural products.[73]

Local entrepreneurs were not satisfied with dominating trade and moved quickly toward manufacturing the machines that hastened natural resource exploitation and transportation. By 1890, the city had become—thanks to plants such as Cyrus McCormick's famous reaper works—the nation's second manufacturing center, surpassed only by New York in terms of the gross value of the products it produced.[74] McCormick and his colleagues were inventing entire new ways of life while devising forward-looking machinery, as evident in the agricultural revolution the reaper wrought around the world.[75] McCormick had chosen Chicago over other possible locations because the city's uncommon transportation facilities enabled him to bring together labor, raw materials, and customers with ease.[76]

Chicago traders earned over $80 million from the lumber business in 1888. Such turnover was itself minuscule in comparison to the

---

[71] Kleppner, *Chicago Divided*, p. 29.

[72] This account is based on Cronon, *Nature's Metropolis*, and Pierce, *A History of Chicago*, Vol. 3, pp. 64–107.

[73] Pierce, *A History of Chicago*, Vol. 3, p. 67.

[74] Ibid., p. 65. Concerning McCormick's plants, see William T. Hutchinson, *Cyrus Hall McCormick*, Vol. 1, *Seed-Time, 1809–1856* (New York: Century, 1930); and William T. Hutchinson, *Cyrus Hall McCormick*, Vol. 2, *Harvest, 1856–1884* (New York: D. Appleton-Century, 1935); as well as McCormick's own *The Century of the Reaper* (Boston: Houghton Mifflin, 1931).

[75] Herbert N. Casson, *Cyrus Hall McCormick: His Life and Work* (Chicago: A. C. McClurg, 1909), pp. 37–53.

[76] Ibid., p. 74.

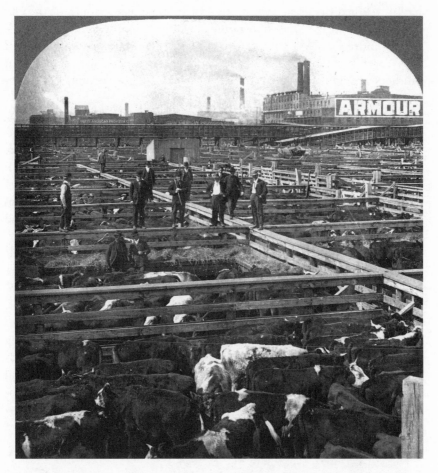

6. Stereograph of the Chicago stockyards, c.1909. Kalley and Chadwick. Library of Congress, Prints and Photographs Division, LC-USZ62-097324.

$195 million in earnings from local slaughterhouses and packing facilities in 1890 alone.[77] Chicago gained a worldwide reputation as a stockyard and smokestack town.[78] Epithets such as "Porkopolis," "Hogbutcher to the World," and "the great bovine city" were well deserved.[79] Three million animals per year were being delivered to their deaths by 1870, just five years after the railroads and packing firms

---

[77] Pierce, *A History of Chicago,* Vol. 3, pp. 103, 108–9.
[78] Kleppner, *Chicago Divided,* p. 15.
[79] Holt and Pacyga, *Chicago: The Loop and South Side,* pp. 28–37, 120–31.

had developed the great Union Stockyard immediately south of the city limits.[80] Nearly five times that number would be "processed" in 1909—adding more than $323 million to the local economy that year.[81] Great "dis"assembly lines awaited the arriving livestock, with immigrant workers providing the final ingredient for this highly profitable slaughtering field.[82]

All told, the Union Stockyard took in nearly $10 billion in income during its first half-century of operation.[83] The world had never seen anything quite like it, and the stockyard became an instant tourist attraction for those with the stomach to witness the carnage. Waste control and pollution became a perennial problem for this most profitable of Chicago's many commercial districts.[84] Large-scale assembly-line production was born in the Chicago shops of the Armours, the Swifts, and the Morrises, rather than in Henry Ford's Detroit.[85]

Chicago's meat barons demanded new rail cars to transport their goods more quickly to new markets, thereby prompting the manufacture in Chicago of the world's first refrigerated rail cars.[86] Local manufacturers and inventors built better rail cars for people as well as for pigs. George M. Pullman's "palace" rail cars established the world standard for luxury rail stock.[87] All sorts of the essentials of daily life were being manufactured for local consumption as well—ranging from washbowls and bathtubs to books, clothes, boots, and shoes—thereby creating North America's most diverse, balanced, and rapidly expanding manufacturing base.[88]

---

[80] Wade, *Chicago's Pride*, pp. 47–60; Stephen Longstreet, *Chicago, 1860–1919* (New York: David McKay, 1973), pp. 56–60.

[81] George Edward Plumbe, *Chicago: Its Natural Advantages as an Industrial and Commercial Center and Market* (Chicago: Civic-Industrial Committee of the Chicago Association of Commerce, 1910), p. 22.

[82] Wade, *Chicago's Pride*, pp. 62–78, 218–40; Miller, *City of the Century*, pp. 198–224.

[83] This estimate is based on data contained in Plumbe, *Chicago: Its Natural Advantages*, p. 22.

[84] Wade, *Chicago's Pride*, pp. 352–69; Charles J. Bushnell, "The Social Problem at the Chicago Stock Yards" (Ph.D. diss., University of Chicago), 1902.

[85] A point made forcefully by James R. Barrett, *Work and Community in the Jungle: Chicago's Packinghouse Workers, 1894–1922* (Urbana: University of Illinois Press, 1987), p. 20. On the special role of Gustavus Swift in these developments, see Glenn Porter, *The Rise of Big Business, 1860–1910* (Arlington Heights, Ill.: Harlan Davidson, 1973), pp. 47–50; on Philip Armour's role, see Arthur Warren, "Philip D. Armour: His Manner of Life, His Immense Enterprises in Trade and Philanthropy," *McClure's Magazine* 2 (December 1893–May 1894), pp. 260–80, for a contemporary account.

[86] Pierce, *A History of Chicago*, Vol. 3, pp. 117–18; Longstreet, *Chicago, 1860–1919*, pp. 71–76; J. Ogden Armour, *The Packers, the Private Car Lines, and the People* (Philadelphia: Henry Altemus, 1906), p. 25.

[87] Pierce, *A History of Chicago*, Vol. 3, pp. 158–61.

[88] Ibid., pp. 161–77.

Chicagoans revolutionized retail trade, as such companies as Sears and Montgomery Ward introduced mail-order shopping on a mass scale.[89] Marshall Field, Carson Pirie & Co., among others, joined the late-nineteenth-century department-store boom that had originated in Paris and New York. Chicago's own retail experience, in turn, spread far and wide. Marshall Field's protégé H. Gordon Selfridge, for example, would revolutionize the carriage trade in distant London.[90] Local retailers quickly perfected the tenets of "scientific advertising," which inexorably extended their reach throughout the continent.[91] The city's domestic design magazine *House Beautiful*, which began publication in December 1896, "became the arbiter of good taste in middle class homes across the nation."[92] A distinguished furniture industry developed at this time as well.[93]

The rise of Chicago was more or less parallel to the ascendancy of the American corporation. Large business organizations emerged during the late nineteenth century as regional commercial networks were stitched into a national market.[94] The railroads—financed by East Coast money and run through networks of middle managers—were among the first nationally integrated corporations in the United States.[95] Individual communities became nodes in a larger, transcontinental economic system staffed by white-collar workers—both mid-level managers and clerical workers. Public and private bureaucracies swelled to previously unimagined size, turning major cities such as Chicago into centers for a new corporate middle class.[96] This new stratum of employees set the tone for American society and culture for much of the twentieth century. Chicago, a leading location for corporate headquarters and regional offices, became an important haven for the new business ethos. Tie-clad clerks competed for urban space with blood-spattered stockyard workers in one of the world's most complex and diverse metropolises.

[89] Ibid., pp. 184–91; as well as Alfred Dupont Chandler, Jr., *The Visible Hand: The Managerial Revolution in American Business* (Cambridge, Mass.: Harvard University Press, 1977), pp. 217–31. Portraits of store founders Aaron Montgomery Ward and Richard Warren Sears may be found in Miller, *City of the Century*, pp. 244–53. Readers may also wish to refer to Nina Brown Baker's popularizing biography, *Big Catalogue: The Life of Aaron Montgomery Ward* (New York: Harcourt, Brace, 1956).
[90] Wayne Andrews, *Battle for Chicago* (New York: Harcourt and Brace, 1946), pp. 208–9.
[91] Duis, *Chicago: Creating New Traditions*, pp. 102–17.
[92] Ibid., p. 117.
[93] Sharon Darling, *Chicago Furniture: Art, Craft, and Industry, 1833–1983* (New York: Norton, 1984), pp. 37–268.
[94] This process of corporate consolidation is explored in Olivier Zunz, *Making America Corporate, 1870–1920* (Chicago: University of Chicago Press, 1990); as well as in Chandler, *The Visible Hand*.
[95] Zunz, *Making America Corporate*, pp. 37–66.
[96] Ibid., pp. 124–48.

PARADIGM OF AMERICAN CIVILIZATON

The great bovine town was becoming a major cultural center as well as an economic dynamo. Its writers—such as L. Frank Baum, Edgar Rice Burroughs, Theodore Dreiser, Upton Sinclair, Will Payne, and Ella Wheeler Wilcox—were leaders of American popular letters.[97] Its philosophers defined American pragmatism.[98] From Dorothy along the yellow brick road to Sister Carrie's discovery of urban realities, from the jungles of Tarzan to those of the South Side's stockyards, Chicagoans redefined the American written word.

Simultaneously, local business leaders of the generation that had fought the Civil War were establishing many of the city's leading cultural institutions during the 1880s and 1890s, including the Art Institute, the Newberry Library, the Chicago Symphony Orchestra, the Field Columbian Museum, the Crerar Library, and the second University of Chicago.[99] These great centers cut across a wide range of artistic and cultural fields, elevating Chicago beyond mere economic existence to the status of American icon.

Chicago combined America's rough-hewn exterior with its boisterous economic—and even social—inventiveness. The city became a focal point for aggressive reform "in virtually every area of local government and public policy, from city charters to public health, from urban planning to labor legislation, from crime control to public education."[100] Unlike continental Europe, Chicago's reform impulse found expression largely through nonstate entities. More than 2,500 men and women supported the work of at least one of some seventy reform groups and agencies between 1892 and 1919, yet only 215 of these Chicagoans participated in the activities of three or more organizations.[101]

The city's reform community was a diverse and only partially overlapping meld of distinct crusades that mobilized a variety of citizens from academic leaders (such as Edith Abbott, Sophonisba P. Breckinridge, John Dewey, Ernst Freund, William Rainey Harper, and Charles E. Merriam) and writers (Dreiser, Lewis, and Robert Herrick) through community organizers (Addams, Florence Kelley, and Ellen Gates Starr) and religious activists (such as William Thomas Stead and the Sisters of the

[97] Heise, *A Sampling of Chicago*, pp. 20–21.
[98] Ibid., pp. 21–22.
[99] Helen Lefkowitz Horowitz, *Culture and the City: Cultural Philanthropy in Chicago from the 1880s to 1917* (Lexington: University Press of Kentucky, 1976), pp. ix–x.
[100] Diner, *A City and Its Universities*, p. 56.
[101] Ibid., p. 56.

Good Shepherd). Chicago's dynamic reformism symbolized the era's "progressivism." Decades later, waves of Chicago academics would join Franklin Delano Roosevelt's "New Deal" in Washington.[102]

Chicago's place as exemplar of a new American civilization—as Oz—reached its apogee with the World's Columbian Exposition of 1893. Walter Benjamin's words about the Paris world's fairs are particularly apropos to the Chicago fair: "World exhibitions are the site of pilgrimage to the commodity fetish."[103] Commodity fetishes were camouflaged by the fair's famous "White City," a neoclassical precursor to today's Epcot Center.

The city had fought so hard with New York City and Washington, D.C., to win the honor of playing host to the fair that Richard Henry Dana of the *New York Sun* coined the sobriquet "the windy city" in trying to capture the "hot air" emanating from Chicago's boosters.[104] Russian correspondents reported home about the bitterness of the competition between first and second city for the privilege of hosting the exposition.[105] Planned and designed by a committee of some of the country's best-known architects under the direction of Daniel Burnham, the World's Columbian Exposition attempted to combine "the city's business values—faith in progress and pride in wealth and in Chicago's growth—and desire for European cultural forms."[106]

WHITE AND GRAY CITIES

The Columbian Exposition was the fifteenth "world's fair," and only the second to be held in the New World.[107] Unlike previous fairs, which had been limited to one or two main halls surrounded by pleasantly landscaped grounds, Chicago's boosters attempted nothing less than to construct an entirely new city parallel to that which had already risen

---

[102] Ibid., p. 176. For further discussion of Chicagoans in the New Deal, see ibid., pp. 176–85.

[103] Walter Benjamin, *Reflections: Essays, Aphorisms, Autobiographical Writings*, trans. Edmund Jephcott (New York: Harcourt Brace Jovanovich, 1978), p. 151.

[104] Sidney Appelbaum, *The Chicago World's Fair of 1893: A Photographic Record* (New York: Dover, 1980), p. 1.

[105] See, for example, Varvara MakGaigin's numerous "Letters from America" columns in *Severnyi Vestnik* throughout 1893, as well as the discussions of the meaning of Chicago in I. M. Veniukov, "Illinois i Chikago," *Nabliudatel'* 1893, no. 5 (May), pp. 257–72.

[106] Robert I. Goler, "Visions of a Better Chicago," in Susan E. Hirsch and Robert I. Goler, eds., *A City Comes of Age: Chicago in the 1890s* (Chicago: Chicago Historical Association, 1990), pp. 90–153: 96–97.

[107] David F. Burg, *Chicago's White City of 1893* (Lexington: University Press of Kentucky, 1976), p. xii.

7. Western view from the Liberal Arts Building of the World's Columbian Exposition, showing Wooded Island, Music Hall, Ferris Wheel, the Horticultural and Women's Buildings, and the dome of the California Building, Chicago, 1893. Photographer unknown. Library of Congress, Prints and Photographs Division, LC-USZ62-089689.

along Lake Michigan. The white hue of the buildings by day and the most extensive use of electrical lighting heretofore seen at night combined with symmetrically balanced classical design to proclaim a new civilization.[108] Yet promoters understood that more than high ideals would be necessary to hold the attention of the hoi polloi. They hired vaudeville impresario Sol Bloom to set up an adult amusement area—the Midway Plaisance—to ensure that visitors parted with sufficient numbers of greenbacks before returning to the real town outside the fairgrounds.[109]

The purposeful contrast between the stodgy yet pristine fairgrounds and the chaotic yet innovative city beyond its gates—and within the fairgrounds between the composed Central Court and the raunchy Midway Plaisance, as hidden from view as possible with George Washington Gale Ferris's gigantic wheel hovering overhead[110]—has sustained a century of high-minded cultural criticism, low-minded literature, and endless scholarly and architectural debates.[111] European visitors of the time were frequently unnerved by the immediate proximity of sacred and profane that accosted them wherever they turned, either at the fair or downtown in the Loop. Chicago in 1893 became, "for hundreds of British, French, and German visitors, an early encounter with tomorrow, an encounter analogous to entering a time warp."[112]

For all the aura of permanence that is still evident a century later in official photographer Charles D. Arnold's exposition images, the Chicago World's Fair was in reality little more than a collection of ramshackle, jerry-built temporary structures. Nearly the entire "White City"

---

[108] John P. Barrett, *Electricity at the Columbia Exposition, Including an Account of the Exhibits* (Chicago: R. R. Donnelley, 1894).

[109] Bloom was refreshingly candid about his contribution to the fair once he had replaced a befuddled Harvard ethnographer—a certain Professor Putnam—who had somehow thought that the "exhibits" along the Midway should instruct. Bloom quickly set out instead to "establish a successful venture in the field of entertainment." Sol Bloom, *The Autobiography of Sol Bloom* (New York: G. P. Putnam, 1948), p. 119.

[110] For a tame overview of the Midway Plaisance, see Miller, *American Apocalypse,* pp. 224–27. On the first Ferris Wheel, see Miller, *City of the Century,* pp. 496–97.

[111] See, for example, Duis, *Chicago: Creating New Traditions,* pp. 44–52; Gilbert, *Perfect Cities,* pp. 75–130; Miller, *American Apocalypse,* pp. 195–250; Carl S. Smith, *Chicago and the American Literary Imagination, 1880–1920* (Chicago: University of Chicago Press, 1984), pp. 140–49; Donald K. Hartman, ed., *Fairground Fiction: Detective Stories of the World's Columbian Exposition* (Kenmore, N.Y.: Motif, 1992); Julie K. Brown, *Contesting Images: Photography and the World's Columbian Exposition* (Tucson: University of Arizona Press, 1994); and R. Reid Badger, *The Great America Fair: The World's Columbian Exposition and American Culture* (Chicago: Nelson-Hall, 1979).

[112] Arnold Lewis, *An Early Encounter with Tomorrow: Europeans, Chicago's Loop, and the World's Columbian Exposition* (Urbana: University of Illinois Press, 1997), p. 4.

burned to the ground in a series of symbolic conflagrations during the harsh depression year that followed the fair's euphoria.[113] Nevertheless, the unrelenting commercial boosterism that prompted the exposition survived both the vagaries of flame and economic downturns.

Chicagoans increasingly turned to their own capital resources to finance their city's rapid growth. Produce exchanges—especially the Chicago Board of Trade's grain market—were among the most important in the world. Established in 1848 to bring order out of market chaos, the Board of Trade was joined by the Chicago Produce Exchange in 1874—which became the Chicago Butter and Egg Board in 1898 before finally emerging as today's powerful Chicago Mercantile Exchange in 1919—and the Midwest Stock Exchange in 1882 to preside over home-grown capital.[114] Major local banks soon followed.[115] Always a secondary capital market to New York, Chicago nonetheless became ever more self-sufficient in financing its extraordinary growth. An important real estate industry was institutionalized by the 1880s.[116] Following the pattern of Chicago entrepreneurs in many economic sectors, bankers and real estate firms revolutionized their activities by explicitly seeking to serve a burgeoning American middle class. Chicagoans perfected mortgages and other financial instruments that sustained the remarkable mass middle-class home-ownership market.[117] This economic vitality and diversity proved to be a strong magnet for new migrants.[118] Laborers flocked to the city to participate in its unprecedented prosperity, even as their actual lives paled in comparison to the Chicago dream.[119] Robert Herrick's description of a streetcar ride down Cottage Grove Avenue in his fair-era *The Web of Life* captures the reality of many Chicagoans' lives:

Block after block, mile after mile, it was the same thing. No other city on the globe could present quite this combination of tawdriness, slackness, dirt, vulgarity, which was Cottage Grove Avenue. India, the Spanish-American countries, might show something fouler as far as mere filth, but nothing so incomparably mean and long. The brick blocks, of many shades of grimy red and fawn color,

---

[113] Especially helpful collections of exposition photographs appeared in 1980 as interest in the White City began to reach a new crescendo that would peak with the fair's 1993 centennial. See Appelbaum, *The Chicago World's Fair*; and Brown, *Contesting Images*, pp. 67–78.

[114] Brief histories of these exchanges may be found in Bob Tamarkin, "Only the Market Knows," *Chicago Times Magazine* 1, no. 2 (November–December 1987), pp. 54–61: 58; and Jonathan Lurie, *The Chicago Board of Trade, 1859–1905: The Dynamics of Self-Regulation* (Urbana: University of Illinois Press, 1979).

[115] Pierce, *A History of Chicago*, Vol. 3, pp. 192–233.

[116] Ibid., p. 207.   [117] Ibid., pp. 207–10.

[118] Abbott, *Boosters and Businessmen*, p. 69.

[119] Pierce, *A History of Chicago*, Vol. 3, p. 240.

thin as paper, cheap as dishonest contractor and bad labor could make them, were bulging and lopping at every angle. Built by the half mile for a day's smartness, they were going to pieces rapidly. . . . Once and again the car jolted across intersection boulevards that presented some relief in the way of green grass and large, heavy fronted houses.[120]

It was at such crossroads that Chicago delineated what would come to be regarded by many as "modern" in the built environment.

ARCHITECTURE FIRMLY PLANTED ON THE GROUND

Postfire Chicago attracted the best of a generation of young architects at a time when unprecedented new construction technologies were coming on-line. The result was a distinctly American residential style—the Prairie School—and a perfection of a new commercial architecture—the skyscraper—that set the stage for the next century's architectural paradigms and debates.[121] Dankmar Adler, Solon Spencer Beman, Daniel Burnham, Henry Ives Cobb, William LeBaron Jenney, John Wellborn Root, Louis Henry Sullivan, and Frank Lloyd Wright are among the best-known American architects of their era.[122] Strikingly different in

---

[120] Robert Herrick, *The Web of Life* (New York: Macmillan, 1900), pp. 198–99. For a description of the "heavy fronted houses" of the rich, see John Drury, *Old Chicago Houses* (New York: Bonanza Books, 1941).

[121] For further discussion of the Chicago School in architecture, see Daniel Bluestone, *Constructing Chicago* (New Haven: Yale University Press, 1991); Carl W. Condit, *The Chicago School of Architecture: A History of Commercial and Public Building in the Chicago Area, 1875–1925* (Chicago: University of Chicago Press, 1964); and John Zukowsky, ed., *Chicago Architecture, 1872–1922: Birth of a Metropolis* (Chicago: Art Institute of Chicago, 1987).

[122] One helpful introduction to the relationships among all of these designers may be found in James F. O'Gorman, *Three American Architects: Richardson, Sullivan, and Wright, 1865–1915* (Chicago: University of Chicago Press, 1991). Also see Sibel Bozdogan Dostoglu, "Towards Professional Legitimacy and Power: An Inquiry into the Struggle, Achievements, and Dilemmas of the Architectural Profession through an Analysis of Chicago, 1871–1909" (Ph.D. diss., University of Pennsylvania, 1983); Wayne Andrews, *Architecture in Chicago and Mid-America: A Photographic History* (New York: Atheneum, 1968); Lewis Mumford, "Towards Modern Architecture," in Donald L. Miller, ed., *The Lewis Mumford Reader* (New York: Pantheon, 1986), pp. 49–72; as well as Donald L. Miller's discussion of skyscraper development in *City of the Century,* pp. 301–53.

Most of these architects outlived perhaps the most talented of their colleagues, Root, who died tragically young in January 1891 at the age of forty-one. For a discussion of Root's pivotal contribution to Chicago architecture, see Donald Hoffman, *The Architecture of John Wellborn Root* (Baltimore: Johns Hopkins University Press, 1973). Readers may also wish to refer to Andrews, *Architecture in Chicago,* pp. 40–43.

Root's demise in the view of many, including Columbian Exposition chronicler David F. Burg, "was a more significant factor in the fate that befell the Chicago school than was the World's Columbian Exposition. . . . Root's death deprived the Chicago movement of its most respected, most articulate, and most original architect." Burg, *Chicago's White City,* p. 306.

temperament and taste, all shared an appreciation of revolutionary design and the practical needs of their clients.[123] Together, these young architects and their commercial clients changed the course of American— and, arguably, international—building and design during the 1880s and 1890s.[124]

Daniel Burnham's grand 1909 Beaux Arts physical plan for the city was not sponsored by any government agency, as it might have been in Europe. Rather, the prestigious Commercial Club of Chicago paid for Burnham's work.[125] Sullivan and Adler's revolutionary opera house, the Auditorium Building—perhaps the highest aesthetic achievement of the era—was a speculative commercial project.[126] Chicago architects never tried to escape the realities of their fast-growing city; they were never isolated from corporate boardrooms, local politicos, or crowds in the street.[127]

The Chicago School defined urban commercial architecture for at least a century, yet the commissions its practitioners took on were not limited to downtown office blocks or urban industrial sites. Chicago emerged full-blown just as the railroads were prompting many thinkers—including William Lever, Ebenezer Howard, and Frederick Law Olmsted—to contemplate the possibility of ideal communities beyond the boundaries of wretched industrial towns.[128] Chicago and its environs witnessed the construction of many a suburban utopia, some of which were built for commercial gain, and others for more lofty ideals. The ultimately unsuccessful industrial new town of Pullman embodied many of the characteristics of both Chicago School pragmatism and garden-city utopianism.[129]

---

[123] Indeed, their clients were often as responsible as the architects for Chicago's innovative styles. See Miles L. Berger, *They Built Chicago: Entrepreneurs Who Shaped a Great City's Architecture* (Chicago: Bonus Books, 1992), pp. 23–194.

[124] Lewis Mumford, *Sticks and Stones: A Study of American Architecture and Civilization* (New York: Boni and Liveright, 1924).

[125] Commercial Club of Chicago, *The Plan of Chicago* (Chicago: Commercial Club of Chicago, 1909). For an interesting discussion of the Chicago plan's impact on subsequent regional planning initiatives, especially in New York, see David A. Johnson, *Planning the Great Metropolis: The 1929 Regional Plan of New York and Its Environs* (New York: E. and F. N. Spon, 1996), pp. 48–55. A somewhat self-serving review of the plan's accomplishments over a decade and a half may be found in Chicago Plan Commission, *The Plan of Chicago in 1925* (Chicago: Chicago Plan Commission, 1925).

[126] Miller, *City of the Century*, pp. 354–77.

[127] Duis, *Chicago: Creating New Traditions*, p. 19.

[128] Robert Fishman, *Bourgeois Utopias: The Rise and Fall of Suburbia* (New York: Basic Books, 1987).

[129] A useful overview of the Pullman story may be found in Buder, *Pullman*.

Built during the early 1880s just ten miles south of Chicago on the Illinois Central railroad, the company town for the Pullman Palace Car Company reflected the megalomaniacal dreams of the company's founder and president, George M. Pullman. Pullman's favorite architect, Solon Spencer Beman, designed a visually congenial industrial town for his master.[130] Beman's design gave physical expression to the widely shared conviction of the era that the family was the critical center of the social order.[131]

Far too much has been written about this failed experiment over the years to repeat here. Much of the discussion following the tragic Pullman strike of 1894 echoed the 1885 article of Richard Ely, who had visited Pullman on his honeymoon.[132]

Ely—a Johns Hopkins University economist at the time—wrote in the popular *Harper's New Monthly Magazine* that the town represented "social experimentation on a vast scale."[133] Pullman represented precisely the combination of aesthetic care and commercial practicality that is the mark of Chicago School architecture everywhere. Mr. Pullman was not alone among his peers in appreciating "the commercial value of beauty."[134]

Pullman and much of the other construction of the era advanced the interest of capital as much as that of beauty. Ely correctly perceived that therein lay the seeds of the experiment's failure: "The Pullman companies retain everything. No private individual owns today a square rod of ground or a single structure in the entire town. No organization, not even a church, can occupy any other than renter quarters. . . . Nobody regards Pullman as a real home and, in fact, it can scarcely be said that there are more than temporary residents at Pullman."[135] Indeed, "In looking over all the facts of the case the conclusion is unavoidable that the idea of Pullman is un-American."[136] Within less than a decade, the 1893–97 depression ensured that neither the respectable authorities nor the industrial-age serf inhabitants of Mr. Pullman's manor would be very pleased. Federal troops brought a bloody end to the Pullman strike that

---

[130] For a quick visual review of Pullman, see Andrews, *Architecture in Chicago*, pp. 34–35. On Berman's role, see Miller, *City of the Century*, pp. 224–40.

[131] Janice L. Reiff, "A Modern Lear and His Daughters: Gender in the Model Town of Pullman," *Journal of Urban History* 23, no. 3 (March 1997), pp. 316–41.

[132] Richard Ely, "Pullman: A Social Study," *Harper's New Monthly Magazine* 70 (February 1885), pp. 453–66. For a subsequent account of his honeymoon travels, see Ely's autobiography: Richard Theodore Ely, *Ground Under Our Feet: An Autobiography* (New York: Macmillan, 1938), pp. 166–71.

[133] Ely, "Pullman," p. 454.

[134] Ibid., p. 461.

[135] Ibid., pp. 462–63.

[136] Ibid., p. 464.

erupted in 1894 in the very "wealthy suburban town" Ely had visited just a decade before.[137]

Whether the Beaux Arts fairgrounds or the neo-Gothic university campus, the Prairie School homes of Oak Park or the commercial towers of the Loop, the bourgeois planned suburbs of Riverside or their proletarian counterparts at Pullman, Chicago architecture and its architects—like so much in their city—were about keeping one's feet planted firmly on the ground, about combining design and profit. The tall office building was made possible both by new building technologies and by new forms of business management that required seeming armies of white-collar workers.[138]

The skyscraper was a technological and organizational wonder to its very core. "Chicago Steel Skeleton Construction" revolutionized all sorts of building and design. As contemporary observer William Birkmire explained to readers in 1894, the skeleton-constructed building represented nothing less than "a new type of structure, which calls for principles entirely different from the old system of cast-iron fronts and cast-doweled columns with wooden girders."[139] Yet steel skeleton frames were not all that was innovative about Chicago's buildings. Skyscraper historian Carl Condit argues that the structures built in Chicago at the end of the nineteenth century were a consequence of an extraordinary change in construction technologies dating back to at least the eighteenth century.[140] Iron framing, wind bracing, watertight caisson foundations, fireproofing, power-operated elevators, central heating, modern plumbing, and induced draft ventilation all predate Chicago's first office towers by decades if not centuries in some instances. Chicago and New York were simply where all of these marvels came together with the requisite desire for financial gain to produce a previously unthinkable feat.[141]

---

[137] Ely subsequently would recall his impressions of Pullman—the town and the industrialist—with the hindsight of an additional four decades of experience, calling Mr. Pullman one of the great industrial leaders of his generation (Richard Theodore Ely, *Ground Under Our Feet. An Autobiography*, p. 170). "It cannot be said of Mr. Pullman," Ely wrote, "that there was any conscientious striving for this excellence. But I believe it can be said that the management of the Pullman Company was really a good deal above the standards that prevailed in business during the past two generations" (Ibid., p. 171).

[138] Zunz, *Making America Corporate*, pp. 103–24.

[139] William H. Birkmire, *Skeleton Construction in Buildings, with Numerous Practical Illustrations of High Buildings* (New York: John Wiley, 1894), p. iii.

[140] Carl W. Condit, "The Two Centuries of Technical Evolution Underlying the Skyscraper," in Lynn S. Beddle, ed., *Second Century of the Skyscraper* (New York: Van Nostrand Reinhold, 1988), pp. 11–24.

[141] Ray Stannard Baker, "The Modern Skyscraper," *Munsey's Magazine* 22 (1899), pp. 48–56.

Economic exigencies rather than aesthetic considerations frequently drove the development of this most fundamentally American of all building types.[142] Chicago and New York were America's—and hence, the world's—only "skyscraper metropolises" until at least the 1940s.[143]

This pair of skyscraper innovators—debate rages to this day over which is most properly identified as the "home" of the skyscraper—offers strikingly different approaches to urban development.[144] Chicago's regulated market was a consequence of the 1893 real estate recession that followed overbuilding during the preceding decade. Chicago's City Council passed a height limit of 130 feet on buildings at that time, a cap that would gradually be raised over the next three decades to 260 feet. The sky was the limit in New York following the lifting of early building restrictions in 1889. Manhattan would boast nearly a thousand buildings of eleven to twenty stories, and fifty-one of between twenty-one and sixty stories by 1913.[145] Chicago's unwillingness to relinquish control and to permit developers to reach for the skies was born of a need to control the market in order to maximize investor return on speculative office buildings (which most skyscrapers then were, as are most today).

Functional requirements, municipal codes, accounting ledgers, and profit rates shaped Chicago's distinctive cityscape of uniformly tall office towers just as much as the aesthetic concerns of what would later become the Chicago School of commercial architecture.[146] Wildly fluctuating land prices and boom-bust cycles similarly wreaked havoc with designers' grand plans.[147]

The commercial nature of the skyscraper proved to be no impediment to beauty.[148] As Root would proclaim, "Beauty is a utility, but not always

---

[142] Carol Willis, *Form Follows Finance: Skyscrapers and Skylines in New York and Chicago* (New York: Princeton Architectural Press, 1995).

[143] As late as 1960, Carol Willis has written, "only three other [American] cities contained more than two buildings taller than twenty-five stories: Detroit had eight, Philadelphia six, and Pittsburgh, five." Ibid., p. 9.

[144] Ibid. Also see Mona Domosh, *Invented Cities: The Creation of Landscape in Nineteenth-Century New York and Boston* (New Haven: Yale University Press, 1996), pp. 76–81; and Sarah Bradford Landau and Carl W. Condit, *Rise of the New York Skyscraper, 1865–1913* (New Haven: Yale University Press, 1996).

[145] Willis, *Form Follows Finance*, p. 9.   [146] Ibid., p. 10.

[147] The dollar value of new construction in Chicago grew from $20.0 million in 1887 to $63.5 million in 1892 (in preparation for the Columbian Exposition), before falling back to $28.5 million in 1893, and just $19.1 million in 1900. A steady increase in the dollar value of new construction followed, reaching a peak of $112.8 million on the eve of World War I, in 1916. Homer Hoyt, *One Hundred Years of Land Values in Chicago: The Relationship of the Growth of Chicago to the Rise in Its Land Values, 1830–1933* (Chicago: University of Chicago Press, 1933).

[148] This was an observation made by Willis, among many, as she drew on the writing of Barr Ferree, an editor of *Engineering Magazine*, in *Form Follows Finance*, p. 15.

8. View of Chicago from 700 ft. above Lake Michigan, 1911. Kaufman, Wiemer, and Fabry Co. Library of Congress, Prints and Photographs Division, Geographical File—Illinois-Chicago.

an obvious utility."[149] Firms such as Holabird and Roche, perhaps the city's most commercially successful and enduring architectural establishment, comprehended the need to blend commerce and art to turn a dollar.[150] Their simultaneous search for beauty and profit characterized much of Chicago life a century ago.

MUNICIPAL GOVERNANCE

Chicago's municipal government was embedded in a federal system that provided for autonomous power structures and fiscal arrangements. The Chicago city government was not directly subordinate to Cook County, state of Illinois, or federal U.S. institutions. Rather, it negotiated with these higher levels of government within the framework of a charter established by the state of Illinois.[151] These arrangements will be discussed in greater detail in Chapter 8. At this point, suffice it to say that legislative and senior executive officials at all four levels of administration—municipal, county, state, and federal—were elected in a system predicated on universal male suffrage. Their administrative counterparts were not elected, but were often appointed by officials who had been.

The fragmentation of competing jurisdictions prompted the establishment of scores of specialized agencies and authorities that managed and operated a variety of services—water, sewer, parks—throughout the Chicago region.[152] Special districts with bonding and taxing authority permitted Illinois cities and counties to circumvent debt limits established by the 1870 state constitution.[153] Existing governments were unable to

---

[149] John Wellborn Root, "A Utilitarian Theory of Beauty," in Donald Hoffman, ed., *The Meanings of Architecture: Buildings and Writings by John Wellborn Root* (New York: Horizon, 1967), pp. 172–74: 172.

[150] Holabird and Roche's accomplishments are only recently receiving the attention they deserve. See, for example, the excellent monograph by Robert Bruegmann, *The Architects and the City: Holabird and Roche of Chicago, 1880–1918* (Chicago: University of Chicago Press, 1997).

[151] For further discussion of these issues, see Flanagan, *Charter Reform*; Charles E. Merriam, *Chicago: A More Intimate View of Urban Politics* (New York: Macmillan, 1929); Paul Michael Green, "The Chicago Democratic Party, 1840–1920: From Factionalism to Political Organization" (Ph.D. diss., University of Chicago, 1975); and Ann Durkin Keating, "Governing the New Metropolis: The Development of Urban and Suburban Governments in Cook County, Illinois, 1831–1902" (Ph.D. diss., University of Chicago, 1984).

[152] A point emphasized by Charles E. Merriam in his classic study of American municipal governance, *Scrambled Government: Who Rules What in Chicagoland?* Chicago, 1934.

[153] According to the Illinois constitution, municipal and county debt could not exceed 5 percent of the assessed valuation of property in a given jurisdiction. Ester R. Fuchs, *Mayors and Money: Fiscal Policy in New York and Chicago* (Chicago: University of Chicago Press, 1992), p. 195.

respond to increasing demands for public services, spinning off special authorities that sometimes crossed municipal boundaries. Republican state legislators were thus able to limit the formal authority of Democratic-dominated city political machines, reducing the Democrats' opportunities for patronage politics in the process.

The result, as Merriam would write, was "scrambled government." Edward C. Banfield, writing a half-century later, went further, noting that "[t]he Chicago area, from *a purely formal standpoint*, can hardly be said to have a government at all. There are hundreds, perhaps thousands, of bodies, each of which has a measure of legal authority and none of which has enough of it to carry out a course of action which other bodies oppose."[154]

Within the city, individual City Council members exercised considerable power and authority over their wards.[155] The mayor was, by and large, a weak figure in terms of formal authority, constantly negotiating with council members, party bosses, state governors, and legislators.[156] Chicago's omnipresent ward bosses controlled more autonomous resources than did the mayor.

The city's revenue system was hurtfully disjoined.[157] Chicago's rapid expansion demanded greater municipal capacity, but its tax system failed to generate the requisite income to support enlarged services. Merriam, in his acclaimed *Report on an Investigation of the Municipal Revenues of Chicago*, prepared for the City Club of Chicago in 1906, observed that Chicago had, among American cities, "the lowest tax-rate, the lowest tax revenue per capita, the lowest total revenue per capita, and the lowest debt per capita."[158] Merriam reviewed a range of revenue-raising authorities collecting taxes in the city, including the state of Illinois, Cook County, the City of Chicago, as well as separate library, school, sanitary, and park commissions.[159] City corporate income, which had constituted half of all tax revenues collected in the city in 1880,

---

[154] Edward C. Banfield, *Political Influence* (Westport, Conn.: Greenwood, 1961), p. 235.
[155] A point vividly explored in Lloyd Wendt and Herman Kogan, *Bosses in Lusty Chicago* (Bloomington: University of Indiana Press, 1967).
[156] For further discussion of this point see Green and Holli, eds., *The Mayors;* Robin L. Einhorn, *Property Rules: Political Economy in Chicago, 1833–1872* (Chicago: University of Chicago Press, 1991); and Frederick Rex, *The Mayors of the City of Chicago, from March 4, 1837, to April 13, 1933* (Chicago: Chicago Municipal Reference Library, 1934).
[157] Flanagan, *Charter Reform*, p. 14.
[158] Charles E. Merriam, *Report on an Investigation of the Municipal Revenues of Chicago* (Chicago: City Club of Chicago, 1906), p. xi.
[159] Ibid., pp. 19–20.

fell to just one-quarter of the taxes gathered by all revenue-raising authorities in 1904. Three-quarters of local administration, when measured in dollar value, thus fell outside the domain of the municipal government.

Nearly half of government expenditures by all revenue-raising agencies—whether under municipal jurisdiction or under the control of county, state, or public-authority administration—supported public health, public safety, and educational services.[160] A relatively low 16.2 percent of Chicago public expenditures went toward the servicing of debts on bonds and loans. Merriam identified the consequent system of municipal public finance as "decentralized, unsystematic, and irresponsible."[161] He concluded that, "[t]he revenue-raising authorities of Chicago constitute one of the most complicated systems of local finance to be found anywhere, certainly the most involved and difficult in the United States."[162]

Successful incumbent mayors emerged as brokers within a highly fractured and decentralized system. Chicago's mayors dominated the system of municipal governance not because of constitutional authority, but because the strength of local allegiances to specific elected candidates was sustained through patronage and political influence.[163]

More than a few Gilded Age Chicago political wizards stood behind emerald screens—pushing, pulling, turning, and twirling various levers, knobs, and wheels to give the appearance of action. Conflict and confrontation often proved to be the order of the day. Unlike L. Frank Baum's Dorothy caught in Oz, however, Chicagoans could not merely click their heels and return to a more peaceful time. The politics of pragmatic pluralism required more than spinning wheels; it took hard work. Those civic leaders who practiced the politics of pragmatic pluralism bequeathed through their labors a number of achievements that continue to serve the city well a century later.

---

[160] Ibid., pp. 29–32. [161] Ibid., p. 35.
[162] Ibid., p. 71.
[163] Bradley and Zald, "From Commercial Elite to Political Administrator," pp. 153–67: 160–61.

3

Russia's Calico Heart

The flames that drove Napoleon's Grand Army from Moscow into a catastrophic and desperate retreat in 1812 destroyed the last vestiges of Moscow's medieval preeminence in Russian life. Formal political power had fled to Peter the Great's new "northern capital" in St. Petersburg a full century before. The imperial system launched by Peter at the beginning of the eighteenth century and perfected by Catherine the Great at that century's end could not tolerate rival political, economic, social, or cultural power centers. Napoleon's blazing departure merely confirmed a decades-long process of decline that had reduced Russia's once preeminent city to mere provincial status. That conflagration nonetheless quite literally cleared the ground for a new Moscow to emerge as a simultaneously bustling and mortifying industrial and commercial giant.

Postfire Moscow's status as Russia's "second city" set a framework for tense relations with imperial administrators for another century, until the outbreak of World War I in August 1914. Home to peasant traders, Old Believer merchants, German and British industrialists, and adventurers of all hues who could never be admitted to Petersburg high society, this "large village" quickly evolved into one of the world's largest cities. It became a metropolis in every sense of that word but one, the political. "Second metropolis" Moscow, in turn, pursued a homegrown agenda of economic advantage and social reform at every opportunity presented by imperial inattention, inactivity, or incompetence. Its economic and cultural leaders looked back to a grander age prior to Peter's arrival when Moscow was, in fact, the single most important place in central Eurasia. The combination of industrial dynamism and philosophical conservatism produced a distinctly Muscovite mélange that remains almost impossible to define to this day. The origins of many of these contradictions lie in the city's initial growth from fringe outpost to primary city during the fourteenth, fifteenth, and sixteenth centuries.

Moscow's early centrality to Russian life was an artifact of the city's position on the periphery of Mongol, Novgorodian, and Lithuanian-Polish territories. Their territory reached by outside invaders only with considerable effort, Moscow's princes skillfully nurtured their resources as their stronghold emerged as the most powerful city of the region. Their rise reflects the insight of Peter Hall's contention that nascent cities that "serve as entrepots between the already-developed world and a frontier region beyond it" have the capacity to emerge as centers of urban innovation and growth.[1]

Moscow first took shape as a discernable place during the long period of decline of the Kievan Rus' state following the death of Yaroslav the Wise in 1054.[2] The world of the East Slavs became increasingly inhospitable as central power in the Kievan state was eviscerated, leaving behind feuding principalities and internecine strife. Seeking the protection of the Upper Volga's wooded lands, some Rus' began migrating to the northeast, establishing a new state centered around the city of Vladimir by the late twelfth century. Within but a half-century, many Rus' would come under siege once more with the arrival of the Mongol horde at the end of the 1230s.

Myth credits Kievan Grand Prince and Suzdal Prince Iurii Dolgorukii ("long arms") with having founded the city of Moscow by constructing a pine-wood fortress, or kremlin, at the confluence of the Moskva and Neglinnaia Rivers in 1147. The site, situated on the edge of the Rostov-Suzdal lands presided over from Vladimir, had probably been inhabited for some time.

With Mongol rulers plundering wealthier towns, Moscow quietly garnered strength while seeming to languish in obscurity. Ivan I, known as Kalita ("moneybags"), consolidated increasing wealth and power between 1325 and 1340, while Moscow Grand Prince Dimitri Donskoi defeated the Mongol Tatars for the first time at the dramatic Battle of Kulikovo Polye in 1380. Donskoi replaced the town's small wooden kremlin with a more substantial stone structure.

---

[1] Peter Hall, *Cities in Civilization* (New York: Pantheon, 1998), p. 302.
[2] Brief accounts of Moscow's early history can be found in Kathleen Berton, *Moscow: An Architectural History* (London: I. B. Tauris, 1990), pp. 11–59; and Ivan Zabielin, *Istoriia goroda Moskvy* (Moscow: I. N. Kushnerev, 1905). An excellent historical overview of the city's development is also found in the opening passages of Timothy J. Colton's monumental *Moscow: Governing the Socialist Metropolis* (Cambridge, Mass.: Harvard University Press, 1995), pp. 11–36.

The principality secured hegemonic control over the lands of the northern Rus' by the time of Ivan III, known as Velikii ("the great"), who ruled between 1462 and 1505. Ivan III built many of the Kremlin's most important religious buildings. Ivan IV, or Groznyi ("the terrible"), cemented Moscow's role as Russia's political and commercial center, declaring himself "tsar," for "Caesar," in 1547. In 1589, only five years after Groznyi's death, the Orthodox Church established a patriarchate in Moscow. The city had now replaced Vladimir as the emerging nation's spiritual center. Moscow's domination of every aspect of Russian life continued until Peter the Great transferred the seat of imperial power to his new capital, St. Petersburg, in 1712.[3]

A THOROUGHLY JUMBLED URBAN ENVIRONMENT

Moscow's character was firmly established during this period of unprecedented power in the sixteenth and seventeenth centuries. Flowing out of the fortress Kremlin and walled Kitai gorod district, Moscow's medieval streets were anything but modern.[4] Visitors, including Russians, transposed this addled cityscape from the built onto the cultural environment. "Ancient Moscow" became viewed by the late eighteenth century as more "provincial" and "backward" than "rational" St. Petersburg to the northwest.[5]

Nineteenth-century cultural critic Vissarion Belinskii popularized such notions, observing in 1845 that Moscow was a city of "patriarchal attachment to family life."[6] American Russianist Sidney Monas would

[3] For a discussion of life in the Moscow lands of this period, see Galina Latysheva and Mikhail Rabinovich, *Moskva i Moskovskii krai v proshlom* (Moscow: Moskovskii rabochii, 1973).

[4] Petr Vasil'evich Sytin, *Iz istorii Moskovskikh ulits (ocherki)*, 3d ed. (Moscow: Moskovskii rabochii, 1958), p. 7.

[5] Nikolai Antsiferov, perhaps Russia's most insightful and eloquent commentator on St. Petersburg, frequently explored the Moscow-Petersburg theme in his essays, especially during the early Soviet period. His major works were republished in 1991 as Nikolai Pavlovich Antsiferov, *"Nepostizhimyi gorod ..." Dusha Peterburga. Peterburg Dostoevskogo. Peterburg Pushkina* (St. Petersburg: Lenizdat, 1991). For a perhaps equally stimulating, yet more contemporary Russian perspective, see Grigorii Kaganov, *Sankt-Peterburg: obrazy prostranstva* (Moscow: Indrik, 1995).

Katerina Clark provides an excellent overview of these issues in her study of St. Petersburg culture during the first third of the twentieth century. See Katerina Clark, *Petersburg: Crucible of Cultural Revolution* (Cambridge, Mass.: Harvard University Press, 1995), pp. 1–73. Priscilla Roosevelt similarly addresses the Moscow-Petersburg debate from the perspective of the Russian provinces in Priscilla R. Roosevelt, *Life on the Russian Country Estate: A Social and Cultural History* (New Haven: Yale University Press, 1995), p. 26.

[6] Vissarion Belinskii, "Peterburg i Moskva" (1845), in V. G. Belinskii and N. A. Nekrasov, eds., *Fiziologiia Peterburga* (Moscow: Sovetskaia Rossiia, 1984), pp. 42–72: 57.

echo Belinskii's characterization of Moscow a dozen decades later, when he noted that the accent in nineteenth-century Moscow life was "on private life, the inclination inward."[7] Vladimir Giliarovskii—one of the greatest publicists of the city, from its street corners and back alleys to its grand ballrooms and parlors—had a character in one story lament that, even after a two-year absence, "I go along the Tverskaia, and everything is just as it was before."[8]

Yet the city did change, and change dramatically, as it absorbed new technologies and attracted new migrants.[9] Built in concentric circles, the city spread out along radials over a landscape that, like Chicago's, was devoid of major topographic obstacles.[10] Moscow established its own distinctive skyline, dominated by church domes and cupolas, including those of the recently constructed Cathedral of Christ the Savior.[11] John Bell Bouton, an American passing through town on "an epicurean journey," described Moscow as if the city were popping up out of a lake: "From [Moscow's] surface, as from a body of water, rose domes, turrets, spires, towers, battlements innumerable."[12]

Exiled liberal leader Paul Miliukov similarly proclaimed his astonishment at this new Moscow. Miliukov noted in his memoirs that he had been disoriented on returning to Moscow in 1905 after years of travel:

I could hardly recognize parts of the city. Thanks to the merchant class, a striking new trend was introduced in Moscow architecture. Amidst the old aristocratic mansions in the Empire style, there arose along the boulevards and side streets the most fastidious imitations of European architectural achievements of various eras. . . . The Tarasovsky mansion on Spiridonovka, for example, reflected the antique classicism of Palladio. Also on Spiridonovka, Ivan

[7] Sidney Monas, "St. Petersburg and Moscow as Cultural Symbols," in Theofanis George Stavrou, ed., *Art and Culture in Nineteenth-Century Russia* (Bloomington: Indiana University Press, 1983), pp. 26–39: 29.

[8] Vladimir A. Giliarovskii, "Sozhzhennaia kniga," in Vladimir A. Giliarovskii, *Sochineniia v 4 tomakh*, gen. ed. V. M. Lobanov, text prep. and notes E. Kiseleva (Moscow: Biblioteka "Ogonek", Izd. "Pravda", 1967), Vol. 3, pp. 315–27: 318. On Giliarovskii himself, see Ia. M. Belitskii and G. N. Glezer, *Moskva neznakomaia* (Moscow: Stroiizdat, 1993), pp. 151–54.

[9] This change is amicably portrayed by Irina Nenarokomova in her sociable post-Soviet biography of merchant art collector Pavel Tretiakov. I. S. Nenarokomova, *Pavel Tret'iakov i ego galereia* (Moscow: Galart, 1994).

[10] For a brief yet comprehensive description of Moscow's physical attributes at this time, see Laura Engelstein, *Moscow 1905: Working-Class Organization and Political Conflict* (Stanford: Stanford University Press, 1982), pp. 43–51.

[11] On the Cathedral of Christ the Savior, see Richard S. Wortman, *Scenarios of Power: Myth and Ceremony in Russian Monarchy*, Vol. 1: *From Peter the Great to the Death of Nicholas I* (Princeton: Princeton University Press, 1995), pp. 384–87.

[12] John Bell Bouton, *Roundabout to Moscow: An Epicurean Journey* (New York: D. Appleton, 1887), p. 251.

Abramovich Morozov built a castle in Gothic style, while on Prechistenka, he built a palace in the style of the Portuguese Renaissance. On Zubovsky Boulevard, his brother, Mikhail, erected his palace with a Classic facade and finished each room in a different historic style.[13]

Moscow's nineteenth-century merchants had transformed their city during the years of Miliukov's absence by rebuilding every space that could be obtained through the sale of property.[14] Five- to ten-story residential and commercial structures replaced older, more modest and staid two- and three-story homes and merchant halls downtown.[15] Henry M. Grove, a visiting Englishman, complained in 1912, "Every year more and more of old Moscow disappears, and the city becomes less and less like the original ancient city. Beyond a very occasional old house and church, the main streets are now composed of modern buildings of three, four, or six stories, whereas Moscow was almost entirely one-storied, with a sprinkling of two-storied houses."[16]

Fearful of proletarians, respectable folk with fewer resources than the great merchant dynasties tended to seek out higher ground to the southwest of the Kremlin. The Sparrow Hills—now the site of Moscow State University—became a favored pastoral rest stop for the rich and the merely well-off.

Building up layer on layer of new rings, the city's diverse and differentiated functions nestled in a circular pattern focused around a single, grand, central landmark, the Moscow Kremlin. These outlines would remain as familiar to Moscow's denizens at century's end as they were at its beginning.

AN OVERGROWN VILLAGE

The boulevards ringing the city's heart sprouted tree-lined promenades; the odd monument appeared, while ubiquitous churches

---

[13] Paul Miliukov, *Political Memoirs, 1905–1917*, ed. Arthur P. Mendel, trans. Carl Goldberg (Ann Arbor: University of Michigan Press, 1967), p. 15.

[14] Richard Wortman, "Moscow and Petersburg: The Problem of Political Center in Tsarist Russia, 1881–1914," in Sean Wilentz, ed., *Rites of Power: Symbolism, Ritual, and Politics since the Middle Ages* (Philadelphia: University of Pennsylvania Press, 1985), pp. 244–71: 246.

[15] For further discussion of this process, see William Craft Brumfield, "Architectural Design in Moscow, 1890–1917," in William Craft Brumfield, ed., *Reshaping Russian Architecture: Western Technology, Utopian Dreams* (Cambridge, U.K.: Cambridge University Press, 1990), pp. 66–110; and Evgeniia Ivanovna Kirichenko, *Moskva na rubezhe stoletii* (Moscow: Stroiizdat, 1977).

[16] Henry M. Grove, *Moscow* (London: Adam and Charles Black, 1912), p. 79.

and monasteries provided guideposts in a thoroughly jumbled urban environment.[17] Newly constructed and redeveloped squares and public spaces provided brief moments of respite for weary Muscovites as well as places for communal activities.[18] Moscow was the sort of place in which "extraordinary sights keep the stranger spell-bound."[19] Ivan Bunin would have one of his characters exclaim that Moscow could even be gloriously beautiful:

I drove towards the Kremlin, a Kremlin lit by the evening sun, went through the Kremlin and past its cathedrals—oh, my God, how beautiful they were!—then along the Ilinka, redolent of paints and oils and already bathed in evening shadow, and along the Pokrovka, already lying beneath the protection of booming, clamouring bells, ringing a blessing upon the happy close of a busy day—I drove, not merely pleased with myself and the world at large, but truly engulfed in the ecstasy of being alive.[20]

Moscow, nonetheless, was simultaneously becoming known as an "overgrown village." As Joseph Bradley has noted, images of European urbanity and Russian village life coexisted, suggesting a duality in the city's social, political, cultural, and economic organization.[21]

By the late nineteenth century, railroads determined Moscow's multiple realities beyond the center-defining Garden Ring boulevards.[22] Factories sought out rail lines to move raw material and finished goods.[23] The concentration of lines to the east required major plants to huddle there. Workers' slums followed, in part because of the paternalism of

[17] A sense of Moscow's tangled streets, alleys, and byways is communicated in Ia. M. Belitskii's 1994 effort to describe various modern-day neighborhoods at the turn of the last century. See Ia. M. Belitskii, *Zabytaia Moskva* (Moscow: Moskovskii rabochii, 1994).

[18] A point emphasized by Leonid Raputov of the Moscow Architectural Institute in several unpublished papers, including "Sovremennaia zhizn' istoricheskikh ploshchadei Moskvy i sokhranenie ikh traditsii" (1994). The continuing power of Moscow's central spaces a century later is explored in O. E. Trushchenko, "Akkumuliatsiia simvolicheskogo kapitala v prostranstve stolichnogo tsentra," *Rossiiskii monitor* 3 (1993), pp. 145–65. For an overview of the city at this time, see I. P. Mashkov, *Putevoditel' po Moskve* (Moscow: Moskovskoe arkhitekturnoe obshchestvo, 1913).

[19] A. S. Rappoport, *Home Life in Russia* (New York: Macmillan, 1913), p. 173.

[20] Ivan Bunin, "Long Ago," trans. Sophie Lund, in Ivan Bunin, *The Gentleman from San Francisco and Other Stories* (New York: Penguin, 1987), pp. 69–76: 76.

[21] Joseph Bradley, *Muzhik and Muscovite: Urbanization in Late Imperial Russia* (Berkeley: University of California Press, 1985), p. 68.

[22] The Garden Ring boulevards had replaced a circle of medieval fortification battlements some two kilometers from the Kremlin walls.

[23] Colton reflects on this growth and the place of the railroad in *Moscow: Governing the Socialist Metropolis*, pp. 35–63.

9. Kremlin Gate, Moscow, 1918. Photographer unknown. Library of Congress, Prints and Photographs Division, LC-USZ62-123212.

some employers who provided a bed in a company barracks, and in part because the chronic inefficiency of public transit required laborers to walk to their jobs.[24]

---

[24] For a discussion of rail transit in the city at the end of the imperial period, see Mashkov, *Putevoditel' po Moskve*, pp. 106–26.

This sprawling worker "village" was remarkably country-like. The city's 4,565 structures three or more stories high in 1912 were almost all located within the Garden Ring. Despite all of the construction downtown, more than 90 percent of Moscow's total building inventory consisted of one- or two-story structures. Small wooden and brick buildings seemed to have been scattered across a landscape that was less than half built up. As late as February 1917, nearly 15 percent of the city's lands were still under cultivation in this sprawling, proletarian, demi-urban world of Moscow beyond the Garden Ring.[25] Not too long before, a network of nearly two hundred ponds provided plentiful water for agricultural activities in the city. The Pure Ponds (*Chistye prudy*) and Patriarch's Ponds, as Mikhail Bul'gakov charmingly reveals in *The Master and Margarita*, provided primarily upscale neighborhoods with a picturesque presence and a reminder of more rural days not so long gone by.[26]

This urban netherworld of Moscow's periphery absorbed most of the city's industrial growth.[27] Although nearly half of the local population lived in central neighborhoods in 1871, by 1917 less than one-quarter of all Muscovites resided in the largely upscale city center.[28] Moscow's outskirts were home to peasant migrants who were increasingly defining the city's character. Only 27.6 percent of Moscow's 1902 population were natives of the city; another one-third had been resident in town for five years or less.[29]

Many of Moscow's workers simply moved back and forth seasonally between the city and their villages, further amplifying the metropolis's transient character.[30] The industrial depression of the 1880s, together with the political crises surrounding the March 1881 assassination of Tsar Alexander II, generally led to a deterioration of social and economic

---

[25] Petr Vasil'evich Sytin, *Kommunal'noe khoziaistvo. Blagoustroistvo Moskvy v sravnenii s blagoustroistvom drugikh bol'shikh gorodov* (Moscow: Novaia Moskva, 1926), pp. 52–53; and E. G. Boldina, "Statisticheskii portret Moskvy na 1910 god," in A. S. Kiselev et al., eds., *Moskovskii arkhiv. Istoriko-kraevedcheskii al'manakh* (Moscow: Moskovskoe gorodskoe ob"edinenie arkhivov, 1996), pp. 162–82.

[26] Mikhail Bul'gakov, *The Master and Margarita*, trans. Diana Burgin and Katherine O'Connor (New York : Vintage, 1996); Petr Vasil'evich Sytin, *Istoriia planirovki i zastroiki Moskvy*, Vol. 3, *Pozhar Moskvy v 1812 godu i stroitel'stvo goroda v techenie 50 let: 1812–1862* (Moscow: Moskovskii rabochii, 1972), p. 311.

[27] Robert Gohstand, "The Shaping of Moscow by Nineteenth-Century Trade," in Michael F. Hamm, ed., *The City in Russian History* (Lexington: University Press of Kentucky, 1976), pp. 160–81: 163–65.

[28] Adol'f Grigor'evich Rashin, *Naselenie Rossii za 100 let (1811–1913gg.). Statisticheskii ocherki* (Moscow: Gosstatizdat, 1956), p. 117.

[29] Ibid., p. 140.

[30] Bradley, *Muzhik and Muscovite*, pp. 27–31.

conditions in the central Russian countryside.[31] Moscow, as the empire's greatest trading and manufacturing center, became the preferred migration destination. The region's decades-long tradition of *otkhodnichestvo* (going away), in which peasants sought temporary employment away from their native villages, conformed to the demands of Moscow industry for a fluid labor force with large numbers of temporary workers.[32] The added mobility provided by a growing national rail system focused on Moscow reinforced such patterns.[33]

Moscow's workers were not necessarily among Russia's most efficient, but they more than served the requirements of Moscow's light-industrial manufacturing base. Tens of thousands of peasants moved into and out of Moscow without severing their ties with agriculture and with village life.[34] Village and factory were not polar opposites in Russia in general, nor in Moscow in particular. Rather, life at the factory in Moscow often represented a stage in one's life, not a permanent change in status.[35]

The preponderance of Moscow's industrial migrants came from the surrounding countryside of the Moscow, Tver, and Yaroslavl provinces (*gubernii*) immediately adjacent to the metropolitan region.[36] The remaining came from a variety of Russia's other European provinces.[37]

Barbara Anderson correctly cautions that it would be inaccurate to assume that all of these arriving peasants were naive country bumpkins. Many were among the most active members of their communities, which

---

[31] P. G. Ryndzhinskii, "K opredeleniiu razmerov agrarnogo perenaseleniia v Rossii na rubezhe XIX–XXv.," in S. L. Tikhvinskii, ed., *Sotsial'no-ekonomicheskoe razvitie Rossii. Sbornik statei k 100-letiiu so dnia rozhdeniia Nikolaia Mikhailovicha Druzhinina* (Moscow: Nauka, 1986), pp. 155–72; and Robert Eugene Johnson, *Peasant and Proletarian: The Working Class of Moscow in the Late Nineteenth Century* (New Brunswick, N.J.: Rutgers University Press, 1979), p. 9.

[32] Johnson, *Peasant and Proletarian*, pp. 12–16; and Jeffrey Burds, *Peasant Dreams and Market Politics: Labor Migration and the Russian Village, 1861–1905* (Pittsburgh: University of Pittsburgh Press, 1998).

[33] Johnson, *Peasant and Proletarian*, pp. 15–21; and E. A. Dudzhinskaia, "Stroitel'stvo zheleznykh dorog v Rossii v ekonomicheskoi programme slavianofilov," in Tikhvinskii, ed., *Sotsial'no-ekonomicheskoe razvitie Rossii*, pp. 172–83.

[34] Johnson, *Peasant and Proletarian*, pp. 20–21, 29, 50–51.

[35] Ibid., pp. 50–52; Burds, *Peasant Dreams*. As late as 1912, there were only 84 women living in Moscow for every 100 men, while only 16.8 percent of the city's population were children. A. Mikhailovskii, "Munitsipal'naia Moskva," in N. A. Geinike, N. S. Elagin, N. A. Efimova, and I. I. Shitts, eds., *Po Moskve. Progulki po Moskvie i eia khudozhestvennym" i prosvietitel'nym" uchrezhdeniiam"* (Moscow: Izdanie M. i S. Sabashnikovykh", 1917), pp. 121–58: 122.

[36] Rashin, *Naselenie Rossii za 100 let*, pp. 136–37.

[37] Barbara A. Anderson, "Who Chose the Cities? Migrants to Moscow and St. Petersburg Cities in the Late Nineteenth Century," in Ronald Demos Lee et al., eds., *Population Patterns in the Past* (New York: Academic, 1977), pp. 277–96: 279.

were themselves often "relatively culturally advanced places."[38] For, as Jeffrey Brooks has demonstrated, Moscow stood at the center of a growing popular culture based increasingly on literacy.[39]

Commercial literature and a booming boulevard press provided a common bond for many among the three-quarters of male and one-quarter of female Muscovites who qualified as literate. Muscovite print magnates Sergei Sharapov, Ivan Sytin, and Nikolai Pastukhov shaped Russian thought with their kopek novellas and newspapers perhaps even more profoundly than did St. Petersburg's high literature. The city housed more bookstores than any other Russian city.[40] Moscow's Nikol'skii Market served as the distribution center for the national book trade.

The same railroads that brought peasants to town and books to the countryside encouraged industrialists to place their plants in a belt of smaller cities surrounding the ancient capital.[41] Such towns as Vladimir, Ivanovo, Yaroslavl, and Tula grew into significant industrial centers tied by the new train lines to Moscow's markets.[42] The resulting central industrial region nearly doubled in population between 1863 and 1914 from a combined 7.6 million residents in Moscow and its surrounding provinces to just over 13 million inhabitants, many of whom were integrated into Moscow's economic orbit.[43]

Railways and factories were new features of the Russian landscape, achievements brought about in partnership with the state.[44] The distinct peculiarities of Russian industrialization lie beyond the scope of this study.[45] The tsar's ministers "exercised a greater control of the economy

[38] Ibid., p. 294.
[39] Jeffrey Brooks, *When Russia Learned to Read: Literacy and Popular Culture, 1861–1917* (Princeton: Princeton University Press, 1985); and V. A. Kumanev, *Revoliutsiia i prosveshchenie mass* (Moscow: Nauka, 1973).
[40] Moscow was home to 205 bookstores in 1890. St. Petersburg, by contrast, supported 142 bookstores in 1890. Brooks, *When Russia Learned to Read*, p. 110.
[41] R. Portal, "Industriels muscovites: le secteur cotonnier (1861–1914),'" *Cahiers du monde Russe et Sovietique* 4, nos. 1–2 (January–June 1963), pp. 5–46: 23–27.
[42] V. Ia. Laverychev, "Moskovskie fabrikanty i sredneaziatskii khlopok," *Vestnik Moskovskogo Universiteta* 9, no. 1 (January–February 1970), pp. 53–72; and Michael Owen Gately, "The Development of the Russian Cotton Textile Industry in the Pre-Revolutionary Years, 1861–1913" (Ph.D. diss., University of Kansas, 1968), p. 34.
[43] The "Moscow Industrial Region" included the Moskovskaia, Vladimirskaia, Tverskaia, Nizhegorodskaia, Kostromskaia, and Yaroslavskaia *gubernii*. Rashin, *Naselenie Rossii za 100 let*, p. 62. Also see Bradley, *Muzhik and Muscovite*, pp. 10–12.
[44] Valerii Ivanovich Bovykin, *Zarozhdenie finansovogo kapitala v Rossii* (Moscow: Izdatel'stvo Moskovskogo universiteta, 1967).
[45] Readers may consult the following classic analyses as a starting point for further investigation of this topic: Alain Besancon, "La Russie et 'l'esprit du capitalisme,'" *Cahiers du monde russe et sovietique* 8, no. 4 (October–December 1967), pp. 509–27; William L. Blackwell, *The Beginnings of Russian Industrialization, 1800–1860* (Princeton: Princeton University Press, 1968); William L. Blackwell, *The Industrialization of Russia: An Historical Perspective* (New York: Thomas Y. Crowell, 1970); Alexander

by [the state's] activities as an authorizer, regulator, producer, and consumer, although it never completely subordinated the economy."[46] Foreign capital, domestic monopolies, and the Russian state played pivotal roles in developing industrial capacity.[47] The Russian experience with industrialization, in these regards, was closer to that of Meiji Japan than to western Europe, let alone North America.[48]

OLD BELIEVER CAPITALISM

Moscow was unusual within this Russian industrial experience for the extent to which a local merchant elite controlled its own finance and manufacturing.[49] Jo Ann Ruckman reports that a "small group of dynasties dominated business participation in the various fields of Moscow cultural, social, and public life and at the same time provided leadership to the business community. The same names recur again and again. . . . Included within this *crème de la crème* were the following families: Abrikosov, Alekseev, Bakhrushin, Botkin, Guchkov, Iakunchikov, Khludov, Konovalov, Krestovnikov, Mamontov, Morozov, Naidenov, Prokhorov, Riabushinskii, Rukavishnikov, Shchukin, Soldatenkov, Tretiakov, Ushkov, and Vishniakov."[50] Family-run firms were especially

Gerschenkron, "Economic Development in Russian Intellectual History of the Nineteenth Century," in Alexander Gerschenkron, *Economic Backwardness in Historical Perspective: A Book of Essays* (Cambridge, Mass.: Harvard University Press, 1962), pp. 152–87; Theodore H. von Laue, *Sergei Witte and the Industrialization of Russia* (New York: Columbia University Press, 1963); and Theodore H. von Laue, *Why Lenin? Why Stalin? A Reappraisal of the Russian Revolution, 1900–1930* (Philadelphia: J. B. Lippincott, 1964).

[46] Jonathan Coopersmith, *The Electrification of Russia, 1880–1926* (Ithaca: Cornell University Press, 1992), p. 11.

[47] Three divergent views touching on key issues concerning both foreign ownership and domestic monopolies in Russian industrialization may be found in V. Ia. Laverychev, "Nekotorye osobennosti razvitiia monopolii v Rossii (1900–1914gg.)," *Istoriia SSSR* 1969, no. 3, pp. 80–97; John P. McKay, *Pioneers for Profit: Foreign Entrepreneurship and Russian Industrialization, 1885–1913* (Chicago: University of Chicago Press, 1970); and Thomas C. Owen, *The Corporation under Russian Law, 1800–1917: A Study in Tsarist Economic Policy* (Cambridge, U.K.: Cambridge University Press, 1991). McKay's and Owen's studies are particularly useful background reading for students of today's economic transition in post-Soviet Russia.

[48] For an informative comparison of the Japanese and Russian experiences with industrialization and modernization, see Cyril E. Black et al., *The Modernization of Japan and Russia: A Comparative Study* (New York: Free Press, 1975).

[49] Isaak Il'ich Levin', *Aktsionernye kommercheskie banki v Rossii* (Petrograd: I. P. Bielopol'skii, 1917), Vol. 1; and S. G. Beliaev, *Banki i finansy Rossii istoriia. Russko-frantsuzskie bankovskie gruppy v periode ekonomicheskogo pod"ema 1909–1914gg.* (Saint Petersburg: AO "eN-Pi," 1995).

[50] Jo Ann Ruckman, *The Moscow Business Elite: A Social and Cultural Portrait of Two Generations, 1840–1905* (DeKalb Northern Illinois University Press, 1984), p. 19.

important in Moscow, particularly those enterprises controlled by a small circle of Old Believer clans and their descendants.

The Old Believers (*staroobriadtsy*) are a schismatic group that separated from the Russian Orthodox Church in a seventeenth-century revolt against rampant centralism in the church and state during the reign of Tsar Aleksei Mikhailovich, the second ruler of the Romanov dynasty.[51] Patriarch Nikon sought to strengthen Muscovite religious culture in the face of foreign influence by reducing what he saw as superstitious practices so as to produce a more coherent and homogeneous faith.[52] Nikon turned to learned and holy men from throughout the Orthodox world for advice and counsel. Convinced of the virtuousness of his cause, the patriarch imposed a number of liturgical and textual changes by decree—including the direction of processions around the church, the spelling of the name Jesus, and increasing the number of fingers used in making the sign of the cross from two to three. These decrees, often issued with imperious enmity, challenged the core of a Muscovite religiosity that had been based on the physicality of icon, incense, and chant rather than written text. The response was profound, with religious dissidents refusing to submit to Nikon's authority.

The Orthodox Church and the tsarist government ferociously persecuted "*raskol'niki*" (schismatics) over the decades to follow—a pattern that intensified as a consequence of the conviction among some Old Believers that Peter the Great was the Antichrist. Constantly at odds with state and ecclesiastic authority—and facing imprisonment, torture, and death—Old Believer colonies were forced to fringe regions of the empire, especially in the far north. Their isolated communities fostered a spirit of pioneer self-reliance blended with a deep communal spirit.

Old Believer families began to move to the Moscow suburbs during a period of religious tolerance under Catherine the Great.[53] This migration increased following the city's destruction during Napoleon's 1812 invasion.[54] The city's postinvasion ruin proved to be a pivotal moment in Moscow's history, as the old order collapsed with the city's buildings into a pile of smoldering ashes. Newcomers, such as future Old Believer

---

[51] For a concise, English-language history of the Old Believer community, see Roy R. Robson, *Old Believers in Modern Russia* (DeKalb: Northern Illinois University Press, 1995).

[52] This discussion is based on James L. West, "A Note on Old Belief," in James L. West and Iurii A. Petrov, eds., *Merchant Moscow: Images of Russia's Vanished Bourgeoisie* (Princeton: Princeton University Press, 1988), pp. 13–18.

[53] A. S. Provorikhina, "Moskovskie staroobriadchestvo," *Moskva v' eia proshlom' i nastoiashchem'* 12, pp. 49–75.

[54] West, "A Note on Old Belief," pp. 16–17.

industrialists, streamed into the city, revitalizing the local economy.[55] The city rebuilt itself behind classical facades.[56] Moscow by 1820 already had become a profoundly different place than it had been in 1810.

More schismatics followed during the mid-nineteenth century as the government of Alexander II reduced civil restrictions on Old Believer communities. Renewed legal constraints and less formal social sanction subsequently compelled some *staroobriadtsy* to convert to official Orthodoxy. Assimilationist pressures would intensify and abate in cycles that continued until the enactment of the 1905 Act of Toleration granting full religious rights to Old Believer communities in the wake of that year's revolution.[57]

The Old Believers' deep adherence to principles of communal support combined with their belief in individual self-reliance to reinforce strong group identity among leading Moscow merchant families of Old Believer background, such as the Riabushinskiis, Morozovs, Guchkovs, and Konovalovs. These characteristics encouraged capital accumulation and mutual assistance, two traits that stood Old Believer families in good stead as the Russian industrial revolution gained momentum at the close of the nineteenth century.[58]

Alexander Gerschenkron explored the Old Believers' apparently contradictory theological conservatism and economic inventiveness in a series of celebrated lectures in 1968. Gerschenkron argued that the origins of Old Believer capitalism lie not in doctrine, but in repression and persecution. Precisely because they were subject to brutal intolerance, Old Believers built up "a feeling of moral superiority to the outsider," which they justified by demonstrations of "cleanliness, honesty, reliability, frugality, industry, and thrift."[59] As James West notes, Old Believer prosperity "served to distinguish true believers in their own

---

[55] Tat'iana Alekseevna Molokova and Vladimir Pavlovich Frolov, *Istoriia Moskvy v pamiatnikakh kul'tury k 850-letiiu stolitsy* (Moscow: Moskovskii litsei, 1997), pp. 172–77; Aleksandr Sergeevich Nikfontov, *Moskva vo vtoroi polovine XIX stoletiia. Stenogramma publichnoi lektsii, prochitannoi 26 marta 1947 goda v lektsionnom zale v Moskve* (Moscow: Izdatel'stvo "Pravda," 1947), pp. 14–15.

[56] Evgeniia Ivanovna Kirichenko, "Arkhitekturno-gradostroitel'noe razvitie Moskvy v seredine XIX–nachale XXvv.," in N. F. Gulianitskii, *Arkhitekturno-gradostroitel'noe razvitie Moskvy. Arkhitekturnoe nasledstvo—42* (Moscow: NIITAG, 1997), pp. 144–84; and Albert J. Schmidt, *The Architecture and Planning of Classical Moscow: A Cultural History* (Philadelphia: American Philosophical Society Press, 1989).

[57] Robson, *Old Believers*, p. 57.

[58] Anthony Serge Beliajeff, "The Rise of the Old Orthodox Merchants of Moscow, 1771–1894" (Ph.D. diss., Syracuse University, 1975); West, "A Note on Old Belief," pp. 16–18.

[59] Alexander Gerschenkron, *Europe in the Russian Mirror: Four Lectures in Economic History* (Cambridge, U.K.: Cambridge University Press, 1970), pp. 14–47: 34.

minds from the less fortunate, and less providential 'Nikonians'."[60] The Old Believers evidenced elements of Weberian capitalist spirit not because of doctrinal belief, but rather as a consequence of survival strategies resulting from fierce state persecution.[61]

A SEARCH FOR RUSSIAN DISTINCTIVENESS

A search for Russian self-identity together with a romantic conservatism that prevailed among Moscow's Slavophile intellectuals found ready attraction to the Old Believer and former Old Believer industrialists.[62] Their families defined themselves by historic opposition to the Westernizing state of the post-Petrine Romanovs (although *not* in opposition to the monarch personally). The roots of genuine "Russian-ness" were thought to predate the Romanovs and their "window on the West" in St. Petersburg.

Conservatives such as Nikolai Naidenov, a longtime Moscow city Duma member, dominated the merchants' political life with a harshly reactionary and nationalistic point of view.[63] An advocate of stridently conservative positions, Naidenov remained the city's quintessential insider until his death in 1905.

Naidenov's at times reactionary views surfaced quite early. In late 1882, for example, he wrote to perhaps the most prominent conservative of the era, Konstantin Pobedonostsev, complaining that the Moscow Duma had "taken on the character of a Socialist rally—and it has become difficult, if not impossible, to accomplish anything."[64] These words were written of a body elected by the very wealthiest of Muscovites. The city Duma nevertheless already had become, in Naidenov's mind, a hotbed

---

[60] West, "A Note on Old Belief," p. 16.
[61] Gerschenkron, *Europe in the Russian Mirror*, p. 46. A similar point is made by Blackwell in *The Beginnings of Russian Industrialization*, pp. 212–27.
[62] For further discussion of the connection between Moscow's merchants and the Slavophiles, see Thomas C. Owen, *Capitalism and Politics in Russia: A Social History of the Moscow Merchants, 1855–1905* (Cambridge, U.K.: Cambridge University Press, 1981), pp. 53–59; 71–106. Also see Andrzej Walicki, *The Slavophile Controversy: History of a Conservative Utopia in Nineteenth-Century Russian Thought*, trans. Hilda Andrews-Ruiecka (Oxford, U.K.: Oxford University Press, 1975), pp. 509–30; V. Ia. Laverychev, *Krupnaia burzhuaziia v poreformennoi Rossii, 1861–1900* (Moscow: Mysl', 1974), pp. 139–53; Wortman, *Scenarios of Power*, Vol. 1: *From Peter the Great to the Death of Nicholas I*, pp. 395–402; Ruckman, *The Moscow Business Elite*, pp. 125–29; and A. Vorob'ev', "Moskovskii universitet," *Moskva v' eia proshlom' i nastoiashchem'* 12, pp. 76–105.
[63] Nenarokomova, *Pavel Tret'iakov*, pp. 131–44; Owen, *Capitalism and Politics in Russia*, pp. 82–95; and Ruckman, *The Moscow Business Elite*, pp. 141–43.
[64] As reported in Laverychev, *Krupnaia burzhuaziia*, p. 155.

of communalistic levelers. Philosophical and cultural conservatism often reinforced economic interests, as in persistent advocacy of high tariffs to protect the city's industries from foreign competition.[65]

The economic success of Old Believer industrialist circles and the relative absence of non-Slavic groups in the city combined with an interest in a medieval past among Slavophile intellectuals to produce an intense, Moscow-led search for a distinct Russian national identity.[66] Pavel Tretiakov, Savva Mamontov, Nikolai Riabushinskii, and other tycoon-collectors created an art market that reveled in Russian themes.[67] Successful Old Believer families formed a nucleus of merchant dynasties around which other *nouveaux riches* could adhere.

Elizabeth Kridl Valkenier correctly cautions that the Old Believer essence of merchant Moscow life can be, and has been, overstated. Old Believer clans, Valkenier argues, "did not remain firm in their Old Belief; some became agnostics, others converted to standard Orthodoxy."[68] Yet the great Old Believer families provided a core around which much of Moscow life revolved, even as that center was itself evolving.

---

[65] Owen, *Capitalism and Politics in Russia*, pp. 59–70; and Owen, *The Corporation under Russian Law*, pp. 102–4.

[66] Boldina, "Statisticheskii portret Moskvy," pp. 167–69.

[67] For further discussion of these developments, see John O. Norman, "Pavel Tretiakov and Merchant Art Patronage, 1850–1900," in Edith W. Clowes, Samuel D. Kassow, and James L. West, eds., *Between Tsar and People: Educated Society and the Quest for Public Identity in Late Imperial Russia* (Princeton: Princeton University Press, 1991), pp. 93–107; John E. Bowlt, "The Moscow Art Movement," in ibid., pp. 108–28; and Nenarokomova, *Pavel Tret'iakov*. For an engaging contemporary account, see Iu. I. Shamurin', "Khudozhestvennaia zhizn' Moskvy v' XIX vek'," *Moskva v' eia proshlom' i nastoiashchem'* 11, pp. 91–116.

    Jo Ann Ruckman explains that this interest in Russian art may not have been driven by nationalist sentiments alone. Tretiakov, for example, initiated his collection with the purchase of European old masters. He evidently was swindled because, thereafter, he wanted to purchase art only from artists whose work could be authenticated—a much easier task if one purchased the paintings directly from the artists themselves. Ruckman, *The Moscow Business Elite*, p. 83.

    Two Moscow collectors—Ivan Morozov and Sergei Shchukin—acquired perhaps the world's best holdings of then-modern French art, including extensive numbers of works by Impressionist painters, Picasso, and other to-be-famous European artists. Their paintings eventually constituted the core holdings of the city's major museums and, in the cases of Morozov and Shchukin, of the Hermitage's magnificent nineteenth- and twentieth-century collections in St. Petersburg, and those of the National Gallery of Art in Washington, D.C. For further discussion of the Morozov and Shchukin collections, see Beverly Whitney Kean, *French Painters, Russian Collectors: The Merchant Patrons of Modern Art in Pre-Revolutionary Russia* (London: Hodder and Stoughton, 1994). For further discussion of the Soviet fates of the Morozov and Shchukin collections, see Geraldine Norman, *The Hermitage: The Biography of a Great Museum* (New York: Fromm International, 1998), pp. 114–32, 179–201.

[68] Elizabeth Kridl Valkenier, "Book Review: *Merchant Moscow: Images of Russia's Vanished Bourgeoisie*. Edited by James L. West and Iurii A. Petrov," *Harriman Review* 10, no. 4 (August 1998), pp. 38–40: 40.

The founders of several Moscow merchant dynasties came from serf stock, as is often the case in upstart and innovative cities.[69] Savva Morozov, the founder of his family's dynasty, arrived in Moscow in the wake of the 1812 conflagration that had destroyed the city after the arrival of Napoleon's Grand Army; Morozov began by selling textiles from door to door.[70] Aleksei Bakhrushin began peddling his leather goods only a short time later, while the Alekseevs, Prokhorovs, Shchukins, Solodovnikovs, and Tretiakovs all descended from small-time peasant entrepreneurs who had come to town during the eighteenth century.[71] They made their way to Moscow where they were able to start new lives as small traders.[72]

Others emerged from the free urban population of *posadskie liudi*.[73] Commerce eventually led these salesmen to production, which by the late nineteenth century had turned into industry. By the early years of the twentieth century, industry and manufacturing were far more important in the portfolios of most of the great Moscow families, although many maintained robust wholesale and retail operations.[74]

Marrying one another, this tight network of merchant families established a complex, multilayered, closely knit hierarchy that dominated nearly every aspect of Moscow life.[75] Pavel and Sergei Tretiakov, for

[69] Hall, *Cities in Civilization*, 302–4.

[70] Belitskii and Glezer, *Moskva neznakomaia*, pp. 175–77; Valentine T. Bill, *The Forgotten Class: The Russian Bourgeoisie from the Earliest Beginnings to 1900* (New York: Praeger, 1959), pp. 16–26; James Lawrence West, "The Moscow Progressists: Russian Industrialists in Liberal Politics, 1905–1914" (Ph.D. diss., Princeton University, 1974), p. 57.

[71] Nenarokomova, *Pavel Tret'iakov*, pp. 10–25; Pavel Buryshkin, *Moskva kupecheskaia: zapiski* (Moscow: Sovremennik, 1991), pp. 102–29; West, "The Moscow Progressists," pp. 76–77; Evgenii Zakharovich Baranov, *Moskovskie legendy: zapisannye Evgeniem Baranovym*, comp. Vera Bokova (Moscow: Literatura i politika, 1993), pp. 165–71. Moscow during the Catherinian Age was surprisingly robust given the city's new "second city" status behind St. Petersburg. For further discussion of the era, see Albert J. Schmidt, "Westernization as Consumption: Estate Building in the Moscow Region during the Eighteenth Century," *Proceedings of the American Philosophical Society* 139, no. 4 (1995), pp. 380–419.

[72] For further discussion of the pre-reform origins of the Moscow merchantry, see V. Ia. Laverychev, *Krupnaia burzhuaziia v poreformennoi Rossii, 1861–1900*, pp. 63–71; as well as Vasilii Kakhrushin, "Opisanie postroeniia khrama sv. Vasiliia ispovednika v Moskve za Rogozhskoi zastavoi v novoe derevne," in A. S. Kiselev, et al., eds., *Moskovskii arkhiv. Istoriko-kraevedcheskie al'manakh*, pp. 131–53.

[73] Valkenier, "Book Review: *Merchant Moscow*," p. 40.

[74] Ruckman, *The Moscow Business Elite*, pp. 49–51.

[75] Bill, *The Forgotten Class*, pp. 99–102. Also see more recent articles, such as Sergei Rogatko, "Botkiny," *Byloe* 1998, no. 2, p. 7; Valerii Osinov, "Reka-kormilitsa," *Byloe* 1998, no. 2, pp. 8–9; Pavel Primachenko, "Napoleon knizhnogo delo'," *Byloe* 1998, no. 2, p. 10; and Elena Shukhova, "Doma deshevykh kvartir," *Byloe* 1998, no. 2, p. 12.

10. The Kremlin wall and tower of the Sacred Gate, Moscow, 1898. Underwood and Underwood. Library of Congress, Prints and Photographs Division, LC-USZ62-073379.

example, established lifelong ties with Anton and Nikolai Rubenstein during childhood late-afternoon swimming expeditions to the Moscow River from their tumbledown Zamoskvorech'e neighborhoods.[76]

Personal connections eventually became institutionalized through trade organizations and other groups, such as the post-1905 Association of Industry and Trade.[77] Their ties extended to other major commercial towns, such as Nizhnii Novgorod, where Moscow merchants dominated

[76] Nenarokomova, *Pavel Tret'iakov*, pp. 18–19.
[77] Ruth AmEnde Roosa, "The Association of Industry and Trade, 1906–1914: An Examination of the Economic Views of Organized Industrialists in Prerevolutionary Russia" (Ph.D. diss., Columbia University, 1967).

the city's famous trade fair.[78] Their banks, which were established with little of the state support so critical for their St. Petersburg competitors, held financial resources second only to those of the capital.[79] And yet, the very complexity of these deep relationships necessarily meant that Moscow remained, in the words of Evgenii Zamiatin, a city unlike St. Petersburg in that "no one's single will directed its growth."[80]

COMPLEX CONTRADICTIONS AND ENIGMAS

Moscow's industries—primarily textiles, metalworking, and machine tools—increased the value of their production by over 300 percent during the latter half of the nineteenth century as a national rail network ferried resources, labor, and workers into the city's interior.[81] Nearly a quarter of the country's industrial turnover and almost 18 percent of trade turnover took place in Moscow and its immediate territory.[82] Local industry looked primarily to domestic markets, hence Moscow's interest in sustaining high protective tariffs. A robust export sector developed over time, especially in textile products manufactured for markets in the Balkans, the Middle East, Mongolia, and those sections of Poland incorporated into the Russian Empire.[83]

Actual production took place both in large factories and in smaller artisanal shops frequently employing fewer than 100 workers. Of the city's 263,078 workers in 1902, 151,359 were classified as being "artisanal" rather than "factory."[84] Textile production of all kinds dominated

---

[78] Laverychev, *Krupnaia burzhuaziia*, pp. 86–108; and Dmitrii Nikolaevich Smirnov, *Nizhegorodskaia starina* (Nizhnii Novgorod: Nizhegorodskaia iarmaka, 1995), pp. 484–518.

[79] On the history of Russian commercial banking, see I. F. Gindin, *Banki i promyshlennost' v Rossii. K voprosu o finansovom kapitale v Rossii* (Moscow: Promizdat, 1927); I. F. Gindin, *Gosudarstvennyi bank i ekonomicheskaia politika tsarskogo pravitel'stva, 1861–1892 gody* (Moscow: Gosfinizdat, 1960); Boris V. Anan'ich, *Bankirskie doma v Rossii, 1860–1914gg. Ocherki istorii chastnogo predprinimatel'stva* (Leningrad: Nauka, Leningradskoe otdelenie, 1991); and V. I. Bovykin and Iu. A. Petrov, *Kommercheskie banki Rossiiskoi imperii* (Moscow: Perspektiva, 1994). On the history of savings associations and banks, see Iu. A. Petrov and S. V. Kalmykov, *Sberegatel'noe delo v Rossii. Vekhi istorii* (Moscow: K.I.T., 1995), pp. 22–68.

[80] Evgenii Zamiatin, *A Soviet Heretic: Essays by Yevgeny Zamyatin*, ed. and trans. Mirra Ginsburg (Evanston, Ill.: Northwestern University Press, 1992), p. 133.

[81] Bradley, *Muzhik and Muscovite*, pp. 70–99; and Berton, *Moscow* (London: I. B. Tauris, 1990), p. 172.

[82] Ruckman, *The Moscow Business Elite*, p. 2.

[83] V. Ia. Laverychev, "K voprosu ob osobennostiakh eksporta tkanei iz Rossii v kontse XIX–nachale XX veka," *Vestnik Moskovskogo universiteta* 9, no. 6 (1965), pp. 58–69; S. B. Ippo, *Moskva i London". Istoricheskie, obshchestvennyi i ekonomicheskie ocherki i issledovaniia* (Moscow: Universitetskaia tipografiia, 1888), pp. 217–58.

[84] Victoria E. Bonnell, *Roots of Rebellion: Workers' Politics and Organizations in St. Petersburg and Moscow, 1900–1914* (Berkeley: University of California Press, 1983), p. 33.

Moscow's economic life, an industrial profile that lent itself to a large number of smaller production facilities. Such dependence on smaller workshops distinguished Moscow from St. Petersburg, where larger plants predominated.[85]

Moscow was essentially a workers' town, with 60 percent of its 1902 workforce classified as factory and artisanal workers, as opposed to less than 20 percent who were labeled as "entrepreneurs" and "professionals."[86] Small production facilities continued to flourish in Moscow up until the outbreak of World War I.[87] A dense net of widely dispersed shops and factories employed relatively stable labor forces next door to the retail and wholesale distributors of their products.[88]

Unions made their appearance, emerging with vigor during the Revolution of 1905. Russia's unions attracted the most urbanized, skilled, and literate among the country's industrial workers as more formal labor organizations emerged from the strike movements of the turn of the century.[89] Unions grew in number throughout 1905, picking up steam following the legalization of trade unions and employer associations on March 4, 1906. Sixty-three unions with over 52,000 members were functioning in Moscow by early 1907, when political and legislative autocratic retrenchment once again undercut labor's right to organize. A modest revival in union activities occurred in Moscow on the eve of World War I.

The imperial government's harsh retaliatory practices forced many disgruntled workers underground, swelling the ranks of radical socialist parties such as the Bolsheviks and Mensheviks and providing fertile soil for right-wing groups as well.[90] Bullying extremist "fighting brotherhoods" took advantage of the general social disorder of 1905–6 to launch some of Moscow's worst pogroms, culminating with the Union of Russian Men's infamous October 16, 1905, riot aimed at killing as many of Moscow's Jews and socialists as could be found.[91] Russia's impending social breakdown lurked just beneath Moscow's sometimes-placid surface throughout the years examined here. Social distance

---

[85] Ibid., p. 39.   [86] Engelstein, *Moscow 1905*, pp. 19–21.

[87] Bonnell, *Roots of Rebellion*, p. 366.

[88] G. Vasilich', "Moskva, 1850–1910g.," *Moskva v' eia proshlom' i nastoiashchem'* 11, pp. 3–28.

[89] Victoria Bonnell, "Radical Politics and Organized Labor in Pre-Revolutionary Moscow, 1905–1914," *Journal of Social History* 12, no. 2 (1979), pp. 282–300.

[90] Don C. Rawson, *Russian Rightists and the Revolution of 1905* (Cambridge, U.K.: Cambridge University Press, 1995).

[91] Ibid., pp. 129–42.

between Moscow's employers and employees nonetheless remained much less than in industrial centers dominated by a few very large factories.

"Abounding in new millionaires," Moscow was home to wealth as well as workers.[92] It was, in fact, Russia's wealthiest city, with the largest number of merchants among all of Russia's towns and cities.[93] Over a quarter of the Russian Empire's "trading houses" were located in Moscow, far in advance of runner-up St. Petersburg, which was home to 13 percent.[94] Moscow similarly led the country by 1910 in the number of individuals earning over 1,000 rubles ($515 in 1903) annually.[95]

Moscow was thus a community in which wealth and poverty coexisted in close proximity.[96] "This architectural and social miscibility, common in Russian cities," Timothy Colton writes, "was more pronounced in Moscow, and historians have used it to help explain Moscow workers' lower degree of class hostility."[97] Moscow was a city of large factories and small workshops, of commerce and industry, of wealth and poverty. The city was noteworthy, in short, for the diversity of its human experience, as may be seen in the variety of its housing stock.

By as early as 1882, Moscow's poor—mostly peasants moving in and out from declining villages—lived where they could, in crowded

[92] Ruckman, *The Moscow Business Elite*, p. 18.
[93] Michael F. Hamm, "The Breakdown of Urban Modernization: Prelude to the Revolutions of 1917," in Hamm, ed., *The City in Russian History*, pp. 182–200: 192. Moreover, the 1897 census categorized 19,491 Muscovites as merchants, ahead of St. Petersburg's 17,411 merchants. A. N. Bokhanov, *Krupnaia burzhuaziia Rossii* (Moscow: Nauka, 1992), p. 31. Although this figure would fluctuate with Russia's and the city's economic fortunes, Moscow retained its lead in the number of merchants until the end of the imperial period. Laverychev, *Krupnaia burzhuaziia*, p. 64.
[94] The actual Moscow percentage in 1904 was 28 percent. Bokhanov, *Krupnaia burzhuaziia Rossii*, p. 99.
[95] This conversion rate is found in Henri Troyat, *Daily Life in Russia under the Last Tsar*, trans. Malcolm Barnes (Stanford: Stanford University Press, 1979), p. 8.
    Moscow's 76,610 thousand-ruble earners edged out the entire St. Petersburg province (*guberniia*) by 285 individuals. Lifliandia (which included the present-day Latvian capital of Riga) came in third with 72,234 thousand-ruble income earners. Warsaw, the Kherson region (including Odessa), and Kyiv followed far behind with between 25,000 and 32,000 equivalent earners, respectively. Not unexpectedly, Petersburg, Moscow, Lifliandia, and Kherson *gubernii* were the empire's most urbanized provinces, with only the two capitals being classified as more than 50 percent "urban." Rashin, *Naselenie Rossii*, p. 101.
[96] As is apparent in Irina Nenarokomova's description of Zamoskvorech'e, on pp. 10–25 of her biography of art collector Pavel Tretiakov (Nenarokomova, *Pavel Tret'iakov*). For a contemporary account, see: G. Vasilich, "Ulitsy i liudi sovremennoi Moskvy," *Moskva v' eia proshlom' i nastoiashchem'* 12, pp. 3–16.
[97] Colton, *Moscow: Governing the Socialist Metropolis*, p. 44.

makeshift lean-tos, basements, barracks, and the infamous *ugol'* (quite literally a rented corner).[98] More well-off proletarian families fared better, perhaps sharing a room or two in a two-story wooden building that contained a dozen apartments housing eighty or so people (with no bath or indoor toilet facilities, and a communal kitchen that required trips to a water tap located on a nearby street).[99] The middle order enjoyed new apartment houses while the wealthy merchants favored "overdesigned, over furnished, and over decorated townhouses" that did not seek "to ape the Russian aristocracy but to build something new."[100] The private spaces of all classes revealed a love of eccentricity, drama, and the unexpected, traits that also spilled out into Moscow's tortuous back alleys, hidden courtyards, twisting lanes, and broad boulevards.[101] The keen eye and expressive prose of Walter Benjamin caught this hodge-podge city as well as anyone. Visiting the city as 1926 became 1927, Benjamin found Moscow's streets curious in a manner that they had been for centuries, with the Russian village playing "hide-and-seek" in them.[102]

Whatever the social group, Muscovites preferred a dramatic gesture over regularity. This love of the unpredictable pervaded local life and remains one of the city's defining characteristics to this day. It also became the physical manifestation of the city's complex contradictions. Timothy Colton's ultimate assessment of Moscow under the old regime captures its profound enigmas. Colton highlights "the mismatch between the complexity and dynamism of [Moscow's] economic and social systems and the ineffectiveness of its political institutions" before concluding that, "[t]hough hardly without its horrors and injustices, the private Moscow responded gamely to intermittent crises and grew in its capacity to meet the needs of most of its inhabitants." Unfortunately,

[98] By 1882 only 26.2 percent of the city's population were Moscow natives. M. Ia. Vydro, *Naselenie Moskvy (po materialam perepisei naseleniia, 1871–1970gg)* (Moscow: Statistika, 1976), p. 11.

[99] Diane Koenker, *Moscow Workers and the 1917 Revolution* (Princeton: Princeton University Press, 1981), pp. 54–55.

[100] John Russell, "The Twilight of the Russian Bourgeoisie," *New York Times*, May 19, 1991, pp. H35–H36.

[101] Iu. I. Shamurin', "Arkhitektura Moskvy," *Moskva v' eia proshlom' i nastoiashchem'* 11, pp. 117–25; G. Baltiskii, "Vnieshnyi vid' Moskvy srediny XIX veka," *Moskva v eia proshlom' i nastoaishchem'* 10, pp. 9–76.

[102] Walter Benjamin, *Moscow Diary*, ed. Gary Smith, trans. Richard Sieburth (Cambridge, Mass.: Harvard University Press, 1986), p. 67. For more on Benjamin's Moscow journey, see Bernd Witte, *Walter Benjamin: An Intellectual Biography*, trans. James Rolleston (Detroit: Wayne State University Press, 1991).

"with the public city, it was a different story."[103] The repercussions of that difference would reverberate for nearly a century.

GOVERNING MOSCOW

Moscow's metropolitan pluralism—like tolerance in many large urban centers—was born not of a desire for interaction so much as of a drive for mutual survival. This would be the case for much of the period under examination, which begins with the 1873 implementation of Alexander II's municipal liberalization of three years earlier.[104] Liberal reform did not last.[105] Counter-reforms in 1892 limited municipal autonomy yet again.[106] More important, class differences became more pronounced. The civil upheavals of 1905–7 exposed deep divisions within Moscow's "congeries of disparate social groups."[107] No social group proved immune to collective action in 1905, and hardly a public or private institution was unaffected by that year's conflicts.[108] Municipal governance itself became an issue during the 1905 Revolution, with popularly supported workers councils—the *sovety*—temporarily replacing formal city administration.[109]

The legalization of political parties in 1905 prompted the emergence of party politics for the first time in Moscow's governing institutions. A

[103] Colton, *Moscow: Governing the Socialist Metropolis*, p. 69.
[104] A. A. Kizevetter, *Miestnoe samoupravlenie v' Rossii. IX–XIX st. Istoricheskii ocherk'* (Moscow: Izd. Moskovskogo universiteta, 1910); Walter Hanchett, "Tsarist Statutory Regulation of Municipal Government in the Nineteenth Century," in Hamm, ed., *The City in Russian History*, pp. 91–114, 196–207; Larissa Zakharova, "Autocracy and the Reforms of 1861–1874 in Russia: Choosing Paths of Development," trans. Daniel Field, in Ben Eklof, John Bushnell, and Larissa Zakharova, eds., *Russia's Great Reforms, 1855–1881* (Bloomington: Indiana University Press, 1994), pp. 19–39; and Valeriia A. Nardova, "Municipal Self-Government after the 1870 Reform," trans. Lori A. Citti, in ibid., pp. 181–96.
[105] Ruckman, *The Moscow Business Elite*, pp. 175–210.
[106] Hanchett, "Tsarist Statutory Regulation," pp. 107–13; Nardova, "Municipal Self-Government," pp. 195–96.
[107] Engelstein, *Moscow 1905*, p. 4.
[108] Ibid., pp. 10–15. For a revealing analysis of social disorder in St. Petersburg during the same period, see Joan Neuberger, *Hooliganism: Crime, Culture, and Power in St. Petersburg, 1900–1914* (Berkeley: University of California Press, 1993). An overview of the 1905 Revolution may be found in Abraham Ascher, *The Revolution of 1905*, 2 vols. (Stanford: Stanford University Press, 1988–92).
[109] On the creation of the *sovety* in general, see Oskar Anweiler, *The Soviets: The Russian Workers, Peasants, and Soldiers Councils, 1905–1912*, trans. Ruth Hein (New York: Pantheon, 1974), which includes a discussion of the Moscow soviets in 1905–7 (pp. 40–64). On the Moscow Soviet in particular, see Robert Melville Slusser, "The Moscow Soviet of Workers' Deputies of 1905: Origin, Structures, and Policies" (Ph.D. diss., Columbia University, 1963).

reactionary "Naidenovskaia" group—led by archconservatives Nikolai Naidenov, Grigorii Krestovnikov, and members of the Botkin family—competed locally with "young," "progressivist" entrepreneurs—centered around the Riabushinskiis and Morozovs.[110] Moscow's Bolsheviks were generally credited with being more tolerant than their revolutionary brethren in Petersburg.[111] The fanaticism of the 1917 revolutions nevertheless swept away many of the city's social rivals.

Municipal governance in Moscow remained embedded within highly centralized imperial bureaucratic and political structures throughout much of the period under review.[112] The optimal fit of municipalities into the imperial order had bewildered Russian sovereigns for decades if not centuries. If, as may be seen in subsequent chapters, some claim of competence is appropriate for American and Meiji local governance of this era, it was far less so for Russia.[113]

Experiments in local self-government continued throughout the imperial era, with alternating periods of greater and lesser local autonomy. In Moscow, the most liberal period in local self-government began with Alexander II's 1870 municipal reform act.[114] Moscow was governed under that law by a rather large (160- to 180-member) policy-making city duma, which in turn elected a small (seven- to nine-member) administrative board, or *uprava*, that had responsibility for establishing the duma agenda and running the city more generally.[115] The mayor, elected by qualified voters, presided over both the duma and the *uprava*. Four of the empire's largest cities—St. Petersburg, Moscow, Odessa, and

---

[110] Ruckman, *The Moscow Business Elite*, pp. 156–57; V. Ia. Laverychev, "Moskovskie promyshlenniki v gody pervoi Russkoi revoliutsii," *Vestnik Moskovskogo universiteta* 9, no. 3 (1964), pp. 37–53; V. Ia. Laverychev, *Po tu storonu barrikad (iz istorii bor'by Moskovskoi burzhuazii s revoliutsiei)* (Moscow: Mysl', 1967); and West, "The Moscow Progressists."

[111] Robert C. Williams, *The Other Bolsheviks: Lenin and His Critics, 1904–1914* (Bloomington: Indiana University Press, 1986).

[112] O. Kuzovleva, "Upravliat' Moskvoi neprosto," in Kiselev et al., eds., *Moskovskii arkhiv*, pp. 183–203.

[113] Anders Henriksson, *The Tsar's Loyal Germans: The Riga German Community: Social Change and the Nationality Question, 1855–1905*, East European Monographs (New York: Columbia University Press, 1983), p. 5.

[114] Hanchett, "Moscow in the Late Nineteenth Century," pp. 45–76; Nicholas J. Astrov, "The Municipal Government and the All-Russian Union of Towns," in Paul G. Gronsky and Nicholas J. Astrov, eds., *The War and the Russian Government* (New York: Howard Fartig, 1973), pp. 129–321: 132–33. For discussion of earlier decentralization efforts, see S. Frederick Starr, *Decentralization and Self-Government in Russia, 1830–1870* (Princeton: Princeton University Press, 1972).

[115] Hanchett, "Moscow in the Late Nineteenth Century," pp. 60–65; Colton, *Moscow: Governing the Socialist Metropolis*, pp. 52–53; and Nardova, "Municipal Self-Government," pp. 183–84.

Riga—also had an assistant mayor. All local officials held four-year terms.

Russian municipal officials were able to draw on charitable donations and bequests to city charity funds to support institutions assisting the poor.[116] By 1900, per capita gifts to charity in Moscow had surpassed similar levels in Paris, Berlin, and Vienna.[117] The Moscow city Duma collected more than 32.5 million rubles in charitable contributions between 1863 and 1912. The Duma established a Department of City Capital and Funds Management in 1912 to administer such charity accounts, which constituted more than a third of the city's budget for assistance activities at that time. Overall, Moscow—in a pattern that was similar to that of other Russian cities—expended the greatest proportion of its municipal budget on health, education, and welfare.[118]

Health, education, and public welfare were also spheres of Russian life in which women established their ability to act. Barbara Alpern Engel acknowledges that, "to be sure, in nineteenth century Russia, as elsewhere in Europe, to be female meant to be a daughter, wife, and almost inevitably mother, and to be subordinate to males in all but the last of these positions." But, she continues,

the content of family roles and the quality of female subordination differed considerably from Western European patterns. In some ways the position of Russian women was more independent, because they retained their rights to property even after marriage, and depending on social position, fulfilled a variety of responsibilities that were vital to maintaining the family's economic and social status.[119]

Engel also observes that Russian women were, in many ways, more "helpless" than their European counterparts as a consequence of an authoritarianism that characterized both Russia's autocratic political system and family relations. Engel notes that many unskilled and usually illiterate village women not unexpectedly found semidependent

[116] Galina Ulianova, "Pages of History: Private Donations in the Municipal Funding of Moscow Charity Institutions at the Beginning of the Twentieth Century," *World of Learning Forum: NGO Law in Brief* 1 (Winter 1995), pp. 9–10. Also see G. N. Ul'ianova, "Blagotvoritel'nost' Moskovskikh predprinimatelei, 1860-e–1914g." (Ph.D. diss., Russian Academy of Sciences, 1995); and M. P. Shchepkin, *Obshchestvennoe khoziaistvo goroda Moskvy v 1863–1887 godakh. Istoriko-statisticheskoe opisanie* (Moscow: Moskovskaia gorodskaia tipografiia, 1890).

[117] Ruckman, *The Moscow Business Elite*, p. 88.

[118] Bradley, *Muzhik and Muscovite*, pp. 37–40.

[119] Barbara Alpern Engel, *Mothers and Daughters: Women of the Intelligentsiia in Nineteenth-Century Russia* (Cambridge, U.K.: Cambridge University Press, 1983), pp. 6–7.

positions as servants, cooks, or nursemaids when they migrated to town.[120]

Hardly every turn-of-the-century Moscow woman was ready or able to sacrifice all for a cause. Yet Russia and Moscow both nurtured significant numbers of exceedingly strong female figures in revolutionary politics, medicine, the arts, and municipal life more generally.[121] Many—and many more than in the rest of Europe—were prepared to advance the health, education, and welfare of their fellow Muscovites, regardless of class. Municipal government's achievements in health, education, and welfare were frequently a direct consequence of the dedication and activism of women, far too many of whose names are lost to history.

IMPERIAL RULES FOR LOCAL GOVERNMENT

An inauspiciously large number of external factors severely limited the scope of Moscow's municipal operations despite some substantial achievements. Provincial (*gubernaiia*) governors appointed by the tsar were empowered to forward municipal decrees to St. Petersburg for review; meanwhile during which time imperial bureaucrats could invalidate local legislative acts or decisions.[122] Moscow's conservative imperial governors used their authority to hold liberal municipal officials in check throughout the last years of the empire.[123]

---

[120] Barbara Alpern Engel, *Between the Fields and the City: Women, Work, and Family in Russia, 1861–1914* (Cambridge, U.K.: Cambridge University Press, 1994), p. 5.

[121] The "women's question" had been firmly placed on Russia's radical agenda by Nikolai Chernyshevsky's landmark 1863 novel, *What Is to Be Done?* Women fought bitter and only partially successful battles to secure full educational rights—with a number of prominent upper- and middle-class women heading to Switzerland for higher education in the mid-nineteenth century. Women's wages were lower than men's, as were their literacy rates. Many women turned to monastic communities and religious life to find opportunities for autonomy, self-development, advancement, and empowerment unavailable in Russian society at large.

For further discussion of these issues, see Richard Stites, *The Women's Liberation Movement in Russia: Feminism, Nihilism, and Bolshevism, 1860–1930* (Princeton: Princeton University Press, 1978), pp. 82–90; Aleksandr Aleksandrovich Kizevetter, *Na rubezhe dvukh stoletii (Vospominaniia 1881–1914)* (Prague: Orbis, 1929), pp. 253–318; and Barbara Alpern Engel and Clifford N. Rosenthal, *Five Sisters: Women against the Tsar* (New York: Knopf, 1975).

[122] Hanchett, "Moscow in the Late Nineteenth Century," pp. 65–70.

[123] Robert William Thurston, "Urban Problems and Local Government in Late Imperial Russia, 1906–1914" (Ph.D. diss., University of Michigan, 1980), pp. 2–3. A genuinely informative discussion of the interrelations among imperial governors and ministers and local officials in the realm of higher education may be found in Guido Hausmann, "Akademische Berufsgruppen in Odessa, 1850–1917," in Charles McClelland, Stephan Merl, and Hannes Siegrist, eds., *Professionen im modernen Osteuropa* (Berlin: Duncker and Humblot, 1995), pp. 427–63.

11. Women selling dry goods, Moscow, 1919. Keystone View Company. Library
of Congress, Prints and Photographs Division, LC-USZ62-080668.

Governors also controlled the police and had the capacity to issue compulsory orders that might contradict local decisions. Prince Vladimir Dolgorukov, Moscow governor-general from 1865 until 1891, was undoubtedly the city's most powerful political figure throughout the 1870 reform period.[124] Given such powers, St. Petersburg–selected governors rather than locally elected mayors were popularly known as the true "town chiefs" (*gorodskoi golova*) throughout Russia.[125] Yet, as Richard Robbins persuasively argues, the governors' power became largely negative—the power of the veto—rather than a capacity to proactively shape their province's or city's future.[126]

The pull and tug between centrally appointed governors and locally elected councils and mayors conforms to a larger pattern throughout late-nineteenth-century Russia and eastern and central Europe.[127] The politics of emergent nationalism frequently became entwined with tussles over local autonomy. The Moscow case both conforms to this broader pattern and marks an important exception. The major protagonists in the ancient capital were generally Russian, so confrontations over centralization were distinct from battles by nationalistic minorities to defend themselves against forced assimilation.

Parallel reform of regional administration established more powerful and generally liberal legislative authorities in the countryside: the zemstvo.[128] Thomas Porter and William Gleason persuasively argue that the zemstvo undermined the regime's paternal rule while leading to the development of a public sphere.[129] Zemstvo councils frequently com-

---

[124] Owen, *Capitalism and Politics in Russia*, p. 78.

[125] The governor's powers were more visible in smaller provincial towns than in the empire's industrial giants. An entertaining fictionalized account of such figures may be found in Vasilii Nemirovich-Danchenko's novel *Gorodskoi golova: roman'* (St. Petersburg: Izd. P. P. Soikina, 1904).

[126] Richard G. Robbins, Jr., *The Tsar's Viceroys: Russian Provincial Governors in the Last Years of the Empire* (Ithaca: Cornell University Press, 1987), pp. 16–17.

[127] A point underscored in Henriksson, *The Tsar's Loyal Germans*, p. ix.

[128] Feodor A. Petrov, "Crowning the Edifice: The Zemstvo, Local Self-Government, and the Constitutional Movement, 1864–1881," trans. Robin Bisha, in Eklof, Bushnell, and Zakharova, eds., *Russia's Great Reforms*, pp. 197–213. For an overview of the extensive scholarship on the zemstvos, see Terence Emmons and Wayne S. Vucinich, eds., *The Zemstvo in Russia: An Experiment in Local Self-Government* (Cambridge, U.K.: Cambridge University Press, 1982).

[129] Thomas Porter and William Gleason, "The Zemstvo and the Transformation of Russian Society," in Mary Schaeffer Conroy, ed., *Emerging Democracy in Late Imperial Russia: Case Studies on Local Self-Government (the Zemstvos), State Duma Elections, the Tsarist Government, and the State Council before and during World War One* (Niwot: University of Colorado Press, 1998), pp. 60–87; and Thomas Porter and William Gleason, "The Democratization of the Zemstvo during the First World War," in ibid., pp. 228–42.

peted with city councils for local tax revenues, a constant source of contention in Moscow throughout this period.[130]

City administrators simultaneously were limited to management of the
"municipal economy."[131] Their authority was largely restricted to provision of basic services and the management of municipal enterprises. In
the case of Moscow, the latter became an ever more important source of
independent revenue in a fiscal system that severely limited local tax collection.[132] Revenues had fallen hopelessly behind expenditures by the
mid-1870s, with an accumulated deficit by 1887 that was roughly equivalent to the entire municipal budget for that year.[133]

By the second decade of the twentieth century, income from municipally owned properties, concessions, and businesses accounted for 40
percent of Moscow city government revenue.[134] Income from slaughterhouses and municipal sewer, water, and transportation services grew ever
more robust, as did property registration fees.[135] City-controlled tram
lines similarly provided enormous profits as ridership grew to over 330
million passengers in 1914.[136] Taxes, meanwhile, accounted for an ever
smaller percentage of municipal revenues.[137]

Moscow's municipal government had the largest operating budget of
any Russian city by the early 1890s. The city's 1892 budget, for example,
was 11.2 million rubles, as compared with 10.3 million rubles for the
St. Petersburg municipal administration. The Odessa government was
third among the empire's cities, with a budget of 3.3 million rubles
that year.[138]

---

[130] For a discussion of duma-zemstvo competition, see Owen, *Capitalism and Politics in Russia*, pp. 95–97. For a zemstvo perspective on these relations, see the memoirs of Moscow Provincial Zemstvo leader Dimitri Shipov: Dmitrii Nikolaevich Shipov", *Vospominaniia i dumy o perezhitom"* (Moscow: Pechatnaia S. P. Iakovleva, 1918).

[131] Hanchett, "Moscow in the Late Nineteenth Century," p. 63.

[132] Astrov, "The Municipal Government," pp. 141–53; Shchepkin', *Obshchestvennoe khoziaistvo goroda Moskvy.*

[133] Shchepkin', *Obshchestvennoe khoziaistvo goroda Moskvy*, pp. 4–6, and accompany-ing charts.

[134] Engelstein, *Moscow 1905*, p. 52; G. Iaroslavskii, "Gorodskoe samoupravlenie Moskvy," *Moskva v' eia proshlom' i nastoiashchem'* 12, pp. 17–48: 38–39.

[135] Mikhailovskii, "Munitsipal'naia Moskva," pp. 124–30.

[136] Ibid., pp. 138–39; E. Kirichenko, "Tramvai i gradostroitel'noe razvitie Moskvy," in Kiselev et al., eds., *Moskovskii arkhiv*, pp. 204–17.

[137] Shchepkin', *Obshchestvennoe khoziaistvo goroda Moskvy*, pp. 4–6, and accompany-ing charts.

[138] V. A. Nardova, *Samoderzhavie i gorodskie dumy v Rossii v kontse XIX–nachale XX veka* (Saint Petersburg: Nauka, 1994), p. 49. For a point of comparison with Moscow, see the discussion of the Odessa municipal budget at the end of the nineteenth century in Patricia Herlihy, *Odessa: A History, 1794–1914* (Cambridge, Mass.: Harvard University Press, 1986), pp. 148–51.

Suffrage was also limited.[139] Moreover, the Ministry of Interior could intervene in this complex electoral system to nullify outcomes viewed as unacceptable in St. Petersburg.

Balloting was organized by *sosloviia* (guild), giving those who paid the most taxes considerably greater weight in the Duma.[140] Such "guilds" bore a superficial resemblance to similar social organizational forms in Europe. Movement from one *soslovie* to another was more open than in the West, with the Russian "estates" proving themselves, in the words of Gregory Freeze, "adaptable to the exigencies of social and economic development."[141]

Russian *soslovie* were narrowly defined in purpose, rather mechanistic in operation, and could formally express opinions about only their own direct concerns.[142] As a result political institutions predicated on *soslovie* were not nearly as dynamic as Russian society itself, even though, to return to Freeze, "the *soslovie* did not inexorably dissolve into classes in the post reform era, as traditionally posited in the estate-class paradigm."[143] This was particularly true in one of Russia's most dynamic cities, Moscow.[144]

All of these various legal provisions and administrative realities resulted in the registration of only a minute proportion of the city's population for participation in municipal elections. The turnout of eligible voters remained shockingly low—just 8 percent of eligible voters bothered to cast their ballots in 1888 and 1889.[145] The municipal political elite produced by such rules of the game became self-perpetuating,[146]

---

[139] The right to vote was granted only to "men 25 years of age and older, holding Russian citizenship, who owned real estate in the city and were subject to municipal real estate taxes, or who maintained a commercial or industrial establishment in the city under the authorization of a merchant guild, or who having lived in the city for two years preceding an election, had paid the relatively low municipal fees for various minor commercial and industrial licenses and permits." Hanchett, "Moscow in the Late Nineteenth Century," pp. 77–78.

[140] Ibid., pp. 84–89.

[141] Gregory Freeze, "The *Soslovie* (Estate) Paradigm and Russian Social History," *American Historical Review* 91, no. 1 (1986), pp. 11–36: 24.

[142] Ruckman, *The Moscow Business Elite*, pp. 25–30.

[143] Freeze, "The *Soslovie* (Estate) Paradigm," p. 36.

[144] Owen, *Capitalism and Politics in Russia*, p. 77.

[145] Ibid., p. 77; Hanchett, "Moscow in the Late Nineteenth Century," pp. 127–34; Colton, *Moscow: Governing the Socialist Metropolis*, pp. 52–53; and Thurston, "Urban Problems," pp. 106–8. Such low turnout was still higher than the national average of 5.5 percent of eligible voters going to the polls in municipal elections in forty Russian cities and towns. Nardova, "Municipal Self-Government," p. 187.

[146] As may be seen quite clearly in Aleksandr Odintsov's photographic portraits and biographical sketches of 1897 Duma deputies. Aleksandr Odintsov, ed., *Moskovskaia gorodskaia duma, 1897–1900* (Moscow: Izdanie Aleksandra Odintsova, 1897).

immune to popular recall yet exposed to arbitrary imperial interdiction.[147] Six of ten Moscow mayors between 1870 and 1917, including four of the last five, were drawn from the Moscow merchants.[148]

Even the limited franchise of 1870 proved too democratic for the tsar's ministers, who in 1892 limited suffrage and municipal authority even further while expanding the capacity of imperial officials to overturn local decisions.[149] In Moscow, the new regulations concerning voter eligibility immediately reduced the electorate from 4.4 percent of the city's total population to 0.6 percent of Moscow residents.[150] Pursuit of any liberal-minded policies in such a system was miraculous. As the case studies to follow indicate, Moscow's municipal government nonetheless proved itself surprisingly concerned with popular welfare at various periods during the half-century leading up to the revolutions of 1917.[151]

PERIODIC SYSTEMIC COLLAPSE

The imperial government's fragile institutional arrangements at all levels of public administration expose the absence of a commitment to systemic change on the part of the tsar and his government. The larger political history of the period was one of an aggressive assertion of autocratic prerogative followed by forced imperial retreat. Space for civic action slowly took shape within the ebb and flow of society's intensifying conflict with the tsar. Christine Ruane captured the essential character of the period when she wrote,

Moscow's new city Duma was heavily dominated by merchants, who constituted two-thirds of all elected deputies. This figure was at the high end of the scale among all Russian municipalities of the era, but behind such councils as Vladimir's, where more than 70 percent of the deputies were local merchants. Nardova, *Samoderzhavie i gorodskie dumy*, pp. 35–39.

[147] Hanchett, "Moscow in the Late Nineteenth Century," pp. 135–79; Colton, *Moscow: Governing the Socialist Metropolis*, pp. 57–61; and Engelstein, *Moscow 1905*, pp. 53–54.

[148] These merchant mayors were I. A. Liamin (1871–73), Sergei Tretiakov (1876–82), Nikolai Alekseev (1885–93), K. V. Rukavishnikov (1893–96), Nikolai Guchkov (1905–12), and Mikhail Chelnokov (1914–17). See Colton, *Moscow: Governing the Socialist Metropolis*, pp. 53, 805.

[149] Hanchett, "Moscow in the Late Nineteenth Century," p. iii; Astrov, "The Municipal Government," pp. 134–37. For a more recent analysis, see V. A. Nardova's excellent in-depth examination of the impact of the 1892 municipal reforms in St. Petersburg and elsewhere: Nardova, *Samoderzhavie i gorodskie dumy*.

[150] Nardova, *Samoderzhavie i gorodskie dumy*, p. 20.

[151] A point most dramatically asserted by Robert W. Thurston in *Liberal City, Conservative State: Moscow and Russia's Urban Crisis, 1906–1914* (Oxford, U.K.: Oxford University Press, 1987).

Despite government inconsistency, increasing numbers of Russians began to participate in the economic, social, and political life of their country as never before. Men and women, educated in the newly reformed schools, sought employment in the expanding sectors of the Russian economy—in industry, commerce, and public service. They were a part of a new, modern Russia, and they wanted to create a new arena where rights could be asserted and defended and where new voices could have legitimacy in shaping "public opinion."[152]

Moscow stood at the center of this elemental clash between state and society. The city's industrialists were among St. Petersburg's harshest critics.[153] The city's intellectuals, peasants, impoverished aristocrats, and workers had their own bills of particulars against the monarchy. Moscow, as this volume will argue, remained a place of surprising accommodation among diverse and fractious social groups, especially in light of the central bureaucracy's intransigence on so many issues.

Systemic collapse occurred twice during these years. The February and October 1917 revolutions mark the beginning of a new Moscow beyond the scope of this study. The 1905 Revolution stands at the heart of many of the concerns under discussion.

Russia's defeat at the hands of an upstart Japan provided the spark that ignited months of social upheaval beginning in October 1905. The violence's deeper antecedents rest, as Abraham Ascher has eloquently argued, in "the government's policy of modernizing the economy without altering social and political institutions," a policy that produced "the simultaneous appearance of organized liberalism and radicalism."[154] The disastrous famine of 1891–92 and the subsequent cholera and typhoid epidemics of 1892–93 further exposed the government's startling ineptitude, as had the calamitous Crimean War two generations before.[155]

A multiplicity of social groups with divergent visions of Russia's future shared hostility toward an autocratic regime that returned their con-

---

[152] Christine Ruane, *Gender, Class, and the Professionalization of Russian City Teachers, 1860–1914* (Pittsburgh: University of Pittsburgh Press, 1994), p. 4–5.

[153] A point explored in Ruth AmEnde Roosa, *Russian Industrialists in an Era of Revolution: The Association of Industry and Trade, 1906–1917*, ed. Thomas C. Owen (Armonk, N.Y.: M. E. Sharpe, 1997).

[154] Ascher, *The Revolution of 1905*, Vol. 1: *Russia in Disarray*, p. 29.

[155] The political importance of late-nineteenth-century Russia's health crisis and the Russian medical community is explored in Nancy Mandelker Frieden, *Russian Physicians in an Era of Reform and Revolution, 1856–1905* (Princeton: Princeton University Press, 1981). Concerning the role of the Crimean War in precipitating the Great Reforms of the early 1860s, see the chapters in Eklof, Bushnell, and Zakharova, eds., *Russia's Great Reforms*.

tempt.[156] Agitation for change, growing for some time, had been held in check despite increasing industrial strife, agrarian unrest, and political assassination—until the humiliating military defeat in 1905.[157] The same war that spawned extraordinary growth in Osaka brought chaos to Moscow.

All of Moscow's social groups were pulled into the maelstrom, with deep wounds festering in the years to follow. The events of 1905 were not quite the "dress rehearsal" for the 1917 revolutions that Lenin later claimed they were. Alternative paths were available to all involved, even after the conservative coup d'état of June 3, 1907, that undermined so many democratic attainments of previous months.[158]

Nicholas II, following the advice of his more reactionary ministers, dissolved the State Duma on that date, leaving many in Moscow—intellectuals, workers, industrialists, and merchants—to fight a series of rearguard actions to preserve what few interests they could. Moscow's municipal achievements under such conditions necessarily reveal a deep local commitment to a broad-based civic vision, predicated on a pluralistic understanding of community rooted in hard-nosed pragmatism.

[156] Alfred J. Rieber, "Interest-Group Politics in the Era of the Great Reforms," in Eklof, Bushnell, and Zakharova, eds., *Russia's Great Reforms*, pp. 58–83.
[157] Ascher, *The Revolution of 1905*, Vol 1: *Russia in Disarray*, pp. 42–45.
[158] This observation is drawn from the work of Abraham Ascher, especially *The Russian Revolution of 1905*, Vol. 2: *Authority Restored*.

4

Kitchen of the Country

Meiji Japan represents an interesting middle ground between a post–Civil War United States, which increasingly defined what it meant to be capitalist, and an imperial Russia, simultaneously attracted and repelled by the nineteenth-century realities all around it. Meiji Japan was as administratively centralized as Russia yet remained more open to the sorts of competitive political institutions, such as political parties and elections, that were the hallmark of the United States. Meiji elites, like their Russian counterparts, often rejected the laissez-faire capitalism that stood at the core of what it seemed to mean to be American during these years. Like Russia, Japan was somehow caught between tradition and modernity. Indeed, Japan's successes and failures provide a context within which Russia comes to appear as not nearly as aberrant as the United States.

Different realities coexisted within Japan. "Tokyo" stood for the same sort of centralizing bureaucratic interference in indigenous development as did "Petersburg" in Russia. "Osaka," in turn, represented a second metropolis that accented the raucous dynamism of unbridled commerce and industry. Osaka in Japan, like Moscow in Russia, rivaled the imperial capital in every measure but one: political power. In any given year, Osaka's factories produced more products, its financiers earned larger profits, its ports handled more trade, its housing held more people than did Tokyo's. Autocratic bureaucratism nonetheless left the "eastern capital" that had once been Edo at the top of the nation's urban hierarchy.

Osaka's role as a leading port, manufacturing, and financial center attracted a more diverse population than was then the norm for Japan. Certain elements of the city's pre-Meiji history, many of which are retold in this chapter, reveal how this had come to be so. Japan's second metropolis was, by the end of the nineteenth century, very much Peter Hall's entrepôt "between the already-developed world and a frontier region beyond it," in which "there is a constant search for the novel; levels of synergy, not only between like-minded individuals but also between quite disparate socio-economic-cultural groups, are very high."[1] Meiji Osaka, Gilded Age Chicago, and Silver Age Moscow were in their own ways the "archetypes of an open society."[2]

Shibamura Atsuki has observed that Osaka was Japan's preeminent industrial city, its leader in both industrialization and industry-related social dislocation.[3] Osaka, which would lead Japan in both population and industrial production between 1925 and 1932, was forced to respond to industrial capitalism before the rest of the country.

Osaka had long been Japan's leading commercial center. Its financiers dominated Tokugawa merchant life, having positioned their trading houses at the center of the nation's all-important rice trade. Inventive and agile, Osaka merchant houses established Japan's first credit system.[4] Osaka banks dominated Japanese commercial life as early as the 1670s with credit mechanisms and methods of exchange that might have outwitted even the most sophisticated 1980s Wall Street trader. "The Osaka rice brokers," one such Wall Street magician, Al Alletzhauser, would write, "gained a well-deserved reputation for being a particularly passionate, underhanded, slippery crowd."[5] It was in seventeenth-century Osaka, for example, and not in nineteenth-century Chicago (as many Americans assume), that commodities traders invented futures trading.[6] The city naturally profited greatly from this Tokugawa-era role as Japan's major staging area and transshipment point for the provisioning of food, household necessities, and luxury goods to the imperial

---

[1] Peter Hall, *Cities in Civilization* (New York: Pantheon, 1998), p. 302.

[2] Ibid.

[3] This point was emphasized by Shibamura Atsuki, professor of history at Momoyama-gakuin University. Shibamura Atsuki, interview by author, Ibaragi, Japan, April 14, 1996.

[4] Kenneth B. Pyle, *The Making of Modern Japan* (Lexington, Mass.: D.C. Heath, 1978), pp. 30–31.

[5] Al Alletzhauser, *The House of Nomura: The Inside Story of the World's Most Powerful Company* (London: Bloomsbury, 1990), p. 27.

[6] The notion that Chicago's Board of Trade is the world's oldest futures market is often repeated in Chicago economic histories. See, for example, Bob Tamarkin, *The New Gatsbys: Fortunes and Misfortunes of Commodity Traders* (New York: Morrow, 1985); and Jonathan Lurie, *The Chicago Board of Trade, 1859–1905: The Dynamics of Self Regulation* (Urbana: University of Illinois Press, 1979), p. 24. The eighty-two businessmen who convened on the first Monday of April 1848 to form the Chicago Board of Trade (Tumarkin, *The New Gatsbys*, p. 19) undoubtedly had no knowledge of the Osaka experience.

capital up the Yodo River at Kyoto, as well as to Edo (Tokyo) much farther away.[7]

American businessman Francis Hall reported on the Tokugawa city's role at the moment of transition to the Meiji era. Hall visited the city just a few years following the 1853 arrival of Commodore Matthew Perry's "Black Armada" in Tokyo Bay. Having freshly arrived in Osaka, Hall observed in an April 26, 1860, journal entry, "In pursuit of business and wealth Oasaca [sic] stands at the head of all places in Nippon. Yedo [sic] is an imperial city, a city for the residences of government officials and the prince of the Empire, Oasaca is the commercial imperium. . . . Thither come the products of the various provinces, to be distributed again as they are wanted."[8]

Osaka had been a significant place ever since Prince Shotoku Taishi established one of Buddhism's earliest Japanese temples in A.D. 593 near what has today become the city's Tennoji district. Osaka was the site of bitter fighting during the civil war era of the early seventeenth century, because it had become a fortified castle town under Toyotomi Hideyoshi at the end of the previous century. Destroyed in 1614 and 1615 by the victorious Tokugawa Ieyasu, the city was rebuilt and expanded within fifteen years to dominate the growing trade of the increasingly peaceful Tokugawa Shogunate. The city grew to 350,000 residents by the Genroku era (1688–1704), specializing in the rapid movement of goods along coastal shipping routes to Edo, thereby bypassing mountainous terrain and inadequate land routes.[9]

Governments from surrounding *hans* (domains) constructed large warehouse compounds in the Osaka port area to facilitate the shipment of their produce to a seemingly insatiable consumer market in Edo.[10] A

---

[7] Reiko Hayashi, "Provisioning Edo in the Early Eighteenth Century: The Pricing Policies of the Shogunate and the Crisis of 1733," in James L. McClain, John M. Merriman, and Kaoru Ugawa, eds., *Edo and Paris: Urban Life and the State in the Early Modern Era* (Ithaca: Cornell University Press, 1994), pp. 211–33; Takeo Yazaki, *Social Change and the City in Japan: From Earliest Times through the Industrial Revolution* (New York: Japan Publications, 1968), pp. 233–40; Takeo Yazaki, *The Japanese City: A Sociological Analysis* (Rutland, Vt.: Japan Publications, 1963); and Jeffrey E. Hanes, "From Megalopolis to Megaroporisu," *Journal of Urban History* 19, no. 2 (February 1993), pp. 56–94: 59–65.

[8] F. G. Notegelfer, ed., *Japan through American Eyes: The Journal of Francis Hall, Kanagawa and Yokohama, 1859–1866* (Princeton: Princeton University Press, 1992), p. 157.

[9] Yazaki, *Social Change and the City*, pp. 233–40; William B. Hauser, "Osaka Castle and Tokugawa Authority in Western Japan," in Jeffrey P. Mass and William B. Hauser, eds., *The Bakufu in Japanese History* (Stanford: Stanford University Press, 1985), pp. 153–72, 242–45.

[10] Francis Hall seems to have been fascinated by this system, as he noted in his journal on April 26, 1860. See Notehelfer, ed., *Japan through American Eyes*, p. 158.

complex system of authorized brokers and wholesalers grew—some 1,300 by 1688 just in the famous Dojima rice market in what is today the centrally located Kita-ku between the Umeda Station complex and Nakanoshima—linked with each other and to the rest of Japan by signal fires, flag communication, and carrier pigeons.[11] Trading, which began each morning at eight, would last as long as a slow-burning rope suspended in a wooden box from a central beam in the Dojima market remained aflame.[12]

Such methods of doing business—and of quoting prices—were used by the rice exchange into the twentieth century. A guidebook prepared for the Fifth National Industrial Exhibition held at Osaka in 1903 reported that foreign tourists should look skyward where, "at fixed times of the day men standing on platforms on the roofs of certain buildings may be seen vigorously waving flags of different colours; a few waves from left to right, a sweep around the head, half a dozen flourishes in the reverse direction and so many market quotations flashed to different offices in the city and in the same way to other stations for repetition to more distant parts of the country—a curious survival of an ancient method in a city where telegraph and telephone wires cross and recross every street."[13] Like Moscow, Osaka at the turn of the twentieth century was struggling to balance the old and new.

Kir Alekseev, an agent of the Russian Ministry of Finance, was fascinated by Osaka's integration of innovation and tradition. In 1902, he reported back to Finance Minister Sergei Witte in St. Petersburg that the city's "visage reflected the development of modern Japanese industry and, simultaneously, maintained its status as a traditional commercial center, price setter, and preserver of national customs." Alekseev, too, was astonished to discover that variously colored flags waved from rooftops communicated information about market transactions in a city transversed by the most modern telephone and telegraph cables.[14]

Osaka thus came to dominate the emerging national rice market and, with it, Japan's capital markets by combining innovation with tradition.

[11] Alletzhauser, *The House of Nomura*, p. 26.

[12] Ibid., p. 27.

[13] Osaka-fu, *The Souvenir Guide to Osaka and the Fifth National Industrial Exhibition (Expressly for the Use of Foreign Visitors)* (Osaka: Hakurankai Kyosankwai, 1903), p. 97.

[14] Communication from K. A. Alekseev to Minister S. Iu. Witte, February 1902 (TsGIA SSSR, f. 460, op. 29, d. 233, 1.1–15), as reported in B. V. Anan'ich, "Foreign Loans and Russia's Economic Development, 1864–1914 (The Gold Standard and Railway Construction)" (paper presented at the Tenth International Economic History Congress, Leuven, Belgium, 1990), p. 21, n. 4.

Nestled among some of Tokugawa Japan's most advanced agricultural lands, Osaka developed close ties to nearby villages and farmers. The city quickly became a major transshipment point for agricultural products—especially rice. Rice and trade brought money in a variety of currencies. By the Kanbun era (1661–73), Osaka money changers were profiting from transactions converting Edo's gold coins into Osakan silver coins, while many brokers dealt in their own copper coins. Osaka financiers controlled the flow of money in Tokugawa Japan much as the city's rice merchants established a monopoly over the country's primary food source.[15]

A CITY OF TOWNSMEN

Osaka remained distinctive among Japan's three major cities—Kyoto and Edo being the other two—in that it was, as William Hauser wrote, "a townsmen city, a city which served the interests of the common people who made up the vast majority of its population."[16] This focus on common townspeople defined Osaka's personality. The relative absence of privileged merchants in Osaka created a more flexible and less restricted climate for merchant expansion and development in the seventeenth century. "Thus, Osaka had neither a long history of privileged merchants associated with aristocratic houses as in Kyoto, nor as large a concentration of warriors and their merchant purveyors as in Edo. Osaka nonetheless developed a more dynamic business culture at the start of the Tokugawa period."[17] Novelist Junichiro Tanizaki once insightfully observed, "Kyoto and Osaka are linked by the Yodo River, but their climates and cultures differ."[18]

Osaka's local ways varied from those of other cities and regions throughout Japan. Coarse, crude, vulgar, and greedy by the standards of Kyoto court and Edo political life, Osaka's merchants and their families were uncharacteristically direct. "Osaka people," as recent travelogue writer Alex Kerr notes, "are impatient and love to disobey rules."[19] They

---

[15] Yazaki, *Social Change and the City*, pp. 233–40.

[16] William B. Hauser, "Osaka: A Commercial City in Tokugawa Japan," *Urbanism Past and Present* 5 (Winter 1977–78), pp. 23–36.

[17] Ibid., p. 24.

[18] Tanizaki Junichiro, *The Reed Cutter and Captain Shigemoto's Mother*, trans. Anthony H. Chambers (New York: Vintage, 1993), p. 10.

[19] Alex Kerr, "Osaka," in Alex Kerr, *Lost Japan* (Oakland, Calif.: Lonely Planet, 1996), pp. 216–28: 217.

cultivated a most unrefined taste for a sort of "gaudy excess" that was atypical for their compatriots elsewhere.[20] This distinctive approach to living was reflected in Osaka's active theater life, the city's unique tradition of Bunraku puppetry, its distinctive local humor, and in its local dialect, an accent that brands an Osaka native even today.[21] Osakans have long found that a good laugh brings people closer together, laughter being an all-important component of merchant relations. In Tokyo— where status and authority dominate—humor is often thought to bring dishonor, insulting one's position in the social hierarchy.[22]

The city's commercial success led one American visitor, Eliza Ruhamah Scidmore, to be reminded of Chicago: "The 'Chicago of Japan' is a fitter title [than the 'Venice of Japan'], for if no pork-packing establishments exist, the whole community is as energetically absorbed in money-making, the yen, instead of the almighty dollar, being the god chiefly worshiped, and Osaka's Board of Trade the most exciting and busy one in the empire."[23]

Like Chicago and Moscow, Tokugawa Osakan commerce was driven by a domestic-oriented mass market. Hauser notes that "[b]y the last decades of the seventeenth century, Osaka had emerged as a city oriented towards a mass consumption economy. The goods produced in the city were intended for popular consumption, not for the tastes of the military and aristocratic elites. Thus processed foodstuff, textiles, books, art, utensils, medicines, and sundries all were designed and produced in quantity to meet the demands of townsmen in Osaka and other cities."[24] Osaka's trade with itself, Hauser argues further, became even more important than the city's famous function as supply house for Edo.[25]

[20] Tanizaki Junichiro, *Quicksand*, trans. Howard Hibbett (New York: Vintage, 1993), p. 38.
[21] Shiraishi Bon, "Merchants of Osaka," *Japan Quarterly* 5, no. 2 (April–June 1958), pp. 169–77: 170–71.
[22] Inoue Hiroshi, "*Rakugo, Manzai* and *Kigeki*: The Arts of Laughter," *Japan Foundation Newsletter* 23, no. 4 (January 1996), pp. 1–4, 15. Shiraishi Bon explained precisely how Osaka merchants were different from other Japanese merchants when he wrote in 1958, "The merchants of Osaka unlike those in Edo and other castle towns, were neither merchants 'by appointment' to samurai families nor were they retailers for the ordinary consumer. Instead they were from the beginning wholesalers or brokers dealing in the products of the whole country: rice, vegetable oil, cotton, medicines, and the like. . . . [They] were different preferring to amass small profits slowly and surely over a long period of time." "Merchants of Osaka," pp. 170–71.
[23] Eliza Ruhamah Scidmore, *Jinrikisha Days in Japan* (New York: Harper, 1897), p. 331.
[24] Hauser, "Osaka: A Commercial City," pp. 23, 26.
[25] Ibid., p. 31.

12. Postcard of Doton-Bori (Theatre Street), Osaka. Photographer unknown, n.d.

MEIJI DECLINE AND INDUSTRIAL REVIVAL

Osakan distinctiveness did not immediately benefit the city and its merchants once Japan entered the modern era. The city had probably already passed its peak at the end of the eighteenth century, and certainly had entered a period of decline by the 1840s.[26] Osaka harbored some remarkable achievers throughout the Tokugawa period, to be sure. Witness, for example, Ogata Koan and his famous School of Dutch Studies.[27] Still, Osaka traders, craftsmen, and manufacturers were fundamentally in trouble long before the new Meiji government set out to stabilize Japan's finances in 1871, the starting point for this study.[28] These additional measures initially hit Osaka particularly hard—most especially local *fudasashi* (rice brokers and agents), who had previously dominated Japan's rice trade.[29] Osaka eventually made a successful transition to a major industrial center, transforming itself from a "sea of roof tiles" to a "forest of smokestacks."[30] Japan's "Venice" (called this because much of its trade moved along an intricate network of canals) would become in just over a quarter-century or so a "city of furnaces, factories, and commerce; the centre of the modern spirit of feverish activity in manufacturing and commercial enterprise."[31] This economic transformation dominates the period under review in this study.

Osaka was not alone in suffering during the earliest Meiji transition; the evolution from Edo to Tokyo similarly traumatized that city's economic and social order.[32] Some notable peculiarities nonetheless distinguish Osaka's Meiji-induced afflictions.

---

[26] Ibid., pp. 32–36. Hauser chronicles Osaka's late-Tokugawa decline in even greater detail in William B. Hauser, *Economic Institutional Change in Tokugawa Japan: Osaka and the Kinai Cotton Trade* (Cambridge, U.K.: Cambridge University Press, 1974).

[27] For a perceptive study of the role of academies of foreign knowledge in Tokugawa Osaka's intellectual life, see Tetsuo Najita, *Visions of Virtue in Tokugawa Japan: The Kaitokydo Merchant Academy of Osaka* (Chicago: University of Chicago Press, 1987).

[28] Milton W. Meyer, *Japan: A Concise History* (Lanham, Md.: Rowman and Littlefield, 1993), p. 151.

[29] Johannes Hirschmeier, *The Origins of Entrepreneurship in Meiji Japan* (Cambridge, Mass.: Harvard University Press, 1964), pp. 28–37; G. V. Navlitskaia, *Osaka* (Moscow: Nauka, 1983), pp. 130–34; and E. Herbert Norman, *Japan: Emergence as a Modern State: Political and Economic Problems of the Meiji Period* (New York: Institute of Pacific Relations, 1940), pp. 54–58, 107–11.

[30] Jeffrey Eldon Hanes, "Seki Hajime and the Making of Modern Osaka" (Ph.D. diss., University of California, Berkeley, 1988), p. 1.

[31] Mortimer Menpes, *Japan: A Record in Colour* (London: Adam and Charles Black, 1905), p. 102.

[32] Henry D. Smith II, "Tokyo as an Idea: An Exploration of Japanese Urban Thought until 1945," *Journal of Japanese Studies* 4, no. 1 (Winter 1978), pp. 53–57.

Osaka initially had been identified as a prime location for a new international port and for the Meiji capital, as it was already the beneficiary of 70 to 80 percent of the nation's profits.[33] Edo-Tokyo eventually won out over Osaka precisely for this reason. Osaka would remain a dominant center regardless of whether it became political capital, it was argued; Edo-Tokyo could not be sustained on its own.

Osaka managed to make the transition to an industrial dynamo with remarkable alacrity, given the magnitude of its economic and social transformation. Industrial development was delayed in Osaka as elsewhere in Japan until the 1880s, when the Japanese government abandoned notions that it could engage directly in industrial production on its own. This lag places developments in Osaka somewhat behind the patterns under review for Chicago and Moscow. The policy shift of the 1880s toward government encouragement of private-sector industrialization through indirect connections with networks of private banks and firms—a system that eventually evolved into the *zaibatsu* system— prepared the way for the country's great leap into the industrial age.[34] Cartelization reduced the displacement generated by erratic market demand and prices while conforming to behavioral expectations rooted in traditional Japanese family-management practices.[35] Osaka, with its dense matrix of interrelated financial houses, was well positioned to take advantage of Meiji Japan's indirect industrial policy.

Osaka was hardly alone in enjoying Japan's astonishing economic launch. Nearly every Japanese participated in their nation's improving living standards throughout the half-century following the consolidation of Meiji power.[36] Not only did individual wealth explode, but consumption patterns became more diverse and discretionary. Outlays for food, heat, and light as a percentage of household income declined significantly between the late 1870s and the early 1920s, while expendi-

[33] Henry D. Smith II, "The Edo-Tokyo Transition: In Search of Common Ground," in Marius B. Jansen and Gilbert Rozman, eds., *Japan in Transition: From Tokugawa to Meiji* (Princeton: Princeton University Press, 1986), pp. 347–74: 353–56; and Michio Umehaki, *After the Restoration: The Beginning of Japan's Modern State* (New York: New York University Press, 1988), pp. 33–51.
[34] A point made in Henry Rosovsky, *Capital Formation in Japan, 1868–1940* (Glencoe, Ill.: Free Press, 1961), p. 21.
[35] W. Mark Fruin, *Kikkoman: Company, Clan, and Community* (Cambridge, Mass.: Harvard University Press, 1983), pp. 51–67.
[36] Hugh Patrick, "An Introductory Overview," in Hugh Patrick, ed., with the assistance of Larry Meissner, *Japanese Industrialization and Its Social Consequences* (Berkeley: University of California Press, 1976), pp. 1–17: 14; Irwin Scheiner, *Christian Converts and Social Protest in Meiji Japan* (Berkeley: University of California Press, 1970), p. 2.

tures for clothing, culture, and entertainment all increased in absolute and relative terms.[37]

The industrial age arrived with a particular vengeance in Osaka, where in 1882 Shibusawa Eiichi launched his massive Osaka Cotton Spinning Company on a site that would be southwest of town once official boundaries were set.[38] Concerned over Japan's unfavorable balance of payments following the Satsuma Rebellion of 1877, Shibusawa viewed cotton and cloth production as a possible means for developing Japan's export markets.[39] Osaka Cotton Spinning used the latest British technologies to power more than ten thousand steam-driven spindles for making thread.[40] By the mid-1880s, Shibusawa had secured Osaka's position as a textile leader and as a factory town—the "Manchester of the Far East."[41]

Shibusawa was himself a formidable force of nature.[42] The son of a rural entrepreneur from Chiaraijima village involved in a variety of local industries, including the indigo trade, young Eiichi had received a samurai education.[43] He managed to secure a spot on the visiting delegation of a Tokugawa prince to France in 1867 at the age of twenty-seven, returning to a prominent position in the new Ministry of Finance a year later.[44] He left government service in 1872 at the age of thirty-two to become president of the First National Bank, and eventually became a leading stockholder or senior official in over 500 Meiji-era banks, as well as a founder of the Tokyo Stock Exchange.[45]

By the late 1870s, Shibusawa was urging his fellow bankers to finance Japan's industrial development.[46] In a Yokohama speech in 1877, for

---

[37] Hiroshi Hazama, "Historical Changes in the Life Style of Industrial Workers," in Patrick, ed., with Meissner, *Japanese Industrialization*, pp. 21–51: 38.

[38] Johannes Hirschmeier, "Shibusawa Eiichi: Industrial Pioneer," in William W. Lockwood, ed., *The State and Economic Enterprise in Japan: Essays in the Political Economy of Growth* (Princeton: Princeton University Press, 1965), pp. 209–47: 215–27.

[39] Ibid., p. 225.

[40] Ibid., p. 226; Yasuzo Horie, "Modern Entrepreneurship in Meiji Japan," in Lockwood, ed., *The State and Economic Enterprise*, pp. 183–208.

[41] Dallas Finn, *Meiji Revisited: The Sites of Victorian Japan* (New York: Weatherhill, 1995), pp. 118–21; Hauser, *Economic Institutional Change*; and E. Patricia Tsurumi, *Factory Girls: Women in the Thread Mills of Meiji Japan* (Princeton: Princeton University Press, 1990).

[42] This discussion is based on Pyle, *The Making of Modern Japan*, pp. 87–88.

[43] William Jones Chambliss, *Chiaraijima Village: Land Tenure, Taxation, and Local Trade, 1818–1884* (Tucson: University of Arizona Press, 1965), pp. 113–22; Kozo Yamamura, *A Study of Samurai Income and Entrepreneurship: Quantitative Analysis of Economic and Social Aspects of the Samurai in Tokugawa and Meiji Japan* (Cambridge, Mass.: Harvard University Press, 1974), pp. 139–43.

[44] Yamamura, *A Study of Samurai Income*, p. 139.

[45] Alletzhauser, *The House of Nomura*, pp. 34–35.

[46] Yamamura, *A Study of Samurai Income*, pp. 140–41.

example, he exhorted bankers to "pay attention to the increasing of their production of the country. . . . Thus may we aid in extending the productions of our country, and if we succeed in doing this, we have all done our duty."[47] This son of a wealthy peasant followed his own advice, mobilizing the capital available through his various banking ventures to launch a textile industry that would dominate global production in but half a century.

Osaka stood at the heart of Shibusawa's textile empire and grew rapidly in Shibusawa's wake. Japan's first generating plant brought electricity to Osaka Cotton Spinning in 1886, a full year ahead of the first provision of electricity for public use in Tokyo.[48] By the turn of the century a city in which there had been nary a factory just over a decade earlier had become home to five thousand plants employing sixty thousand men and women. The Osaka rice, cotton, sugar, and oil exchanges set national prices and Osaka's stock exchange competed directly with that of Tokyo.[49] The construction industry expanded as well, with the city's population tripling in just twenty years.[50] The municipality's official territorial limits expanded in 1897 with the annexation of three and a half times the city's previous land area.[51]

Development continued following the turn of the century, with the local manufacturing base becoming ever more diversified. Shibusawa was hardly alone in his wealth. The Sumitomo clan successfully moved from Tokugawa merchant riches to industrial capitalist wealth; Baron Fujita Denzaburo built a spectacular empire (and Asian art collection). By 1912, there were 6,415 registered factories in the city manufacturing "cotton, wool, metals, oils, ships, matches, machinery, soap, tobacco, medicines, brushes, rolling stock, clothing, umbrellas, toilet goods, paint, furniture, paper, candles, canned goods, lacquer, carpets, bags, safes, casks, fans, flowers, musical and sporting goods, ice, clocks, and many other things."[52] Twenty-seven banks maintained their headquarters in the

---

[47] As quoted in Charles Lanman, *Leading Men of Japan with an Historical Summary of the Empire* (Boston: D. Lothrop, 1883), pp. 216–20.

[48] Ryoshin Minami, "The Introduction of Electric Power and Its Impact on the Manufacturing Industries: With Special Reference to Smaller Scale Plants," in Patrick, ed., with Meissner, *Japanese Industrialization*, pp. 299–325.

[49] In addition, 20,000 weaving establishments with over 30,000 hand looms churned out over 3.5 million pieces of cotton cloth annually. The city's 900 warehouses contained 74,214 cubic feet of storage capacity, while textile, copper goods, and curio production dominated the local industrial scene. *Souvenir Guide to Osaka*, p. 51.

[50] From 332,425 in 1882 to 921,617 in 1901, a growth that demanded expansion of the housing stock from 88,978 units to 211,313 units during the same years. Ibid., p. 54.

[51] Yazaki, *Social Change and the City*, p. 469.

[52] Osaka Hotel Company, *A Guide to Osaka Japan* (Osaka: Osaka Shiyakusho, 1913), p. 35.

THE COMMUNICATION IS ORDERLY
AT THE POINT OF NAGABORI-BASHI, OSAKA.
甚大の殷地繁荣と点又交梢相長る大繁栄道突 （阪 大）

13. Postcard of the Point of Nagabori-Bashi, Osaka. Photographer unknown, n.d.

city at this time.[53] This was precisely the period when the total value of Osaka industrial production exploded—increasing by 400 percent between 1901 and 1907.[54] Growth continued in textiles, with the value of cloth production increasing by 186.7 percent during this time. The city's industrial base diversified, with machine-tool production growing by 436.8 percent in value, chemicals by 464.3 percent, and food production by 699.7 percent.[55] New utilities—gas and electric—increased their value of production by an astonishing 5,097 percent, reflecting both the relatively late arrival of such services in Osaka and the city's stormy growth. Another spurt prompted by the "Great War" in Europe would leave 21,600 factories of various sizes working away by 1923.[56]

FINANCIAL BARONS

Industrialist bankers such as Shibusawa were joined in the world of finance by prodigies such as Osaka Stock Exchange founder Godai Tomoatsu and the legendary Nomura brothers Tokushichi (also known as Shinnosuke) and Jitsusaburo. Godai, who had attended the Paris International Exposition of 1867 with Shibusawa, was widely regarded as the most important business leader in early Meiji Osaka.[57] Like Shibusawa, Godai launched his career in government and eventually took his early network of connections with him to the world of commerce. Hardly a major Osaka business was operating by the 1890s that did not involve Godai in one manner or another.[58]

[53] *Present-day Osaka* (Osaka: Osaka Shiyakusho, 1915), p. 35.

[54] Yuzo Mima, "Meiji Koki Osaka no Kogyo," in Shinshu Osakashishi Hensei Iinkai, *Shinshu Osakashishi* 7 (Osaka: Osaka City Government, 1994), ch. 2, sec. 2, sub. 1, pp. 234–46: 235.

[55] Ibid.

[56] *Great Osaka: A Glimpse of the Industrial City* (Osaka: Osaka Shiyakusho [municipal office], 1925), p. 45.

[57] Sugihara Shiro and Nishizawa Tamotsu, "In the 'Commercial Metropolis' Osaka: Schools of Commerce and Law," in Chuhei Suguyama and Hiroshi Mizuta, eds., *Enlightenment and Beyond:. Political Economy Comes to Japan* (Tokyo: University of Tokyo Press, 1988), pp. 189–207.

[58] Ibid., pp. 190–92. Godai was born in the clan of Satsuma in southeastern Japan in 1835, a time when the region was under the "enlightened lord" Shimazu Nariakira. Godai studied at Nagasaki's Naval Training School, coming under the mentorship of Scottish merchant Thomas Glover. His early exposure to Westerners convinced Godai that Japan could become strong only by competing successfully at the West's own economic game. He would later become instrumental in sending Japanese students abroad for study, and in the founding of the Osaka Commercial School, a precursor to today's Osaka City University.

Godai arrived in Osaka in February 1868 as a supervisor for the Foreign Affairs Office. He was a leader in the founding of both the Osaka Mint and the Osaka Stock

Godai was less entrepreneurial than Shibusawa. He was rather, in the words of Sugihara Shiro and Nishizawa Tamotsu, "a bureaucrat or an administrator . . . who was in non-governmental circles."[59] Men such as Godai who could serve as brokers between government and the private sector were indispensable in an era in which "rapid but primitive accumulation" took place under the strong direction of the state.

If Shibusawa's tale was that of the peasant boy made good and Godai's was that of an enlightened provincial leader's early patronage, the Nomura saga has an even more distinctly Osakan flavor.[60] Shinnosuke and Jitsusaburo's father—Tokushichi I—had been born into a distinguished line of samurai in 1850. His father, the keeper of Osaka Castle, had been one of the richest men in Japan. Unfortunately for Tokushichi, his mother was a mere servant girl in his father's household. Tokushichi was disowned by his father and turned over to a wealthy landowner paid to take care of him. Young Nomura began life at a disadvantage despite his father's distinguished lineage.

Tokushichi undertook an apprenticeship with Yahei Osakaya, an Osaka money changer, at the age of ten. Tokushichi performed all of the menial tasks expected of an apprentice, and must have done so well. Osakaya adopted the twenty-one-year-old Nomura Tokushichi in 1871, a year before Osakaya passed away. Tokushichi founded Nomura Shoten (the "Nomura shop") the following year, taking over Osakaya's money-changing business, and married the heir of a dispossessed samurai family who was herself knowledgeable in the world of finance. The family lived the life of modest commercial wealth, poised at the edge of the Meiji economic miracle.

The younger Nomura Tokushichi—or Shinnosuke—was born in 1878, the year his father joined the newly established Osaka Security Exchange. He was one of five children, including younger brother Jitsusaburo. Shinnosuke completed the Osaka Commercial School and, until he took over the family business in 1904, led something of a

Exchange. Godai consistently encouraged the city's industrialization along the Western model. Together with Nakano Goichi, Hirose Saihei, Kato Yuichi, and Shibakawa Matahei, Godai founded the Osaka Chamber of Commerce in July 1877, a body that strongly advocated the extension of Western business practices throughout the local economy together with large-scale industrialization. These efforts brought Godai into close contact with the emerging Sumitomo cartel. Godai conveyed an entrepreneurial attitude to Osaka, even as he failed as an entrepreneur on his own, leaving a debt of one million yen at the time of his death.

[59] Ibid., p. 190.
[60] This account of the Nomura empire's early years is based on Alletzhauser, *The House of Nomura*, pp. 25–38, 36–51.

dissipated existence. He rode his bicycle all over the back streets of Osaka, trying to find stock buyers by going door-to-door. He and his brother helped to develop futures trading in stocks, playing the 1906 bull market that followed the Russo-Japanese War just right. The Nomuras and their customers survived the January 1907 stock market crash, thereby securing unwavering client loyalty.[61] Their successors would build Nomura Securities into one of the world's largest brokerage houses by the 1980s.

The Nomura saga is a classic Osaka story. Schooled in the city's robust financial markets long before capitalism took flight, the Nomura family overcame disadvantage through guile and brazenness to create and capture staggering wealth. As in Chicago, Nomura and many other Osaka entrepreneurs explicitly sought out the merely well-to-do as clients. Shinnosuke's forays on his two-wheeler through Osaka streets to find new customers was the Japanese equivalent of the Armours, Swifts, Morrisses, Fields, and Wards, all playing to a new American middle class. Osaka and Chicago market heroes found their share of their nations' exploding wealth by defining new needs for those whose climb above subsistence had been relatively recent. Their stories tell of their cities' commercial genius at a time when mass marketing was just beginning to emerge. Not in existence in 1870, such new Japanese classes were well on their way to security by the 1910s.

The Nomuras came to represent a new merchant elite that became increasingly separated from the city's life.[62] The local upper crust was becoming ever more differentiated, just as the rest of Osaka subdivided into new social groupings unheard of before the Meiji era. The city's industrial elite—or, to be more precise, the owners of the small and medium-sized plants that dominated employment patterns—lived close to their production facilities and to their workers. In a pattern reminiscent of Moscow, labor relations in such enterprises remained largely paternalistic, yet congenial. Labor strife arose first and foremost at the large plants outside of the traditional city core, factories owned by the Shibusawas, Nomuras, and others who had moved on from production to finance. Meanwhile, new white-collar clerical and professional groups were being lured by new commuter rail lines out to more distant suburban communities.

---

[61] Markets were falling around the world that year; Japan was particularly hard hit as its combined stock values plummeted by 88 percent.

[62] I would like to thank Hotta Akio, deputy director of the Osaka City History Editor's Office, for offering these observations during a conversation in Osaka on April 11, 1996.

The city's decentralization accelerated into the 1920s as jobs and people followed the rail lines out in all directions. This pattern is hardly unique to Osaka, to Japan, or to the cities under review here.[63] The whir of the electric tram was decentralizing cities around the world, well before the internal combustion engine finished the job.[64] Such expansion was even more rapid in nearby suburbs, where both private speculative development and government-sponsored garden cities were pulling Osakans out into the countryside.[65]

Decentralization was widely viewed as the optimal solution to over-crowded conditions in town. In 1921, the Osaka City Labor Investigation Department's housing investigation reported that local workers had an average per capita living space allocation of 5.1 square yards (4.8 square meters), while schoolteachers were hardly better off, with 7.5 square yards (6.3 square meters). Teachers, however, paid a higher percentage of their income for housing—23.1 percent as opposed to 15.6 percent for workers. The department's report concluded, "No matter how narrowly compared to the teachers, workers' housing is extremely inferior in every way. What is more, if compared to that of classes higher than the teachers, one would even see a much larger difference."[66] Migration to the suburbs became a favored nostrum for social welfare advocates in Osaka, as elsewhere.

Osaka changed both physically and socially during the decade following the Russo-Japanese War, in a pattern that would acc-

---

[63] James R. Scobie's account of the impact of electric traction on the physical shape and settlement patterns of Buenos Aires a decade or so earlier could be easily applied to Osaka. "The development of suburbs signaled a new era for the city.... By 1910 only 10% of the city's 1,230,000 inhabitants lived in the Central City." James R. Scobie, *Buenos Aires: Plaza to Suburb, 1870–1910* (Oxford, U.K.: Oxford University Press, 1974), pp. 191–92. For other perspectives on the Argentine capital's growth, see Charles S. Sargent, *The Spatial Evolution of Greater Buenos Aires, Argentina, 1870–1930* (Tempe: Center for Latin American Studies, Arizona State University, 1974); as well as a collection of articles on the legacy of the architect Martin Noel, a volume that includes several articles about the evolving physical and social evolution of Buenos Aires during the early twentieth century. Ramon Gutierrez, Margarita Gutman, and Victor Perez Escolano, eds., *El arquitecto Martin Noel: Su tiempo y su obra* (Seville: Junta de Andalucia, 1995).

[64] In Osaka, central wards such as Higashi-ku, Nishi-ku, Minami-ku, Naniwa-ku, and Tennoji-ku were either stable in their populations or actually declining by the 1920s, while the populations of outer wards such as Nishiyodogawa-ku, Higashiyodogawa-ku, and Higashinariwari-ku were increasing their populations by another one-third to one-half. Shibamura Atsuki, "Dai-Osaka no Kensetsu," in Shinshu Osakashishi Hensei Iinaki, *Shinshu Osakashishi*, vol. 7, chp. 1, sec. 1, sub. 1, pp. 3–25: 4–6.

[65] Toru Kodama, "The Experimentation of the Garden City in Japan," *Kikan Keizai Kenkyu* 16, no. 6 (Summer 1993), pp. 22–46.

[66] Ibid., pp. 40–41.

elerate in the 1920s and 1930s. The city was transforming itself from a traditional, large Japanese town into a twentieth-century "megaroporisu."[67]

A NEW AND AN OLD MINORITY

The 1910s were further notable for the arrival of the forerunners of Osaka's large—and Japan's leading—Korean community.[68] That community's origins rest with the Japanese imperial experiment that would culminate in the Great Pacific War. The Korean peninsula had become a prize in an expanding Japanese empire that was taking shape following successful wars fought against China (1894–95) and Russia (1904–5). Having achieved "great power" status—and having emerged as the "Leader of Asia"—Japan sought to spread "enlightenment" to Korea through annexation in 1910.[69] The peninsula had been a point of contention between China and Russia dating back to the 1880s. Sensing an opportunity for action, the Japanese government extended colonial rule, bringing various forms of imperial administration to Korea that had been tested fifteen years previously in Taiwan.

Supposed cultural affinities and an education system predicated on assimilation masked harsh realities that remained just beneath the surface of Japanese rhetoric. Korea "was to be regarded as a colonial possession, and its people as culturally and politically inferior to the Japanese."[70]

Koreans could now migrate to Japan freely, as they were no longer foreign subjects. In debt to absentee landlords with little chance for advancement, the peninsula's subsistence farmers fled their farms to seek employment elsewhere. Japan's flourishing factories—especially during the World War I boom years—pulled Korea's impoverished as much as their neglected fields pushed them away. If, in 1910, only a small handful of Koreans lived in Japan, their numbers surpassed 400,000 by the mid-1930s, and more than 2,000,000 Koreans were living in Japan by the end of World War II.[71] More than half of Osaka's Koreans migrated from

---

[67] As Jeffrey E. Hanes observes, the Japanese "megaroporisu" offers a distinctly Japanese accent to the familiar "megalopolis" pattern of urban expansion. See Hanes, "From Megalopolis to Megaroporisu."

[68] A rare English-language history of Japan's Korean community may be found in Michael Weiner, *The Origins of the Korean Community in Japan, 1910–1923* (Atlantic Highlands, N.J.: Humanities Press International, 1989).

[69] Ibid., pp. 3, 17–18.   [70] Ibid., p. 22.

[71] Ibid., p. 43.

Cheju, taking advantage of a new direct passenger route between that island and Osaka that began operation in 1923.[72]

Osaka's Settsu Cotton Spinning Plant was the first Japanese factory to hire Korean immigrants in 1911.[73] The city quickly became home to Japan's largest Korean community by the early 1920s, with 21,984 residents (all but 57 of whom were blue-collar workers in Osaka's massive factories).[74] Koreans remain a prominent feature of Osakan life to this day, frequently impoverished and sometimes ostracized.

Korean marginality was especially apparent at moments of social breakdown, such as the tense days following the 1923 Great Kanto Earthquake centered around Tokyo. U.S. diplomatic reporting of the period revealed widespread harassment of Koreans throughout Japan, with "hundreds of Koreans massacred and thousands interned with insufficient supplies," including 250 poor souls "bound hand and foot in groups of five, placed on an old junk, covered with oil and burned alive."[75]

The arrival of so many poor, typically illiterate, and culturally distinct migrants altered the nature of Osaka poverty. Poor Korean rural migrants could not escape up the socio-economic ladder from their growing ghettos in Osaka and elsewhere to nearby suburbs.[76]

The Koreans were joined by additional groups of Osakan dispossessed, the *Hinin* (itinerants, beggars, prostitutes, and castoff commoners known as "nonpeople") and the untouchable *Eta*.[77] Outcastes had existed in Japan for nearly a thousand years, being identified by a set of occupational specializations tied to the slaughtering of animals, butchering, and tanning of hides. The *Eta* had been somewhat protected by the feudal lords who depended on their services in the Tokugawa castle towns. They were emancipated in August 1871 as part of the early Meiji modernization program but, in the process, lost historical monopolistic privileges and tax exemptions.[78] They soon became scapegoats for the economic traumas of the initial Meiji transition.

---

[72] Shibamura Atsuki interview.

[73] Weiner, *The Origins of the Korean Community*, p. 57.

[74] Ibid., p. 63.

[75] Letter from Floyd W. Tomkins (president, League of the Friends of Korea, Philadelphia, Pennsylvania) to Charles Evan Hughes, Secretary of State, November 20, 1923, Department of State, General Records, RG59.894.4016/3, National Archives, pp. 1–6.

[76] Weiner, *The Origins of the Korean Community*, p. 202.

[77] John Price, "A History of the Outcaste: Untouchability in Japan," in George De Vos and Hiroshi Wagatsuma, eds., *Japan's Invisible Race: Caste in Culture and Personality* (Berkeley: University of California Press, 1966), pp. 6–30.

[78] George O. Totten and Hiroshi Wagatsuma, "Emancipation: Growth and Transformation of a Political Movement," in De Vos and Wagatsuma, eds., *Japan's Invisible Race*, pp. 33–68.

Now known as *Burakumin*, the outcastes began to organize themselves, with various homegrown associations and community groups
advocating literacy, cooperation, thrift, and diligence as strategies for
greater acceptance. Outcaste settlements were—and remain—spread
throughout Japan. The Kansai cities of Kyoto, Nara, Kobe, and Osaka
historically have been home to disproportionately large *Hinin, Eta*, and
later, *Burakumin* communities.[79] Such *Burakumin* groups became increasingly radicalized in the years leading up to World War I, particularly in
Osaka.

Angry and with little to lose, increasingly radicalized "others" became
shock troops for Japan's expanding labor and student movements.[80] As
in Chicago, where a growing African-American community was simultaneously challenging previous assumptions about the nature of the city,
Osaka's socially disadvantaged groups denied myths of cultural homo-
geneity by their very presence. The Koreans' increasing visibility throughout the 1910s, and especially in the interwar years ahead, necessarily
meant that Osaka was fragmented by more than class. Municipal peace
required the practice of pragmatic pluralism.

INTERNATIONAL AND PAROCHIAL

Osaka's profiting from World War I indicates that the city not only industrialized and diversified its economy, but also became ever more integrated into the international economy. Exports increased fivefold in yen
value and imports doubled between 1914 and 1918, in a pattern that
had first become apparent during the Sino-Japanese and Russo-Japanese
wars a decade or two earlier.[81] Local economic development was driven
by expanding cotton-goods production and export growth. Osaka
emerged by the end of World War I as the city that determined the movement of finance and the shape of industrial development throughout
Japan. It stood at the center of Japanese economic integration.

[79] At the beginning of the nineteenth century, 4,423 outcastes resided in Osaka, as opposed
to less than a thousand at the time in Tokyo. Ibid. By 1920, Osaka was home to 47,909
Burakumin, approximately twice the number of Koreans living in the city at that time.
This figure may also be compared to 107,608 *Burakumin* living in Hyogo that same
year; 69,345 in Fukuoka; 42,179 in Kyoto; 32,676 in Nara; and 7,658 in Tokyo. Hiroshi
Wagatsuma and George De Vos, "The Ecology of Special Buraku," in De Vos and
Wagatsuma, eds., *Japan's Invisible Race*, pp. 112–28: 115–16.
[80] Weiner, *The Origins of the Korean Community*, pp. 99–126; Totten and Wagatsuma,
"Emancipation."
[81] Yazaki, *Social Change and the City*, p. 469.

Osaka's economic success came at considerable social cost. A deep rift between the city's haves and have-nots erupted in July and August 1918, when a series of rice riots that had begun in a small fishing village on the coast of Toyama Bay spread nationwide from Hokkaido to Kyusho.[82] The disturbances, which arose in response to the spiraling cost of Japan's basic foodstuff, were particularly pronounced in Osaka, where a quarter-million protestors battled with police and military authorities. As with Chicago's race riots in 1919 and Moscow's revolutionary convulsions in 1917, Osaka's rice riots both close the period under review and demonstrate the limits of metropolitan tolerance and pragmatic pluralism. Social, political, and economic accommodation must transcend mere form. Successful inclusionary politics requires a transfer of resources as well as gestures of goodwill.

Osaka remained a profoundly Japanese city despite its growing importance in—and reliance on—international trade and Korean migrant labor.[83] The treaties concluded by Commodore Perry in 1854 had provided for foreign settlements with the entitlement of extraterritoriality. An Osaka settlement opened to foreigners on January 1, 1868, and would remain a small, self-governed enclave until the revision of the unequal treaties in July 1899.[84] Most merchants and diplomats moved to Kobe at the end of the 1870s, relinquishing Osaka settlement lands to missionaries who established churches, schools, seminaries, orphanages, and hospitals—many of which still serve the city. Chinese nationals constituted the largest single foreign group within the settlement, although, as non-Westerners, they remained "merely bystanders" in settlement administration throughout the period.[85] The international community in Osaka thus never gained the visibility and commanding

---

[82] These events are explored in Michael Lewis, *Rioters and Citizens: Mass Protest in Imperial Japan* (Berkeley: University of California Press, 1990).

[83] There were only 418 foreign men and 72 foreign women officially registered as Osaka residents in 1900, and three times that number a decade and a half later. This includes 14 Englishmen and 18 Englishwomen, 26 American men and 24 American women, 6 French men and 3 French women, 369 Chinese men and 27 Chinese women, 2 Swiss men, and 1 Korean man (although there almost certainly were more Korean residents living in the city at this time). *The Souvenir Guide to Osaka*, p. 96. The number of foreign residents had increased by 1916 to 1,538 (including 1,380 Chinese, 75 Americans, 37 British, 16 French, 16 German, 9 Swiss, 2 Portuguese, and 1 Dane, 1 Dutch, and 1 Belgian). "Foreign Population of Osaka," *The Japan Chronicle* (Kobe), January 13, 1916, p. 50.

[84] Jon Vandercammen, "The Osaka Foreign Settlement: A Study of the Osaka Municipal Council Based upon the Minutes of the Council Meetings, 1869–1899" (Osaka, 1996), pp. 1–8.

[85] Ibid., pp. 8–9.

presence that Westerners had been able to establish in Kobe and Yokohama.

Beyond quantitative measures, Osaka and nearby Kyoto became the focal point for intellectual movements that privileged non-Western experience. Baron Fujita Denzaburo's elegant collection of Asian art emphasized distinctiveness from the West, much as the collections and patronage of the Tretiakovs and Mamontovs had in Moscow. Naito Konan, Japan's leading Sinologist prior to World War II, initially set forth positions that later would justify Japanese hegemonic control in Asia while working as a writer during the 1890s for the *Osaka Asahi Shimbun*.[86] Naito became best known in the West for his periodization of Chinese history, a schema that would become widely recognized around the world.[87] He championed East Asia's cultural superiority from his position at Kyoto University, where, in 1907, he assumed that school's first lectureship in East Asian history. He and many others found the Kansai metropolises of Osaka and Kyoto more congenial precisely because the modernizing state and Western influences were further away than in the imperial capital.[88]

Osaka, like Moscow and Chicago, benefited from an increasingly international economy while simultaneously sustaining distinctively national value systems. They all stood, to borrow once again from Peter Hall's *Cities in Civilization*, at the junction of the known and unknown worlds.

In the case of Osaka, local values at times called into question an undue reliance on money as the arbiter of human relations. Thorstein Veblen's 1915 observation about turn-of-the-century Japan as a whole applied to Osaka in particular. Japan's borrowed achievements, Veblen wrote, have not "seriously begun to dismantle and reshape those matters of imputation that make up the working specifications of the institutional fabric, the ethical (sentimental) values and conventional principles of conduct by force of which it holds true that 'men live not by bread alone.' "[89] The precise extent to which Osakans refused to believe that humans live by bread alone became apparent in the local initiatives to improve their community that will be examined in chapters to come.

---

[86] Joshua A. Fogel, *Politics and Sinology: The Case of Naito Konan (1866–1943)* (Cambridge, Mass.: Harvard University Press, 1984), pp. 61–77.

[87] Ibid., pp. xv–xxiv.   [88] Ibid., pp. 115–16.

[89] Thorstein Veblen, "The Opportunity of Japan," in Thorstein Veblen, *Essays in Our Changing Order*, ed. Leon Ardzrooni (New York: Augustus M. Kelley, 1964), pp. 248–66: 252.

GOVERNING MEIJI AND TAISHO OSAKA

The Meiji emperor moved in 1890 to expand the power of Japan's prefectural assemblies, which had been established in 1878. The national Imperial Diet had been created by the February 11, 1889, constitution and began operation in November the following year.[90] The convening of a national assembly in 1890 had been announced in 1881, with the imperial government requiring nearly a decade to prepare for the assembly's inauguration.[91] The Meiji founders viewed the Diet as a safety valve for political and social unrest as well as a means for fostering national unity.[92] Parliamentary assemblies denoted Japan's entry into the ranks of "civilized" democracies. Suffrage, however, remained limited, with all Japanese male citizens over the age of twenty-five obtaining the right to vote only in 1925.[93]

Prefectures became more than administrative departments within the national bureaucracy for the first time in the 1890s. The basic parameters of Meiji-era local government were established by various laws passed between 1871 and 1888 setting forth new institutions for local and regional administration.[94] Like so much of Meiji governance, regional and local administration was shaped through an iterative process that remained complex and haphazard. Reality dictated form as much as the other way around as the Meiji transition moved forward fitfully.[95] The

---

[90] Kenneth B. Pyle, *The New Generation in Meiji Japan: Problems of Cultural Identity, 1885–1895* (Stanford: Stanford University Press, 1969), p. 44.

[91] Bernard S. Silberman, "The Structure of Bureaucratic Rationality and Economic Development in Japan," in Hyung-ki Kim, Michio Muramatsu, T. J. Pempel, and Kozo Yamamura, eds., *The Japanese Civil Service and Economic Development* (Oxford, U.K.: Clarendon, 1995), pp. 135–73; Nobutaka Ike, *The Beginnings of Political Democracy in Japan* (Baltimore: Johns Hopkins University Press, 1950), pp. 70–101; and George Akita, *Foundations of Constitutional Government in Modern Japan, 1868–1900* (Cambridge, Mass.: Harvard University Press, 1967).

[92] Andrew Fraser, "The House of Peers (1890–1905): Structure, Groups, and Role," in Andrew Fraser, R. H. P. Mason, and Philip Mitchell, *Japan's Early Parliaments, 1890–1905: Structure, Issues, and Trends* (London: Routledge, 1995), pp. 8–36.

[93] Sally Ann Hastings, *Neighborhood and Nation in Tokyo, 1905–1937* (Pittsburgh: University of Pittsburgh Press, 1995), p. 11.

[94] This discussion is based on Shibamura, interview. Readers may wish to consult Neil L. Waters, *Japan's Local Pragmatists: The Transition from Bakumatsu to Meiji in the Kawasaki Region* (Cambridge, Mass.: Harvard University Press, 1983), pp. 82–87; James C. Baxter, *The Meiji Unification through the Lens of Ishikawa Prefecture* (Cambridge, Mass.: Harvard University Press, 1994), esp. pp. 161–200; and the more contemporary account found in Walter Wallace McLaren, *A Political History of Japan during the Meiji Era, 1867–1912* (New York: Scribner's, 1916), pp. 112–52.

[95] Baxter, *The Meiji Unification*, p. 3.

break with the pre-Meiji past was never complete; individuals and institutions transmuted themselves through a prolonged process of re-invention.[96]

Prefectures and municipalities gained limited autonomy under these new laws, with the imperial government in Tokyo retaining dominance in nearly all spheres of local life. Modeled after the Napoleonic prefectural system as interpreted through recent German experience, the 1888 legislation in particular ensured that local administration would remain embedded in a national unitary state. Local officials, for example, were employees of the central government rather than local and regional institutions.

Local notables, especially those who became mayors and members of local assemblies, retained a degree of informal autonomy. This was especially the case in rural areas in which landowners continued to hold sway over the local citizenry. Suffrage was limited to those males who were able to pay a direct tax of fifteen yen per year, thereby ensuring that traditional elites would continue to exercise power and authority in their local domains.[97]

Tokyo, Kyoto, and Osaka—Japan's three largest cities at the time— were exempted from the 1888 municipal reforms and continued to be managed directly by the central government until 1898.[98] These urban centers were deemed as being too important to be granted even the limited autonomy provided for by the 1888 reforms. Central authorities also found urban merchant elites less-reliable agents of central control than their landowning rural counterparts.

Municipal prerogatives were finally extended to Tokyo, Kyoto, and Osaka in 1898.[99] Under the new arrangements—which are generally considered to be the beginning of local self-government in Osaka— a restricted electorate of male taxpayers selected members of a Municipal Assembly, which at various times included upwards of ninety deputies. The Municipal Assembly, in turn, selected a smaller Executive Committee of six members, including a mayor who presided at Executive Committee sessions. The mayor, as the city's chief executive, was

---

[96] This point is made in considerable detail in Michio Umegaki, *After the Restoration: The Beginning of Japan's Modern State* (New York: New York University Press, 1988).

[97] Marius B. Jansen and Gilbert Rozman, "Overview," in Jansen and Rozman, eds., *Japan in Transition*, pp. 2–36: 19.

[98] Shibamura interview.

[99] *Great Osaka*, pp. 6–8; *An Outline of Municipal Administration of the City of Osaka, 1930* (Osaka: Osaka Shiyakusho, 1930), pp. 9–10.

thus elected by the Municipal Assembly but assumed his post only with the permission of the minister of interior.[100] He was assisted in his duties by a councillor, or *sanyo,* and a number of deputy mayors and revenue officers, all of whom served four-year terms upon appointment by the mayor and approval by the prefectural governor. The city was subdivided into a number of administrative units, each with chief responsibility for such obligations as census registration, tax collection, and education.[101]

Education had been made a local governmental responsibility in 1892.[102] Osaka had been divided at that time into thirty-six self-financing school districts. As these districts collected their own tax revenues, they—and not the city's electoral districts—became the keystone of local politics. Local educational agencies were often quite parochial in their outlook, given to corrupt practices, and in the hands of small groups of minor and middling merchants who were among those few taxpayers who had the right to vote in local elections. These networks were already in place by the time the first Municipal Assembly elections were conducted in 1898. Cliques, formed around school agencies at the ward level, established alliances that brought their own members to the Municipal Assembly. Once there, the assembly delegates easily ensured the selection of Executive Committee members loyal to ward-level constituencies.

The Osaka mayor's authority was undermined from two directions: by imperial and gubernatorial intervention from above and by ward and educational-agency bosses from below. The mayor's only authority was as chair of the Municipal Assembly Executive Committee, a body on which the mayor held but a single vote among six. Small and medium-sized merchants and factory owners dominated the initial home-rule government until 1912, with the mayor being little more than a facade. None of Osaka's first four mayors between 1898 and 1912 completed their terms of office.[103] Ward bosses and their Municipal Assembly cronies meanwhile engaged in corrupt behavior that might have made even their Chicago counterparts blush. With an eligible electorate of never more than 20 percent of the city's population, few mechanisms were in place for citizen oversight and accountability.

---

[100] Akizuki Kengo, "Institutionalizing the Local System: The Ministry of Home Affairs and Intergovernmental Relations in Japan," in Kim, Muramatsu, Pempel, and Yamamura, eds., *The Japanese Civil Service,* pp. 337–66: 339.
[101] *Great Osaka,* p. 9.   [102] Shibamura interview.
[103] Ibid.

WARD LORDS

In Osaka, as in Chicago, power was diffuse, with ward leaders—both formal and informal—holding decisive power and extensive resources until 1910–20.[104] Subject to unruly neighborhood bosses below and imperious Tokyo bureaucrats above, Japanese cities and prefectures developed their own local political subcultures.[105] In Osaka, the mayor's job was fundamentally one of seeking common ground among local power brokers and social groups. Success was predicated on the practice of pragmatic pluralism.

Whatever power resided in the hands of Osaka ward and educational-agency bosses, central bureaucratic agencies remained the linchpin of the Japanese system of governance. The Home Ministry, the Education Ministry, and other Tokyo-based bureaucracies ran a variety of programs and sponsored a number of local groups that extended their sometimes overly paternalistic reach deep into every Japanese community. They were "participation bureaucrats" whose proactive vision was one in which all imperial subjects could share the benefits and responsibilities of empire.[106]

Bureaucratic activism extended throughout the Japanese system.[107] The changing realities of a city in the midst of an industrial explosion forced Osakans to alter their conduct of city affairs, as evident in an examination of local government expenditures. Shibamura Atsuki has argued persuasively that local expenditures not only increased by over 300-fold, but further, that the structure of activities and expenditures became more "modern."[108]

---

[104] I thank Osaka City University political science professor Kamo Toshio for bringing this pattern to my attention during an April 11, 1996, conversation.

[105] A point underscored for postwar Japan in Ronald Aqua, "Mayoral Leadership in Japan: What's in a Sewer Pipe?" in Terry Edward MacDougall, ed., *Political Leadership in Contemporary Japan* (Ann Arbor: Center for Japanese Studies, University of Michigan, 1982), pp. 115–26.

[106] Hastings, *Neighborhood and Nation in Tokyo*, pp. 12–13; and T. J. Pempel and Michio Muramatsu, "The Japanese Bureaucracy and Economic Development: Structuring a Proactive Civil Service," in Kim, Muramatsu, Pempel, and Yamamura, eds., *The Japanese Civil Service*, pp. 19–76.

[107] Sally Ann Hastings reports in reference to Tokyo that "[e]spousing the principal that the state was responsible for the well-being of all its citizens, the bureaucratic staff of the municipal government extended its functions to encompass control over employment opportunities, emergency shelter, welfare payments, the distribution of gifts to the needy, and access to subsidized medical care—all the services that the political bosses of American cities employed to secure the loyalty of voters." Hastings, *Neighborhood and Nation in Tokyo*, p. 4.

[108] Osaka municipal expenditures increased from 2,813,000 yen between 1889 and 1893 (i.e., prior to the formation of the Osaka city government) to 312,118,000 yen between 1920 and 1924. Shibamura Atsuki, "Gyozaisei no Kozo Henka," in Shinshu Osakashishi Hensei Iinkai, *Shinshu Osakashishi* (Osaka: Osaka City Government, 1994), vol. 6, chp. 1, sec. 5, sub. 1, pp. 120–34: 124.

Special public works projects consumed the preponderance of municipal funds throughout this era: port renovation in the years 1898–1902, for example, and water and sewer construction between 1907–11. The city assumed responsibility for a modern electric tram and rail system, introduced city planning, and expanded its role in education, while sustaining investment in health care.[109] The profile of municipal responsibilities at the close of World War I was that of a twentieth-century metropolis. The municipality's expenditures conformed to more traditional patterns of unsystematic investment in a handful of particular projects just two decades before. The number of municipal employees similarly increased by a factor of twelve between 1900 and 1920.[110] Osaka experienced a revolution in municipal administration and local governmental capacity even as formal structures had evolved with at times excruciating tardiness. The city could be proactive in 1920 in ways that it could not have been in 1900, and even in 1910.[111]

This expansion of municipal functions moved forward in fits and starts. Municipal revenues were often insufficient and, as in Chicago and Moscow, local officials had few revenue-producing measures at their disposal. By the late 1910s, various city services generated about 40 percent of municipal revenues, with the new city-owned tram system quickly emerging as Osaka's leading public revenue producer.[112] This change in regime was assisted by the passage of a new municipal statute in Tokyo.

THE ARRIVAL OF STRONG MAYORS

The 1911 law on local government greatly strengthened the executive powers of mayors while limiting the power of municipal assemblies. The Osaka mayor, like his counterparts across Japan, became a chief executive officer for the first time. This move clarified the flow of power within the Japanese administrative system and bolstered the central authority's

[109] Ibid. The Osaka municipal government gradually asserted its authority over education in the 1920s, following the failure of local school districts to sustain quality education throughout the city. Shibamura interview.

[110] Shibamura interview. Concerning the profile of Osaka public employees during the 1920s, see Shibamura Atsuki, "Zaisei Kiki no Sinko to Osakashi Zaisei," in Shinshu Osakashishi Hensei Iinkai, *Shinshu Osakashishi*, vol. 7, chp. 1, sec. 1, sub. 2, pp. 25–41: 31.

[111] Hotta Akio, "Shushi jijo to Shichosha no Kensetsu," in ibid., vol. 6, chp. 1, sec. 1, sub. 3, pp. 19–33: 28–29; Nakao Toshimitsu, "Dai_gokai Naikoku Kangyo Hakurankai to Shisei," in ibid., chp. 1, sec. 2, sub. 1, pp. 34–48: 38–39; Nakao Toshimitsu, "Senso to Gyozaisei," in ibid., chp. 1, sec. 2, sub. 2, pp. 48–63: 50–51; and Shibamura Atsuki, "Gyozaisei no Kozo Henka," pp. 124, 128–29.

[112] Shibamura interview.

14. Postcard of the Dojima Building, Osaka. Photographer unknown, n.d.

ability to exercise control over local affairs. According to Osaka historian Shibamura Atsuki, the 1911 reforms had the additional consequence of opening up municipal administration to professional consultants who could serve at the pleasure and discretion of the mayor.[113] By limiting the role of the assemblies, the 1911 law inhibited the increasingly corrupt practices of Osaka's ward bosses and Municipal Assembly deputies.

Osaka was in the midst of disruptive social change. The city's textile industry led Japan's entry into the industrialized world. Osaka fast became Japan's largest, wealthiest, and most productive urban center. Its recently modernized port benefited from Japan's imperial adventures. Seventy percent of Osaka port trade in 1910, for example, was with Asia—mostly Japanese-controlled Asia. The city reflected all of the problems, conflicts, and contradictions of the Industrial Revolution. Osaka was hit first and hardest by Japan's capitalist industrial adventure. Local government had to respond.

Raging industrialization produces entirely new social strata. Osaka's largely disenfranchised workers sought political expression through an emergent union movement and manifestations of urban violence. Osaka, like Tokyo, was racked by rioting following a peace settlement to the

[113] Ibid.

Russo-Japanese War that many viewed as unfair to Japan. Outbreaks of civic violence reached a crescendo with the 1918 rice riots. New middle-management groups and white-collar professionals demanded governmental reform and an end to the insider wheeling and dealing of corrupt ward bosses, much as their counterparts in the United States demanded "progressive" reform and "good" city government. A search for democracy in which Osakans fully participated and shared dominated the Taisho era, which began in 1912.

The 1911 municipal reforms created a legal context within which Osaka's pragmatic leaders could balance these competing concerns. A new, "urban professional specialist regime," to borrow from Shibamura's terminology, took shape. This regime was both made possible and aided by Osaka's two exceptional mayors of the era, Ikegami Saburo and Seki Hajime, who held local power between 1913 and 1935—a period during which Tokyo elected eight mayors, Kyoto six, and Nagoya and Kobe three each. Ikegami and Seki successfully institutionalized a new specialist regime, one that completed Osaka's transition from Tokugawa Japan's mercantile center to Showa industrial giant.

Ikegami witnessed Osaka's social upheavals firsthand as a street cop and later as a senior police official charged with maintaining social control in the sprawling Kansai metropolis.[114] His police work made him value the constructive role of experts and professionals. Moving to consolidate the powers newly granted to mayors by the 1911 municipal reforms, Ikegami recruited some of Japan's leading specialists on hygiene, public health, transportation, and social research. Seki Hajime, who arrived in Osaka in 1916 to serve as deputy mayor, was one such recruit. Together Ikegami and Seki constructed an alliance among senior businessmen, professional elites, and academic specialists to establish an "expert regime" in Osaka. Political parties played an increasing role on the Osaka scene, especially after the extension of voting rights to all adult males over the age of twenty-five nationally in 1925 and locally in 1926.

The Ikegami-Seki professional administration and its pragmatic ethos of control through social reform grew deep roots in the Osaka political

---

[114] Ibid. The Ikegami story is a remarkable tale. The son of a lesser samurai in eastern Japan, young Ikegami fought as a soldier with the losing Tokugawa forces against the Meiji Restoration. Having been in the defeated army, Ikegami sought to reinvent himself by moving to Osaka and joining the police force. He rose steadily through the ranks from foot patrol to chief of the Osaka constabulary, the position he held immediately prior to becoming mayor in 1913. His granddaughter would later marry into the imperial family.

soil. This system favored an authoritarianism of professional specialists who presumed to know what was best for their community, yet remained democratic in the sense that this strategy embraced the social concerns and needs of Osaka's residents. It was the sort of benign or enlightened bureaucratic despotism American urban progressives often sought but, in the case of Chicago, failed to achieve in the face of universal male suffrage.

Osaka mayors thus succeeded by manipulating ministerial and local parochial jealousies to secure central resources for themselves and their community as a whole. The primary task of running the city became one of bargaining with bureaucratic overseers from Tokyo while mobilizing local resources at home. Osaka politics were closer to those of Moscow than of Chicago in that ultimate authority rested with central imperial power. Yet Osaka's electorate was larger than that of Moscow and continued to expand during the period under consideration. Imperial approval of local decisions became more perfunctory, with community decisions less subject to arbitrary interference from the capital than was the case in Russia.[115] Political parties and the other accouterments of competitive elections became increasingly significant in the functioning of the city.[116] Professionals played an ever expanding role in local administration.

Osaka provides an intermediary case between the more extreme popular rule of Chicago and the highly centralized authoritarian governance structures of Moscow. Quasi-democratic institutions brought more and more Osakans into the political fray. Community leaders reached out to dissimilar partners in pragmatic, issue-specific coalitions. The city's politics became a breeding ground for the practice of pluralism based on hard-nosed practicality.

---

[115] Akizuki, "Institutionalizing the Local System."
[116] On the emergence of Japanese national parties, see Peter Duus, *Party Rivalry and Political Change in Taisho Japan* (Cambridge, Mass.: Harvard University Press, 1968).

Part II

Tales of Success and Excess

5

Transit Tussles

Nearly four decades after his epic confrontation with streetcar tycoon Charles Tyson Yerkes, five-time Chicago mayor Carter Henry Harrison, Jr., would recall his battle for public control over transit contracts as "the supreme fight" of his life.[1] The "traction wars" dominated Chicago politics for over half a century, becoming, in many ways, the defining struggle between public and private visions of the city.[2] Between 1901 and 1908 alone, Chicago voters went to the polls eleven times to decide the question of public ownership of the city's streetcar lines. They voted for municipal ownership every time except on the decisive last referendum.[3]

Chicago's trolley battles were central to how the city came to terms with its own growth: pragmatic political leaders sought compromise—and graft—whenever possible; private investors looked for new ways to maximize profits; labor leaders pursued strategies for democratizing the workplace; engineers wanted more efficient operating systems; and straphangers merely wanted a commodious means for moving about a huge, sprawling metropolis. There were few, if any, shared interests, no matter how loudly Chicagoans proclaimed the need to advance the public good.

---

[1] Carter H. Harrison, Jr., *Growing Up with Chicago* (Chicago: Ralph Fletcher Seymour, 1944), p. 289.

[2] The centrality of the traction wars in establishing the boundaries and balance between public and private interests in Chicago life is explored in Georg Leidenberger, "Working-Class Progressivism and the Politics of Transportation in Chicago, 1895–1907" (Ph.D. diss., University of North Carolina, Chapel Hill, 1995). This perspective is also touched on by Perry Duis in his exhibition catalogue for the Chicago Historical Society's 1976 bicentennial exhibition. Perry R. Duis, *Chicago: Creating New Traditions* (Chicago: Chicago Historical Society, 1976), p. 49.

[3] David Macrum Maynard, "The Operation of the Referendum in Chicago" (Ph.D. diss., University of Chicago, 1930), p. 6.

Many historians look back at this episode with dismay. Transit specialists detect the precise moment when public transportation in Chicago was dealt its ultimately losing hand in future competition with automobiles and highways. Progressive labor historians detect the instant when warfare over the fundamental meaning of democracy was successfully reduced by Wall Street capital to mere tiffs over consumer preferences. More conservative interpretations view the same outcome as a victory in which a series of half-measures permitted Chicagoans to step out of a zero-sum battle in which the winners would have won all and the losers would have squandered all. The traction wars are a litmus test for how one views Chicago's larger meaning during the period. Moreover, they are a grand story replete with the full range of human emotions and foibles. Indeed, these battles often spilled over city boundaries, frequently involving deception in Springfield (the Illinois state capital), and eventually reached the hallowed chambers of the United States Supreme Court. A consequence of a ninety-nine-year giveaway of transportation franchises in 1865, the question of municipal control over Chicago's streetcars was both a tale of local intrigue and reflective of larger confrontations throughout Progressive Era urban America over the precise contours of private interest in the provision of public utilties.[4]

The Chicago traction wars were about graft, corruption, and patronage within a highly factionalized political culture. Numerous philosophical and ideological fissures run through this political episode, as well.[5] Chicago's diverse economic, social, ethnic, and political groupings came up with a number of strikingly different proposals to resolve the question of how best to protect public and private interests in the provision of passenger transportation. On one extreme stood the streetcar companies themselves, claiming an untouchable right to set their own business and operating standards; on the other were advocates of public ownership who included in their ranks increasingly radicalized trade unionists.[6] This contest over public utilities, it should be added, was being played out in cities and towns all around the United States.[7]

---

[4] A point made effectively, for example, in Paul Barrett, *The Automobile and Urban Transit: The Formation of Public Policy in Chicago, 1900–1930* (Philadelphia: Temple University Press, 1983); and Ernest S. Griffith, *A History of American City Government: The Progressive Years, 1910–1920* (New York: National Municipal League; Lanham, Md.: University Press of America, 1983), pp. 85–99.

[5] A point emphasized by contemporary observer Hugo Grosser in "The Movement for Municipal Ownership in Chicago," *Annals of the American Academy of Political and Social Science*, January 1906, pp. 72–90.

[6] Leidenberger, "Working-Class Progressivism."

[7] Samuel P. Hays, *The Response to Industrialism, 1885–1914*, 2d ed. (Chicago: University of Chicago Press, 1995), pp. 130–32.

The traction struggle lasted as long as it did—ruining a score of political careers in the process—precisely because the lines of battle had been drawn so tautly. Little neutral turf seemed to exist on the traction issue, and yet those civic leaders who practiced the politics of compromise and pluralism eventually found safe ground in public oversight rather than outright municipal ownership. The resolution of Chicago's streetcar wars demonstrates how inclusive political strategies during periods of intense social fragmentation can advance community interests.

The battle was primarily over money. Who would profit from the inconvenience of the Chicago straphanger? By how much? Who in the municipal and state governments would be enriched by arranging for franchise rights? What would the price be for such services? Which neighborhoods would grow and flourish, and which real estate developers would have access to those neighborhoods? Which neighborhoods would atrophy, dragging down whose real estate investment? How would streetcar franchises be tied to other lucrative utility franchises such as gas, water, and later, electricity?[8] Savvy entrepreneurs and corrupt politicians recognized scores of ways to enrich themselves at this particular public trough.

Chicago's traction struggle—with its arcane legal battles, conflicting audits, wild city council and state legislature sessions, "boodle" (the local term for bribes) on an unimaginable scale, and towering characters worthy of Shakespearean invention—proved to be literally the material of novels. Theodore Dreiser drew directly from this saga when he wrote *The Financier* in 1912 and *The Titan* in 1914, both of which were based on the career of Chicago streetcar mogul, Charles Tyson Yerkes. Dreiser's Yerkes—Frank Algernon Cowperwood—was "innately and primarily an egoist and intellectual, though blended strongly therewith was a humane and democratic spirit. We think of egoism and intellectualism as closely confined to the arts. Finance is an art. And it presents the operations of the subtlest of intellectuals and egotists."[9] Cowperwood, for Dreiser, was meant to be something of a personification of Chicago itself, as apparent in the blurring of the distinction between central character and city in *The Titan*. "The city of Chicago," Dreiser wrote, "with whose development the personality of Frank Algernon Cowperwood was soon

---

[8] Harold. L. Platt's *The Electric City: Energy and the Growth of the Chicago Area, 1880–1930* (Chicago: University of Chicago Press, 1991) provides a parallel tale in Chicago's franchising of electrical services; Ann Durkin Keating discusses the development of the local water system in "Governing the New Metropolis: The Development of Urban and Suburban Governments in Cook County, Illinois, 1831–1902" (Ph.D. diss., University of Chicago, 1984), pp. 213–28.

[9] Theodore Dreiser, *The Financier* (1912; reprint New York: Signet, 1967), p. 120.

to be definitively linked! . . . This singing flame of a city, this all America, this poet in chaps and buckskin, this rude, raw, Titan, this burns of a city!"[10]

To Carter Harrison, Jr., his old nemesis Yerkes possessed "a brilliant mind joined to a vivid imagination and an attractive personality."[11] However, as in a Greek tragedy, Harrison's engaging protagonist had a dark side. "Yerkes in his arrogant cynicism," Harrison reports further, "was riding to a fall. For all his brilliancy, his years of contact with men of education and breeding, the Baron never completely found himself."[12]

Harrison, for his part, was another of the many remarkable characters in the traction saga. Described by contemporary and subsequent critics as the pampered, indolent, irresolute son of a famous father (who had himself been a five-term Chicago mayor), Carter, Jr., nonetheless governed Chicago with sufficient skill to win office five times and, in the process, established a new standard by which Chicago mayors could be judged. Garry Wills points out that the behavior of Carter, Jr., could be summarized by a credo equally honored by Richard J. Daley and many other of the Harrisons' successors: "I use the crooks, but I'm not a crook."[13]

Harrison was at war not only with Yerkes. As with so much in Chicago, white hats were frequently interchangeable with black hats. Harrison's ultimate bane was Roger Sullivan, a tough ward boss who, unlike the wealthy Harrison, needed to earn a profit from his political dealings in order to sustain his personal standard of living.[14]

Sullivan left rural Illinois at the age of nineteen in 1879 to work in Chicago's West Side rail yards.[15] He had considerable organizational skill and worked quietly to meld business and politics in a manner

[10] Theodore Dreiser, *The Titan* (New York: John Lane, 1914), p. 6.
[11] Carter Henry Harrison [Jr.], *Stormy Years: The Autobiography of Carter H. Harrison, Five Times Mayor of Chicago* (Indianapolis: Bobbs-Merrill, 1935), p. 111.
[12] Ibid., p. 151.
[13] Garry Wills, "Sons and Daughters of Chicago," *New York Review of Books*, June 9, 1994, pp. 52–59: 52.
[14] The relationship between Sullivan and Harrison is discussed in Ralph R. Tingley, "From Carter Harrison II to Fred Busse: A Study of Parties and Personages from 1896 to 1907" (Ph.D. diss., University of Chicago, 1950); Paul Michael Green, "The Chicago Democratic Party, 1840–1920: From Factionalism to Political Organization" (Ph.D. diss., University of Chicago, 1975); Paul Michael Green, "Irish Chicago: The Multi-Ethnic Road to Machine Success," in Melvin G. Holli and Peter d'A Jones, eds., *Ethnic Chicago* (Grand Rapids, Mich.: William B. Eeridmas, 1984), pp. 412–59; as well as Loomis Mayfield, "The Reorganization of Urban Politics: The Chicago Growth Machine after World War II" (Ph.D. diss., University of Pittsburgh, 1996), pp. 51–53.
[15] Bill Granger and Lori Granger, *Lords of the Last Machine: The Story of Politics in Chicago* (New York: Random House, 1987), pp. 40–45.

increasingly associated with the city of Chicago. He teamed up with elected politicians such as Republican alderman Martin B. Madden and, most prominently, John P. Hopkins to pursue material gain from city contracts. The acerbic Harold L. Ickes describes Madden, who would die several years later while serving as chair of the Appropriations Committee of the U.S. House of Representatives, as "just the unscrupulous captain of a crew of piratical racketeers."[16]

The bogus Ogden Gas Company owned by Sullivan, Hopkins, and Madden prompted the younger Harrison to label Sullivan "the gas man," an irksome moniker that would remain with Sullivan for the rest of his life. Sullivan occasionally managed to rise above purely material interest, as in 1912, when he helped bring the Democratic presidential nomination to Woodrow Wilson because Sullivan's son, who had been a student at Princeton University during Wilson's tenure as president there, considered the New Jerseyan to be a "great man."[17] Chicago aficionados Bill and Lori Granger compare Sullivan with the Prohibition Chicago gangster Al Capone, noting that both men created a "non-family-based syndicate of men devoted to like-minded goals."[18]

Hopkins, who had become mayor following the elder Harrison's assassination, and Sullivan did all that they could to mobilize Chicago's Irish against the Harrison machine, especially following the junior Carter's initial election as mayor. Nearly a half-century later, Ickes recalled that Hopkins and Sullivan would lure local journalists into their offices and "curse Carter Harrison and all of his works. And what lurid expletives for eager ears! Not only had Harrison barred them all from real participation in the political affairs of the city, he had also made it impossible for their followers to collect graft in their own right."[19]

The "handsome, unmarried, and rich" Hopkins had arrived from Buffalo, New York, at the age of twenty-two.[20] He quickly found work with the Pullman Palace Car Company, rising from timekeeper to head paymaster.[21] Hopkins then jumped into Hyde Park politics and moved onto the Chicago scene once that community had been annexed into the larger city. For Hopkins, local politics was largely about making money. He once claimed, for example, that city aldermen could readily collect $1 million for themselves in any twenty-four-hour period.[22]

[16] Harold L. Ickes, *The Autobiography of a Curmudgeon* (New York: Reynal and Hitchcock, 1943), p. 83.
[17] Granger and Granger, *Lords of the Last Machine*, p. 45.
[18] Ibid., p. 58.   [19] Ickes, *Autobiography*, p. 37.
[20] Ibid., p. 35.   [21] Green, "Irish Chicago," pp. 426–30.
[22] Ickes, *Autobiography*, p. 90.

Sullivan, Hopkins, and their West Side Irish friends undercut Harrison's ethnic political base, enlisting Johnny "de Pow" Powers' powerful Nineteenth Ward machine in the process. The younger Harrison thwarted Sullivan's bid to become the ultimate overlord of the Chicago Democratic Party when Harrison appropriated his father's saloon-keeper political base.[23]

Harrison and Sullivan would remain at war until Sullivan's death in 1920—with Harrison preventing Sullivan from getting elected mayor and U.S. senator, and Sullivan destroying Harrison's lifelong dream of becoming his party's presidential nominee. Harrison and Sullivan, in the words of Paul Michael Green, "were political foes and personal enemies. Each man not only wanted to eliminate the other from Democratic politics but to humiliate and destroy him in the process. Like the knightly jousters of feudal England, Harrison and Sullivan verbally prodded, poked, and stabbed each other in full public view. Their duels clouded local politics and delayed the creation of a unified Democratic party."[24]

Sullivan was a political ally of Hopkins, who had been elected mayor following the assassination of Carter Harrison, Sr. Hopkins, in turn, was tied to Yerkes. Hence, the junior Harrison and Yerkes would have been sworn political enemies regardless of on whose side virtue lay.

The career of Mayor Hopkins demonstrates the volatility of political alliances in the topsy-turvy world of 1890s Chicago. Hopkins had once been a favored employee of the Pullman Company and a resident of George Pullman's model worker community south of Chicago. As mayor, he nevertheless emerged as one of labor's strongest partisans and benefactors during the bitter Pullman strike of 1894.[25]

Such personalistic factionalism bedeviled both major political parties, becoming an ingrained feature of Chicago political life until local party organizations emerged supreme at the time of World War I.[26] These twists of personal ties help to explain the enthusiasm with which low-life ward heelers such as "Bathhouse" John Coughlin and Michael "Hinky Dink" Kenna would stay the reform course in their opposition to Yerkes rather than pursuing their direct personal economic interests by accepting Yerkes's munificent bribes.

---

[23] Green, "The Chicago Democratic Party," p. 1–3, 204–358.
[24] Ibid., p. 85.
[25] Janice L. Reiff, "A Modern Lear and His Daughters: Gender in the Model Town of Pullman," *Journal of Urban History* 23, no. 3 (March 1997), pp. 316–41: 330–34.
[26] Tingley, "From Carter Harrison II to Fred Busse," p. 227; Mayfield, "The Reorganization of Urban Politics," pp. 51–53.

Greed explains much of the traction story, but not all. Underlying the desire to maximize profits were profound differences over the meaning of public good and private gain. Deeply held beliefs about the appropriateness and efficacy of private ownership of public services and thoroughfares infused the traction wars with an ideological dimension that precluded easy buyouts and compromises.[27] As elsewhere in nineteenth-century urban America, advocates of unbridled free enterprise stood in opposition to "municipal socialists" who found private profit at public expense to be profoundly wrong.[28]

Despite surface similarities with streetcar franchise battles in a number of other American cities, the Chicago experience had its own peculiar twists.[29] The city's sheer physical size, the speed of its population growth, its flat topography, and the distinctiveness of local laws and legislative practice meant that the Chicago traction story, while illustrative of the turn-of-the-century urban political economy in the United States, is a tale well worth telling on its own terms.[30]

Clay McShane points to one seemingly minor departure from "normal" practice in almost all American cities that illustrates this point. According to McShane, Chicago was unusual in requiring street railways to acquire consent for their franchise privileges from both the City Council and the owners of two-thirds of the frontage property along their proposed routes.[31] This practice exposed the street railway companies to protracted negotiations with City Council aldermen, ward bosses, and property owners. Not surprisingly, every possible private interest

[27] Ralph E. Heilman, "Chicago Traction: A Study of the Efforts of the Public to Secure Good Service," *American Economic Association Quarterly* 9, no. 2 (1908), pp. 313–409.

[28] John D. Fairfield, *The Mysteries of the Great City: The Politics of Urban Design* (Columbus: Ohio State University Press, 1993), pp. 83–86; Leidenberger, "Working-Class Progressivism." For a discussion of the simultaneous debates over public and private finance for subways in New York, see David C. Hammack, *Power and Society: Greater New York at the Turn of the Century* (New York: Russell Sage Foundation, 1982), pp. 243–51. The construction of the New York system is another good example of the politics of pragmatic pluralism at the municipal level.

[29] Paul Barrett, *The Automobile and Urban Transit: The Formation of Public Policy in Chicago, 1900–1930* (Philadelphia: Temple University Press, 1983), pp. 5–8.

[30] Such disputes were not limited to the United States. In Japan, Tokyo experienced similarly bitter conflicts over public and private ownership of tram lines. The Osaka Municipal Assembly preempted the issue when it moved to construct the city's first streetcar line with its own funds and, furthermore, to operate all future tram lines within Osaka's city limits. Streetcar profits provided the city with indispensable revenues well into the 1930s. Shibamura Atsuki, interview with the author, April 14, 1996.

[31] Clay McShane, "Transforming the Use of Urban Space: A Look at the Revolution in Street Pavements, 1880–1924," *Journal of Urban History* 5, no. 3 (May 1979), pp. 279–307: 287.

15. Cermak Station, between State and Wabash Streets, on the South Side, Chicago. Photographer unknown, n.d. Courtesy Chicago Historical Society, ICHi-30088.

became entangled in such negotiations. At a less venal level, every shade of the political spectrum between the polar opposites of complete laissez-faire and public ownership was also represented in Chicago traction politics. This entire game was played out at a time when elected city officials stood for office every two years, thereby heightening the electorate's participation in this ongoing struggle.

Money, ideology, and electoral and personal politics came into conflict with one another whenever the slightest action on street railway franchises required public resolution—a stormy brew for controversy. Freshly arriving Chicagoans by the thousands injected a dynamism of demand beyond the capacity of any of the era's transit systems. There were simply too many new riders each year for even the best-intentioned street railway to have served its customers well—and no Chicago streetcar company had the best intentions. Technological change similarly forced action, frequently expensive action, to keep up with a cutting edge that evolved from horsepower through cable lines to electric stanchions within the working career of a streetcar executive or a city alderman.[32]

Reformers, for their part, were intent on using streetcar service to disperse Chicago's population, alleviating center-city congestion and density by spreading the middle class and immigrant workers out across the expanses of prairie.[33] Streetcars became an integral component of social reform, far too important to leave to the avarice of laissez-faire capitalists and their purchased political agents.[34]

"The streetcar corporation emerged as the main villain in Chicago's political discourse during the 1890s and dominated the political agenda until well into the first decade of the twentieth century," Georg Leidenberger reminds us in his penetrating 1995 dissertation on Chicago's transportation politics of the era.[35] "Almost all Chicagoans, perhaps with the exception of the streetcar owners," Leidenberger continues, "agreed on the need to counteract the company's powers and political dealings,

---

[32] Cable power began to replace Chicago's horsecar lines in early 1882; electric traction arrived a decade and a half later. Brian J. Cudahy, *Cash, Tokens, and Transfers: A History of Urban Mass Transit in North America* (New York: Fordham University Press, 1990), pp. 22–34, 74–75.

[33] Leidenberger, "Working-Class Progressivism," pp. 1–15; Fairfield, *The Mysteries of the Great City*, pp. 83–86; Keating, "Governing the New Metropolis," pp. 242–78, 330–38; and Ann Durkin Keating, *Building Chicago: Suburban Developers and the Creation of a Divided Metropolis* (Columbus: Ohio State University Press, 1988), pp. 3–12, 22–26.

[34] Early provision of electrical service to suburban areas similarly played a pivotal role in suburban growth. See Platt, *The Electric City*.

[35] Leidenberger, "Working-Class Progressivism," p. 25.

yet by the end of the decade they articulated very divergent solutions to the problem."

The popular discontent over poor trolley service provided a social and political base for civic reform through which the distribution of urban political and economic power could be altered.[36] Dreiser was correct: the half-century-long Chicago traction wars were the material of high drama.

THE NINETY-NINE-YEAR LEASES

The story began innocently enough in 1855 and 1856 when the Chicago City Council authorized the operation of the city's first horse-drawn streetcars for twenty-five years with the stipulation that the operating companies gain permission from property owners along their routes.[37] When permission was not forthcoming, the aldermen changed the rules of the game in the first of a score of policy revisions: the City Council permitted the companies to proceed with their rail lines without seeking permission from abutting property owners. This act was overridden by the first of many court injunctions, at which point (1859) the Illinois state legislature chartered the Chicago City Railway Company. That company was endowed with the requisite powers to set down tracks and operate horsecars on any South Side or West Side street for a period of up to twenty-five years with the approval of the City Council. The legislature shortly thereafter chartered the similarly empowered North Chicago City Railway Company and, in 1861, created the Chicago West Division Railway Company, which took for itself the City Railway Company's rights for the city's West Side.[38] These actions blurred the lines between public and private, state and city authority to a degree that made litigation inevitable.

By the middle of the Civil War, Chicago was served by three major horsecar companies, each operating in one of the geographic divisions created by the meandering Chicago River (i.e., north, south, and west of the river; there was no "East Side," for such a unit would have been under the waters of Lake Michigan).[39] The Chicago City Railway

[36] Platt, *The Electric City*, p. 94.
[37] Alfred Theodore Andreas, *History of Chicago*, vol. 2 (Chicago: A. T. Andreas, 1885), pp. 118–21; Robin L. Einhorn, *Property Rules: Political Economy in Chicago, 1833–1872* (Chicago: University of Chicago Press, 1991), pp. 217–18; and Henry P. Weber, comp., *An Outline History of Chicago Traction* (Chicago: Chicago Railways Company, 1936), pp. 5–7.
[38] Andreas, *History of Chicago*, vol. 2, pp. 118–21.
[39] Alfred Theodore Andreas, *History of Chicago*, vol. 3 (Chicago: A. T. Andreas, 1886), pp. 164–66; Keating, *Building Chicago*, pp. 23–24.

Company, the North Chicago City Railway Company, and the Chicago West Division Railway Company each operated horsecar lines under a franchise charter granted by the State of Illinois and scheduled to expire in February 1884.[40] Seeking greater advantage, the three companies returned to the Illinois legislature in Springfield during the winter of 1865, when nineteen and twenty-one years still remained on their respective franchise charters. There they undertook a quiet campaign to extend their franchise agreements for ninety-nine years. In what Charles E. Merriam, the University of Chicago political scientist, reform city alderman, and mayoral candidate, would describe as "the high spot in a series of minor betrayals," the state legislature acceded to the companies' demands.[41] Carter Harrison, Jr., Merriam's longtime adversary, was more blunt. "Innocuous on the surface yet freighted with future menace," Harrison would recall in 1935, "the three companies joined in asking the legislature an extension of their franchise life, making it ninety-nine years. That the act was cunningly devised becomes evident from its being passed corruptly over the veto of Governor Richard Yates, becoming the first of the outright boodle traction grants."[42]

As Harrison's memoirs recall, the law that passed on February 6, 1865, extended "horse railway franchises in the City of Chicago" until 1954.[43] It was rushed through both houses of the legislature before Chicago officials could travel to Springfield and was passed over a gubernatorial veto with equal haste (and, undoubtedly, no small amount of money changing hands).[44] Governor Yates himself later claimed to have been offered $100,000 not to veto this law once it reached his desk.[45]

The Ninety-Nine-Year Act greatly complicated traction policy.[46] It aroused considerable public anger and mistrust. The act was poorly written, opening up enormous room for legal battles—not the least of which would revolve around the question of whether these companies and their successor franchise holders owned operating rights for anything other than horse-drawn streetcars. Finally, this act of corrupt folly prompted inclusion of language in the 1870 State of Illinois Constitution recognizing local power in franchise approvals.[47]

[40] Samuel Wilber Norton, *Chicago Traction: A History Legislative and Political* (Chicago, 1907), pp. 16–25.
[41] Charles E. Merriam, *Chicago: A More Intimate View of Urban Politics* (New York: Macmillan, 1929), p. 14.
[42] Harrison, *Stormy Years*, p. 109.   [43] Einhorn, *Property Rules*, pp. 220–22.
[44] Heilman, "Chicago Traction," pp. 315–19.
[45] Ibid., p. 315.
[46] Weber, comp., *An Outline History of Chicago Traction*, pp. 8–9.
[47] Ibid., pp. 318–19; Norton, *Chicago Traction*, pp. 28–45.

Ignoring the Ninety-Nine-Year Act, city authorities acted as if the original franchise agreements would expire in 1884 and 1886. The companies, for their part, put their faith in claims extending their franchise more than halfway into the next century. A number of smaller companies were also operating in the city, and cable was soon to replace horsepower. Legally, nothing was clear.

Harrison, Sr., first came to office in 1879 as the leader of a city of 491,516 souls. That figure would grow to 760,000 by the time he left office for the first time in 1887.[48] Harrison, Sr., struggled with many vexing issues, including the bloody Haymarket Square bombing of 1886. Traction was not at the top of his agenda.

The city of Chicago had imposed a $50 annual tax on each streetcar the year prior to Harrison's election as mayor.[49] The transit companies were fighting the imposition of this tax, appealing to a lower-court decision favorable to the city that was on appeal to the U.S. Supreme Court. Harrison calculated that he could not ensure victory on either this case or the legal questions posed by the ninety-nine-year franchises. He decided, therefore, to act as if nothing had happened since the original streetcar railway franchises had been granted in 1859 and 1861. The mayor moved to open negotiations over a twenty-year extension of the original franchises.[50] Meanwhile, a number of utility franchises in gas and the new electrical services were coming due, creating ample opportunity for Chicago aldermen to enrich themselves.[51]

Harrison successfully negotiated new streetcar franchise agreements in July 1883 by cajoling the companies and city aldermen into agreements whereby the companies would pay a $25 per annum car tax for a five-year period beginning in 1878, after which time the city would levy a $50 fee. All ordinances then in force were extended until 1903.[52] Harrison thus kept the cars operating, tax revenues flowing, and avoided expensive and unpredictable litigation on the Ninety-Nine-Year Act. He played the politics of compromise to buy time. But time could not be bought. Transit service had to be extended to new outer neighborhoods, cable technologies were about to be introduced on a mass scale, and ridership and customer complaints grew daily. Moreover, Yerkes would soon arrive in town with pockets and bank accounts bulging with Eastern money.

---

[48] Frederick Rex, *The Mayors of the City of Chicago from March 4, 1837, to April 13, 1933* (Chicago: Municipal Reference Library, 1934), pp. 65–69.
[49] Ibid., p. 67; Heilman, "Chicago Traction," pp. 319–20.
[50] Harrison, *Stormy Years*, pp. 110–11.   [51] Platt, *The Electric City*, pp. 41–51.
[52] Heilman, "Chicago Traction," pp. 320–23.

CHARLES YERKES ARRIVES

Yerkes was already well into his forties by the time he came to Chicago in the 1880s.[53] He had won and lost fortunes in his native Philadelphia, where he had served jail time in 1871 for the misuse of funds. He was by all accounts forceful, charming, intelligent, and amoral. Chicago chronicler Stephen Longstreet once wrote that "that dreadful Mr. Yerkes" was daring even by comparison to his contemporary robber barons. "Yerkes showed skill, were it the dubious franchises of watered stock (in one batch of $518 million of securities he offered, $72 million were water based, or of no value) or hiring court bailiffs to bribe jurors to bring in verdicts against victims of trolley accidents in damage suits. . . . Yerkes' boldness was outstanding."[54] Yerkes died in London in 1905, where he had gone to help develop that city's Underground subway system.

Yerkes drew on social grace and connections to obtain capital from Philadelphia and New York financiers. He represented a Philadelphia streetcar syndicate backed by Peter Widener and William Elkins, who were looking to secure control over transit in America's—indeed, the world's—fastest-growing city.[55] Yerkes soon emerged as the majority stockholder in the Chicago streetcar companies and set out to maximize dividends by providing minimal services. He eventually would count many of Chicago's best families among his stockholders and backers.[56] Yerkes did not limit his activities to streetcar railways; he was also a pivotal speculator in the city's lucrative gas franchises.[57]

Yerkes moved to exercise monopolistic control over Chicago's streetcars.[58] He gained majority control of stock issued by those companies operating in the North and West Divisions. He incorporated the North Chicago Street Railway Company, which, on May 24, 1886, secured a 999-year lease on all property, rights, franchises, and privileges

[53] Wayne Andrews, *The Battle for Chicago* (New York: Harcourt and Brace, 1946), pp. 176–85; Donald L. Miller, *City of the Century: The Epic of Chicago and the Making of America* (New York: Simon and Schuster, 1996), pp. 268–73.

[54] Stephen Longstreet, *Chicago, 1860–1919* (New York: David McKay, 1973), p. 81.

[55] Cudahy, *Cash, Tokens, and Transfers*, p. 131.

[56] Harrison, *Stormy Years*, pp. 110–242; Frederic Cople Jaher, *The Urban Establishment: Upper Strata in Boston, New York, Charleston, Chicago, and Los Angeles* (Urbana: University of Illinois Press, 1982), pp. 481–82.

[57] Platt, *The Electric City*, pp. 50–51.

[58] This account is based on Norton, *Chicago Traction*, pp. 61–64; and Bessie Louise Pierce, *A History of Chicago*, Vol. 3: *The Rise of a Modern City, 1978–1893* (Chicago: University of Chicago Press, 1957), pp. 216–20.

16. Bust of Charles Tyson Yerkes. K. K. Campbell, N.Y. Manhattan Publishing Co., n.d. Courtesy Chicago Historical Society, ICHi-13106.

of the previous companies. He did the same on October 20, 1887, in the West Division by establishing the West Chicago Street Railway Company. These two companies would themselves be consolidated on June 1, 1899, as the Chicago Union Traction Company. His firms eventually secured a 999-year lease from the West Chicago Street Railroad Tunnel Company for control of the city's yet-to-be-constructed Jackson Street tunnel.

Yerkes's companies quickly introduced cable technology, while integrating and coordinating fragmented North and West Side traction services. By 1898, he had financed, organized, built, and opened the famous elevated "loop" railway around downtown Chicago, a two-mile line connecting four "L" lines. The city's initial elevated rail transit system had opened on the South Side in time for the World's Columbian Exposition in 1893. Other Ls followed, with the Metropolitan West Side Elevated Railway inaugurating the country's first elevated electric railway service in 1895.[59] Eighty miles of elevated railway would be built between 1892 and 1906 in a self-contained system regulated by a different set of laws and government agencies from those with jurisdiction over the streetcar railways.[60] Yerkes's Union Elevated—and its famous Loop route duplicating old cable-powered street-level loops—bound these various elevated railways into a single service.

Such efforts have led some later commentators to credit Yerkes with bringing about a necessary modernization of the Chicago streetcar system.[61] His methods, however, relied on graft and the sale of watered-down stock issues—hardly tactics intended to advance community interests. To the average citizen, Yerkes was a devil who owned numerous local politicians. Whatever the reality, appearances confirmed this impression. DeWitt C. Creiger, the city's mayor between 1889 and 1891, had served previously as superintendent of Yerkes's West Chicago Street Railway Company.[62]

Yerkes's traction companies failed to gain monopolistic control over Chicago transit: his reach did not extend to the South Side, for example. Yerkes's companies nonetheless secured more than their fair share of the 164 paid streetcar rides taken on average throughout 1890 by every adult and child in the city.[63]

---

[59] Cudahy, *Cash, Tokens, and Transfers*, pp. 70–75; Brian J. Cudahy, *Destination: Loop: The Story of Rapid Transit Railroading in and around Chicago* (Brattleboro, Vt.: Stephen Greene, 1982), pp. 10–42; and James Leslie Davis, *The Elevated System and the Growth of Northern Chicago*, Northwestern University Studies in Geography no. 10 (Evanston, Ill.: Northwestern University Department of Geography, 1965), pp. 1–17.

[60] Barrett, *The Automobile and Urban Transit*, pp. 15–16; Rex, *The Mayors of the City of Chicago*, pp. 70–72; and Pierce, *A History of Chicago*, Vol. 3, pp. 219–20.

[61] See, for example, Barrett, *The Automobile and Urban Transit*, pp. 16–17.

[62] Rex, *The Mayors of the City of Chicago*, pp. 73–75.

[63] Barrett, *The Automobile and Urban Transit*, pp. 15–16. Interestingly, this figure would rise to 319 rides on mass transport per average Chicagoan by 1946, and fall back to 163 in 1956. Edward C. Banfield, *Political Influence* (Westport, Ct.: Greenwood, 1961), p. 92.

By the early 1890s, Yerkes, though already "traction baron," sought further advantage.[64] The stage was set for yet another confrontation with reform-minded politicians. Conveniently, the early 1890s was a period of "the deepest degradation of both the city council of Chicago and the state legislature in Illinois."[65] Legislators at both state and municipal levels regularly sold their votes, while the forces of reform were only just beginning to mobilize. The traction issue provided reformers with precisely the issue they needed to attract a broad base of citizen support. As will be discussed in greater detail in Chapter 8's examination of a proposed revision of the city charter, franchise battles over streetcar railways and gas and electricity utilities provided all-important flash points around which newly formed reform organizations such as the Municipal Voters' League could rally support.[66]

LEGISLATIVE REMEDIES

The situation on the ground was hardly clear-cut. Yerkes had built his own empire through a pyramid of leases, underfunded stocks and bonds, and pure guile. In addition to a number of commuter rail lines,[67] Chicagoans at the outset of the 1890s could choose among the services of eighteen streetcar companies operating 41.95 miles of cable traction lines, 255.64 miles of electrified lines, and 18.46 miles of horsecar lines. The new elevated trains would add even more miles.[68] The legal net of franchise agreements was hopelessly tangled, with the validity of the 1865 Ninety-Nine-Year Act yet to be tested in court.

The companies made the first move in the next chapter of the traction saga in 1895, inducing State Senator Charles H. Crawford of Cook County to propose legislation that would provide city councils the right to grant railway franchises for up to ninety-nine years instead of the twenty years then allowed by state law. Crawford's bill also extended the rights and privileges of existing franchise agreements, giving the current franchise holders an advantage in future negotiations. The bill passed

---

[64] Grosser, "The Movement for Municipal Ownership," pp. 73–76.

[65] John A. Fairlie, "The Street Railway Question in Chicago," *Quarterly Journal of Economics* 21 (1907), pp. 371–404.

[66] Norton, *Chicago Traction*, pp. 70–75; Heilman, "Chicago Traction," pp. 323–25; and Pierce, *A History of Chicago*, Vol. 3, pp. 221–25.

[67] Chicago is unusual for a city of its size in that it came into being more or less at the same time as the railroad. Thus commuter rail service has always played a large role in shaping the metropolitan region. For further discussion of the commuter rail lines, see Keating, "Governing the New Metropolis," pp. 116–24.

[68] Rex, *The Mayors of the City of Chicago*, p. 87.

both houses of the state legislature but was vetoed by Governor John Peter Altgeld, who proclaimed, "I love Chicago and am not willing to help forge a chain which would bind her people hand and foot for all time to the wheels of monopoly and leave them no chance of escape."[69] Years later, Edward F. Dunne, who as Chicago mayor and later Illinois governor would play his own leading role in the traction saga, recalled a chat he had with Altgeld in a "cheap" Chicago restaurant. According to Dunne, Altgeld told him that as governor he (Altgeld) "could have gotten without any danger whatsoever of prosecution to himself $500,000 if he had permitted that bill [the Crawford bill] to become law."[70]

Altgeld held the line despite personal financial setbacks suffered as a result of the 1893 depression, his preoccupation with official duties, and chronic invalidism.[71] A last-minute effort to override the governor's veto collapsed on the floor of the legislature's lower house. This failed initiative inflamed public opinion in Chicago, ensuring that future legislative initiatives could not take place in secret.

Nearly two years later, in February 1897, the companies moved to bypass city officials altogether by prompting State Senator John Humphrey to introduce a bill that would have established a three-member state commission to regulate traction service and grant transit franchises.[72] The Humphrey Act would have extended existing franchises for fifty years beyond December 1897 and, in a populist gesture, would have frozen fares at five cents per ride. The companies did not hide their roles in the preparation of the Humphrey Act. Rather, they launched an 1890s-style media blitz to gain its passage. The Illinois Senate passed the bill, but the Illinois House defeated the proposed act following a month of public denunciations of the Senate action.

The companies concluded at this point that it would be impossible to ride roughshod over the city of Chicago. They abandoned their strategy

---

[69] Norton, *Chicago Traction*, p. 70.

[70] Edward F. Dunne, *Illinois: The Heart of the Nation*, 5 vols. (Chicago: Lewis, 1933), Vol. 3, p. 219.

[71] Harvey Wish, "Altgeld and the Progressive Tradition," *American Historical Review* 46, no. 4 (July 1941), pp. 813–31: 823–30. Altgeld's principled stance is not surprising given his courageous pardon of three Haymarket anarchists who had not been executed by the time he had come to office. For further contemporary readings on Altgeld's career, see Waldo R. Browne, *Altgeld of Illinois: A Record of His Life and Work* (New York: B. W. Huebsch, 1924). Altgeld's Haymarket pardon, explained in John Peter Altgeld, *Reasons for Pardoning Fielden, Neebe, and Schwab* (Springfield, Ill.: Governor's Office, 1893), remains one of the strongest condemnations of the misuse of judicial power in the history of American jurisprudence.

[72] Grosser, "The Movement for Municipal Ownership," pp. 74–75; and Heilman, "Chicago Traction," pp. 325–28.

of seeking protection from the Illinois legislature. The traction interests now moved to have all powers transferred to the City Council, where, they were confident, they could purchase a sufficient number of aldermen to ensure passage of whatever plan they advocated. The period was probably one of the city's low points in political ethics; journalists such as Ickes widely commented that the City Council "was forever on the auction block—ready to go to the highest bidder."[73]

Immediately upon the defeat of the Humphrey Act, Illinois House delegate G. A. Allen introduced what became widely known as the Allen Law.[74] Ralph E. Heilman summarized the Allen Law's major provisions as follows:

The bill . . . provided that local authorities might give street privileges to street railway companies for any period not exceeding fifty years, but all grants were to be conditional upon the consent of more than one-half of the owners of land fronting the parts of streets to be used, although this signature once given could not be revoked. Five cents was to be the regular rate of fare, which could not be changed during the life of any existing ordinance of franchise, and, in case of the extension of any existing ordinance, the rate was to be five cents for the first twenty years. For new privileges granted, the Council was to fix the fare, which could not exceed five cents; but which, when once fixed, was not to be changed for twenty years.[75]

The Allen Law passed both houses and was signed into law by Governor John Tanner in June 1897. The Speaker of the legislature's lower chamber was absent for the key vote, claiming that "he was suffering from a carbuncle."[76]

THE HARLAN COMMISSION

With the passage of the Allen Law in Springfield, the action shifted back to Chicago. Within two weeks, Republican reform alderman John Maynard Harlan (son of Justice John Harlan of the U.S. Supreme Court, and father of another future justice, also named John Harlan) played the role of responsible compromiser. Harlan was six feet tall, the very picture of the college football star he had been when he played center at Princeton.[77] He had the sort of overly proper style that would today be labeled "uptight." He nonetheless established himself as a major reform leader within local Republican politics.

---

[73] Ickes, *Autobiography*, p. 82.
[74] Ibid., pp. 328–33; Norton, *Chicago Traction*, pp. 91–93.
[75] Heilman, "Chicago Traction," p. 328.   [76] Harrison, *Stormy Years*, p. 146.
[77] Ickes, *Autobiography*, p. 82.

Local Republican boss William Lorimer—the "blond boss of Chicago"—was Harlan's primary intraparty antagonist, as well as a major nemesis of Republican reformer Merriam.[78] Lorimer, whose family fled Manchester, England, during the 1865 depression, worked his way up through the lower ranks of the West Side's "river ward" (the Sixth) from laundry solicitor and coal hauler to gambling-house helper and meat-packing laborer. He eventually landed a prized streetcar job in 1880 and used the ties he developed there to move laterally into Republican politics. Lorimer had emerged as Cook County's most powerful Republican leader by the mid-1890s, just as the party was benefiting from nationwide mass desertions from the Democratic Party following the Panic of 1893. John "Farmer" Humphrey, who had introduced Yerkes's ill-fated bill in the Illinois Senate, was a Lorimer man.

Lorimer served in the U.S. House of Representatives between 1895 and 1901, and again between 1903 and 1909, before being elected on the ninety-fifth ballot by the Illinois General Assembly to the U.S. Senate. Lorimer was subsequently thrown out of the Senate in 1912 as a result of an investigation that alleged that the "blond boss" had purchased the votes in the Illinois legislature that had carried him over the top and into the nation's highest deliberative body. Lorimer received a hero's welcome back in Chicago, organized by his rising protégé, future mayor and Capone buddy "Big" Bill Thompson.

Harlan, meanwhile, had lost a close race against Carter Harrison, Jr., in the 1897 mayoral contest. He had "barnstormed the city," making an especially vigorous run only to be undercut by his own party's bosses.[79] Harlan turned around and quickly proposed that the City Council establish a five-person commission to review the status of all streetcar franchises. The Harlan Commission would eventually produce a comprehensive report that was submitted to the City Council on March 28, 1898.[80] Meanwhile, the political waters were reaching full boil.[81]

The 1898 state and municipal elections were catastrophic for Yerkes and the supporters of the Allen Law. A dozen Senate sponsors and

---

[78] This discussion of Lorimer is based on Joel Arthur Tarr, *A Study in Boss Politics: William Lorimer of Chicago* (Urbana: University of Illinois Press, 1971).

[79] Ickes, *Autobiography*, pp. 85–88.

[80] Dunne, *Illinois*, Vol. 2, pp. 221–23; Grosser, "The Movement for Municipal Ownership," p. 74; Weber, comp., *An Outline of Chicago Traction*, pp. 24–25; and *Report of Special Committee of the City Council of Chicago on Streetrail Franchises and Operations* (Chicago: Chicago City Council, 1898).

[81] Heilman, "Chicago Traction," pp. 329–33.

sixty-four members of the House who had voted for the Allen Law in the state legislature were defeated in their re-election bids.[82] Of equal significance, forty-two candidates for the Chicago City Council's sixty-eight aldermanic seats who had declared opposition to Yerkes won office, drastically changing the balance of power on the council.[83] Nineteen aldermanic candidates among the twenty-one who had been supported by the Municipal Voters' League were among this group—securing a firm proreform bloc on the City Council.[84] Harrison, Jr., was learning the levers of power available to his new post. Harrison loathed Yerkes, who, as already noted, was closely linked with Roger Sullivan, Harrison's archrival in the local Democratic Party.

The traction wars now reached a fevered pitch—with three major battles shaping up simultaneously. First, Alderman Harlan and his four colleagues on the recently formed Harlan Commission were examining all information that could be secured about the history to date of traction franchises in Chicago. Second, Chicagoans were lobbying in Springfield for repeal of the Allen Law. Third, Yerkes and his allies were seeking a new set of franchises directly from the Chicago City Council.

The Harlan Commission's report provided a complete, detailed review of all aspects of street railroad franchises, focusing on capitalization, earnings, dividends, franchise ordinances, and passenger services. It provided a firm base for the subsequent debates in the City Council, equipping reformers with much-needed information about their traction opponents.[85] Harlan and his colleagues embodied the potentially positive role that a commission subordinate to the City Council might play in developing future traction policy. The Harlan Commission eventually became the model for the City Council Street Railway Commission, established in December 1899, and its successor, the powerful Committee on Local Transportation, which was established in May 1901.[86]

These legislative commissions demonstrated that efforts to find common ground could advance everyone's interests further than the continual bickering of the previous four decades. The Street Railway

---

[82] Ibid., pp. 332–33; Maureen A. Flanagan, *Charter Reform in Chicago* (Carbondale: Southern Illinois University Press, 1987), pp. 43–44; Leidenberger, "Working-Class Progressivism," pp. 36–43.

[83] Barrett, *The Automobile and Urban Transit*, pp. 21–22.

[84] Norton, *Chicago Traction*, pp. 99–100.

[85] Heilman, "Chicago Traction," pp. 331–32.

[86] Norton, *Chicago Traction*, pp. 100–110; Grosser, "The Movement for Municipal Ownership," pp. 86–89.

Commission's 1900 report, for example, favored the establishment of a legal basis for municipal ownership of the lines in the future while opposing immediate city operation of the street railways. "In fact," the commissioners wrote, "the Commission is quite distinctly of the opinion that it would be unwise for the city of Chicago to attempt at the present time to operate its street railways. Nor has the Commission any notion that the people of Chicago, if given the opportunity through the referendum to express themselves upon the subject, would at present favor municipal operation."[87]

Repeal of the Allen Law itself was a relatively straightforward affair following the election debacle of 1898. The law was repealed by a nearly unanimous vote in March 1899. With Allen repealed, the streetcar battle passed back to the Chicago City Council. The clock was ticking on the 1883 and 1884 twenty-year franchise grants; the stage was set for a climactic showdown at the Chicago City Council.[88]

THE NOOSES WERE HUNG FROM THE BALCONY WITH CARE

Yerkes and his colleagues had purchased many ward bosses and their aldermen and fully expected to win the franchise extensions on their own terms. Yerkes's man on the City Council, John ("Johnny de Pow") Powers of the Irish-Italian Nineteenth Ward, was proud of his reputation as "prince of the Boodlers."[89] Alderman "de Pow"—a Sullivan man—detested the Harrisons, father and son, both of whom headed a vaguely reformist faction within the Democratic Party that was limiting the boodle prince's field of play. Powers, described at the time as "cool-headed, cunning, and wholly unscrupulous," was also known for "good-fellowship" and "good heartedness."[90] "Imagine a short, stocky man with a flaring gray pompadour," the *Outlook* observed in 1898, "a smooth-shaven face, rather heavy features and a restless eye, standing at the front of the Council Chamber with one finger aloft to catch the Mayor's eye, and you have a good picture of 'Johnny' Powers."[91] Powers ruled his fiefdom through a shrewd combination of benevolence and

---

[87] Chicago City Council Street Railway Commission, *Report of the Street Railway Commission to the City Council of the City of Chicago* (Chicago: Chicago City Council, 1900).

[88] Heilman, "Chicago Traction," pp. 234–35; Norton, *Chicago Traction*, pp. 100–05.

[89] Lloyd Wendt and Herman Kogan, *Bosses in Lusty Chicago: The Story of Bathhouse John and Hinky Dink* (Bloomington: Indiana University Press, 1967), pp. 38–39.

[90] Ray Stannard Baker, "Hull House and the Ward Boss," *Outlook* 58 (March 26, 1898), pp. 769–71: 769.

[91] Ibid.

intimidation. His band of rowdies, for example, once threatened to physically force Harlan from the podium at a Nineteenth Ward speaking engagement, only to be stared down by the "muscular" Harlan.

Harrison was not without his own shady allies—most notably "Bathhouse" Coughlin and "Hinky Dink" Kenna.[92] It perhaps would be reassuring to see Harrison's City Council victory over Yerkes as a clear-cut victory of reform over graft. This was not the case, however. As Paul Michael Green writes, "the notion of good guys (reformers) versus bad guys (politicians) does not appear in Chicago for several reasons. The Harrison family clouded historical animosities because of their appeal to both sides."[93]

Harold L. Ickes, later to be Franklin Delano Roosevelt's henchman in the White House, was cutting his teeth on Chicago politics as a young reporter at this time. He mastered the ins and outs of local factional politics and generally found Harrison to be a respectable character. "No one ever accused him of dipping his fingers into the graft till," Ickes would write in his autobiography. "But the Democratic machine, under the leadership of Bobby Burke, was a pretty unsavory institution. It was a political cesspool that no amount of activated sludge treatment could deodorize."[94] Harrison, Coughlin, and Kenna were part of a single package.

Coughlin and Kenna, for their parts, stayed the course with Harrison despite tempting offers to jump on the Yerkes juggernaut. Their loyalty was prompted by their own conflicts with the likes of de Pow and Sullivan. Yet, as historian Edward Kantowicz has observed, had Harrison's "motivation been totally cynical, he wouldn't have taken so strong and visible a stand."[95]

Harrison drew on solid support in more respected circles as well. *Daily News* publisher Victor Lawson was perhaps Yerkes's most tenacious opponent.[96] He was joined in his negative press coverage of the Yerkes traction empire by Joseph Medill's *Chicago Tribune* and Herriman Kohlsaat's *Chicago Times-Herald.*[97]

---

[92] Wendt and Kogan, *Bosses in Lusty Chicago*, pp. 171–83.

[93] Green, "The Chicago Democratic Party," p. 2.

[94] Ickes, *Autobiography*, pp. 89–90.

[95] Edward R. Kantowicz, "Carter Henry Harrison II: The Politics of Balance," in Paul M. Green and Melvin G. Holli, eds., *The Mayors: The Chicago Political Tradition* (Carbondale: Southern Illinois University Press, 1987), p. 26.

[96] John Franch, "Opposite Sides of the Barricade," *Chicago History* 24, no. 2 (Summer 1995), pp. 39–57.

[97] Ibid. This is the same Medill who had sponsored the entry into politics of Carter Henry Harrison, Sr., in 1871.

Harrison—with the help of his allies Kenna and Coughlin—turned back the Yerkes franchise extension at a raucous City Council meeting in mid-December 1898.[98] Harrison would later recall this colorful session as having been played out to an overflowing crowd.[99] The balconies were crammed; in the front row sat assorted Harrison supporters with hangman's nooses that they dangled over the balcony railing at key moments in the debate. Mayor Harrison waved a noose himself as he held forth on the floor, while the crowd yelled "Hang 'em! Hang 'em!"[100] A German band paraded outside of City Hall playing patriotic marches; it was followed by an angry throng of torch- and club-bearing citizens. Flash photographers snapped away all the while at the bar hall–like crowd.[101]

The nineteenth century closed with a series of defeats for Yerkes: at the hands of Harrison forces at the City Council in December 1898 and by opponents of the Allen Law in Springfield the following March. The traction baron soon left Chicago for good. Harrison would remain in office, riding the crest of his successful fight with Yerkes, until 1905, and served yet another term as mayor from 1911 to 1915. Harrison never moved to resolve the traction issue once and for all, apparently content to savor his victory over Yerkes.[102]

In many ways, the ultimate victor at this stage was Alderman Harlan. His commission had demonstrated the advantages of confronting the complex technological, engineering, and legal issues involved in the traction debates by fostering a far less emotionally charged atmosphere.[103]

THE HONEST JUDGE DUNNE

With Yerkes gone and various legislative ploys by the traction companies in both Springfield and Chicago spent, attention now turned to possible public takeover of the streetcar lines. Harrison's political authority was dissipated, a fact he reluctantly acknowledged by not standing for re-election in 1905.[104]

---

[98] Andrews, *Battle for Chicago*, p. 184.

[99] Harrison, *Stormy Years*, p. 174. This story may also be found in Ickes, *Autobiography*, p. 38.

[100] Longstreet, *Chicago*, p. 92.

[101] Harrison, *Stormy Years*, p. 174; Andrews, *Battle for Chicago*, p. 184; Cudahy, *Cash, Tokens, and Transfers*, pp. 131–33.

[102] Richard Edward Becker, "Edward Dunne, Reform Mayor of Chicago: 1905–1907" (Ph.D. diss., University of Chicago, 1971).

[103] Norton, *Chicago Traction*, pp. 105–8; Weber, comp., *An Outline History of Chicago Traction*, pp. 24–25; Dunne, *Illinois*, Vol. 2, pp. 221–23.

[104] Tingley, "From Carter Harrison II to Fred Busse," pp. 168–84.

Meanwhile, an increasingly radical and broad-based "new unionism" was taking shape in Chicago. In 1902, John Fitzpatrick led a group of young progressive reformers in seizing control of the Chicago Federation of Labor from an older band of corrupt union officers.[105] Under Fitzpatrick's leadership, which would continue until his death in 1946, the local unions began to use municipal ownership as an important means of attack against the corporations they viewed as controlling their city.

Georg Leidenberger attributes the return of the traction issue to the front page of Chicago's newspapers to the city's "new unionism."[106] Leadership of the municipalization movement shifted from the middle-class progressives so evident in the settlement-house movements to just-organized elementary school teachers, teamsters, glove-makers, and typographers who were coming to dominate the Chicago Federation of Labor. Labor's efforts to organize previously un-unionized groups were turning Chicago into the "trade union capital of the world," in which teachers and teamsters were leading the way to broad-based unions including workers of all trades and all skill levels, of both sexes and, to some extent, of all races. The municipal ownership issue provided an opening for the unions to demand a new democratic relationship between capital and community, in addition to a means to address more limited concerns tied to traditional employer-employee relations.

Local companies responded to the municipalization movement with a vengeance, especially when various groups affiliated with the Chicago Federation of Labor began to honor one another's picket lines. Harold Barton Myers, in an extensive 1929 dissertation reviewing the policing of labor disputes in Chicago, argued that "[i]n few other cities have the methods used by labor and employer in industrial disputes been so drastic, so violent, so cruel, and so unscrupulous as in Chicago."[107] Reviewing police action in nearly two dozen major strikes between 1877 and 1925, Myers concludes that "[a]fter 1898 came a period of highly favorable industrial prosperity. Unions grew rapidly and, beginning about 1902, came the most serious era of strikes Chicago [had] ever experienced. Between 1902 and 1906 Chicago was in constant turmoil.

---

[105] Julia Wrigley, *Class Politics and Public Schools: Chicago, 1900–1950* (New Brunswick, N.J.: Rutgers University Press, 1982), pp. 26–27.
[106] Leidenberger, "Working-Class Progressivism," pp. 44–232.
[107] Howard Barton Myers, "The Policing of Labor Disputes in Chicago: A Case Study" (Ph.D. diss., University of Chicago, 1929), p. 5.

The strikes of the period, while not as numerous as those of 1886, were far more serious."[108]

Myers would also note that "[t]he apathy, lack of training, and incompetency which are frequently observed in the actions of the public prosecutors and the judges of the lower courts, and the frequent failure of the mayor of Chicago and the various administrative officers of the city or state to perform the duties of their offices, are part of the general problem of inefficient and corrupt local government."[109]

A strike by the South Side's traction workers in late 1903 sent shock waves through town as it took police dispatched by Mayor Harrison to return order to the streets.[110] Edward Dunne emerged as the leading politician representing the union reformers' views on a number of issues, including the traction wars. The turning point came with a particularly aggressive confrontation between labor and capital during a bitter 1905 strike by the teamsters that had erupted over the issue of open (i.e., nonunion) shops. While reflecting national labor relations trends of the era, the Chicago confrontations nonetheless were among the most brutal and divisive anywhere in the United States. Employer reliance on African-American strikebreakers—many of whom had been unable to join the white-dominated unions in the first place—poisoned Chicago's race relations for over a generation and led to even more destructive racial confrontations in the future. The employers eventually dominated this round of Chicago's labor wars—and would continue to do so until after World War I.[111]

Judge Edward F. Dunne, a strong advocate of municipal ownership of franchises, was elected mayor in April 1905 with solid labor support. Dunne also represented the growing number "of 'lace-curtain' (well-to-do) Irish residents living in the city's better neighborhoods."[112] A final resolution of the traction wars appeared to be at hand.

Dunne came to power as a leading proponent of public ownership of major public utilities, including the city's transit system.[113] "I have no hesitation," he announced in March 1902, "in declaring that I am in favor of municipal ownership and operation of Chicago's street railways,

[108] Ibid., p. 1192. The Depression-era labor wars of the 1930s had not yet occurred when Myers defended his dissertation.
[109] Ibid., p. 1187.
[110] Ibid., pp. 384–432; Leidenberger, "Working-Class Progressivism," pp. 131–46.
[111] The subsequent rise of organized labor in Chicago is explored in Lizabeth Cohen, *Making a New Deal: Industrial Workers in Chicago, 1919–1939* (Cambridge, U.K.: Cambridge University Press, 1990).
[112] Green, "Irish Chicago," p. 427.   [113] Dunne, *Illinois*, Vol. 2, pp. 224–55.

17. Mayor Edward F. Dunne, 1913. Moffett Co. Library of Congress, Prints and Photographs Division, Biographical File.

telephone system, gas and electric lighting plants, providing always that they be managed under an honest and rigid civil service. The public demands and will be content only with two essentials in the operation of these public utilities: first, efficiency and comfort in service; second, operation at the lowest cost commensurate with efficiency and comfort."[114]

Dunne defeated Republican alderman John Harlan by just over 35,000 votes in an election that had become a referendum on municipal ownership of the streetcar railways.[115] Harlan's highest ambition had been to be elected Chicago's mayor, especially following his close race against Harrison in 1897. However, he never appreciated the extent to which his own party's leaders could not forgive past "political irregularities."[116] Harlan was crippled in the end by his battles with the local Republican Party machine led by "Blond Boss" Lorimer.[117]

Dunne, a fifty-two-year-old former circuit court judge, was born of Irish immigrant parents.[118] He had spent most of his life in Illinois, save for a brief period as a student at Trinity College in Dublin, where he had been unable to complete his coursework due to severe financial losses suffered by his family back in the States. Dunne is widely regarded as having been honest and intelligent, if somewhat intractable. Paul Michael Green noted that Dunne had "neither Sullivan's organizational ability nor Harrison's capacity to instill loyalty."[119] He should not be viewed solely as an advocate of reform, however, as his electoral success in the 1905 mayoral race and the 1912 gubernatorial contests rested on an alliance with boodle boss Sullivan.[120]

Dunne's two-year term would be remembered as a difficult one in which radical reformers failed to prove themselves capable of governance. Dunne was the last Chicago mayor to serve for two years.

---

[114] Edward F. Dunne, "Advantages of Public Ownership and Operation of Utilities: Statement to the Public, March 29, 1902," in Edward F. Dunne, *Dunne: Judge, Mayor, Governor*, comp. and ed. William L. Sullivan (Chicago: Windemere, 1916), p. 137.

[115] A point emphasized by Hugo Grosser, among many observers during this period. See Grosser, "The Movement for Municipal Ownership," p. 81.

[116] Ickes, *Autobiography*, p. 90.

[117] Tingley, "From Carter Harrison II to Fred Busse," pp. 181–84.

[118] Rex, *The Mayors of the City of Chicago*, pp. 93–97; Becker, "Edward Dunne, Reform Mayor of Chicago"; and John D. Buenker, "Edward F. Dunne: The Limits of Municipal Reform," in Green and Holli, eds., *The Mayors*, pp. 33–49.

[119] Green, "The Chicago Democratic Party," pp. 111–20.

[120] Ibid, pp. 111–21, 169–218; Becker, "Edward Dunne, Reform Mayor of Chicago"; and Michael F. Funchion, "The Political and Nationalist Dimensions," in Lawrence J. McCaffrey, Ellen Skerrett, Michael F. Funchion, and Charles Fanning, eds., *The Irish in Chicago* (Urbana: University of Illinois Press, 1987), pp. 61–97: 66–69. Dunne's personal secretary during his governorship was the younger brother of another "Boss" Sullivan, Judge John J. Sullivan of the "back of the yards" Fourteenth Ward Democratic organization near the great Union Stockyards. Robert A. Slayton, *Back of the Yards: The Making of a Local Democracy* (Chicago: University of Chicago Press, 1986), p. 153–54.

Four-year terms were enacted in November 1905, taking effect at the time of the April 1907 mayoral election.[121]

Chicago under Mayor Dunne "was widely regarded as 'the most radical city in America,' one presided over by a 'socialist' mayor who loaded his administration with 'long haired friends and short haired women.'"[122] His unrelenting demand for municipal ownership of the street railways brought the traction wars to closure. Using partisan, class, and ethno-cultural appeals, Dunne managed to mobilize Democratic Party faithful to his cause in 1905 and sought to build on that electoral base once in City Hall. Even as cynical an observer as Ickes credited Dunne with attempting "in all sincerity to make good on his promises."[123] He challenged the local power elite with a blend of "advanced Catholic social thought and populist Democracy."[124] In the end, his administration failed.

Subsequent observers, such as historian John D. Buenker, have expressed doubt that Dunne ever could have achieved his transit goals. "It is highly unlikely," Buenker wrote, "that a majority of Chicago voters ever unequivocally supported the notion [of immediate municipal ownership]."[125] While appearing to polarize the issue between "democratic idealists who advocated municipal ownership" and "business pragmatists who favored regulation,"[126] Dunne's forcing of the issue created a middle space for compromise. This is the moment at which the Harlan-prompted City Council commissions came into play.

The Council's Street Railway Commission immediately set out to determine the feasibility of municipal ownership of the city's street railway lines.[127] As part of that process, the commission undertook a review of the Ninety-Nine-Year Act, the validity of which had never been tested in a court of law. A number of questions hung in the air, not the least of which was whether or not that act had pertained only to horse-drawn transit vehicles. By 1901, City Council aldermen had been sufficiently impressed with the commission's work that its status was elevated to a permanent committee with jurisdiction over all local transportation. This new Committee on Local Transportation would remain a focal point for Chicago transit policy well into the twentieth century. The committee came as close as Chicago ever would come prior

[121] Rex, *The Mayors of the City of Chicago*, p. 96.
[122] Buenker, "Edward F. Dunne," p. 33.   [123] Ickes, *Autobiography*, p. 107.
[124] Buenker, "Edward F. Dunne," p. 34.   [125] Ibid., p. 43.
[126] A formulation proposed by Platt in *The Electric City*, p. 124.
[127] Norton, *Chicago Traction*, pp. 105–7; Weber, comp., *An Outline History of Chicago Traction*, pp. 35–41.

to World War II to having a transportation planning and policy-making agency.[128]

FROM ALLEN TO MUELLER

As one of its first actions, the Committee on Local Transportation commissioned an engineering report from Bion J. Arnold reviewing "all financial and scientific facts, practical matters and statistics" relating to existing street railway services as well as the initiation of new services by the city.[129] Arnold's report, which was completed on November 19, 1902, made several important contributions to the traction debate.[130] First, it set forth an action plan for initiating new routes that would be followed as late as the 1930s. Second, it underscored the desirability and practicality of eliminating divisional lines between the North, West, and South Sides. Third, it strongly advocated a single-fare system for the entire network of streetcar lines. Fourth, it demonstrated the financial feasibility of a public takeover of existing lines. Fifth, it turned many of the conflict's most vexing questions into engineering problems to be solved by experts rather than politicians. Arnold thereby created the political space for compromise.[131]

The reform-oriented Civic Federation of Chicago simultaneously sponsored its own report on the transit system. Following the Allen Law defeat, the Civic Federation invited Yerkes and his fellow street rail-road owners to open their books to a full audit. The owners complied.[132] The resulting exhaustive report, prepared by Milo Roy Maltbie with accompanying company audits conducted by Edmund F. Bard, set forth the companies' intricate financial maneuverings.[133] Arnold's and Maltbie's efforts created an unusually high level of transparency in street railway operations.[134] The companies, for their part, scrambled to accommodate middle-class demands for openness in a strategy to avoid falling prey to labor's more radical injunctions. A number of key legal

---

[128] Barrett, *The Automobile and Mass Transit*, p. 23.
[129] Norton, *Chicago Traction*, p. 118.
[130] Bion Joseph Arnold, *Report of the Engineering and Operating Features of the Chicago Transportation Problem, Submitted to the Committee on Local Transportation of the Chicago City Council in November 1902* (New York: McGraw, 1905).
[131] Barrett, *The Automobile and Urban Transit*, pp. 28–31.
[132] Norton, *Chicago Traction*, pp. 113–14; Heilman, "Chicago Traction," pp. 335–38.
[133] Milo Roy Maltbie, ed., *The Street Railways of Chicago: Report of the Civic Federation of Chicago with an Accountant's Report by Edmund F. Bard* (Chicago: Civic Federation of Chicago, 1901).
[134] Lloyd Henry Demarest, *The Chicago Traction Question* (Chicago: George Waite Pickett, 1903).

issues remained obscured, especially the status of the ninety-nine-year franchises.

Another round of franchise and lease consolidation had taken place by this time, and the newly formed Chicago Union Traction Company had subsumed the North and West Chicago Street Railway Companies. The South Side lines remained under separate ownership. A complex set of legal issues arose during the putting together of these companies, including questions concerning the validity of the Ninety-Nine-Year Act in those jurisdictions that had been annexed by the city of Chicago subsequent to that law's enactment. Lower-court rulings were ambiguous, and in 1905 litigation reached the U.S. Supreme Court. The Court's ruling on March 12, 1906, upheld the city's stance, thereby giving municipal authorities practical control over most of the street railway system (with the exception of a few lines in the West and South Divisions).[135] The Ninety-Nine-Year Act had finally been put to rest.

The major inheritor of the Yerkes operation, the Chicago Union Traction Company, had fallen into bankruptcy receivership. The receivers negotiated a temporary twenty-year franchise extension—the Tentative Ordinance of 1904—pending the resolution of various legal cases.[136] The primary actors on both sides were beginning to seek a compromise.

The Illinois state legislature put into place the final precondition for resolution of the traction wars in May 1903.[137] The Mueller Law, which had passed that month, gave Illinois cities—including Chicago—the power to own and operate street railways through direct title as well as through leasing arrangements. The law further required that cities receive the approval of three-fifths of their electorates prior to assuming responsibility for transit operations. Cities were granted authority to borrow funds for the purpose of assuming control of their car lines.[138] The Chicago City Council immediately acted and, on April 5, 1904, the city electorate approved municipal acquisition of street railways under the provisions of this law.[139]

[135] Harrison, *Stormy Years*, pp. 242–45; Norton, *Chicago Traction*, pp. 193–202; Weber, comp., *An Outline History of Chicago Traction*, p. 55; Leidenberger, "Working-Class Progressivism," pp. 206–7.

[136] Norton, *Chicago Traction*, p. 191.

[137] Weber, comp., *An Outline History of Chicago Traction*, pp. 46–52; Demarest, *The Chicago Traction Question*.

[138] Heilman, "Chicago Traction," pp. 339–45; Willard E. Hotchkiss, "Chicago Traction: A Study in Political Evolution," *Annals of the American Academy of Political and Social Science* 28, no. 3 (November 1906), pp. 27–46.

[139] Heilman, "Chicago Traction," pp. 344–45; Hotchkiss, "Chicago Traction," pp. 37–38.

All was ready, then, for a municipal takeover of the transit lines as Mayor Dunne came to power. In accepting the nomination to run for mayor, Dunne had announced his intention to move quickly. "[M]unicipal ownership and operation is no idle dream," he bellowed. "We need not discuss the theories of municipal ownership, or municipal ownership alone in the abstract. . . . We know that, where it is in force, it has resulted in reduced fares, in more rapid, constant, and efficient service, in increased wages to traction employees, and the unqualified endorsement of the public."[140] Lingering legal issues had been resolved by judicial and legislative action, financial and engineering feasibility studies had been completed, and financial arrangements were being moved into place. The time to act had finally arrived.

At Dunne's prompting, the City Council approved the issuance of $75 million worth of Mueller Law street railway certificates to enable the city to execute the purchase of existing lines.[141] Issuance of such bonds was subsequently approved by Chicago voters in a referendum held in April 1906. City ownership seemed imminent, especially with the coming to power of a mayor who so strongly advocated a public takeover of the street railway lines. Both the Chicago Federation of Labor and William Randolph Hearst, who had himself run for mayor of New York on the Municipal Ownership League ticket, added their considerable weight to the Chicago municipal ownership campaign.[142] Service, meanwhile, was deteriorating almost daily.

"Streetcars Here World's Dirtiest." "Thousands Wait; Cars Packed Full." "Make Chicagoans Human Sardines." "Let Car Service Be Bad." Thus proclaimed the era's headlines in the *Chicago Tribune*.[143] Yerkes's old paper, *The Inter-Ocean*, while it presented riding conditions more favorably, proved no more forgiving of the politicians. That paper's headlines declared, "Council Demands Traction Question End in a Month," "Injunction Suit Adds to Traction Tangle," "Council Threatened by Mob with Ropes."[144] Chicagoans were exasperated;

---

[140] Edward F. Dunne, "Accepting Nomination as Mayor of Chicago: Address before Chicago Democratic Convention, February 25, 1905," in Dunne, *Dunne: Judge, Mayor, Governor*, pp. 177–85: 177.

[141] Heilman, "Chicago Traction," pp. 347–54.

[142] Cudahy, *Cash, Tokens, and Transfers*, p. 128. On Hearst's national campaign for municipal transit ownership, see Michael W. Brooks, *Subway City: Riding the Trains, Reading New York* (New Brunswick, N.J.: Rutgers University Press, 1997), pp. 74–105.

[143] *Chicago Tribune*, November 11, 1906, p. 1; November 14, 1906, p. 7; November 29, 1906, p. 2; January 12, 1907, p. 1.

[144] *The Inter-Ocean*, December 4, 1906, p. 1; January 27, 1907, p. 4; January 28, 1907, p. 4.

they wanted action—a demand reinforced each morning and evening rush hour.

Electoral support for municipal ownership had never been stronger, yet the voters could be fickle. Unlike Dunne, who was ideologically committed to public ownership of all utilities, Chicago's riding public principally wanted a more commodious ride to and from work. The citizenry was ready to support any plan that had a likelihood of success, as measured by the quality of their own experience as straphangers.

Authorized by referendum to issue Mueller Act certificates in preparation for a municipal takeover of the street railway companies, Mayor Dunne set forth his next moves in an April 27, 1906, letter to the chair of the Committee on Local Transportation, Charles Werno.[145] The "Werno letter" underscored Dunne's intention to bring about "prompt and thorough improvement" of service through municipalization of the street railways.[146] The mayor proposed to encourage the companies to upgrade service in preparation for sale to the city. At the top of Dunne's list of recommended changes in service were unification of the services provided by various companies, through routes that did not terminate downtown, and universal transfers.[147] He also urged Werno's committee to initiate negotiations for a municipal buyout.

Werno began negotiations as instructed, with somewhat different results than Dunne had anticipated.[148] As can sometimes happen in municipal management, professional and expert staff may not necessarily reach the same conclusions as their political overlords.[149] Werno's experts and, in the end, his committee reported two ordinances to the City Council on January 15, 1907, following an arduous, complex, and at times confusing set of discussions.[150] The proposed ordinances granted twenty-year franchises to the companies in return for immediate rehabilitation of rolling stock and adherence to performance standards specified in the proposed agreements. The companies would advance the city $5 million to initiate construction of a subway line downtown to be

---

[145] Norton, *Chicago Traction*, p. 215.

[146] The Werno letter is reproduced in Dunne, *Dunne: Judge, Mayor, Governor*, pp. 286–94.

[147] Heilman, "Chicago Traction," pp. 354–56.

[148] Becker, "Edward Dunne," p. 119; Weber, comp., *An Outline History of Chicago Traction*, pp. 58–79.

[149] Cathleen M. Giustino explores the tensions between emerging expert communities and municipal politicians in Prague of this period. Cathleen M. Giustino, "Architects and the Task of Urban Planning in Late Imperial Czech Prague, 1866–1900: Winning Jurisdiction 'From Below' " (manuscript, 1995).

[150] Heilman, "Chicago Traction," pp. 357–77.

owned by the city.[151] A newly established Board of Engineers would supervise the companies' operations to ensure compliance with agreed goals, including the annual construction of a specified amount of new track.[152] Werno's committee thus proposed a compromise involving private ownership with public supervision. An irate Dunne vetoed the ordinances, a move that the City Council overrode on the night of February 11, 1907, by a vote of 57 to 12.[153] The entire issue was now turned over to Chicago voters for approval by referendum.

April 2, 1907, was a momentous election day for Chicago, and an extremely disappointing one for Mayor Dunne. Not only did Dunne lose the mayor's race to Fred A. "Fat Freddie" Busse—by a vote of 151,779 for the incumbent, 164,702 for his Republican challenger, and 19,449 votes cast for other candidates—but the Compromise Ordinances Dunne had so vehemently opposed passed by a tally of 167,367 votes in favor and 134,281 against.[154] What had appeared assured when Dunne entered office—municipalization of the street railway companies—had become virtually impossible. Another nail was added to the coffin of municipal ownership sixteen days after the election when the Illinois Supreme Court declared that the proposed sale of $75 million Mueller Law railway certificates had been unconstitutional, as that sale would have increased the city's indebtedness beyond limits set by the state constitution.[155]

Dunne's defeat was total, brought about in part by his own stubbornness. Dunne and one of his traction counsels, Clarence Darrow, never sought compromise.[156] They turned their backs on the politics of pragmatic pluralism. In so doing, they defeated themselves. Dunne would recall from retirement that he had left "the Mayor's Office with a clear conscience, with hands untainted, with a clear record, with a stout heart, and with confidence that I had kept every trust reposed in me by the people. I had done my duty and I had not broken a single pledge."[157]

---

[151] Various proposals to construct a subway to supplement street and elevated transit lines had been under consideration since the early 1890s. See the discussion in John W. Stamper, *Chicago's North Michigan Avenue: Planning and Development, 1900–1930* (Chicago: University of Chicago Press, 1991), pp. 2–5.

[152] Heilman, "Chicago Traction," pp. 377–83.

[153] The text of Mayor Dunne's veto message may be found in Dunne, *Dunne: Judge, Mayor, Governor*, pp. 329–35; as well as in Dunne, *Illinois*, Vol. 2, pp. 281–88.

[154] Rex, *The Mayors of the City of Chicago*, p. 98.

[155] Heilman, "Chicago Traction," p. 387.

[156] Darrow's own account of these events may be found in Clarence S. Darrow, "The Chicago Traction Question," *International Quarterly* 12 (October 1905), pp. 13–22.

[157] Dunne, *Illinois*, Vol. 2, p. 197.

Dunne went on to be a successful Illinois governor, elected in 1912 as a Woodrow Wilson Democrat with support from labor as well as from ward boss—and Harrison antagonist—Roger Sullivan.[158] The Compromise Ordinances he so abhorred had been victorious after some of the most extensive campaigning undertaken in Chicago at that time.[159] He had lost the mayoral race in 1907 to an undistinguished Lorimer-faction Republican, "Fat Freddie" Busse.[160] Short and rotund, Busse drew on a political base in the German North Side to win the election despite being unable to campaign due to injuries suffered in a train accident at the outset of the election season.[161]

Busse was a "rough, profane" North Side "ward politician extraordinary" who had served as state treasurer and state senator.[162] His ward encompassed Lake Shore Drive's "Gold Coast" and a territory farther inland "composed largely of slums, pockmarked by saloons, gambling houses, and brothels."[163] It was in this "transitional zone" west of Clark Street that Busse felt most at ease. His "natural associations were the dives. He was a barroom tough."[164] To keen observer Ickes, Busse's fundamental political challenge—one that Busse had mastered in his own ward—was to remain "a rough-and-ready politician" while convincing his wealthier constituents along the lake that he also "understood the problems and aspirations of those born to the purple and linen."[165] Busse offered a stark contrast to his predecessor, the pontifical reform-judge-turned-mayor Dunne.

Dunne's intransigence on the traction issue—despite some waffling as the Compromise Ordinances moved to approval—opened the possibility of compromise between the Committee on Local Transportation and the street railway companies. Walter Fisher, another of Dunne's traction counsels, led the way in searching for a settlement. (Fisher would go on to serve as U.S. Secretary of the Interior in the Taft administration.[166]) Committee members were joined by other local notables—such as Harrison, Ickes, Arnold, and even the sainted University of Chicago

[158] Dunne, *Dunne: Judge, Mayor, Governor*, p. 1; Dunne, *Illinois*, Vol. 2, pp. 308–79; Green, "The Chicago Democratic Party," pp. 169–89.

[159] Heilman, "Chicago Traction," pp. 38–39.

[160] Tarr, *A Study in Boss Politics*, pp. 172–99.

[161] Maureen A. Flanagan, "Fred A. Busse: A Silent Mayor in Turbulent Times," in Green and Holli, eds., *The Mayors*, pp. 50–60; and Rex, *The Mayors of the City of Chicago*, pp. 98–102.

[162] James W. Errant used these adjectives to describe Fred Busse in "Trade Unionism in the Civil Service of Chicago" (Ph.D. diss., University of Chicago, 1939), p. 6.

[163] Ickes, *Autobiography*, p. 93.   [164] Ibid., p. 107.

[165] Ibid., p. 93.

[166] Barrett, *The Automobile and Urban Transit*, pp. 37–45.

football coach Amos Alonzo Stagg—in support of the ordinances. Coalition politics brought to conclusion a nearly half-century-long struggle to define an appropriate balance between the public good and private gain.

The Compromise Ordinances, as they came to be known, established a Board of Supervisory Engineers, initially headed by Arnold. Arnold was considered by a vast majority of Chicagoans to be beyond reproach. Yet the board's supervisory authority was never precisely defined— leaving some troublesome loose ends to be tied in the future. The new system was not sufficiently flexible to sustain quality service in bad times as well as good.

Writing on the career of electricity magnate Samuel Insull, Harold L. Platt evaluated the period 1905–7 as a turning point in Chicago political history: "[T]he heated debate over the future of the city reached a climax. Older patterns of political loyalty broke down, spawning a major realignment that would gradually shift power to the ethnic leadership of Anton Cermak, and the Democratic Party. . . . The battle for municipal reform was over."[167]

Platt's assessment is based on a number of developments in the Chicago body politic, including the simultaneous City Charter contest discussed in Chapter 8. Reform never remained a binary choice between "good" and "evil." Chicagoans were discovering the necessity of giving up power to keep power in a fragmented, rapidly changing urban world. They were becoming pragmatic pluralists.

TROLLEYS AND AUTOMOBILES

Initial evidence pointed to service improvements on the city's street railways following the enactment of the Compromise Ordinances. An immediate upgrading of rolling stock and other equipment began, for example, and miles of new track were brought into service.[168] Writing with the hindsight of three-quarters of a century, transit historian Paul Barrett is less charitable to the Chicagoans of the era.[169] For him, the Chicago

---

[167] Platt, *The Electric City*, p. 136. In addition to Platt's excellent book, readers may wish to refer to Wayne Andrews's earlier work, *Battle for Chicago*, for a brief yet informative discussion of Samuel Insull's career and acquittal in a famous 1930s trial (pp. 257–87).

[168] Weber, comp., *An Outline History of Chicago Traction*, pp. 380–420; Alan R. Lind, *Chicago Surface Lines*, 3d ed. (Park Forest, Ill.: Transport History Press, 1979), pp. 26–33.

[169] Barrett, *The Automobile and Urban Transit*.

traction wars were merely another local episode in a larger sorting out of public transit policy throughout urban America, a process in which mass transit became "a regulated, privately owned utility" while "facilities for the automobile were publically subsidized."[170] Turn-of-the-century political victories by those intent on regulation thus dealt transit a losing hand in its future battle with the automobile.

Barrett disparages Mayor Harrison (the junior) as a "dapper, smooth talking and personally honest" politician who "tolerated a measure of graft and vice" and "had no clear position in the transportation issue aside from a steadfast opposition to Yerkes."[171] The historian is drawn to Dunne's advocacy of municipal ownership because Dunne was committed and, unlike the dilettante Harrison, deeply knowledgeable about the issues at hand.

Barrett acknowledges that Dunne was "seriously overconfident of the public's commitment to public ownership and hopelessly intolerant of opposition to his most cherished goal."[172] "Mayor Dunne," Barrett continues, "left no room for honest disagreement, and Republicans and Harrison Democrats alike took umbrage at his slurs on their integrity."[173] Barrett is also more positive about Yerkes than were many who lived through these battles. Barrett views the transit boss as the person who was able "to consolidate and rationalize the city's transit system."[174]

Barrett acknowledges that the public was angry, but he tends to view such ire as misplaced. The fundamental problem, as Barrett sees it, was that Chicago was growing too quickly and its central business district remained too compact for service improvements to keep pace with increasing demand. He argues against municipal ownership as a possible solution. Rather, he points to the success of the East Coast "big three"—Boston, New York, and Philadelphia—which combined public investment with public oversight of private transit companies.[175] Such mixed approaches created transportation infrastructures that are still functioning a century later. In other cities, where little or no public investment accompanied state regulation, transit companies were never able to separate their lines from the street surface—by subway or elevated tracks and restrictive rights-of-way. Their streetcars thus quickly found themselves in a losing competition with the private automobile for street

---

[170] Ibid., p. 6.
[172] Ibid., p. 35.
[174] Ibid., p. 16.
[171] Ibid., p. 22.
[173] Ibid., p. 36.
[175] For a concise overview of public-private cooperation and conflict surrounding transit issues in New York, see Clifton Hood, *722 Miles: The Building of the Subways and How They Transformed New York* (New York: Simon and Schuster, 1993).

18. Caricature of Carter H. Harrison, Jr. *Verdict Supplement* no. 34, n.d. Library of Congress, Prints and Photographs Division, Biographical File.

space. Chicago's "L"—with its own separate legal status—is the exception that proves his case.[176]

Barrett's analysis is compelling from the perspective of someone concerned first and foremost with rational transportation policy. The 1907 Compromise Ordinances were never more than a temporary solution to Chicago's transit wars. Harold Platt reminds his readers that the transit companies were "still hamstrung by the political legacy of Charles Yerkes" a decade after the ordinances had been ratified.[177] Harold G. Gosnell, in a study of Depression-era Chicago politics, similarly reports that the traction issue continued to fester throughout the 1930s.[178] For his part, Barrett would have preferred a more coherent and internally consistent approach to traction than compromisers such as Harrison could ever have provided.

Barrett's work is a forceful reminder that great policy victories often appear to have been Pyrrhic in hindsight—a phenomenon that is hardly unique to early-twentieth-century America, as anyone who has reviewed the fate of postwar public housing and 1950s urban-renewal policies in the United States can attest.[179] The passage of time, the accumulation of new knowledge, and technological, political, and social change can make the most "rational" policy suspect just a quarter-century later.

More recently, Georg Leidenberger's authoritative examination of Chicago's traction wars criticized the 1907 Compromise Ordinances from a different direction.[180] Leidenberger's work demands the attention of all scholars interested in this intriguing chapter of Chicago history. He connects the traction wars' final chapter to the larger saga of an increasingly radicalized "new unionism" that was emerging in Chicago during

---

[176] Barrett, *The Automobile and Urban Transit*, p. 26. On the history of the L, see Bruce G. Moffatt, *The "L": The Development of Chicago's Rapid Transit System, 1888–1932* (Chicago: Central Electric Railfans' Association, 1995); and George Krambles and Arthur H. Peterson, *CTA at 45: Recollections of the First 45 Years of the Chicago Transit Authority* (Oak Park, Ill.: George Krambles Transit Scholarship Foundation, 1993).

[177] Platt, *The Electric City*, p. 218.

[178] Harold F. Gosnell, *Machine Politics: Chicago Model* (1937; reprint, New York: AMS, 1969), pp. 142–44.

[179] Another interesting instance of combatants at the time being proven shortsighted by history is the case of business and political opposition to Aaron Montgomery Ward's tenacious efforts to stop construction on the downtown Lake Michigan waterfront in order to keep it clear as open parkland. Lois Willie provides an engaging account of this saga in *Forever Open, Clear, and Free: The Historic Struggle for Chicago's Lakefront* (Chicago: Henry Regnery, 1972), pp. 71–81. Readers might also refer to Dennis H. Cremin, "Chicago's Front Yard," *Chicago History* 37, no. 1 (Spring 1998), pp. 22–44.

[180] Leidenberger, "Working-Class Progressivism."

this period, as well as to the aggressive antilabor stance such activism prompted among local corporations. The Chicago Federation of Labor and the city's quickly growing teamsters' and teachers' unions struggled to expand organized labor's influence beyond more traditional craft-oriented workers' associations. "Immediate municipal ownership" became a potent slogan for reaching out to laborers.

The bitter 1905 teamsters' strike and mayoral campaign moved confrontation over traction lines to center stage in local politics. Dunne's election was not merely a fluke tied to Mayor Harrison's decision not to seek re-election. The 1905 elections were the crest in a wave of working-class progressivism that advocated greater citizen empowerment. Labor began to organize cooperative strikes throughout this period as stronger unions such as the teamsters often struck in sympathy for the work stoppages of less secure unions, such as that of waitresses.[181]

For Leidenberger—and for the labor activists about whom he writes—immediate municipal ownership was about extending democracy. Leidenberger argues that the municipal ownership fight pitted a local community against large financial trusts and corporations that were providing essential services to the community. Chicago's traction wars fall into the narrative of a larger populist battle for democratization of American capitalism. In the view of the era's more radical elements, municipal ownership would loosen Wall Street's stranglehold over peoples' lives. "In fact," Leidenberger writes, "the battle over Chicago's streetcars, culminating in the 1907 election, was fought over political control and different conceptions of democracy. During these two years [1905–7], conservative civic reformers aligned with streetcar as well as real estate interests and major employer groups to mount an effective offensive against a popular movement for public control."[182]

Leidenberger concludes that the passage of the Compromise Ordinances marked the new unionism's failure to extend democracy. Corporate power ultimately proved able to mobilize conservative middle-class reformers around transit policies based on public regulation rather than public ownership, thereby transforming—and even degrading—democratic citizenship into consumerism. In Leidenberger's account, Mayor Harrison emerges as merely the loutish son of a rich and famous father. Alderman Harlan and transit expert Arnold—together with the

---

[181] See, for example, the discussion of the milk-wagon drivers' union's support of a waitress strike in March 1902 in Dorothy Sue Cobble, *Dishing It Out: Waitresses and Their Unions in the Twentieth Century* (Urbana: University of Illinois Press, 1991), pp. 66–67.

[182] Leidenberger, "Working-Class Progressivism," p. 199.

other specialists rallying behind the ordinances—became an extension of American capital. Chicago's citizenry—or at least the male minority that enjoyed voting privileges—squandered a historic moment in which it could have brought about meaningful democratic reform to municipal life.

For Leidenberger, Barrett, and many other authorities on public transportation, the Compromise Ordinances represent yet another unfortunate example in a line of Chicago's failures at pursuing an optimal policy outcome. In the case of Barrett, optimization would have involved the implementation of measures rendering the transit system efficient from a transportation specialist's point of view. In the case of Leidenberger, the optimal outcome would have involved the implementation of procedures rendering local political life more democratic from the point of view of those who advocate citizen participation.

The argument offered here moves in a different direction, suggesting that the ability to transform a battle over fundamental democratic philosophies into one of mere consumer preferences constitutes a victory rather than a defeat for the era's Chicagoans. The alternative to such half-measures would have been the continuation of a zero-sum battle in which the winners would have won everything. Those who were sufficiently unfortunate to have found themselves on the losing side would have squandered all. The cases discussed in Part III of this volume illustrate some of the calamitous consequences of such all-or-nothing politics.

For many Chicagoans, if not a majority—and certainly for the majority who voted on April 2, 1907—the Compromise Ordinances *did* represent a consumer issue. Many Chicagoans of the time appear to have been interested primarily in being able to walk to the nearest streetcar stop; be offered frequent, commodious, comfortable travel to their destination; and return home in clean and efficient streetcars, as well. The traction companies fended off municipalization of their assets simply by agreeing to improve streetcar service.

The capacity to convert fundamental disagreements over values into a range of decisions revolving around consumer preferences stands at the core of a viable and stable democratic system. The transformation of profound altercations among unremitting principles into the mere regulation of a public service creates the space within which a number of individuals and communities with widely divergent philosophies can live with one another without being forced to defend their most closely held beliefs.

The politics of pragmatic pluralism that stands at the center of this volume constituted a strategy that achieved a result that a more "progressive" observer such as Leidenberger abhors: converting citizens into consumers. Pragmatic pluralism resolves profound divisions over policy and value in highly fragmented societies by rendering them trivial. Individuals and communities win less, perhaps, but they lose less as well.

Leidenberger correctly identifies such an approach as fundamentally "conservative" in that it does not seek to restructure the underlying bases of power in society. Forces other than municipal politics may achieve such a result. Nontraditional elites secured positions of wealth and power in all three cities under review in this book during the half-century beginning in 1870. Economic restructuring and technological change, rather than municipal politics, picked new winners and losers in each society. Alas, these outcomes were not always the most appealing of all possible outcomes. But alternatives could well have been even more monstrous, as can be seen in the case of Moscow in Chapter 9.

Barrett's and Leidenberger's analyses diminish the political difficulties of forging coherent policy in the fragmented metropolis. Chicago's traction wars may be viewed as policy "successes" in that the key players—such as the socialite Harrison, the publisher Victor Lawson, and the princely Harlan—were able to find common ground at the end of the day, while more professional planners and progressive politicians could not. The fact that subsequent municipal leaders were unable to adjust to the new realities and protect mass transit service in the age of the automobile is regrettable. But it does not undermine the genuine achievements of those public figures who tried as best they could to practice the politics of pragmatic pluralism in turn-of-the-century Chicago.

6

﹋﹌﹋﹌﹋﹌﹋﹌﹋﹌﹋﹌﹋﹌﹋﹌﹋﹌

Educating Moscow's Workers

Mass education loomed over Silver Age Moscow as an issue of major public concern that managed to bring together Moscow's aspiring civic society and fumbling municipal administration, often in an alliance against reactionary overseers from the imperial Ministry of Education. Education was a sphere in which individual Muscovites could convert into practice long-held cultural and religious teachings about the meaning of charity and piety without undercutting their own self-interest. Public education in Moscow—quite unlike the situation in Chicago at the same time—became one realm in which broad agreement and concerted action often transcended ideological concerns and narrow social interest. Radicals and conservatives alike advocated teaching the city's residents to read and write. Education was often an area of fin de siècle Moscow life in which civic awareness transcended class consciousness.

The 1861 emancipation of the serfs placed public education squarely on the Russian political and social agenda. Freed men and women must be literate to survive. The end of servitude presented relatively concise moral, political, social, and economic quandaries. The maintenance of millions of peasants able to travel about was a far more complex undertaking.

Emancipated Russian peasants were never as free as they might have wished. They frequently remained tied to their villages through intricate systems of mutual obligation and social attachment. Peasants, nonetheless, were increasingly pushed off the land as central Russian agriculture continuously failed to sustain viable rural communities.[1]

---

[1] For more on these issues, see Joseph Bradley, *Muzhik and Muscovite: Urbanization in Late Imperial Russia* (Berkeley: University of California Press, 1985); Jeffrey Burds, *Peasant Dreams and Market Politics: Labor Migration and the Russian Village, 1861–1905* (Pittsburgh: University of Pittsburgh Press, 1998); and Robert E. Johnson,

Mass literacy rates remained deplorably low as late as 1914, when 9.8 percent of the Russian Empire's peasant women and 25.1 percent of peasant men could read and write.[2] The situation in Moscow was more positive: male literacy in Moscow *guberniia* rose from 33 to 76.2 percent between the 1880s and 1908, and literacy among women workers increased from 4.7 to 26 percent during the same period. Educational levels remained generally higher within the city itself throughout the period. According to some later estimates, eight out of ten Moscow males could read by the outbreak of World War I, as could over half of the city's women.[3]

Although the precision of such calculations remains open to question, the general pattern is quite apparent: vast swaths of the Moscow population were literate and used their reading and writing skills on a daily basis. General literacy represents a substantial achievement in Russian society, in which basic education for peasant children in the countryside, as well as for adult peasants in towns and cities, endured as an elemental concern.

Russians were hardly passive about the state of their public education. Numerous attempts were made to improve general literacy, "to close the oft-cited gap between educated Russians and the people, seen as backward, culturally bereft, and potentially dangerous."[4] The motivations behind such efforts were as diverse as the programs themselves, ranging from a concern over social order through a desire to improve industrial productivity to an aspiration to foster the fulfillment of human capacity.

Attempts to elevate the educational level of working Russians both in the countryside and in the city were hardly abject failures. The overall level of school saturation in European Russia, measured by school enrollments as a percentage of the general population, increased from 1.5 percent in 1880 to 4.5 percent in 1911. This achievement paled in comparison to other industrializing states of the era such as the United States, where the classroom saturation level between 1900 and 1910 reached 19.4 percent, or Great Britain (17.4 percent), Germany (17 percent),

Peasant and Proletarian: The Working Class of Moscow in the Late Nineteenth Century (New Brunswick, N.J.: Rutgers University Press, 1979).
[2] Rose L. Glickman, *Russian Factory Women: Workplace and Society, 1880–1914* (Berkeley: University of California Press, 1984), pp. 111–12.
[3] Adol'f Grigor'evich Rashin, *Naselenie Rossii za 100 let (1811–1913gg). Statisticheskie ocherki* (Moscow: Gosstatizdat, 1956), p. 299.
[4] Susan Bronson, "Enlightening the Urban Poor: Adult Education in Late Imperial Russia, 1859–1914" (Ph.D. diss., University of Michigan, 1995), p. 1.

Austria-Hungary (15.7 percent), France and Sweden (14.2 percent), and Japan (11 percent).[5] The proverbial late-imperial Russian educational glass was both half full *and* half empty.

Educational accomplishment became especially visible among specific segments of the population. Jeffrey Brooks reports in his distinguished study of late-imperial Russian literacy, *When Russia Learned to Read*, that common literacy increased substantially in Russia between the serf emancipation and the Bolshevik Revolution.[6] Literacy among army recruits, for example, advanced from 21 percent in 1874 to 68 percent by 1913.[7] A 1920 census of European Russian twelve- to sixteen-year-old children representing the last prerevolutionary school cohort showed that 71 percent of the boys and 52 percent of the girls could read and write, a dramatic if insufficient advancement since 1861.[8]

Yet, education—whether by rural zemstvo, Orthodox parish, or state-supported public school—often remained primitive at best. Working adults in cities such as Moscow required additional training and skills to meet the demands of ever more advanced industries. Moscow merchants and industrialists invested considerable money on their own in adult education programs to ensure that their workers and employees could read and write. These efforts supplemented national educational initiatives, marking a conscious effort on the part of the city's wealthiest families to reach out to some of the community's poorest members.

THE 1861 GREAT REFORMS AND EDUCATION

The 1861 serf emancipation was accompanied by a series of additional reforms that sought to transform tsarist society, including major statutes governing primary education in 1864 and a decade later, in 1874.[9] These reform laws encompassed changes in primary, secondary, and higher education throughout the Russian Empire. Of particular note here, basic

---

[5] Ben Eklof, *Russian Peasant Schools: Officialdom, Village Culture, and Popular Pedagogy, 1861–1914* (Berkeley: University of California Press, 1986), p. 292.

[6] Jeffrey Brooks, *When Russia Learned to Read: Literacy and Popular Culture, 1861–1917* (Princeton: Princeton University Press, 1985).

[7] Ibid., p. 4.   [8] Ibid.

[9] This discussion of the 1864 and 1874 educational reforms is based on Eklof, *Russian Peasant Schools*, pp. 50–69; and Jeffrey Brooks, "The Zemstvo and the Education of the People," in Terence Emmons and Wayne S. Vucinich, eds., *The Zemstvo in Russia: An Experiment in Local Self-Government* (Cambridge, U.K.: Cambridge University Press, 1982), pp. 243–78.

primary education was substantially overhauled as a result of national legislation and various accompanying edicts and decrees.

The transformation of primary instruction was tied to the establishment of the zemstvo, as education and health care were among the primary responsibilities of these newly created elected rural councils.[10] A dozen years were required to establish local self-government councils following the ratification of the original zemstvo statute on January 1, 1864. Debates over the meaning of the zemstvos began almost immediately following the enactment of that law and have continued until today. Were the zemstvos an extension of autocratic government deeper into the Russian countryside? Or did these councils support completely new lines of citizenship? Could the zemstvos shape policy? Or did they merely control local administration of policies established elsewhere? How genuine were their elections? How captive of central officials were their full-time employees?

Ben Eklof notes that "much ink has been spilled in arguments over the origins and functions of the zemstvos, but we should not lose sight of the fact that they were created to fill an administrative vacuum in the countryside."[11] There is little doubt that, with very few exceptions, zemstvos were not representative of local society, especially following 1890, when the system of electing peasant delegates directly by their communities was changed.

Education represented an area of zemstvo achievement. Basic instruction had long constituted a major void in rural administration prior to 1864, an absence that the zemstvos managed to address. For Brooks, for example, "primary schooling was the area of greatest zemstvo achievement, and on the eve of World War I education was the largest item in zemstvo budgets."[12]

The zemstvos raised revenues from levies imposed on lands, factories, taverns, commercial enterprises, and residences, and from a number of incidental fees.[13] The zemstvos relied on local police for tax collection and were required to receive government approval for their budgets. Consequently, zemstvos were frequently underfunded, with taxes often in arrears.

---

[10] For further discussion of zemstvo self-government, see the articles contained in Emmons and Vucinich, eds., *The Zemstvo in Russia*; as well as S. Frederick Starr, *Decentralization and Self-Government in Russia, 1830–1870* (Princeton: Princeton University Press, 1972).
[11] Eklof, *Russian Peasant Schools*, p. 56.   [12] Brooks, "The Zemstvo," p. 243.
[13] Eklof, *Russian Peasant Schools*, p. 63.

The zemstvos were but one provider of education in the Russian countryside.[14] A variety of private, religious, and ministerial schools competed with zemstvo-run classes for students and for financial support. The Ministry of Education placed inspectors of primary educational institutions in each province to coordinate the activities of all of these educational institutions under a law ratified in 1869.[15] The result was a highly fragmented rural educational system in which the quality of instruction varied greatly. Such divergence in rural educational quality came to the city with peasants looking for work.

Urban leaders became ever more aware of the social and economic consequences of illiteracy within a few decades of mass peasant migration to Russian cities. Literacy committees sprang up around the country, promoting basic primary education in many Russian communities. In 1894, Vasilii Vakhterov, an inspector of schools for the city of Moscow as well as a member of the Moscow Zemstvo's Commission on Education, called for the introduction of universal education throughout Russia.[16]

Vakhterov's speech, subsequent accounts of it, and other publications "electrified" public opinion, bringing a strong sense of urgency to the literacy issue.[17] Combining questions of school accessibility, cost, and compulsory education, School Inspector Vakhterov argued that Russia could afford universal education. He contended that compulsory education could no longer be viewed as a utopian ideal but was, in fact, a prerequisite for social well-being. Such views led to his dismissal as a school inspector in 1896. Vakhterov subsequently left Moscow, teaching in a series of provincial towns and cities. He helped to organize the Teachers' Union following the 1905 Revolution and ended his career during the early 1920s instructing Red Army soldiers on how to read and write.

Vakhterov's 1894 speech provides but one small indication of how much the attitudes and opinions of educated Russians toward their compatriots' lack of literacy had evolved since the Great Reforms of the 1860s. He captured the views of his fellow Muscovites as well. Vakhterov

---

[14] Brooks, "The Zemstvo," pp. 245–46.
[15] Eklof, *Russian Peasant Schools*, pp. 66–67.
[16] For a discussion of Vakhterov's remarks and the national attention they brought to this issue, see ibid., pp. 110–15.
[17] Ibid., p. 110; and "Vakhterov, Vasilii Porfir'evich," in Joseph L. Wieczynski, ed., *The Modern Encyclopedia of Russian and Soviet History*, 61 vols. (Gulf Breeze, Fla.: Academic International, 1976–97), Vol. 41, p. 157.

and his associates on the Moscow Literacy Committee were part of a general movement to fill in those educational lacunae left by faulty government and religious institutions through a social activism that would have been immediately recognizable to Chicagoan and Osakan proponents of educational betterment.

Moscow merchant families joined with city officials to improve popular literacy on a number of fronts. They supported primary educational institutions for children, took an interest in official and unofficial institutions of higher learning, and generally encouraged reading and writing. Wealthy Muscovites and the merely well-to-do launched a number of creative initiatives to educate adults both in basic literacy and in more specialized skills. They were frequently joined in their efforts by political activists, labor organizers, and religious leaders.

Moscow's literacy rates improved, exceeding national Russian norms and approaching international standards. The city's society and culture were transformed by rising levels of basic schooling in a manner that was at times overlooked in the wake of the revolutions and social unrest of the early twentieth century. Mass general education proved to be one arena in which a remarkable variety of Muscovites at the turn of the last century showed themselves to be pragmatic pluralists. It was also a domain in which the Moscow *haute* bourgeoisie came into direct conflict with more conservative officials in the imperial Ministry of Education.[18]

THE VERY DEFINITION OF REACTIONARY AUTOCRACY

Late-imperial ministers of education represent a sluggers' row of reactionary autocratic ideologues. Former St. Petersburg school superintendent and university founder Sergei Uvarov—who served as Nicholas I's minister of education between 1833 and 1848—defined the precise concept of autocracy when he penned a missive to all school officials proclaiming "Orthodoxy, Autocracy, and Nationality" as authoritative state ideology.[19] Count Dmitrii Tolstoi, minister from 1866 until 1882,

---

[18] This conflict is explored in some depth in Robert W. Thurston, *Liberal City, Conservative State: Moscow and Russia's Urban Crisis, 1906–1914* (Oxford, U.K.: Oxford University Press, 1987), pp. 154–80.

[19] James T. Flynn, "Tuition and Social Class in the Russian Universities: S. S. Uvarov and 'Reaction' in the Russia of Nicholas I," *Slavic Review* 35, no. 2 (1976), pp. 232–48; and James T. Flynn, "Uvarov, Sergei Semenovich," in Wieczynski, ed., *Modern Encyclopedia*, Vol. 41 (1986), pp. 147–51: 147.

was the model Russian reactionary who saw every university student as a potential terrorist.[20] He resigned his education post to become *ober-procurator* of the Holy Synod and, from 1882 until his death in 1889, served as both the empire's chief of internal security and the president of its Academy of Sciences.

Count Tolstoi implemented a reactionary system of education associated with his name against which reformers would rail until the 1905 Revolution finally brought the "Tolstoi system" to a welcomed end.[21] Early-twentieth-century British educational specialist Thomas Darlington viewed Tolstoi as a pivotal figure in Russian educational history. "The year 1866 in which Count Dmitri Tolstoi succeeded Golovin as Minister of Public Instruction," Darlington wrote in 1909, "may be fixed as the turning point in the educational history of the reign. The policy of the man at the helm of educational affairs previously to this year had been to pay the utmost possible deference to the opinion of educated society, and to allow the widest practicable scope of local initiative and self-government. With the advent of Tolstoi to office, this policy was completely reversed."[22]

Tolstoi generally restricted access to secondary and higher education, reducing the number of students as a means to ensure social order.[23] He was "not an original thinker," but accepted and promoted Uvarov's credo of "Orthodoxy, Autocracy, and Nationality" while considering nearly all of the Great Reforms as a tragic mistake.[24] Tolstoi vigorously advocated the Russification of non-Russian peoples in the empire. He was, in brief, "the archetypical conservative bureaucrat of nineteenth-century Russia."[25]

Tolstoi's ideological soul mate Konstantin Pobedonostsev exerted a similarly strong influence over Russian education during this era, even though he was never formally education minister. Pobedonostsev was involved in many ministerial commissions while serving as the highest

---

[20] Patrick K. Alston, *Education and the State in Tsarist Russia* (Stanford: Stanford University Press, 1969), pp. 107–17; William H. E. Johnson, *Russia's Educational Heritage* (Pittsburgh: Carnegie Press, 1950), pp. 148–53; and James C. McClelland, *Autocrats and Academics: Education, Culture, and Society in Tsarist Russia* (Chicago: University of Chicago Press, 1979), pp. 9–17.

[21] Alston, *Education and the State*, pp. 153–65.

[22] Thomas Darlington, *Education in Russia*, Special Reports on Educational Subjects (London: Great Britain Education Board, 1909), p. 90.

[23] Nicholas A. Hans, *History of Russian Educational Policy (1701–1917)* (New York: Russell and Russell, 1931), pp. 110–30.

[24] William L. Mathes, "Tolstoi, Dmitrii Andreevich," in Wieczynski, ed., *Modern Encyclopedia*, Vol. 39, pp. 101–5.

[25] Ibid., p. 101.

lay official of the Russian Orthodox Church from 1880 until 1905, just two years before his death.[26] The tutor to two tsars—Alexander III and Nicholas II—Pobedonostsev was noted for a "bleak and gloomy view of human nature and the flawed institutions of mankind."[27] He worked hard behind the scenes to promote the most conservative educational policies possible at every turn. In the process, he became a hated symbol of the tsarist regime, surviving five assassination attempts.

Pobedonostsev was instrumental in the appointment of Ivan Delianov as education minister in 1882.[28] Delianov, who was personally something of a liberal, previously had served as director of the Imperial Public Library. He played a critical role in gaining imperial approval for the progressive 1863 University Statute.[29] Delianov struggled to rationalize Russia's overly complex educational system by advocating vocational education, uniform standards of instruction, and peasant literacy.[30] Simultaneously, however, he fought to place the educational system under the control of Pobedonostsev's Holy Synod, promoted Russification, and bitterly opposed granting permission to women to enter higher educational institutions. Delianov remained committed to the fundamental principles of faith, order, and autocracy until a heart attack in 1897 forced him from office just prior to his death the following year.

If Tolstoi's coming to power in the ministry had marked a turning point in Russian educational history for Darlington, Delianov's passing similarly provides a watershed in this history. For American historian James C. McClelland, Delianov's departure came at a portentous moment for Russian oppositionists. "The policies of Tolstoi, Pobedonostsev, and Delianov," McClelland argues, "had engendered bitter opposition among teachers, pupils, and much of the educated public as a whole. But these ministers could well afford to ignore such opposition, which at first was weak in numbers, disunited, and unrecognized."[31] This would no longer be the case as Russia hurtled toward revolution in 1905.

Delianov's successor, Nikolai Bogolepov, would pay with his life for such changed circumstances. Bogolepov, who had taught law at Moscow

[26] Hans, *History of Russian Educational Policy*, pp. 140–64; and Robert D. Warth, "Pobedonostsev, Konstantin Petrovich," in Wieczynski, ed., *Modern Encyclopedia*, Vol. 28, pp. 139–42.

[27] Warth, "Pobedonostsev," p. 141.

[28] Paul W. Johnson, "Delianov, Ivan Davidovich," in Wieczynski, ed., *Modern Encyclopedia*, Vol. 9, pp. 34–37.

[29] Johnson, *Russia's Educational Heritage*, pp. 153–83.

[30] Johnson, "Delianov."

[31] McClelland, *Autocrats and Academics*, p. 29.

University, was widely seen at the time of his appointment as another "reactionary stooge of Pobedonostsev."[32] As minister, he never openly dissented from the Tolstoi system, which dealt harshly with university demonstrators (leading one expelled student to assassinate Bogolepov in early 1901). Unlike his predecessors, Bogolepov acknowledged that there was cause for such tumult.[33]

Officials associated with the Ministry of Education and other imperial government agencies often preferred to limit educational opportunities to schools linked with the official Russian Orthodox Church. They confronted a hostile international environment in which Russia could not continue to play the role of great power without profound internal changes; yet internal transformation undermined the very stability at home that was required for such stature abroad. Education was one fulcrum for the deepest of Russia's incongruities.[34]

Pobedonostsev's demise, the rise of Sergei Witte, and the Revolution of 1905 combined to bring greater state resources to bear on literacy. Orthodox parish schools became increasingly marginal after 1905, with the Church proving itself incapable of providing sufficiently robust levels of funding and instruction to sustain a national educational network.[35] Moscow's local educational contest was a manifestation of these larger confrontations.

WHY EDUCATION MATTERS

Moscow's better-off supporters of education often were less interested in human development and personal fulfillment than in the creation of a sufficiently skilled and disciplined labor force to sustain their factories. Support for adult and vocational education reflected the peculiarities of late-imperial Russian educational policies. Historian Nicholas Hans notes that, although reaction and vocational education are not necessarily connected in themselves, they seem to have been so in Russia. Those reactionaries who generally viewed education with suspicion tried to divert thirst for knowledge into vocational channels. Their motives, Hans proposes, were "rather more political than educational.

---

[32] James T. Flynn, "Bogolepov, Nikolai Pavlovich," in Wieczynski, ed., *Modern Encyclopedia*, Vol. 5, pp. 34–36.
[33] Ibid.; and Johnson, *Russia's Educational Heritage*, pp. 183–86.
[34] Eklof, *Russian Peasant Schools*, p. 119.
[35] Ibid., p. 168; Brooks, "The Zemstvo."

The industrial evolution of Russia demanded thousands of skilled craftsmen and foremen, but the satisfaction of these needs was really subordinated to political aims."[36] Russian liberals, meanwhile, remained suspicious of educational programs not tied to the general educational curriculum.[37]

Vocational education was initiated at a national level following an 1878 order from Alexander II to the minister of finance to prepare a financial plan for additional trades-related curricula at existing schools.[38] A new set of primary, secondary, and higher technical courses and schools came into being with imperial assent a decade later, in March 1888.[39] Meanwhile, as is often the case, Russian society was developing and evolving more rapidly than official policy.

If vocational education was viewed as reactionary, more general adult education programs were often seen as revolutionary. Susan Bronson perceptively argues that adult education was "for all activists, an effort to socially construct the people according to particular visions of a future Russia."[40] Russia's "working classes" were the activists' targets, with adult education becoming "a ground of contestation over the capacity to reform or transform the working classes."[41] As tsars and their ministers pursued narrow vocational education as a means to limit the impact of literacy and its accompanying social change, their liberal and socialist opponents pursued the provision of broader educational programs for children and adults alike.

The initial wave of bottom-up adult education initiatives began informally throughout the 1870s and 1880s with the creation of Sunday schools offering training for basic literacy.[42] Ministerial meddling limited the Sunday school movement, closing many such efforts by the 1890s. Education advocates moved on to more formal programs, establishing literacy committees that sought to educate the previously illiterate in a variety of informal venues.[43] Models for extension classes, open "people's universities," informal women's courses, and public lecture and discussion forums drifted into Russia from abroad.[44] A book by

---

[36] Hans, *History of Russian Educational Policy*, p. 151.
[37] McClelland, *Autocrats and Academics*, p. 32.
[38] Hans, *History of Russian Educational Policy*, pp. 151–52.
[39] Ibid. Descriptions of courses of instruction may be found in Darlington, *Education in Russia*, pp. 460–97, 505–28.
[40] Bronson, "Enlightening the Urban Poor," p. 2.
[41] Ibid., p. 5.   [42] Ibid., pp. 25–33.
[43] Ibid., pp. 87–91.   [44] Ibid., p. 87.

Columbia University Teachers College President James Russell, *The Extension of University Teaching in England and the United States*, appeared in Russian in 1897, while a variety of prototypes ranging from British extension courses to the American Chautauqua movement were tried out in the empire's larger towns. St. Petersburg and Moscow led the way as a nascent Russian civil society challenged imperial authority time and again over who had the right to teach the previously untaught.

Pressure for new and innovative approaches toward mass education grew as the nineteenth century became the twentieth. Educational policy became entwined with an ever more intricate competition among Russian liberals, conservatives, radicals, and reactionaries. Advocates of widespread literacy and training—especially teachers—seized the political moment in 1905 to press for educational reform at every possible opportunity.[45]

NATIONAL RETRENCHMENT AND MUNICIPAL EXPANSION

The Stolypin coup of June 3, 1907—when conservatives, led by Prime Minister Petr Stolypin, gutted liberal election laws forced on the tsar during the upheavals of 1905–6—marked a dramatic retreat from progressive social policy. Reaction was especially vigorous in labor relations as moderate to radical labor groups were forced underground—leading to social explosions following the April 4, 1912, slaughter of miners in the Lena gold fields.[46] Ironically, the years 1907–14 constituted something of an era of achievement in Russian public education for adults as well as for children.

The national education law of May 3, 1908, at long last set Russia on a path toward universal compulsory primary education.[47] In keeping with the era's caution, the tsar and his legislators charted a course that would not have been completed until 1922, even had World War I and two revolutions not intervened. Imperial bureaucrats retained their right to intercede with local authorities, but much of the financial burden for schools was transferred to local governments.[48]

---

[45] Scott J. Seregny, "Professional Activism and Association among Russian Teachers, 1864–1905," in Harley D. Balzer, ed., *Russia's Missing Middle Class: The Professions in Russian History* (Armonk, N.Y.: M. E. Sharpe, 1996), pp. 169–96.

[46] Bronson provides a useful chronology of educational reform and reactionary retrenchment during these years in "Enlightening the Urban Poor," pp. 171–75.

[47] Robert William Thurston, "Urban Problems and Local Government in Late Imperial Russia, 1906–1914" (Ph.D. diss., University of Michigan, 1980), p. 203.

[48] Thurston, *Liberal City, Conservative State*, pp. 154–80.

Stolypin moved against Moscow's educational reformers on a different front in 1911.[49] The conservative prime minister fired Moscow University's rector and two prorectors after they had failed to enforce a central government prohibition against student meetings. That ban, in turn, had been imposed after a series of student demonstrations in Moscow and elsewhere protesting capital punishment following the death of Leo Tolstoy the previous fall.[50] Student meetings honoring Tolstoy had led to general class disruptions within days. More than four thousand Moscow students rallied against the death penalty despite warnings from university officials that they would face expulsion. Street battles between students and police led to a strike that virtually closed down Moscow and other Russian universities. The official response was to expel approximately 5 percent of Russia's university students.[51] Many of those expelled were from Moscow University. These actions, in turn, touched off further protests by students and faculty alike, leaving the university's senior administration in disarray.

Stolypin maintained that he had the right to act against state employees—the university's senior administration and faculty—who had engaged in political demonstrations. One-third of the Moscow University professorate—including twenty-five full and seventy-four assistant professors—resigned from the university faculty. Most found positions in those Moscow institutions of higher education beyond the control of the Ministry of Education, such as the Moscow Commercial Institute and the newly formed Shaniavskii People's University (the significance of the latter institution will be discussed below).

Moscow's municipal administration struggled to meet its expanding educational responsibilities against this backdrop of conflict and commotion. Municipal expenditures on education nearly quadrupled between 1905 and 1913, while the student population more than doubled.[52] Local programs broadened beyond the classroom. The city was spending 199,000 rubles a year by 1913 on breakfasts for students "without means"—nearly half of the student population.[53]

Central ministries provided but 10 percent, more or less, of overall education costs in Moscow, with the city being responsible for the

---

[49] This account is based on Samuel Kassow, "Professionalism among University Professors," in Balzer, ed., *Russia's Missing Middle Class*, pp. 197–222.

[50] The significance of Leo Tolstoy's opposition to the death penalty is discussed in Jeffrey Peter Brooks, "Liberalism, Literature, and the Idea of Culture: Russia, 1905–1914" (Ph.D. diss., Stanford University, 1972), pp. 200–220, 460–73.

[51] Ibid., pp. 469–70.   [52] Thurston, "Urban Problems," p. 203.

[53] Thurston, *Liberal City, Conservative State*, p. 157.

balance.[54] The city Duma enforced the goal of free primary education in 1909, raising budgetary expenditures to 7.5 million rubles by 1916 (as compared to 6.9 million in larger St. Petersburg).[55] For all of these achievements, Moscow provided education by 1910 to only 2.7 percent of its total population, as compared to educational programs in Philadelphia offering schooling to 10 percent of that city's similarly sized population.[56]

Many of Moscow's successes in education at this time were a direct consequence of Mayor Nikolai Guchkov's leadership.[57] Mayor Guchkov had been elected to his post on November 19, 1905, just a few weeks before his city descended into nearly total anarchy. Guchkov remained in office until December 18, 1912, seeking valiantly to heal social, physical, economic, and psychic wounds inflicted by revolutionary disorder.

Guchkov came from a formerly Old Believer merchant family descended from Fyodor Guchkov, a cloth merchant who left an enserfed village to gain prominence and wealth in Moscow around the turn of the eighteenth century.[58] The Guchkovs maintained close ties throughout the city's merchant circles, joining the official Orthodox Church and heading a number of factories, banks, and business associations. Nikolai, who served as the chair of the Russian-American Chamber of Commerce for some time, was known to have had especially warm relations with several conservative members of the prominent Botkin family, among many.[59]

Mayor Guchkov participated in civic politics for over a decade prior to his elevation by fellow city Duma members to the post of mayor. He had represented the city on the Moscow provincial zemstvo and had been active in commissions to assist the poor. He eventually fought with the Whites during the Civil War and died in obscurity in Paris in 1935 at the age of seventy-five.

[54] The Russian government provided 11 percent of the Moscow elementary school budget, and 9 percent of all educational expenditures in the city in 1913. Ibid.

[55] Nicholas J. Astrov, "The Municipal Government and the All-Russian Union of Towns," in Paul G. Gronsky and Nicholas J. Astrov, eds., *The War and the Russian Government* (1929; reprint, New York: Howard Fartig, 1973), pp. 129–321, 156.

[56] Thurston, *Liberal City, Conservative State*, p. 158.

[57] Liubov' Fedorovna Pisar'kova, "Gorodskie golovy Moskvy (1863–1917gg.)," *Otechestvennaia istoriia* 1997, no. 2, pp. 3–19: 12–14.

[58] I. F. Gindin, "Guchkov Family," in Wieczynski, ed., *Modern Encyclopedia*, Vol. 13, pp. 187–88.

[59] O. V. Terebov, D. B. Pavlov, and A. N. Bokhanov, "Guchkovy," in S. O. Shmidt et al., eds., *Moskva entsiklopediia* (Moscow: Nauchnoe izdatel'stvo 'Bol'shaia Rossiiskaia entsiklopediia,' 1997), pp. 240–41.

As Mayor, Guchkov viewed educational policy as a sphere within which he could mobilize a variety of diverse social groups (another, similar realm being physical infrastructure development, which his administration favored generously). Guchkov acknowledged that the poor needed education to advance, noted that many among the more well-to-do were philosophically predisposed to support education for all, and understood that industrialists required literate and competent workers. Guchkov used the force of his personality to cajole action, even when financial resources could not meet the task. The result was a dramatic expansion in the city's school system during his tenure as mayor.

The conventional image of Guchkov's fellow merchants during this period is hardly one of enlightenment. Moscow merchants often have been portrayed as shunning the public eye, being reticent and absorbed in their businesses.[60] Concern over education was one meeting place in which merchants, professionals, local government officials, intellectuals, and even radicals rubbed shoulders. Paradoxically, the merchants' deep cultural conservatism established the preconditions for their at times more enlightened views on the value of education.

MOSCOW CHARITY

Moscow society's philosophical conservatism was evident in the presence of a large and well-to-do Old Believer community, as well as in the local high regard for Slavophilic philosophical views. Russian Orthodoxy, as Adele Lindenmeyr asserts, "neither condemned nor celebrated wealth, but subscribed to the concept of stewardship. As a gift from God, riches did not signify superiority; on the contrary, they imposed an obligation to use them for the general good—specifically, to give to charity."[61] Such stewardship could—and did—lapse into degrading paternalism. Based on a notion of exchange between provider and recipient, Muscovite charity tended toward those activities that implied exchange, such as support for education.

Silver Age Muscovites with resources were remarkable philanthropists. By early in the second decade of the twentieth century,

[60] See, for example, Joseph C. Bradley, "Merchant Moscow After Hours: Voluntary Associations and Leisure," in James L. West and Iurii A. Petrov, eds., *Merchant Moscow: Images of Russia's Vanished Bourgeoisie* (Princeton: Princeton University Press, 1998), pp. 133–43: 133.

[61] Adele Lindenmeyr, *Poverty Is Not a Vice: Charity, Society, and the State in Imperial Russia* (Princeton: Princeton University Press, 1996), p. 8.

Lindenmeyr reports, Moscow merchants "supported twelve almshouses, a hospice for nuns, two institutions providing free housing, a hospital with 150 beds, and six schools and, in 1899, it handed out more than 107,000 rubles in monetary aid."[62]

The issue at hand is not whether Muscovites with money were, for the most part, wild advocates of radical educational policies; they certainly were not. Nor were they particularly interested in knowledge for knowledge's sake. Literacy activist Lev Kleinbort complained in his memoirs that, whereas prewar Moscow spent millions on primary schools, it opened only forty public libraries (in a town that supported more than 1,400 beer and wine stalls).[63] Economic interests supported adult and vocational education programs rooted in a deep pragmatism that transcended ideology.

Muscovite charitable support for schools of all sorts, as well as for hospitals and poorhouses, sustained a proto-civic sphere that was rare in imperial Russia: one governed by an unusual blend of pragmatism and belief that, at the same time, could be surprisingly radical and profoundly conservative. Local support for adult education—including basic literacy instruction and vocational courses, as well as more advanced training— becomes significant within this context.

SCHOLARLY OUTREACH

Moscow's intellectual life revolved first and foremost around the local university. Founded by Mikhail Lomonosov in 1755, Moscow University was Russia's leading institution of higher learning well into the nineteenth century. St. Petersburg and Kazan' universities overtook Moscow by midcentury in a number of specific disciplines; Moscow University at the time was not the home base for scholars of the stature of St. Petersburg's chemist Dmitrii Mendeleev and Kazan' mathematician Nikolai Lobachevskii. But Moscow University arguably had greater depth in the quality of faculty and students across a wider range of disciplines than did Kazan' University or even St. Petersburg University.[64]

Russian universities remained generally inferior to European institutions of higher learning well into the nineteenth century. By midcentury,

[62] Ibid., p. 58.
[63] L. M. Kleinbort, *Ocherki rabochei intelligentsii*, Vol. 1: *1905–1916* (Petrograd: Nachatki znanii, 1923), p. 49.
[64] William L. Blackwell, *The Beginnings of Russian Industrialization, 1800–1860* (Princeton: Princeton University Press, 1968), pp. 354–64.

European students were still unlikely to travel east to receive their education, and many Russians went abroad to secure professional qualifications. However, Russian universities no longer were forced to hire foreign professors from abroad to ensure qualified teachers for their students. Russian professors were contributing to mainstream European science, lecturing and publishing in the West. Moscow University was strong in mathematics, physics, chemistry, geology, and biology, with many professors justifiably earning international reputations. The university was already a center of intellectual and political ferment by the 1830s.

Moscow University, more than any other in the Russian Empire, emphasized the technical, industrial, and applied nature of the scientific endeavor with a curriculum that accented a practical orientation shared by many university professors. Faculty members were swift to establish laboratories tied to pragmatic problem-solving following the university reform of 1835. As in Chicago, scholarship was about doing as well as understanding. And, as in Chicago, the university was embedded in its community.

Moscow University's lively intellectual life firmly tied to its surrounding community cultivated a broad liberalism and love of inquiry that extended beyond isolated academic careers. The university led all Russian institutions of higher learning in reaching out to society at large. University faculty offered public lectures as early as 1804 and remained active in civic outreach throughout the nineteenth century. They were joined in such efforts by other members of the Moscow educated public, with factory owners supporting literacy classes and more general instruction for community members. Nearly two dozen factory schools were training more than a thousand worker-students in or near Moscow factories as early as the mid-1840s.[65] Nineteenth-century Moscow University reflected its times and community while simultaneously shaping its environment in return.

The Moscow Literacy Society, which had been founded in 1847 by the Moscow Agricultural Society, was joined fourteen years later by the St. Petersburg Committee on Literacy, established by Sergei Loshkarev and the Imperial Free Economic Society in 1861.[66] Both societies supported a variety of efforts to improve literacy among local workers and promoted local and national discussion of education issues throughout

[65] V. Ia. Laverychev, *Tsarizm i rabochii vopros v Rossii, 1861–1917* (Moscow: Mysl', 1972), p. 16.
[66] Bronson, "Enlightening the Urban Poor," pp. 15–42.

the second half of the nineteenth century. Such initiatives brought their members into frequent conflict with the Ministry of Education, which finally assumed managerial responsibility for the Petersburg and Moscow literacy committees in November 1895.

Moscow officials remained sympathetic to local literacy activists and their goals, however. City Duma member Mikhail Dukhovskii, for example, mobilized city funds to launch a school for factory workers in the Prechistenskie District.[67] These projects reached beyond the geographic confines of the neighborhoods of the well-to-do, often extending deep into worker communities.

Dukhovskii also taught criminal law at Moscow University, where he was a popular professor. His worker school, which opened on October 12, 1897, received contributions from several Moscow industrialists. More than three hundred workers showed up for classes the first day, with larger crowds to follow as word of the program spread. Abandoned buildings, elementary schools, and factory kitchens were turned over in several industrial districts to provide space for literacy training from 8:00 until 10:00 in the evening. By 1902, successor programs to Dukhovskii's Prechistenskie worker schools offered instruction in geometry, chemistry, physics, history, and literature, as well as in basic literacy.

Other Muscovites were copying American settlement houses and British, German, and French "people's palaces" in alternative efforts to reach out and educate the city's adults.[68] Prominent economist and Moscow University professor of finance law Ivan Ianzhul emerged as a leading education activist. Ianzhul and fellow Moscow education leaders seized control of part of the program for the December 1895–January 1896 Second Congress of Russian Activists for Technical and Professional Education, which was held in the city, to advance a movement promoting broad literacy and adult education.[69]

Teaching workers to read and the less well-off to do more than read was a major concern for many in the nineteenth-century Moscow education establishment. Not every Moscow University professor engaged in these efforts, not every Moscow industrialist supported adult education programs. But a significant number of each did. Concern over the ability of Moscow workers to read and write became one area in which

---

[67] Ibid., pp. 60–64; and Victoria E. Bonnell, *Roots of Rebellion: Workers' Politics and Organizations in St. Petersburg and Moscow, 1900–1914* (Berkeley: University of California Press, 1983), pp. 69–72.
[68] Bronson, "Enlightening the Urban Poor," pp. 64–73.
[69] Ibid., pp. 74–76.

differing political and philosophical views could be translated into specific action. Education for women was another such area. Once again, Muscovites figure prominently among late-nineteenth-century advocates for opening up Russian educational opportunities.

UNIVERSITY WOMEN

The issue of education for women became tied to a radical political agenda with the 1862 publication of Nikolai Chernyshevsky's novel, *What Is to be Done?*[70] Chernyshevsky presented strong female characters who personified the benefits of hard work and self-reliance. His work touched off heated discussion among the Russian intelligentsia over the country's future, debates that quickly polarized around the "women's question," among many points of contention. Chernyshevsky's novel—together with real-life models provided by those wives of the leaders of the 1825 Decembrist revolt, who had followed their husbands into Siberian exile—served to secularize female self-sacrifice. Chernyshevsky converted women's emancipation into a revolutionary pursuit.

The issue of how much and what kind of education could be deemed appropriate for women of various social classes had been largely ignored prior to 1861, at least in official circles. A few secondary schools for the daughters of gentry families and merchants opened following the establishment by Catherine the Great of the Society for the Training of Well-Born Girls, housed at the village of Smolnyi, which at the time was on St. Petersburg's fringes.[71]

Many well-off families relied on private tutors to train their daughters in the appropriate ways of the world. There were no public girls' schools until the 1860s, although 27,000 girls were being educated in such schools by the mid-1870s. Only a handful of young Russian women earned the formal education required for university entrance.

The imperial government would not permit the admission of even the best-trained Russian woman to a university in any event. Russian women in search of higher education had but two options. The first involved

[70] Lindenmeyr, *Poverty Is Not a Vice*, pp. 127–30.
[71] Richard Stites, *The Women's Liberation Movement in Russia: Feminism, Nihilism, and Bolshevism, 1860–1930* (Princeton: Princeton University Press, 1978), p. 4. The society's Smolnyi Institute served as Bolshevik headquarters during the fall of 1917, becoming Lenin's headquarters during his successful October coup against the provisional government. The site subsequently served as the city's Communist Party headquarters until 1991, when it passed into the hands of the municipal government.

convincing a university professor to let her audit his course for no credit; the second required going abroad. In either case, young women whose social pedigrees entitled them to privilege came into direct conflict with officialdom.

Some Russian women gave up altogether on the possibility of bringing about reform and joined the era's populist (*narodniki*) and other radical and revolutionary movements. A few sought out sympathetic educational institutions at home, such as the country's leading medical school, the St. Petersburg Medical-Surgical Academy. Many more trundled off to Zurich, where they entered degree programs at the Polytechnical School. The staid Swiss banking town thus became a major center of Russian radicalism.[72] Young women trained in medicine and engineering were returning home to Russia from Switzerland as early as the mid-1870s.[73]

The Russian university establishment intermittently attempted to respond to the increasing demand for higher education among well-off women. Kazan' University organized women's courses in 1876, followed by St. Petersburg and Kyiv universities two years later.[74] Ministerial officials in St. Petersburg did their best to limit such courses, denying degrees to women despite their attendance and achievement. In Moscow, university professors led by Vladimir Ger'e (Guerrier) circumvented these restrictions by organizing courses outside of the control of the ministry.

Ger'e was a leading professor of European history at Moscow University from 1868 until his retirement in 1904 (he died in 1919 at the age of 82).[75] Ger'e had completed his university education at Moscow University before studying abroad for three years in Germany, Italy, and Paris. He returned to Moscow to complete his graduate training with the First Cadet Corps. Ger'e's historiography emphasized a broad cultural approach, while his teaching won many kudos. He is credited, for example, with having introduced university seminars in Russia for the study of history.

Ger'e was a liberal who rejected his country's radical movement. He supported local self-government, advocated the liberal University Statute of 1863, and founded what became Russia's most important seminars

---

[72] Ibid., pp. 79–84.

[73] An English-language translation of the memoirs of five female medical-student radicals is to be found in Barbara Alpern Engel and Clifford N. Rosenthal, *Five Sisters: Women against the Tsar* (New York: Alfred A. Knopf, 1975).

[74] Stites, *The Women's Liberation Movement*, pp. 82–84.

[75] Christine Johanson, "Ger'e (Guerrier), Vladimir Ivanovich," in Wieczynski, ed., *Modern Encyclopedia*, Vol. 12, pp. 149–51.

19. Two students in the Public Higher Courses for Women (Ger'e courses) during the early 1900s. Photographer unknown. Photo collection of Mikhail Zolotarev, Moscow.

for women. Between 1872 and 1888, when the imperial government forced the seminars to shut down, Ger'e operated open advanced courses for women in the humanities and social sciences. Ger'e remained the prime mover behind the establishment of "public higher courses for women in Moscow" throughout the period. He succeeded with the sustained financial support of wealthy Muscovites who donated money, and Moscow University colleagues who donated time.[76]

Never able to gain official recognition, Ger'e's courses remained an initiative of Moscow civic society and culture. Ger'e re-established the courses in 1900, and directed the program until 1905.[77] Difficulties remained in the provision of higher education to Russian women, drawing critical comment from Darlington as late as 1909.[78]

As already noted, national literacy rates among Russian women were abysmally low. Moscow became something of an exception to this pattern in large part because numerous auxiliary educational initiatives launched and supported by the city and local merchants were open to women. The city Duma, for example, continually discussed women's primary and secondary education well into the first decade of the twentieth century.[79]

Self-interest remained a factor in merchant concern over female literacy. Many of Moscow's light industries depended on a relatively cheap female workforce. Patriarchal rural communities controlled land through communal action. Women could claim an allotment only in exceptional cases, and village men were the most likely to leave for a life in town. As Barbara Alpern Engel has established, exceptions to such general rules mounted following emancipation, as the opportunity to earn a living at home contracted.[80] Village women, though poorly equipped for urban life, went to town in increasing numbers throughout the 1890s, 1900s, and 1910s. Once there, women migrants left behind both the restrictions and the protections of village life. Opportunities for domestic employ-

---

[76] Ar. Krasheninnikova, "Vysshee zhenskoe obrazovanie v' Moskvie," *Moskva v eia proshlom' i nastoiashchem'* 12, pp. 106–20.

[77] Johanson, "Ger'e (Guerrier)."

[78] Darlington, *Education in Russia*, pp. 426–59.

[79] For a small sampling of the decrees about women's educational issues during this period, see the materials from city Duma meetings held on February 8, 1900, March 21, 1900, January 23, 1901, February 6, 1901, February 20, 1901, September 28, 1901, December 18, 1901, February 5, 1902, and February 12, 1902, as published in *Stenograficheskie otchety o sobraniiakh" Moskovskoi gorodskoi dumy* (Moscow: Gorodskaia duma, 1889–1908) for these dates.

[80] This discussion is based on Barbara Alpern Engel, *Between the Fields and the City: Women, Work, and Family in Russia, 1861–1914* (Cambridge, U.K.: Cambridge University Press, 1994).

ment and jobs in burgeoning textile factories lured many central Russian women to Moscow. The investment of Moscow merchants and industrialists in a modicum of education for the city's women was an investment in their own labor force.

Justified though such cynicism may be, it tells only part of the story. Secular and religious women were especially active in Russian philanthropy in general and Moscow philanthropy in particular. As Adele Lindenmeyr notes, "[i]t is difficult to exaggerate the major role women played in reform-era voluntarism, charity, and social reform movements. . . . For many women, organized charity continued to offer an officially approved outlet for their piety or patriotism."[81] Women of middle-stratum origin similarly became teachers, especially in primary schools.[82] Women's education at all levels became a natural arena for voluntarism among already active Muscovite women.

Women's education brought together many of the elements of Moscow's pragmatic pluralism. Those with greater resources helped those with fewer in order to help themselves. The cumulative effect was substantial, raising women's literacy well above the national norm. Moscow's women were active in philanthropy and in political life in the broadest sense—including union, radical, and revolutionary movements. Moscow's women contributed immeasurably to their community's nascent civic culture, sustaining the social space required for alliances to be built that could transcend traditional class and guild boundaries.

A PEOPLE'S UNIVERSITY

As the conflicts over women's education reveal, confrontations over mass education stood at the nexus of many of turn-of-the-century Moscow's most pressing challenges. The absorption of thousands of peasant workers affected how the city's factories and neighborhoods functioned as well as how everyone would be able to live their lives. Literacy meant higher skill levels on the job. Reading ability was a precondition for entry into Moscow's burgeoning commercial urban culture. Social activists, liberal professors, pragmatic municipal politicians, and reactionary emissaries from St. Petersburg became entangled in protracted struggles over means and ends. The results were an uncommon blend of frustration and achievement, culminating in a number of grand accomplishments and

---

[81] Lindenmeyr, *Poverty Is Not a Vice*, p. 125.
[82] Christine Ruane, *Gender, Class, and the Professionalization of Russian City Teachers, 1860–1914* (Pittsburgh: University of Pittsburgh Press, 1994), pp. 32–33.

immense failures. Moscow sustained a literate metropolitan culture by 1910—even as the educational accomplishments of many cities in Europe and North America were arguably greater.[83]

Success depended on the activities of broad civic coalitions that engaged municipal politicians on questions of literacy and mass education. City leaders energetically encouraged more-established Muscovites to act to improve education. Often, however, praiseworthy results were undercut by limited municipal resources, bureaucratic intervention from above, and larger social and political contestation.

The founding of the Shaniavskii People's University demonstrates much that was exemplary as well as deficient in the city's approaches to general education. The university represented what would today be known as a public-private partnership—as was the case with another of Moscow's crowning achievements of the period, the Tretiakov Gallery. Such institutions helped uncover an alternative path to the Russian future that was subsequently overwhelmed by growing social and political polarization, factionalism, and intolerance.

Al'fons Shaniavskii—unlike art collector Pavel Tretiakov—was not a doyen of the city's Old Believer merchant elite. A Pole who traveled to Siberia in service to the Imperial Army, Shaniavskii entered the gold trade following his military retirement in 1875. He soon made a lucrative association with Vasilii Sabashnikov, father of brothers Mikhail and Sergei who eventually would found one of Moscow's more prestigious academic publishing houses.[84]

Shaniavksii and the Sabashnikovs exemplify a different Moscow reality from that of Old Believer merchant Moscow. They epitomized precisely the sort of energetic and accomplished *haute* bourgeoisie whom burgeoning cities often attract. Shaniavskii and Sabashnikov archetypes sprinkle the Chicago and Osaka chapters in this volume as well. Their presence in Moscow illustrates that city's growing heterogeneity, a diversity that Shaniavskii's bequest to his adopted town both acknowledged and promoted.

Shaniavskii was born in 1837 on a family estate near the Polish city of Sedl'tse. The son of a noble family, his parents dispatched Al'fons at the age of nine to study at the Tula Cadet Korpus.[85] He completed his military education at the General Staff Academy in St. Petersburg, graduating with honors in 1861. Shaniavskii turned down an offer to remain

[83] A point forcefully made by Jeffrey Brooks in his landmark study, *When Russia Learned to Read*.

[84] S. V. Belov, "Sabashnikovy," in Shmidt et al., eds., *Moskva entsiklopediia*, pp. 710–11.

[85] Evgenii Kniazev, "Vol'nyi universitet," *Vash Vybor* 1995, no. 1, pp. 34–36.

in the capital as a military school professor and headed east to explore the Amur district in an expedition headed by Count Nikolai Murav'ev-Amurskii. Shaniavskii would stay in Siberia and the Far East throughout his military career, retiring with the rank of major general.

Shaniavskii had been inculcated by Russia's 1860s generation's belief in progress through knowledge.[86] He actively supported public education while in Siberia. He married Lidiia Alekseevna Podstvenna, a pioneer feminist whose family owned several small Siberian gold fields.[87] He and his wife drew on the income from their gold operations to support philanthropic work. An initial foray into the field of education—the establishment of a local school for Buriats—ended when the minister of education, Count Tolstoi, prohibited the beginning of classes.

Al'fons and Lidiia eventually settled in Moscow, living off income from their gold businesses and local Moscow real estate.[88] They were beneficent supporters of women's education, generously contributing to programs such as the Ger'e courses from their grand home on the Arbat.[89]

The Shaniavskiis sensed an opportunity to advance public higher education in the wake of governmental collapse in 1905. Al'fons's health failed, and he died that year before he could see the couple's final project through to completion. He bequeathed Moscow real estate and 300,000 rubles to the city government with the stipulation that the city Duma establish an institution of higher education that would remain beyond the reach of the Ministry of Education and would offer admission to all citizens over the age of sixteen regardless of estate, religion, or educational background.[90] He wisely imposed a deadline on his bequest—a stipulation that forced the Duma to act.[91]

The Shaniavskiis' vision for their university was in keeping with a larger movement for the establishment of people's universities during the 1905 Revolution.[92] The Society of Civil Engineers had founded the

---

[86] Shaniavskii's contemporaries emphasize his strong belief in progress and freedom, which they viewed as emblematic of an 1860s generation belief in social advance. See, for example, A. A. Kizevetter, *Na rubezhe dvukh stoletii (Vospominaniia 1881–1914)* (Prague: Orbis, 1929), pp. 471–74; and A. Mikhailovskii, "Munitsipal'naia Moskva," in N. A. Geinike, N. S. Elagin, E. A. Efimova, and I. I. Shitts, eds., *Po Moskvie. Progulki po Mosvkie i eia khudozhestvennym" i prosvietitel'nym" uchrezhdeniiam"* (Moscow: Izdanie] M. i S. Sabashnikovykh", 1917), pp. 151–58.

[87] Kizevetter, *Na rubezhe dvukh stoletii*, p. 474.

[88] Ia. M. Belitskii and G. N. Glezer, *Moskva neznakomaia* (Moscow: Stroiizdat, 1993), pp. 208–11.

[89] Ia. M. Belitskii, *Zabytaia Moskva* (Moscow: Moskovskii rabochii, 1994), pp. 16–17.

[90] Bronson, "Enlightening the Urban Poor," p. 109.

[91] Kizevetter, *Na rubezhe dvukh stoletii*, pp. 478–79.

[92] Bronson, "Enlightening the Urban Poor," pp. 105–9.

20. Al'fons Shaniavskii. Photographer unknown, n.d. Photo collection of Mikhail Zolotarev, Moscow.

All-Russian Society of People's Universities in December 1905, with the Moscow Society of People's Universities being created the following spring. Proponents envisioned these institutions as autonomous organizations promoting out-of-school education and knowledge through professional courses, public lectures, excursions, access to libraries and reading rooms, and the like. The Shaniavskiis intended their people's university to go one step further by offering their graduates the full rights and privileges granted to the graduates of state universities.

The city Duma accepted the Shaniavskii bequest, establishing a blue-ribbon commission chaired by Prince Vladimir Golitsyn—and including Lidiia Shaniavskaia and family friend Mikhail Sabashnikov—to bring the plan to fruition.[93] A number of generous financial contributions were made and members of local academe offered their services as instructors.[94] The Ministry of Education balked at certifying the proposed school, touching off a protracted battle that continued into 1908.[95] The university was denied the right to grant degrees and was placed under the ministry's supervision as the price for its opening. Open admissions policies were affirmed, with courses being offered to all interested students over the age of sixteen regardless of previous educational experience.[96] This political maneuvering was completed in time for the school's first classes to convene on October 2, 1908.[97]

The school was an immediate success. Shaniavskii People's University was organized into three departments—social science, history-philosophy, and natural science—that offered public lectures as well as more formal academic training. The lecture courses were intended for students who had not yet completed secondary school, with workers constituting nearly half of registered students. The academic track provided the equivalent of a university degree in three years. Enrollments grew to 1,735 students in 1910 and to more than 7,000 by 1916.[98] Its library grew to contain 35,000 volumes.[99]

The city Duma and private donors eventually constructed a grand *moderne* building designed by Ilarion Ivanov-Shits on Miusskoi Square to house their university.[100] The new facilities opened to public acclaim in 1912. The Bolsheviks took over the building when they closed the university in late 1918, using it for their own educational purposes. The Miusskoi Square complex housed several Communist Party educational institutions throughout the Soviet period before being ceded in 1991 by

---

[93] Many of the relevant city Duma resolutions and actions can be found in *Stenograficheskie otchety o sobraniiakh" Moskovskoi gorodskoi dumy* on January 10, 1906, February 21, 1906, May 30, 1906, June 13, 1906, June 20, 1906, August 22, 1906, September 5, 1906, February 13, 1907, May 29, 1907, August 21, 1907, November 6, 1907, and November 27, 1907.
[94] "Shaniavskii universitet," in Shmidt et al., eds., *Moskva entsiklopediia*, p. 908.
[95] McClelland, *Autocrats and Academics*, pp. 93–94.
[96] "Shaniavskii universitet," p. 908.
[97] Bronson, "Enlightening the Urban Poor," pp. 114–15.
[98] Evgenii Kniazev, "Vol'nyi universitet," p. 36.
[99] Bronson, "Enlightening the Urban Poor," p. 184.
[100] "Shaniavskii universitet," p. 908.

the Moscow Soviet to the newly formed Russian State Humanities University.

Shaniavskii People's University remained a barb in the Ministry of Education's hide throughout the school's existence. Ministry officials increasingly viewed the university as a hotbed of radical politics. Shaniavskii University hired many protesting faculty members from Moscow University following Prime Minster Stolypin's 1911 battle with that institution. Many of the city's liberal intelligentsia lectured at Shaniavskii or joined its faculty, including agronomists Kliment Timiriazev and Aleksandr Chaianov, biologist Nikolai Kol'tsov, chemist Nikolai Zelinskii, geochemist Aleksandr Fersman, geophysicist Petr Lazarev, historians Aleksandr Kizevetter and Nikolai Speranskii, hydro- and aerodynamics specialist Nikolai Zhukovskii, jurist Anatoli Koni, literary scholar Matvei Rozanov, neuropathologist Vladimir Rot, physicist Petr Lebedev, the poet Sergei Esenin, and Shaniavskii confidant and scientific publisher Mikhail Sabashnikov.

Together, these scholars and their colleagues created autonomous space for intellectual inquiry within an educational system and society increasingly dishonored by doctrinal intolerance. Kizevetter, for example, looked back at his years at Shaniavskii as among the most glorious of his distinguished career—a view seemingly held by many Shaniavskii students and faculty.[101]

Shaniavskii People's University represented a capstone to Moscow's public and private efforts to address the inadequacies of national education policy. It succeeded through the partnership of municipal government, local wealth, and a vibrant intellectual community. Shaniavskii's very existence—together with that of the Prechistenski workers' school, the Ger'e higher courses for women, and various outreach programs run through Moscow University—testifies to the emergence of a civic culture in Moscow that nurtured space for social initiative beyond governmental control.

The Shaniavskii story and a multitude of other educational programs just beyond the reach of the Ministry of Education's bureaucrats echoed the dissenting academies and parallel literary and philosophical societies active in Manchester and Scotland on the eve of the Industrial Revolution in Great Britain. Peter Hall contends in his study of innovation in cities that such peripheral educational and intellectual establishments nurture the cerebral space within which outside entrepreneurs, who so

---

[101] Kizevetter, *Na rubezhe dvuky stoletii*, pp. 468–501.

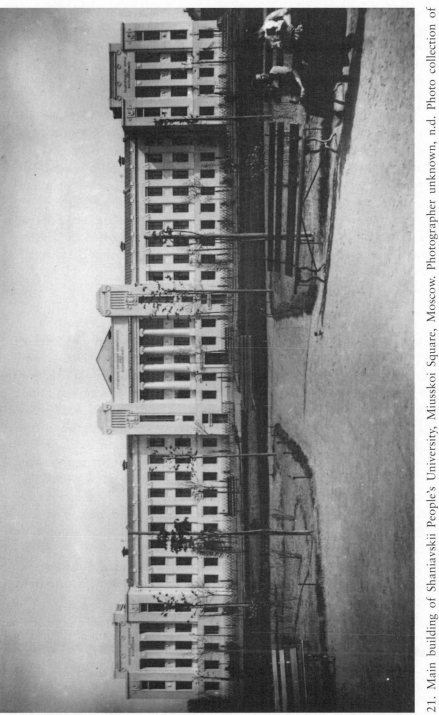

21. Main building of Shaniavskii People's University, Miusskoi Square, Moscow. Photographer unknown, n.d. Photo collection of Mikhail Zolotarev, Moscow.

often spark technological breakthroughs, are able to thrive. For Hall, the presence in Lancashire of Nonconformists, Dissenters, Congregationalists, and Independents, together with their associations and academies, provided Manchester with an invaluable resource that permitted that town to "score a clear advantage over its rivals" at the outset of the Industrial Revolution.[102]

The support of Moscow's rising merchant class for similar fringe educational programs and philosophical currents bespoke the influence of both a pious interest in charity and a hard-nosed economic pragmatism that rested on the need to improve the quality of local workers. The success of municipal politicians at bringing competing and contentious social forces together behind such educational programs affirms an ability to foster compromise generally thought to have been absent during tsarist Russia's last years. Pragmatic pluralists often carried the day whenever questions of mass literacy and public education demanded attention.

MOSCOW'S LITERATE URBAN CULTURE

The works of scholars, such as Jeffrey Brooks, Daniel Brower, Stephen Frank, Rose Glickman, Louise McReynolds, and Mark Steinberg, who have examined issues of literacy and reading patterns amplify the significance of Moscow's municipal and philanthropic educational initiatives. Such research suggests that, despite the dislocations inherent in any transition from agrarian to industrial society, pre-revolutionary Moscow was hardly mired in some primitive, premodern, "peasant" culture.

Glickman, for example, demonstrates that one-fifth of the Russian industrial workforce was female by 1914, a startling increase from older, patrimonial patterns and one that undermined entrenched family relationships.[103] Women's wages were closer to those of men than one might think. Women workers in cotton, woolen, and linen production received between two-thirds and three-quarters of men's wages at the outbreak of World War I. Furthermore, as demonstrated earlier in this chapter, literacy rates in Moscow were close to those of North Atlantic societies.

Literacy and interest in the printed word ran deep among Muscovites of all classes. The sly and somewhat crude Nikolai Pastukhov became very rich playing to the new reading public in his popular boulevard

---

[102] Peter Hall, *Cities in Civilization* (New York: Pantheon, 1998), pp. 336–42.
[103] Glickman, *Russian Factory Women*, p. 2.

newspaper, *Moskovskii listok*. Full of vivid articles and advice, *Moskovskii listok* and other urban papers in Moscow and St. Petersburg did not lose a step on the popular journalism of American and European cities.[104] Mark Steinberg and Stephen Frank correctly assert that "reading had become an integral part of working-class culture by the turn of the century."[105]

Jeffrey Brooks explored the depth of Moscow's book culture in *When Russia Learned to Read*. However much Moscow and Muscovites kept one boot in a pre-industrial past, the other was as firmly planted in the "modern" world of industrial capitalism. Moscow had become the focal point of a commercial, mass-based print culture that produced more than a few fortunes. Several Moscow press kingpins emerged from humble backgrounds to obtain great wealth through the sale of books and newspapers.[106] Publisher Ivan Sytin, the "Russian Joseph Pulitzer," fought his way up from the village to control the country's largest publishing house and the widely respected liberal newspaper *Russkoe slovo*.[107] Newspaper mogul Nikolai Pastukhov became the epitome of the rough-and-tumble self-made man.[108]

Russia published 133,561,886 copies of books in 1914, triple the number published just two decades earlier.[109] This popular press was increasingly "secular, rational, and cosmopolitan," and the ideas of the Enlightenment and industrial Europe reached deep into the Russian mind through Moscow's boulevard press. The spread of popular literacy and metropolitan newspapers also points to the emergence of a Muscovite civic consciousness that was capable of transcending other group allegiances.

Peter Fritzsche's assertions about the community-building role of the daily press in Berlin are directly applicable to Moscow. Fritzsche writes that "the metropolitan newspaper gave its readers choices for moving about the city without compelling a particular itinerary. While the city was presented as the locus of spectacle, the word city could be rummaged

---

[104] Louise McReynolds, *The News under Russia's Old Regime: The Development of a Mass Circulation Press* (Princeton: Princeton University Press, 1991); and Daniel R. Brower, "The Penny Press and Its Readers," in Stephen P. Frank and Mark. D. Steinberg, eds., *Cultures in Flux: Lower-Class Values, Practices, and Resistance in Late Imperial Russia* (Princeton: Princeton University Press, 1994), pp. 147–67.

[105] Mark D. Steinberg and Stephen P. Frank, "Introduction," in Frank Steinberg, eds., *Cultures in Flux*, pp. 3–10: 4.

[106] Brooks, *When Russian Learned to Read*, pp. 94–104.

[107] A tale told in Charles A. Ruud, *Russian Entrepreneur: Publisher Ivan Sytin of Moscow, 1851–1934* (Montreal: McGill–Queen's University Press, 1990).

[108] Brooks, *When Russia Learned to Read*, pp. 118–29.

[109] Ibid., p. 61.

in diverse ways. Middle-class women, white collar commuters, and proletarians all made their own way. . . . But the idea that the city was a fabulous place where its multiple actors could take journeys, collect impermanent images, and construct a sense of themselves does give modern diversity a common, inclusive note."[110]

The "fabulous city" of Moscow was home to a culture of consumption that transformed the Russian big-city streetscape, especially in Moscow. Peasants, peasant-workers, and the upper and middle strata of society were all barraged by signs that, in the words of Jeffrey Burds, spread "the new gospel of consumerism."[111] Up-to-date clothing became a source of pride for the urban bourgeoisie and village peasant alike. To consume was to move up the social scale.

The emergence of a new Russian urban culture became particularly evident in changing patterns of alcohol consumption. Drinking emerged as an integral aspect of urban life, touching off an "alcohol wave" that swept across Russia during the 1890s.[112] Alcohol production and consumption moved from a handicraft basis to an industrial footing, with the city tavern and bar defining urbanity just as much as the boulevard press. Nikolai Gorin argues that the very character of Russian drinking habits changed during the period, becoming less tied to the seasonal festivals and ceremonies of the rural countryside.[113] Drunkenness became more permanent and omnipresent in Moscow and other large Russian cities.

Glickman's literate women workers, McReynolds's and Brower's press magnates, Brooks's penny press readers, Steinberg's proletarian poets, Burds's consumers, and Gorin's drinkers all participated in an urban civic culture that went beyond group divisions to produce a broad civic consciousness that often challenged more narrow class identities. Moscow's urbanity was of a rough-and-tumble sort. The servants of autocracy rightly considered Moscow's urban vitality a threat to their own order. Russian industrialization was rife with tensions that could not always find accommodation. Moscow's pragmatic pluralists, however, negotiated their troubled times more effectively than did most other Russians.

---

[110] Peter Fritzsche, *Reading Berlin, 1900* (Cambridge, Mass.: Harvard University Press, 1996), p. 49.
[111] Burds, *Peasant Dreams and Market Politics*, p. 147.
[112] Nikolai Gorin, "Russkoe p'ianstvo kak sotsial'no-kul'turnyi fenomen," *Vlast'* 1998, no. 3, pp. 50–57.
[113] Ibid.

PRAGMATIC SUCCESS

Mass education emerged during the period under review as an issue of public concern that brought together Moscow's aspiring civic society and fumbling municipal administration, often in an alliance against reactionary overseers from the imperial Ministry of Education. As was the case with labor relations and public health, general education became one of many litmus tests for the attitudes of well-to-do and merely well-off Muscovites toward their less-fortunate neighbors. Education was a sphere in which Muscovites could convert into practice long-held cultural and religious teachings about the meaning of charity and piety without undercutting their own self-interests. Unlike other, more divisive local issues, public education in Moscow—quite unlike the situation in Chicago at the same time—came to represent a realm in which broad agreement and concerted action could transcend ideological concerns and narrow social interest. Radicals and conservatives alike advocated teaching the city's residents how to read and write.

Whether one looks to basic literacy training for workers, education at all levels for women, or public access to university education, it is possible to identify skillful community leaders and inventive activists who forged constructive and effective alliances in the face of seemingly insuperable odds. Their successes, in turn, brought many well-heeled Muscovites into bitter conflict with national officials from the Ministry of Education and elsewhere, who all too often viewed any form of education as a dangerous confederate to political radicalism.[114]

Nonetheless, many prominent supporters of these various programs were also defenders of the imperial regime. At a minimum, they were not the radicals and revolutionaries officialdom feared. Like the heroes of Chicago's traction wars, Vasilii Vakhterov, Mikhail Dukhovskii, Vladimir Ger'e, Nikolai Guchkov, Al'fons Shaniavskii, and their less well-known supporters were not initially interested in restructuring the underlying bases of power in society. Rather, they were fundamentally conservative; their primary objective was to make the society within which they lived function better.

Moscow's education activists were pragmatic pluralists very much in keeping with Carter Harrison, John Harland, and Bion Arnold in Chicago and, as in Chicago, their success was of a limited sort. Literacy

[114] Thurston, *Liberal City, Conservative State.*

spread and reading became ever more central to Moscow's urban culture among all social groups, even as the education system as a whole tottered on the brink of breakdown.

The imperial government in St. Petersburg moved at every opportunity to restrict local initiative while the Muscovites pressed their case forward. St. Petersburg's entrenched reaction appeared to be in retreat at the end of the 1905 Revolution, only to return even more ferociously following Stolypin's June 3, 1907, parliamentary coup. Vakhterov eventually ended up teaching Red Army soldiers how to read under the new Bolshevik government in the 1920s. Ger'e died in a Moscow torn by revolution and civil war, ever loyal to his liberal principles. Guchkov joined the Whites and fought the Soviets until his death as an émigré in the 1930s. The Bolsheviks shut down Shaniavksii People's University despite the school's manifest success. Such fates exemplify the collapse of Russia's political center under the stress of military defeat, political obtuseness, and gross administrative incompetence.

The failure of pragmatic pluralism on the national political stage in Russia renders even more remarkable the local achievements described here. Education policy in Moscow was marked by a pragmatic pluralism that benefited the city generally and many of its individual residents in particular. Education remained one area in Silver Age Moscow in which civic awareness truly managed to transcend class consciousness, even if only for a while.

7

Prosperity's Harbor

Large-scale urban development projects rest of necessity in compromise. Construction of new cityscapes requires large-scale investment of labor, capital, and intellect. Cities are the product of powerful forces of systemic, technological, and economic change as well as of individual preference. This is especially so in cities seeking to redefine their identities, an arena in which presumptions and compromises are cast in brick, stone, steel, and concrete. Not surprisingly, therefore, appropriate urban development remained a major issue of dispute in Japan throughout the half-century under discussion.

Reform-minded journalists such as Suzuki Shikajiro began writing about the human degradation of Osaka's Nagomachi slum as early as 1888.[1] Numerous other journalists and reformers followed, often drawing heavily on the calls of the urban visionary Ebenezer Howard in England for the establishment of self-contained "garden cities" that would draw city residents out into the countryside.[2] Suburbanization— in its commercial mode as much as with its reformist face—would be aided in Osaka, as elsewhere in the world, by the development of an extensive commuter railway system. Eleven major routes opened between 1893 and 1900, greatly increasing centrifugal forces that, by the beginning of the twentieth century, encouraged the city to sprawl into surrounding prefectures.[3]

---

[1] Jeffrey Eldon Hanes, "Seki Hajime and the Making of Modern Osaka" (Ph.D. diss., University of California, Berkeley, 1988), pp. 204–5; Chubachi Masayoshi and Taira Koji, "Poverty in Modern Japan: Perceptions and Realities," in Hugh Patrick, ed., with Larry Meissner, *Japanese Industrialization and Its Social Consequences* (Berkeley: University of California Press, 1976), pp. 391–437: 403–4.

[2] Hanes, "Seki Hajime," pp. 206–9, 303–21, 343–51.

[3] Takeo Yazaki, *Social Change and the City in Japan: From Earliest Times through the Industrial Revolution* (Tokyo: Japan Publications, 1968), p. 471.

Electrified commuter service and street trams spread throughout the city, though not without controversy, profit-mongering, and graft at a level no less ambitious than that of Charles Yerkes and his partners in Chicago.[4] One of the most dramatic controversies resulted in Mayor Uyemura's resignation in 1912 after a dispute over the alteration of the tram route between Kujo and Kozu.[5] The proposed route changes were blocked from Tokyo following an insider deal with a gas company that sought unfettered control over a bridge on the proposed route. Citizen groups quickly organized to protest Tokyo's refusal to grant the necessary charters and permissions.[6] The issue became increasingly convoluted when, in August 1912, five notables were arrested for purportedly bribing members of the Municipal Assembly on behalf of the gas company.[7]

The Osaka Municipal Assembly initially backed Mayor Uyemura, condemning the gas company and its agents while renominating him as mayor.[8] The story dragged on through the autumn. Finally, in January 1913, the Municipal Assembly gathered to elect the city's new mayor. The stormy proceedings erupted in violence with "something of a free fight" breaking out as Baron Kimotsuki was elected and Uyemura was pushed aside.[9] As in Chicago, such political shenanigans provide color. Nevertheless, the expansion of tram and commuter rail service continued unabated. This unrelenting growth made urban expansion ever more feasible.[10]

---

[4] See, for example, the following articles in the *Japan Weekly Chronicle* (Kobe): "Osaka-Nara Electric Railway: Another Charter Refused," September 6, 1906, p. 306; "The Osaka City Electric Railway: Who Is to Undertake the Enterprise?" November 22, 1906, p. 653; "The Hanshin Electric Railway. Municipal Difficulty at Osaka," February 21, 1907, p. 247; "Another Electric Railway Scheme: Charter Refused," February 6, 1908, p. 161; "Osaka Tramways," June 4, 1908, p. 699; "Opening of Osaka Electric Tram Service: Incidents in the Celebrations, Cost of the Line," August 13, 1908, p. 239; "Osaka Municipal Corruption: Alteration of Electric Tramway Route," February 17, 1910, p. 271; "The Osaka Tramway Dispute: Enthusiastic Public Demonstration," August 29, 1912, p. 381; "Baiting the Mayor: An Osaka Municipal Appointment," November 27, 1913, p. 927; and "Illuminated Tramcars in Osaka: Municipal Celebrations," May 10, 1917, p. 750.

[5] "The Osaka Municipality and the Government: Growing Indignation, Mayor Resigns," *Japan Weekly Chronicle*, July 25, 1912, p. 174.

[6] "The Osaka Municipality and the Government: Growing Indignation, Arrangements for Mass Protest Meeting," *Japan Weekly Chronicle*, August 1, 1912, p. 222.

[7] "The Osaka Municipality and the Government: Leading Residents Arrested," *Japan Weekly Chronicle*, August 15, 1912, p. 305.

[8] "The Osaka Electric Tramway Question: Excited Meeting of Municipal Assembly: The Vacant Mayoral Chair," *Japan Weekly Chronicle*, August 22, 1912, p. 339.

[9] "The Election for Mayor at Osaka: Stormy Proceedings," *Japan Weekly Chronicle*, January 16, 1913, p. 111.

[10] *An Outline of Municipal Administration of the City of Osaka* (Osaka: Osaka Shiyakusho, 1930), p. 74.

PUBLIC WORKS

Such traditional aspects of urban planning as urban and suburban expansion were only a limited component of a much larger effort by Osakan elites to integrate economic development and physical planning. Planners, politicians, and real estate developers sought spatial relationships that would be better suited to the industrial age. Osaka became a quite different place than it had ever been.

Osakan leaders failed to achieve a consensus over the most appropriate policies to manage the spatial dimension of economic and urban development. Some local leaders—beginning with longtime Mayor Ikegami Saburo—were able to forge a program of major infrastructural construction that benefited a wide range of Osakan citizens. Ikegami—who was attacked by opponents in 1913 for being "too honest and pure to be a successful mayor of Osaka"[11]—understood better than many of his peers that local politics had become a multidimensional game, with public and private players coming from Osaka and Tokyo as well as from industry, the unions, and small businesses. The Osaka story is one of a successful mobilization of resources around a limited number of highly visible and much-needed construction projects.

As with the traction wars in Chicago, success may be seen with historical hindsight to have been somewhat illusory. Water and sewerage projects never quite managed to keep pace with demand, and the city's massive harbor redevelopment became outmoded almost as soon as it was completed. Critics of these initiatives had more than sufficient basis for their assaults. These now nearly century-old civil works projects continue to serve the city and region despite their numerous shortcomings, even after the massive destruction of World War II and, more recently, the Great Kansai Earthquake of 1995.

Osaka's first city plan, the 1899 Yamaguchi Plan—named for the civil engineer dispatched from Tokyo to oversee the project—culminated a more than decade-long campaign of urban improvements. Sewer pipes were set down in the Senba and Shimanouchi districts in 1894; a new waterworks came on line in 1895.[12] The first waterworks was able to serve 610,000 Osakans when it opened, and sewer service was provided to virtually the entire city by 1901.[13] The massive port-improvement

[11] "Honesty a Disqualification," *Japan Weekly Chronicle*, September 18, 1913, p. 509.
[12] Johannes Hirschmeier, *The Origins of Entrepreneurship in Meiji Japan* (Cambridge, Mass.: Harvard University Press, 1964), pp. 38–9.
[13] *An Outline of Municipal Administration*, pp. 62–4.

program of 1897, which will be discussed in greater detail below, turned Osaka into an important international shipping center.

MEIJI MUNICIPAL ADMINISTRATION

Local city planning initiatives were embedded in a highly centralized political structure that undercut municipal power and authority. The Meiji Restoration brought about a general centralization of administrative functions throughout Japan, especially following the institutionalization of core regime practices and relationships throughout the 1880s.[14]

Local elites had expanded their power and authority during the long enfeeblement of the previous regime. Tetsuo Najita has suggested that Osaka merchants "could analyze the structure and content of political economy with greater accuracy and insight than the ruling aristocracy," thereby maximizing their own position in relation to the formal structures of Tokugawa power.[15] The Meiji Restoration reversed this relationship. Centralized administrative arrangements became a product of —and, in turn, reinforced—the new regime's attempts to integrate the country as a precondition for economic modernization.[16]

Centralization was aided by the relatively small number of losers during the tumultuous year of 1868. Local elites, even in those domains that had supported the losing side, accepted the revolutionary changes that were engulfing their country.[17] Their acquiescence to Meiji centralization became one of the hallmarks of the transition to a new regime system. Marius B. Jansen and Gilbert Rozman have argued that a highly centralized administrative system had been put into place by the end of the 1880s to guide Japan along a "modern" course.[18] The ultimate goal was to turn Japan into a "first rate nation."[19]

Prefectural assemblies and the Imperial Diet at the national level had been included in the Meiji Constitution, promised in 1881 and enacted

---

[14] Marius B. Jansen and Gilbert Rozman, "Overview," in Marius B. Jansen and Gilbert Rozman, eds., *Japan in Transition: From Tokugawa to Meiji* (Princeton: Princeton University Press, 1986), pp. 2–36: 6.

[15] Tetsuo Najita, *Visions of Virtue in Tokugawa Japan: The Kaitokydo Merchant Academy of Osaka* (Chicago: University of Chicago Press, 1987), p. 287.

[16] Ibid., pp. 7–8, 10.

[17] A point explored in Michio Umegaki, "From Domain to Prefecture," in Jansen and Rozman, eds., *Japan in Transition*, pp. 91–110.

[18] Jansen and Rozman, "Overview," p. 18.

[19] Kozo Yamamura, "The Role of Government in Japan's 'Catch-Up' Industrialization: A Neo-Institutionalist Perspective," in Hyung-ki Kim, Michio Muramatsu, T. J. Pempel, and Kozo Yamamura, eds., *The Japanese Civil Service and Economic Development* (Oxford, U.K.: Clarendon, 1995), pp. 102–32: 111–13.

in 1889.[20] The Japanese electorate was limited at the national level to those males able to pay a direct, fifteen-yen national tax—coincidentally, producing almost precisely the same number of voters as the tally of samurai family heads under the old regime.[21] The new political class remained tightly constricted until after the new century had dawned. Considerable informal power rested with ward-level leaders and local businessmen, as well, so municipal governance took place within a highly centralized state system and a tendentious local environment that permitted only restricted political maneuvering. Osakan political processes thus combine features found in both Moscow and Chicago at the time.

Between 1860 and 1890, some 260 domains of widely varied size and complexity were reorganized throughout Japan into three metropolitan cities and forty-two more or less uniform prefectures.[22] Towns and villages as well as urban and rural districts were created within the prefectures as the standard units for elected assemblies, schools, police, and the like. Such local administrative units were to conform to national standards of operation established by officials in Tokyo. Suffrage for local assemblies was limited to adult male taxpayers. Osaka, together with Tokyo and Kyoto, became officially designated "metropolitan cities," with a prefectural-type government structure provided for each.

By 1898, however, central administrators had concluded that the three metropolitan cities had outgrown their initial administrative configurations. Accordingly, the Diet enacted special municipal regulations under which all three cities were to be placed under new governing arrangements.[23] Osaka's prefectural governor assumed the duties of mayor until eligible Osakans could elect their mayor and a newly created Municipal Assembly. Local self-governance in Osaka is said to date from this time.

The mayor, as chief executive, was elected by the Municipal Assembly but assumed his post only with the sanction of the Ministry of Interior in Tokyo through the approval of the Osaka prefectural governor. Significantly, governors were themselves increasingly becoming the representatives of national power to Osaka, rather than the reverse. Whereas none of the thirteen Osaka prefectural governors who served

[20] Bernard S. Silberman, "The Structure of Bureaucratic Rationality and Economic Development in Japan," in Kim et al., eds., *The Japanese Civil Service*, pp. 135–73: 157–58.
[21] Jansen and Rozman, "Overview," p. 19.
[22] Andrew Fraser, "Local Administration: The Example of Awa-Tokushima," in Jansen and Rozman, eds., *Japan in Transition*, pp. 111–31: 111.
[23] *Great Osaka: A Glimpse of the Industrial City* (Osaka: Osaka Shiyakusho [municipal office], 1925), pp. 6–8; *An Outline of Municipal Administration*, pp. 9–10.

between 1867 and 1905 were graduates of Tokyo University, eight of nine Osaka governors between 1905 and 1925 had completed Tokyo University and, hence, were part of central patronage networks.[24]

The new personnel system led to rapid turnover of executive officials in many Japanese cities. Osaka, in fact, became noteworthy for the stability of its executive personnel. Mayor Ikegami served for more than a decade, as did his successor, Seki Hajime.[25] The city was divided into administrative wards, each with a ward chief responsible for census registration, tax collection, and education.[26]

MODERN OSAKA TAKES SHAPE

Despite the weakness of local authorities within the centralized Meiji administrative system, Osaka leaders from time to time managed to cajole central officials into granting operational authority for various projects. More important, municipal expenditures grew exponentially, outstripping even the city's rapid economic and population growth. In 1889, prior to the establishment of a municipal government by the 1898 municipal regulations, local Osaka government agencies expended 197,043 yen for their operations. This figure had risen to 3,098,318 yen a year by the time of "self-governance" in 1898 and continued to increase, reaching 9,152,798 a decade later and 20,084,725 at the end of the "war boom" in 1918.[27] Municipal revenues increased in tandem with expenditures throughout the period. Of perhaps equal significance, funding for city-shaping activities assumed a higher proportion of municipal expenditures as the city's capacity to plan increased. The transportation budget line, which had not even existed prior to 1903, expanded to 34.7 percent of the city budget during 1907–11, when tram service was being introduced, before stabilizing at 26.0 percent during 1920–24.[28] A modest city-planning administration began operation in 1918; it would grow to a 6,000,000-yen-per-year operation by the early 1920s, consuming 7.3 percent of all city expenditures during

[24] Tetsuo Najita, *Hara Kei in the Politics of Compromise, 1905–1915* (Cambridge, Mass.: Harvard University Press, 1967), p. 33. The emerging dominance of Tokyo University graduates was systemwide rather than specific to Osaka. See Silberman, "The Structure of Bureaucratic Rationality," pp. 153–55, 168–70.

[25] *An Outline of Municipal Administration*, p. 10.

[26] *Great Osaka*, p. 9.

[27] *An Outline of Municipal Administration*, pp. 17–18.

[28] Shibamura Atsuki, "Gyozaisei no Kozo Henka," in Shinshu Osakashishi Hensei Iinkai, *Shinshu Osakashishi* (Osaka: Osaka City Government, 1994), vol. 6, chp. 1, sec. 5, sub. 1, pp. 120–34: 124.

1920–24.[29] Government capacity increased in the health and education spheres as well.

City planning initiatives were conducted under the aegis of a municipal system that ceded final decision-making authority to Tokyo, usually to the national Home Ministry. This arrangement required local officials to mobilize support for initiatives being brought before at times hostile bureaucrats in Tokyo. As might be imagined, given the city's complex economic and social structure, such ventures were not always neat and tidy affairs.

Osaka's place as a center of economic integration assured its niche in an emerging national structure uniting economic and political power.[30] Japanese governmental and economic leaders appropriated capitalist structures and techniques through calculated and planned action. Integrated financial cliques disproportionately benefited from the country's successes. In Osaka, Japanese victories over the Chinese (1894–95) and the Russians (1904–5), together with the country's careful alignment with World War I victors, generated great wealth, which was in turn reinvested in the city's dynamic industrial base. The city's economic elites also enriched themselves through their control of trade with Japan's expanding Asian colonies.

The Osaka bourgeoisie not only invested in their factories. Like their counterparts elsewhere, it seems, they sought to beautify their surroundings—frequently by pushing the poor and their slums out of sight. Chubachi Masayoshi and Taira Koji's description of Osakan planners' beautification projects could easily be taken, with a few changes in proper nouns, from accounts of Baron Georges-Eugène Haussmann's grand Paris boulevards, Robert Moses's U.S. highways, or Mao Zedong's Tiananmen Square.[31]

"The City of Osaka," Chubachi and Taira begin, "for many years after the Meiji Restoration remained a small area well within the bounds of the present day National Railway Loop (*Osaka kanjo-sen*). In 1888, Osaka became a modern 'city' under new legislation. In order to reach 'city standards' in housing, slum clearance was actively pursued. Osaka expanded in 1897 by taking in some areas both inside and outside the loop."

[29] Ibid.
[30] The emergence of the *zaibatsu* system has been examined by numerous observers of the Japanese scene. This discussion is based on the work of Takeo Yazaki, who relates the growth of integrated financial cliques to the evolution of Japanese cities in general, and Osaka in particular. Yazaki, *Social Change and the City*, pp. 384–409.
[31] Chubachi and Taira, "Poverty in Modern Japan," pp. 403–5.

"At the beginning of modern Japan," Chubachi and Taira continue, "about one-sixth of the Osaka population was said to be 'destitute'. Osaka also enjoyed dubious fame for having the worst slum in all of Japan, commonly known as Nagomachi, a corruption of Nagomacho of the Tokugawa period. Today, this area is fashionable Nihonbashi-suji, running south from the well-known Dotonbori area to the Tenoji Park. . . . In 1899, there were 2,255 households with 8,532 persons in Nagomachi, almost twice as many as in the largest of Tokyo's ghettos." The situation had "improved markedly after the police began a program of stiff supervision of public sanitation."[32]

THE POOR REMAIN

The poor hardly disappeared—they never do as a consequence of such "beautification" projects. Instead, pockets of poverty and clusters of day laborers' cheap inns (*doya*) came to ring the city. Strict building codes made the Osakan streetscape decent and orderly, while appalling conditions merely moved indoors. "Rooms were occupied by more than one person per tatami [straw mat]," Chubachi and Taira add. Meanwhile, "the incongruity between appearance and substance in these areas was a consequence of Osaka's urban face-lifting policy."[33]

The poor did not always go quietly into their hidden "pockets" within the great city. Traditional master-client relations did not continue unaffected by the forces of market capitalism. The city's industrial workforce—especially in larger firms—became increasingly restive, joining Japan's expanding union movement. Osakan professionals similarly sought independence and autonomy. The antagonisms of industrial capitalism were omnipresent.

Capital became increasingly concentrated at the top of the financial pyramid in a small group of expanding corporations that sought monopolistic control over their economic sectors. Cartel arrangements grew through a complex system of holding companies, which married industrial monopolists with the financial giants that were simultaneously consuming the banking sector. Interlocking banking and industrial capital sought political partners in Tokyo. By World War I, five large banks (Mitsui, Mitsubishi, Yasuda, Sumitomo, and Daiichi) stood at the core of what would become known as the *zaibatsu* system.[34] Of these,

[32] Ibid., p. 403.   [33] Ibid.
[34] Yazaki, *Social Change and the City*, pp. 387–95.

Sumitomo was based in Osaka. Meiji financial and industrial organization paralleled the centralization of government administration and politics.

The *zaibatsu* monopolies concentrated in large cities, extending their control over industry, finance, and politics from their family and corporate headquarters. Most *zaibatsu* groups capitalized on close ties with early Meiji authorities who had permitted them to buy government firms and factories at low prices. Founding households and holding companies expanded their power from these initial state-sponsored purchases. Capital grew through rapid accumulation and heightened concentration in a pattern quite unlike that of European and North American capitalist development.

A number of *zaibatsu* were based in Tokyo, further strengthening that city's centrality in Japanese life. The giant Mitsui, Mitsubishi, and Yasuda *zaibatsu* were headquartered there, together with a number of medium-sized and small cartel groups. Osaka's Sumitomo *zaibatsu* was the sole non-Tokyo cartel with the power and size of these Tokyo giants. Osaka was simultaneously home to Baron Fujita Denzaburo's multifaceted operations, the Nomura and Yamaguchi groups in financing, and the Okazaki and Yamashita shipping cartels. Such businesses and financial organizations were national and international in scope; Osaka was merely their place of origin. Sumitomo, in particular, which could trace its origins to a successful merchant clan in early Tokugawa Osaka, sustained an active interest in municipal affairs. Local political leaders could no more afford to ignore this power than they could turn their back on imperial authorities in Tokyo.

The game of governing Osaka became one of balancing the competing interests of the central government, the local *zaibatsu*, other powerful yet more localized business interests, trade unions and other social organizations, ward heelers, growing political parties, and various factions within the prefectural and city administrations. All major planning initiatives—such as the grand harbor revitalization project to be discussed below—demanded the construction and maintenance of fragile alliances extending through these competing and, at times, antagonistic groups. Success required politicians to build coalitions that could be sustained through the life of a project. The more grand and complex the undertaking, the more difficult it was for the politician and the planner to reach a consensus.

To be successful, local planning required the participation of powerful political or business godfathers, as may be seen in Mayor Tsuruhara

Sadakichi's pivotal role in launching the 1903 Fifth National Industrial Exhibition at Tennoji, or in businessman Nishimura Sutezo's stewardship of the vast harbor revitalization project.[35] Tennoji—located directly south of the Osaka Castle—would become the city's first major park and site of the city's zoo upon the completion of these projects in 1909 and 1915.[36] Those Osakan politicians of the period remembered today for having brought about important projects were practitioners of the compromise politics of metropolitan pluralism.

MEIJI TOWN PLANNING

"Modern" urban planning initiatives reached Meiji Japan through Tokyo, where a number of projects were undertaken during the 1880s to make the capital city more rational, more secure, and more presentable to foreign visitors. Tokyo was "not deconstructed and remade" so much as it was "subjected to a rash of successive experiments in planning which left the city a hodgepodge of the old and the new."[37] Rather than explore indigenous traditions, Meiji planners—especially at the powerful Home Ministry—looked to Paris and European planning traditions for ways to blend the country's new industrial development with urban life.

The Home Ministry used powers from the Municipal Improvement Act of 1888 to expand planning activities in Tokyo. The ministry did not look beyond the capital until 1899, when ministry officials led by Yamaguchi Hanroku began to tackle Osaka's urban sprawl. The Yamaguchi Plan of 1899 called for an ambitious holistic approach, expanding the city's area from 15 to 56 square kilometers, thereby increasing the population within its jurisdiction from 500,000 to 750,000, and proposing the construction of 212 new roads, 20 canals, and 29 parks in addition to various road-widening schemes and harbor-improvement projects.[38]

Yamaguchi and his Tokyo colleagues proposed the sort of comprehensive town planning that was already the vogue among Osaka elites. City leaders had approved new building codes, sponsored limits on new construction, and launched their water, sewer, and harbor projects long

[35] Hanes, "Seki Hajime," pp. 277–79.

[36] David M. Dunfield, *Exploring Osaka: Japan's Second City* (New York: Weatherhill, 1993), pp. 51–53; "The New Osaka Park: Opening Ceremony," *Japan Weekly Chronicle*, October 21, 1909, p. 744; "The Value of Public Parks," *Japan Weekly Chronicle*, October 28, 1909, pp. 760–61.

[37] Hanes, "Seki Hajime," p. 195.   [38] Ibid., p. 201.

before the Home Ministry became interested in Osaka's development. The Osaka Prefectural Assembly established a planning committee in 1886, which immediately set out to restrict hazardous industries and to reorient the city around a road system linking the city's entrances at Umeda in the north and Namba in the south.

Yamaguchi's appearance and the Home Ministry's newfound attention to the city gave Osaka leaders the bureaucratic and political support they needed to turn such grand plans into reality. The Paris-trained engineer-planner preferred developing grand "avenue designs" rather than wrestling with the dynamic socio-economic processes that lay below the surface of Osaka's dramatic economic and industrial growth. Yamaguchi and his successors' bullish pursuit of wider streets frequently won them the enmity of local landlords and residents.[39] In this regard, Yamaguchi and other Osaka planners were neither better nor worse than many of their counterparts elsewhere in the late-nineteenth- and early-twentieth-century urban world.

Local officials opposed Yamaguchi's plans for their city's periphery, plans that they feared would lead to substandard housing and inadequate roads for outlying neighborhoods.[40] The Municipal Assembly developed its own programs in 1900 and 1901 to force developers building on the city's outskirts to improve the quality of their work. Rising military expenditures leading up to the Russo-Japanese War drained funds required to launch various planning initiatives. Osakan authorities eventually returned to the issue of suburban development in the early 1910s, just as local developers and railroads were launching a number of "garden city" suburbs for the city's rising middle class.[41]

White-collar residents were beginning to be pushed out of the city at about this time by rising rents, which were among the highest in Japan.[42] The number of satellite communities with populations above 10,000 increased from two in 1911 to nineteen in 1920. These towns,

---

[39] As was the case when landlords and tenants protested plans to widen streets to accommodate new streetcar lines in 1908 and again in 1911. See "The Osaka Tramway Scheme: Compulsory Removal of Houses," *Japan Weekly Chronicle*, May 28, 1908, p. 670; "The Osaka Electric Tramway: Compulsory Removal of Houses," *Japan Weekly Chronicle*, June 18, 1908, p. 773; "Osaka Municipal Electric Tramways: A Remarkable Protest," *Japan Weekly Chronicle*, October 1, 1908, p. 500; "Osaka Electric Tramways: The Question of Street Widening," *Japan Weekly Chronicle*, August 10, 1911, p. 237; and "Dispute Between Landlords and Tenants: An Osaka Grievance," *Japan Weekly Chronicle*, August 24, 1911, p. 333.

[40] Hanes, "Seki Hajime," p. 293.   [41] Ibid., pp. 294–95.

[42] "City Life in Japan: The Exodus to the Suburbs," *Japan Weekly Chronicle*, April 8, 1909, p. 560; "The Price of Land in Osaka," *Japan Weekly Chronicle*, April 18, 1918, p. 596.

which were set out in an arc to the east of Osaka, centered on pre-viously existing agricultural villages and independent towns. They quickly developed specialized functions—being home to medium-sized industrial establishments in some instances, to white-collar families in others.[43]

THE NAKANOSHIMA PUBLIC CENTER

Nakanoshima was one place where local bravura and the Home Ministry's sponsorship of model neighborhoods coincided. Between 1903 and 1921 Osaka built an imposing new public center on this island along the city's new Umeda-Namba axis.[44] The effort was reminiscent—though on a considerably grander scale—of the Imperial Mint project that had opened with great fanfare during the early Meiji years on a river site near Osaka Castle.[45]

The mint was one of the first major "Western" buildings to be built in Japan. Designed by British surveyor-architect Thomas J. Waters between 1868 and 1871, the mint and its grounds became an instant "must visit" for citizens and tourists alike.[46] The building, and the newly industrialized minting processes it housed, became an immediate symbol of the city's modernity.[47] This status was quite appropriate, as Waters's mint was both a technical and an architectural achievement.[48] Behind an elegant neoclassical facade symbolizing the nation's commitment to Westernization churned state-of-the-art Watt steam engines, Krupp steel rollers, and Thonnelier coining presses originally intended for a failed British mint in Hong Kong. A nearby guest house on the mint's grounds—the Sempukan—hosted numerous foreign and imperial digni-taries in its Victorian-style halls and grand verandas reminiscent of the British Raj.[49]

---

[43] Yazaki, *Social Change and the City*, pp. 470–71.

[44] Hanes, "Seki Hajime," pp. 286–87.

[45] *The Souvenir Guide to Osaka and the Fifth National Industrial Exhibition* (Osaka: Hakurankai Kyosankai [municipal office], 1903), pp. 74–75; *A Guide to Osaka* (Osaka: Osaka Hotel Company, 1913), pp. 12–13.

[46] Dunfield, *Exploring Osaka*, pp. 25–26.

[47] For a provocative discussion of the importance of the Imperial Mint in Meiji Japan's Westernization drive, see Roy Seijun Hanashiro, "The Establishment of the Japanese Imperial Mint and the Role of Hired Foreigners: 1868–1875" (Ph.D. diss., University of Hawaii, 1988).

[48] For further discussion of the Osaka mint, see Dallas Finn, *Meiji Revisited: The Sites of Victorian Japan* (New York: Weatherhill, 1995), pp. 18–21.

[49] Botond Bognar, *The Japan Guide* (New York: Princeton Architectural Press, 1995), p. 215.

堂會公央中るあに園公島之中　(所名阪大)
Central Public Hall at Nakanoshima Park. (Famous Place in Osaka)

22. Postcard of Central Hall, Nakanoshima Koen, Osaka. Photographer unknown, n.d.

The placement of a major park (the Nakanoshima Koen), the new Bank of Japan building, the prefectural library, Central Hall, and City Hall on Nakanoshima—and a concomitant reorientation of water- and street-transportation services around the island—pulled the city's epicenter to the east and shifted the city from an east-west axis focused on the castle and an extensive canal system to a north-south flow of roads built over old canals running between the Umeda and Namba railway stations.[50] This transformation was aided by the castle's status as the center of a considerable military reservation. The Imperial Army had effectively removed the castle district from city life just as the new rail hubs were attracting that life elsewhere.

The Nakanoshima park opened in 1890 on the island's eastern end. Nakanoshima's major development followed more than a decade later with construction of Tatsuno Kingo's neo-Renaissance Bank of Japan Building (1903), Nagouchi Magoichi's Roman-revival Osaka Prefectural Library (1904), and Okada Shinichiro's quirkily neo-classical Central Hall (1918).[51] All three men were among the first generation of

[50] Hanes, "Seki Hajime," pp. 286–87.
[51] Dunfield, *Exploring Osaka*, pp. 27–32; "Osaka Municipal Building: Details of Plans," *Japan Weekly Chronicle*, May 11, 1911, p. 805.

Japanese architects to be trained in Western design and construction methods, with Tatsuno becoming the best known of the group.[52] His firm, the Tatsuno-Kansai Architectural Firm, designed such prominent Tokyo landmarks as the Shimbashi Station.[53]

Tatsuno's Bank of Japan was one of Meiji Japan's most important architectural achievements.[54] A mélange of Western styles—fundamentally classical with a touch of the baroque—the bank featured a central dome and copper-domed cupolas that established a somewhat idiosyncratic silhouette against the Osaka sky. Its inlaid wood paneling, parquet floors, silk wallpaper, pedimented doors, and red velvet upholstery all communicated power, status, and the latest in turn-of-the-century fashion. Tatsuno would build thirty-seven more banks across Japan, with a final corpus of close to two hundred Western-styled structures.

Nagouchi's prefectural library was more firmly neo-classical, surprisingly reminiscent of Ithiel Town and Alexander Jackson Davis's 1833–40 State Capitol building in Raleigh, North Carolina. Both the building's architecture and its function were very much American in inspiration.[55] Leader Sumitomo Kichizaemon XV of the famous Osaka *zaibatsu* funded its construction and the purchase of its original collections after a visit to the 1893 World's Columbian Exposition in Chicago.[56] Following Andrew Carnegie's example—as well, perhaps, as that of Manchester's industrialists in Britain—Sumitomo decided to build a civic library to make knowledge more available to a wider community of Osakans. The brick-and-iron skeleton structure was covered with granite, bedecked with grand Corinthian columns, and topped off with the requisite copper dome. Nagouchi's efforts were enhanced by Asai Chu's interior artwork and Asahira Funio's bronze reliefs.

Okada's Central Hall, while less satisfying aesthetically, fulfilled a major social function.[57] Okada's original 1912 design was subsequently modified by architects Tatsuno and Kataoka Yasushi, who were asked by stock-market speculator Iwamoto Einosuke to perfect the building's initial plan. Iwamoto had commissioned and financed the structure in an

[52] Dunfield, *Exploring Osaka*, pp. 27–32. For more on Tatsuno and his rivalry with fellow Westernizing architect Tsumaki Yorinaka, see Finn, *Meiji Revisited*, pp. 191–92.
[53] Hiroyuki Suzuki and Toharu Hatsuda, *Urban Architecture in Taisho: A Visual Anthology* (Tokyo: Kashiwa-shobo, 1992), p. 122.
[54] Finn, *Meiji Revisited*, pp. 192–96; and Bognar, *The Japan Guide*, p. 207.
[55] Bognar, *The Japan Guide*, p. 207.   [56] Finn, *Meiji Revisited*, pp. 181–82.
[57] Suzuki and Hatsuda, *Urban Architecture*, pp. 186–88; and Bognar, *The Japan Guide*, p. 208.

outburst of civic pride. For years the city's largest auditorium, Central Hall offered a congenial venue for the numerous meetings, lectures, concerts, recitals, rallies, and other civic events that gave Osaka its metropolitan feel. Central Hall became Osaka's great public forum for the period. A man of many styles, Okada also designed the massive neo-Gothic Takashimaya department store in Osaka, as well as the neo-Japanese Kabuki theater and the neo-classical Municipal Art Gallery in Tokyo.[58]

Kataoka's five-story neo-Renaissance City Hall secured the island's status as Osaka's central place when it was completed in 1918 on a site between the Bank of Japan and the prefectural library. Designed in conjunction with architects Ushimura Kiyu and Imabayashi Hikotaro, this domed, fire- and earthquake-proof, steel-reinforced building proudly proclaimed Osaka's "metropolitan" pretensions.[59] It was joined across the narrow channel separating Nakanoshima from the Umeda district to the north by Yamashita Keijiro, Yokohama Tsutomu, Kanehashi Shintaro, and Ushimura Kiyu's imposing 1916 brick High Court of Justice, which would have fit quite snugly—tower and all—into a small English city of the period.[60] The emergence of a new city center on Nakanoshima soon drew traffic away from the city's traditional merchant neighborhoods, still stretched out on a seventeenth-century grid oriented around Osaka Castle.

The Westernizing stylistic impulse so grandly on display on Nakanoshima was present in the private sphere as well. Several banks were constructed in the latest contemporary styles of the period, as were insurance-company headquarters and stores.[61]

A pair of young Osaka architects—Nagouchi (of prefectural library fame) and Hidaka Yutaka—would draw on the Sumitomo *zaibatsu*'s backing to establish reputations as Japan's leading practitioners of Art Nouveau.[62] Although many of their buildings were constructed elsewhere, Osaka's visual environment nurtured Nagouchi and Hidaka, as did Sumitomo-backed craftsmen and financial support. Their work evolved toward a British Arts and Crafts style. The private homes and richly styled furniture they produced led the way in introducing the latest European designs to Japan just as Japanese design was shaping the aesthetic sensibilities of such prominent Western architects as Chicagoan

[58] Suzuki and Hatsuda, *Urban Architecture*, pp. 102–4, 116–21, 176–79.
[59] Ibid., pp. 18–19; Hanes, "Seki Hajime," p. 285.
[60] Suzuki and Hatsuda, *Urban Architecture*, pp. 8–10.
[61] Ibid., pp. 48–49, 74–75, 94–95.   [62] Finn, *Meiji Revisited*, pp. 214–18.

Frank Lloyd Wright.[63] Nagouchi and Hidaka participated fully in the development of a Taisho style that reflected "the maturing of the understanding of the historical style which advanced parallel with the emergence of avant-garde architecture" and an "awareness of the architectural traditions of Japan."[64]

Beyond architecture, Osaka's urban planning continued fitfully throughout the 1910s. Transit planning grew ever more ambitious, especially following the inauguration of streetcar service in 1903.[65] The internal combustion engine was making its impact felt; the first efforts to regulate automobile traffic came about by the middle of the decade.[66] Comprehensive planning lagged behind the city's development until the enactment of the national Urban Planning Law of 1919, which established more comprehensive planning policies for the entire country.[67] As will be discussed later in this book, Osaka's deputy mayor Seki Hajime was a central figure in the preparation of that national planning law.

THE GREAT HARBOR PROJECT

The city's mammoth harbor redevelopment project was perhaps the most important city-building project of the era. Bringing together local business interests with municipal politicians, the project was carried out despite opposition in Tokyo. It was completed only with the implicit and explicit support of all major social groups in the city. As Jeffrey Hanes reports, the project "became something of a civic obsession. Indeed, when it came time to select a municipal crest in 1894, the City Assembly rejected such obvious suggestions as the abacus in favor of its distinctive channel markers."[68] For better or, as many critics charged, for worse, the Osaka port stood at the center of the city's politics for a generation.

The initial years of the Meiji Restoration were difficult for Osaka. After the failure of an early attempt to have the new national capital placed in their city, Osakan merchant families faced the realities of reduced status and government policies directed at destroying their

[63] Kevin Nute, *Frank Lloyd Wright and Japan: The Role of Traditional Japanese Art and Architecture in the Work of Frank Lloyd Wright* (New York: Van Nostrand Reinhold, 1993).

[64] Suzuki and Hatsuda, *Urban Architecture*, pp. 3–4.

[65] *The City Transit System in Osaka, 1966* (Osaka: City of Osaka, 1966), p. 1.

[66] "Regulation of Traffic in Osaka: Creation of New Bureau," *Japan Weekly Chronicle*, December 13, 1917, p. 962; and "Taxis for Osaka: New Scheme," *Japan Weekly Chronicle*, May 2, 1918, p. 688.

[67] Hanes, "Seki Hajime," pp. 311–31.   [68] Ibid., p. 277.

monopoly positions in finance and trade. The realization that the local harbor was unsuited to modern shipping was among many disturbing discoveries of the period.

Osaka had dominated coastal trade throughout the Tokugawa period. However, its silty harbor was not deep enough for oceangoing vessels. The harbor's unnavigability contributed to the early Meiji decision to develop nearby Kobe as the Kansai region's link to the outside world. Osaka was beginning to feel the double bind of needing to modernize its port facilities to stay alive and to compete with a nearby port into which central government money was being poured. Realization of this stark reality forced local elites to find common ground.

By the mid-1870s, a loose alliance of local business and political leaders began to cooperate in economic development strategies that would keep Osaka competitive with the new open ports of Kobe and, farther away, Yokohama. Osaka's rivalry with Kobe for international shipping became an open economic war, one that, to some extent, has lasted to this day.

Osakans were forced to develop plans and raise money on their own as a consequence of Kobe's Tokyo allies. Only coalitions and cooperation could bring massive projects such as the harbor revitalization to fruition. Osakans—be they old merchant families such as the Sumitomo clan or members of the new Meiji economic elite such as Baron Fujita Denzaburo and Osaka Stock Exchange founder Godai Tomoatsu— sought common ground.

A number of private initiatives during the 1880s attempted to improve the city's harbor facilities and to bring rail lines deeper into Osaka's industrial and port areas.[69] Finally, during the 1890s, the newly empowered municipal administration took over the project as its own through a public-private partnership under the direction of powerful local businessman Nishimura Sutezo.[70]

The basic plan was to create a new harbor by extending a huge breakwater into Osaka Bay, straightening the curving Yodo River, dredging deep channels into its delta to new dock and warehouse facilities, and linking these facilities to the national freight network through newly

---

[69] The railroads arrived relatively late in Japan; the initial Tokyo-to-Yokohama route opened only in 1872. Railway development was quite rapid thereafter. The first rail line in the Kansai region linked Kobe and Osaka in 1874, and was extended to Kyoto in 1877. Thomas C. Smith, *Political Change and Industrial Development in Japan: Government Enterprise, 1868–1880* (Stanford: Stanford University Press, 1955), pp. 42–45.

[70] Ibid., p. 277.

FINE VIEW OF ESTUARY OF THE RIVER AJIKAWA, OSAKA.
觀盛の口川る也裝幅客船賃 （阪 大）

23. Postcard of the estuary of the Ajikawa River, Osaka. Photographer unknown, n.d.

constructed rail lines. The project would have to be self-financing, as the municipality could not depend on steady support from Tokyo ministries. Local financiers floated the initial loans to start the project; future construction, it was hoped, would be paid for by revenues from the sale and rental of new landfill areas to local developers. This approach continued on an even grander scale the city's expansion into the bay through land-reclamation projects reaching back at least to the seventeenth century.

The scheme more or less worked, although not without pushing and shoving among local officials, war-related delays in 1904–5 and 1914–18, battles with central authorities when it became necessary to float bonds on the international market, and more than a scent of scandal. The project almost pulled the city into financial ruin on more than one occasion.[71] The port consumed between one-third and one-half

[71] Data substantiating this discussion may be found in Hotta Akio, "Shushi Jijo to Shichosha no Kensetsu," in Shinshu Osakashishi Hensei Iinkai, *Shinshu Osakashishi* (Osaka: Osaka City Government, 1994), Vol. 6, chp. 1, sec. 1, sub. 3, pp. 19–33: 28–29; Toshimitsu Nakao, "Dai-gokai Naikoku Kangyo Hakurankai to Shisei," in Shinshu Osakashishi Hensei Iinkai, *Shinshu Osakashishi*, vol. 6, chp. 1, sec. 2, sub. 1, pp. 34–48: 38–39; Toshimitsu Nakao, "Senso to Gyozaisei," in Shinshu Osakashishi Hensei Iinkai, *Shinshu Osakashishi*, Vol. 6, chp. 1, sec. 2, sub. 2, pp. 48–63: 50–51; and Shibamura, "Gyozaisei no Kozo Henka," pp. 124, 128–29.

of the entire city budget every year from the municipality's establishment in 1898 until 1904, not including an astonishing 70.9 percent of all expenditures in fiscal year 1899. Municipal revenues fell following the Russo-Japanese War and only slowly recovered in the decade beginning in 1910. Bonds sold to finance the harbor and other smaller projects began to come due at the height of this post-1905 recession, so servicing bond interest accounted for well over a quarter of the city's budget until the end of World War I. Interest on bond payments consumed 48.9 percent of Osaka's 1916 budget at the peak of yet another harbor-induced fiscal crisis. In all, the municipality invested over 27 million yen in port-related expenditures over a twenty-year period beginning in 1897.

Osaka sustained its share of trade in its ceaseless competition with Kobe by constantly modernizing its port facilities.[72] The city successfully established a niche in Japan's trade with Korea and China.[73] Over 70 percent of its trade in 1910 was with other Asian ports beyond the islands of Japan.[74] The new harbor became integrated into a rail system that encouraged the further development of Japan's largest industrial complex—the Osaka metropolitan region—throughout the period prior to World War II.

The port's impact was already being felt long before the project's completion in the late 1910s. Kobe leaders were becoming concerned by 1904 that their government-subsidized harbor facilities were being increasingly overshadowed by Osaka's municipal port.[75] Their fear led Kobe to undertake its own port-modernization effort, which in turn spurred the Osaka group on to further construction efforts.[76]

The massive Osaka harbor project was plagued by a number of logistical difficulties. Three problems in particular shed light on tensions infusing the project, resulting from the need to keep various partners working in tandem: financing remained vexing, frequently bringing Osakans into conflict with central authorities in Tokyo; corruption

[72] *A Guide to Osaka Japan*, p. 5.
[73] "Governor Takasaki on Osaka Harbour," *Japan Weekly Chronicle*, October 15, 1908, p. 581.
[74] Shibamura Atsuki, interview by author, Ibaragi, Japan, April 14, 1996.
[75] "Osaka Harbour Facilities," *Japan Weekly Chronicle*, August 4, 1904, p. 136.
[76] "Osaka Harbor Works: A Warm Debate: The Ethics of Ministerial Influence," *Japan Weekly Chronicle*, August 9, 1906, p. 165; "The Osaka Harbour Works," *Japan Weekly Chronicle*, February 20, 1908, p. 236; "The Kobe Harbour Works," *Japan Weekly Chronicle*, March 5, 1908, p. 281; "The Future of Kobe," *Japan Weekly Chronicle*, July 29, 1909, pp. 181–83; and "Osaka and Kobe Shippers," *Japan Weekly Chronicle*, March 29, 1917, p. 518.

ran rampant at various stages in the project, especially in connection with the disposition of the landfill areas; and modern port facilities were worthless unless they could be connected to the Japanese interior by rail.

IGNOMINY, INIQUITY, AND DEBT

Municipal authorities quickly exhausted local capital markets in financing the harbor modernization. Failing to gain sufficient investment from either the prefectural or the imperial administrations, city officials were forced to turn to international capital markets. To do so, they needed the approval of the Finance Ministry in Tokyo. Such permission was not always forthcoming. Local plans brought Osaka into conflict with an increasing number of central ministries (Home, Finance, Communications, etc.), all of which had their own jurisdictional battles with one another.[77] Moreover, as the *Japan Weekly Chronicle* in Kobe reported, the central government in Tokyo "always regard[ed] Osaka Municipality as bankrupt, and senseless."[78]

The city entered into negotiations in late 1906 with Japan Credit Mobilier to secure 27 million yen to be used in completion of various city capital projects, including the harbor.[79] The Finance Ministry initially withheld approval of the loan due to what ministry bureaucrats found to be unfavorable conditions in European money markets.[80] The final go-ahead was given in early 1907, but only after considerable shuttling back and forth by municipal and port officers between Osaka and Tokyo.[81] Such constant struggle for funding necessitated a short-term crisis-management approach to the project at the expense of long-term planning for the overall dock area and its ties with the rest of the city.[82]

[77] "The Future of Osaka Harbour: Speech by Dr. Sakatini: The Kobe Breakwater," *Japan Weekly Chronicle*, September 27, 1906, p. 394.

[78] "The Osaka Engineering Scandal: Accused Committed for Trial," *Japan Weekly Chronicle*, November 22, 1906, p. 653.

[79] "Osaka Improvements: Warm on Waterworks Scheme: Huge Foreign Loan," *Japan Weekly Chronicle*, July 19, 1906, p. 85; "The Osaka Foreign Loan: Curious Action by the Government," *Japan Weekly Chronicle*, August 16, 1906, p. 216; "The Osaka Municipal Loan: An Arrangement Arrived At," *Japan Weekly Chronicle*, December 20, 1906, p. 778; and "Osaka Municipal Loan: Government Approval," *Japan Weekly Chronicle*, March 21, 1907, p. 406.

[80] "The Osaka Foreign Loan: Curious Action by the Government," p. 216.

[81] "Osaka Municipal Loan: Government Approval," p. 406; "The Osaka Municipal Loan: Government Approval Granted," *Japan Weekly Chronicle*, April 30, 1908, p. 549.

[82] "Osaka Harbour Works: Another Scheme Formulated," *Japan Weekly Chronicle*, October 4, 1906, p. 422.

As mentioned above, the city had intended to promote real estate development in landfill areas to generate funds for further harbor development. The possibilities for misallocation of funds from such a scheme transcend time, place, and culture. Osakan city leaders were no less reluctant in using the city's real estate for personal gain than were their Chicago contemporaries who sold streetcar franchises on a block-by-block basis.

City and prefectural authorities—especially members of the Osaka Prefectural Assembly—had multiple opportunities to profit from these land deals. They controlled access to decisions about which areas of landfill would be developed first, enjoyed insider information about planned infrastructure development, had opportunities to reduce registration fees, and the like. Scandal hung in the air as accusations circulated widely about various assembly members and city bureaucrats.[83]

Osakan ignominy reached its height in late 1908, when half the members of the Prefectural Assembly were implicated in the inappropriate disposal of waterfront property. Elaborate kickback schemes had been organized by Nishio Teppu, an Osaka barrister, who had joined with law clerk Kojima Fukutaro to extort "a large sum" from timber merchants.[84] Once the scheme became public, several prominent politicians—including eleven Prefectural Assembly members—were charged with various criminal acts. A number of members of the assembly's committee for oversight of the harbor project reserve fund were sentenced to jail terms or fined. Assembly members Ose Hansaburo, Takada Minoru, Yamashita Yoshitaro, and Nishio Teppu expressed incredulity at their sentences, despite the open discussions being held of their dealings with timber trusts. Simultaneous attempts to develop amusement areas and licensed quarters on the new lands similarly raised the eyebrows of local

---

[83] See, for example, "Municipal Scandal at Osaka: Leakage in the Tax Office," *Japan Weekly Chronicle*, June 13, 1907, p. 777; "Official Corruption in Japan: Remarkable Revelations in Osaka," *Japan Weekly Chronicle*, July 22, 1909, p. 152; "Corruption in Osaka: Grave Charge against a Tax Official," *Japan Weekly Chronicle*, March 31, 1910, p. 539; "Alleged Corrupt Land Deal: Osaka Official Arrested," *Japan Weekly Chronicle*, November 13, 1913, p. 87; "Violation of the Election Law: Curious Case in Osaka," *Japan Weekly Chronicle*, February 25, 1917, p. 271; "Official Corruption in Osaka," *Japan Weekly Chronicle*, March 22, 1917, p. 474; "The Osaka Engineering Scandal: Fresh Developments," *Japan Weekly Chronicle*, March 29, 1917, p. 507; "The Osaka Engineering Scandal: Accused Committed for Trial," *Japan Weekly Chronicle*, October 18, 1917, p. 639; and "Municipal Corruption in Osaka: Another Scandal Disclosed," *Japan Weekly Chronicle*, February 28, 1918, p. 319.

[84] "The Osaka-Fu Assembly Scandal," *Japan Weekly Chronicle*, July 16, 1908, p. 97; "The Osaka-Fu Assembly Scandal: Decision of Preliminary Court," *Japan Weekly Chronicle*, October 22, 1908, p. 627; "The Osaka-Fu Assembly Scandal: Accused Sentenced," *Japan Weekly Chronicle*, December 31, 1908, p. 1003.

24. Postcard of the Osaka Harbor construction. Photographer unknown, n.d.

enforcers of probity.[85] Port officials were caught extracting bribes for freeing illegally seized ships.[86]

A year after the mass resignations from the assembly, Mayor Yamashita and Deputy Mayor Fujimara were forced to step down in yet another scandal, this time over the location of a streetcar route.[87] Municipal Assembly members allegedly accepted bribes from licensed businesses to alter the route to enhance their own interests.[88] A number of senior officials were convicted of corruption charges, including former senior deputy mayor Matsumura Toshio.[89] Public outrage and calls for election reform reached a crescendo during this uproar, with at least one member of the Municipal Assembly being physically assaulted by the local citizenry for his role in the scandal.[90]

[85] "The Osaka Harbour Works," *Japan Weekly Chronicle*, June 4, 1908, pp. 697–98.
[86] "Corruption in Osaka: Allegations against Officials of Marine Office," *Japan Weekly Chronicle*, September 17, 1908, p. 423.
[87] "The Osaka Municipal Assembly: Question of New Municipal Council: Alteration of Electric Tram Route," *Japan Weekly Chronicle*, December 30, 1909, p. 1169.
[88] "Osaka Municipal Corruption: Alteration of Electric Tramway Route," *Japan Weekly Chronicle*, February 17, 1910, p. 271.
[89] "The Osaka Municipal Scandal: Opening of Public Trial," *Japan Weekly Chronicle*, July 21, 1910, p. 124; "The Osaka Municipal Scandal Case: Judgement," *Japan Weekly Chronicle*, August 18, 1910, p. 297.
[90] "Sequel to Osaka Municipal Scandal: Assault on Member of Council," *Japan Weekly Chronicle*, January 20, 1910, p. 124.

WORKING ON THE RAILROAD

Inadequate rail service to the new docks proved to be a more significant problem for the harbor project than were continuing innuendo and municipal iniquity. This planning misadventure was in part a consequence of the short-term horizons of municipal officials who were constantly fighting budgetary brush fires, and in part a result of the city's failure to secure support from officials in Tokyo.

By 1910, however, the inconvenience to shippers could no longer be ignored if Osaka was to continue to compete with the port at Kobe. Debate erupted over the site and over ownership of a trunk railway connecting the port to the main Japanese rail system. A northern route was eventually chosen because it could also serve the city's primary industrial areas.[91] Financing once again proved to be a prime obstacle as the central government withheld funds slated for rail construction.[92] Home Ministry officials agreed to invest in the project only in early 1911, with the stipulation that a southern route be followed instead of the link through northern industrial neighborhoods.[93] Local officials concluded that such a shift would guarantee that the Osaka port would be transformed "into one for local use only."[94]

Bureaucratic bickering between Osaka municipal planners and Home Ministry bureaucrats continued for the next five years, during which time not a kilometer of new rail line could be constructed.[95] In March 1916, three private businessmen from Osaka—all of whom owned warehouse facilities at the port—bought the requisite land and built the line on their own.[96] By the 1920s, with the harbor improvements finished and the port thriving, national and local officials joined with the private railroad to upgrade the port's rail yards, securing Osaka's place as an important international port.

[91] "Osaka Harbour: The Question of Railway Connection," *Japan Weekly Chronicle*, May 26, 1910, p. 911.
[92] "Osaka Harbour Works: Statement by Director of Engineering Bureau," *Japan Weekly Chronicle*, June 9, 1910, p. 985; "The Osaka Harbour Works: Estimate of Cost," *Japan Weekly Chronicle*, October 20, 1910, p. 700; "Osaka Harbour Works: Question of Railway Extension," *Japan Weekly Chronicle*, January 5, 1911, p. 13.
[93] "Osaka Harbour Works: Question of Railway Extension," p. 13; "The Osaka Harbour Works: The Question of Railway Connection," *Japan Weekly Chronicle*, April 27, 1911, p. 729.
[94] "The Osaka Harbour Works: The Question of Railway Connection," p. 729.
[95] "Osaka Harbour Works Railway: Discussion in Diet Committee," *Japan Weekly Chronicle*, February 3, 1916, pp. 171–72.
[96] "Osaka Harbour Facilities: Proposed Undertakings by Merchant Princes," *Japan Weekly Chronicle*, March 16, 1916, p. 431.

The harbor improvement program never lacked for critics, despite its ultimate success in attracting to Osaka a significant portion of Japan's trade with Asia. Several factors gave testy contemporary observers more than sufficient grounds for criticism: the project's slow pace of construction; lulls and stoppages linked to the cyclical rise and fall of prosperity in a market economy; recurring charges of graft, corruption, and waste; managerial dimwittedness; and cost overruns. Osaka's competitors in Kobe certainly did all that they could to make the project fail. More thoughtful critics, such as Seki Hajime, merely argued that this was the wrong sort of economic and urban development project, one that squandered large amounts of public money for limited commercial gain.[97]

The final cost of the only major Japanese harbor built with municipal funds—27 million yen—was roughly twenty times the annual expenditure of Osaka's municipal governments during that era.[98] The harbor sustained Osaka as a viable metropolitan center throughout the decades leading up to World War II. This project—together with associated infrastructure development and city building initiatives—transformed Osaka into one of the world's leading industrial centers. This would not have been the case were it not for the coalition politics that lie at the core of pragmatic pluralism.

[97] Hanes, "Seki Hajime," p. 247.
[98] *The City of Osaka: Its Government and Administration* (Osaka: Osaka Shiyakusho, 1953), p. 2; *An Outline of Municipal Administration*, pp. 82–83.

Part III

Riots and Revolution

8

Charter Failure

Between 1902 and 1914, pious citizens' groups and their political front men managed to draft—and, in the first instance, to bring before Chicago's electorate—three revisions of the city's governing charter. Their initiatives went down to ignominious defeat every time. On the surface, exasperated citizens could well have joined with muckraking journalist Lincoln Steffens in asking, "Do we Americans really want good government? Do we know it when we see it?"[1] Beneath the surface, the absence of a will to compromise and to accommodate difference produced a policy outcome in Chicago that set the stage for a new, more exclusionary era in the city's politics. One of the most potent political machines in American history would eventually emerge to fill the widening breach between the formal capacities of administrative and political structures on the one hand, and the complex realities of metropolitan life on the other. Compromise and accommodation yielded to the stark choices between "machine" and "reform." A mind-set prone to binary choices came to be imposed on an increasingly racially divided city. The ultimate failure of Chicago's politics and practice of pragmatic pluralism could no longer be hidden following intense racial strife and warfare during the "red summer" of 1919. The price of failure was too evident and too high to ignore.

The movement for charter reform united the middle and professional classes who were part of a larger Progressive Era reform crusade throughout urban America. The key to their failure on the Chicago city charter issue rested in a local political culture long polarized by labor, class, and ethnic strife.[2] On one side stood a group of men who

---

[1] Originally in *McClure's Magazine* in 1903, this quote is taken from Justin Kaplan, *Lincoln Steffens: A Biography* (New York: Simon and Schuster, 1974), p. 123.

[2] Unless otherwise noted, this discussion of Chicago's failed charter reform movement is based on Maureen A. Flanagan, *Charter Reform in Chicago* (Carbondale: Southern Illinois University Press, 1987).

"talked primarily to themselves," believing that "the impulse toward urban reform came exclusively from within their ranks" and assuming that "all reform in the city should be guided by them."[3] On the other were less-refined ethnic groups, laborers, and as yet disenfranchised women who remained skeptical of codes of morality that served to solidify the status quo, had become contemptuous of self-appointed defenders of probity, and generally proved themselves to be more tolerant of moral ambiguity—at least when it came to saloons, prostitution, and the ubiquitous "boodle" that greased Chicago's emerging political machine.

All Chicagoans shared a common antagonist in "downstate" Illinois farmers and their legislators. Leaders practicing the politics of inclusion—such as the Carter Harrisons (senior and junior)—could define common ground. The self-righteous bourgeois advocates of charter reform, however, preferred to characterize their opponents as "selfish, corrupt, or narrow minded," hardly a winning strategy when ballots are to be cast.[4] As Alfredo Rodriguez and Lucy Winchester would observe nearly a century later about Latin American cities, "[a]bove all, reinventing the government of the city means creating a shared vision of the city and a long-term commitment to it."[5] The charter reformers lacked both the common vision and the staying power needed to transform the government.

CHICAGO'S "SCRAMBLED GOVERNMENT"

Chicago's mercurial growth had outdistanced its political institutions nearly from the city's founding.[6] By the beginning of the twentieth century, the city functioned under an antiquated set of governing institutions and principles established during the 1860s, when four hundred thousand Chicagoans inhabited the metropolis that forty years later would be home to nearly two million souls.[7]

---

[3] Ibid., pp. 38–39.   [4] Ibid., pp. 47–63.

[5] Alfredo Rodriguez and Lucy Winchester, "The Challenges for Urban Governance in Latin America: Reinventing the Government of Cities," in Patricia K. McCarney, ed., *Cities and Governance: New Directions in Latin America, Asia, and Africa* (Toronto: University of Toronto Press, 1996), pp. 23–38: 30.

[6] A point emphasized by reformers of the era. See, for example, Jane Addams, "Problems of Municipal Administration," *American Journal of Sociology* 10, no. 4 (January 1905), pp. 425–44.

[7] A point explored in Ann Durkin Keating, "Governing the New Metropolis: The Development of Urban and Suburban Governments in Cook County, Illinois, 1831–1902" (Ph.D. diss., University of Chicago, 1984), pp. 2–15.

The Civic Federation of Chicago, in a 1902 report setting forth the case for charter reform, lamented the outdated and fractured machinery of local governance.[8] "It is universally conceded," the federation's spokesperson wrote, "that the multiplication of independent bodies for local governmental purposes in this community has gone far beyond the bounds of economy or good public service. . . . The Charter of Chicago is antiquated, and not suited to its present size and conditions."[9] Calling for geographic expansion of city boundaries, extension of constitutional limits on municipal indebtedness, reform of the local justice system, consolidation and unification of local government agencies, and reform of the ward system, the federation's report declared that the business of municipal governance "may be performed with greater economy, efficiency, and fairness to all concerned."[10] The federation then endorsed amendment procedures for the state constitution that would enable the city to draft a new charter, perhaps along the lines of the recent (1897–98) merger of New York City's five boroughs.[11]

The Illinois Constitution of 1870 had not chartered individual towns and cities but rather had created identical incorporation procedures for all communities regardless of their size. This system favored rural and small-town Illinoisans who both feared the "evil" cosmopolitan metropolis by the lake and fought to keep their state's scarce tax revenues closer to home.[12]

Prior to the Great Fire of 1871 Chicago, like many American municipalities, was run essentially as a business in which those who benefited directly from government services paid the bill.[13] In a remarkable study based on long-lost City Council records, Robin L. Einhorn labels this privatization of municipal governance as the "segmented system." "The documents showed," Einhorn reports, "a period in Chicago's history

---

[8] *Preliminary Report on Need for New City Charter* (Chicago: Civic Federation of Chicago, 1902).

[9] Ibid., p. 2.   [10] Ibid., p. 4.

[11] Ibid., pp. 15–16, 27–28.

[12] Flanagan, *Charter Reform*, pp. 1–9. The issue of downstate competition for tax revenues dates back almost to the city's founding and would be fought over and over by Chicago mayors from at least the era of "Long John" Wentworth during the 1850s and 1860s. See Don E. Fehrenbacher, *Chicago Giant: A Biography of "Long John" Wentworth* (Madison, Wisc.: American History Research Center, 1957), pp. 185–87.

[13] Concerning the management of other American cities, see Amy Bridges, *A City in the Republic: Antebellum New York and the Origins of Machine Politics* (Cambridge, U.K.: Cambrdge University Press, 1984); Sam Bass Warner, Jr., *The Private City: Philadelphia in Three Periods of Its Growth* (Philadelphia: University of Pennsylvania Press, 1968); and Terrence J. McDonald, *The Parameters of Urban Fiscal Policy: Socioeconomic Change and Political Culture in San Francisco, 1860–1906* (Berkeley: University of California Press, 1987).

when its government was clean enough to satisfy even the most fastidious of urban reformers, the self-consciously elitist 'structural reformers'
of the late nineteenth century, the men who compared cities to private
corporations in order to condemn municipal governments as inappro-
priately democratic."[14] Owners of taxable real property paid for and
controlled city services.

The change from a Jacksonian "segmented system"—in which local
governments did little more than build a variety of public works and
infrastructural projects paid for by users—to Gilded Age ambition was
prompted in part by the evolving scale and content of American government following the Civil War.[15] Expanding demand for government
services prompted the informal centralization of political institutions in
order to increase revenues and coordinate government efforts.[16] Civil
engineers—often in government employ—planned towns and neighborhoods through their massive projects, thereby undercutting notions that
American cities such as Chicago were the creations merely of market
forces.[17] By the 1870s in Chicago, at least, the segmented system was
being replaced by "a system that used government to redistribute wealth
in accordance with public policy decisions made through power politics
and inter-group competition."[18]

Facing increasing demands for public services, Chicago's city leaders
initially sought to expand their revenue base by extending their reach
into surrounding areas.[19] Between 1880 and 1890, the city—often acting
with the support of leading local business interests[20]—annexed several

[14] Robin L. Einhorn, *Property Rules: Political Economy in Chicago, 1833–1872* (Chicago:
   University of Chicago Press, 1991). Einhorn's research is based on the documentary
   records of the Chicago City Council from 1833 to 1871, which were believed to have
   been lost in the conflagration. These missing records resurfaced in a Chicago warehouse
   during a state records inventory.
[15] This change in government involvement in physical improvements may be detected in
   Chicago in an insatiable appetite for federal funding of expensive harbor improvements.
   See, for example, Joan E. Draper, "Chicago: Planning Wacker Drive," in Zeynep Celik,
   Diane Favro, and Richard Ingersoll, eds., *Streets: Critical Perspectives on Public Space*
   (Berkeley: University of California Press, 1994), pp. 259–76; and Robin L. Einhorn,
   "A Taxing Dilemma: Early Lake Shore Protection," *Chicago History* 18 (Fall 1989),
   pp. 34–51.
[16] Einhorn, *Property Rules*, p. 24.
[17] This point is made by Donald L. Miller, *City of the Century: The Epic of Chicago and
   the Making of America* (New York: Simon and Schuster, 1996), pp. 59–60.
[18] Einhorn, *Property Rules*, p. 229.
[19] For further discussion of the annexation movement, see Ann Durkin Keating's informative discussion in her *Building Chicago: Suburban Developers and the Creation of a
   Divided Metropolis* (Columbus: Ohio State University Press, 1988), pp. 98–119.
[20] Frederic Cople Jaher, *The Urban Establishment: Upper Strata in Boston, New York,
   Charleston, Chicago, and Los Angeles* (Urbana: University of Illinois Press, 1982),
   p. 503.

surrounding communities, including an 1889 land rush that nearly quadrupled the city's area.[21] Neighboring communities were already experiencing population growth faster than that of the city. A number of major local employers, such as the Union Stockyard, had been situated beyond city limits up until this time.[22] The annexation movement ran out of steam following the 1893 inclusion of the northern townships of Rogers Park and West Ridge. The city's boundaries have remained essentially unchanged ever since.

Chicago and Cook County officials took advantage of provisions in Illinois statutes to create a number of special-purpose administrative and fiscal agencies and districts to handle shared concerns such as water, sewerage, parks, education, and libraries.[23] The resulting patchwork eventually grew to encompass over 1,600 independent legal jurisdictions in a system that one of the most enduring local reformer-practitioners, Charles E. Merriam, would describe as "scrambled government."[24] According to Merriam, the community of Chicago was governed at the end of the 1920s by 4 states, 16 counties, 203 cities, 166 townships, 59 park districts, 10 sanitary districts, 188 drainage districts, and 1,027 other miscellaneous government agencies.[25]

Chicago was hardly unique among American cities in developing such a quilt of overlapping governments and state agencies. Ernest S. Griffith argues that the complexity and incoherence of such structures remained a fundamental weakness of American urban governance throughout the latter part of the nineteenth century—leading to what he argued was a

---

[21] The 1889 annexation included the towns of Jefferson and Lake, the city of Lake View, and the village of Hyde Park. Irving Cutler, *Chicago: Metropolis of the Mid-Continent*, 3d ed. (Dubuque, Iowa: Kendall/Hunt, 1982), p. 33. For further discussion of annexation, see Keating, "Governing the New Metropolis," pp. 307–20; and Edith Abbott, *The Tenements of Chicago, 1908–1935* (Chicago: University of Chicago Press, 1936), pp. 9–14.

[22] Flanagan, *Charter Reform*, p. 13.

[23] Ibid., pp. 22–24. This pattern is also discussed in Richard Schneirov, "Class Conflict, Municipal Politics, and Governmental Reform in Gilded Age Chicago, 1871–1875," in Hartmut Keil and John B. Jentz, eds., *German Workers in Industrial Chicago, 1850–1910: A Comparative Perspective* (DeKalb: Northern Illinois University Press, 1983), pp. 183–205: 184–87; as well as in Ester R. Fuchs, *Mayors and Money: Fiscal Policy in New York and Chicago* (Chicago: University of Chicago Press, 1992), p. 195.

[24] Charles E. Merriam, *Scrambled Government: Who Rules What in Chicagoland?* (Chicago: League for Industrial Democracy, 1934). For Merriam, "government" in this context referred to "an agency which independently exercises the powers of initiating tax levies and assuming indebtedness, and has legally constituted officials responsible for certain services within a defined area" (p. 3).

[25] Charles E. Merriam, *Chicago: A More Intimate View of Urban Politics* (New York: Macmillan, 1929), pp. 90–93.

"conspicuous failure."[26] David Rusk would be able to make quite similar claims a century later in his widely selling volume *Cities without Suburbs*.[27] As Loomis Mayfield contends, however, the consequences of suburban growth in the early 1900s were "quite different from [those of] the modern period. City economies before World War II were not affected as severely nor in as uniform a fashion as they would be later on. . . . Even without annexation, the city economic network could and often did expand into outlying areas, and many independent suburban providers of industrial and consumer services were supplanted and replaced by city institutions with the increasing integration of metropolitan areas."[28]

Merriam's point is nonetheless important for this particular discussion, for it helps to explain some of the ways in which the governance of Chicago differed from that of Moscow or Osaka. He rightly argued, for example, that Chicago's complex system converted the process of governance into one of managing and manipulating the highly conflictual interactions among various governing bodies. "Vivid personalities," Merriam observed, "are woven through the complex scene, binding together or tearing apart social groups and attitudes and giving them expression for the time."[29] Moreover, as Ann Durkin Keating would write six decades later, "the confused state of water, sewerage, street, and sidewalk improvements in Chicago left ample opportunity for corruption and graft."[30]

CHARLES E. MERRIAM AND CIVIC REFORM

Merriam's bitter and unsuccessful candidacy for mayor in 1911 represented the high-water mark of Chicago's Progressive movement.[31] As winner of the Republican primary, Merriam, who was an alderman as well as a University of Chicago political science professor, led a reformist charge against Democrat Carter Henry Harrison, Jr.[32]

[26] Ernest S. Griffith, *A History of American City Government: The Conspicuous Failure, 1870–1900* (New York: National Municipal League; Lanham, Md.: University Press of America, 1983), pp. 4, 52–96.

[27] David Rusk, *Cities without Suburbs* (Washington, D.C.: Woodrow Wilson Center Press, 1993).

[28] Loomis Mayfield, "The Reorganization of Urban Politics: The Chicago Growth Machine after World War II" (Ph.D. diss., University of Pittsburgh, 1996), p. 14.

[29] Merriam, *Chicago*, p. 94.   [30] Keating, *Building Chicago*, p. 48.

[31] A point explored in Steven J. Diner, *A City and Its Universities: Public Policy in Chicago, 1892–1919* (Chapel Hill: University of North Carolina Press, 1980), pp, 154–75.

[32] Concerning Merriam's own political career, see Barry D. Karl, *Charles E. Merriam and the Study of Politics* (Chicago: University of Chicago Press, 1974), pp. 61–83.

Merriam was the son of an Iowa politician and had pursued graduate study in politics and government at New York City's Columbia University before joining the Department of Political Science at the University of Chicago in 1900.[33] Merriam quickly took an interest in local politics and prepared numerous studies for Chicago reform groups. He was elected a Chicago alderman in 1909 by the Hyde Park community surrounding the university and quickly established himself as a champion of reform. Merriam took advantage of Republican mayor Fred A. Busse's retirement in 1911, as well as divisions within the Illinois Republican Party, to win that party's nomination primary over the opposition of state boss William Lorimer.[34] These divisions in 1911 within the local party foreshadowed the split a year later among national Republicans between party regulars and the reformers who would found the Progressive Party. After losing the mayoral contest, Merriam won back his City Council seat in 1913 as an Independent over strong resistance from Republican regulars. He would run for mayor again, but never came as close to winning as he did against Harrison in 1911.

Merriam biographer Barry D. Karl argues that Harrison and Merriam were, in fact, more similar than either would admit.[35] Both were reformers who drew on factions that cut across party lines to mobilize support for their candidacies. Merriam and Harrison had each defeated his party's political machines in heated primary battles, and each could appeal to a number of different ethnic groups—especially the Irish and the Germans—for support, often using the German language to do so.[36] Harrison, however, had more political experience, especially at managing factions and coalitions.[37] His own skill as a campaigner and a healer in the diverse and divided city carried Harrison over the top and kept him in power until 1915.[38]

Advocates of municipal home rule and a new city charter appreciated the limits of short-term administrative strategies based on the annexation of neighboring jurisdictions and the creation of stopgap specialized regional authorities. The archaic structure of Chicago's government needed to change, they knew, to meet the challenges of the world's

---

[33] Diner, *A City and Its Universities*, pp. 33–34.
[34] Ibid., pp. 169–71. [35] Karl, *Charles E. Merriam*, pp. 68–69.
[36] Harrison's relationship with German voters is discussed in Schneirov, "Class Conflict," pp.199–200.
[37] Karl, *Charles E. Merriam*, pp. 68–69.
[38] Edward R. Kantowicz, "Carter H. Harrison II: The Politics of Balance," in Paul M. Green and Melvin G. Holli, eds., *The Mayors: The Chicago Political Tradition* (Carbondale: Southern Illinois University Press, 1987), p. 28.

fastest-growing and perhaps most technologically advanced metropolis.[39] The reformers, however, proved far better at the theory than at the practice of politics.

PROGRESSIVE WOMEN

By the late 1890s, a number of different groups were trying to position themselves as the most appropriate spokespersons for reform. As early as the 1870s, various citizens had banded together to form the Citizens Association—a self-proclaimed monitor of local government.[40] The settlement-house movement—led by Jane Addams, Ellen Gates Starr, and, a little later, Florence Kelley at Hull House—sought to mobilize middle-class and more proletarian reform elements through work with immigrants and laborers.[41] For some, Addams—who would share the 1931 Nobel Peace Prize with the educator Nicholas Murray Butler—is the quintessential Chicagoan of the era, exerting a powerful influence over the most diverse elements of local society.[42] For others, Kelley—the daughter of a privileged Philadelphia Republican member of Congress, translator and confidant of Friedrich Engels, and president of the National Consumer League—personifies many of the virtues of the first generation of college-educated women in the United States.[43]

Social reformers tied to the new University of Chicago and to Northwestern University established the Chicago Commons as well as univer-

---

[39] These arguments are set forth, for example, in Chicago New Charter Movement, *Why the Pending Constitutional Amendment Should Be Adopted*, Text A (Chicago: New Charter Campaign Committee, 1904); and Chicago New Charter Movement, *Why the Pending Constitutional Amendment Should Be Adopted*, Text B (Chicago: New Charter Campaign Committee, 1904).

[40] Flanagan, *Charter Reform*, pp. 35–36; and Schneirov, "Class Conflict," pp. 183–205.

[41] Jane Addams, *Twenty Years at Hull-House* (1910; reprint, New York: New American Library, 1961); Helen Lefkowitz Horowitz, *Culture and the City: Cultural Philanthropy in Chicago from the 1880s to 1917* (Lexington: University Press of Kentucky, 1976), pp. 126–44; Allen F. Davis and Mary Lynn McCree, eds., *Eighty Years at Hull-House* (Chicago: Quadrangle, 1969); Elizabeth Wilson, *The Sphinx in the City: Urban Life, the Control of Disorder, and Women* (Berkeley: University of California Press, 1991), pp. 71–75; Abbott, *The Tenements of Chicago*, pp. 30–33; and Miller, *City of the Century*, pp. 416–25, 455–67.

[42] Garry Wills, "Sons and Daughters of Chicago," *New York Review of Books*, June 9, 1994, pp. 52–59: 55, 58–59.

[43] See, for example, Kathryn Kish Sklar, *Florence Kelley and the Nation's Work*, Vol. 1: *The Rise of Women's Political Culture, 1830–1900* (New Haven: Yale University Press, 1995). Readers may also refer to Kelley's autobiography, *Notes of Sixty Years: The Autobiography of Florence Kelley*, ed. Kathryn Kish Sklar (Chicago: C. H. Kerr, 1986); or to some of Kelley's numerous reports, such as *First Report of the Factory Inspectors of Illinois on Small-Pox in the Tenement House Sweatshops of Chicago* (Springfield, Ill.: H. W. Rokker, State Printer and Binder, 1894).

25. Jane Addams with children at Hull House, Chicago. Photographer unknown, n.d. Courtesy Chicago Historical Society, ICHi-09375.

sity settlement programs of their own during the 1890s.[44] For example, Margaret Dreier Robins, leader of the Women's Trade Union League, took up residence a few blocks from the Northwestern University

[44] Perry R. Duis, *Chicago: Creating New Traditions* (Chicago: Chicago Historical Society, 1976), pp. 57–81; Robert A. Slayton, *Back of the Yards: The Making of Local Democracy* (Chicago: University of Chicago Press, 1986), pp. 172–87; and Wilson, *The Sphinx in the City*, pp. 71–75.

Settlement following a stint at Hull House.[45] Social reform in Chicago fostered a tradition of activist social inquiry, one that dominated many departments at the University of Chicago, especially under the institution's founding president, William Rainey Harper, who served between 1892 and 1906.[46]

Growing concern among these citizens over the need to strike an appropriate balance between public and private interest prompted various strata of society to try to foster a new civic consciousness. At least 2,500 Chicagoans joined one or more of the seventy reform groups active in the city between 1892 and 1919.[47]

Upper-class women were among Chicago's leading reform activists more often than in other American cities.[48] Women—most especially Sophonisba P. Breckinridge and Edith Abbott—played a particularly important role in establishing a distinctive "Chicago School" in social work, an approach to community services based on extensive empirical research in the city's disparate neighborhoods.[49] Social-science language and methods—data collection, detatched observation, and an emphasis on prevention—proved congenial to reform-oriented women.[50] Jane Addams, for example, worked closely with sociologists George H. Mead, W. I. Thomas, and their colleagues at the University of Chicago in examining social behavior and the capacity for social change within communities.[51] She participated fully in the emergence of American academic sociology, contributing regularly to the debates that were shaping the discipline.[52]

The role of established women in Chicago political and social activism thus deserves special mention. Having been excluded from electoral

[45] Elizabeth Anne Payne, *Reform, Labor, and Feminism: Margaret Dreier Robins and the Women's Trade Union League* (Urbana: University of Illinois Press, 1988), p. 44.
[46] The connection between social activism and social research in Chicago during this era is the theme of Steven J. Diner's exceptional study, *A City and Its Universities.* On Harper, see pp. 15–19.
[47] Ibid., p. 56.
[48] Jaher, *The Urban Establishment,* p. 508; and Bessie Louise Pierce, *A History of Chicago,* Vol. 3: *The Rise of a Modern City, 1871–1893* (Chicago: University of Chicago Press, 1957), pp. 487–90. This point is made in a more journalistic mode in Wills, "Sons and Daughters of Chicago."
[49] Diner, *A City and Its Universities,* pp. 44–47.
[50] A point emphasized in Paula Baker, "The Domestication of Politics: Women and American Political Society, 1780–1920," *American Historical Review* 89, no. 3 (1984), pp. 620–47: 634.
[51] Mary Jo Deegan, *Jane Addams and the Men of the Chicago School, 1892–1918* (New Brunswick, N.J.: Transaction, 1988), pp. 105, 309–28.
[52] See, for example, the materials published in Jane Addams, *The Social Thought of Jane Addams,* ed. Christopher Lasch (Indianapolis: Bobbs-Merrill, 1965).

politics, nineteenth-century American women sought influence through voluntary associations and reform groups. Women and men alike used such organizations, Sara Evans reports, "not only as active forums for public discussion but also as schools for civic action. Women found there a new kind of free space, which offered the possibility of action outside the domestic sphere but not in formal, governmental arenas from which they were banned."[53]

Maureen Flanagan contends further that, by ignoring women as political reformers during the Progressive Era, historians have frequently run the risk of denying women their political history.[54] Her own research points in precisely the opposite direction.

Flanagan's comparative study of the civic activism of members of Chicago's City Club and Woman's City Club reveals that women's participation in local Chicago political and social reform extended well beyond the settlement-house movement. "Because of their different relationships to the urban power structure, to daily life within the city, and to other individuals," Flanagan writes, "when members of the Woman's City Club confronted these problems [of municipal incapacity], they came to a vision of a good city and specific proposals of how best to provide for the welfare of its residents that were very different from those of their male counterparts in the City Club."[55]

The contrast between the two city clubs is especially striking since both recruited members from the same upper-middle-class segments of local society. Members of the male City Club, which was established in 1903, were predominantly businessmen or professionals; their counterparts in the Woman's City Club, established in 1910, were often their wives.[56] Both clubs took positions on major municipal reform issues of the day: garbage control, public education, vocational education, and police and labor issues, for example. For the men, citywide reform became a means for improving Chicago "primarily as an arena in which to do business, and they advocated municipal reforms intended to protect and further the aims of business."[57] Woman's City Club members, on the other hand, sustained a citywide vision that required municipal agencies

---

[53] Sara M. Evans, "Women's History and Political Theory: Toward a Feminist Approach to Public Life," in Nancy A. Hewitt and Suzanne Lebsock, eds., *Visible Women: New Essays on American Activism* (Urbana: University of Illinois Press, 1993), pp. 119–39: 128.

[54] Maureen A. Flanagan, "Gender and Urban Political Reform: The City Club and the Woman's City Club of Chicago in the Progressive Era," *American Historical Review* 95, no. 4 (October 1990), pp. 1032–50.

[55] Ibid., p. 1033.   [56] Ibid., p. 1034.

[57] Ibid., p. 1044.

to guarantee "the well-being of everyone within the city, regardless of the immediate implications for business."[58]

Flanagan argues persuasively that this difference in viewpoint arose from the different daily experiences of the members of the two clubs. For the majority of City Club members, life was experienced through their professional activities. Most middle-class women, conversely, experienced Chicago through their homes. "Women were used to organizing a home environment that ensured the well-being of everyone in the family," Flanagan contends.[59] "When they entered the political arena," she continues, "they sought to achieve the same objective." In short, Woman's City Club members "seldom equated the good of the business community with the good of the citizenry as a whole," despite their elevated social status.[60] This difference greatly enriched Progressive Era reform efforts of various kinds—social, political, and economic—within Chicago.

Catholic women also worked to alleviate the suffering of Chicago's immigrant poor, although they used methods rather different from those of their better-off Protestant sisters. Catholic social and educational institutions tended to serve their own communities rather than to promote broad social reform. Steven J. Diner has observed that such a "parochial stance stemmed from the ostracism of American Catholics by the nation's Protestant majority."[61] St. Ignatius College (renamed Loyola University in 1909) and St. Vincent's College (renamed DePaul University in 1907), for example, never championed the social activism so evident at the University of Chicago and Northwestern University.

Suellen Hoy has noted that Catholic religious orders were long active in service to Chicago's poor. Hoy acclaims this work even though the record of Catholic religious charities was "little known outside Catholic circles" and was overshadowed by the city's more famous settlement houses.[62] The almost exclusively Irish and Irish-American Sisters of Our Lady of Charity of the Good Shepherd, for example, ministered to women in need, including single mothers with their children as well as "abandoned," "fallen," and "penitent" women. The Sisters of the Good Shepherd had arrived in town in 1859 and grew under the dynamic leadership of Mother Mary Nativity Noreau, Mother Mary of St. Angelique Cleary, and Mother Mary of the Holy Cross McCable. By 1911, the order was providing shelter, religious instruction, vocational training,

---

[58] Ibid.
[59] Ibid., p. 1046.
[60] Ibid., p. 1050.
[61] Diner, *A City and Its Universities*, p. 24.
[62] Suellen Hoy, "Caring for Chicago's Women and Girls: The Sisters of the Good Shepherd, 1859–1911," *Journal of Urban History* 23, no. 3 (March 1997), pp. 260–94: 260–61.

and job placement to scores of women. The sisters' Chicago Industrial School quickly became one of the city's leading vocational education programs for women.

African-American women similarly had their own clubs that pushed for social reform and suffrage.[63] African-American women pursued a wide variety of causes, ranging from kindergartens and child welfare to literacy and housing. Beyond an agenda that they shared with their Progressive white counterparts, members of such groups as the Phyllis Wheatley Club, the Alpha Suffrage Club, and the Frederick Douglass Woman's Club consciously engaged in political causes promoting the advancement of African-American Chicagoans. Their efforts helped, for example, secure Oscar de Priest's victory as Chicago's first African-American alderman.

Women very actively shaped the metropolis. They found inventive ways for making their opinions known and felt and expanded the local—and national—economy. Women fought their way into relatively well-paying clerical positions: the number of female clerical workers in Chicago jumped from just 9 in 1870 to 96,963 a half-century later, in 1920.[64] The city's overall female labor force increased during the same period, from 35,600 in 1880 to 407,600 in 1930.[65] The metropolis is incomprehensible without a full appreciation of the enormous contributions of Chicago's women to public economic, cultural, and political life.

CIVIC ASSOCIATIONS

If women reformers found a variety of outlets for their activism through clubs, schools, and settlement houses, men were able to pursue more "traditional" means of influence through organized political parties and organizations. The "better" elements of local male society rallied around such organizations as the Union League Club of Chicago to protect the "purity of the ballot box."[66] Founded in 1879 and functioning since 1880, the Union League was the local affiliate of a national movement.

---

[63] Anne Meis Knupfer, "For Home, Family, and Equality: African American Women's Clubs," *Chicago History* 27, no. 2 (Summer 1998), pp. 5–25.

[64] Relatively well paying and stable clerical jobs had been another male domain until the beginning of the twentieth century. Lisa M. Fine, *The Souls of the Skyscraper: Female Clerical Workers in Chicago, 1870–1930* (Philadelphia: Temple University Press, 1990), p. 48.

[65] Joanne J. Meyerowitz, *Women Adrift: Independent Wage Earners in Chicago, 1880–1930* (Chicago: University of Chicago Press, 1988), p. 5.

[66] Bruce Grant, *Fight for a City: The Story of the Union League Club of Chicago and Its Times, 1880–1955* (Chicago: Rand McNally, 1955).

They sought to recapture the spirit of Civil War–era organizations of a similar name that had defended the Union against the "traitorous" activities of Southern sympathizers—known as "copperheads"—in Illinois and other northern states. Bringing together the likes of the McCormicks, the Medills, and the Fields, the Union League opposed ethnically based political groups, advanced the cause of "reform," promoted such boosterish activities as the World's Columbian Exposition, and generally engaged in the elevated gatherings of a local social elite. Their efforts came into conflict with a system of ward-level politics predicated on the boodle.[67]

Two of the larger reform-minded civic groups of the era—the Civic Federation of Chicago and its spin-off, the Municipal Voters' League—played instrumental roles in the preparation of a new charter to bring before city and state authorities and, eventually, to the Chicago electorate. These groups promoted the "pragmatism with a conscience" that Ernest Griffith argues so characterized Progressive Era city politics in many American cities.[68]

The Civic Federation emerged almost full-blown from a raucous rally presided over by British journalist and moral crusader William Thomas Stead, author of a sharply critical and widely read tract, *If Christ Came to Chicago!*[69] Stead had come to town to visit the World's Columbian Exposition but apparently spent far more time seeking out lowlifes among Chicago's numerous saloons, groggeries, and houses of prostitution than at the fair. Outraged by the city's corruption, depravity, and profligacy, Stead held forth at rallies, eventually publishing his account of what would happen if Judgement Day came to Sodom by the Lake.

The rally in question—attended by a diverse group of the city's virtuous, including various representatives of the monied classes, social reformers, union organizers, and religious leaders—convened at the much-used Central Music Hall on November 12, 1893.[70] Future Civic Federation leader Douglas Sutherland would recall the event a half-century later: "The Columbian Exposition of 1893 had just closed its

---

[67] Robert I. Goler, "Visions of a Better Chicago," in Susan E. Hirsch and Robert I. Goler, eds., *A City Comes of Age: Chicago in the 1890s* (Chicago: Chicago Historical Society, 1990), pp. 90–153.

[68] Ernest S. Griffith, *A History of American City Government: The Progressive Years and Their Aftermath, 1900–1920* (New York: National Municipal League; Lanham, Md.: University Press of America, 1983), p. 9.

[69] William T. Stead, *If Christ Came to Chicago! A Plea for the Union of All Who Love in the Service of All Who Suffer* (Chicago: Laird and Lee, 1894).

[70] Stead's own description of these events may be found in ibid., pp. 465–71.

doors. The impact of the nationwide 'hard times' of that year (from which Chicago had been largely shielded because of the great amount of local employment which the construction and maintenance of the 'World's Fair' had afforded and the flood of money-spending brought by the swarms of visitors from all parts of the globe) was then being fully realized. . . . Establishments of vice and gambling, ranging from palatial to sordid, flaunted open doors in the districts immediately adjoining the business heart of the city."[71] Moved by Stead's call to virtue, the crowd launched a "Battle of Chicago" designed to bring salvation to the city through civic action.[72]

Five of those present, including Hull House's Jane Addams, were appointed to draw up a plan of action.[73] Those plans, in turn, were presented to a larger group of rally participants at a session convened in the Auditorium Recital Hall on December 12, 1893. The Central Relief Association (CRA), which was created that evening, would eventually pursue good works under the umbrella of the Civic Federation, which the CRA launched, in turn, on February 3, 1894.[74]

The new Civic Federation's Moral Department was hard at work within weeks, engaging the services of Pinkerton detectives to carry out a crusade against vice that Mayor John P. Hopkins and the Chicago Police Department had been reluctant to launch on their own.[75] Fundamentally pro-business, the Civic Federation sought to arbitrate between labor and management during the brutal May 1894 Pullman strike. That confrontation eventually exploded in bitter violence when President Grover Cleveland sent in federal troops over the objections of local officials.[76]

By 1896, the federation's Political Department was independently incorporated as the Municipal Voters' League.[77] The league was more politically activist in orientation, seeking civic redemption by direct political action rather than through the production of chronicles of ethical abuse.[78] The league drew on the CRA's findings to mobilize support for and opposition to various candidates for political office. The league also nurtured the thoughts of several of its members who were committed to

---

[71] Douglas Sutherland, *Fifty Years on the Civic Front: A History of the Civic Federation* (Chicago: Civic Federation of Chicago, 1943), p. 4.
[72] Ibid., pp. 4–7; Miller, *City of the Century*, pp. 533–41.
[73] Addams, *Twenty Years at Hull-House*, pp. 122–23.
[74] Sutherland, *Fifty Years on the Civic Front*, pp. 8–9.
[75] Ibid., p. 10.   [76] Flanagan, *Charter Reform*, p. 36.
[77] Sutherland, *Fifty Years on the Civic Front*, p. 16.
[78] Flanagan, *Charter Reform*, p. 37.

even broader municipal reform—a group that came together in 1903 to organize the City Club of Chicago.

Many of these reform organizations were Protestant, pro-business, and highly self-assured; they supported public moral probity and individual responsibility. They viewed the city as "a corporation of which all citizens are members, and in which they all have a proprietary interest. If the corporation is well managed they are all gainers. If it is badly conducted, they are all losers."[79] Like Republicans of the 1990s, the civic federation movement of a century before believed that the best government was limited government. One way to measure the wellness of government, the movement's leaders argued, was to ensure minimal and "fair" taxation policies.[80] Rather than build coalitions within Chicago's complex ethnic and class mix, local reform organizations of the period stood on a rather limited social base. Samuel Hays has argued that Progressive Era municipal reformers throughout the United States did not wish "simply to replace bad men with good; they proposed to change the occupational and class origins of decision-makers."[81] Reformers wanted fellow businessmen to enter local government because, talking primarily to themselves, "they believed that the impulse toward urban reform came exclusively from within their ranks."[82] Their insularity proved fatal in the charter reform battle ahead.

THE FIGHT TO EXPAND HOME RULE

A number of proposals for extending local home rule and streamlining the intricate web of State of Illinois, Cook County, and City of Chicago agencies had been surfacing for several years prior to 1902.[83] By that time, the Civic Federation had convinced itself that the only effective means for ending overlapping government agencies, restructuring the out-of-control City Council, and gaining enhanced fiscal responsibility would be a total overhaul of the city's organizing principles. Federation

---

[79] Lucius S. Richardson, *The Civic Federation and the Municipal Government* (St. Louis: Civic Federation of St. Louis, 1896), pp. 15–16.

[80] See, for example, such Civic Federation pamphlets as *Tax Inequalities in Illinois* (Chicago: Civic Federation of Chicago, 1910), and Douglas Sutherland, *Federal "Aid"* (Chicago: Civic Federation of Chicago, 1921).

[81] Samuel P. Hays, "The Politics of Reform in Municipal Government in the Progressive Era," *Pacific Northwest Quarterly* 55, no. 4 (October 1964), pp. 157–69: 163.

[82] Flanagan, *Charter Reform*, p. 38.

[83] Several of these proposals are contained in Edmund J. James, *The Charters of the City of Chicago*, Part 2: *The City Charters, 1838–1851* (Chicago: University of Chicago Press, 1899).

members called for a new city charter—one that had to meet the approval of both a hostile state legislature in Springfield and an impulsive local electorate. Finally, at the federation's prompting, seventy-four men from the city's business and social elite gathered on October 28, 1902, as the Chicago New Charter Convention.[84] Business organizations such as the Board of Trade, the Chicago Bar Association, the Illinois Manufacturers' Association, the Municipal Voters' League, and the Real Estate Board were well represented, as were elite clubs such as the Commercial Club, the Country Towns' Association, the Illinois Club, the Marquette Club, and the Union League Club.[85] Mayor Harrison appeared as an ex officio member of the Charter Convention's Executive Committee. Otherwise, leadership positions were held by elite reformers, except for George J. Thompson of the Chicago Federation of Labor, who was added to the convention's Executive Committee along with the Board of Trade's B. A. Eckhart soon after the group's initial meeting. Despite the presence of the odd labor and political leader, the New Charter Convention consisted primarily of successful businessmen and professionals.

The Civic Federation's pro-business orientation and lingering hostility among local unions over the close-down of the Pullman strike eight years before almost guaranteed that any event so closely identified with the federation could never be truly representative. Labor's concerns were heightened when, in November 1904, the Chicago School Board gave the federation access to local classrooms to promote charter reform while initially shutting the unions out of the same local schools.[86]

The New Charter Convention prompted various failed efforts in Springfield and on the Chicago City Council to convene a formal convention to draft a new city charter.[87] As might be expected, Republicans and Democrats, laborites and commercial interests all advocated charter convention plans that would have extended their own control over the

[84] Flanagan, *Charter Reform*, p. 50.
[85] Chicago New Charter Convention, *Proceedings* (Chicago: New Charter Convention, 1902), pp. 3–4.
[86] Flanagan, *Charter Reform*, pp. 55–56.
[87] The New Charter Convention's activities were discussed by Civic Federation of Chicago President Bernard E. Sunny in a comprehensive address to the Union League Club on April 14, 1904. See Bernard E. Sunny, *The Proposed Amendment to the Constitution of the State of Illinois and a New Charter for Chicago* (Chicago: Civic Federation of Chicago, 1904). Readers may also wish to consult Chicago New Charter Convention, *Report of the Executive Committee, to Be Submitted to the Convention at Its Next Meeting, December 15, 1902* (Chicago: New Charter Convention, 1902).

26. Hotel guests doing their own chores during waiters' strike, Chicago, 1903. *Chicago Daily News*. Courtesy Chicago Historical Society, DN-000637.

proceedings. Republicans in the Sixth and Seventh Wards, for example, established twenty-five committees that convened every Saturday in joint session at the Union Restaurant "to hear and consider the report of some committee or committees."[88] These groups conducted "public meetings in clubs, churches or convenient places of assembly, where general discussion of the problems of Chicago government will be undertaken."[89] In this manner, the Wards Six and Seven Republicans sought "to present, primarily to [their] own legislators, a series of carefully considered measures which are representative of popular sentiment."[90] A serious group of people, these committees included Merriam and journalist Harold L. Ickes, together with University of Chicago professors and prominent Republican reformers.

A Republican-dominated City Council finally approved a plan in 1905 whereby a number of key local entities appointed delegates to a charter convention. In the end, as Maureen Flanagan reports, "by occupation there were 26 lawyers, 32 businessmen, 2 social workers, one professor and one minister. Many of these men were the same ones who had been active in the previous reform movements of the Civic Federation and the Municipal Voters League. Even the few ethnic delegates were mostly well-to-do businessmen; only two delegates were members of the CFL [Chicago Federation of Labor], and one delegate was a black businessman. Mayor [Edward F.] Dunne had appointed these last three members."[91]

The convention's conveners produced a 150-page draft bill around which discussions could revolve.[92] The assembly's deliberations were somewhat anticlimactic given the maneuvering that had preceded its convocation on November 30, 1906.[93] The delegates carefully reviewed past legal and administrative practices in Illinois and elsewhere in the United States.[94] A few issues prompted sharp dispute: the lengthening of aldermanic terms from two years to four, the delineation of the taxation and

---

[88] Sixth and Seventh Ward Charter Committee (Republican), *Plan and Purpose* (Chicago: Sixth and Seventh Ward Charter Committee, 1904), p. 3.

[89] Ibid.   [90] Ibid., p. 4.

[91] Flanagan, *Charter Reform*, p. 61.

[92] *Bill for an Act to Provide a Charter for the City of Chicago* (Chicago: City Charter Convention, 1905); *An Act to Provide a Charter for the City of Chicago* (Chicago: Chicago Charter Convention, 1905).

[93] Flanagan, *Charter Reform*, pp. 64–97.

[94] These reviews were based on several remarkable compilations of American and international municipal administration practices of the era. See, for example, August Raymond Hattan, *Digest of City Charters Together with Other Statutory and Constitutional Provisions Relating to Cities* (Chicago: Chicago Charter Convention, 1906); and Merriam, *Report of an Investigation*.

decision-making powers of the City Council, the extent of local home rule, women's suffrage, and prohibition.

The forces of moderate reform and a pro-business cast of mind carried the day on each of these issues, although sometimes with considerable acrimony. On the education front—a staple of Chicago's political, class, ethnic, and culture wars—the proposed charter waved a red flag before teachers, their unions, and a number of parent associations. Teachers and parents were to be excluded from educational decision-making, as school board members would be appointed rather than elected and internal administration would be centralized.[95] Businessmen feared that the charter's provisions would eventually lead to higher taxes, yet another flaw for many voters. Meanwhile, discussion of the city's most contentious issues—municipal suffrage for women, municipal regulation of liquor sales, and municipal ownership of public utilities—was put off until late December 1906.

On the question of women's suffrage, the delegates concluded that the question was beyond their reach. Several warned that suffrage would give the women of the wrong social class access to the ballot box.[96] Regarding liquor regulation, convention delegates simply had no place to hide. The temperance issue—like the struggle over abortion a century later—served as a touchstone in disagreement over social values.[97] The issue had emerged as a cultural battlefield between old-line Protestant elites and newly arriving immigrant groups.[98] It stood at the core of calls for moral revival.[99] Those favoring temperance wanted liquor regulation to be decided in the rural-dominated Illinois state legislature in Springfield; advocates of more liberal policies argued for "home rule" on this question.

Charter Convention delegates proposed separate bills governing the sale of alcoholic beverages, thereby removing charter reform from the fight over prohibition. Perry Duis notes, however, that morality was only half of the battle. Liquor-license fees produced indispensable revenues for Chicago and other municipalities throughout Illinois.[100] Duis cites figures ranging from $3 million in municipal revenues collected during

[95] Julia Wrigley, *Class Politics and Public Schools: Chicago, 1900–1950* (New Brunswick, N.J.: Rutgers University Press, 1982), pp. 105–10.

[96] Flanagan, *Charter Reform*, p. 85.

[97] This conflict is examined in Perry R. Duis, *The Saloon: Public Drinking in Chicago and Boston, 1880–1920* (Urbana: University of Illinois Press, 1983).

[98] The German community, for example, was quite active in the antitemperance movement. Andrew Jacke Townsend, "The Germans of Chicago" (Ph.D. diss., University of Chicago, 1927), pp. 140–42.

[99] Flanagan, *Charter Reform*, pp. 87–92.   [100] Duis, *The Saloon*, p. 115.

1886 for the entire state to $8 million added annually to the City of Chicago's municipal coffers by 1910.[101] Given that the Illinois state legislature had prohibited the city from either raising tax rates or floating bond issues, "[s]aloon license fees were the only means of averting municipal bankrupcy."[102]

Chicago politicians such as the irrepressible Anton "Tony" Cermak were building powerful political machines through their opposition to Prohibition. Cermak, who as mayor would be assassinated in early 1933 while riding with President-elect Franklin Roosevelt in a Florida motorcade, used ethnic opposition to Prohibition to establish what became (with further refinement by Mayors Edward J. Kelly and Richard J. Daley) the great Democratic machine of twentieth-century Chicago.[103] This son of a Bohemian miner was known for his "force, firmness, persistence, and shrewdness" despite a number of rough edges.[104] Cermak was precisely the sort of politician Civic Federation members saw as reprehensible.

The campaign for municipal ownership of public utilities was similarly well underway when the Charter Convention convened. Once again, many delegates thought they could find a safe middle path through this municipal minefield.[105] The conventioneers added provisions for greater municipal regulation and oversight of utilities—including traction companies—while eschewing demands for public ownership.

Two major battles lay ahead before the convention's draft city charter could be brought to Chicago's voters. First, the mayoral election of 1907 had to be held in early spring; second, the Illinois state legislature had to ratify the proposed charter. These events sealed the proposed charter's fate.

THE 1907 REFERENDUM

The 1907 mayoral race pitted the Democratic incumbent and "radical" Edward F. Dunne against the noncontroversial Republican Chicago postmaster, Fred A. Busse. Busse, as noted in Chapter 5, had been injured in

---

[101] Duis's figures are consistent with Merriam's estimate that the City of Chicago received $3,759,555 from the sale of saloon licenses in 1904 alone. Merriam, *Report of an Investigation*, p. 114.

[102] Duis, *The Saloon*, p. 115.

[103] On the career of Cermak, see Alex Gottfried, *Boss Cermak of Chicago: A Study of Urban Political Leadership* (Seattle: University of Washington Press, 1962).

[104] Harold F. Gosnell, *Machine Politics: Chicago Model* (1937; reprint, New York: AMS, 1969), p. 13.

[105] Flanagan, *Charter Reform*, pp. 90–92.

a train accident at the outset of the election season and remained in a sickbed until the polls opened.

Dunne had run in 1905 on a promise to implement municipal ownership of the street railways, a campaign pledge that he had been unable to keep. He had become a harsh critic of the powerful City Council. He told the prestigious Commercial Club, for example, "The experience of the last thirty or forty years that we have had with corrupt and profligate legislators and common councils has forced upon reflecting citizens the conviction that a check upon legislative corruption and profligacy is absolutely necessary."[106] Mayor Dunne's efforts at reform of the Chicago school system similarly touched some of the most sensitive nerve endings of the local body politic.

Busse pledged to gain home rule for the city on the liquor question. Never forced to appear in public as a consequence of his accident, Busse rode an anti-Dunne wave into office. He immediately set out to gain support for charter reform from the Illinois General Assembly. In the process, he and his fellow Chicagoans retreated on several key issues, the first of which was a proposed statewide local option bill that temperance supporters saw as an opening for total prohibition. The legislature redrew ward boundaries and reversed proposed provisions for direct primaries, thereby imperiling delicate compromises that had stood at the center of Charter Convention deliberations.[107] The Chicago delegation beat back a proposed permanent restriction on the number of state representatives to be elected from Cook County. The amended charter passed the General Assembly on May 7, the state Senate on May 12, and was sent back to the city for a September 1907 referendum.

Debate raged in the local media all summer, with the legislature's meddlesome gerrymandering of ward boundaries gaining increasing attention.[108] The city's respectable Protestant business elite remained confident that, whatever its imperfections, their beloved charter would pass. Reform proponents attempted to minimize the significance of the state legislature's changes and modifications.

"It is regrettable," a Civic Federation of Chicago report noted,

that the redistricting for the new ward plan should have raised a political issue in connection with the charter. It was pretty generally agreed that the act reducing the number to fifty, with a corresponding number of wards, was wise. It will

[106] Edward F. Dunne, "On the Chicago Charter: Address to Commercial Club, March 12, 1904," in Edward F. Dunne, *Dunne: Judge, Mayor, Governor*, comp. and ed. William L. Sullivan (Chicago: Windemere, 1916), pp. 150–56: 156.

[107] William Booth Philip, "Chicago and the Downstate: A Study of Their Conflicts, 1870–1934" (Ph.D. diss., University of Chicago, 1940), p. 61.

[108] Flanagan, *Charter Reform*, pp. 110–35.

concentrate responsibility and facilitate legislative business. In redistricting, the conditions had to be encountered of the large outlying wards growing in population, while the tendency of the inlying wards is to decrease or remain stationary. As a matter of fact Democratic leaders were in the conference with Republicans when redistricting was done, and it is reliably asserted that they for the most part assented to it. There were individual Democratic grievances, as there were individual grievances.[109]

All very rational, orderly, and "apolitical," one would have thought from the Civic Federation's account. It turned out, however, that the ward bosses about to lose their power bases were less reasonable.

The draft represented a "good start" for local rule, especially as the city's "best and brightest" had participated in its creation. The City Club of Chicago's luncheon meetings that summer largely ignored those who stood in opposition to the proposed charter. Yet, as Flanagan notes, opposition ran deep: "What is relevant is that many of the opponents of the charter had conceptualized municipal government and the city as a whole in a way that conflicted with the views of those backing the charter."[110]

Charter supporters denied the legitimacy of many of their opponents' views. The Civic Federation's advocacy in favor of passage of the new charter must have insulted many less-fortunate participants in the Chicago political process. The proposed charter's alleged "defects," the federation argued,

depend altogether upon the angle of view. They are mainly bogies, such as the charge that the charter is framed in the interest of corporations; that it is inimical to the public schools; that it makes a czar of the mayor; that it gives him too much authority over the Board of Education, and authorizes him to call out the militia in case of riot or insurrection; that it imposes upon the city political ring rule, that the consolidation of the parks is "dangerous." Some of these are too puerile for serious attention, and others can be objections only in the minds of those who are self-seeking or have peculiar ideals not generally endorsed as to what would best subserve the interests of the city and *all*—not a particular class—of its citizens.[111]

The Civic Federation evidently failed to appreciate the extent to which its own membership was perceived by many as having "self-seeking" ideals that would best serve a very particular class of Chicago citizens.

---

[109] *The New Chicago Charter: Why It Should Be Adopted at the Special Election, September 17* (Chicago: Civic Federation of Chicago, 1907), p. 10.
[110] Flanagan, *Charter Reform*, pp. 115–16.
[111] *The New Chicago Charter*, pp. 10–11.

By ignoring opposing views, proponents had doomed the charter to certain defeat. Had they reached out to incorporate opposing views more fully in their deliberations, they might not have appeared nearly as remote from their fellow Chicagoans as Cook County residents felt themselves from the "downstaters." Arrogantly ignoring strategies of inclusion, the Civic Federation–City Club crowd plowed ahead, oblivious to the growing chorus of grievance from labor, ethnic groups, women's organizations, William Randolph Hearst's Independence League, and other, less proper citizens. The final tally in the referendum was 121,935 votes against the proposed charter, and just 59,786 in favor of the reform package.[112]

A second charter assembly convened in September 1908, this one was more open to opposing viewpoints. The hostility from the previous year's debacle lingered on, however. Once again, the conventioneers rejected demands for municipal women's suffrage. The liquor question degenerated into yet another boundless clash between Protestant and Catholic cultures. Once again, Springfield meddled. In the end, the second proposed charter reform failed to clear the state legislature.[113] Those middle and professional classes most committed to reform had begun, by this time, to forsake the dissolute city for the more superficially upstanding communities in Chicago's suburban belt.[114] A third attempt at drafting a charter for Chicago died with a whimper in 1914, and an effort to rewrite the state constitution during the early 1920s likewise collapsed under upstate-downstate rivalries.[115]

Maureen Flanagan convincingly argues that

[t]he reason Chicagoans failed to agree upon and implement any type of charter reform lay deeply rooted in their past political culture. It did not lie in "reformer" versus "bosses" antagonisms or in hostility toward reform. Each side in the charter battle had different ideas about the correct priorities of municipal government. Those in favor of the charter valued strict fiscal controls over all sectors of the municipal government. The opponents of the charter, in contrast, believed that public utilities and public schools, for instance, should be conceived of as vital services provided by the city to assure and constantly improve the quality

[112] Flanagan, *Charter Reform*, p. 135.
[113] For the text of this version of a new Chicago municipal charter, see Chicago Charter Convention, *Resolutions and Communications Received at Meeting held January 19, 1909* (Chicago: City Charter Convention, 1909); and Chicago Charter Convention, *An Act to Provide a Charter for the City of Chicago* (Chicago: City Charter Convention, 1909).
[114] A point underscored by Wayne Andrews in *The Battle for Chicago* (New York: Harcourt and Brace, 1946), pp. 319–21.
[115] Flanagan, *Charter Reform*, pp. 146–48.

of life for all the people of the city. They ultimately turned against the 1907 charter because they believed that it would implement a municipal government dedicated to using the wrong means to achieve the wrong ends.[116]

Such an explanation, while persuasive, fails to reveal how Carter Harrison, Jr., had been able just a few years before to close a similarly deep gulf between proponents and opponents of municipal ownership of the streetcar system. The charter reform movement failed because it at best ignored, and at worst denied, the legitimacy of those who were not part of it. Progressive reformers had failed to practice the politics of metropolitan pluralism. Meanwhile, Chicago lived on. Personal ties rather than institutions and formal legal arrangements came to fill organizational voids left by antiquated constitutional arrangements.

Republican "Big Bill" Thompson and Democrats Cermak, Kelly, and Daley took advantage of precisely such organizational ambiguity later in the century to build their powerful political machines.[117] Flanagan concludes, "The political machine ultimately provided a way around this otherwise ungovernable structural mess left by the failure of charter reform. The machine brought centralized government to Chicago; it found a way to implement the control over the entire municipal system that had not been accomplished by the structural reform of overlapping authorities or attained through the institution of home rule."[118]

The machine and its patronage system thus brought informal order to Chicago's formal chaos, and continues to do so to this day, albeit in a much truncated form. As Ester Fuchs proposes, the party machine "guaranteed Chicago mayors a loyal vote on election day and assured that the City Council would follow the mayor's lead on the budget."[119] "It was the machine," she continues, "that gave Chicago mayors extralegal control over important budget decisions," and, she might add,

---

[116] Ibid., p. 148.

[117] On Thompson, see Douglas Bukowski, "Big Bill Thompson: The 'Model' Politician," in Green and Holli, eds., *The Mayors*, pp. 61–81. On Cermak, see Paul M. Green, "Anton J. Cermak: The Man and His Machine," in ibid., pp. 99–110; as well as Gottfried, *Boss Cermak*. On Kelly, see Roger Biles, "Edward J. Kelly: New Deal Machine Builder," in Green and Holli, eds., *The Mayors*, pp. 111–25; as well as Gosnell, *Machine Politics*. On Daley, see John M. Allswang, "Richard J. Daley: America's Last Boss," in Green and Holli, eds., *The Mayors*, pp. 144–63; as well as Mike Royko, *Boss: Richard J. Daley of Chicago* (New York: E. P. Dutton, 1971). On the collapse of the machine following Daley's death, see Gary Rivlin, *Fire on the Prairie: Chicago's Harold Washington and the Politics of Race* (New York: Henry Holt, 1992). The return of the Daley family to power following Mayor Harold Washington's death with the accession of Richard J.'s son, Richard M. Daley, to the mayor's post suggests the lingering though muted influence of the great Chicago machine during the 1990s.

[118] Flanagan, *Charter Reform*, p. 155.   [119] Fuchs, *Mayors and Money*, p. 6.

critical power on other issues as well.[120] The rise of the Chicago political machine, in turn, was a direct consequence of the failure of pragmatic pluralism during the great charter reform debates of 1907, Mayor
Dunne's unsuccessful tenure in office between 1905 and 1907 (see the
discussion in Chapter 5), and Merriam's defeat in the 1911 mayoral race.

THE GREAT MIGRATION

Pragmatic pluralism would decline further in the decade to follow.
The expanding pace of African-American migration from the rural
South added a new dimension to Chicago's political and social mix
that touched off distinctly more volatile chemical reactions in the city's
streets.

Chicago quickly became a primary destination for black Southern participants in the "great migration" of the late 1910s and 1920s. The city
was a "land of hope" for poor African-American farmers being pushed
off the land in Mississippi, Louisiana, Alabama, Texas, Arkansas, and
parts of Tennessee and Georgia.[121] Up the Illinois Central rail routes they
traveled—pushed by racism and discriminatory Jim Crow laws, declining returns on Southern agricultural products, and a general desire to see
more of the world; pulled by the greater superficial freedom and industrial riches of the North. Moving along the sort of classic traditional
kinship networks that sustain migrants everywhere, black Southerners
were drawn—and, more important, confined by racial prejudice—to "a
narrow strip of land known to whites as the Black Belt" on the city's
South Side.[122] These restricted and crowded neighborhoods housed 78
percent of Chicago's African Americans by 1910. Such segregation was
a dramatic change in settlement patterns for a city where, as late as 1898,
only slightly more than one-fourth of the black residents had lived
in precincts in which African Americans constituted a majority, and
more than 30 percent lived in neighborhoods that were at least 95
percent white.

James R. Grossman reports in his exceptional study of Chicago and
the great migration, *Land of Hope*, that the flow of blacks from the rural
South began in 1916 as World War I choked off immigration routes
across the Atlantic Ocean.[123] Increasing industrial production for the war

[120] Ibid., p. 8.
[121] James R. Grossman, *Land of Hope: Chicago, Black Southerners, and the Great Migration* (Chicago: University of Chicago Press, 1989), p. 6.
[122] Ibid., p. 123.   [123] Ibid., pp. 3–6.

effort heightened labor demand in manufacturing centers such as Chicago, with recruiters heading south in search of inexpensive labor. From 1916 to 1919, between 50,000 and 70,000 African Americans relocated to Chicago, and untold thousands more passed through its train stations and burgeoning black neighborhoods. The river of migrants would not attenuate until the Great Depression closed off employment opportunities in Chicago and other northern cities.

The arrival of so many African Americans in such a brief period unleashed many of the most pathological forces the American psyche can conjure. Social reformers concerned over the plight of the white poor often simply ignored the needs of impoverished blacks.[124] White real estate agents and owners were hardly passive, frequently conspiring to restrict African Americans to a well-defined area on the South Side. Some whites, when duplicity failed, turned to violence. In the two years prior to the 1919 riots, at least twenty-six bombs exploded at the homes of African Americans in previously all-white neighborhoods and at the offices of the realtors who had sold those houses.[125] Such bombings would persist for decades. Their impact was immediate. If none of the city's African Americans had lived in a census tract that was more than 75 percent black in 1910, 35.7 percent of Chicago's blacks lived in such divisions by 1920.

Chicago finally exploded on July 27, 1919, in a two-week binge of open racial warfare rather mildly known today as the "Chicago Race Riot of 1919." Race riots being as American as apple pie, this title obscures the horror of one of the worst incidents of metropolitan intolerance the United States has ever experienced. The name domesticates these horrible days by placing them within the context of a well-known narrative.

In his powerful account of the 1919 events, William M. Tuttle, Jr., wrote, "The origins of the Chicago Race Riot of 1919 are to be found, not in high-level policy, but in gut-level animosities between black and white people who were generally inarticulate and presentist-oriented, and who did not record their motivations or feelings for posterity. . . . The truly bitter and functional animosities were thus not at the top, but

---

[124] Jane Addams was a notable exception, speaking out about the race issue on numerous occasions. See Elisabeth Lasch-Quinn, *Black Neighbors: Race and the Limits of Reform in the American Settlement House Movement, 1890–1945* (Chapel Hill: University of North Carolina Press, 1993), pp. 1–10.

[125] William M. Tuttle, Jr., "Contested Neighborhoods and Racial Violence: Chicago in 1919: A Case Study," in Kenneth T. Jackson and Stanley K. Schultz, eds., *Cities in American History* (New York: Knopf, 1972), pp. 232–48.

at the bottom, at the common denominators at which races coexisted—
at the shop level in industry, at the block level, at the neighborhood recre-
ational level."[126]

The origins of the 1919 riots are, in short, at that point when pragmatic tolerance breaks down. Race became Chicago's pivotal issue
that summer, replacing class and ethnicity as the leitmotif of local
politics. The tragic July–August events in 1919 close a remarkable period
in the city's history when the game of power expanded to incorporate
many disadvantaged groups. The riots demonstrate the alarming
consequences of exclusionary politics in communities of intense social
fragmentation.

THE "RED SUMMER" OF 1919

July 1919 had been a particularly warm and sultry month for Chicago.[127]
Large crowds of blacks and whites were drawn to the city's lakeshore to
cool off. A number of minor but ugly interracial incidents had already
taken place before July 27, when John Harris, a fourteen-year-old
African American, and four companions named Williams (two brothers,
Charles and Lawrence, and two unrelated friends, Eugene and Paul)
drifted offshore over an invisible but firm dividing line between the South
Side's 25th Street beach, frequented by African Americans, and the 29th
Street beach, preferred by whites. It was their misfortune to have crossed
this line just as a racial fight was breaking out on shore. A biracial pair
of police on foot patrol quickly lost control of the situation, with fists
and stones flying. One of the boys, Eugene Williams, was hit by a brick
thrown by a white man onshore, and drowned as a result.[128] This tragic
incident was compounded by the white police officer's refusal to allow
the brick-thrower to be arrested, and the situation spiraled out of control
when he arrested a black man instead on a separate complaint. Another
black man fired a gun at the police who had come to take the arrested

---

[126] William M. Tuttle, Jr., *Race Riot: Chicago in the Red Summer of 1919* (New York:
Atheneum, 1970), p. viii.

[127] Unless otherwise noted, this account is based on ibid., pp. 3–10.

[128] The Cook County Coroner's Office tells a very different story, claiming that Eugene
Williams drowned of exhaustion after clinging to a railroad tie for hours, waiting for
the melee on land to cease, and that his death did not involve any stones or anything
thrown. This rumor, the coroner's report notes, was a major trigger for the riots that
followed. The coroner's report also gives different numbers of casualties than Tuttle
does, with the coroner's count of fatalities standing at "23 blacks and 15 whites, with
291 wounded and maimed." Peter M. Hoffman, *The Race Riots*. Available at
http://cpl.lib.uic.edu/004chicago/disasters/riots_race.html, accessed December 1, 1999.

27. Man being stoned during race riots, Chicago, 1919. Jun Fujita. Courtesy Chicago Historical Society, ICHi-22861.

man into custody. The police fired back, and suddenly bullets were flying everywhere. Chicago's race riots had begun. Two weeks, and the intervention of 6,200 state militia troops, would be required to bring a modicum of order back to Chicago's streets, by which time 38 Chicagoans (including 33 blacks) had perished, and another 537 (including 342 blacks) had sustained major injuries.

The year had already been a difficult one for the city.[129] A postwar recession hit this manufacturing center particularly hard. African Americans, especially doughboys returning from Europe, were loath to surrender their wartime gains in earning power and personal freedom.[130] Returning white veterans wanted their old jobs back, generating tensions throughout Chicago factories. Whites were also suspicious of blacks for their willingness to cross strike barricades to work as scabs—apparently failing to understand why African Americans might be less than willing to honor picket lines tossed up by unions that had excluded them.[131]

[129] Ibid., pp. 12–31. [130] Ibid., pp. 208–41.
[131] The issue of white racism in Chicago's unions is tellingly explored in Grossman, *Land of Hope*, pp. 208–45.

Chicago employers, for their part, were always more than willing to seek gain by manipulating such differences within the Chicago laboring class.[132] Most of the city's industrial employers were large: 70 percent of Chicago's 400,000 industrial wage earners in 1919 labored for plants that employed at least 100 workers; almost a third worked in factories with more than a thousand workers.[133] The city of small workshops had disappeared, and with it any sense of shared fates among class and ethnic groups.[134]

Race and class relations were deteriorating across the United States for many of the same reasons. The Ku Klux Klan was on its way to peak strength; lynchings of African Americans were almost a daily occurrence in the South. Both national and local trends were driving Chicago's races to conflict.

The city's white workers had other reasons for concern as well. The summer of 1919 also saw the anti-Bolshevik "red scare," an outburst of antisocialist hysteria prompted by events in Moscow, among many European centers. The red scare played nicely into union-busting campaigns, placing white laborers under greater economic threat. Many of the nations living through actual communist revolutions in Europe—both successful, as in Russia, and failed, as in Germany—were well represented in the slums and middle-class neighborhoods of Chicago. Ethnic Chicagoans were concerned about their relatives' welfare back home and were themselves choosing sides in Europe's class battles. All of these pressures were being placed on a city that, having been predominantly German just a half-century before, had been stigmatized during the war as suspiciously non-native.

The air was thus full of anxiety that summer, even before whites sought to drive blacks off of "their" public beaches. To this more immediate air of conflict was added the steady increase in racial hostility that accompanied a decade-long migration of African Americans up the Mississippi to the great mid-American metropolis. As already noted, more and more blacks were forced by local custom, white violence, and racist real estate agents to live on top of one another in carefully delineated neighborhoods. Black tenements, already some of Chicago's worst housing, became even less inhabitable under the strain of receiving far too many migrants. Chicago's African-American community thus

---

[132] Tuttle, *Race Riot.*
[133] Lizabeth Cohen, *Making a New Deal: Industrial Workers in Chicago, 1919–1939* (Cambridge, U.K.: Cambridge University Press, 1990), p. 15.
[134] Ibid., p. 29.

had its own "bill of particulars" against their white neighbors. The Chicago of 1919 was, in short, a powder keg ready to explode. Chicago had become a perfect laboratory for racial, ethnic, and class intolerance and violence.

Local politicians contributed their own touch to this brew. Mayor and Republican boss "Big Bill" Thompson depended on African-American voters to sustain his edge over a Democratic machine that was building up steam.[135] Thompson—who served as mayor from 1915 to 1923 and again from 1927 to 1931—was no stranger to corrupt machine politics. He was "the machine politician first elected on a harmony ticket with two Bull Moose Progressives, the nationally discredited figure courted by presidential candidates, and the alleged ally of Al Capone the Justice Department never prosecuted."[136] The rotund and buffoonish boss tied to his city's violent gangster underworld seized control of the local Republican Party from reformers such as Addams and Merriam in 1915 and never looked back. He pandered initially to middle-class interests by breaking municipal unions and closing down the infamous "Levee" saloon-brothel district from which the Harrisons had drawn so much political sustenance.

Big Bill found himself maneuvered during his first term into a public alliance with de Priest, Chicago's first black alderman, and with the African-American community more generally. Thompson also drew on his position as mayor of "the sixth largest German city in the world" to criticize American entry into World War I. Corruption charges and rumors of ties to organized crime also began to surface during this initial term. Such "negatives" cost Thompson a U.S. Senate seat in 1918 and turned away his once-solid middle-class voter base. African-American and German voters, however, returned his loyalty, keeping him in office for a second term. Second Ward blacks accounted for over half of his margin of victory in 1919, when he defeated the perennial reformer Merriam in the Republican primary, and Democrat Robert Sweitzer and Independent Maclay Hoyne in the general election.[137]

Thompson sat out the 1923 election, returning to power in 1927 by defeating his good-government reform Democrat successor, William Dever.[138] By 1931, however, Thompson could no longer hold together

---

[135] For an informative yet brief discussion of the relationship between Thompson and African-American voters, see Grossman, *Land of Hope*, pp. 176–79.
[136] Bukowski, "Big Bill Thompson," p. 61.
[137] Ibid., pp. 74–76.
[138] See John R. Schmidt, "William E. Dever: A Chicago Political Fable," in Green and Holli, eds., *The Mayors*, pp. 82–98.

his power base in the face of the massive Depression-era desertion of the Hoover-led Republican Party in favor of the Democrats. Thompson's final term was dominated by unrelenting rumors of his ties to Prohibition-enriched Chicago mobsters such as Al Capone.[139]

Cermak followed as mayor, launching a white, blue-collar, Democratic "machine" that would vanquish meaningful opposition for half a century. Cermak and his successor, Kelly, courted Chicago's African-American voters, but later Democratic mayors Martin H. Kennelly and Richard J. Daley would increasingly play the "race card" during the post–World War II era.[140] The city's racial divide lay just beneath the surface of a machine-induced political calm.[141]

The legacy of July–August 1919 would last a very long time, markedly altering Chicago's civic life. George Herbert Mead—who, together with his University of Chicago colleague John Dewey, had led the development of the Chicago school of pragmatist philosophy—immediately viewed the class and racial strife of 1919 as the "bankrupt end" of Chicago's Progressive reform movement.[142] The politics of pragmatic pluralism enjoyed diminishing success after that "red summer." Like the 1907 failure to adopt a new city charter, the 1919 riots set the stage for a new, more exclusionary era in Chicago politics.

[139] Bukowski, "Big Bill Thompson" pp. 76–77; Milton L. Rakove, *Don't Make No Waves, Don't Back No Losers: An Insider's Analysis of the Daley Machine* (Bloomington: Indiana University Press, 1975), pp. 25–26.

[140] The issue of race and its relationship to the Democratic machine during the Richard J. Daley years is explored in depth in Roger Biles, *Richard J. Daley: Politics, Race, and the Governing of Chicago* (DeKalb: Northern Illinois University Press, 1995).

[141] For a discussion of the complex relationship between the Democratic machine of Cermak, Kelly, and Daley, see Rakove, *Don't Make No Waves,* pp. 256–81.

[142] Andrew Feffer, *The Chicago Pragmatists and American Progressivism* (Ithaca: Cornell University Press, 1993), p. 1.

9

The Worst-Housed City in Europe

Moscow was the most poorly housed of Europe's major urban centers at the turn of the twentieth century, surpassed only by St. Petersburg for the title of the continent's least healthy city. Only the Russian capital could compete with Moscow's depleted housing stock, exhausted public health facilities, and devastating outbreaks of infectious disease. The inability of Moscow municipal officials to address such social ills contributed to growing tensions among the city's various social groups, a strain that eventually would erode and overwhelm any middle ground for compromise and accommodation. This radicalization was brought about as much—and arguably more—by events outside of Moscow. Social polarization intensified class hostility and heightened a shared perception of irreconcilability on all sides. Pragmatic solutions to intractable problems became impossible in a world increasingly intent on ideological clarity. Politics moved onto the streets of Moscow with a violence that revealed the unbearable price of failed pluralism. Revolutionary warfare destroyed the vibrant merchant Moscow that had blossomed following the 1861 Great Reforms. Inadequate housing is a revealing chapter within the almost cosmic revolutionary story of twentieth-century Russia.

To be a poor European anywhere was dreadful during this era, but nowhere on the continent was poverty more destructive than in Russia's great industrial towns and cities. Deplorable housing conditions were marked both by limited space and by poor sanitary standards. Harshly cold winters exacerbated matters, as did a heavy reliance on wooden as opposed to brick and stone construction. The failure of Russian authorities at all levels to alleviate such horrid conditions fed social unrest every bit as much as did employer parsimony, greed, and denigrating paternalism, and imperial arrogance and obtuseness.

265

According to Stepan Alaverdian—an Armenian graduate student at the Moscow Commercial Institute whose frustration with authorities over the suppression of his 1915 dissertation on Moscow housing conditions led to his helping to found the Armenian Communist Party—8.7 Muscovites crowded into each apartment in 1912, as opposed to 4.3 Parisians, 3.9 Berliners, 4.2 Viennese, and 4.5 Londoners in apartments in their respective cities.[1] Canadian geographer James Bater reports in his authoritative study of St. Petersburg that the number of persons per apartment in that city stood at 7.4 in 1910—far above European levels but meaningfully less than the situation in Moscow at the same time.[2] Joseph Bradley has argued that Moscow's density of population per housing unit exceeded European norms, even though the city's overall population density per unit of land was relatively low.[3]

Moscow's most crowded rooms were in places in which other Europeans rarely ever lived. Some 10 percent of the city's apartments were in basements; the proportion of the city's total population living below ground increased by half between 1882 and 1912.[4] Another 40 percent of the city's workers—some 180,000 Muscovites in 1899—lived in apartments in which they rented only part of a room—often only a cot.[5] The smaller the apartment, in fact, the greater the number of residents per room.[6] In 1912, the average number of residents per one-room apartment stood at 6.5 people, as opposed to 3.9 for two-room apartments, 2.2 for three-room apartments, and 2.7 for four-room apartments.[7]

Over 200,000 Muscovites that same year were living in employer-provided housing, nearly a third inhabiting barracks where they could lay claim to no more than a cot.[8] An indeterminate number of Muscovites and visitors sought accommodations in the notorious flophouses of the Khitrov district—a warren of crime, diseases, and infamous inns just over a kilometer east of the Kremlin—where a cot cost five to seven

---

[1] Stepan Karapetovich Alaverdian, *Zhilishchnyi vopros v Moskve* (Yerevan: Izdatel'stvo A. N. Armianskoi S. S. R., 1961), p. 34.
[2] James H. Bater, *St. Petersburg: Industrialization and Change* (Montreal: McGill–Queen's University Press, 1976), p. 329.
[3] Joseph Bradley, *Muzhik and Muscovite: Urbanization in Late Imperial Russia* (Berkeley: University of California Press, 1985), pp. 196–97.
[4] Ibid., p. 197.
[5] Ibid., p. 211; William Gleason, "Public Health, Politics, and Cities in Late Imperial Russia," *Journal of Urban History* 16, no. 4 (August 1990), pp. 341–65: 350.
[6] Bradley, *Muzhik and Muscovite*, p. 210.   [7] Alaverdian, *Zhilishchnyi vopros*, p. 34.
[8] Bradley, *Muzhik and Muscovite*, pp. 199–204.

kopecks a night.[9] Here were Maxim Gorky's "lower depths," hellholes as bad as any on the European continent, and arguably worse.

Sanitary conditions, not surprisingly, were inferior in urban Russia to those found in urban Europe or America, and the rates of infectious disease were higher. Recurring outbreaks of cholera, tuberculosis, and typhus amplified the failure of Russian local officials to assure adequate living conditions for their fellow citizens. As already noted above—but worthy of repetition—Moscow trailed only its own capital, St. Petersburg, as Europe's least healthy major city.[10]

Moscow's municipal authorities permanently housed an insignificant two thousand residents in public housing by 1913.[11] This was at a time when deplorable housing conditions throughout industrialized Europe and North America prompted philanthropists and government officials to consider how to house the urban poor. Studies, regulation, and the construction of subsidized housing were becoming the order of the day elsewhere, but not in Russia.[12]

The compressed nature of Russia's mass urbanization—which began only after the Great Reforms of 1861, much later than in western Europe—combined with Moscow's inadequate fiscal base and the heavy hand of imperial bureaucrats to thwart many municipal plans and programs intended to ameliorate local housing and health conditions.[13] Moscow's inability to forge an effective consensus over how best to address the city's housing crisis demonstrates the failure of pragmatic pluralism just as the local commitment to education reveals its success.

DIFFERENT HOMES FOR DIFFERENT FOLKS

The reality of Moscow's homes at this time was more diverse than descriptions of slums might imply. Moscow's rapidly expanding population was becoming ever more differentiated by socio-economic category.

[9] Alaverdian, *Zhilishchnyi vopros*, pp. 45–50; Robert W. Thurston, *Liberal City, Conservative State: Moscow and Russia's Urban Crisis, 1906–1914* (Oxford, U.K.: Oxford University Press, 1987), p. 16.

[10] Bater, *St. Petersburg*, pp. 342–53.

[11] A. Mikhailovskii, "Munitsipal'naia Moskva," in N. A. Geinike, N. S. Elagin, N A. Efimova, and I. I. Shitts, eds., *Po Moskve. Progulki po Moskvie i eia khudozhestven-nym" i prosvietitel'nym" uchrezhdeniiam"* (Moscow: Izdanie M. i S. Sabashnikovykh", 1917), pp. 121–58: 147–48.

[12] Nancy Steiber, *Housing Design and Society in Amsterdam: Reconfiguring Urban Order and Identity, 1900–1920* (Chicago: University of Chicago, 1998).

[13] A point argued persuasively in Gleason, "Public Health."

A hereditary aristocracy contended with a rising merchant class for power and prestige. Small-scale business owners competed with local oligarchs for the benefits of trade and commerce. Peasant artisans came and went in the city's bustling markets, while workers slaved away in factories large and small. Educated women rubbed shoulders with their illiterate sisters; union members fought with police-supported scabs. The city was bursting with Russians of all sorts, and more than a few non-Russians as well. These various groups found their own niches within the local housing hierarchy.

A walk around the city a century ago would have revealed a glimpse of precisely how heterogeneous Moscow's population had become. Half of the city's nearly 40,000 residential buildings in 1902 were wooden, another third were constructed of brick and stone, while the remainder combined building materials in one way or other.[14] More significant, by 1912 approximately 45 percent of Moscow's apartments—home to more than 400,000 people—contained more than one room per inhabitant.[15] The city's new middle order lived in such apartments, worse off than higher-status residents inhabiting their own houses perhaps, yet significantly better housed than 55 percent of the apartment dwellers who were forced to live with more than one neighbor in each room.

Central Moscow's helter-skelter alleyways within the Garden Ring contained scattered survivors of a prereform city dominated by ancient aristocratic families. Charming classical *osobniaki* (detached town houses) leaned and creaked in their diminutive homage to St. Petersburg's grand palaces.[16] Many stone-and-stucco townhouses built in the years following the fires of 1812 were painted in the same burnt-yellow hue as their larger models in the capital. A few hearty wooden survivors of the previous era mimicked imperial grandeur as best they could with broad timbers, log columns, and carved woodland pediments.

Moscow's aristocracy had been in a prolonged decline following the emancipation of the serfs and the slow impoverishment of nobles' country estates.[17] Their grand townhouses' tatty charm was increasingly

---

[14] E. G. Boldinoi, "Statisticheskaia portret Moskvy na 1910 god," in A. S. Kiselev et al., eds., *Moskovskii arkhiv. Istoriko-kraevedcheskii al'manakh* (Moscow: Moskovskoe gorodskoe ob"edinenie arkhivov, 1996), pp. 162–82: 165.

[15] Alaverdian, *Zhilishchnyi vopros*, p. 33.

[16] For a discussion of Moscow's classical period, see Albert J. Schmidt, *The Architecture and Planning of Classical Moscow: A Cultural History* (Philadelphia: American Philosophical Society Press, 1989).

[17] Concerning the estate life of the Russian aristocracy, see Priscilla R. Roosevelt, *Life on the Russian Country Estate: A Social and Cultural History* (New Haven: Yale University Press, 1995).

28. House of a wealthy merchant, Moscow, 1902. H. C. White Co. Library of Congress, Prints and Photographs Division, Stereograph Collection.

overwhelmed by the more assertive and theatrically extravagant mansions of the rising merchant class. Turn-of-the-century Moscow's dominant stratum—the merchants of the city's industrial boom—favored a grandeur and eclecticism that would have been out of place in the more sedate years of an age gone by.

The great merchant clans slowly but steadily abandoned their fortress-like compounds in the Zamoskvorech'e district across the Moscow River, where they had lived for decades near their factories and workers.[18] They built ever more impressive homes in the latest fashionable style, ranging from an animated art nouveau to an ersatz Gothic, from something known as *neo-russkie* to an increasingly conservative grand classicism in the years following the social disruptions of 1905.[19] "Weirdly climbing plants" spiraled their sculpted tendrils up building sides, bentwood windows peered out onto the street, "and colored tiles ingeniously" attracted the passing eye.[20] No aristocratic refinement and good taste here. Such homes were built to impress with size and wonderment.

If Moscow prior to the 1870s was, in the words of architectural observer Kathleen Berton Murrell, "a rambling city full of empty plots of land and small wooden houses rarely more than two storeys high, each with its own garden," private developers had done their best to fill in the city center within the Garden Ring with apartments for the newly emerging middle strata.[21] The speculative apartment—the *dokhodnyi dom,* or "income house"—transformed both St. Petersburg and Moscow.[22]

St. Petersburg apartments retained some of the trappings of imperial display—grand lobbies and staircases, servant stairways tucked out of sight, and the like. Moscow's developers rarely wasted their money on such amenities. Here were the Russian versions of the efficient mid-level quarters that were popping up across urban Europe and North America. They were as stylistically theatrical as the nearby mansions of the city's

[18] Dmitri Chvidkovski [Shvidkovskii], "Le monde du 'Zamoskvoretche' dans la culture de Moscou," in Olda Morel et al., eds., *La maison Igoumnov: Residence de l'ambassadeur de France à Moscou* (Paris: Les amis de la maison Igoumnov, 1993), pp. 33–41, 140–43: 140.

[19] William Craft Brumfield, "Redesigning the Russian House, 1895 to 1917," in William Craft Brumfield and Blair A. Ruble, eds., *Russian Housing in the Modern Age: Design and Social History* (Cambridge, U.K.: Cambridge University Press; Washington, D.C.: Woodrow Wilson Center Press, 1993), pp. 25–54.

[20] Kathleen Berton Murrell, *Moscow Art Nouveau* (London: Philip Wilson, 1997), p. 6.

[21] Ibid., pp. 105–6.

[22] William Craft Brumfield, "Building for Comfort and Profit: The New Apartment House," in Brumfield and Ruble, eds., *Russian Housing,* pp. 55–84.

merchants—often built in a florid art nouveau that proclaimed "modern" and "European" at one and the same time.

Moscow's housing changed rapidly as one moved out beyond the center-defining Garden Ring, especially to the industrial east along the city's major rail lines. Here, in a semi-urban wooden demi-world of peasants in workers' clothing and workers' families living on the edge of dire poverty, dwelled more than half of the city's population. Servants lived with the wealthy, while artisans and construction laborers were spread throughout Moscow. Factory workers, by contrast, were concentrated beyond the Garden Ring.[23] Poorly constructed wooden homes (shacks, really) provided shelter for the better off who could afford to maintain a vegetable garden and a farm animal or two. By 1917, close to 300,000 workers lived in fetid barracks provided by their employers: "workers on different shifts sometimes doubled up on the beds, which were often nothing more than a series of boards built across a room. The rows of beds occupied virtually the entire floor space. Workers in the young women's barracks at Trekhgorka had no place else to go during their free time, so they read, sewed, and gossiped on these beds."[24]

Such were the lives of employees at Moscow's more enlightened factories. Many workers simply time-shared a cot in a corner of a private house or a cellar. The city's worst-off moved from flophouse to flophouse in the Khitrov district, or wandered homeless—no mean chore in a city where winter conditions lasted for half the year.

Moscow's pre-Soviet housing picture is difficult to fully assess a century later. Conditions would deteriorate further during Stalin's industrialization drive of the 1930s—with the crowded conditions of prerevolutionary Moscow's poorest becoming the norm for all but a privileged few.[25] Subsequent Soviet failures to house the city's population adequately cast a perhaps more favorable light on pre-Soviet Moscow's private developers.

Housing construction steadily improved throughout the half-century leading up to World War I. The proportion of wooden buildings within city limits declined.[26] More significant, the number of housing units with

[23] Thurston, *Liberal City*, p. 17.
[24] Diane Koenker, *Moscow Workers and the 1917 Revolution* (Princeton: Princeton University Press, 1981), p. 54.
[25] Stephen Kotkin, "Shelter and Subjectivity in the Stalin Period: A Case Study of Magnitogorsk," in Brumfield and Ruble, eds., *Russian Housing*, pp. 171–210; and William J. Chase, *Workers, Society, and the Soviet State: Labor and Life in Moscow, 1918–1929* (Urbana: University of Illinois Press, 1987).
[26] Bradley, *Muzhik and Muscovite*, pp. 195–96.

indoor plumbing and flush toilets grew from a mere 15,496 units in 1882 (or 22 percent of those for which figures were available), to more than 800,000 (or almost 60 percent of the city's population) by 1912. This included more than 90 percent of the residents in the city's central districts.[27]

Many Muscovites of the era remained wretchedly poor, with the average worker spending approximately half of his or her income on food alone in the years leading up to the revolutions of 1917 (and up to 70 percent in the civil war year of 1918).[28] The city's failure to adequately provide for its worst-off was often most immediately visible in the very housing in which Muscovites lived.

MOSCOW'S MARKET FAILURE

Several factors combined to exacerbate conditions in the city's poorest districts. The speed of Moscow's growth was of obvious importance, neither the city nor private developers being quite able to keep pace with a city "growing not by the day but by the hour."[29] The number of housing units in the city grew by 8.8 percent between 1907 and 1912, while the number of city residents increased almost twice as rapidly (rising by 16.1 percent during the same period).[30] Moscow was hardly alone in the rapidity of its expansion; in fact, its growth lagged behind that of the other two cities under examination in this volume.

Overall population density in Moscow was less than in such urban centers as London, Paris, Vienna, or Milan. Buildings throughout the city's outer reaches often nestled picturesquely in a surrounding yard (*dvor*) full of weeds and barnyard animals. Yet nowhere else in Europe were people more densely packed into each building and room than in Moscow.

Economic and technological backwardness contributed to Moscow's housing scene. Public transportation developed slowly in Russia, with electrified streetcar lines coming to Moscow only in 1904, well after they had appeared in the rest of Europe and in North America. Moscow's transit development lagged behind that of Osaka, as well. Consequently, Muscovites were forced to live close to their places of employment, leading to intense overcrowding in manufacturing districts.[31] Such neighborhoods were segregated by income and wealth, producing explosive

[27] Ibid., p. 197.
[28] Koenker, *Moscow Workers*, p. 56.
[29] Alaverdian, *Zhilishchnyi vopros*, p. 25.
[30] Thurston, *Liberal City*, p. 19.
[31] Bater, *St. Petersburg*, pp. 318–20, 326–42.

29. A Russian house on Sparrow Hills, Moscow, 1903. William H. Ram. Library of Congress, Prints and Photographs Division, LC-USZ62-123210.

concentrations of poorly paid and overworked laborers.[32] Peasant migratory patterns reproduced village connections within the city as peasant-workers settled together with their brethren from back home, living and working with their formerly rural neighbors in tight, closed urban networks well given to conspiratorial organization.[33]

Muscovites maintained strong ties to their villages. Aristocrats tried to keep their estates, while workers came and went according to the local demand for labor. Abundant religious holidays encouraged a constant coming and going between town and country. "Hundreds of thousands of peasants," Robert Johnson reports, "traveled annually to and from the cities and factories without ever severing their ties to the village."[34]

Much of Moscow remained a transient worker settlement—with only 70 women for every 100 men in 1871 and but 84 women for every 100 men by 1912.[35] Many workers maintained their families in the countryside, bifurcating household structures.[36] Few sharply drawn distinctions—such as between "peasant" and "worker"—could be made among Russia's unprivileged. Elise Kimerling Wirtschafter correctly reminds late-twentieth-century readers that "heightened migration, urbanization, and industrialization destroyed important structures of economic, social, and cultural life, erecting new ones in their stead. But indeterminate definitions, fluctuating identities, and insecure legal moorings were abiding patterns in Russian society. . . . In any of their traditional or new occupations, urban 'citizens' might, as they had in the past, live permanently in one city or wander between cities."[37]

Social relations retained more than a hint of the collective mentality of village life. Over time, connections survived, even though many merchants who had for decades lived together with their workers began to move away into their own neighborhoods in the city center as the proletariat was increasingly banished to Moscow's periphery. Some factory owners rejoiced in their own peasant ancestors, claiming a tie to their workers rarely evident in St. Petersburg, Europe, or North

---

[32] Koenker, *Moscow Workers*, p. 53.
[33] For a discussion of these central Russian *zemliaki* networks in Moscow, see Robert E. Johnson, *Peasant and Proletarian: The Working Class of Moscow in the Late Nineteenth Century* (New Brunswick, N.J.: Rutgers University Press, 1979), pp. 79–87.
[34] Ibid., p. 29.
[35] Mikhailovskii, "Munitsipal'naia Moskva," p. 122.
[36] Johnson, *Peasant and Proletarian*, p. 56.
[37] Elise Kimerling Wirtschafter, *Social Identity in Imperial Russia* (DeKalb: Northern Illinois University Press, 1997), p. 136.

America. Others retained patriarchal and paternalistic attitudes shaped by custom and tradition long eclipsed in other "modern" societies. Social distance was growing but had not been totally breached as late as World War I. "Though among the elites of Merchant Moscow there were occasional descendants from other social strata," Mikhail Shastillo reports, "the majority of the most prominent entrepreneurial families claimed peasant ancestors. The founders of future merchant dynasties resembled the peasants in every detail: their dress, lifestyle, and vernacular speech."[38]

Moscow was slowly becoming a more settled family town by the outbreak of World War I. In addition to the increasing presence of women, the percentage of children within the general population grew during this same period, from 10.6 percent to 16.8 percent.[39] Russian families were larger than in Europe. As Johnson explains, "[i]n Russia, where land tenure was often communal and a father's inheritance was divided among his sons, different patterns [from those in Europe] prevailed: Households were larger, marriages were earlier, and bachelorhood and spinsterhood were extremely rare."[40] When families moved to town together, more family members piled into ramshackle homes and flats than was the case farther west.

Broad swaths of the Moscow cityscape remained the domain of peasant men who had left their families in the village. They lived in temporary quarters—barracks, "corners," and the like—giving the city a transitory feel. The market failed to provide adequate housing for far too many Muscovites. Housing conditions for most continued to deteriorate throughout the 1910s.[41] Local officials, for their part, failed to respond to the growing gap between minimal standards and daily reality.

Municipal agencies were awash in a sea of housing and health problems. Building codes were poorly written and laxly enforced, and public housing assistance failed to alleviate the shortcomings in the accommodation of the poor. City budgets remained inadequate to the challenges at hand; bureaucrats tied to the national government limited local autonomy and authority; jurisdictional lines among competing agencies were often murky; the traditional slovenliness and corruption of Russian

---

[38] Mikhail K. Shastillo, "Peasant Entrepreneurs and Worker Peasants: Labor Relations in Merchant Moscow," in James L. West and Iurii A. Petrov, eds., *Merchant Moscow: Images of Russia's Vanished Bourgeoisie* (Princeton: Princeton University Press, 1998), pp. 85–93: 86.

[39] Johnson, *Peasant and Proletarian*, p. 56.   [40] Ibid., p. 51.

[41] Thurston, *Liberal City*, pp. 17–18.

officialdom impeded those potentially beneficial policies that had been set forth by city officials.[42] Late-imperial Russia had become a "society of formal privileges and obligations—economic, social, and political—imposed by the monarchy on its subjects yet limited by the government's institutional weakness, which prevented effective implementation."[43] Moscow's slums quickly became a breeding ground for revolution.

POOR HOUSING, POOR HEALTH

The city's housing ills in and of themselves were not of particular concern to the better off. As elsewhere in Europe and North America, seemingly reasonable explanations were readily available for the tawdriness and absence of fortune experienced by the unprivileged. Such were the forces of the market and nature at work. Nevertheless, Moscow's better-off could not afford to ignore the social ills that accompanied poor housing and that rarely stayed confined to slums: lax morals, crime, and disease.

The Khitrov market—with its taverns, alehouses, brothels, and cheap transient lodgings—represented all that typified a "sin quarter" at the turn of the last century. Peasants and indigents arriving in town always knew a cot could be had there for a few kopecks. Disaffected youths hung out on Khitrov street corners learning local criminal trades. Alcohol flowed freely and cheaply. Khitrov was a distinctly nasty part of town with little of the randy charm ascribed to Chicago's levee district. It was, in the words of an 1898 city commission, "the most horrible ulcer of the whole city."[44] Illegitimacy ran twice the city average—perhaps a third of all births in the area being out of wedlock—and thousands fell prey to its "life of drunkenness, debauchery, and crime."[45]

Moscow could not have existed without the Khitrov district, however. Its cheap taverns and inns sustained job seekers streaming into town from an ever impoverished countryside. Many naive country boys found dissolution and depravity within crumbling Khitrov walls, but many more gained a toehold on a new urban life, moving on to other neigh-

---

[42] Issues explored further in Bradley, *Muzhik and Muscovite;* as well as in Robert William Thurston, "Urban Problems and Local Government in Late Imperial Russia: Moscow, 1906–1914" (Ph.D. diss., University of Michigan, 1980).

[43] Wirtschafter, *Social Identity,* p. 169.

[44] From *Sovremennoe khoziaistvo goroda Moskvy,* as reported in Koenker, *Moscow Workers,* p. 16.

[45] Ibid., p. 17.

borhoods wiser if not necessarily richer. Khitrov was a machine for inducting the uninitiated into city life.

Thousands passed through Khitrov every year, bringing not only hopes but germs as well. Transient dormitories and cheap flophouses bred disease. Once again, Khitrov led the way. Moscow endured epidemics of infectious diseases every year—typhus, typhoid, diphtheria, scarlet fever, measles, cholera, sexually transmitted maladies, and more. All too frequently, Khitrov was ground zero in whatever the contagion of the moment might have been.[46] Simply walking Khitrov's streets increased one's chances of death.

Crime and prostitution and alcoholism could be contained to some extent within such down-at-the-heels neighborhoods as Khitrov and the worker districts farther away from the city center. Germs proved far more mobile. The tragic famine of 1891–92—while not directly apparent in Moscow—drove tens of thousands of Russian peasants from their homes. Cholera accompanied hunger, traveling to town with migrant refugees.[47] Moscow's tuberculosis rates were by far the highest in Europe.[48]

The city persisted in its infirmities throughout the half-century leading up to World War I. Aside from St. Petersburg, Moscow remained Europe's deadliest metropolis during the entire span from 1881 to 1910. Robert Thurston has calculated, for example, that the city's death rate in 1910 was higher than the average rate for other major European cities in 1881–85.[49] Though Moscow's death rate declined by 17.1 percent between 1881 and 1910, this improvement lagged far behind that of other major European cities during the same period.[50] Moscow's 1909 infant mortality rate was one-third higher than that of Madrid, nearly twice as high as that of Vienna and even Odessa.[51]

Moscow's public health failures were massive. Death and disease rates were significantly higher than elsewhere in Europe, and continued to be so for years. As Thurston suggests, the city "faced a situation in public health [in 1906] that had not changed substantially, compared to the very low level of 1881."[52]

---

[46] Thurston, *Liberal City,* p. 19.
[47] Adele Lindenmeyr, *Poverty Is Not a Vice: Charity, Society, and the State in Imperial Russia* (Princeton: Princeton University Press, 1996), p. 5.
[48] The death rate from tuberculosis in 1911 per 100,000 population was 17.6 in London, 18.6 in Rome, 20.0 in Berlin, 38.7 in Paris, 42.7 in Vienna, 44.1 in St. Petersburg, and 45.6 in Moscow. Thurston, *Liberal City,* p. 19.
[49] Ibid., pp. 19–20.
[50] Death rates in St. Petersburg fell during this same period by 22.3 percent; in Paris, by 28.3 percent; in London, 33.0 percent; and in Berlin, 41.5 percent. Ibid., p. 196.
[51] Ibid.   [52] Ibid., p. 20.

30. The great Sunday market, Moscow, 1898. Underwood and Underwood. Library of Congress, Prints and Photographs Division, LC-USZ62-123209.

Local society and officialdom might be able to turn a blind eye to disreputable morals and decrepit lodgings, or a deaf ear to the cries of the defeated. They could not, and did not, ignore the rampant disease that such conditions nurtured. The municipality expended large sums on health programs to little effect.[53] Programs focused narrowly on health concerns—all too often providing little more than traditional almshouses and orphanages to the needy (facilities that often spread disease further). Public relief efforts routine elsewhere in Europe at the time were ignored as economic and social change and recurring rural crises overwhelmed town and country alike.[54]

The municipality's commitment to poverty relief grew steadily throughout the 1890s following the brutal famine and horrendous cholera outbreak of 1891–92.[55] Unfortunately, the absence of consensus among local elites about what sorts of poverty alleviation programs were appropriate and effective reduced the impact of those city initiatives that were undertaken. Meanwhile, as Adele Lindenmeyr has noted,

government officials and outside experts engaged in reform ran up against one of the most bitter conflicts of late Imperial politics: the struggle between the central and local governments. The financial question also seemed intractable; given Russia's relative economic backwardness, where could sufficient funds for effective public assistance be found? Poverty itself proved difficult to define; in such a poor country, who actually should be entitled to public assistance? Finally, the reform effort revealed deep disagreements over the social significance and moral purpose of public relief.[56]

The intellectual breakthroughs shaping social policies in Chicago and even Osaka had a more muted impact in Moscow. Opinion and attitudes evolved, yet reform advocates were too often isolated within specialist communities and increasingly sequestered liberal political circles. Housing policy languished even though improvement in Muscovite dwellings could well have alleviated the urgency of the city's public health crisis. The consensus that drove large-scale public and philanthropic investment in education evaporated in housing policy. Pragmatic pluralism failed to resolve one of late-imperial Moscow's most pressing problems—where and how people lived. The consequences were apparent in the city's public health statistics, which placed Russia's heartland metropolis beyond the bounds of contemporary European experience.

[53] This argument is developed eloquently in ibid., pp. 19–20.
[54] Lindenmeyr, *Poverty Is Not a Vice*, pp. 62–63.
[55] Ibid., p. 68.   [56] Ibid., p. 74.

TOO LITTLE, TOO LATE

Moscow's academic and political leaders were well aware of changing intellectual fashions abroad. The local professorate was particularly well informed of developments in German universities. Inquiry into social issues was well known to Muscovites. As elsewhere, Moscow's leaders turned to surveys and inventories of social reality as a means for defining a course of action. All too often, however, the local political system was prevented from acting on such studies by inadequate fiscal resources as well as by the intrusive attention of bureaucratic overseers in St. Petersburg.

Russian efforts to enumerate indicators of social change began in the field of public health. The zemstvo, already described in Chapter 6, developed an ambitious program for gathering social statistics. Frequently led by zemstvo physicians, such measurement efforts focused primarily on health and environmental concerns. Zemstvo medicine had emerged by the turn of the century as a "pioneering system of rural health protection."[57] Health professionals valued the zemstvo's means of providing model health care through a set of institutions that potentially bypassed the reach of central institutions. The zemstvo became an arena in which physicians could assert their own professional standards with relatively less interference from the tsarist state. Such efforts were especially evident during the years leading up to 1905 when physicians and zemstvo deputies found an uneasy common ground in their shared desire to combat disease.

Zemstvo medicine was widely praised by contemporary observers as well as by both Russian and foreign historians. Reality proved more enigmatic, as the profound difficulties of Russian rural life frequently meant that peasants "continued to live in a squalid environment which fostered high rates of chronic and epidemic disease."[58]

Zemstvo ambitions appealed to a broad spectrum of Russian professionals and intellectuals even though practice rarely matched zemstvo ambition. Significantly for housing and health policies in Moscow, zemstvo health services encouraged the joint participation of activists and technical experts in local efforts to ameliorate public health

---

[57] Nancy M. Frieden, "The Politics of Zemstvo Medicine," in Terence Emmons and Wayne S. Vucinich, eds., *The Zemstvo in Russia: An Experiment in Local Self-Government* (Cambridge, U.K.: Cambridge University Press, 1982), pp. 315–42: 315.

[58] Samuel C. Ramer, "The Zemstvo and Public Health," in Emmons and Vucinich, eds., *The Zemstvo in Russia*, pp. 279–314: 279.

standards.[59] As Nancy Frieden accurately notes, "physicians in pre-Revolutionary Russia shared many of the characteristics of the educated elite. As social reformers they served the common folk in both remote villages and urban slums, as technical experts they devised and implemented pioneering community health programs, and as political activists they helped to precipitate the Revolution of 1905."[60]

Russian physicians traditionally had been employed in salaried, official positions, lacking the independence associated in Europe with a "free profession." Health care became a branch of Russian public administration. The community-based zemstvo health system provided physicians with a middle ground between full autonomy and service to the central state. Doctors sought ways to serve the broader public and, in the process, extend their own professional autonomy. One such physician, Dr. Nicholas Pirogov, came to hold an especially honored place in the Russian public and medical mind precisely because he redefined what it meant to practice medicine in imperial Russia.

Pirogov, who died at the age of seventy-one in 1881, encouraged physicians to become social activists. He sponsored and organized a series of societies through which medical schools, hospitals, clinics, and individual physicians could treat the less advantaged. The fiftieth anniversary of the Pirogov Societies in May 1881—shortly before his death—became an occasion for general celebration. The new tsar, Alexander III, sent the good doctor a congratulatory telegram and the city of Moscow named Pirogov an "honored citizen."[61]

Other physicians emerged as leading advocates of public health services as well. Evgenii Osipov, for example, proposed ambitious health services tied to local community needs at an 1873 zemstvo convention held in Samara.[62] Osipov advocated the wide collection of health statistics and the mapping of local medical topography. The president of the Moscow provincial zemstvo, Dimitrii Naumov, a Moscow University–trained jurist, established Russia's most successful medical statistics program in conjunction with Osipov following the latter's elevation to director of the Moscow provincial Public Health Council in 1875.[63] The collection of basic data was intended as a precondition for

[59] Nancy Mandelker Frieden, *Russian Physicians in an Era of Reform and Revolution, 1856–1905* (Princeton: Princeton University Press, 1981), p. xiii.
[60] Ibid.
[61] Ibid., pp. 5–11; and Gleason, "Public Health," pp. 347–48.
[62] Frieden, *Russian Physicians*, pp. 91–93.   [63] Ibid., p. 93.

the creation of widespread hygiene and public health education programs—though such aspirations often remained unfulfilled.

The model Moscow province health official became something of
a minor cultural icon by the end of the nineteenth century. Frieden
explains, for example, that "Dr. Astrov in Chekhov's 'Uncle Vanya' may
strike the Western reader as strangely preoccupied with the local ecology,
but he personified the Moscow zemstvo physician whose tasks included
the correlation of disease with geographic factors."[64] Dr. Chekhov
himself collected medical histories of prison inmates during his famous
sojourn to Sakhalin in 1890.[65] Moscow provincial medical statisticians
eventually produced nineteen volumes of statistical data evaluating
health conditions in the wake of industrialization.[66]

Laudable though zemstvo commitment to community medicine may
have been, rural Russia's public health realities remained appalling.
Russian public health standards fell to calamitous levels during such
times as the 1891 famine and the subsequent cholera epidemic. Underfunded zemstvo councils were grievously ineffectual in confronting
famine and pestilence. Meanwhile, rural statistical gathering forged a
path for the collection of health and other social data in cities such as
Moscow.

Such efforts in the countryside were paralleled by increasingly activist
urban doctors and health officials.[67] Community, journalistic, and professional advocacy for improved urban health conditions reached a peak
during the early years of World War I as the All-Russian Union of Towns,
a voluntary association of several hundred municipalities, lobbied
aggressively for expanded public health initiatives.[68]

Moscow city officials had long before sponsored an extensive survey
of local housing conditions.[69] An 1899 city survey had included both statistical data and descriptive material to advance an explicit connection
between substandard housing and the city's frightening tendency toward
infectious disease.[70] In 1912, the city issued another description of
housing patterns based on the census of 1902.[71] Social scientists—such
as the above-mentioned Alaverdian—drew on these data in their studies

[64] Ibid.   [65] Ibid.
[66] Ibid., p. 101.
[67] As may be seen in the pages of the journal *Gorodskoe delo*. For an examination of these
articles, see Gleason, "Public Health."
[68] Ibid.
[69] Thurston, *Liberal City*, pp. 17–19, 138–39.
[70] Ibid.; and Alaverdian, *Zhilishchnyi vopros*.
[71] Thurston, *Liberal City*, p. 17.

of Moscow housing conditions (though Alaverdian's dissertation was suppressed in part for his reliance on this information).[72]

Moscow civic leaders knew precisely how bad conditions were in their city, as did many officials in St. Petersburg. The city's squalid circumstances—as well as similarly unpalatable conditions in the capital—provided ammunition for an increasingly radicalized opposition. The city and its socially concerned civic leaders were never able to unite behind a concerted program designed to improve local housing conditions.

INADEQUATE POLICIES, INADEQUATE HOUSING

Municipal activism in the housing sphere moved ahead on two distinct yet related tracks. First, a number of Moscow's well-to-do supported philanthropic efforts to improve the lives of the city's worst-off. Second, city authorities endeavored to improve conditions through strengthened regulation of private housing and the construction and operation of public housing facilities.

Moscow's wealthy had long lent private support to poorhouses, workhouses, and orphanages. The Imperial Foundling Home (which was established in 1763 and granted royal patronage in 1797 by Tsar Paul I's second wife, Maria Fedorovna) was chartered to house the offspring of destitute parents, orphans up to the age of thirteen, and illegitimate infants.[73] The Foundling Home benefited from its connection to the royal family as well as generous private support. By the end of the nineteenth century, it had grown to become Moscow's largest philanthropic organization. Numerous smaller private and religious institutions, including hospitals, similarly sought to serve Moscow's poor.

The Moscow Workhouse and its related agencies became the city's and the region's second-largest institution of poor relief following its transfer from private to municipal control in the 1890s.[74] The Foundling Home limited its programs primarily to the care and education of children. Its officials rarely sought to attack the origins of the poverty that brought children to its doors in the first place. The Workhouse, which was modeled after the poor laws of medieval Europe, traded maintenance for labor through arrangements that were punitive at times. Administrators began to modify their programs only at the very end of

[72] Alaverdian, *Zhilishchnyi vopros*.
[73] Bradley, *Muzhik and Muscovite*, pp. 260–66.
[74] Ibid., pp. 267–72.

the nineteenth century, following the creation of a vocational center for Workhouse residents.

The city's numerous religious-supported shelters, indigent homes, and services for the poor similarly reached out to those seen to be pious and worthy. Private housing initiatives rarely accomplished more than providing a down-and-out Muscovite or traveler with a clean bed for a night at a local shelter.

The inadequacy of private philanthropy could no longer be ignored by the late 1880s, no matter how meritorious and commendable individual programs and institutions may have been. The scale of Moscow's poverty, health, and housing distress was too apparent to all. The tsar's ministers considered welfare provision to be a police problem best left to the Ministry of Internal Affairs. That ministry, in turn, reviewed the empire's welfare system, paying particular attention to the deficiencies of Moscow's response to the growing cascade of indigent peasants arriving in the city looking for work. The ministry and the State Council approved the transfer of a number of charitable organizations, almshouses, and hospitals to city control in 1887. A Moscow Duma commission chaired by Ivan Mamontov reviewed municipal management of private, public, and state welfare institutions within city boundaries the following year.[75] The City of Moscow subsequently expanded the scope of its activities to embrace housing, health, and welfare.

The city government's first initiative in housing had been the opening of a shelter in 1879 to stem the spread of infectious disease by lessening overcrowding in privately run flophouses.[76] It grew from a capacity of 510 people at its opening to provide up to 1,305 needy with a clean bed, a bath, and a meal by 1886. The city would open additional shelters by 1912, accommodating up to 5,650 homeless each night for free, for a nominal charge, or in exchange for labor from able-bodied persons, depending on the facility in question. This was at a time when private facilities housed 7,500 indigents each evening. In 1913, municipally run lodgings turned away 55,823 people in the course of a year—one sure indication of the inadequacy of city programs.

City officials also attempted to reign in some of the most deleterious practices in private-sector housing. The city's administration issued regulations on fire safety and sanitation for private lodging in 1910, making a concerted effort to upgrade the Khitrov district inns throughout 1912.[77]

[75] Ibid., p. 309.				[76] Thurston, *Liberal City*, pp. 138–39.
[77] Ibid., pp. 140–42.

Many Muscovites understood the need for regulation of public and private shelters, especially as a means for controlling the spread of disease. Supervision of other forms of housing—including the notorious worker dormitories in the city's east end—proved to be less successful. Laws and regulations covering factory housing issued by the Ministry of Finance and the Russian Duma as well as by city officials remained little more than declarative statements.

City leaders meanwhile made a conscious decision not to regulate housing conditions more broadly. Robert Thurston notes that "in 1911 the city Commission on Housing Problems decided that strict rules on conditions in cot-closet apartments would only force many to close, pushing thousands of people onto the streets. In view of the extremely tight housing market in the city, the commission was undoubtedly correct. The only effective solution to the problem was to build a great deal more housing, either privately or publicly."[78]

The entrance of city and national government agencies into the housing market was taking place at this time in numerous communities across Europe and around the world.[79] Many Muscovites were aware of such programs. The wealthy Solodovnikov family bequeathed over seven million rubles to the city in 1901 to support the construction of inexpensive apartments for small families and single residents.[80] The Solodovnikov gift was in excess of that of Al'fons Shaniavskii for the founding of his People's University, but the result was far less beneficial. The city had managed to build only two of the mandated apartment buildings by 1909 due to the municipality's poor administration of the funds. By the time that World War I broke out, Solodovnikov houses were occupied by approximately 2,000 people, many of whom were low-level white-collar workers rather than the truly impoverished.

Meanwhile, the city was spending its own funds on housing for the poor in accordance with a 1911 plan to upgrade local housing conditions. Subsequent plans undermined by the war foresaw the construction of public housing for city employees. Thurston estimates that Moscow's pre-Soviet municipal administration eventually built sixty apartment houses with a capacity of 39,000 people—an achievement which pales before both the contemporary demands of the market, and the housing programs of many cities throughout Europe.[81]

The grave and grievous nature of Moscow's public health, housing, and poverty crises at the turn of the last century were readily apparent

[78] Ibid., pp. 142–43.
[80] Thurston, *Liberal City*, pp. 143–44.
[79] Steiber, *Housing Design*.
[81] Ibid.

to many who cared to look. Numerous scholarly studies and manifold literary texts documented what was before everyone's eyes. Moscow was Europe's worst-housed and least healthy city—and had been so for some time. City officials charged with improving the situation had few resources with which to respond. Budgetary allocations were low and, of perhaps equal importance, few civic leaders stepped forward to make the case for city-run programs. Imperial officials from St. Petersburg further undermined local action when seen as pandering to groups long held to be in opposition to the regime. There was no broad consensus for action as there had been in the educational sphere. Municipal efforts to alleviate public health risks and improve housing conditions were too little, too late. Pragmatic pluralism failed. The result was festering neighborhoods that would prove themselves to be ideal breeding grounds for precisely the sort of political radicalism so feared by the tsarist regime.

DEFEAT AND REVOLT

The Russian state collapsed twice during the period under review. The first breakdown followed Russia's humiliating defeat at the hands of the Japanese in 1905. The second took place during even more punishing setbacks in World War I. The chaos unleashed by state implosion was national in scale, transcending local conditions. The suffering and degradation of Moscow's massive population of impoverished and disenfranchised peasant workers together with the deep alienation of the city's intellectuals and merchants from the imperial regime induced the simultaneous collapse of local government institutions. Health and housing conditions such as those described here cultivated thousands of shock troops for Russia's various radical and revolutionary causes. The Moscow of this study would be swept into oblivion by the maelstrom unleashed in 1917. The local aristocracy and merchant class ceased to exist; the city's idealist intelligentsia and irascible workers would face crucibles of their own making.

By the middle of World War I, Moscow politics, like that of the Empire as a whole, had turned into a series of binary choices. People were for the monarchy or enemies of it, for the "people" or against the "people," for or against this or that class or ethnic group. The middle ground in which pragmatic pluralism could thrive through a politics of compromise had given way to a new psychology: If you are not "for us," you are "against us." Such simple notions would lead to the extermination of thousands of Muscovites and millions of Russians in the decades ahead.

Organized labor was absent from local civic councils—thanks in large part to the obstinacy of imperial labor policies and the brutality of the tsarist police. Legal unions first appeared during the 1905 Revolution, although a number of underground labor organizations and revolutionary parties had existed previously.[82] The diversity of the city's economy led to an assortment of trade unions. Unions tended to align themselves with ideologically based political parties, conforming more to European patterns than to those of organized labor in the United States.

Moscow unions emerged from the strike movement of October–November 1905, growing to number more than 100 with more than 30,000 members by the time of the December uprising several weeks later.[83] Radical labor movements peaked in Moscow at this time. Disturbances had broken out in a number of Russian cities and towns throughout 1905 as a reaction to the privations brought on by Russia's defeat. The situation deteriorated steadily after troops had fired on Father Georgii Gapon's peaceful demonstrators in St. Petersburg's Palace Square on January 22, 1905, a day that would forever be known as "Bloody Sunday."

Strikes and demonstrations took on political meaning as the imperial government lost control over its own subjects. Revolutionary unrest focused on St. Petersburg, but soon spread to Moscow and elsewhere in the empire. Social and political groups of all hues sought advantage from the resulting chaos, with hardly any element of Russian society managing to avoid turmoil and upheaval.[84]

The eight-hour October 20, 1905, funeral procession for the slain revolutionary Nikolai Bauman through Moscow's streets attracted between 30,000 (the government estimate) and 150,000 marchers (the estimate of some labor leaders).[85] Bauman had been shot and beaten to death by workers sympathetic to the right-wing Black Hundreds. The confrontation among pro-government forces, right-wing nationalists, constitutional liberals, and radical revolutionaries gained momentum throughout

---

[82] Victoria Bonnell, "Radical Politics and Organized Labor in Pre-Revolutionary Moscow, 1905–1914," *Journal of Social History* 12, no. 2 (1979), pp. 282–300: 282.

[83] Ibid., p. 284.

[84] On the role of Moscow teachers in the local union movement, for example, see Christine Ruane, *Gender, Class, and the Professionalization of Russian City Teachers, 1860–1914* (Pittsburgh: University of Pittsburgh Press, 1994), pp. 128–63.

[85] Abraham Ascher, *The Revolution of 1905*, Vol. 1: *Russia in Disarray* (Stanford: Stanford University Press, 1988), pp. 262–64.

the fall. Both sides moved inexorably toward a test of strength in December, a trial that would take place in the streets of Moscow.[86]

The city had been relatively peaceful, with a smaller percentage of its workers on strike than was the case in the capital. St. Petersburg's larger plants, especially in heavy industry, were more union-oriented than the smaller, family-run textile mills in Moscow. No revolutionary *"soviet"* (council) had been formed in the city until late November, though universities and high schools had long been centers of unrest. Some 340,000 Moscow workers went on strike as the year was coming to an end. Moscow's radical left moved to seek advantage during the waning weeks of 1905, with the army, police, and roving bands of right-wing thugs responding. The left lost a series of pitched battles; according to some estimates more than a thousand Muscovites lost their lives.[87] Local authorities subsequently launched brutal retaliations, arresting workers and students and carrying out executions without formal trial. Only a few of Moscow's largest unions survived such retribution.[88]

Moscow union organizers moved quickly to take advantage of the March 4, 1906, regulations legalizing labor and employer associations. Sixty-three unions acquired legal status in Moscow over the next fifteen months, with more than 50,000 workers joining labor unions during this time. The unions became actively involved in electoral politics and began to seek advantage in expanded municipal elections. The movement suffered crippling setbacks, however, following the "Stolypin coup" of June 3, 1907 (when Prime Minister Petr Stolypin forced the dissolution of the Duma and secured new parliamentary elections under far more restrictive voting laws).[89] Union membership fell to some 20,000 in Moscow. Local unions would remain weak until after the April 1912 massacre of striking workers at the Lena gold fields, an event that sparked another wave of labor radicalism throughout the Russian Empire.

Tsar Nicholas II and his ministers were able to reassert their authority through compromise with liberal-minded reformers. A number of changes made in Russia's political organization held out the promise of genuine democratization. Local government was made stronger and more vigorous, labor laws were strengthened, employer associations were formed, university curricula liberalized, and political parties were authorized to participate in national parliamentary elections. Russia

---

[86] Ibid., pp. 304–22.   [87] Ibid., p. 322.
[88] Bonnell, "Radical Politics," pp. 284–85.
[89] Abraham Ascher, *The Revolution of 1905*, Vol. 2: *Authority Restored* (Stanford: Stanford University Press, 1992), pp. 355–68.

emerged from its social upheavals with a set of political and social institutions well along an evolutionary path to a more European model.
Autocracy was on the run. Nicholas nevertheless refused to view his compromises as more than tactical maneuvering once he regained political
strength. He moved with renewed confidence to undercut many newly
established institutions—most importantly, the Duma.[90] The Stolypin
coup of June 3, 1907, cleared the way for the autocratic state to steadily
reassert its power.

1917

Russia's ruinous defeats in World War I shattered the regime's under-
pinnings once and for all. Popular patience ran out early in 1917 when
hungry workers took to the streets of St. Petersburg. Palace guards were
unwilling to fire yet again on civilian demonstrators. Nicholas was forced
to abdicate on March 15, 1917, ending more than three centuries of
Romanov rule. No one picked up his crown. A constitutional Provisional
Government initially led by Prince George Lvov, and later by Aleksandr
Kerensky, assumed power. The war continued, privation grew more
severe, and radical political movements sought advantage.

Moscow initially remained tranquil during the spring of 1917, especially in comparison to St. Petersburg. Prior to March, as Diane Koenker
has argued, strikes had been overt political acts directed against the government as much as or more than mere actions against factory management.[91] After the fall of the tsar, a strike was merely a strike.

Labor-management relations nonetheless continued to deteriorate
throughout the year. Koenker calculates that at least 269 strike actions
involving over 257,000 workers occurred between March and October.[92]
Yet, to return momentarily to Georg Leidenberger's work on Chicago's
transit wars, Moscow's post-February strikes no longer represented confrontations over fundamentally different conceptions of democracy and
the state.[93] They were, more simply, battles over money. Fundamental
disagreements over values were being converted into a range of disputes revolving around wages and shop-floor management practices.
Moscow's strikers throughout 1917 tended to be highly paid, urban-born
workers from large factories, in search of material gain.

[90] An argument forcefully developed in ibid.
[91] Koenker, *Moscow Workers,* p. 293.   [92] Ibid., p. 295.
[93] Georg Leidenberger, "Working-Class Progressivism and the Politics of Transportation
in Chicago, 1895–1907" (Ph.D. diss., University of North Carolina, 1995), pp. 165–99.

Nicholas's abdication thus initially opened the way for a reemergence of Moscow's propensity for pragmatic solutions to pressing problems. The number of strikes taking place in the city peaked in May; the number of workers actually on strike in any month rose steadily until July, when labor disputes began to recede once more.[94] Broader political concerns were being pushed aside as summer arrived. Developments elsewhere in Russia, especially in St. Petersburg, were less recuperative. Various political factions continued their contest for power, as radical parties initially cast aside by the naming of the Provisional Government sought an appropriate moment to seize the day.

The inability of Moscow's municipal officials to address the social ills described in this chapter contributed to the growing tensions among the city's various social groups. As Ron Suny has argued, Russia's deepening social cleavage heightened fear and suspicion, hope and despair.[95] Social polarization intensified class hostility, which underscored a perception of irreconcilability on all sides. This radicalization brought about by events outside as well as within Moscow eroded opportunity for the practice of pragmatic pluralism within the city. The radicalization of city life and of Russian society at large converted a wide menu of political options into the binary choices of revolution.

Moscow's Bolsheviks had remained more moderate than their comrades in St. Petersburg. They reluctantly moved to support the new revolutionary regime in the capital.[96] The Moscow Soviet established a Military Revolutionary Committee on October 25 to defend themselves against the Committee of Public Safety representing forces aligned with many in the city Duma. Both sides negotiated, seeking to avoid confrontation even as street skirmishes began to erupt on October 27. Bolshevik leader Viktor Nogin was arrested on October 28 as he left Soviet headquarters for a negotiating session. Anti-Bolshevik forces hunkered down in the Kremlin while the Military Revolutionary Committee armed for combat. Forces loyal to Lenin took the Kremlin at 4 in the afternoon on November 3, after hours of heavy fighting. Although no precise figures are available, the Bolsheviks claimed to have lost at least a thousand men in the Moscow fighting. Their opponents undoubtedly suffered even higher casualties.

---

[94] Koenker, *Moscow Workers*, pp. 296–98.
[95] Ronald Grigor Suny, "Toward a Social History of the October Revolution," *American Historical Review* 88, no. 1 (February 1983), pp. 31–52: 49.
[96] This account is based on Koenker, *Moscow Workers*, pp. 332–55.

The October violence did not halt plans for the election of the national Constituent Assembly. Voting was set in the capital for November 12, and for November 19–21 in Moscow. Polling took place elsewhere throughout the second half of November. Moscow workers, who largely had stayed away from the barricades on November 3, went to the polls in large numbers to vote for their assembly delegates. The agrarian-based Socialist Revolutionaries, who would win the national vote, won less than 8 percent of the vote in Moscow. The Bolsheviks polled 47 percent of the ballots cast in Moscow, while the liberal Kadets gained 35 percent of the Moscow tally.

Ballot boxes mattered little. Armed Bolsheviks simply closed down the Constituent Assembly as it gathered in St. Petersburg's Tauride Palace on January 5, 1918, sending home those deputies who had guilelessly tried to convene their duly elected parliament. The Bolsheviks would control Russia's commanding heights from that point forward despite a fiercely fought civil war and years of endemic unrest.

Lenin fled St. Petersburg in early 1918, moving his capital to Moscow in order to gain distance from the various international expeditionary forces that were coming to the aid of his opponents. The vibrant merchant Moscow that had grown inexorably during the years following the 1861 Great Reforms expired as Lenin stepped onto the platforms of Moscow's Nicholas Station on March 11, 1918.

10

Poverty and Riots

By the early years of the twentieth century Osakans understood that industrial capitalism was accompanied by a seemingly irrevocable breach between those who owned factories and those who worked in their factories. This rift became increasingly contentious despite a seemingly relentless increase in aggregate income and consumption levels throughout Japan.[1] Many Japanese viewed industrial patterns of human relations with consternation even as they simultaneously consumed wealth on a scale never before seen, generated by the very same industrialization process.

Such concerns were justified as an inability to confront growing social inequality erupted in unprecedented street violence throughout Japan during the summer of 1918. For Osaka, that summer's "rice riots" mark a moment in which opposing sides lost sight of their rivals' basic human dignity. The use of violence on both sides marked the end of a long process of political accommodation. The rice riots helped set the stage in Osaka—as well as in Japan as a whole—for right-wing authoritarian rule at home and expansionist militarism abroad. Institutions and codes of political conduct predicated on a plurality of interests failed to hold the center ground at the national level, undercutting a local political culture of pragmatic pluralism in Osaka.

The Japanese discovery of urban poverty had taken place a generation or so earlier, when journalists and intellectuals "descended into the ghettoes of Japan's major cities partly to verify the social consequences of capitalist development . . . and partly to gain a more complete picture

---

[1] Alan H. Gleason, "Economic Growth and Consumption in Japan," in William W. Lockwood, ed., *The State and Economic Enterprise in Japan: Essays in the Political Economy of Growth* (Princeton: Princeton University Press, 1965), pp. 391–444.

of the type of society that was unfolding in Japan."[2] Poor city-dwellers had struggled in Japan prior to the Meiji industrial revolution. An 1870 survey of Osaka, for example, identified 18 percent of the city's population—nearly 57,000 residents—as poor.[3] But poverty among able-bodied, adult males—be they displaced samurai, rural migrants, or the working poor of Osaka's growing factories—represented something new and seemingly non-Japanese.

THE SOCIAL ROOTS OF POVERTY

The notion that chronic poverty has social roots that lie in the destructive consequences of structural change rather than in individual moral deficiencies emerged in Japan only in the 1880s and 1890s with pathbreaking accounts by investigative journalists such as Hara Kei, unrelenting social activism by Christian and Buddhist social reformers such as Abe Isoo, and paternalistic interventionism by agile bureaucrats such as Goto Shimpei.[4] David Howell noted in his study of the Hokkaido fishing industry that "life under capitalism is not necessarily better and not necessarily worse, but it is necessarily different."[5] The new reliance on cash and contractual bonds, Meiji Japan's initial romanticism about and celebration of relentless market rationality, and an unprecedented freedom to ignore the wishes of elders shocked many Japanese.

Urban industrial poverty presented a moral enigma as well as an economic problem. "The endogenous dependency that prevailed in precapitalist villages throughout Japan," Howell writes, "while hardly static, was nevertheless in place for many generations. As a result, a kind of moral economy had evolved to regulate human interaction. The social equilibrium thereby engendered could not, however, survive the emergence of capitalism because it could not compensate for the exploitative mechanism inherent in capitalist relations of production."[6] The search for a new moral as well as economic equilibrium in labor relations would continue throughout the period under review.

---

[2] Koji Taira, "Urban Poverty, Ragpickers, and the 'Ants' Villa' in Tokyo," *Economic Development and Cultural Change* 17, no. 2 (January 1969), pp. 155–77: 156.

[3] W. Dean Kinzley, "Japan's Discovery of Poverty: Changing Views of Poverty and Social Welfare in the Nineteenth Century," *Journal of Asian History* 22, no. 1 (1988), pp. 1–24: 4.

[4] Kinzley, "Japan's Discovery"; Taira, "Urban Poverty."

[5] David L. Howell, *Capitalism from Within: Economy, Society, and the State in a Japanese Fishery* (Berkeley: University of California Press, 1995), p. 6.

[6] Ibid., p. 8.

31. Slums in Osaka. Photographer unknown, n.d. Osaka City Government and Yuhikaku Publishing Company.

Jeffrey Hanes succinctly captures Osaka's grim indigence in his study of reform mayor Seki Hajime. "Industrial laborers bore the brunt of unchecked urban expansion," Hanes wrote, "as they crowded into tenement neighborhoods lacking even the most basic amenities. Indoor plumbing, sewers, dampproofing, ventilation, and sunlight were the exception rather than the rule on the outskirts of Osaka. Tuberculosis was rife among slum residents, and cholera epidemics were a fact of life (and death). Deprived of parks, playgrounds, and adequate transportation, the slumdweller was a virtual prisoner of the urban blight which daily intensified at Osaka's ragged edge."[7]

Trade unions and radical labor movements grew in scale and scope; capitalist factory owners responded with union-busting intent. The process was hardly linear; social reformers enjoyed some success during the late 1890s and again two decades later during World War I.[8] Desperately poor factory workers, with little education and often feeling resented and ostracized in a social order clinging to agrarian norms of

[7] Jeffrey Eldon Hanes, "Seki Hajime and the Making of Modern Osaka" (Ph.D. diss., University of California, Berkeley, 1988), pp. 1–2.
[8] Andrew Gordon, *The Evolution of Labor Relations in Japan: Heavy Industry, 1853–1955* (Cambridge, Mass.: Harvard University Press, 1985), pp. 47–50.

the past, were easy prey for rapacious managers. They were described even by sympathetic observers such as future Communist Katayama Sen as "a hard-drinking, fighting, gambling type with no care for saving for the future."[9] Advancement, to the extent it was possible, was a consequence of switching employers rather than movement up through the ranks. Turnover was high, class consciousness low, and the state ever ready to resort to force and intimidation. This pattern of advance and retreat by management, labor, and state alike may be seen on the shop floors of Osaka.

Reformers began to look beyond the factory gates for solutions to the workers' desperate plight. Industrial laborers came to be viewed as part of a larger category of the working urban poor.[10] Labor disputes spread throughout Osaka and Japan during 1906.[11] That summer, at the nadir of an industrial downturn following the Russo-Japanese War, a protest by eight hundred workers who had just been laid off at the Osaka Military Arsenal ended when officers of the local constabulary escorted the newly unemployed to their homes.[12] All was not in order in proletarian neighborhoods once workers reached them. The plague broke out among the city's most tightly packed industrial districts, with 463 inhabitants of 103 warrenlike homes falling victim to the disease in July of that year.[13] Such conditions forced city officials to open Japan's first Municipal Hygienic Laboratory to promote the prevention of communicable diseases.[14]

THE OSAKA LABOR FORCE

The large number of dependent laborers on the Osaka labor market undercut worker demands. One-quarter of all workers in a 1901 survey of twenty-one industrial facilities around the city were under fourteen years of age.[15] Over half the workers in Osaka's celebrated textile plants were minors from poor families; a majority of the young female laborers in match factories were between ten and fifteen years old.

---

[9] Katayama offered this observation in 1897, as summarized in ibid., p. 29.

[10] Ibid., pp. 26–27.

[11] Takeo Yazaki, *Social Change and the City in Japan: From Earliest Times through the Industrial Revolution* (Tokyo: Japan Publications, 1968), p. 408.

[12] "The Osaka Military Arsenal: Dismissal of Workers and the Consequence," *Japan Weekly Chronicle* (Kobe), July 12, 1906, p. 48.

[13] "Factory Life in Japan: The Treatment of Operatives," *Japan Weekly Chronicle*, August 2, 1906, p. 152.

[14] *Great Osaka: A Glimpse of the Industrial City* (Osaka: Osaka Shiyakusho, 1925), pp. 16–17.

[15] Yazaki, *Social Change*, p. 407.

Though extreme, one could find six- and seven-year-olds working in match factories.[16] Overall, 80 percent of the city's textile workers were women, many from struggling tenant-farm households in impoverished rural villages, others from slum districts within the great industrial metropolis itself.[17] A system of "free lodging" in plant dormitories made some workers even less willing to risk "losing all" in an unsuccessful strike.[18]

Shibusawa Eiichi's 10,500-spindle Osaka Cotton Spinning Company, which opened in 1882, set the pace for textile labor relations throughout the city and the nation. Shibusawa drew on his contacts from an earlier tour of duty at the Imperial Ministry of Finance to raise an enormous sum—250,000 yen—in private capital to back his venture.[19] Guaranteeing his stockholders lavish profits, Shibusawa intended to produce high-quality cloth for the international market at low Japanese wages. Shibusawa drew on a seemingly bottomless labor pool of dispossessed farmers—especially the daughters of such farmers.[20]

Women constituted 62 percent of Japan's factory labor force in 1909.[21] Their dominant presence is, in part, an artifact of the commanding role of textile manufacturing in the nation's overall industrial economy.[22] The textile industry employed 61.2 percent of all industrial workers that year, with food and beverage manufacturing in a distant second place at 11.2 percent.[23] The share of factory employment in textiles would drop to a still preeminent 55.6 percent in 1920 as a consequence of the rapid increase in metal and machinery manufacturing.[24]

Female textile workers were difficult to unionize. Often younger than twenty, unmarried, intending to work for only a short period before mar-

---

[16] Ibid.
[17] E. Patricia Tsurumi, *Factory Girls: Women in the Thread Mills of Meiji Japan* (Princeton: Princeton University Press, 1990), pp. 5, 42.
[18] Yazaki, *Social Change*, p. 407.   [19] Tsurumi, *Factory Girls*, pp. 39–45.
[20] For a discussion of the Osaka textile industry's labor force over time, see Gary R. Saxonhouse, "Productivity Change and Labor Absorption in Japanese Cotton Spinning, 1891–1935," *Quarterly Journal of Economics* 16, no. 2 (May 1977), pp. 195–219.
[21] Hiroshi Hazama, "Historical Changes in the Life Style of Industrial Workers," in Hugh Patrick, ed., with the assistance of Larry Meissner, *Japanese Industrialization and Its Social Consequences* (Berkeley: University of California Press, 1976), pp. 21–51: 29.
[22] Gary R. Saxonhouse, "Country Girls and Communication among Competitors in the Japanese Cotton-Spinning Industry," in Patrick, ed., *Japanese Industrialization*, pp. 97–125.
[23] Robert E. Cole and Ken'ichi Tominaga, "Japan's Changing Occupational Structure and Its Significance," in Patrick, ed., *Japanese Industrialization*, pp. 53–96: 59.
[24] Metal and machinery workers moved into second place in terms of the number of workers employed by 1920, constituting 17.2 percent of the manufacturing workforce. This new labor force was primarily male. Ibid.

rying, Osaka's "factory girls" were far from their rural homes, usually living in company dormitories.[25] Nearly half remained at their job for less than a year in 1897, and over 95 percent would switch jobs, marry, or enter prostitution before five years were out. This number would fall off slightly by 1918, when nearly 11 percent of cotton textile workers remained at their workstations for five years or more.[26] These patterns— which were extreme by international standards of the period—persisted into the 1920s despite management's ever more paternalistic welfare practices.[27]

Japan's textile "factory girls" should not be portrayed "merely as the victims of exploitation."[28] Many—like their counterparts long before in other textile centers such as Lowell, Massachusetts, and Moscow— viewed their jobs as opportunities for personal improvement. Personal autonomy for female workers was growing, especially in the later Taisho era following World War I. Some women mill workers in Osaka and elsewhere actively pursued better working and living conditions, higher wages, and greater personal freedom on Japan's shop floors. They were nonetheless largely untouched by mainstream unionism, especially during the initial years of Meiji-era industrialization. The predominance of young women workers in Osaka's largest factories benefited mill owners, who purposefully sought out the most vulnerable employees whenever possible.

Shibusawa, for example, initially chose Osaka as the site for his mill in order to maximize recruitment from the impoverished Kansai countryside. Japanese farmers were increasingly being driven off the land, with the land area cultivated by tenant farmers growing from just 30 percent of total cultivated land in 1868 to over 45 percent in 1913.[29] This was particularly the case in the Kansai region.

Shibusawa's complex wage-grade classification, harrowing night shifts, and insatiable demand for poorly paid, unskilled laborers undercut traditional Japanese notions of mutual obligations between employers and employees. Shibusawa's management techniques brought both modern accounting and stock dividends as well as late-nineteenth-century labor relations to the new industrial heart of Osaka. Osaka Cotton

---

[25] Hazama, "Historical Changes," p. 29.   [26] Saxonhouse, "Country Girls," p. 101.
[27] Ibid., pp. 102–6.
[28] A point made in Barbara Molony, "Activism among Women in the Taisho Cotton Textile Industry," in Gail Lee Bernstein, ed., *Recreating Japanese Women, 1600–1945* (Berkeley: University of California Press, 1991), pp. 217–38.
[29] Thomas R. H. Havens, *Farm and Nation in Modern Japan: Agrarian Nationalism, 1870–1940* (Princeton: Princeton University Press, 1974), p. 35.

Spinning attracted a poor, proto-proletariat to the city, and the underlying social base of a European-style labor movement. Shibusawa and his plant helped to make "the Manchester of the Far East" possible.

STRIKES AND UNIONS

The power balance in Osakan industrial relations shifted from year to year. Workers increasingly turned to the strike as a weapon in improving their living conditions. The Osaka Guild of Cereal Dealers acceded to laborer demands for higher salaries in August 1907.[30] The Kwan Steamship Union successfully bargained for a 20 percent increase in shipyard wages that same summer, with workers at nearby freight switching yards quickly following suit.[31] Two thousand Osaka printers went on strike for higher wages in Osaka at about the same time,[32] while another two thousand hat- and cap-industry laborers walked out in late September.[33] Strikes erupted with greater frequency throughout Japan and especially in Osaka during 1907.[34] Yet the pendulum would swing back in favor of the owners once more. By year's end the owners of the Horigoshi Printing Works closed their plant rather than meet their workers' demand for a 30 percent wage increase.[35]

Strikes continued into mid-1908 before the market completed its cycle and turned in the owners' direction.[36] A slumping economy in 1909 assisted those employers who wanted to reduce their workforces.[37] And so it went, strikes and lockouts, settlements and layoffs, the normal fare of capitalist industrial relations—except that in Japan in general and Osaka in particular, reformers and labor activists began to look for solutions well beyond the factory gates.

[30] "The Labour Question in Japan: More Dissatisfied Miners: Osaka Coolies Demand Higher Wages," *Japan Weekly Chronicle*, August 1, 1907, p. 137.

[31] "The Labour Question in Japan: Another Strike: Increase of Wages at Osaka," *Japan Weekly Chronicle*, September 5, 1907, p. 303.

[32] "The Labour Question in Japan: More Strikes," *Japan Weekly Chronicle*, September 19, 1907, p. 370.

[33] "Labour Troubles in Japan: Big Strike at Osaka," *Japan Weekly Chronicle*, 26 September 1907 p. 405.

[34] "The Labour Question in Japan: Growing Frequency of Strikes," *Japan Weekly Chronicle*, September 12, 1907, p. 332.

[35] "The Labour Question in Japan: More Demands for Increased Wages in Osaka," *Japan Weekly Chronicle*, December 5, 1907, p. 729.

[36] "Labour Troubles in Osaka: Ferry-Boat Men on Strike," *Japan Weekly Chronicle*, May 28, 1907, p. 673; "The Labour Question: Strike in Osaka," *Japan Weekly Chronicle*, June 25, 1908, p. 812.

[37] "Unemployed Mercantile Officers and Seamen: Serious Situation in Osaka," *Japan Weekly Chronicle*, March 25, 1909, p. 475.

Labor reformers such as Seki Hajime and Fukuda Tokuzo were lobbying for national labor law reform at the very time the above strikes were taking place in Osaka.[38] Caught in the middle between laissez-faire ideologues and rapacious industrialists, advocates of industrial reform became ever more forthright in their demands for safety regulations, shorter working hours, and higher wages.[39]

Anti-urban agrarian idealists joined the fray, arguing that Japan's culture and its workers could be preserved only by an exodus back to the countryside.[40] Typical of many societies undergoing the transition from village agriculture to urban industry, agrarianism emerged throughout the Meiji era as an alternative vision to the increasingly "modern" world of the city. *Nohonshugi*, or "agriculture-as-the-essence-ism," offered an alternative vision of the new Japan. Thomas R. H. Havens reports that radicals and reactionaries, officials and farmers, soldiers and civilians, utopians and pragmatists, city dwellers and rural residents would all be drawn at various times to *Nohonshugi* ideology until World War II.[41] This movement, Havens continues, resonated with particular salience among post–World War I bureaucrats.[42]

Labor reformers, facing attack from such a variety of quarters, began to view what happened to workers at home as being as much a part of the overall labor problem as what happened to workers at the plant. Most of the hallmarks of the paternalistic Japanese industrial system would reach maturity during the 1920s and 1930s. Strategies to reduce labor turnover, undermine union authority, and increase productivity through managerial initiatives aimed at treating the worker as a total human being first emerged during the period under investigation.[43] As the country's leading industrial city, Osaka was at the center of such efforts.

Industrial workers, as has been noted, had become something of social outcasts in Meiji Japan, as they did not fit neatly into the four major status groups of the Tokugawa era—samurai, peasants, artisans, and merchants.[44] The product of social fragmentation and economic upheaval, factory workers personified the dramatic transformation of the Meiji era.[45] Their very existence fostered anxiety. Workers, in response

---

[38] Hanes, "Seki Hajime," pp. 164–65.   [39] Ibid., pp. 166–90.

[40] Henry D. Smith II, "Tokyo as an Idea: An Exploration of Japanese Urban Thought until 1945," *Journal of Japanese Studies* 4, no. 1 (winter 1978), pp. 58–59.

[41] Havens, *Farm and Nation*, pp. 1–10.   [42] Ibid., p. 9.

[43] T[homas] C. Smith, "The Right to Benevolence: Dignity and Japanese Workers, 1890–1920," *Comparative Studies in Society and History* 26, no. 4 (October 1984), pp. 587–613.

[44] Ibid., pp. 589–90.   [45] Tsurumi, *Factory Girls*, pp. 105–6.

to rejection, demanded higher status and improved treatment not merely to satisfy economic needs—which were considerable—but also to establish their worth as human beings.[46] Industrial disputes became not merely battles between labor and capital, but rather struggles among Japanese on the fringe of society with their culture's primary status groups.[47] Labor reformers and activists sought more than higher wages and better worker conditions. They demanded recognition of workers as full members of Japanese society. The social programs run by municipal officials for proletarian neighborhoods were critical components of a labor relations strategy that did not end at the shop floor.

THE CASE AGAINST LAISSEZ-FAIRE

Prominent intellectuals and bureaucrats—initially in Tokyo but followed quickly in other cities such as Osaka—debated precisely how Japanese capitalism might differ from what they were seeing in the West.[48] Some leading politicians, such as Taisho-era premier Okuma Shigenobu, resisted laissez-faire approaches to economic development.[49] Important scholars and opinion-makers, such as Kyoto University Sinologist and Osaka polemicist Naito Konan, argued strongly that there was a distinct East Asian approach to development that transcended Western-style social relations.[50] Influential groups such as the Social Policy Association (*Shakai Seisaku Gakkai*) argued that responsible social policies not only could reconcile groups at odds with one another, but must also distinguish Japan from the laissez-faire capitalism of the West.[51] Japan could

---

[46] This observation is repeated with increasing conviction by Thomas C. Smith in his various studies of Japanese industrialization. See, for example, Smith, "The Right to Benevolence," pp. 549–95; Thomas C. Smith, "Japan's Aristocratic Revolution," *Yale Review* 50 (Spring 1961), pp. 370–83; and Thomas C. Smith, *Native Sources of Japanese Industrialization, 1750–1920* (Berkeley: University of California Press, 1988), pp. 236–70.

[47] Smith, "The Right to Benevolence," p. 597.

[48] Kenneth B. Pyle, "The Technology of Japanese Nationalism: The Local Improvement Movement, 1900–1918," *Journal of Asian Studies* 33, no. 1 (November 1973), pp. 51–66.

[49] Joyce C. Lebra, *Okuma Shigenobu: Statesman of Japan* (Canberra: Australian National University Press, 1973), pp. 137–40.

[50] For further discussion of Naito Konan's views, see Joshua A. Fogel, *Politics and Sinology: The Case of Naito Konan (1866–1934)* (Cambridge, Mass.: Harvard University Press, 1984).

[51] Pyle, "The Technology of Japanese Nationalism," p. 54. These issues arose quite early during the Meiji transformation. See, for example, the discussion of early parliamentary debates concerning poverty in R. H. P. Mason, "The Debate on Poor Relief, 1890," in Andrew Fraser, R. H. P. Mason, and Philip Mitchell, *Japan's Early Parliaments, 1890–1905: Structure, Issues, and Trends* (London: Routledge, 1995), pp. 67–90.

chart its own path by devising policies that would moderate social differentiation.[52] These sentiments were related to a broader effort within Japanese intellectual circles to establish a historical sense related to but distinct from the development of Europe.[53] They mark a distinct turn in Japanese thinking over the decade that begins about 1885 away from mere imitation of the West toward a definition of Japanese uniqueness that nonetheless enabled Japan to compete successfully on the world stage.

Kenneth B. Pyle captured this transformation in his study of generational change during precisely this period. "Somewhere in the terrain of the late 1880s and early 1890s," Pyle wrote in 1969, "lies a major watershed in Modern Japanese history. On one side lies a Japan occupied with domestic reform; a curious, self-critical, uncertain Japan, a Japan still in the making. . . . On the other side lies a Japan with a renewed sense of order and discipline in her national life; a Japan less tractable, less hospitable to social reform, less tolerant to new values . . . above all, a Japan with a heightened sense of her own unity and exclusiveness."[54]

Many Japanese intellectuals and central bureaucrats had been attracted to German thinking about economic development for some time.[55] Returning to Japan in 1890 after four years of study in Germany, the popular Tokyo Imperial University professor Kanai Noburu maintained ever more forcefully that the nation was an organism in which no segment could be permitted to remain diseased.[56] Goto Shimpei—who would serve as civilian governor of Taiwan, president of the South Manchurian Railway Company, foreign minister, and mayor of Tokyo—was similarly influenced by his time in Berlin as a young Japanese Home Ministry bureaucrat.[57] Goto and his compatriots were drawn to the

[52] For a stimulating discussion of how the modernizer's demand for improved working conditions can be transformed into a plea for national particularity, even superiority, see R. P. Dore, "The Modernizer as a Special Case: Japanese Factory Legislation, 1882–1911," *Comparative Studies in Society and History* 11, no. 4 (October 1969), pp. 433–50.

[53] This theme is elaborated further in Stefan Tanaka, *Japan's Orient: Rendering Pasts into History* (Berkeley: University of California Press, 1993).

[54] Kenneth B. Pyle, *The New Generation in Meiji Japan: Problems of Cultural Identity, 1885–1895* (Stanford: Stanford University Press, 1969), p. 188.

[55] This point is underscored in, among many places, Nobutaka Ike, *The Beginnings of Political Democracy in Japan* (Baltimore: Johns Hopkins University Press, 1950), pp. 115–18.

[56] Sally Ann Hastings, *Neighborhood and Nation in Tokyo, 1905–1937* (Pittsburgh: University of Pittsburgh Press, 1995), pp. 22–23.

[57] Yukiko Hayase, "The Career of Goto Shimpei: Japan's Statesman of Research, 1857–1929" (Ph.D. diss., Florida State University, 1974), pp. 20–24; Kinzley, "Japan's Discovery of Poverty," pp. 18–19.

anti-laissez-faire inclinations of the German Historical School. Such views found immediate resonance among Japanese thinkers who were terrified by the specter of industry-induced social revolution. German openness to state intervention and discussion of morality in economic development found a ready audience in Japan.[58]

LOCAL IMPROVEMENT MOVEMENTS

Anti-laissez-faire attitudes naturally fed into efforts to foster political community at the local level. Tensions caused by the postwar recession in 1907 contributed to a sense of urgency among those who counseled social reconciliation.[59] The resulting Local Improvement Movement (*Chiho Kairyo Undo*) shifted the weight of response to industrial inequality from employers to governments and urban philanthropic groups. The 1911 law governing factory labor relations pointed in the same direction.[60] It would not be long before the "municipal socialist" ideals circulating in the West would find an audience in Japan in general, and in Osaka in particular.

Advocates of the Local Improvement Movement remained ambivalent toward the city as a social form. Reformers who viewed the metropolis as an integral part of the Japanese future took the additional step of urging their fellow citizens not to shun urban growth. Alleviate suffering in the city itself, they demanded. For such activists, labor reform, social reform, and urban reform became synonymous.[61]

By the early twentieth century, reformers were imploring the Japanese state to undertake a more energetic stance toward the problems of the cities.[62] Identifying with American and English activists of similar appellation, these "municipal socialists" (*toshi shakaishugisha*) opposed central government intervention into urban life even as they advocated greater public involvement in alleviating the ills of the industrial town.[63]

Katayama Sen and Abe Isoo, among many theorists, vigorously advocated shifting responsibility for reform to the local level.[64] They were

---

[58] Kenneth B. Pyle, "Advantages of Fellowship: German Economics and Japanese Bureaucrats, 1890–1925," *Journal of Japanese Studies* 1, no. 1 (Autumn 1974), pp. 127–64.
[59] Pyle, "The Technology of Japanese Nationalism," pp. 55–57.
[60] Ibid.   [61] Hanes, "Seki Hajime," pp. 186–90.
[62] Such activism was apparent in Japanese colonial administration as well, as evidenced by Goto Shimpei's performance as civilian governor of Taiwan and as president of the South Manchurian Railway Company. Hayase, "The Career of Goto Shimpei," pp. 40–128.
[63] This discussion is based on Hanes, "Seki Hajime," pp. 208–33.
[64] For a more contemporary account of Katayama and Abe's role—among those of many participants—in these discussions, see A. Morgan Young, *Japan in Recent Years, 1912–1926* (New York: William Morrow, 1929), pp. 48–69.

following a philosophical path that would lead from Christianity through "municipal socialism" to more radical forms of socialism—and, in the case of Katayama, eventually to a leadership position in the Communist International in Moscow (and burial in the Kremlin wall).[65]

Katayama and Abe asserted that the city is where citizens actually live out their lives. Katayama and Abe continued that municipal management should seek to benefit a city's citizenry in its entirety.[66] This goal could be achieved by the transfer of authority to local government units and by an accompanying shift to municipal ownership of utilities and transportation facilities.[67] Reform strategies, they proposed, would lead to an improvement in the provision of basic human services.[68] In this regard, Katayama and Abe sounded very much like Chicago's Mayor Edward F. Dunne. They were playing a slightly different game, however. To draw on a distinction made by John Boyer between German and Austrian municipalization models during the same era, Dunne and his fellow Chicagoans, like their German counterparts, were primarily in pursuit of social reform.[69] In Osaka, as in Vienna, "municipal socialists" were at least as interested in promoting municipalization as a means for protecting local communities from state intervention by central authorities.

Katayama was both representative of reform intellectuals of his era and something of a rebel. The son of poor peasants from Okayama in southwestern Japan, his organizing activities led him into exile in the United States, Mexico, and, eventually, the Soviet Union.[70] "A pioneer in the social movement, a founder of professional social work, and a leader in the early trade union movement," Katayama was also the editor of Japan's first labor newspaper and Japan's first Bolshevik.[71] Katayama joined the Communist International's Executive Committee while residing in Moscow and played a principal role in the establishment of the

---

[65] For an important discussion of the role Christian social thought played in the early intellectual development of both men, see Irwin Scheiner, *Christian Converts and Social Protest in Meiji Japan* (Berkeley: University of California Press, 1970), pp. 243–47.

[66] Ibid., p. 210.

[67] Ibid., pp. 211–12. Municipal ownership of trams became a particularly contentious issue, as it had in Chicago. See, for example, "Electric Municipalisation in Osaka: Some Curious Manoeuvres," *Japan Weekly Chronicle*, July 17, 1913, p. 127; "Electric Municipalisation in Osaka: The Scheme Rejected," *Japan Weekly Chronicle*, July 24, 1913, p. 169; and "Osaka Electric Supply: Municipalisation Scheme Rejected," *Japan Weekly Chronicle*, July 31, 1913, p. 195.

[68] Hanes, "Seki Hajime," pp. 212–13.

[69] John W. Boyer, *Political Radicalism in Late Imperial Vienna: Origins of the Christian Social Movement, 1848–1897* (Chicago: University of Chicago Press, 1981), pp. 420–21.

[70] Michiko Sawada, *Tokyo Life, New York Dreams: Urban Japanese Visions of America, 1890–1924* (Berkeley: University of California Press, 1996), pp. 126–40.

[71] Hyman Kublin, *Asian Revolutionary: The Life of Sen Katayama* (Princeton: Princeton University Press, 1964), p. ix.

Japanese Communist Party in 1922.[72] His increasing radicalism was driven in part by the failure of Japanese authorities to respond to industrial labor as anything other than a social menace.

Katayama became an outspoken advocate of "municipal socialism" during the early years of the twentieth century. Having studied Christian theology at Yale University, Katayama returned home and was soon publishing a number of articles on municipal self-management in Europe and the United States.[73] He wrote compassionately about the need to place communal values above narrow economic considerations.[74] "The city must not only be a place of trade and gain," he observed, "an arena of the embittered struggle between free competitors. From the place of the fight for profit, such as it is now, the city must be transformed into a place of the flourishing of trade and industry, a place of joy where there will be a more full acceptance of the most recent achievements of culture and the entire urban population will be able to conduct peaceful lives in conditions of fulfillment and tranquility."[75]

Katayama was based primarily in Tokyo while in Japan, but was frequently forced into exile in the United States. He traveled extensively around the United States (spending significant time in Chicago), speaking, writing, studying, working as a day laborer, and even managing several-hundred-acre rice farms in Texas.[76] Katayama gained notoriety with his leadership of Tokyo's 1911 streetcar strike, which marked the turning point in labor conflict from small local affairs to major social and political events. He remained in close contact with Osaka socialists, such as Oi Kentaro (publisher of the city's first labor paper, the *Osaka Weekly*), and "Comrade" Morichika (publisher of the socialist-leaning *Osaka Heimin*).[77] For Katayama, like many Tokyoites, Osaka was "the most conservative city in Japan."[78]

Abe, for his part, was a prominent convert to Protestant Christianity and an advocate of socialist-oriented reform.[79] A professor at Waseda

---

[72] Katayama Sen, *Vospominaniia* [translation of a Japanese text] (Moscow: Nauka, 1964), pp. 3–5.

[73] Smith, "Tokyo as an Idea," p. 60.

[74] Shiro Sugihara, "Economists in Journalism: Liberalism, Nationalism, and Their Variants," in Chuhei Sugiyama and Hiroshi Mizuta, eds., *Enlightenment and Beyond: Political Economy Comes to Japan* (Tokyo: University of Tokyo Press, 1988), pp. 237–53: 252–53.

[75] Katayama, *Vospominaniia*, pp. 440–43.   [76] Sawada, *Tokyo Life*, pp. 126–40.

[77] Katayama, *The Labor Movement in Japan* (Chicago: Charles H. Kerr, 1918), pp. 54–55, 129–32.

[78] Ibid., p. 131.

[79] Scheiner, *Christian Converts*, pp. 188–93; Sawada, *Tokyo Life*, pp. 99–101.

University and widely known as the "father of Japanese baseball," Abe had been introduced to Western municipal governance while studying theology in the United States.[80] He went further than Katayama by advocating public ownership of all urban land.[81] For Abe, cities were like homes and needed to be governed by the same principles as was family life. It was not sufficient to generate income to have a suitable home. Rather, health, convenience, livability, and congenial relations with one's neighbors all contributed to domestic bliss. Abe contended that hierarchical, semi-"feudal" notions of authority must be replaced by "enterprise-based" authority (*taijigyo kankei*) that would promote loyalty through equality.[82] Solutions to urban problems could be found, Abe argued, by thinking of the enterprise and the city as a home.[83]

Japanese municipal socialists tried to develop a "moderate utilitarian approach" to urban problems with "a reliance on proven Western techniques."[84] As in the United States, the idealism of the municipal socialist agenda frequently ran afoul of pragmatic politics.[85] Home Ministry bureaucrats in Tokyo attempted to appropriate the reform agenda for their own purposes.[86]

Unlike in the United States, they also ran counter to more radical forces on the left, such as those led by social activist Kotoku Shusui, that pursued more intellectual and elitist approaches to Japan's emerging capitalism.[87] Nonetheless, even the leading Japanese Marxist Kawakami Hajime arrived at his most radical stances only after flirtations with Confucian, Buddhist, and Christian thought, German historicism, and Anglo-American social reformism.[88]

In the end, the municipal socialists left a rich legacy of urban research in their wake by couching many of their arguments in the new idiom of social science.[89] Reform programs and institutions implemented by

---

[80] Hastings, *Neighborhood and Nation*, p. 182; Smith, "Tokyo as an Idea," p. 60.

[81] Smith, "Tokyo as an Idea," p. 60.   [82] Smith, *Native Sources*, p. 260.

[83] Hanes, "Seki Hajime," pp. 214–15.   [84] Smith, "Tokyo as an Idea," p. 59.

[85] Hanes, "Seki Hajime," pp. 215–17.   [86] Ibid., pp. 219–22.

[87] Kotoku—who would be executed in January 1911 for the crime of high treason as a consequence of his pacifist activities—juxtaposed "materialistic" radicalism to the "Christian humanism of men like Katayama Sen." For further discussion of the internecine conflicts within the Japanese left of the period, see F. G. Notehelfer, *Kotoku Shusui: Portrait of a Japanese Radical* (Cambridge, U.K.: Cambridge University Press, 1971), pp. 93–105.

[88] Gail Lee Bernstein's admirable intellectual biography of Kawakami demonstrates the power of such conflicting trends in Japanese social thought at the beginning of this century. See Gail Lee Bernstein, *Japanese Marxist: A Portrait of Kawakami Hajime, 1879–1946* (Cambridge, Mass.: Harvard University Press, 1976).

[89] As did reforming bureaucrats such as Goto Shimpei. Hanes, "Seki Hajime," pp. 222–33; Hayase, "The Career of Goto Shimpei," pp. 179–99.

Osakans in particular sought to make the municipality the central focus of efforts to alleviate social suffering.

Municipal socialists and reformers such as Seki Hajime came to view planning as essential for nurturing livable cities by combining the best ideas and programs from within Japan and from the West.[90] Japanese thinkers were drawn to French aesthetics, British social policies, German eclecticism, and American pragmatism, together with local traditional notions of social relations and obligations. Class conflict became viewed as an obstacle to economic progress. The reformers did not wish to inhibit private enterprise so much as they wanted to enhance its effectiveness by adding considerations beyond profit to the bottom line.

Recognizing the weakness of available entrepreneurial talent and resources, some reform thinkers—such as Seki Hajime for example—advocated the establishment of limited liability corporations, thereby liberating factory owners from the constraints of traditional personalistic financing schema. He argued that social safety nets were important to factory owner and worker alike. He observed that industrial materialists should not be permitted merely to maximize profit for personal gain. State regulation should secure public benefit from private investment, thereby assuring more balanced capitalist development than was found in the laissez-faire West.[91] Factory owners should be subject to greater regulation because they had the upper hand in their relations with workers. Success, for Seki, could not be reduced to quantitative measures, for a community's "moral economy" transcended bookkeeping accounts.[92]

Reformers looked to industrialists to reach beyond selfish gain, and to municipalities to help factory owners achieve social goals. Social stability became a more important goal than profit maximization.[93] Local autonomy became an essential ingredient for bringing about the reformers' agenda.[94]

MUNICIPAL SOCIAL ACTIVISM

Efforts to transcend profit orientations through philanthropic and municipal activism began in Osaka before the reformer Seki Hajime arrived in 1914 to begin his term as the city's deputy mayor. Municipal

[90] This discussion is based on Hanes, "Seki Hajime," pp. 9, 96–110, 131–33, 161, and 231–39.
[91] Ibid., pp. 96–110.   [92] Ibid., pp. 131–32.
[93] Ibid., p. 161.   [94] Ibid., pp. 233–39.

programs encouraged charitable undertakings, such as relief to the poor, free medical treatment to those in need, and the education of foundlings and orphans.[95] By 1915, the city had 1,585 sanitary associations, voluntary groups working under municipal direction to reduce the incidence of contagious disease.[96] Such groups frequently coordinated their efforts with the Municipal Hygienic Laboratory, which had been established in 1906.[97]

Seki's arrival in the city added greater impulse to local efforts to alleviate the ills suffered by the proletariat. For Seki, these concerns were paramount even before the 1918 rice riots made social services "a matter of political necessity."[98] He was attracted to Osaka by the opportunity to "administer a prophylactic to the social illnesses of industrial Japan."[99] He made social reform one of his top priorities as deputy mayor.

Osaka established its Municipal Industrial Research Laboratory in 1916 with funds provided by the emperor.[100] The laboratory conducted various technical studies designed to guide manufacturers toward more effective and humane labor policies. It immediately initiated a number of living-standard surveys that would become a model for all similar Japanese research.[101]

Consonant though they may have been with the philosophies of urban planners and municipal socialists, Osaka's initiatives hardly made a dent in the plight of the city's poor. Income was distributed unevenly, with the fluctuation of prices and wages creating new winners and losers throughout Japanese society.[102] Industrial pay was low and remained that way despite Japan's World War I boom.[103] In the end, municipal officials—no matter how well intentioned—could not change the underlying structural realities of Japan's industrial development.

"Japanese labor," wrote Osaka's British consul general Oswald White in 1920, "is usually summed up as being cheap in price and poor in

[95] *Present-Day Osaka* (Osaka: Osaka Shiyakusho, 1915), pp. 8–10.
[96] Ibid., p. 11.
[97] *An Outline of Municipal Administration of the City of Osaka* (Osaka: Osaka Shiyakusho, 1930), p. 14.
[98] Hanes, "Seki Hajime," p. 11.   [99] Ibid., p. 128.
[100] *An Outline of Municipal Administration*, pp. 33–34.
[101] Oswald White, *Report on Japanese Labor* (London: His Majesty's Stationary Office, 1920).
[102] W. Mark Fruin, *Kikkoman: Company, Clan, and Community* (Cambridge, Mass.: Harvard University Press, 1983), pp. 67–68.
[103] *Report of Labor Research*, Series X: *Cost of Living among Laborers in Osaka Japan* (Osaka: Municipal Bureau of Labor Research of Osaka, 1921); Young, *Japan in Recent Times*, pp. 110–19.

quality and, as a rough generalization, this judgement may be accepted."[104] Drawing on the work of the Osaka Municipal Industrial Research Laboratory, White noted that Japanese manufacturers favored labor-intensive methods of production, which, although wasteful of resources, demanded lower capital investment than new technologies and machinery. Laborers worked long hours—ten to twelve hours per shift, on average—with very few days off—perhaps two to four days a month.[105] Child and female labor predominated in several industries, especially spinning and weaving plants, where some 100,000 "girls" were employed by Osakan industrialists.[106] Taxes on consumer staples placed a disproportionate burden on the poor as well.[107] In a highly competitive and capital-starved economy such as Japan's, labor received low wages, suffered poor living conditions, and reacted accordingly. "At the same time," White added, "the development of industry and trade in Japan adds to the wealth of the country, and all classes benefit, even if disproportionately so that it would be a mistake to regard the working class as standing still."[108]

The economic boom of World War I exposed the fallacies of reformers who had believed that municipal and philanthropic intervention could sufficiently alleviate the suffering of the Osaka poor. The Japanese elite generally sensed that a crisis was growing, feared social disintegration, and was drawn to responses predicated on national mobilization and suppression rather than reform.[109] Foreigners also noticed these trends. White observed, for example, that "the pay received in various industries has increased steadily year by year; during the war it nearly doubled. . . . Unfortunately, prices have risen too as the salaried worker finds to his cost. In fact, there is little doubt that in Japan prices have risen first and wages after."[110]

White's U.S. counterparts similarly reported back to Washington that labor problems were on the horizon. An unidentified American diplomat cabled home that

wages have been inconceivably low. . . . As long as the articles which the workmen produced were mostly sold in Japan, and the food which they consumed was produced at home, there was an economic balance between the two, which enabled the laborer to maintain his family without real suffering, although

---

[104] White, *Report on Japanese Labor*, p. 5.
[105] Ibid., p. 12.   [106] Ibid., p. 11.
[107] Ibid., p. 13.   [108] Ibid., p. 5.
[109] Kenneth B. Pyle, *The Making of Modern Japan* (Lexington, Mass.: D. C. Heath, 1978), pp. 124–27.
[110] White, *Report on Japanese Labor*, p. 13.

with the strictest economy. The result of the war was, however, to raise prices in Japan, as well as elsewhere, to a great extent but the employers retained the advance in price and declined to raise wages to any great extent. At the same time, other countries bought in Japan, rice, beans, oil and other foods, thus raising the cost of living, while incomes of the workers remained nearly stationary.[111]

The result, the American concluded, would be widespread social unrest.

The U.S. government's emissary reported further, in language that echoed that of the Japanese municipal socialists, that industrial conflict was becoming an urban problem. Recounting a visit to the Osaka spinning mills, the diplomat continued: "A little quiet investigation developed the fact that part, at least, of the trouble is due to insufficient food and improper living quarters. As very many girls are recruited from distant farming districts, many of the factories board and lodge their female employees in dormitories inside the factory fences. . . . There are practically no amusements and the life consists only of hard, monotonous work, devoid even of rest and recreation. The male operatives live mostly in cheap lodging houses, covering whole blocks, absolutely destitute of all the conveniences and comforts of life, crowded into inadequate and unsanitary quarters."[112]

Osaka's approach to the consequent urban poverty was not only a case of "too little, too late"; its shortcomings underscored the reformers' collective failure to convince industrialists to manage their operations differently. They failed in part because pro-proletarian politicians and urban reformers largely spoke among themselves rather than reaching out to incorporate a wider range of Osakans into their discussion. As White's analysis makes clear, labor reform could have drawn on the enlightened self-interest of factory owners who would have benefited disproportionately from any improvement in the technological level of their operations.

RIOTING OVER RICE

The breakdown in pragmatic pluralism erupted into view in August 1918, when rioting left an unbridgeable divide between labor and capital, city and peasant, haves and have-nots that would traumatize

---

[111] "Present Economic Conditions," report by the U.S. Embassy, Tokyo, n.d. [probably late 1918], National Archives and Records Administration, Department of State General Records, Class 8, Country 94, Record Group 59.894.00, pp. 37–44: 38–39.
[112] Ibid., p. 42.

Japan for a generation. The riots, for example, strengthened an anti-capitalist drift within the Nohonshugi agrarianism movement in the countryside.[113] The rebellion against rising rice prices did not begin, nor did it end, in Osaka. But Osaka was especially traumatized, as the riots left little doubt that the anti-laissez-faire intellectuals were correct. Without more enlightened social policies, capitalist industrialization would lead to the breakdown of social order.

Rice riots were nothing new in Japan. Edo had experienced three major mutinies over Japan's most important foodstuff in the eighteenth century alone.[114] The 1918 riots nonetheless marked a major turning point in Japanese—and, especially, Osakan—social policy.

Osaka officials had been struggling to alleviate the suffering created by rising rice prices for some time. Municipal raids had sought to end price gouging as early as September 1911, after which philanthropist Kimura Nisaburo joined the city in providing funds for five thousand destitute Osakans to purchase grain.[115] Families were forced from time to time to take their children out of school and put them to work in factories merely to earn money to purchase rice.[116] As late as March 1918, city officials were trying to establish municipal-run farmers' markets to drive down food and vegetable prices through competition.[117] By mid-August, a quarter-million Osakans nonetheless took to the streets, rioting, looting, and generally battling the police and the military, all as a consequence of high rice prices.[118]

The story began on the evening of July 22, 1918, far away in a small fishing village on the coast of Toyama Bay, where housewives who had

---

[113] Havens, *Farm and Nation*, pp. 9–10.

[114] Anne Walthall, "Edo Riots," in James L. McClain, John M. Merriman, and Kaoru Ugawa, eds., *Edo and Paris: Urban Life and the State in the Early Modern Era* (Ithaca: Cornell University Press, 1994), pp. 407–28. A number of rural disturbances occurred during the 1880s that, although not rice riots per se, similarly displayed desperation and impoverishment. See, for example, Roger W. Bowen, *Rebellion and Democracy in Meiji Japan: A Study of Commoners in the Popular Rights Movement* (Berkeley: University of California Press, 1980).

[115] "Raid on Osaka Rice-Brokers: Breaking Up the 'Bull' Ring," *Japan Weekly Chronicle*, September 7, 1911, p. 415; "An Osaka Philanthropist: Free Rice for the Poor: Proposed Municipal Grant to the Destitute," *Japan Weekly Chronicle*, September 14, 1911, p. 461.

[116] "The High Price of Rice: Effect on School Attendance in Osaka," *Japan Weekly Chronicle*, March 14, 1912, p. 487.

[117] "The High Price of Rice: Effect on School Attendance in Osaka," *Japan Weekly Chronicle*, March 7, 1918; "Public Markets in Osaka: Successful Experiments," *Japan Weekly Chronicle*, July 4, 1918, p. 19.

[118] "The Riots in Osaka: Police Reinforced by Military," *Japan Weekly Chronicle*, August 18, 1918, p. 251; "Casualties and Arrests in Osaka," *Japan Weekly Chronicle*, August 29, 1918, p. 297.

gathered for a cool evening's socializing grew angrier and angrier over the spiraling cost of rice.[119] The U.S. Embassy in Tokyo was already reporting that real hunger could be found in the country and, further, that "violence and bloodshed were the inevitable results of the failure of the Government to devise adequate measures of relief."[120]

Over the course of the next eight weeks, these initially peaceful meetings would lead to demonstrations and armed clashes from Hokkaido to Kyushu, in villages, rural hamlets, and major metropolitan centers alike. The riots have come to be viewed as "no more than ephemeral events" despite their enormous scale and unprecedented reach.[121] Rice prices hardly fell, central and local authorities re-established their control over society, and more than five thousand convicted rioters quietly served their sentences with "barely a murmur of dissent."[122] Riots, it seems, do not fit neatly into consensus-oriented historiography on Japan.

Osaka experienced one of the most violent outbreaks of rioting of any locale. Initially, demonstration leaders in Osaka—as in Kyoto and Kobe—led their followers on visits to retail rice dealers to force them to lower prices.[123] "Riots started in Osaka at 8 o'clock P.M. on August 12th at the signal of a bell in one of the principal temples," American diplomats informed their superiors in Washington. "Ten groups of people went to different villages," the report continues, "took rice from the owners and carried it away in sacks and in wagons. The chief of police estimated the number of rioters at 150,000. There were 70,000 in one district alone. They offered stubborn resistance to the police and troops, but were finally scattered with considerable difficulty."[124]

The high degree of self-control evident during the demonstrations' initial days slowly eroded as attacks on and by police became more frequent. In Osaka and other cities, "crowds expanded their attacks beyond rice merchants to include other 'economic' enemies, such as residential landlords, pawnbrokers, loan sharks, and real estate agencies."[125] A spontaneously formed strike committee eventually gained a congenial

---

[119] Michael Lewis, *Rioters and Citizens: Mass Protest in Imperial Japan* (Berkeley: University of California Press, 1990), p. xvii.

[120] "Labor Unions," report by the U.S. Embassy, Tokyo, n.d. [probably late 1918], National Archives, Department of State General Records, Class 8, Country 94, Record Group 59.894.00, pp. 47–48.

[121] Lewis, *Rioters and Citizens*, p. xviii.   [122] Ibid., p. xvii.

[123] Ibid., p. 97–98.

[124] "Osaka Riots," report of the U.S. Embassy, Tokyo, n.d. [probably late 1918], National Archives, Department of State General Records, Class 8, Country 94, Record Group 59.894.00, p. 61.

[125] Lewis, *Rioters and Citizens*, pp. 104–5.

32. Rice riots, Osaka, 1918. Photographer unknown. *Asahi Shimbun.*

audience with Osaka's provincial governor Hayashi Ichizo and the city's mayor Ikegami Saburo, only to be arrested by central police authorities immediately following that meeting.[126]

Excesses followed. "In some cases," the U.S. Embassy in Tokyo dispatched word home, "the wealthy defended themselves by hiring bodies of guards, armed with fire arms, and by spraying sulphuric acid from hoses on the crowds. As might be expected, this action was bitterly resented by the crowds, which promptly endeavored to set fire to the buildings in which the rich merchants had taken refuge."[127] The practice of accommodation and inclusion that constitutes pragmatic politics is predicated on the recognition of the human value of people unlike oneself. The decision to spray a crowd with sulfuric acid marks a moment when this was no longer the case. The use of violence and violent responses to protest marks the end of a process of political

[126] Ibid., pp. 109–11.
[127] "The Rice Riots," report by the U.S. Embassy, Tokyo, n.d. [probably late 1918] National Archives, Department of State General Records, Class 8, Country 94, Record Group 59.894.00, pp. 54–56: 55.

accommodation. Not surprisingly, "the vengeful hatred of the lower classes towards the nobility" heightened with each day.[128]

"The resentment against these rice merchants," another diplomatic observer reported, "is naturally very great, not only among the poor and middle classes who are suffering from the shortage, but even among the small store keepers and rice retailers who see their stocks sold at half price, dumped in the street, while the real criminals, the stock market gamblers, quietly slip away in disguise or join the mob."[129]

As this account indicates, the riots were noteworthy for the characteristics of those who took to the streets. Rioters were seldom among the city's very poor, but rather were "family supporting men long employed in the traditional trades."[130] Such "middling" groups had been excluded from union movements on the one hand, and from wealthy merchant guilds on the other. Left to their own wits to survive the storm of unbridled capital accumulation, this local equivalent of what might today be called the lower middle class had been excluded from Osaka's politics of social fragmentation. They had never been the object of charity by self-proclaimed "municipal socialists" and urban reformers. Their broad participation in the riots demonstrates the failure of a local politics of pragmatic pluralism.

IN THE RIOTS' WAKE

A wave of repressive laws and rightist movements followed throughout Japan in the wake of the long hot summer of 1918.[131] These actions had the immediate effect of quieting mass action.[132] Not surprisingly, Osaka's labor movement made use of its new opportunities to further radicalize unionized workers.[133]

---

[128] This phrase was used by an unidentified U.S. diplomat in his reports back about the riots. "The Profiteers (The *Narikin*)," report by the U.S. Embassy, Tokyo, n.d. [probably late 1918], National Archives, Department of State General Records, Class 8, Country 94, Record Group 59.894.00, pp. 45–46: 45.

[129] "The Causes of the Rice Riots," report by the U.S. Embassy, Tokyo, n.d. [probably late 1918], National Archives, Department of State General Records, Class 8, Country 94, Record Group 59.894.00, pp. 49–53: 50.

[130] Lewis, *Rioters and Citizens*, pp. 117–24.

[131] Ibid., pp. 240–46.

[132] "Report," U.S. Embassy, Tokyo, September 6, 1918, National Archives, Department of State General Records, Class 9, Country 94, Record Group 59.894.50/5a, pp. 1–9.

[133] "Radicalism in Japanese Labour Unions: Restraining Influence of Mr. Kagawa: Moderation Unpopular," *Japan Weekly Chronicle*, October 21, 1920, p. 574; "The Socialist and Labour Movement in Japan: IV. The Rise of the Labour Unions," *Japan Weekly*

33. Vigilantes preparing to engage rioters, Osaka, 1918. Photographer unknown. *Asahi Shimbun.*

Another sort of reaction may have been more significant over the medium term. As Michael Lewis has noted, "[t]he riots contributed to the establishment of special divisions within prefectural governments concerned exclusively with social welfare. Osaka prefecture and Osaka city, which before the riots had established welfare agencies, took the lead in upgrading small government sections or subsections into full fledged divisions. Within a few years of the organization of Osaka city's Social Division, all of Japan's major cities had similar agencies."[134]

The rice riots marked a watershed in Japanese policies toward the poor.[135] Coming as they did so close to the Bolshevik Revolution, the 1918 riots broke through the consciousness of even the most hardened

Chronicle, December 2, 1920, p. 761; "The Socialist and Labour Movement in Japan: V. The Growing Power of the Labour Movement," *Japan Weekly Chronicle*, December 9, 1920, pp. 796–97; "The Socialist and Labour Movement in Japan: VIII. The Labour Movement—Recent Development," *Japan Weekly Chronicle*, December 30, 1920, pp. 898–900.

For an explicitly Marxist interpretation along similar lines, see Katayama Sen's 1933 article on the 1918 rice riots: "K 15-letiiu risovykh buntov 1918 goda v Iaponii," in Katayama Sen, *Sen Katayama. Stat'i i memuary (k stoletiiu so dnia rozhdeniia)* (Moscow: Izd. vostochnoi literatury, 1959), pp. 121–39.

[134] Lewis, *Rioters and Citizens*, p. 247.
[135] Masayoshi Chubachi and Koji Taira, "Poverty in Modern Japan: Perceptions and Realities," in Patrick, ed., *Japanese Industrialization*, pp. 391–437: 427.

reactionary.[136] Social welfare had been placed firmly on the Japanese policy agenda. The Japanese Home Ministry moved from merely encouraging the private sector to practice philanthropy to becoming actively engaged in the administration of assistance to the poor.[137] Osaka Prefecture led the way, with Governor Hayashi establishing Japan's first welfare committees in October 1918.[138]

Ogawa Shigejiro, a scholar who assisted Hayashi in this effort, argued that the committees—which had 527 members in 35 districts—were designed to both bring relief to the poor and supervise (e.g., exercise surveillance over) antisocial behavior. Sally Ann Hastings reports that Ogawa intended committee members to establish relationships with members of poor households, much as American probation officers worked with their ex-convict clients over time.[139] The committee member—almost always from the middle class—would follow a Confucian ideal, mentoring the poor as a parent would a child, an elder brother would a younger brother, a lord would his retainer, or a friend would a friend.

At the municipal level, spending on health and education programs increased markedly as city authorities strove to respond to social unrest. Public health expenditures had edged upward from 98,000 yen in fiscal year 1897 to 796,000 yen in 1907, and 931,000 yen a decade later.[140] Funding for health programs would then double by 1919, rising to 2,758,000 yen by fiscal year 1922, while city expenditures for education rose twenty-seven-fold between 1917 and 1922 as the city assumed new responsibilities from failing neighborhood school agencies.[141]

With a dozen years of hindsight, Osaka's city leaders would come to recognize that the "rice riots" in 1918 mark[ed] a turning point in social welfare work in Japan. It is true that even before then various forms of relief work were carried out by individual philanthropists or local public bodies, on a very small scale.

[136] Michael Weiner, *The Origins of the Korean Community in Japan, 1910–1923* (Atlantic Highlands, N.J.: Humanities Press International, 1989), p. 101.
[137] Hastings, *Neighborhood and Nation*, pp. 85–87.
[138] Ibid.   [139] Ibid., p. 87.
[140] Hotta Akio, "Shushi jijo to Shichosha no Kensetu," in Shinshu Osakashishi Hensei Iinkai, *Shinshu Osakashishi* (Osaka: Osaka City Government, 1994), Vol. 6, chp. 1, sec. 1, sub. 3, pp. 19–33: 28–29; Natao Toshimitsu, "Dai-gokai Naikoku Kangyo Hakurankai to Shisei," in Shinshu Osakashishi Hensei Iinkai, *Shinshu Osakashishi*, Vol. 6, chp. 1, sec. 2, sub. 1, pp. 34–48: 38–39; Natao Toshimitsu, "Senso to Gyozaisei," in Shinshu Osakashishi Hensei Iinkai, *Shinshu Osakashishi*, Vol. 6, chp. 1, sec. 2, sub. 2, pp. 48–63: 50–51; and Shibamura Atsuki, "Gyozaisei no Kozo Henka," in Shinshu Osakashishi Hensei Iinkai, *Shinshu Osakashishi*, Vol. 6, chp. 1, sec. 5, sub. 1, pp. 120–34: 128–29.
[141] Ibid.

But they were too inadequate, in their form and quality, to be called social welfare work in the modern sense of the word. To-day [in 1930], however, they are being pursued on a far larger scale than before, a considerable sum of money being spent annually, and keeping perfect unity with one another.[142]

Ironically, the rice riots combined with the emergence of Seki as Osaka's leading political figure to ensure the implementation of precisely those policies of inclusion that had failed prior to 1918. Seki would go on to become "the father of modern Osaka," and Osaka itself would launch what arguably became Japan's most ambitious program of municipally supported social services and social research.[143]

The last years prior to World War II may well have been Osaka's post-Tokugawa golden age. Local industrialists and merchants had come to realize that they could no longer win on every issue. Osaka's fragmented social groups would come to appreciate the power of the politics of pragmatic pluralism only after the period presently under review.

[142] *An Outline of Municipal Administration*, p. 41.
[143] A strong countercase can be made for Tokyo's having led the way, especially after the establishment of the Tokyo Institute of Municipal Research in 1922 during the administration of Goto Shimpei. The American political scientist Charles Beard played an important role in shaping that institute's initial research agenda. Hayase, "The Career of Goto Shimpei," pp. 179–99; and Charles A. Beard, *The Administration and Politics of Tokyo: A Survey and Opinions* (New York: Macmillan, 1923).

Part IV

Conclusion

11

+‍≻‍≺‍+ +‍≻‍≺‍+ +‍≻‍≺‍+ +‍≻‍≺‍+ +‍≻‍≺‍+ +‍≻‍≺‍+ +‍≻‍≺‍+ +‍≻‍≺‍+ +‍≻‍≺‍+

Successful Pragmatic Pluralists: The Practice of Politics without Hegemony

The preceding case studies highlight the effectiveness of political strategies based on the pragmatism and tolerance of metropolitan pluralism
in urban communities of spectacular size, deep fragmentation, and rapid
transmutation. Failure, in turn, often rested on a desire to ride roughshod
over—or to merely ignore—various competing groups obstructing the
path to policy change. What is perhaps most striking is the fact that,
despite so many differences among these three cities, similar patterns
emerge.

Writing about American Progressivism, Richard L. McCormick
observed that Progressives owed much of their success "to a distinctive
method of reform, variations of which were adopted by the leaders of
nearly every cause. They typically began by organizing a voluntary association, investigating a problem, gathering relevant facts, and analyzing
them according to the precepts of one of the newer social sciences."[1]
Reformers in both Moscow and Osaka followed a similar prescription
for action, frequently citing German rather than American experience as
their operational model. Educators and health care activists in all three
cities under review relied heavily on social research to justify their causes.
Moscow's Old Believers often behaved in a manner remarkably similar
to that of Chicago's Protestants. More strikingly, successful municipal
leaders pursued quite comparable tactics based on bringing a plurality
of interests into line with their own positions.

Four commanding politicians from these three cities—Carter H.
Harrison, Sr., Carter H. Harrison, Jr., Nikolai Alekseev, and Seki
Hajime—personify such strategies of pragmatic pluralism in their com-

[1] Richard L. McCormick, "Public Life in Industrial America, 1877–1917," in Eric Foner,
   ed., *The New American History* (Philadelphia: Temple University Press, 1990), pp.
   93–117: 107.

munities. Different in personality and national culture, in training and social status, these four leaders successfully sought practical solutions to pressing problems within the context of enormous, deeply divided, and rapidly changing industrial cities at the height of their capitalist explosion. They succeeded at a time when many of their rivals and contemporaries failed. Their careers reveal similar commitments to compromise, pragmatism, and moderate reform despite markedly different backgrounds. These similarities and differences combine to reveal some of the strengths and weaknesses of political strategies seeking pragmatic and pluralistic solutions to urban problems.

THE HARRISONS

Writing in 1929 about his experiences in local politics, University of Chicago political scientist, Chicago alderman, and sometime mayoral candidate Charles E. Merriam observed that his hometown had managed to avoid the excesses of American municipal corruption between 1879 and 1915 thanks in large measure to the leadership of Carter H. Harrison, Jr. and Sr.[2] Both Harrisons pursued the politics of inclusion while holding back the worst indulgences of a corrupt city council.[3] The elder Harrison found that "his most loyal adherents belonged to classes of society which were not represented in his parlor."[4] Harrison the younger professed that his "sympathies have always been with the underdog,"[5] a feeling that in part explains his close association with such infamous ward-heelers as Michael "Hinky Dink" Kenna and "Bathhouse" John Coughlin.[6]

The origins of the Harrison family brought both Carter Harrisons into close contact with very different communities and people, and their political styles emerged from this contact. The Carter Harrisons were descen-

---

[2] Charles E. Merriam, *Chicago: A More Intimate View of Urban Politics* (New York: Macmillan, 1929), pp. 19–21, 190–92.

[3] For an informative discussion of the practice of "boodling," whereby local alderman sold public franchises for their own gain, see Lloyd Wendt and Herman Kogan, *Bosses in Lusty Chicago: The Story of Bathhouse John and Hinky Dink* (1943; reprint, Bloomington: Indiana University Press, 1967), pp. 34–35.

[4] Claudius O. Johnson, *Carter Henry Harrison I: Political Leader* (Chicago: University of Chicago Press, 1928), p. 185.

[5] Carter H. Harrison, [Jr.,] *Stormy Years: The Autobiography of Carter H. Harrison, Five Times Mayor of Chicago* (Indianapolis: Bobbs-Merrill, 1935), p. 51.

[6] Kenna and Coughlin are the subject of Wendt and Kogan's classic study, *Bosses in Lusty Chicago*. On the subject of the connection between saloons and politics in urban America at the turn of the last century, see Perry R. Duis, *The Saloon: Public Drinking in Chicago and Boston, 1880–1920* (Urbana: University of Illinois Press, 1983), pp. 114–42.

dants of the Harrison and King Carter families of Virginia, who had dominated Tidewater society from early in the seventeenth century. The Harrison side of their lineage furnished many leaders of Colonial Virginia as well as "a signer of the Declaration of Independence, two presidents, mayors of Chicago for a generation."[7] Moving west to Kentucky, the elder Carter's parents became prominent members of Lexington society.[8] Carter himself graduated from Yale (class of 1845) and studied law at Lexington's Transylvania University. The elder Harrison managed to bring "to his pioneer heritage," as his son would write, "from two years in the Latin Quarter of Paris continental ways and ideas, and a liberal attitude toward what is termed necessary evils, such as alcohol, gambling, prostitution."[9] Harrison eventually moved to Chicago via St. Louis, a transfer prompted in part by what the younger Carter would call his father's "natural bent of opposition to the idea of slavery."[10] Carter Senior settled with a number of other Kentuckians in a semirural corner of the growing city, earning a more than modest income from his real estate dealings.[11] There, in a community near what would eventually become Union Park, Harrison and his neighbors lived "a staid, proper, socially active life within their homes. These homes were immune from the ills of the city; the miseries of the poor did not disturb the view from the bay windows of the mansions or town houses, nor were the signs of commerce present in any noxious form."[12]

Drawn into politics by the debacle of the Great Fire in 1871, Carter Henry Harrison, Sr., eventually became the first professional politician to occupy Chicago's City Hall.[13] He initially served for three years as a county commissioner on Republican Joseph Medill's "fireproof ticket," followed by a stint in Congress as a Democrat, before getting himself elected as mayor for the first time in 1879.[14] His early connection with Medill seems somewhat paradoxical in retrospect, as *Chicago*

[7] Johnson, *Carter Henry Harrison I*, pp. 3–6.
[8] For a brief biographical sketch of Carter Henry Harrison, Sr., see Donald L. Miller, *City of the Century: The Epic of Chicago and the Making of America* (New York: Simon and Schuster, 1996), pp. 439–40.
[9] Carter H. Harrison, Jr., *Growing Up With Chicago* (Chicago: Ralph Fletcher Seymour, 1944), p. 259.
[10] Harrison, *The Stormy Years*, p. 17.
[11] Harrison, *Growing Up With Chicago*, p. 11.
[12] Richard Sennett, *Families against the City: Middle Class Homes of Industrial Chicago, 1872–1890* (Cambridge, Mass.: Harvard University Press, 1970), p. 22.
[13] A point made by Paul Michael Green in "The Chicago Democratic Party, 1840–1920: From Factionalism to Political Organization" (Ph.D. diss., University of Chicago, 1975), p. 1.
[14] Johnson, *Carter Henry Harrison I*, pp. 62–71.

Tribune editor and publisher Medill would pummel Harrison later on in the mayor's career. Medill, like many of the city's Protestant elite, accused Harrison of appealing to the worst elements of Chicago society: anarchists, socialists, saloon and brothel keepers, and unsavory ward bosses. Medill remained Harrison's personal friend despite the former's censure for the future mayor's youthful support of the Democratic ticket in the historic election of 1860.[15] Harrison's magnetism, wit, generosity, courage, and vitality could win over even his most ardent political antagonists. Commenting on Harrison's career immediately following the mayor's 1893 assassination, Medill told a reporter from the *Los Angeles Times* that Harrison "was the most remarkable man—and I believe that will be the popular verdict—that our city has ever produced."[16]

Harrison was a consummate politician who proved to be particularly favored among immigrant groups, with whom he overtly identified despite his own Anglo-Saxon lineage.[17] The elder Harrison, as Paul Kleppner has noted, "was attuned to ethnic group sensitivities, and his ability to campaign in several languages evoked a strong bond of psychological rapport between him and some ethnic groups that usually gave only lukewarm support to Democratic candidates."[18] Harrison is said to have personified Chicago's "freewheeling, optimising spirit of individualism."[19] His social tolerance certainly "reflected the strange tolerance of a city that put the pragmatic ethics of the marketplace ahead of any need to express the ethnic, religious, and racial hatreds they assuredly held."[20] Put differently, Harrison believed that the moral standards of a New England village were unenforceable in cosmopolitan Chicago.[21]

[15] Miller, *City of the Century*, pp. 437–39.

[16] Ibid., p. 437.

[17] Green, "The Chicago Democratic Party," pp. 37–44. Edward Herbert Mazur reports that Harrison was particularly favored by poor Jewish immigrants because he could "be counted on to prevent the blue-nosed Protestants and Reform Jews who celebrated the Sunday Sabbath from imposing their narrow views on ghetto dwellers." Edward Herbert Mazur, "Minyans for a Prairie City: The Politics of Chicago Jewry, 1850–1940" (Ph.D. diss., University of Chicago, 1974), p. 99.

[18] Paul Kleppner, *Chicago Divided: The Making of a Black Mayor* (DeKalb: Northern Illinois University Press, 1985), p. 22.

[19] R. Reid Badger, *The Great America Fair: The World's Columbian Exposition and American Culture* (Chicago: Nelson-Hall, 1979), p. 89.

[20] Bill Granger and Lori Granger, *Lords of the Last Machine: The Story of Politics in Chicago* (New York: Random House, 1987), p. 28.

[21] A point underscored by his friend Willis John Abbott in a postassassination biography of the martyred mayor. Willis John Abbott, *Carter Henry Harrison: A Memoir* (New York: Dodd, Mead, 1895), pp. 235–41.

34. Carter H. Harrison, Sr. Photographer unknown, n.d. Library of Congress, Prints and Photographs Division, LC-BH826-2686.

Harrison's first mayoral inaugural address on April 28, 1879, made clear that his support from immigrants would in no way imperil the interests of his old business partners. "Real estate, the foundation of wealth, which furnishes four-fifths of the city's revenues, has been laid under a heavy load of taxation," he declared. "This stifles energy," he continued, "detracts investments and will, unless checked, dry up these sources of revenue."[22]

Rather than becoming merely the favorite of the less well off, the genteel Harrison was a benefactor of real estate and business interests as well. Harrison may well not have seen any contradiction in his diverse political support. "It was as an urban imperialist, not as a social reformer," Donald L. Miller comments, "that Carter Harrison believed he could be of greatest assistance to the average Chicago workingman."[23] Promoter of the business community's economic interests, Harrison also protected and tolerated the gambling, drinking, and womanizing of the local immigrant working class.[24] His formula for governing embraced unapologetic use of the spoils system yet ensured that qualified people were appointed to positions of real responsibility. "While holding on to his working-class support, he won over hesitant businessmen—'silk-stocking' Democrats and some Republicans—with his record of economy and efficiency in the administration of municipal funds and by promoting improvements in the downtown area that merchants and real estate dealers like Owen Aldis considered essential."[25] Harrison was, in the lingo of the late twentieth century, a social liberal and fiscal conservative.

Harrison met electoral defeat in 1887, a failure due in part to a previous unsuccessful gubernatorial bid as well as to his alleged liberality in dealing with socialists and anarchists following the Haymarket bombing.[26] Harrison left the city government on a sound financial basis.[27] He quickly departed on a round-the-world tour, returning triumphantly to Chicago two years later. His popular account of that journey, *A Race with the Sun,* revealed the elder Harrison to be a discerning observer and a talented writer.[28]

[22] Alfred Theodore Andreas, *History of Chicago* (Chicago: A. T. Andreas, 1884–86), Vol. 3, p. 856.

[23] Miller, *City of the Century*, p. 444.   [24] Ibid., p. 448.

[25] Ibid., p. 441.

[26] Abbott, *Carter Henry Harrison*, pp. 139–44. Harrison had been at Haymarket Square earlier in the afternoon and, judging the crowd orderly, had departed prior to the bombing. For a succinct account of these events, see Ray Ginger, *Age of Excess: The United States from 1877 to 1914*, 2d ed. (New York: Macmillan, 1975), pp. 59–60; as well as Ray Ginger, *Altgeld's America: The Lincoln Idea versus Changing Realities* (1958; reprint, New York: Markus Wiener, 1986), pp. 42–48. The perhaps definitive account of the Haymarket affair is found in Paul Avrich, *The Haymarket Tragedy* (Princeton: Princeton University Press, 1984).

[27] Frederick Rex, *The Mayors of the City of Chicago, from March 4, 1837, to April 13, 1933* (Chicago: Chicago Municipal Reference Library, 1947), pp. 65–69.

[28] Carter H. Harrison, [Sr.,] *A Race with the Sun* (New York: G. P. Putnam; Chicago: W. E. Dibble, 1889).

Of interest for this particular study, Carter Senior visited both Osaka and Moscow on his global jaunt. His description of Osaka from October 17, 1887, is combined with an overview of Tokyo and Kyoto, all three of which he concluded "are great hives of people, and bewilder one who rides or walks through them. Each has its castle or central palace, each has great temples, and densely populated, narrow streets."[29] His week in Moscow commanded considerably more attention in his diary, with an entry dated June 12, 1888, noting that "there is probably no city in Christendom laid out with more absolute irregularity than Moscow."[30]

Harrison ran for mayor again as a rogue Democrat in 1891, only to be narrowly defeated in a multicandidate race. He regained office in 1893 just in time to host the World's Columbian Exposition.[31] Carter Senior "frankly asserted his right to be mayor of the city in its greatest hour."[32] He presided over the fair with grace. Impresario Sol Bloom found Harrison to be "an ideal mayor during the fair. As a welcomer of visiting royalty and other distinguished guests no other man could have equaled him. He personified Chicago to all important strangers, and his contributions to favorable publicity could hardly be overestimated."[33]

The elder Harrison fell to an assassin's bullet on the last day of the exposition's last full week, after having returned home following his appearance at the "American Cities Day" ceremonies on October 28, 1893.[34] He had been in fine form that day, declaring that Chicago "never could conceive what it would not attempt, and yet has found nothing that it could not achieve."[35] Such braggadocio typified a man who "bore his sixty-eight years with the lightness of a lad of twenty."[36] Having just announced his impending marriage, Harrison declared that he intended to live for almost another half-century, while his audience appeared to forget "that this man was already within two years of the Scriptural limit

[29] Ibid., p. 78.   [30] Ibid., p. 387.
[31] Abbott, *Carter Henry Harrison*, pp. 190–98; Miller, *City of the Century*, pp. 482–87.
[32] Wendt and Kogan, *Bosses in Lusty Chicago*, p. 59.
[33] Sol Bloom, *The Autobiography of Sol Bloom* (New York: G. P. Putnam, 1948), p. 132.
[34] For further discussion of the elder Harrison, see Johnson, *Carter Henry Harrison I*. For the story of his October 28, 1893, assassination at the Harrison house by disappointed office-seeker Patrick Eugene Prendergast, see Abbott, *Carter Henry Harrison*, pp. 225–35; Carl S. Smith, *Urban Disorder and the Shape of Belief: The Great Chicago Fire, the Haymarket Bomb, and the Model Town of Pullman* (Chicago: University of Chicago Press, 1995), pp. 266–68; Badger, *The Great America Fair*, p. 129; and Edward R. Kantowicz, "Carter H. Harrison II: The Politics of Balance," in Paul M. Green and Melvin G. Holli, eds., *The Mayors: The Chicago Political Tradition* (Carbondale: Southern Illinois University Press, 1987), p. 19.
[35] Abbott, *Carter Henry Harrison*, p. 232.   [36] Ibid., p. 226.

of three-score years and ten."[37] His funeral—and its purposeful procession from City Hall to the Graceland Cemetery—turned into one of the city's grandest and most solemn events ever.[38]

"A lusty, prideful, imposing man, an urban expansionist who loved the diversity and drive of big-city life," Harrison personified his town.[39] Reform-minded and Roger Sullivan–supported Edward Dunne overcame whatever animosities he retained toward the Harrison clan when, in his 1933 memoirs, he observed that Carter H. Harrison, Sr., "was probably as able, progressive, and honorable a mayor as Chicago has ever had."[40] Most Chicagoans of the era would have concurred.

Writing more than six decades later, Donald L. Miller was more direct. Miller concludes

that no politician in Chicago history, with the possible exception of the elder Richard Daley, appealed to as broad a spectrum of the citizenry as Carter Harrison. Workers, including a good number of socialists, voted for him because he appointed union leaders as factory and health inspectors, supported labor's right to organize, strike, and demonstrate, and refused, on several occasions, to use police against strikers despite heavy pressure from powerful capitalists. . . . But many Republican businessmen with smaller operations and big investors in downtown real estate continued to back him because he remained committed to infrastructure improvements that fueled urban growth and rising real estate values, creating thousands of new jobs for people in all walks of life.[41]

Carter H. Harrison, Jr., enjoyed considerable electoral success on his own terms, despite being a rather different man than his father. The younger Carter was more thoughtful and less gregarious than his father, making him a less effective speaker. He shared his father's mastery of the details of city administration, however, always made himself available to the public, and never missed a City Council meeting during his five terms.[42]

Carter *fils* served as mayor between 1897 and 1905 and for another four years after defeating Republican reformer Merriam in 1911.[43] Professor Merriam had taken advantage of both Republican mayor Fred

---

[37] Ibid.   [38] Miller, *City of the Century*, pp. 434–37.
[39] Ibid., p. 437.
[40] Edward F. Dunne, *Illinois: The Heart of the Nation* (Chicago: Lewis Publishing, 1933), Vol. 2, p. 203.
[41] Miller, *City of the Century*, p. 444.
[42] Edward R. Kantowicz, *Polish-American Politics in Chicago, 1888–1940* (Chicago: University of Chicago Press, 1975), p. 72.
[43] For an account of the 1911 election, see Steven J. Diner, *A City and Its Universities: Public Policy in Chicago, 1892–1919* (Chapel Hill: University of North Carolina Press, 1980), pp. 154–75.

A. Busse's surprise decision not to seek re-election and a new Illinois law requiring nomination through primaries to mobilize Theodore Roosevelt Progressives, reform-minded businessmen—such as industrialist Charles R. Crane, newspaper magnate Victor F. Lawson, and Julius Rosenwald, president of Sears, Roebuck, and Company—disgruntled middle-class professionals in suburbanizing neighborhoods, and longstanding do-gooders such as Hull House's Jane Addams to snatch the Republican nomination away from party regulars.[44] Harrison, who had faced his own intraparty battles, retained his long-standing working-class base of electoral support. Supporters of West Side Republican boss and U.S. senator William Lorimer largely sat the election out, permitting Harrison to squeak by Merriam 177,923 votes to 160,791. The local Republican feuds would be played out a year later at the national level when party bosses denied Theodore Roosevelt their presidential nomination despite a string of primary victories. Roosevelt's consequent run as a Bull Moose guaranteed the defeat of Republican incumbent William Howard Taft, and the election of Democratic Progressive Woodrow Wilson.

A man of comfortable means, the younger Harrison was frequently photographed with his hands in his pockets, an image accompanied by the slogan "Chicago is fortunate in having a mayor who keeps his hands in his own pockets."[45] Whether his followers managed the same trick is a different story. As journalist Harold L. Ickes explained to the readers of his *Autobiography of a Curmudgeon,* the Harrison

> organization was dominated by Robert E. ("Bobby") Burke. Burke was built like a hogshead—as round and not much, if any, taller. He was secretary of the county committee, of which Tom Gahan was chairman and Fred Elred treasurer. Tom Carey, from "back of the yards", "Hinky Dink" Kenna, "Bathhouse" John Coughlin, Jimmy Quinn, and others of their stripe were prominent in the group. They were, believe me, cash-value realists. Politics was their living, their fortunes—yes, their very lives. . . . These wolves and jackals Mayor Harrison, generally speaking, permitted to roam unmolested in the highways and byways of the city to pick up anything that wasn't nailed down.[46]

Carter Junior, who had been educated for a while at a German *gymnasium,* ignored his father's entreaty to attend Yale. He chose instead to

---

[44] Michael P. McCarthy, "Prelude to Armageddon: Charles E. Merriam and the Chicago Mayoral Election of 1911," *Journal of the Illinois State Historical Society* 67, no. 5 (November 1974), pp. 505–18.

[45] Harrison, *The Stormy Years,* caption to photograph dated 1897 following p. 88.

[46] Harold L. Ickes, *The Autobiography of a Curmudgeon* (New York: Reynal and Hitchcock, 1943), p. 35.

remain in Chicago and study at Jesuit-run St. Ignatius College (later Loyola University).[47] The sporting life was not unknown to young Carter before he settled down in marriage to New Orleans socialite Edith Ogden.[48] His home at Ashland and Jackson Streets was long one of Chicago's centers of high society.[49]

The patrician younger Harrison managed, as had his father, to secure a firm political base in Chicago's ethnic communities.[50] He and his father also enjoyed considerable popularity among the city's growing African-American community.[51] Like his father, Carter Junior could not always convert his personal appeal into support for the Democratic Party; the Democrats held a majority in the City Council for only four of his twelve years as mayor.[52]

Harrison Junior's tolerance of cultural difference combined with a "judicious distribution of patronage" to win him support at the polls from a number of non-native groups.[53] Reminiscing in his eighty-fourth year about his ties to the likes of George "Red" Brennan and "Hinky Dink" Kenna, Harrison quite unapologetically explained that Chicago's ward leaders had remained loyal during the supreme traction battle with Charles Tyson Yerkes and never asked anything in return.[54] "The nostrils of a pink-livered reformer might well have lifted gingerly, with a supercilious sniff, when brought close to eighteenth ward political doings," Harrison wrote. "Hinky Dink and the Bath House had a way of handling their political chores, against which purists in politics at times have filed a more than casual protest."[55] However, Brennan and Kenna "always passed with me a coin of the realm, of honest worth and undebased fineness. This is a tribute I cannot pay to a lot of pretentious members of the so-called better classes, with whom I have rubbed elbows on my journey through life."[56]

"Hinky Dink and the Bath House" have passed into local lore as the quintessential Chicago rapscallions. Kenna and Coughlin were products

---

[47] Harrison, *The Stormy Years*, p. 26.
[48] Harrison, *Growing Up with Chicago*, pp. 56–76; Green, "The Chicago Democratic Party," pp. 74–78.
[49] John Drury, *Old Chicago Houses* (New York: Bonanza, 1941), pp. 157–202.
[50] Miller, *City of the Century*, pp. 441–46.
[51] Charles Branham, "Black Chicago: Accommodationist Politics before the Great Migration," in Melvin G. Holli and Peter d'A. Jones, eds., *Ethnic Chicago*, rev. ed. (Grand Rapids, Mich.: William B. Eeridmas, 1984), pp. 338–79: 376–77.
[52] Kleppner, *Chicago Divided*, p. 22.
[53] Mazur, "Minyans for a Prairie City," p. 139; Kantowicz, *Polish-American Politics*, pp. 57–85.
[54] Harrison, *Growing Up with Chicago*, p. 289.
[55] Ibid., p. 213.   [56] Ibid., pp. 211–12.

35. Carter H. Harrison, Jr., 1911. Moffett Co. Library of Congress, Prints and Photographs Division, Biographical File.

of Chicago's notorious Levee vice district, where they held forth as purveyors of pleasures and votes. Their neighborhood was known for providing "the city's wildest entertainment for those seeking gambling places,
dance halls, barrelhouse joints, hock shops, tintype picture galleries,
penny arcades, voodoo goofer dust, charms, gyp auctions, livery stables"
and the like.[57] It was a part of town in which "there was an absence of
morals bordering on genius."[58] And Democratic Party precinct captains
and City Council aldermen, Kenna and Coughlin ruled the realm. Their
"First Ward Balls" raised money for themselves and their political friends.
Surveying one such gathering, Kenna is reported to have proclaimed of
"the vast gathering of madams, police captains, saloonkeepers, dips, and
second-story workers, whores and sweating waiters," that "[I]t's a lolla-
palooza! . . . Chicago ain't no sissy town."[59] "Pretentious members of the
so-called better classes" indeed "filed a more than casual protest" before
prohibition finally closed the Levee down during the 1910s.

Recently, historians have been more sympathetic to Harrison's assessment of his ward buddies.[60] Late-twentieth-century historians such as Jon
Teaford, Terrence J. MacDonald, and Ann Durkin Keating have argued
that considerable achievement in urban infrastructure and even fiscal
management outweighed the corruption and inefficiency of American
city politics a century earlier.[61] This success is all the more remarkable
when one recalls, as John M. Allswang does, that the Progressive Era
(1890–1915) "was a time when more and more groups—economic,
social, cultural—turned to government to deal with problems" as a consequence of the challenges of industrial and urban change.[62] To draw on
Teaford's memorable work, whatever problems there were, the "bright
side of the municipal endeavor" takes on special meaning when "one
recognizes some of the challenges that municipal leaders faced during the
period 1870 to 1900."[63] American municipalities succeeded in meeting

---

[57] Stephen Longstreet, *Chicago, 1860–1919* (New York: David McKay, 1973), p. 353.
[58] Ibid., p. 354.   [59] Ibid., p. 358.
[60] A point noted in David P. Thelen's 1979 review essay on then-recent works in Ameri-
can urban history. David P. Thelen, "Urban Politics: Beyond Bosses and Reformers,"
Reviews in American History 7, no. 3 (September 1979), pp. 406–12.
[61] Jon C. Teaford, *The Unheralded Triumph: City Government in America, 1870–1900*
(Baltimore: Johns Hopkins University Press, 1984); Terrence J. McDonald, *The
Parameters of Urban Fiscal Policy: Socioeconomic Change and Political Culture in San
Francisco, 1860–1906* (Berkeley: University of California Press, 1987); and Ann Durkin
Keating, *Building Chicago: Suburban Developers and the Creation of a Divided Metropolis* (Columbus: Ohio State University Press, 1988).
[62] John M. Allswang, *Bosses, Machines and Urban Voters* (Baltimore: Johns Hopkins University Press, 1986), pp. 14–15.
[63] Teaford, *The Unheralded Triumph*, p. 4.

"the challenges of diversity, growth, and finance with remarkable success. By century's close, American city dwellers enjoyed, on the average, as high a standard of public success as any urban residents in the world."[64]

Harrison Junior's 1897 entrance into politics had been tumultuous, with the Democratic convention that nominated him to his initial run for the mayoralty ending with fists flying in a Chicago-style melee between his supporters and those of "Boodle Boss" Sullivan.[65] Such violence was hardly unusual for the era. Hundreds were reported to have been injured during the November 1894 elections, with one Chicagoan being killed during an election-related riot of city employees.[66]

Harrison eventually suffered a humiliating primary defeat in 1915 after having tried unsuccessfully the previous year both to reform the streetcar franchises yet again and to close down many of the saloons, gambling dens, and houses of ill repute that had provided the bulk of his ward-level allies' incomes.[67] Prohibition of the sale of alcoholic beverages and the Mann Act (Illinois Congressman James Mann's bill outlawing the transport of a woman across a state line for "immoral purposes") would soon thereafter finish the Levee district for good.[68] Only in his early forties, Harrison never returned to elected office (though he eventually served under Franklin Roosevelt as the federal government's appointed collector of internal revenue at Chicago).[69]

The Harrisons "were petty bosses," Merriam would write, "but no great boss could spring up. There were minor peculations," he continued, "and there were gamblers and prostitutes, not pursued if they kept to the rear, but there was no room for a thoroughly organized system of political corruption of the type that had become familiar in American cities."[70] Merriam continued on in admiring terms about his old opponent's skillful approach to the city's diverse and competing communities. "Like his father," Merriam argued, "the younger Harrison was not an

[64] Ibid., p. 6.
[65] Wendt and Kogan, *Bosses in Lusty Chicago*, pp. 59–67.
[66] Ray Stannard Baker, "The Civic Federation of Chicago," *Outlook* 52 (July 27, 1895), pp. 132–33.
[67] Kantowicz, "Carter H. Harrison II," p. 30; Harold F. Gosnell, *Machine Politics: Chicago Model* (1937; reprint New York: AMS, 1969), pp. 142–44.
[68] Wendt and Kogan, *Bosses in Lusty Chicago*, pp. 336–39; Paul S. Boyer, *Urban Masses and Moral Order in America, 1820–1920* (Cambridge, Mass.: Harvard University Press, 1978), p. 191; Herbert Asbury, *Gem of the Prairie: An Informal History of the Chicago Underworld* (New York: Knopf, 1940), pp. 281–319.
[69] Harrison, *Growing Up with Chicago*, p. 289; Green, "The Chicago Democratic Party," pp. 219–54.
[70] Merriam, *Chicago*, p. 20.

idealist, but a political realist, hostile however to the growth of a boss-controlled spoils and grafting machine, and antagonistic to such formidable spoilsmen as aspired to complete domination of the city."[71] He tried to avoid antagonizing both reform forces and immigrant groups, "interpreting the spirit of a cosmopolitan community."[72] The Harrisons were, in brief, "consummate politicians riding the stormy waves of a metropolitan community with unparalleled success."[73]

One reason for the absence of a single great political machine during this era was that Chicago was awash with small, competing machines. American political allegiances at this time were based on religion and ethnicity, so it is hardly surprising that Chicago, a city of diverse population, would spawn scores of small alliances rather than a single commanding political organization.[74] In the social science lingo of M. Craig Brown and Charles N. Halaby, Harrison's Chicago was home to a number of "factional machines" rather than the preserve of one "dominant" machine.[75] "Jobs and neighborhoods were parceled out by ethnic division," Garry Wills reports, "and politics naturally followed. There were as many subordinate 'machines' as there were clusters of potential voters."[76] As difficult as it may be to acknowledge today, such machines not only prevented the emergence of a single, antidemocratic large machine, but made the city a fertile ground for compromise and a politics that was predicated on the city's diversity. Social fragmentation reinforced rather than undercut pluralism.

Despite sharply different personalities—the father cutting "a picturesque figure, with his white horse and his broad-brimmed hat" to become "one of the characters of the town," the son being "less magnetic in personality" but a political tactician of unequaled skill[77]— both Harrisons pursued what Edward R. Kantowicz has called "the politics of balance."[78] Successful politicians in a city with a weak party system, the Harrisons drew on personal popularity and a capacity to reach out to a plurality of social, economic, ethnic, and political

---

[71] Ibid., p. 21.   [72] Ibid., pp. 21–22.
[73] Ibid., pp. 190–91.
[74] For further discussion of the commanding importance of religion and ethnicity in nineteenth-century U.S. politics, see Paul Kleppner, *The Third Electoral System, 1853–1892: Parties, Voters, and Political Cultures* (Chapel Hill: University of North Carolina Press, 1979); and Richard Jensen, *The Winning of the Midwest: Social and Political Conflict, 1888–1896* (Chicago: University of Chicago Press, 1971).
[75] M. Craig Brown and Charles N. Halaby, "Machine Politics in America, 1870–1945," *Journal of Interdisciplinary History* 17, no. 3 (Winter 1987), pp. 587–612: 595–96.
[76] Garry Wills, "Sons and Daughters of Chicago," *New York Review of Books*, June 9, 1994, pp. 52–59: 52.
[77] Merriam, *Chicago*, p. 20.
[78] Kantowicz, "Carter H. Harrison II," pp. 16–32.

constituencies.[79] John M. Allswang suggests that they alone may have accounted for a considerable degree of their party's success during this period. Allswang's analysis "points to the popularity of the Carter H. Harrisons, father and son; their popularity was considerable with all ethnic groups (for example, the low Democratic vote in 1891 when the senior Harrison ran as an independent; and the Democratic majorities among all seven [ethnic] groups [under consideration] in 1911 when the junior Harrison reentered local politics for the last time)."[80]

The Harrisons' understanding of politics represented the epitome of pragmatic pluralism and converted the city's stark fragmentation and diversity into invaluable political capital for the gain of themselves and their city. They "accepted Chicago for what it was, a battleground of competing classes and ethnic groups, each with its own share of power."[81] The mayor, in their conception, was the central deal maker who kept the divided city running. The Harrisons were consummate pragmatic pluralists.

Only the legendary Richard J. Daley surpassed Harrison Senior and Junior in a 1989 ranking of Chicago's mayors by local political observers and historians.[82] Even for as jaundiced an observer of American urban governance as Ernest Griffiths, the elder Harrison "historically stands as the best symbol of his age—a compromiser, certainly, tolerant, but withal a great public servant and a great humanitarian. The combination resulted in an empathy and rapport with the masses of the people, which a more orthodox reformer could never enjoy at the time."[83] The Harrisons "were able," Edward Kantowicz concludes, "to accommodate, with amazing dexterity and flexibility, the explosive growth and bewildering diversity of Chicago at the turn of the century."[84]

NIKOLAI ALEKSEEV

Moscow's "Harrison" could well have been Nikolai Alekseev, who, like Carter Harrison, Sr., fell to an assassin's bullet—in this instance, at the

[79] Of twenty-five elections in the city held between 1890 and 1916, the Democrats won ten, the Republicans nine, the two parties shared the victory in three, and other parties emerged victorious in three contests. See John M. Allswang, *A House for All Peoples: Ethnic Politics in Chicago, 1890–1936* (Lexington: University Press of Kentucky, 1971), pp. 23–24, 34–35.
[80] Ibid., p. 34.   [81] Miller, *City of the Century*, p. 486.
[82] Melvin G. Holli, "Ranking Chicago's Mayors: Mirror, Mirror, on the Wall, Who Is the Greatest of Them All?" in Green and Holli, eds., *The Mayors*, pp. 202–11.
[83] Ernest S. Griffith, *A History of American City Government: The Conspicuous Failure, 1870–1900* (New York: National Municipal League; Lanham, Md.: University Press of America, 1983), pp. 103–4.
[84] Kantowicz, "Carter H. Harrison II," p. 17.

City Duma on March 11, 1893.[85] Like the Harrisons, Alekseev's contemporaries might be surprised to see the adjective "pluralist" attached
to his name. Yet, just as Kantowicz labels the younger Harrison a
"reform boss" because of his capacity to bring many reform policies to
fruition despite alliances with "a motley crew of ward bosses and immigrant politicos,"[86] Alekseev used heavy-handed means to achieve what
for Moscow at that time may be considered to have been reform-
oriented and pluralistic ends.[87] Unlike Harrison, Alekseev did not have
to face a large electorate.[88]

By the time of Nikolai's birth on October 15, 1852, the Alekseev
family had already emerged among the most established Moscow merchant clans. As with many, but hardly all, merchant dynasties of the era,
the Alekseevs had come to Moscow as peasant serfs (in their case, in
1746 from the Yaroslavl region). Late-eighteenth- and early-nineteenth-
century Moscow was an engine for social mobility for serfs and recently
freed peasants as well as for the free urban population (*posadskie liudi*).[89]
Elise Kimerling Wirtschafter reports in her exceptional study *Social Identity in Imperial Russia* that the absence of traditional European-style
guild structures combined with long winters, short growing seasons, and
unpredictable agricultural surpluses to compel Russian peasants to enter
into handicraft production and trade for survival.[90]

A number of Moscow's most prominent families at the end of the
nineteenth century had descended from such humble yet vibrant entrepreneurial origins. Catherine the Great's encouragement of commerce
(1762–96) and Napoleon's destruction of Moscow in 1812 were "seismic
disruptions" that "apocalyptically burned" Moscow's established mer-

---

[85] I would like to thank Galina Ulianova of the Russian Academy of Sciences' Institute of
History for her advice and counsel during the preparation of this discussion of Nikolai
Alekseev's life and career.

[86] Kantowicz, "Carter H. Harrison II," p. 22.

[87] An overall assessment of Alekseev's mayorship in English may be found in Walter S.
Hanchett, "Moscow in the Late Nineteenth Century: A Study in Municipal Self-
Government" (Ph.D. diss., University of Chicago, 1964), pp. 137–42.

[88] Amy Bridges reminds us that one of the most distinctive aspects of nineteenth-century
American urban politics was the hotly contested elections and primaries that provided
the opportunity for "the first generation of industrial workers, and their artisan fore-
bears before them" to vote. Amy Bridges, *A City in the Republic: Antebellum New York
and the Origins of Machine Politics* (Cambridge, U.K.: Cambridge University Press,
1984), p. 8.

[89] Elizabeth Kridl Valkenier, "Book Review: *Merchant Moscow: Images of Russia's Vanished Bourgeoisie*, edited by James L. West and Iurii A. Petrov," *Harriman Review* 10,
no. 4 (August 1998), pp. 38–40: 40.

[90] Elise Kimerling Wirtschafter, *Social Identity in Imperial Russia* (DeKalb: Northern Illinois University Press, 1997), pp. 78–79.

chants to the ground, wiping the local socio-economic slate clean for a new wave of small-scale peasant traders.[91] As James L. West recounts the tale, "it was among these rough peasant-traders that most all of the founders of the great industrial dynasties of Merchant Moscow emerged. Well positioned in the 1820s to take advantage of the technological revolution of steam power then belatedly occurring in Russia, the most aggressive of these early entrepreneurs, a few dozen at most, rode a short-lived economic escalator to wealth and well being quickly enough to pioneer a whole new industry in cotton production."[92]

Wirtschafter, who intends her focus to be as broad as the entire imperial Russian social system, places the Moscow experience within the larger framework set by the peculiarities of Russian servitude. Wirtschafter reminds her readers that "before and after emancipation, any man with adequate economic resources who obtained a release from his master or community of origin was free to enroll as a townsman."[93] Such releases could be purchased with the earnings of nonagricultural endeavors such as handicraft trade. Serf traders sufficiently successful to save the capital required to buy their freedom frequently had one foot already firmly planted in town. Resting in the traditional Russian heartland, Moscow—as Russia's wholesale and retail commercial center—was a destination of choice for peasant craftsmen and tradesmen both newly freed and, as yet, indentured.[94] The consequent socio-economic hierarchy was variable and open-ended, with newly arriving mercantile overachievers forcing out more-established merchant elites.[95]

The Alekseevs were among the small group of families that managed to enter the first-guild world early and hold on until all such social formations collapsed in the wake of 1917. Nikolai was a fifth-generation Muscovite on the Alekseev side and a seventh-generation native on his mother's side. His wife's mother was a member of the even more

---

[91] James L. West, "Merchant Moscow in Historical Context," in James L. West and Iurii A. Petrov, eds., *Merchant Moscow: Images of Russia's Vanished Bourgeoisie* (Princeton: Princeton University Press, 1998), pp. 3–12: 7.

[92] Ibid.   [93] Wirtschafter, *Social Identity*, p. 132.

[94] Irina V. Potkina, "Moscow's Commercial Mosaic," in West and Petrov, eds., *Merchant Moscow*, pp. 37–44.

[95] In Moscow, 26 of the 382 first-guild merchant families registered in 1748 remained in the last two decades of that century, as did only 10 of the 235 families registered in 1766–67. Of 137 first-guild Moscow families identified at the end of the eighteenth century, 21 maintained that position in 1815. In 1873, only 108 of 623 first-guild Moscow merchants traced their origins to eighteenth-century merchant families; the ancestors of 185 had entered the guild from other social categories between 1800 and 1861. See Wirtschafter, *Social Identity*, p. 72.

illustrious Tretiakov family.[96] By the time of Nikolai's generation, the Alekseevs had become tied through marriage, business, social engagement, and mentorship to the powerful Chertvertikovs, Mamontovs, and Tretiakovs.[97]

Pulling peasant artisans together from villages in nearby Moscow *guberniia*, dynasty founder Semyon Alekseev established a traditional handicraft workshop in the city's Old Believer Rogozhskii district (although the Alekseevs were not, themselves, practitioners of the Old Rite).[98] Semyon purchased the stone house of former Moscow city chief Vasili Zhigarev just a few months prior to Napoleon's destruction of the city. The house (which was next door to the homes of such Old Rite magnates as the Soldatenkovs, Simonovs, and several Morozovs) was the birthplace of both Nikolai and his second cousin, future Moscow Art Theater co-founder Konstantin Stanislavskii-Alekseev.[99] It eventually was donated by the Alekseev family to the Moscow Merchant Society for construction of the Nikolaevskii House for the Care of Widows and Orphans.

The disastrous Moscow fire of "the French year"—1812—had breached Moscow's floodgates for a swarm of peasant traders and petty merchants from the Russian hinterland.[100] Napoleon's devastation of the city coincided with a time of relatively less repression for Old Believer communities, so that Morozovs, Riabushinskiis, Guchkovs, Soldatenkovs, Khludovs, and members of other future Old Believer merchant dynasties could join "this motley population of itinerant peddlers" in transforming Moscow.[101] The Old Believers nestled into two self-

---

[96] I would like to thank Galina Ulianova for sharing this information with me from her extensive database on the philanthropic activities among Moscow entrepreneurial families: "Blagotvoritel'nost' moskovskikh predprinimatelei, 1869–1914," database, 1998.

[97] Thomas C. Owen, *Capitalism and Politics in Russia: A Social History of the Moscow Merchants, 1855–1905* (Cambridge, U.K.: Cambridge University Press, 1981), pp. 221–22; Pavel Buryshkin, *Moskva kupecheskaia: zapiski* (1954; reprint, Moscow: Sovremennik, 1991), pp. 129–30. For a discussion of the illustrious Sheremetev family, see M. I. Pyliaev, *Staraia Moskva* (1891; reprint, Moscow: Svarog, 1995), pp. 162–86.

[98] Buryshkin, *Moskva kupecheskaia*, pp. 129–30; Alfred J. Rieber, *Merchants and Entrepreneurs in Imperial Russia* (Chapel Hill: University of North Carolina Press, 1982), p. 205. Concerning the Old Believer community at Rogozhskoe, see Roy R. Robson, *Old Believers in Modern Russia* (DeKalb: Northern Illinois University Press, 1995), pp. 53–74.

[99] I would like to thank Galina Ulianova for information about this early Alekseev house.

[100] James L. West, "A Note on Old Belief," in West and Petrov, eds., *Merchant Moscow*, pp. 13–18: 16–17.

[101] Ibid., p. 17; Iu. A. Petrov, *Dinastiia Riabushinskikh* (Moscow: Russkaia kniga, 1997), pp. 8–10.

contained communities outside of the city's official boundaries, just across the Yauza River.

Banned from living in town following a plague epidemic in 1771, the Bezpopovtsy (or "priestless" sect) formed a community around Preobrazhenskii Cemetery near today's Preobrazhenskaia metro station. The Popovtsy (or "priestly" sect) took up residence slightly more to the south, near the Rogozhskii Cemetery along what is today Enthusiasts' Highway.[102] Rogozhskii churches served some sixty-eight thousand parishioners during the mid-1820s. Both communities thrived after the 1831 cholera outbreak, which largely passed over the hygienic-minded Old Believers.

Semyon Alekseev, like many other Rogozhskii Orthodox and Old Believer entrepreneurs, lived with his workers and generally treated the entire operation as an extension of his family—an approach continued by his son Vladimir. The high quality of the family's silk and gold thread production—which was valued as far away as Central Asia, the Caucasus region, and Iran—enabled the Alekseevs to accumulate considerable capital reserves, import English workers, and enter the Moscow merchant elite.[103] Aleksandr Alekseev led the local government during the 1840s.[104]

Nikolai's mother, Elizaveta, was the daughter of Mikhail Bostandzhoglo, a tobacco magnate from the Greek community of Nezhin in the Chernigov region, some 125 kilometers northeast of Kyiv. Her father had established what would become Moscow's largest tobacco factory in 1820. This plant was being run by Elizaveta's brothers (Nikolai's uncles) at the time of Nikolai's prominence in Moscow social, economic, and political life.[105]

The energetic Nikolai became impatient with his family's old-fashioned production methods and, when given the opportunity, mechanized the Alekseevs' textile plants. Nikolai could do so because uniform and growing economic distress was forcing most men—and, in time, a large number of women—throughout the central industrial region surrounding Moscow into wage labor.[106]

---

[102] Galina Ulianova, "Old Believers and New Entrepreneurs: Religious Belief and Ritual in Merchant Moscow," in West and Petrov, eds., *Merchant Moscow*, pp. 61–71: 67–68.

[103] Rieber, *Merchants and Entrepreneurs*, p. 205.

[104] Buryshkin, *Moskva kupecheskaia*, p. 130.

[105] I would like to thank Galina Ulianova for this information about Nikolai Alekseev's mother.

[106] Rose L. Glickman, *Russian Factory Women: Workplace and Society, 1880–1914* (Berkeley: University of California Press, 1984), p. 45.

Shared peasant origins had long sustained a connection between owner and worker in many Moscow-region factories such as those of the Alekseevs.[107] Social distances grew, with production tied closer and closer to machinery, while workers increasingly lived in barracks far from the fancy new homes of plant owners.

Nikolai took over the family business just as traditional labor relations were being depreciated by "modern" production and organizational schemes being imported from Europe. Nikolai was uncommonly successful, and ruthless, in introducing the latest management systems to the family's far-flung factories—as distant as Khar'kiv (and, eventually, Australia and South Africa). These business successes provided Alekseev with the moniker of "dynamic reformer" before he had even contemplated entering politics.

Although Nikolai grew up in Rogozhskii, his childhood was closely connected through family and social ties with the Zamoskvorech'e district (immediately south of the Moscow River and just across from the Kremlin) when that neighborhood was still the focal point of merchant life.[108] Late-twentieth-century architectural historian Dmitri Shvidkovskii describes that special world well in his study of the Igoumnov Mansion, now the residence of France's ambassador to Russia. Zamoskvorech'e was "really unusual with a wealth of traditions; a singular life and an unduplicated exceptional 'world' full of old Russian customs and beliefs. It was the heart of Russia, the essence of its real character . . . the 'most' Russian section of the ancient city, where it preserved the soul of its strangeness, where it staggered foreigners, indeed all people of European culture, who were captivated by a lively persistent force and an authentic beauty."[109]

Nikolai and his childhood friends escaped their closed world, abandoning caftans for business suits, giving up private card games at home for vibrant social clubs, and moving from fortress-like Zamoskvorech'e family compounds to lushly theatrical art nouveau mansions across town

[107] Mikhail L. Shastillo, "Peasant Entrepreneurs and Worker Peasants: Labor Relations in Merchant Moscow," in West and Petrov, eds., *Merchant Moscow*, pp. 85–93.

[108] For further discussion of Zamoskvorech'e life, see Ia. M. Belitskii, *Zabytaia Moskva* (Moscow: Moskovskii rabochii, 1994), pp. 190–280; and Mikhail Mikhailovich Novikov, *Ot Moskvy do N'iu-Iorka. Moia zhizn' v nauke i politike* (New York: Chekhov Press, 1952), pp. 18–25.

[109] Dmitri Chvidkovski [Shvidkovskii], "Le monde du 'Zamoskvoretche' dans la culture de Moscou," in Olda Morel et al., eds., *La maison Igoumnov: Residence de l'ambassadeur de France à Moscou* (Paris: Les amis de la maison Igoumnov, 1993), pp. 33–41, 140–43: 140.

36. Nikolai Alekseev. Photographer unknown, n.d. Photo collection of Mikhail Zolotarev, Moscow.

along Malaia Bronaia and Bolshaia Nikitskaia Streets near Patriarch's Pond.[110] The Alekseevs, for example, moved to Prechistenskii Boulevard near the location of today's Kropotkinskaia metro station.

Nikolai and childhood friend Sergei Tretiakov (the brother of the art collector Pavel Tretiakov and himself mayor of Moscow from 1876 to

---

[110] Christine Ruane, "Caftan to Business Suit: The Semiotics of Russian Merchant Dress," in West and Petrov, eds., *Merchant Moscow*, pp. 53–60; William Craft Brumfield, "Aesthetics and Commerce: The Architecture of Merchant Moscow," in West and Petrov, eds., *Merchant Moscow*, pp. 119–31; Joseph C. Bradley, "Merchant Moscow after Hours: Voluntary Associations and Leisure," in West and Petrov, eds., *Merchant Moscow*, pp. 133–43; Edith W. Clowes, "Merchants on Stage and in Life: Theatricality and Public Consciousness," in West and Petrov, eds., *Merchant Moscow*, pp. 147–59; and Elena Chernevich and Mikhail Anikst, in collaboration with Nina Baburina, *Grafica Russa, 1880–1917* (Florence: Cantini Editore, 1990).

1882) especially enjoyed each other's company well beyond the political sphere. Together, they became major patrons of the Moscow musical scene, activists in the local Imperial Russian Musical Society, and supporters of the newly formed Moscow Conservatory.[111] Nikolai also had extensive social and business dealings with the Chertverikovs.[112]

Alekseev, however, was anathema to many other prominent merchant families and figures, such as the archconservative Moscow city Duma leader Nikolai Naidenov and the city's governor-general, Vladimir Dolgorukov.[113] Naidenov headed his family's mighty Trade Bank, as well as the city's powerful Moscow Exchange Committee, which represented old-line industrialists (including Nikolai Alekseev's father).[114] Naidenov was a self-proclaimed conservative who remained sympathetic to Slavophile perspectives throughout his life.[115] His animosity for Mayor Alekseev seems to have been based in part on a profound distrust of Nikolai's youth and dynamism.[116]

In keeping with local Moscow civic culture, members of such families as the Alekseevs routinely distrusted anything that was associated with St. Petersburg. Drawing income from textiles and railroads, these families supported Russian and Slavic culture.[117] Their cultural conservatism did not prevent individual family members either from learn-

---

[111] Jo Ann Ruckman, *The Moscow Business Elite: A Social and Cultural Portrait of Two Generations, 1840–1905* (DeKalb: Northern Illinois University Press, 1984), p. 103; E. I. Kazanskii, "Muzyka v' Moskvie," *Moskva v' eia proshlom' i nastoiashchem'*, Vol. 11, pp. 60-90; V. Ger'e, "O Moskovskoi gorodskoi dume," in A. S. Kiselev et al., eds., *Moskovskii arkhiv. Istoriko-kraevedcheskii al'manakh* (Moscow: Moskovskoe gorodskoe ob"edinenie arkhivov, 1996), pp. 421–38; and V. P. Ziloti, *V dome Tret'iakova* (New York: Chekhov Press, 1954), pp. 161–87.

[112] Rieber, *Merchants and Entrepreneurs*, p. 205. Sergei Chetverikov's warm remembrance of Nikolai Alekseev may be found in Sergei's memoirs, *Bezvozvratno ushedshaia Rossiia. Neskol'ko stranits iz knigi moei zhizni* (Berlin: Moskva-Logos, 192?), pp. 83–94.

[113] Liubov' Fedorovna Pisar'kova, "Gorodskie golovy Moskvy (1863–1917gg.)," *Otechestvennaia istoriia* 1997, no. 2, pp. 3–19: 8–10.

[114] Iurii A. Petrov, "'Moscow City': Financial Citadel of Merchant Moscow," in West and Petrov, eds., *Merchant Moscow*, pp. 45–50: 46. Information about the Alekseev family from Ul'ianova, "Blagotvoritel'nost' moskovskikh predprinimatelei."

[115] As may be immediately discerned in Naidenov's memoirs: Nikolai A. Naidenov, *Vospominaniia o vidennom, slyshannom i isputannom. Moscow: 1903–1905* (Newtonville, Mass.: Oriental Research Partners, 1976).

[116] Owen, *Capitalism and Politics*, pp. 86–87.

[117] A number of lively memoirs from the period recall the merchants' sponsorship of the arts. See, for example, Valerii Briusov, *Dnevniki, 1891–1910* (Moscow: Izdanie M. i S. Sabashnikovykh, 1927); Valerii Briusov, *Iz moei zhizni. Moia iunost', Pamiati* (Moscow: Izdanie M. i S. Sabashnikovykh, 1927); Chetverikov, *Bezvozvratno ushedshaia Rossiia*; V. S. Mamontov, *Vospominaniia o Russkikh khudozhnikakh* (Moscow: Izd. Akademii khudozhestv S.S.S.R., 1950); Vladimir Nemirovitch-Dantchenko, *My Life in the Russian Theatre*, trans. John Cournos (Boston: Little, Brown, 1936); and Ziloti, *V dome Tret'iakova*.

ing foreign languages (in Nikolai Alekseev's case, French, German, and some English) or from becoming generally educated in the ways of the West. They fearlessly imported Western technologies and managerial philosophies.[118] Merchant Moscow established a system of commercial education that "clearly met world standards and sometimes even surpassed them." Aleksei Vishniakov's Moscow Commercial Institute, founded in 1902, was arguably the world's first graduate-level commercial school.[119] Others, such as Nikolai's second cousin Stanislavskii-Alekseev, gained international fame as innovators in their chosen fields of endeavor.[120]

Their hostility to the Roman Catholic and Protestant worlds of Europe focused squarely on a Westernizing state that had been "imposed" by Peter the Great on a "true" Russia. These merchant families sustained an intense dislike for a nobility that lived off of that state, and they feared any distortion of "genuinely Russian" values, such as those that had been sustained by the patriarchal structures of their own families. Moscow merchant clans, including the Alekseevs, sought to sustain an "authentic" Russia even as they nurtured industries, banks, and cultural institutions that undermined this same older Slavic world. This fundamental contradiction both reflected and nurtured Russia's merchants' deep ambivalence toward their own political capital and the West.[121] Their political stances, it should be added, always stopped far short of disloyalty or opposition to the imperial family.[122]

Moscow's aloofness from imperial elites in St. Petersburg distinguished the old capital and its surrounding region from the rest of Russia, helping to foster a singular brand of entrepreneurship that was rooted more on grassroots initiative and capital formation than on subservience

---

More scholarly accounts may be found in Stuart Ralph Grover, "Savva Mamontov and the Mamontov Circle, 1870–1905: Art Patronage and the Rise of Nationalism in Russian Art" (Ph.D. diss., University of Wisconsin, Madison, 1971); and Beverly Whitney Kean, *French Painters, Russian Collectors: The Merchant Patrons of Modern Art in Pre-Revolutionary Russia* (London: Hodder and Stoughton, 1994).

[118] Ruckman, *The Moscow Business Elite*, pp. 128–29.

[119] Sergei V. Kalmykov, "Commercial Education and the Cultural Crisis of the Moscow Merchant Elite," in West and Petrov, eds., *Merchant Moscow*, pp. 109–16.

[120] Nemirovitch-Dantchenko, *My Life in the Russian Theatre*, pp. 115–17, 149. For an engaging contemporary account of the early years of the Moscow Art Theater, see Z. I. Zhamurina, "Moskovskie teatry v' XIX viekie," *Moskva v' eia proshlom' i nastoiashchem'* 11, pp. 29–59.

[121] A point emphasized by Boris V. Anan'ich in "The Economic Policy of the Tsarist Government and Enterprise in Russia from the End of the Nineteenth through the Beginning of the Twentieth Century," in Greg Guroff and F. V. Carstensen, eds., *Entrepreneurship in Imperial Russia and the Soviet Union* (Princeton: Princeton University Press, 1983), pp. 125–39.

[122] Rieber, *Merchants and Entrepreneurs*, pp. 165–170, 285.

to the state and reliance on state and foreign capital.[123] As Thomas C. Owen has observed, Moscow-style capitalism reflected an uneasy accommodation of traditional Russian culture and European business methods.[124] Moscow economic leaders were both "thoroughly modern" and experienced practitioners of premodern trading methods.[125] Nikolai Alekseev, a product of this milieu, remained throughout his life both a modernizing promoter of organizational and infrastructural innovation and an autocratic, closed-minded traditionalist.

Local Moscow political machinery was far from what even the most hidebound Chicagoan would have considered to be democratic. The city had been granted a degree of autonomy by a new municipal statute in 1870, although even this reform would be partially rolled back in 1892.[126] Less than 1 percent of the local population could participate in the city Duma elections prior to 1905.[127] The Duma, in turn, elected the mayor from among its own ranks.

---

[123] A point explored by William Blackwell in his essay "The Russian Entrepreneur in the Tsarist Period: An Overview," in Guroff and Carstensen, eds., *Entrepreneurship in Imperial Russia*, pp. 13–26.

[124] Thomas C. Owen, "Doing Business in Merchant Moscow," in West and Petrov, eds., *Merchant Moscow*, pp. 29–36: 32.

[125] Thomas C. Owen, "Entrepreneurship and the Structure of Enterprise in Russia, 1800–1880," in Guroff and Carstensen, eds., *Entrepreneurship in Imperial Russia*, pp. 59–83: 72.

[126] Ruckman, *The Moscow Business Elite*, p. 115.

[127] Laura Engelstein, *Moscow 1905: Working-Class Organization and Political Conflict* (Stanford: Stanford University Press, 1982), pp. 51–53.

According to governing arrangements prior to 1870, the local city council had consisted of representatives of the five-town *sosloviia* (the Russian arrangement of social organization reminiscent of the old French estates system). After 1870, three new curia were established within the city Duma based on property qualifications. Following the 1892 statutes, all curia were eliminated, with voting rights being granted to members of the merchantry's "first guild" as well as to qualified property owners. Voting rights were essentially denied to all who did not own their own houses—although, in contrast to Chicago and Osaka, qualified property-owning women could participate in elections through designated proxies.

More specifically,

> regardless of estate, city taxpayers owning immovable property and individuals paying specific duties on trade and industry received the right to participate in elections. Furthermore, legal entities such as various government agencies, institutions, associations, companies, churches, and monasteries also held voting rights. Men who had reached the age of twenty-five could vote, but women meeting the prescribed voter qualifications could participate in elections solely through the use of designated proxies. Hired laborers (the overwhelming majority of the population owning no real estate) were deprived of the right to vote, as were educated white-collar people such as engineers, physicians, teachers and bureaucrats (Valeriia A. Nardova, "Municipal Self-Government after the 1870 Reform," trans. Lori A. Citti, in Ben Eklof, John Bushnell, and Larissa Zakharova, eds., *Russia's Great Reforms, 1855–1881* [Bloomington: Indiana University Press, 1994], pp. 181–96: 184).

One speaks with difficulty of a politics of inclusion or pluralism under such conditions. Yet Nikolai Alekseev managed to mobilize various groups within his small Moscow world behind his pet projects—while simultaneously holding what for the period were liberal views on such questions as labor relations.

The Duma's dominant *kuptsy* (merchants) elected one of their own to the post of mayor for the first time in 1876—Sergei Tretiakov. Tretiakov never managed to reach agreement over means and ends with the Duma's representatives of both the *meshchanie* (a Russian social category somewhat reminiscent of the French *petit bourgeoisie*) and the *kustarniki* (handicraftsmen). He resigned in disgust in 1882 and was succeeded by an economics professor with permanent residence in Tambov, Boris Chicherin.[128]

Chicherin, who proved ineffectual as mayor, kicked up considerable controversy when he purchased a rickety shack on the city's outskirts in order to qualify as a local voter and office-holder in Moscow.[129] Chicherin quickly tangled with the conservative Moscow governor-general, Prince Vladimir Dolgorukov, who was able to persuade the newly appointed and reactionary Minister of Internal Affairs, Count Dmitrii Tolstoi, to remove the liberal-minded professor from office.[130] Before leaving office, Chicherin managed to make several speeches demanding that local administration be reformed through the "full inclusion of all legal segments of society."[131] He also forced the Duma to initiate the establishment of several service-oriented enterprises that would eventually provide the municipality of Moscow with much-needed revenues.[132] Chicherin was followed as mayor by a bland local official named S. A. Tarasov, whom Alekseev replaced in 1885.

Jo Ann Ruckman argues that the city Duma's failure to find an adequate mayor during the first decade and a half following the 1870 municipal statues lies both in a paralyzing struggle on the city Duma between the *kuptsy* and the *meshchanie*, and in the Duma's general lack of purpose and vision. The absence of suitably dynamic leaders among the *kuptsy* surely contributed to this failure.[133] Alekseev's dynamism,

[128] Iurii Luzhkov, "Moskva—stolitsa patriarkhal'naia," *Obshchaia gazeta* 1994, no. 26 (July 1–7), p. 16.
[129] Valeriia A. Nardova, "Municipal Self-Government after the 1870 Reform," p. 184.
[130] Ger'e, "O moskovskoi gorodskoi dume," pp. 424–25.
[131] Aleksandr Aleksandrovich Kizevetter, *Na rubezhe dvukh stoletii (Vospominaniia 1881–1914)* (Prague: Orbis, 1929), p. 19.
[132] Pisar'kova, "Gorodskie golovy Moskvy," pp. 7–8.
[133] Ruckman, *The Moscow Business Elite*, pp. 115–16.

intelligence, and organizational competence combined with an ability to secure unity of action through compromise when possible and autocratic directive when not. He totally transformed local politics. Ruckman observes that Alekseev's "election initiated one of the stormiest and most creative periods in the history of Moscow self-government."[134]

Alekseev became Moscow's mayor at the age of thirty-three and immediately set out to recast municipal services.[135] The city was just entering one of its most dynamic periods, leading St. Petersburg scientist Dmitrii Mendeleev to report that Moscow concentrated "so many enterprising people and forms . . . that it will long remain at the head of the extensive manufacturing development destined for Russia."[136]

Alekseev moved to build coalitions supporting the enlargement of the city's water supply, the inauguration of an ambitious street paving program, the construction of Moscow's first underground sewer system, and expansion of municipal slaughterhouses.[137] He achieved all of these goals while bringing fiscal rigor to municipal operations. A tough administrator who was not always admired by local liberals, Alekseev proved to be a consummate mediator and coalition builder.[138]

Nikolai Astrov, secretary of the Moscow city Duma in 1897 and later mayor for four months during 1917, describes that body's highly formal modes of discourse in his 1941 memoirs, published in emigration.[139] "The Moscow Duma," Astrov reports, "had its own strict morals, customs, and rules, the violation of which was not possible. So, far from all the delegates were able to speak freely in the Duma. . . . Younger members spoke carefully as they met an inattentive reception, as their views were not taken kindly, while the Duma welcomed those who were ice cold, who did not demand the attention of the Duma for long."[140] The young, petulant, and impulsive Alekseev set this tame deliberative

---

[134] Ibid., p. 116.

[135] For further discussion of Alekseev's tenure as mayor, see Rieber, *Merchants and Entrepreneurs*, pp. 205–6; as well as Alla Belousova and Nikolai Laman, "Moskovskoi gorodskoi golova. K 100-letiiu so dnia smerti Nikolaia Aleksandrovicha Alekseeva," *Nezavisimaia gazeta*, March 17, 1993, p. 5.

[136] D. I. Mendeleev, "Introduction," *The Industries of Russia*, Vols. 1–2: *Manufactures and Trade*, trans. John M. Crawford (Chicago: World Columbian Exposition, 1893), p. xix.

[137] These activities gained wide attention. See, for example, Pisar'kova, "Gorodskie golovy Moskvy," pp. 8–10; and I. P. Mashkov, *Putevoditel' po Moskve* (Moscow: Moskovskoe arkhitekturnoe obshchestvo, 1913), pp. 85–106. Mashkov featured the city's water and sewer system in a guide to Moscow architecture prepared for participants in the Fifth Congress of Architects, convened in the city in 1913.

[138] See Luzhkov, "Moskva."

[139] Concerning Astrov's own tenure as mayor, see Pisar'kova, "Gorodskie golovy Moskvy," pp. 15–16.

[140] Nikolai Ivanovich Astrov, *Vospominaniia* (Paris: YMCA Press, 1941), Vol. 1, p. 261.

body on edge. Local government in Moscow could never be the same once Alekseev had become mayor.

Extravagant in a style befitting a Moscow merchant of the era, Alekseev drew strength from his own background.[141] He utilized his strong backing from his childhood chums, the powerful Tretiakovs, to mobilize shifting elite support for his favorite projects.

Nikolai was himself a generous philanthropist, providing gifts from his own pocket to a range of adult-education programs as well as to the Alekseev family's favorite charity, the Nikolaevskii House for the Care of Widows and Orphans. His widow, Aleksandra, who would outlive Nikolai by a decade, similarly contributed to the Nikolaevskii House (as had his father and his brothers). Aleksandra also provided charitable contributions to a number of psychiatric hospitals and child health-care facilities, perhaps in recognition of the hardships suffered by one of her and Nikolai's three daughters, who had been an invalid since childhood.[142]

Many of Alekseev's achievements, especially in the fiscal sphere, were rooted in the coming of age of reforms and civil service appointments undertaken by Tretiakov and the much-maligned Chicherin.[143] Alekseev's authoritarian streak, combined with an energy that lent itself to impatience, complicates any discussion of his tenure in office. He had, in the words of fellow civic leader Vladimir Ger'e, "a powerloving temperament," a sharp temper in dealing with people, and "both energy and lust for power."[144]

Alekseev's successes were considerable, from successful battles against Moscow *guberniia* tax grabs and the founding of a municipal fire insurance society, to the construction of a new Duma building (1890–92) and the Upper Trading Rows (1886–93), which later became the Soviet-era GUM department store that dominates Red Square to this day.[145] Pavel Tretiakov further credited Alekseev with having played an instrumental role in bringing his family's famous gallery of Russian art under municipal control.[146]

---

[141] Theatricality was a major aspect of Moscow merchant life. See Clowes, "Merchants on Stage."

[142] Ul'ianova, "Blagovoritel'nost' moskovskikh predprinimatelei."

[143] Owen, *Capitalism and Politics*, p. 87.

[144] Ger'e, "O Moskovskoi gorodskoi dume," pp. 427–29. This point is echoed in Mikhail Novikov's memoirs of the same period, *Ot Moskvy do N'iu-Iorka*, pp. 11–12.

[145] G. Iaroslavskii, "Gorodskoe samoupravlenie Moskvy," *Moskva v' eia proshlom' i nastoiashchem'* 12, pp. 17–48; Brumfield, "Aesthetics and Commerce."

[146] Iu. Aleksandrov, "Gogolevskii bul'var," in Kiselev, et al., eds., *Moskovskii arkhiv*, pp. 95–106. Also see Pavel Tretiakov's letter of December 11, 1893, to V. V. Stasov concerning the establishment of the Tretiakov Gallery: "Pis'mo No. 162 P. M. Tret'iakov–

Thomas Owen captures Alekseev's flamboyant style with an anecdote befitting any Chicago "boss." According to Owen, the mayor worked hard to secure sufficient funds (about 1.5 million rubles) to build Moscow's first and Europe's finest insane asylum. "As usual," Owens writes, "rich merchants were invited to contribute. When one wealthy trader offered 10,000 rubles, Alekseev addressed him loudly at a party in the presence of many important merchants, saying that 10,000 was shamefully little. But if 50,000 were pledged, Alekseev announced, he would bow down before the donor in public. The merchant replied that it would be worth such a financial sacrifice to humble the mayor of Moscow. Alekseev immediately dropped to his knees and said, 'I won't stand up until you write out a check for 50,000 rubles.' The embarrassed merchant had no choice but to comply. Alekseev stood up, pocketed the check, and dusted off his trousers, saying, 'There, you see how it turned out; you know, I had almost decided to kneel down for only 25,000!' The flustered donor left the party amid general laughter."[147]

A modern-day Moscow mayor, Iurii Luzhkov, enjoyed an Alekseev story or two, as in a 1996 display of unabashed self-promotion in which he attempted to draw a direct parallel between himself and "the ideal city mayor," Nikolai Alekseev.[148] According to Luzhkov, Alekseev would substitute Duma protocols with his own decrees prior to sending them forward to higher authorities for final approval, authorize construction projects prior to Duma sessions at which he faced certain defeat, and generally avoid the Duma whenever he understood that its members would beat him.

Like the Harrisons in Chicago, and Luzhkov a century later for that matter, Alekseev was not a classical liberal reformer. He was frequently attacked by the era's reformers among the local intelligentsia as being a

---

V. V. Stasovu," in N. G. Galkina and M. N. Grigor'eva, eds., *Perepiska P. M. Tret'iakova i V. V. Stasova, 1874–1897* (Moscow: Iskusstvo, 1949), pp. 171–74, 263–65. Alekseev's concern and active engagement in gallery affairs was also acknowledged in a letter dated August 12, 1891, from the famous painter Ilya Repin to Pavel Tretiakov: "Pis'mo No. 197. I. E. Repin–P. M. Tret'iakovu," in M. N. Grigor'eva and A. N. Shchekotova, eds., *Pis'ma I. E. Repina. Perepiska s P. M. Tret'iakovym. 1873–1898* (Moscow: Iskusstvo, 1946), p. 148. Another account is found in the memoirs of Pavel Tretiakov's daughter, Aleksandra: Aleksandra Pavlovna Botkina, *Pavel Mikhailovich Tret'iakov v zhizni i iskusstve* (Moscow: Izdatel'stvo Tret'iakovskoi galerei, 1951), pp. 249–59.

[147] Owen, *Capitalism and Politics*, p. 87. Another English-language account may be found in Valentine T. Bill, *The Forgotten Class: The Russian Bourgeoisie from the Earliest Beginnings to 1900* (New York: Praeger, 1959), p. 171. A Russian-language account of this story may be found in Buryshkin, *Moskva kupecheskaia*, p. 130.

[148] Luzhkov, "Moskva"; Iurii Luzhkov, *My deti tvoi, Moskva* (Moscow: Vagrius, 1996), pp. 199–208.

boss in his own right. He was also known to be anti-Semitic. Indeed, Alekseev's complex relationships with his city's and country's Jewish community expose a number of important contradictions within the practice of pragmatic pluralism and, for that reason, are essential to the story told in this volume.

Alekseev enthusiastically supported various proposals from imperial authorities in St. Petersburg to expel Jews from Moscow. This advocacy rightly earned him the eternal hostility of Russian Jewry.[149] That expulsion, which occurred unexpectedly in 1891, forced between 10,000 and 20,000 Jewish merchants to resettle in the Pale of Settlement in the western lands of the empire.[150] Yet, Alekseev took a different stance when he joined with Finance Minister Sergei Witte in opposing similar decrees restricting the commercial activities of Jews in Bukhara.[151] This shift in stance reflected the different interests of the Moscow merchant class of which Alekseev was a member: Bukhara's Jewish merchants facilitated the cotton trade with Moscow's mill owners, whereas Jewish traders closer to home represented competition. His position suggests different

---

[149] Hanchett, "Moscow in the Late Nineteenth Century," p. 141.

[150] Timothy J. Colton, *Moscow: Governing the Socialist Metropolis* (Cambridge, Mass.: Harvard University Press, 1995), p. 35; Hans Rogger, *Jewish Policies and Right-Wing Politics in Imperial Russia* (Berkeley: University of California Press, 1986), p. 69. For further discussion of imperial Russia's policies toward the Jewish populations brought into the empire following the annexation of Poland, see Solomon M. Schwarz, *The Jews in the Soviet Union* (Syracuse: Syracuse University Press, 1951); T. B. Geilikman, *Istoriia obshchestvennogo dvizheniia Evreev v Pol'she i Rossii* (Moscow: Gosudarstvennoe izdatel'stvo, 1930); and Iulii I. Gessen, *Istoriia evreiskago naroda v Rossii* (St. Petersburg: Tipografiia L. Ia. Ganzburga, 1916).

According to M. S. Kupovetskii, "Evreiskoe naselenie Moskvy (XV–XXvv.)," in E. M. Pospelov et al., eds., *Etnicheskie gruppy v gorodakh Evropeiskoi chasti SSSR (formirovanie, rasselenie, dinamika kul'tury)* (Moscow: Moskovskii filial Geograficheskogo obshchestva S.S.S.R., 1987), pp. 58–71, the Russian Empire's Jewish population largely originated from the capture of lands in Belorus', Ukraine, and Poland beginning in the seventeenth century. Jews had been present in Moscow for some time, but began to arrive in large numbers only during the nineteenth century. Fewer than 300 Jews were estimated to have been living in Moscow at the time of the emancipation of the serfs in 1861. Moscow's Jewish population grew quite rapidly over the next three decades, reaching perhaps as many as 35,000 at the time of the 1891 expulsion decree. Some Jews simply moved to surrounding areas beyond the city boundaries, but most evidently returned to their designated reserves in and around Poland.

Jewish merchants of the first guild were permitted to come back to Moscow following 1899 upon receiving permission from the minister of finance in St. Petersburg and the local governor-general in Moscow. Significant numbers of Jewish students moved to town as well, numbering some 3,000 university students by 1916. Sixty thousand Jewish residents were estimated to have been living in Moscow at the time of the 1917 revolutions, constituting approximately 3 percent of the city's total population. Also see Rogger, *Jewish Policies*, p. 69.

[151] Owen, *Capitalism and Politics*, p. 103.

strategies for a mayor who could become more open to pragmatism and pluralism when it suited his purposes.

Alekseev's contradictory career illustrates some of the essential characteristics of the leadership strategy labeled here as "pragmatic pluralism." It underscores the more noxious aspects of a public policy predicated first and foremost on ruthless pragmatism. Alekseev's career, in this regard, is perhaps more illustrative of the strengths and weaknesses of this leadership style than that of a more explicitly liberal—and, as generally acknowledged, lovable—pluralist mayor such as Prince Vladimir Golitsyn, who served as Moscow's mayor from 1897 until 1905.

In the end, Alekseev's accomplishments advanced a broadly reformist agenda—including numerous improvements in public health facilities. As with Carter Harrison the younger's battles with Yerkes, Alekseev dealt with unsavory allies and used questionable methods to achieve lasting results that, more than a century later, appear to have advanced the cause of municipal reform within the specific environment in which he worked.

Alekseev supported numerous liberal causes despite the limitations imposed by his own social milieu and by his city's weak municipal government. His endorsement of adult education for workers won him the lasting enmity of some fellow factory owners. His vigorous advocacy of local self-government brought him into conflict with Petersburg centralizers. Many of these positions were undoubtedly motivated, as Owen has expressed it, by "narrow concern for economic gain" rather than by principled belief.[152]

Nikolai's actions divided local politics into pro-and-anti-Alekseev camps.[153] Alekseev was mayor at a time in his city's history when action was in and of itself reform—and action required not just despotic rule but also the mobilization of diverse interests behind specific projects. His concern for education, public health, and commerce necessarily advanced segmented social interests.

Alekseev and his fellow Moscow merchant elites were arguably "the freest and most energetic people ever to live in Russia."[154] Subsequent pre-Soviet Moscow social, economic, and political masters (frequently from the same entrepreneurial and social stratum) similarly succeeded at mobilizing resources behind their favorite initiatives, including charity-supported hospitals, public libraries, new parks, expanded educational

[152] Owen, *Capitalism and Politics*, p. 103.
[153] Ruckman, *The Moscow Business Elite*, p. 117.
[154] West, "Merchant Moscow in Historical Context," p. 5.

opportunities, and free higher education for workers.[155] Late-imperial mayors such as the beloved Golitsyn, Moscow University law professor Nikolai Guchkov, and future Serb hero Mikhail Chelnokov were constantly at odds with St. Petersburg as they fought to implement liberal policies, especially in the field of education.[156] Their victories were often predicated on the capacity of local officials to negotiate effectively with central ministries.[157] Middle-ranking groups became increasingly involved in the process of municipal administration throughout this period, far more than was ever the case in rival St. Petersburg.

Moscow liberalism, especially among the "young industrialists" and "progressists" around such groups as the "Riabushchinskii circle," placed city leaders in opposition to both the more conservative imperial government based in the northern capital and the increasingly radicalized socialist movement demanding revolution from below.[158] Russian liberalism's ultimate failure would come, of course. That collapse would be yet another quarter-century away on the day that Alekseev was shot.

SEKI HAJIME

Osaka mayor Seki Hajime also personified the politics of pragmatic pluralism. Jeffrey Hanes reports in an accomplished dissertation focusing on Seki that the economist, labor relations specialist, transportation

---

[155] Robert W. Thurston, *Liberal City, Conservative State: Moscow and Russia's Urban Crisis, 1906–1914* (Oxford, U.K.: Oxford University Press, 1987), pp. 154–80; M. P. Shchepkin, *Obshchestvennoe khoziaistvo goroda Moskvy v 1863–1887 godakh. Istoriko-statisticheskoe opisanie* (Moscow: Moskovskaia gorodskaia tipografiia, 1890).

[156] Pisar'kova, "Gorodskie golovy Moskvy," pp. 10–15.

[157] On the function of imperial ministries during this period, see Hans Rogger, *Russia in the Age of Modernisation and Revolution, 1881–1921* (London: Longman, 1983), pp. 27–43.

[158] Petrov, "'Moscow City'"; James L. West, "Visions of Russia's Entrepreneurial Future: Pavel Riabushinsky's Utopian Capitalism," in West and Petrov, eds., *Merchant Moscow*, pp. 161–70; James L. West, "The Fate of Merchant Moscow," in West and Petrov, eds., *Merchant Moscow*, pp. 173–78; James L. West, "Merchant Moscow in Historical Context," in West and Petrov, eds., *Merchant Moscow*, pp. 3–12; James Lawrence West, "The Moscow Progressists: Russian Industrialists in Liberal Politics, 1905–1914" (Ph.D. diss., Princeton University, 1974), pp. 57–64; Ruth AmEnde Roosa, *Russian Industrialists in an Era of Revolution: The Association of Industry and Trade, 1906–1917*, ed. Thomas C. Owen (Armonk, N.Y.: M. E. Sharpe, 1997); Ruth AmEnde Roosa, "Russian Industrialists during World War I: The Internationalization of Economics and Politics," in Guroff and Carstensen, eds., *Entrepreneurship in Imperial Russia*, pp. 159–87; and Ruth AmEnde Roosa, "The Association of Industry and Trade, 1906–1914: An Examination of the Economic Views of Organized Industrialists in Prerevolutionary Russia" (Ph.D. diss., Columbia University, 1967).

planner, and social reformer left Tokyo in 1914 to accept a position as deputy mayor of Osaka after having tired of life in academe.[159] Seki served in that position until he was appointed mayor in 1924, a post that he would hold until his death in 1935.[160] His two decades of service to Japan's second city would earn him the appellation "the father of Osaka."

On the surface, Seki appears to have been a rather different sort of political leader and human being than were the Harrisons and Alekseev. An economics professor by profession, Seki represented precisely the sort of "progressive" intellectual that the earthier Harrisons and young Alekseev held in high contempt.

For its part, Osaka enjoyed only a modicum of electoral politics. Kyoto, Osaka, and Tokyo, as "metropolitan prefectures," were not permitted to have mayors prior to 1898 and, thereafter, could choose their municipal leaders only indirectly through city councils that were themselves selected by a highly restricted electorate.[161] The councils named three candidates, one of whom was appointed mayor by imperial decree following a recommendation from the Ministry of Interior. Bureaucratic infighting within municipal offices and battling with Tokyo's central ministries naturally remained far more important under such a system than was the case with Moscow's personalistic politics or Chicago's multi-constituency public political games. No colorful tales of Seki's use and misuse of power appear, whereas one readily discovers them when researching the Harrisons and Alekseev.

Similarities emerge on closer examination, however. Like the Harrisons, Seki spent time at German universities. Like Alekseev, his profound interest in national revival balanced his European experiences. Like both Harrisons and Alekseev, Seki was a pragmatist, willing to pick up whatever tools of urban management were at his disposal. Like all three, Seki saw that his nation's future success lay in the economic achievements of its cities.

Seki had no illusions about the nature of the city he governed. Indeed, he was attracted to Osaka precisely because it was a sprawling industrial behemoth so unlike his own intellectual and social community in

---

[159] This account is based on Jeffrey Eldon Hanes, "Seki Hajime and the Making of Modern Osaka" (Ph.D. diss., University of California, Berkeley, 1988), pp. 1–11.

[160] "Mayor of Osaka [Mr. Ikegami Saburo]: Impending Resignation," *Japan Weekly Chronicle* (Kobe), November 15, 1923, p. 687; "Mayor of Osaka: Retiring Bonus," *Japan Weekly Chronicle*, December 13, 1923, p. 829.

[161] Edward Seidensticker, *Low City, High City: Tokyo from Edo to the Earthquake* (New York: Knopf, 1983), p. 30.

Tokyo.[162] More fundamentally, Seki believed in the politics of gradual reform from within, of compromise, and of bringing as many of Osaka's fragmented social forces into alliances that might temper the politics of difference.

The eldest of four children, Seki was born on September 26, 1873, in a remote temple near the Izu Peninsula on Japan's western coast.[163] His father, who would die when Hajime was still a teenager, was a mathematics tutor and teacher; his mother similarly taught in a variety of private and public schools. The elder Sekis moved their family to the Asakusa district in Tokyo when Hajime was four. He led a quintessentially Restoration Tokyo childhood.

Seki Hajime was, like many children and young adults of his generation, both fascinated by the West and concerned over Japan's possible loss of distinctiveness. He was trained at the Tokyo Commercial School, a Meiji institution that sought to inculcate Western knowledge. The school, which eventually attained university status, remained Seki's touchstone until his departure for Osaka in 1914. He completed secondary, university, and graduate training there before joining the faculty at the age of twenty-four.

Prior to teaching, Seki and five Tokyo Commercial colleagues were packed off to study in Europe for some two years.[164] Every bit the model of a serious Japanese exchange student, Seki appears to have done little more than study diligently during his stay in the West. He drew a placement studying transportation planning and economics in Belgium, where he developed a specialization that would serve him well until the end of his career. Seki mastered French, German, and English during this period, and completed his European sojourn with a grand tour of Germany, England, and, on his way home, the United States. Most meaningfully for his future intellectual development, Seki evidently enrolled in lectures at the University of Berlin. He also managed a stop at North America's transportation hub (Chicago), where he was much taken with the city's new network of elevated commuter trains.

Seki and many of his Tokyo Commercial School classmates became ever more skeptical of economic theory that advanced laissez-faire principles within a social and cultural vacuum. They preferred historical approaches to economic development that incorporated cultural, political, and social context into economic thinking. Seki, in this regard, was

---

[162] Hanes, "Seki Hajime," p. 2.   [163] Ibid., pp. 25–27.
[164] Ibid., pp. 29–33.

thoroughly familiar with the writings of the German Historical School, even to the point of establishing a Berlin Association within the Tokyo Commercial School.[165]

Seki became increasingly skeptical of unfettered market development. He was, in fact, an economist who today would be associated with the label "Keynesian." Left to their own devices, Seki would argue, financiers became mere "procurers of capital" rather than builders, managers, and true "capitalists."[166] Reason and moderation dictated, he would write, that management and labor both compromise to advance the national interest.[167] Furthermore, the "livable city" could be achieved only through the creation of a moral economy based on social justice.[168] Seki's actions were the essence of a pragmatic pluralist who demonstrated, as had the Harrisons and Alekseev, a penchant for compromise that would serve him well once he entered the rough-and-tumble world of urban politics in Osaka.

Seki's Tokyo life was undistinguishable from that of other professors of the period.[169] He taught, wrote several books and nearly fifty articles, participated on the edges of various student strikes and arguments with central authorities, and consulted for a number of government and nongovernment entities. A well-respected economist, Seki gained considerable theoretical expertise. He eventually grew tired of academic grandstanding, back-biting intramural politics, and pointless mind games. Committed to labor reform, Seki wrote more popular tracts as well as his scholarly treatises, became a trustee of a trade union, and founded the *Kokumin Keizai Zasshi* (Journal of National Economics). Responding to a number of newspaper articles about Osaka's search for a deputy mayor—and probably prompted by prominent Osaka banker Koyama Kenzo, whom Seki would have known when Koyama had headed the Tokyo Commercial School—Seki made a definitive move from the world of ideas to the world of public affairs.[170] Seki was elected deputy mayor by a unanimous vote of the Osaka Municipal Assembly with the enthusiastic recommendation of Mayor Ikegami Saburo.[171]

As with other Japanese reformers of the era—and, indeed, their counterparts in such cities as Chicago and Moscow—Seki was not of the

---

[165] Ibid., pp. 38–46, 67.   [166] Ibid., p. 101.
[167] Ibid., pp. 6–8.   [168] Ibid., pp. 2–5.
[169] Ibid., pp. 67–95.   [170] Ibid., pp. 251–55.
[171] "New Deputy-Mayor for Osaka: Dr. Seki Recommended," *Japan Weekly Chronicle*, July 16, 1914, p. 137.

37. Seki Hajime (seated, at center) celebrating having become mayor of Osaka. Photographer unknown, n.d. From Shibamura Atsuki, *Seki Hajime: Toshi Shiso No Paionia* (Kyoto: Shoraisha, 1989), p. 150.

laboring classes and may even have argued against their right to vote. He feared an outbreak of massive social and class conflict and gradually grew frustrated by the failure of attempts to reform society solely through changing labor relations. He was a reformer out of pragmatism as much as or more than out of idealistic conviction. Concluding that the source of the "worker problem" lay in the nature of workers' living environments, Seki rejected the notion that reform should begin and end at the factory gate. Rather, he believed that reform should extend to worker housing, eventually encompassing the entire industrial city.

Upon arriving in Osaka in early 1914, Seki was bent on bringing more reason to the urban bedlam that was turn-of-the-century Osaka. He immediately tackled a number of significant urban problems with considerable success, especially in his sphere of greatest expertise, transportation. He focused on streetcar safety and, following the arrival of the automobile, highway construction.[172]

Seki emerged as a leading participant in the preparation of the 1919 national Urban Planning Law.[173] Seki and fellow reformers in other cities (such as Otsuki Ryuji in Kyoto and Yamazaki Ryutaro) had been inspired by British and American urban reformers. These "municipal socialists" advocated planning as a tool for confronting Japan's growing urban ills. Yet the central government remained suspicious of granting too great a degree of autonomy to local administrators and governments. Maintaining control over municipal budgets, the central government choked off planning objectives that went beyond narrowly defined physical improvements in existing urban areas. As in Chicago and especially in Moscow, the underdevelopment of local institutions subverted reform initiatives.[174] Central bureaucrats in provincial (or, in the American context, "state") and national capitals protected their turf. Underfunded and underinstitutionalized, Osaka municipal agencies could not sustain a politics of pragmatic pluralism in the face of opposition from an increasingly authoritarian imperial government in Tokyo.

Different as they were in personality and national culture, in training and social status, the Carter Harrisons (father and son), Nikolai

---

[172] Hanes, "Seki Hajime," pp. 322–23.   [173] Ibid., pp. 208–33, 322–31.

[174] See, for example, the discussion in Charles A. Beard's 1923 report on municipal administration for Tokyo mayor Goto Shimpei's newly established Tokyo Institute of Municipal Research. Beard's report deals with many issues of Japanese city management overall. Charles A. Beard, *The Administration and Politics of Tokyo: A Survey and Opinions* (New York: Macmillan, 1923). Concerning Goto Shimpei's career, see Yukiko Hayase, "The Career of Goto Shimpei: Japan's Statesman of Research, 1857–1929" (Ph.D. diss., Florida State University, 1974).

Alekseev, and Seki Hajime successfully wrestled with the practical problems of governing enormous, deeply divided, and rapidly changing industrial cities at the height of their capitalist explosions. They did so in an era when many of their predecessors and successors failed at the same task. Despite their differences, their careers reflect a similar commitment to compromise, pragmatism, and moderate reform. All four were practitioners of a pragmatic pluralism that advanced their communities' interests and improved their constituents' quality of life in innumerable ways.

12

The Practice of Pragmatic Pluralism:
The City, Transitional Capitalism, and the
Meaning of Moscow

Chicago, Moscow, and Osaka at the turn of the twentieth century all
could have been described equally well by Lincoln Steffens's characterization of Chicago as "first in violence, deepest in dirt; loud, lawless,
unlovely, ill-smelling, irreverent, new; an overgrown gawk of a village,
the 'tough' among cities, a spectacle for the nation."[1] All three communities represented a new type of urban phenomenon: highly adaptive,
complex, differentiated, metropolitan-scale urban centers created by, and
in turn recreating, private capital driven by innovative technologies.[2]

Chicago—and Moscow and Osaka as well—has often been portrayed
as a rough, tough town. The Midwest metropolis was the sort of place
that could drive Rudyard Kipling to proclaim in 1899, "Having seen it,
I urgently desire never to see it again. It is inhabited by savages. Its water
is the water of the Hughli [the river that flows through Calcutta], and
its air is dirt."[3] Kipling need not have bothered to malign the city, for as
longtime journalistic observer of the local scene George Ade once wrote,
"The town is never satisfied with itself."[4]

Feral toughness is not all Chicago—or Moscow and Osaka—
was about. Chicago became viewed as the quintessential American city

---

[1] Lincoln Steffens, *The Shame of the Cities* (1904; reprint, New York: Hill and Wang, 1992), p. 163.

[2] Indeed, they confirm Henry D. Smith II's maxim, "the city is never what we think it is: it is always far more complex and changeable than our ideas about it." Henry D. Smith II, "Tokyo and London: Comparative Conceptions of the City," in Albert M. Craig, ed., *Japan: A Comparative View* (Princeton: Princeton University Press, 1979), pp. 49–99: 49.

[3] Rudyard Kipling, "How I Struck Chicago, and How Chicago Struck Me: Of Religion, Politics, and Pig-Sticking, and the Incarnation of the City among Shambles," in Bessie Louise Pierce, comp., *As Others See Chicago: Impressions of Visitors, 1673–1933* (Chicago: University of Chicago Press, 1933), p. 251.

[4] George Ade, *Stories of the Streets and of the Town: From the Chicago Record, 1893–1900*, ed. Frank J. Meine (Chicago: Caxton Club, 1941), p. 104.

precisely because of its newness, its boldly utilitarian purpose, and its bewildering roughness. Yet a vibrant artistic and cultural life always coexisted alongside commerce and industry.[5] Late-twentieth-century American social observer Garry Wills hit close to the mark when he observed, "Chicago has had its full share of atrocities and enormities— reaction to the Haymarket Riot, or the Saint Valentine's 'massacre,' or the splitting of the atom at the University of Chicago's Stagg Field. But it is time to give up on barroom mysticisms about this 'male city'—all those shoulders on the brain. What mattered is that Chicago had, from the outset, a brain on its shoulders. It was primarily a technological and commercial mind, but also a reforming, even a socially creative, intel-lect."[6] Moscow and Osaka were also home to technologically inventive, commercially adept, socially creative, and artistically talented intellects at the turn of the last century. These were all cities full of movers and shakers.

Chicago, Moscow, and Osaka of a century ago were similar types of cities embedded in dissimilar nations and political systems. The distinc-tiveness of those larger national systems explains the differences in the subsequent development of all three towns. At the time covered by this book, Chicago, Moscow, and Osaka were simultaneously large com-mercial cities at the height of major social, technological, economic, and political transitions. Their shared characteristics made the three cities more similar at times to one another than they were to the national soci-eties from which they emerged. They nurtured alternative approaches to the organization of human existence from those found elsewhere in the United States, Russia, and Japan.

The collective failure to institutionalize the exercise of pragmatic pluralism eventually eroded the long-term legacies of these great private metropolises. This approach to power is sufficiently fluid, as it must become embedded in collective memory as much as in legal statute. Legends about Chicago's rapacious politicians are as central to the survival of a politics of compromise and accommodation as are city charters and state-legislated norms. Similarly, the Bolshevik eradication of collective memory concerning the prerevolutionary period under-mined the practice of pragmatic pluralism in Moscow every bit as much

---

[5] A point eloquently and forcefully argued in Helen Lefkowitz Horowitz, *Culture and the City: Cultural Philanthropy in Chicago from the 1880s to 1917* (Lexington: University Press of Kentucky, 1976).

[6] Garry Wills, "Chicago Underground," *New York Review of Books,* October 21, 1993, p. 22.

38. Business section and the new post office, Chicago, 1906. H. C. White Co.
Library of Congress, Prints and Photographs Division, LC-USZ62-055105.

as did changes in the city's legal status. Nonetheless, such ultimate failure does not negate the power of comparison for the period under scrutiny here.

THREE LARGE CAPITALIST CITIES IN TRANSITION

Peter Hall argues that creative cities share many characteristics through-out history.[7] Size becomes important to the extent that large scale fosters

---

[7] Peter Hall, *Cities in Civilization* (New York: Pantheon, 1988), pp. 282–87.

complexity and diversity. Living conditions are often appalling. Intensely creative cities tend to be in transition toward "new and unexplored modes of organization."[8] Spare wealth attracts migrants "from the four corners of their worlds."[9] Hall continues that "probably, no city has ever been creative without continued renewal of the creative bloodstream."[10]

Chicago, Moscow, and Osaka shared these features with the dozens of cities about which Hall writes in his magisterial *Cities in Civilization*. They were precisely the sort of wide-open, nonhierarchical towns that Hall argues are the keys to creativity and civilization. Coarse and abrasive communities in which large numbers of people who did not have any particular reason to like one another were forced to find ways to live together, socially fragmented and spatially impacted—they were breeding grounds for pragmatic pluralism.

Chicago's property owners were able to use government institutions and policies to protect their considerable investments. Ironically, perhaps, their successes were rooted in a half-century of social, economic, and political fragmentation. Chicago landowners learned coalition politics as multiple class and ethnic pyramids replaced more unitary social systems. They preserved power where it counted—in their ability to manage their own property—by relinquishing power when it did not matter.

Constantly shifting multipolar political games created surprising coalitions—as may be seen in the seven-decades-long Chicago traction wars. Aristocratic reformers joined ethnic political machines, union bosses sought out corporate supporters, middle-class society tugged and pulled at neighboring social groups, "downstate" collaborated with "upstate," the Irish with the Germans with the Poles with the Jews.

No single group could dominate the rapidly shifting worlds of Chicago—as became apparent in the city charter debacles of the early years of the twentieth century. The evolving political structures and practices of these years rendered the city's extreme fragmentation more benign by expanding opportunities for all. Moreover, they ensured that the city's most successful politicians—such as the Carter Harrisons—were required to master the politics of compromise. The booming local and national economy assisted this process, to be sure—nurturing an increasing economic base that seemed to provide endless opportunities for improving one's life. As Ester Fuchs has noted, American urban

---

[8] Ibid., p. 284.   [9] Ibid., p. 285.
[10] Ibid.

politics became distinctly more conflictual once the fundamental issue
was no longer who gets which piece of an expanding pie, but rather who
gets less pie.[11]

Unlike the burgeoning prosperity of the United States, the imperial
Russian economy collapsed. Tsar Nicholas II's ministers rarely felt compelled to accommodate new social forces. National political institutions
rejected expanded political participation. Cunning bureaucrats and
imperial fiat subverted those half-measures toward the establishment of
more pluralistic institutions that had been taken in the wake of the 1905
Revolution.[12] Pragmatic pluralism lost out.

Moscow's local political life had become surprisingly tolerant as the
city's economy and population became ever more diverse. Effective mer-
chant-mayors—such as Nikolai Alekseev—succeeded in extending local
authority by expanding municipal services. Philanthropists and civic
leaders scrambled to create educational, health, and social organizations
to help absorb the city's new workers. Local political folkways and
customs reflected the tempestuousness of Moscow's economic life.

The imperial government and its officers and agents in Moscow,
together with local conservatives, subverted many emerging institutions
and traditions. Reform-minded Moscow merchants and landowners
found fewer and fewer allies on either the left or the right in an era of
gathering political confrontation. The politics of diversity failed as those
striving for power sought monopolistic power. The very groups that had
contributed so much to the dynamism of turn-of-the-century Moscow
disappeared as Russia entered its Soviet period.

Osaka enjoyed a period of moderate reform at the end of the nineteenth century. Local politics benefited from an expanding national
economy, as production and real incomes throughout Japan virtually
doubled between 1890 and 1914.[13] Osaka's most successful politicians—
such as Seki Hajime—were similarly proponents of compromise and
practitioners of a politics of inclusion. Their achievements were considerable and, at times, tangible, as was the case with the city's mammoth
harbor-development project.

Breakdown, when it came at moments like the 1918 rice riots, proved
to be a product of the failure to incorporate many among Osaka's busi-

[11] Ester R. Fuchs, *Mayors and Money: Fiscal Policy in New York and Chicago* (Chicago:
University of Chicago Press, 1992).
[12] For further discussion of autocratic retrenchment, see Abraham Ascher, *The Revolution
of 1905*, Vol. 2: *Authority Restored* (Stanford: Stanford University Press, 1992).
[13] Thomas R. H. Havens, *Farm and Nation in Modern Japan: Agrarian Nationalism,
1870–1940* (Princeton: Princeton University Press, 1974), p. 87.

ness leaders into civic coalitions committed to the amelioration of industrialization's abundant scourges. Pluralism's ultimate collapse in Osaka took another direction from that of Moscow—toward right-wing authoritarian rule at home and expansionist militarism abroad. Institutions and codes of political conduct predicated on a plurality of interests failed to hold the center ground at the national level, undercutting a local political culture of pragmatic pluralism in Osaka.

The stormy political life of Chicago, Moscow, and Osaka thus demonstrates that pragmatic local leaders may serve as critical buffers between their constituents and the more destructive aspects of change at times of intense social, economic, and political transition. Pragmatic politicians practicing the art of inclusion and coalition-building around specific issues can ameliorate tensions arising from the fragmentation of previously secure social, political, economic, and cultural hierarchies. To do so, however, local politicians must pursue the interests of their regions and their communities in addition to personal profit and political gain. Local political machines must do more than forage for the wealth of others if they are to "add value" by shielding their communities from the worst ravages of economic uncertainty, resource scarcity, and structural change.

To borrow an idea from Joan Clos i Matheu, mayor of Barcelona at the end of the twentieth century, cities are rooted in a complexity that is, itself, the product of thousands of human relationships.[14] Politicians must accept complexity and remain humble in their ambition, as success is transitory and financial resources are finite. Alliances among disparate groups remain among the few building blocks at the disposal of urban managers over the medium to long term. Clos, his predecessor (the legendary Pasqual Maragall), and their colleagues proved themselves to be among the twentieth century's most effective urban managers precisely because of their pragmatic, process-oriented approach to Barcelona's management.[15] The insights gleaned from their achievements transcend time and place, being perhaps never more fitting than was the

[14] Joan Clos i Matheu, "The Barcelona Model of Urban Success," lecture delivered at the Conference on the Real and Imagined City, Center for Contemporary Culture of Barcelona, Barcelona, October 11, 1997. Revised text published as Joan Clos, "Barcelona: patrimoni, creacio, qualitat," in Pep Subiros, ed., *Debat de Barcelona (III): Ciutat real, ciutat ideal* (Barcelona: Centre de Cultura Contemporania de Barcelona, 1998), pp. 113–16.

[15] For a review of Barcelona's successes during the 1980s and 1990s, see Joan-Eugeni Sanchez, "Barcelona: The Olympic City," in Chris Jensen-Butler, Arie Shachar, and Jan van Weesep, eds., *European Cities in Competition* (Brookfield, Vt.: Avebury, 1997), pp. 179–208.

case in the exploding industrial metropolises of the late nineteenth century.

The eventual failures of nascent democratic institutions in Moscow and Osaka together with the rise of a predatory political machine in Chicago at the close of World War I mark the limits of pragmatic pluralism. Like Hall's innovative cities more generally, politics predicated on bringing together dissimilar groups demands constant attention. The veneer of stability offered by pragmatic pluralist politicians proves illusory in the face of an ever-changing environment. The retention of power in periods of rapid social and economic dislocation is "an extraordinarily fragile and delicate balancing act."[16] The staying power of the Chicago Democratic machine in particular—holding control of the mayor's chair from 1931 until 1979—was a remarkable political accomplishment.

Pragmatic pluralism emerges as an especially powerful political strategy during difficult periods of social and economic transition. Writing about the impact of the Meiji revolution in provincial Kawasaki, Neil L. Waters penned a line that would apply equally well to Chicago, Moscow, and Osaka; "Economic diversity and powerful regional leadership would prove to be surprisingly effective armor against the more objectionable aspects of the transition to Meiji."[17]

Though Kawasaki's Meiji rulers were "on paper functionaries of a rigidly centralized system," Waters continues, "they were in fact willing and generally able to modify the programs they were charged to enforce in accordance with their perceptions of local interests."[18] The result was not the undoing of Meiji reform, but just the opposite. "The ability of local leaders to shield the Kawasaki region from some of the short term deleterious effects of early Meiji administrative and economic changes," Waters contends, "helps to explain why the region weathered the transition from Bakumatsu to Meiji without violent incidents."[19]

Violence was omnipresent in all three cities under consideration in this volume. Especially potent challenges to reformist pragmatic pluralistic politics came from authoritarian populists proclaiming national uniqueness. In his examination of creative cities, Hall observes that

---

[16] Robert A. Slayton, "Labor and Urban Politics: District 31, Steel Workers Organizing Committee, and the Chicago Machine," *Journal of Urban History* 23, no. 1 (November 1996), pp. 29–65: 31.

[17] Neil L. Waters, *Japan's Local Pragmatists: The Transition from Bakumatsu to Meiji in the Kawasaki Region* (Cambridge, Mass.: Harvard University Press, 1983), p. 55.

[18] Ibid., p. 81.   [19] Ibid., p. 76.

[b]ecause these were all societies in economic transition, they were also societies in the throes of a transformation in social relationships, in values, and in views about the world. As a massive generalization, but one that stands up surprisingly well, they all were in a state of uneasy and unstable tension between a set of conservative forces and values—aristocratic, hierarchical, religious, conformist—and a set of radical values which were the exact opposite: bourgeois, open, rational, skeptical. These were societies troubled about themselves, societies that were in the course of losing the old certainties but were deeply concerned about what was happening to them.[20]

Once Moscow is approached within the comparative context of other like cities, it—and Russia, for that matter—does not appear to be quite as peculiar and distinctive as nationalist myth suggests.

MOSCOW AND THE NATURE OF RUSSIAN "DIFFERENCE"

Many of the stories told in this volume seem at first to confirm that Russia and Moscow were different from societies along the North Atlantic littoral. The managerial revolution that produced the Chicago of the same era emerged in response to the growing national middle-class markets of the United States. The city's leading innovators—Pullman, McCormick, Field—provided goods and services tied to an unprecedented mass middle market. Osaka's leading innovators—such as Shibusawa and Nomura—also responded to the middling wealth of most Japanese. Old Believer textile merchants in Moscow, on the other hand, kept their eye for much longer than one would have thought prudent on a largely unchanged, rural, peasant market.

The middle strata so important in Chicago and Osaka initially appear to have been "missing" in the Russian case.[21] Harley Balzer argues the opposite, namely that professionals were coming to constitute the "largest component of Russia's nascent middle class by 1900, and professionals played a more important role in political activity than did the commercial or industrial bourgeoisie."[22] Yet, "divisions along lines of geography, economic sector, and market orientation largely precluded making common cause."[23] This was so even in Moscow, perhaps Russia's most autonomous economic center for the reasons discussed in this volume.

[20] Hall, *Cities in Civilization*, p. 285.
[21] Kendall E. Bailes, "Reflections on Russian Professions," in Harley D. Balzer, ed., *Russia's Missing Middle Class: The Professions in Russian History* (Armonk, N.Y.: M. E. Sharpe, 1996), pp. 39–54: 41.
[22] Harley D. Balzer, "Conclusion: The Missing Middle Class," in Balzer, ed., *Russia's Missing Middle Class*, pp. 293–320: 293.
[23] Ibid., pp. 293–94.

Such argumentation, Christine Ruane proposes, misses a larger point. "Because Russian professionals do not appear to conform to the criteria of the Anglo-American model," she writes, "most Western scholars have seen Russian professionalization as a failure." She suggests that "Russian professionals were involved in an exciting and important process of social transformation" even as they did not create Western-style professions.[24] This book has told a similar tale.

Subordinate to a state that stifled entrepreneurship, caught in a precarious caste (*soslovie*) system, and prone to use nationalist fervor to cover their deficiencies as modern capitalists, some among Moscow's merchants never transcended the foibles of their old-fashioned ways.[25] Rather, they converted their old ways into "traditionalism in business practice, conservatism in politics, and nationalism in culture."[26]

Russia was different, and not the least because Russian autocracy seems to have been different.[27] Russia's emerging professionals sustained an ideal of state service rooted in an earlier era.[28] Its workers were similarly caught between town and country—at times, quite literally, as they shuttled back and forth between farm and factory.[29] The feebleness of Moscow's labor supply crippled innovation, interrupted production, and, in the minds of some observers, unalterably reduced the city's capacity as a manufacturing center. The city's appearance remained almost uniquely traditional well into the twentieth century.[30]

Comparisons with Osaka are most instructive. Certainly, Osaka merchants had more than their fair share of tiffs and disagreements with imperial officials in Tokyo, as has been shown in this volume. But the Meiji and Taisho regimes, at their core, were committed to making Japan into

---

[24] Christine Ruane, *Gender, Class, and the Professionalization of Russian City Teachers, 1860–1914* (Pittsburgh: University of Pittsburgh Press, 1994), p. 9.

[25] Ibid., p. 4. This argument is also developed by Thomas C. Owen in *Russian Corporate Capitalism from Peter the Great to Perestroika* (Oxford, U.K.: Oxford University Press, 1995); and "Entrepreneurship and the Structure of Enterprise in Russia, 1800–1880," in Greg Guroff and F. V. Carstensen, eds., *Entrepreneurship in Imperial Russia and the Soviet Union* (Princeton: Princeton University Press, 1983), pp. 59–83.

[26] William Blackwell, "The Russian Entrepreneur in the Tsarist Period: An Overview," in Guroff and Carstensen, eds., *Entrepreneurship in Imperial Russia*, pp. 13–26: 18.

[27] Marc Raeff, *Understanding Imperial Russia: State and Society in the Old Regime*, trans. Arthur Goldhammer (New York: Columbia University Press, 1984), pp. 188, 223.

[28] Ruane, *Gender, Class*, p. 9.

[29] The effect of the dependence of Moscow factories on temporary hires from surrounding villages is tellingly explored in Robert E. Johnson, *Peasant and Proletarian: The Working-Class of Moscow in the Late Nineteenth Century* (New Brunswick, N.J.: Rutgers University Press, 1979).

[30] Irina V. Potkina, "Moscow's Commercial Mosaic," in James L. West and Iurii A. Petrov, eds., *Merchant Moscow: Images of Russia's Vanished Bourgeoisie* (Princeton: Princeton University Press, 1998), pp. 37–44: 41.

39. The great vegetable market, Moscow, 1902. H. C. White Co. Library of Congress, Prints and Photographs Division, LC-USZ62-056576.

a capitalist industrial power. The emperors and their advisers embraced the notion of transforming Japan into a "modern" state just like the European powers (even though it wasn't always clear precisely which European model was to be followed, or what a "power" might really be).

The Romanovs never unambiguously embraced such goals.[31] Their interest was different—how to keep Russia in the game of European

---

[31] Much to the chagrin of many leading Russian entrepreneurs and industrialists who, according to Cyril Black and Ruth AmEnde Roosa, argued vigorously for state-supported economic reinvigoration. See Cyril E. Black, "Russian and Soviet Entrepreneurship in a Comparative Context," in Guroff and Carstensen, eds., *Entrepreneurship*

power without altering key authority relationships at home. Nicholas II retreated from reform at every opportunity following the calamities of 1905–7.[32] Ambiguous signals from the top paralyze centralized systems such as that of the Romanov dynasty. An inept and incompetent imperial elite, rather than a missing social stratum, made Russia different from Japan and America, even as Moscow revealed striking similarities with urban communities elsewhere.

UNFINISHED BUSINESS

Seeking equivalence of Moscow with European and North American cities—and of Russia with the West—cannot, in and of itself, shed new light on Russian development. The cases for and against Russia's uniqueness have been made ad nauseam. The strategy employed here has tried to step outside of that century-long debate by approaching Russia through a handful of Russia's multiple discrete realities. In this case, Moscow has been examined in relation to historiography on urban community power in the United States and elsewhere, as well as from the perspective of debates over the relationship between inventiveness and urbanity.

Accumulated studies such as those offered in this volume will make explicit definitions and assumptions about the urban experience that, over time, will expand theoretical approaches to the place of the city in civilization. Lewis Mumford's classics, *The Culture of Cities* and *The City in History*, as well as Peter Hall's massive *Cities in Civilization*, set high standards toward which future studies must strive.[33]

At the moment, scholars less ambitious and capable than Mumford and Hall may contribute discrete case studies out of which general histories and theories might be constructed. What remains important, as David Hammack so successfully demonstrated in his work on New York

in Imperial Russia, pp. 3–11; Ruth AmEnde Roosa, "The Association of Industry and Trade, 1906–1914: An Examination of the Economic Views of Organized Industrialists in Prerevolutionary Russia" (Ph.D. diss., Columbia University, 1967); Ruth AmEnde Roosa, "Russian Industrialists during World War I: The Internationalization of Economics and Politics," in Guroff and Carstensen, eds., *Entrepreneurship in Imperial Russia*, pp. 159–87; and Ruth AmEnde Roosa, *Russian Industrialists in an Era of Revolution: The Association of Industry and Trade, 1906–1917*, ed. Thomas C. Owen (Armonk, N.Y.: M. E. Sharpe, 1997).

[32] Marc Raeff, "The Bureaucratic Phenomena of Imperial Russia, 1700–1905," *American Historical Review* 84, no. 2 (April 1979), pp. 399–411: 411.

[33] Lewis Mumford, *The Culture of Cities* (New York: Harcourt, Brace, 1938); Lewis Mumford, *The City in History: Its Origins, Its Transformations, and Its Prospects* (New York: Harcourt, Brace and World, 1961); and Hall, *Cities in Civilization*.

City, is that the composite points of analysis involve major decisions and figures.[34] The six case studies and four mayors examined here address Hammack's concern for importance in that they significantly affected how large numbers of Chicagoans, Muscovites, and Osakans lived their lives. In the best case, they contribute a few meager additions to the comparative literature on the city.

Turn-of-the-century Russia was unlike Europe and North America and Japan even as Moscow was similar in important ways to fin de siècle Chicago and Osaka. But how much so? For all the difference between Russia and the West, for all the distance between Moscow corporate leaders and their peers in Chicago, or between acquiescent Moscow workers and their truculent brethren in Chicago, or between Orthodox-infused Slavophile intellectuals and the practitioners of Deweyan instrumentalism, Moscow was hardly "more backward" than Chicago or Osaka. At a minimum, Muscovites Anton Chekhov, Aleksandr Gorskii, Vasili Kandinskii, Anton Rubenstein, and Konstantin Stanislavskii-Alekseev, to name but a few, arguably made more enduring contributions to high culture than did comparable Chicagoans or Osakans.

Muscovite achievements in culture and the arts were hardly an accident.[35] Quite the opposite: they are a direct result of Moscow's unpolished commercialism, social turbulence, political volatility, and transitional capitalism. Moscow's cultural accomplishments were grounded in the same soil as the city's pragmatically pluralistic approach to social difference. Attainment was a direct consequence of the confrontation between talent and city, a point proudly proclaimed by Stanislavskii-Alekseev in his celebrated memoirs, *My Life in Art:* "Fate has been kind to me all through my life. It has surrounded me with people and society. To begin with, I began my life at a time when there was considerable animation in the spheres of art, science, and aesthetics. In Moscow, this was due to a great degree to young merchants who were interested not only in their businesses, but also in art."[36]

Elise Kimerling Wirtschafter correctly maintains that Russia in general and Moscow in particular were unusually dynamic in comparison to

---

[34] David C. Hammack, *Power and Society: Greater New York at the Turn of the Century* (New York: Russell Sage Foundation, 1982), p. 22.

[35] Indeed, Aaron Joseph Cohen argues that the art scene was itself an emerging civil society. See Aaron Joseph Cohen, "Making Modern Art National: Mass Mobilization, Public Culture, and Art in Russia during the First World War" (Ph.D. diss., Johns Hopkins University, 1998).

[36] Konstantin Stanislavskii[-Alekseev], *My Life in Art* (Moscow: Foreign Languages, 1958), p. 36.

most of the world. This was so despite—or, perhaps, because of—the absence of constitutional self-government, extensive state involvement in industrial development, and the persistent images of urban stagnation that have informed much reporting and scholarship about the weaknesses of local capitalist development.[37] Turn-of-the-century Muscovite realities, mentalities, and psychoses ultimately proved to be those of millions of twentieth-century human beings. Moscow was every bit a harbinger of the twentieth century as were Chicago and Osaka.

BACK TO THE FUTURE

A futurologist in 1900 would have had difficulty predicting the diverse twentieth-century fates of Chicago, Moscow, and Osaka. Much that happened, in fact, would have been well beyond human imagination a century ago. The developmental trajectories of these great second cities took quite different directions following World War I.

All three cities grew in population, to be sure: metropolitan Chicago reaching over eight million souls by the 1990s, Moscow approximately nine million, and Osaka ten million. All three remained economic powerhouses, producing more wealth each year than all but a handful of nations. All three cities continue to serve as major international transportation hubs. Nevertheless, Chicago and Osaka are not nearly as important to their nations as they were a century ago. Moscow, on the other hand, has become a leading world city with no competitor in the urban hierarchy for hundreds of miles west to Berlin and thousands of miles east to Beijing.

The turn-of-the-century built environment of each of these cities suffered greatly during subsequent decades. Chicago's Loop retains many of the revolutionary skyscrapers of the city's heroic age. Upscale retail moved north along a revitalized Michigan Avenue, and the city has spread deeper into the prairie along interstate highways. The Pullman plant and stockyards—so prominent in the life of the late-nineteenth-century city—have long closed, leaving enormous scars cutting across the city's South Side.

The Red Army stopped Hitler's *Wehrmacht* just short of Moscow, saving the city from certain destruction during World War II. Pockets of merchant Moscow survived megalomaniacal Soviet-era plans that turned

---

[37] Elise Kimerling Wirtschafter, *Social Identity in Imperial Russia* (DeKalb: Northern Illinois University Press, 1997), p. 75.

the old commercial city into a totalitarian imperial capital. Old mansions along Spiridonovka, Malaia Bronia, Bolshaia Nikitskaia, and other streets now serve as embassies for foreign powers. The wooden city that constituted so much of turn-of-the-century Moscow is but a distant memory for the city's oldest residents, having been replaced during the 1960s and 1970s by low-grade, prefabricated apartment towers.

With the exception of a handful of prominent public buildings on or near Nakanoshima—such as the Bank of Japan, the prefectural library, Central Hall, and the Imperial Mint—the Osaka of old has been destroyed by American bombs and rapacious real estate development. Today's Osaka is a sea of cement and bad taste.

Population growth and many of the physical changes wrought by a century of development could well have been comprehensible to a nineteenth-century mind. The complex social and economic transformations of Chicago, Moscow, and Osaka would not have been as predictable. Following 1920, all three cities became profoundly different places than they had been before, with Chicago and Osaka remaining more alike while Moscow was transfigured into a dissimilar urban form.

Three fundamental changes within Chicago have made the city distinct from of its 1900 self. Demographically, the arrival of tens of thousands of African Americans who rode the rail lines up from the South made race an essential factor in Chicago life. Ethnicity and religion remain salient, to be sure. The racial divide nonetheless has bleached all previous ethnic divisions into a sea of whiteness that all too often stands in opposition to the world of African-American Chicagoans. Politically, the divided and raucous competition among dozens of small machines that marked the tales recorded here gave way to the half-century ascendancy of one large machine. As with race, machine politics converted a fractious town into a city of stark choice—white versus black, machine versus reform opposition, suburb versus central city.

Economically, Chicago ceased being the place where future became present by the 1920s. The Sunbelt replaced the Midwest as North America's driving economic force. Chicago formally fell to "third city" status in terms of population (yielding to Los Angeles) by the 1980s after having relinquished economic power long before. The city's economic base stagnated in relative terms, and now confronts the multiple traumas of the postindustrial transition brought by a globalized economy. Battles over streetcar lines are as forgotten as the streetcars themselves; city charter reform seems an almost quaint battle in a world dominated by Washington bureaucrats and international bankers. The issues animating Chicago political life at the turn of the twenty-first century are profoundly different from those of the turn of the twentieth.

Osaka similarly faces the conundrums of a postindustrial globalized economy. Textiles and other industries predicated on cheap labor are merely a remembrance. The city physically rebuilt itself following near-total destruction during World War II, a quarter-century effort topped off by the Expo-70 World's Fair in 1970. The war left less visible yet more profound wounds. Osaka's port had been oriented toward Japan's Asian empire—a hinterland lost in 1945. Some of Osaka's inner-city neighborhoods are among Japan's most dangerous. The city's heavy industries became less competitive over the postwar period, leaving Osaka's leaders a number of festering socio-economic dilemmas faced by such cities as Chicago, Manchester, and Marseilles.

The increasingly centralized postwar Japanese state poses a more pernicious problem for Osaka. Political and economic power has come to rest ever more squarely in Tokyo, drawing all but a few symbolic corporate headquarters and much-needed financial capital away from Osaka. By the 1990s, Tokyo's neighbor Yokohama had surpassed Osaka as Japan's second-largest city. Like Chicago, Osaka is no longer a place where future becomes the present.

Moscow's twentieth-century history is more enigmatic than that of either Chicago or Osaka. Moscow's east side faces many of the same difficulties of failing heavy industry with all of the accompanying social problems that postindustrial transitions bring. Moscow's primary story line, however, has been one of imperial political ascendancy.

Lenin's 1918 transfer of political power from St. Petersburg was intended to be a temporary measure imposed by the exigencies of civil war. Nothing in life proves to be as permanent as that which is thought to be temporary. Soviet power remained based in Moscow, with the city growing along with Bolshevik might. Moscow became the headquarters and command center for an ideological empire that extended to nearly every continent; it oversaw massive military and prison kingdoms of a previously unknown scale; it became the showcase for all that was thought to be good about Soviet-style socialism. Both socialism and the city's capital status transformed the city, creating a new culture of absolute power—of *kto kogo* (who and whom)—which left no room for the politics of accommodation so evident just a few years before.[38]

---

[38] For further discussion of this transformation, see Blair A. Ruble, "Failures of Centralized Metropolitanism: Inter-war Moscow and New York," *Planning Perspectives* 9, no. 4 (1994), pp. 353–76; and Timothy J. Colton, *Moscow: Governing the Socialist Metropolis* (Cambridge, Mass.: Harvard University Press, 1995).

Moscow emerged as the primary city of an enormous hinterland covering a dozen time zones while Chicago and Osaka were slipping from second- to third-city status. Clocks from Prague to Pyongyang marked Moscow time. No soothsayer in 1900 could have predicted such a future.

The collapse of the Soviet Union has done little to reduce Moscow's predominance of the Central Eurasian plain. Economically, Moscow is even more different today from the rest of Central Eurasia than it was a decade ago. Contemporary Moscow busily tries to bully its way into the very top of the global urban hierarchy. The Moscow of today is an urban imperialist in a manner that Muscovites of the 1890s could never have dreamed possible.

For all of these changes, contemporary Moscow's political agenda is more similar to that of a century ago than is the case in either Chicago or Osaka. Soviet power did not destroy the world of the early 1900s so much as it froze that world in amber. Scores of dinosaur eggs have begun to hatch now that the amber has cracked. Today's Muscovites fiercely debate issues of inequality, philanthropy, and education, much as did their predecessors described in this study. The fundamental issue for today's Moscow remains the same as a century ago: How does Russia play the West's games well enough to remain a great power without turning its back on past traditions, customs, and folkways? Muscovites are plumbing their history for answers, hoping that their future can be found in their past. The events and issues explored in this study resonate in contemporary Moscow life. Unlike Chicago and Osaka, Moscow remains a place where the future is to be found in the past.

Bibliography

++≻=≺+ +≻=≺+ +≻=≺+ +≻=≺+ +≻=≺+ +≻=≺+ +≻=≺+ +≻=≺+ +≻=≺+

GENERAL AND COMPARATIVE

Books and Articles

Banfield, Edward C. *Civility and Citizenship in Liberal Democratic Societies.* New York: Paragon House, 1992.

Barker, Theo. "London: A Unique Megalopolis?" In Theo Barker and Anthony Sutcliffe, eds., *Megalopolis: The Giant City in History*, 43–60. London: St. Martin's, 1993.

Barker, Theo, and Anthony Sutcliffe, eds. *Megalopolis: The Giant City in History.* London: St. Martin's, 1993.

Benjamin, Walter. *The Correspondence of Walter Benjamin.* Ed. and annotated Gershom Scholem and Theodor W. Adorno. Trans. Manfred R. Jacobson and Evelyn M. Jacobson. Chicago: University of Chicago Press, 1994.

———. *One-Way Street and Other Writings.* London: N.L.B., 1979.

———. *Reflections: Essays, Aphorisms, Autobiographical Writings.* Trans. Edmund Jephcott. New York: Harcourt Brace Jovanovich, 1978.

Black, Cyril E., et al. *The Modernization of Japan and Russia: A Comparative Study.* New York: Free Press, 1975.

Boyer, John. *Political Radicalism in Late Imperial Vienna: Origins of the Christian Social Movement, 1848–1897.* Chicago: University of Chicago Press, 1981.

Buchanan, William. "Glasgow Art, Glasgow Craft, Glasgow International." In William Buchanan, James Macaulay, Andrew MacMillan, George Rawson, and Peter Trowles, eds., *Mackintosh's Masterwork: Charles Rennie Mackintosh and the Glasgow School of Art*, 147–58. San Francisco: Chronicle, 1989.

Buchanan, William, James Macaulay, Andrew MacMillan, George Rawson, and Peter Trowles, eds. *Mackintosh's Masterwork: Charles Rennie Mackintosh and the Glasgow School of Art.* San Francisco: Chronicle, 1989.

373

Celik, Zeynep, Diane Favro, and Richard Ingersoll, eds. *Streets: Critical Perspectives on Public Space*. Berkeley: University of California Press, 1994.

Cohen, Michael A., Blair A. Ruble, Joseph S. Tulchin, and Allison M. Garland, eds. *Preparing for the Urban Future: Global Pressures and Local Forces*. Washington, D.C.: Woodrow Wilson Center Press, 1996.

Davis, Diane E. *Urban Leviathan: Mexico City in the Twentieth Century*. Philadelphia: Temple University Press, 1994.

Demetz, Peter. *Prague in Black and Gold: Scenes from the Life of a European City*. New York: Hill and Wang, 1997.

Fainstein, Susan S. *The City Builders: Property, Politics, and Planning in London and New York*. Oxford, U.K.: Blackwell, 1994.

Ferguson, Priscilla Parkhurst. *Paris as Revolution: Writing the Nineteenth-Century City*. Berkeley: University of California Press, 1994.

Fredrickson, George M. "In Black and White: Review of *Studies in Social and Economic History of Witwatersraand, 1886–1914*, Vol. 1: *New Babylon*; Vol. 2: *New Nineveh*, by Charles van Onselen," *New Republic*, February 27, 1984: 37–39.

Fritzsche, Peter. *Reading Berlin, 1900*. Cambridge, Mass.: Harvard University Press, 1996.

Giner, Salvador. "Political Economy, Legitimation, and the State in Southern Europe." In Guillermo O'Donnell, Philippe C. Schmitter, and Laurence Whitehead, eds., *Transitions from Authoritarian Rule. Southern Europe*, 11–44. Baltimore: Johns Hopkins University Press, 1986.

Giustino, Cathleen M. "Architects and the Task of Urban Planning in Late Imperial Czech Prague, 1866–1900: Winning Jurisdiction from Below." In Charles McClelland, Stephan Merl, and Hannes Siegrist, eds., *Professionen im modernen Osteuropa*, 464–91. Berlin: Duncker and Humblot, 1995.

———. "Architects and the Task of Urban Planning in the Late Imperial Czech Prague, 1866–1900: Winning Jurisdiction 'From Below.'" Paper presented at the Workshop for Young Scholars in East European Studies, sponsored by the American Council of Learned Societies and the Woodrow Wilson International Center for Scholars, Washington, D.C., August 1994.

Gutierrez, Ramon, Margarita Gutman, and Victor Perez Escolano, eds. *El arquitecto Martin Noel: Su tiempo y su obra*. Seville: Junta de Andalucia, 1995.

Gutman, Margarita. "Martin Noel y el neocolonial en la Argentina: inventando una tradicion." In Ramon Gutierrez, Margarita Gutman, and Victor Perez Escolano, eds., *El arquitecto Martin Noel: Su tiempo y su obra*, 41–57. Seville: Junta de Andalucia, 1995.

Halfani, Mohamed. "Marginality and Dynamism: Prospects for the Sub-Saharan African City." In Michael A. Cohen, Blair A. Ruble, Joseph S. Tulchin, and Allison M. Garland, eds., *Preparing for the Urban Future: Global Pressures and Local Forces*, pp. 83–107. Washington, D.C.: Woodrow Wilson Center Press, 1996.

Hall, Peter. *Cities in Civilization*. New York: Pantheon, 1998.

Haneck, Peter. *The Garden and the Workshop: Essays on the Cultural History of Vienna and Budapest*. Princeton: Princeton University Press, 1998.

Hohenberg, Paul M., and Lynn Hollen Lees. *The Making of Urban Europe, 1000–1994*. Cambridge, Mass.: Harvard University Press, 1995.

Jensen-Butler, Chris, Arie Shachar, and Jan van Weesep, eds., *European Cities in Competition*. Brookfield, Vt.: Avebury, 1997.

Jordan, David P. *Transforming Paris: The Life and Labors of Baron Haussmann*. Chicago: University of Chicago Press, 1995.

Kaplan, Temma. *Red City, Blue Period: Social Movements in Picasso's Barcelona*. Berkeley: University of California Press, 1992.

Klima, Ivan. *The Spirit of Prague and Other Essays*. Trans. Paul Wilson. New York: Granta, 1994.

Kriedte, Peter, et al., eds. *Industrialization before Industrialization: Rural Industry in the Genesis of Capitalism*. Cambridge, U.K.: Cambridge University Press, 1981.

Landes, David S. *The Wealth and Poverty of Nations: Why Some Are So Rich and Some So Poor*. New York: Norton, 1998.

Lee, R. D., Richard D. Easterlin, Peter H. Lindert, and Etienne van de Walle, eds. *Population Patterns in the Past*. New York: Academic Press, 1977.

Lindblom, Charles E. *Politics and Markets: The World's Political-Economic Systems*. New York: Basic Books, 1977.

Linz, Juan J. "Transitions to Democracy." *Washington Quarterly* 13, no. 3 (Summer 1990): 143–64.

———. "Crisis, Breakdown, and Reequilibration." In Juan J. Linz and Alfred Stepan, eds., *The Breakdown of Democratic Regimes*, 3–124. Baltimore: Johns Hopkins University Press, 1978.

Linz, Juan J., and Alfred Stepan, eds. *The Breakdown of Democratic Regimes*. Baltimore: Johns Hopkins University Press, 1978.

Maier, Charles S. *Recasting Bourgeois Europe: Stabilization in France, Germany, and Italy in the Decade after World War I*. Princeton: Princeton University Press, 1975.

McCarney, Patricia K., ed. *Cities and Governance: New Directions in Latin America, Asia, and Africa*. Toronto: University of Toronto Press, 1996.

McClelland, Charles, Stephan Merl, and Hannes Siegrist, eds. *Professionen im modernen Osteuropa*. Berlin: Duncker and Humblot, 1995.

McNeill, William H. "The Changing Shape of World History." In Philip Pomper, Richard H. Elphick, and Richard T. Vann, eds., *World Historians and Their Critics*, 8–26. Middletown, Conn: Wesleyan University, 1995.

———. "The Eccentricity of Wheels, or Eurasian Transportation in Historical Perspective." *American Historical Review* 92, no. 5 (December 1987): 1111–26.

Medick, Hans. "The Proto-Industrial Family Economy." In Peter Kriedte et al., eds., *Industrialization before Industrialization: Rural Industry in the Genesis of Capitalism*. Cambridge, U.K.: Cambridge University Press, 1981.

Mendels, Franklin. "'Proto-Industrialization': The First Phase of the Industrialization Process." *Journal of Economic History* 32, no. 1 (1972): 241–61.

Meyerling, Anne C. "Workers in European Cities, 1880 to 1950." *Journal of Urban History* 23, no. 4 (1997): 513–22.

Michels, Robert. *Political Parties: A Sociological Study of the Oligarchical Tendencies of Modern Democracy*. New York: Hearst's International Library, 1915.

Missac, Pierre. *Walter Benjamin's Passages*. Trans. Shierry Weber Nicholsen. Cambridge, Mass.: MIT Press, 1995.

Moore, Barrington, Jr. *Injustice: The Social Bases of Obedience and Revolt*. White Plains, N.Y.: M. E. Sharpe, 1978.

Mumford, Lewis. *The City in History: Its Origins, Its Transformations, and Its Prospects*. New York: Harcourt, Brace, and World, 1961.

———. *The Urban Prospect*. New York: Harcourt Brace Jovanovich, 1956.

———. *The Culture of Cities*. New York: Harcourt, Brace, 1938.

O'Donnell, Guillermo. "Introduction to the Latin American Cases." In Guillermo O'Donnell, Philippe C. Schmitter, and Laurence Whitehead, eds., *Transitions from Authoritarian Rule: Latin America*, 3–18. Baltimore: Johns Hopkins University Press, 1986.

O'Donnell, Guillermo, and Philippe C. Schmitter. "Tentative Conclusions about Uncertain Democracies." In Guillermo O'Donnell, Philippe C. Schmitter, and Laurence Whitehead, eds., *Transitions from Authoritarian Rule: Prospects for Democracy*, Part 4, 3–78. Baltimore: Johns Hopkins University Press, 1986.

O'Donnell, Guillermo, Philippe C. Schmitter, and Laurence Whitehead, eds. *Transitions from Authoritarian Rule: Comparative Perspectives*. Baltimore: Johns Hopkins University Press, 1986.

———. *Transitions from Authoritarian Rule: Latin America*. Baltimore: Johns Hopkins University Press, 1986.

———. *Transitions from Authoritarian Rule: Prospects for Democracy*. Baltimore: Johns Hopkins University Press, 1986.

———. *Transitions from Authoritarian Rule: Southern Europe*. Baltimore: Johns Hopkins University Press, 1986.

Polanyi, Karl. *The Great Transformation*. New York: Farrar and Rinehart, 1944.

Pomper, Philip, Richard H. Elphick, and Richard T. Vann, eds. *World Historians and Their Critics*. Middletown, Conn.: Wesleyan University, 1995.

Porter, Roy. *London: A Social History.* Cambridge, Mass.: Harvard University Press, 1995.

Prendergast, Christopher. *Paris and the Nineteenth Century.* Cambridge, Mass.: Blackwell, 1992.

Prislei, Leticia. "Los intelectuales argentinos ante el problema de la modernizacion y de la seleccion de tradiciones (1900–1920)." In Ramon Gutierrez, Margarita Gutman, and Victor Perez Escolano, eds., *El arquitecto Martin Noel: Su tiempo y su obra,* 59–69. Seville: Junta de Andalucia, 1995.

Przeworski, Adam. "Some Problems in the Study of the Transition to Democracy." In Guillermo O'Donnell, Philippe C. Schmitter, and Laurence Whitehead, eds., *Transitions from Authoritarian Rule: Comparative Perspectives,* 47–63. Baltimore: Johns Hopkins University Press, 1986.

Rex, John. *Race, Colonialism and the City.* London: Routledge and Kegan Paul, 1973.

Richie, Alexandra. *Faust's Metropolis: A History of Berlin.* New York: Carroll and Graf, 1998.

Rodriguez, Alfredo, and Lucy Winchester. "The Challenges for Urban Governance in Latin America: Reinventing the Government of Cities." In Patricia K. McCarney, ed., *Cities and Governance: New Directions in Latin America, Asia, and Africa,* 23–38. Toronto: University of Toronto Press, 1996.

Sanchez, Joan-Eugeni. "Barcelona: The Olympic City." In Chris Jensen-Butler, Arie Shachar, and Jan van Weesep, eds., *European Cities in Competition,* 179–208. Brookfield, Vt.: Avebury, 1997.

Sargent, Charles S. *The Spatial Evolution of Greater Buenos Aires, Argentina, 1870–1930.* Tempe: Center for Latin American Studies, Arizona State University, 1974.

Sassen, Saskia. *Cities in a World Economy.* Thousand Oaks, Calif.: Pine Forge Press, 1994.

Saunier, Pierre-Yves. "Center and Centrality in the Nineteenth Century: Some Concepts of Urban Disposition under the Spot of Locality." *Journal of Urban History* 24, no. 4 (May 1998): 435–67.

Schmitter, Philippe C. "An Introduction to Southern European Transitions from Authoritarian Rule: Italy, Greece, Spain, and Turkey." In Guillermo O'Donnell, Philippe C. Schmitter, and Laurence Whitehead, eds., *Transitions from Authoritarian Rule: Southern Europe,* 3–10. Baltimore: Johns Hopkins University Press, 1986.

———. "Speculations about the Prospective Demise of Authoritarian Regimes and Its Possible Consequences." Latin American Program Working Papers, no. 60. Washington, D.C.: Woodrow Wilson International Center for Scholars, 1979.

Scobie, James R. *Buenos Aires: Plaza to Suburb, 1870–1910.* Oxford, U.K.: Oxford University Press, 1974.

Shain, Yossi, and Juan J. Linz. "The Power-Sharing Model." In Yossi Shain and Juan J. Linz, eds., *Between States: Interim Governments and Democratic Transitions,* 41–51. Cambridge, U.K.: Cambridge University Press, 1995.

Shain, Yossi, and Juan J. Linz, eds. *Between States: Interim Governments and Democratic Transitions.* Cambridge, U.K.: Cambridge University Press, 1995.

Sharpe, William, and Leonard Wallock, eds. *Visions of the Modern City: Essays in History, Art, and Literature.* Baltimore: Johns Hopkins University Press, 1987.

Steiber, Nancy. *Housing Design and Society in Amsterdam: Reconfiguring Urban Order and Identity, 1900–1920.* Chicago: University of Chicago, 1998.

Stepan, Alfred. "Paths toward Redemocratization: Theoretical and Comparative Considerations." In Guillermo O'Donnell, Philippe C. Schmitter, and Laurence Whitehead, eds., *Transitions from Authoritarian Rule: Comparative Perspectives,* 64–84. Baltimore: Johns Hopkins University Press, 1986.

Sutcliffe, Anthony. "Introduction: The Giant City as a Historical Phenomenon." In Theo Barker and Anthony Sutcliffe, eds., *Megalopolis: The Giant City in History,* 1–13. London: St. Martin's, 1993.

Sutcliffe, Anthony, ed. *Metropolis, 1890–1940.* Chicago: Universtity of Chicago Press, 1984.

Szelenyi, Ivan. *Urban Inequalities under State Socialism.* Oxford, U.K.: Oxford University Press, 1983.

Tilly, Louise. *Politics and Class in Milan, 1881–1901.* Oxford, U.K.: Oxford University Press, 1992.

Wechsler, Diana. "Las ideas esteticas en Buenos Aires: entre nacionalismo y cosmopolitismo (1910–1930)." In Ramon Gutierrez, Margarita Gutman, and Victor Perez Escolano, eds., *El arquitecto Martin Noel: Su tiempo y su obra,* 71–79. Seville: Junta de Andalucia, 1995.

Whitehead, Laurence. "International Aspects of Democratization." In Guillermo O'Donnell, Philippe C. Schmitter, and Laurence Whitehead, eds., *Transitions from Authoritarian Rule: Comparative Perspectives,* 3–46. Baltimore: Johns Hopkins University Press, 1986.

Wilentz, Sean, ed. *Rites of Power: Symbolism, Ritual, and Politics since the Middle Ages.* Philadelphia: University of Pennsylvania Press, 1985.

Wilson, Elizabeth. *The Sphinx in the City: Urban Life, the Control of Disorder, and Women.* Berkeley: University of California Press, 1991.

Witte, Bernd. *Walter Benjamin: An Intellectual Biography.* Trans. James Rolleston. Detroit: Wayne State University Press, 1991.

Young, David M. *Chicago Transit: An Illustrated History.* DeKalb: Northern Illinois Press, 1998.

Dissertations

Giustino, Cathleen M. "Architecture and the Nation: Meanings of Modern Urban Design and Possibilities for Political Participation in Czech Prague 1900." Ph.D. diss., University of Chicago, 1997.

CHICAGO AND AMERICAN CITIES

Newspapers

The Chicago Tribune
The Inter-Ocean
The New York Times

Books and Articles

Abbott, Carl. "Thinking About Cities: The Central Tradition in U.S. Urban History." *Journal of Urban History* 22, no. 6 (September 1996): 687–701.
———. *Boosters and Businessmen: Popular Economic Thought and Urban Growth in the Antebellum Middle West.* Westport, Conn.: Greenwood, 1981.
Abbott, Edith. *The Tenements of Chicago, 1908–1935.* Chicago: University of Chicago Press, 1936.
Abbott, Willis J[ohn]. "The Harrison Dynasty in Chicago." *Munsey's Magazine,* September 1903.
———. *Carter Henry Harrison: A Memoir.* New York: Dodd, Mead, 1895.
Abu-Lughod, Janet L. *New York, Chicago, Los Angeles: America's Global Cities.* Minneapolis: University of Minnesota Press, 1999.
An Act to Provide a Charter for the City of Chicago. Chicago: City Charter Convention, 1909.
An Act to Provide a Charter for the City of Chicago. Chicago: Chicago Charter Convention, 1905.
Addams, Jane. "Problems of Municipal Administration." *American Journal of Sociology* 10, no. 4 (January 1905): 425–44.
———. *The Social Thought of Jane Addams.* Ed. Christopher Lasch. Indianapolis: Bobbs-Merrill, 1965.
———. *Twenty Years at Hull-House.* 1910. Reprint, New York: New American Library, 1961.
———. *The Second Twenty Years at Hull-House: September 1909 to September 1929, with a Record of a Growing World Consciousness.* New York: Macmillan, 1930.
———. *The Spirit of Youth and the City Streets.* New York: Macmillan, 1909.
Ade, George. *Stories of the Streets and of the Town: From the Chicago Record, 1893–1900.* Ed. Frank J. Meine. Chicago: Claxton Club, 1941.

Allswag, John M. *Bosses, Machines and Urban Voters*. Baltimore: Johns Hopkins University Press, 1986.

——. *A House for All Peoples: Ethnic Politics in Chicago. 1890–1936*. Lexington: University Press of Kentucky, 1971.

Altgeld, John Peter. *Reasons for Pardoning Fielden, Neebe, and Schwab*. Springfield, Ill.: Governor's Office, 1893.

Andreas, Alfred Theodore. *History of Chicago*, 3 vols. Chicago: A. T. Andreas, 1884–86.

Andreas, Simon. *Chicago, the Garden City: Its Magnificent Parks, Boulevards, and Cemeteries*. Chicago: F. Gindele, 1893.

Andrews, Wayne. *Architecture in Chicago and Mid-America: A Photographic History*. New York: Atheneum, 1968.

——. *The Battle for Chicago*. New York: Harcourt and Brace, 1946.

Anton, Thomas J. "Power, Pluralism, and Local Politics." *Administrative Science Quarterly* 7, no. 4 (March 1963): 425–57.

Appelbaum, Sidney. *The Chicago World's Fair of 1893: A Photographic Record*. New York: Dover, 1980.

Armour, J. Ogden. *The Packers, the Private Car Lines, and the People*. Philadelphia: Henry Altemus, 1906.

Arnold, Bion Joseph. *Report of the Engineering and Operating Features of the Chicago Transportation Problem, Submitted to the Committee on Local Transportation of the Chicago City Council in November 1902*. New York: McGraw, 1905.

Arnold, Isaac N., and J. Young Scammon. *William B. Ogden and Early Days in Chicago*. Chicago: Fergus, 1882.

Asbury, Herbert. *Gem of the Prairie: An Informal History of the Chicago Underworld*. New York: Knopf, 1940.

Avrich, Paul. *The Haymarket Tragedy*. Princeton: Princeton University Press, 1984.

Badger, R. Reid. *The Great America Fair: The World's Columbian Exposition and American Culture*. Chicago: Nelson-Hall, 1979.

Bahl, Roy W. *Metropolitan City Expenditures: A Comparative Analysis*. Lexington: University Press of Kentucky, 1969.

Bailey, Alice W. *Mark Heffron: A Novel*. New York: Harper, 1896.

Baker, Nina Brown. *Big Catalogue: The Life of Aaron Montgomery Ward*. New York: Harcourt, Brace, 1956.

Baker, Paula. "The Domestication of Politics: Women and American Political Society, 1780–1920." *American Historical Review* 89, no. 3 (1984): 620–47.

Baker, Ray Stannard. "The Modern Skyscraper." *Munsey's Magazine* 22 (October 1899): 48–56.

——. "Hull-House and the Ward Boss." *Outlook* 58 (March 26, 1898): 769–71.

——. "The Civic Federation of Chicago." *Outlook* 52 (July 27, 1895): 132–33.

Banfield, Edward C. *The Unheavenly City: The Nature and Future of Our Urban Crisis.* Boston: Little, Brown, 1968.

———. *Political Influence.* New York: Greenwood, 1961.

Banfield, Edward C., and James Q. Wilson. *City Politics.* Cambridge, Mass.: Harvard University Press, 1967.

Bardach, Eugene. *The Skill Factor in Politics: Repealing the Mental Commitment Laws in California.* Berkeley: University of California Press, 1975.

Barrett, James R. *Work and Community in the Jungle: Chicago's Packinghouse Workers, 1894–1922.* Chicago: University of Illinois Press, 1987.

———. "Immigrant Workers in Early Mass Production Industry: Work Rationalization and Job Control Conflicts in Chicago's Packinghouses, 1900–1904." In John B. Jentz and Hartmut Keil, eds., *German Workers in Industrial Chicago, 1850–1910: A Comparative Perspective,* 104–26. DeKalb: Northern Illinois University Press, 1983.

Barrett, John P. *Electricity at the Columbian Exposition, Including an Account of the Exhibits.* Chicago: R. R. Donnelley, 1894.

Barrett, Paul. *The Automobile and Urban Transit: The Formation of Public Policy in Chicago, 1900–1930.* Philadelphia: Temple University Press, 1983.

Barth, Gunther Paul. *City People: The Rise of Modern City Culture in Nineteenth-Century America.* Oxford, U.K.: Oxford University Press, 1980.

Beedle, Lynn S., ed. *Second Century of the Skyscraper.* New York: Van Nostrand Reinhold, 1988.

Bennett, Larry. *Fragments of Cities: The New American Downtowns and Neighborhoods.* Columbus: Ohio State University Press, 1990.

Berger, Miles L. *They Built Chicago: Entrepreneurs Who Shaped a Great City's Architecture.* Chicago: Bonus Books, 1992.

Biles, Roger. *Richard J. Daley: Politics, Race, and the Governing of Chicago.* DeKalb: Northern Illinois University Press, 1995.

Bill for an Act to Provide a Charter for the City of Chicago. Chicago: City Charter Convention, 1905.

Birkmire, William H. *Skeleton Construction in Buildings, with Numerous Practical Illustrations of High Buildings.* New York: John Wiley, 1894.

Bloom, Sol. *The Autobiography of Sol Bloom.* New York: G. P. Putnam, 1948.

Bluestone, Daniel. *Constructing Chicago.* New Haven: Yale University Press, 1991.

Bodnar, John. *Remaking America: Public Memory, Commemoration, and Patriotism in the Twentieth Century.* Princeton: Princeton University Press, 1992.

Bornstein, Daniel J. "Competitive Communities on the Western Frontier." In Kenneth T. Jackson and Stanley K. Schultz, eds., *Cities in American History,* 9–15. New York: Knopf, 1972.

Boulay, Harvey, and Alan DiGaetano. "Why Did Political Machines Disappear?" *Journal of Urban History* 12, no. 1 (November 1985): 25–49.

Boyer, Paul. *Urban Masses and Moral Order in America, 1820–1920.* Cambridge, Mass.: Harvard University Press, 1978.

Bradley, Donald S., and Mayer N. Zald. "From Commerical Elite to Political Administrator: The Recruitment of the Mayors of Chicago." *American Journal of Sociology* 71:2 (September 1965): 153–67.

Branham, Charles. "Black Chicago: Accommodationist Politics before the Great Migration." In Melvin G. Holli and Peter d'A. Jones, eds., *Ethnic Chicago*, rev. ed., 338–79. Grand Rapids, Mich.: William B. Eeridmas, 1984.

Brazer, Harvey E. *City Expenditures in the United States.* New York: National Bureau of Economic Research, 1959.

Bridges, Amy. *A City in the Republic: Antebellum New York and the Origins of Machine Politics.* Cambridge, U.K.: Cambridge University Press, 1984.

Brooks, Michael W. *Subway City: Riding the Trains, Reading New York.* New Brunswick, N.J.: Rutgers University Press, 1997.

Brown, Julie K. *Contesting Images: Photography and the World's Columbian Exposition.* Tucson: University of Arizona Press, 1994.

Brown, M. Craig, and Charles N. Halaby. "Machine Politics in America, 1870–1945." *Journal of Interdisciplinary History* 17, no. 3 (Winter 1987): 587–612.

Browne, Waldo R. *Altgeld of Illinois: A Record of His Life and Work.* New York: B. W. Huebsch, 1924.

Brubaker, C. William. "Evolution of the Skyscraper: A History of the Tall Building in Chicago." In Lynn S. Beedle, ed., *Second Century of the Skyscraper*, 33–52. New York: Van Nostrand Reinhold, 1988.

Bruegmann, Robert. *The Architects and the City: Holabird and Roche of Chicago, 1880–1918.* Chicago: University of Chicago Press, 1997.

Buder, Stanley. *Pullman: An Experiment in Industrial Order and Community Planning, 1880–1930.* Oxford, U.K.: Oxford University Press, 1967.

Buenker, John D. *Urban Liberalism and Progressive Reform.* New York: Charles Scribner's Sons, 1973.

Buhle, Paul. "German Socialists and the Roots of American Working-Class Radicalism." In Hartmut Keil and John B. Jentz, eds., *German Workers in Industrial Chicago, 1850–1910: A Comparative Perspective*, 224–35. DeKalb: Northern Illinois University Press, 1983.

Burg, David F. *Chicago's White City of 1893.* Lexington: University Press of Kentucky, 1976.

Burgess, Ernest Watson, and Charles Newcomb. *Census Data of the City of Chicago, 1920.* Chicago: University of Chicago Press, 1931.

Burnett, Frances Hodgson. *Two Little Pilgrims' Progress: A Story of the City Beautiful.* New York: Charles Scribner's Sons, 1895.

Burnham, Clara Louise (Root). *Sweet Clover: A Romance of the White City.* Boston: Houghton, Mifflin, 1894.

Butterworth, Hezekiah. *Zigzag Journeys in the White City, With Visits to the Neighboring Metropolis.* Boston: Estes and Lauriat, 1894.

————. *Zigzag Journeys on the Mississippi: From Chicago to the Islands of the Discovery.* Boston: Estes and Lauriat, 1892.

Cain, Louis P. *Sanitation Strategy for a Lakefront Metropolis: The Case of Chicago.* De Kalb: Northern Illinois University Press, 1978.

Candeloro, Dominic. "Suburban Italians: Chicago Heights, 1890–1975." In Melvin G. Holli and Peter d'A. Jones, eds., *Ethnic Chicago*, rev. ed., 239–68. Grand Rapids, Mich.: William B. Eeridmas, 1984.

Cappetti, Carla. *Writing Chicago: Modernism, Ethnography, and the Novel.* New York: Columbia University Press, 1993.

Casson, Herbert N. *Cyrus Hall McCormick: His Life and Work.* Chicago: A. C. McClurg, 1909.

Chafe, William H. "Women's History and Political History: Some Thoughts on Progressivism and the New Deal." In Nancy A. Hewitt and Suzanne Lebsock, eds., *Visible Women: New Essays on American Activism*, 101–18. Urbana: University of Illinois Press, 1993.

Chandler, Alfred Dupont, Jr. *The Visible Hand: The Managerial Revolution in American Business.* Cambridge, Mass.: Harvard University Press, 1977.

Chicago City Council New Charter Committee. *How She Will Get That New Dress.* Chicago: City Council of the City of Chicago, 1904.

Chicago City Council Street Railway Commission, *Report of the Street Railway Commission to the City Council of the City of Chicago.* Chicago: Chicago City Council, 1900.

Chicago New Charter Convention. *Proceedings.* Chicago: New Charter Convention, 1902.

Chicago New Charter Movement. *Why the Pending Constitutional Amendment Should Be Adopted.* Text A. Chicago: New Charter Campaign Committee, 1904.

Chicago New Charter Movement. *Why the Pending Constitutional Amendment Should Be Adopted.* Text B. Chicago: New Charter Campaign Committee, 1904.

Cigliano, Jan, and Sarah Bradford Landau, eds. *The Grand American Avenue, 1850–1920.* San Francisco: Pomegranate Artbooks, 1994.

City of Chicago Board of Education. *Suggestions to Instructors on a Course in Citizenship and Language Adapted to Adults Having Little Command of English Who Are Applicants for Citizenship.* Chicago: Board of Education, 1921.

————. *A Tentative Program for Community Centers.* Chicago: Board of Education, 1919.

————. *Reports on Underfed Children*. Chicago: Board of Education, 1908.

Clarke, Jane H. "Epilogue: Thirteen Projects in Progress in the 1990s." In Pauline A. Saliga, ed., *The Sky's the Limit: A Century of Chicago Skyscrapers*, 290–93. New York: Rizzoli, 1990.

Cobb, Weldon J. *A World's Fair Mystery*. Chicago: Melbourne, 1892.

Cobble, Dorothy Sue. *Dishing It Out: Waitresses and Their Unions in the Twentieth Century*. Urbana: University of Illinois Press, 1991.

Cohen, Lizabeth. *Making a New Deal: Industrial Workers in Chicago, 1919–1939*. Cambridge, U.K.: Cambridge University Press, 1990.

Condit, Carl W. "The Two Centuries of Technical Evolution Underlying the Skyscraper." In Lynn S. Beedle, ed., *Second Century of the Skyscraper*, 11–24. New York: Van Nostrand Reinhold, 1988.

————. *The Chicago School of Architecture: A History of Commercial and Public Building in the Chicago Area, 1875–1925*. Chicago: University of Chicago Press, 1964.

Conzen, Kathleen Neils. "Community Studies, Urban History, and American Local History." In Michael Kammen, ed., *The Past Before Us: Contemporary Historical Writing in the United States*, 270–91. Ithaca: Cornell University Press, 1980.

————. "Immigrants, Immigrant Neighborhoods, and Ethnic Identity: Historical Issues." *Journal of American History* 66, no. 3 (1979): 603–15.

Conzen, Michael P. "A Transport Interpretation of the Growth of Urban Regions: An American Example." *Journal of Historical Geography* 1, no. 4 (1975): 361–82.

Cook County (Ill.) Coroner's Office. *Biennial Report 1918–1919 and Official Record of Inquests on the Victims of the Race Riots of July and August, 1919*. Chicago: Cook County Coroner's Office, 1920.

Couvares, Francis, G. *The Remaking of Pittsburgh: Class and Culture in an Industrializing City, 1877–1919*. Albany: State University of New York Press, 1984.

Creese, Walter L. *The Crowning of the American Landscape: Eight Great Spaces and Their Buildings*. Princeton: Princeton University Press, 1985.

Cremin, Dennis H. "Chicago's Front Yard." *Chicago History* 37, no. 1 (Spring 1998): 22–44.

Cromie, Robert. *The Great Chicago Fire*. New York: McGraw-Hill, 1958.

Cronon, William. *Nature's Metropolis: Chicago and the Great West*. New York: Norton, 1991.

Cudahy, Brian J. *Cash, Tokens, and Transfers: A History of Urban Mass Transit in North America*. New York: Fordham University Press, 1990.

————. *Destination Loop: The Story of Rapid Transit Railroading in and around Chicago*. Brattleboro, Vt.: Stephen Greene, 1982.

Cummings, John. "The Chicago Teamsters Strike." *Journal of Political Economy* 13 (1905): 536–73.

Cutler, Irving. "The Jews of Chicago: From Shtetl to Suburb." In Melvin G. Holli and Peter d'A. Jones, eds., *Ethnic Chicago*, rev. ed., 69–108. Grand Rapids, Mich.: William B. Eeridmas, 1984.

———. *Chicago: Metropolis of the Mid-Continent.* 3d ed. Dubuque, Iowa: Hunt, 1982.

Dahl, Robert. *Who Governs? Democracy and Power in an American City.* New Haven: Yale University Press, 1961.

———. *A Preface to Democratic Theory.* Chicago: University of Chicago Press, 1956.

Darling, Sharon. *Chicago Furniture: Art, Craft, and Industry.* New York: Norton, 1984.

Darrow, Clarence S. "The Chicago Traction Question." *International Quarterly* 12 (October 1905–January 1906): 13–22.

David, Henry. *The History of the Haymarket Affair.* New York: Farrar and Rinehart, 1936.

Davis, Allen F., and Mary Lynn McCree, eds. *Eighty Years at Hull-House.* Chicago: Quadrangle, 1969.

Davis, James Leslie. *The Elevated System and the Growth of Northern Chicago.* Northwestern University Studies in Geography, no. 10. Evanston, Ill.: Northwestern University Department of Geography, 1965.

Dawley, Alan. *Class and Community: The Industrial Revolution in Lynn.* Cambridge, Mass.: Harvard University Press, 1976.

Deegan, Mary Jo. *Jane Addams and the Men of the Chicago School, 1892–1918.* New Brunswick, N.J.: Transaction, 1988.

Demarest, Lloyd Henry. *The Chicago Traction Question.* Chicago: George Waite Pickett, 1903.

Diner, Steven J. *A City and Its Universities: Public Policy in Chicago, 1892–1919.* Chapel Hill: University of North Carolina Press, 1980.

Domosh, Mona. *Invented Cities: The Creation of Landscape in Nineteenth-Century New York and Boston.* New Haven: Yale University Press, 1996.

Dorsett, Lyle W. "The City and the Reformer: A Reappraisal." *Pacific Northwest Quarterly* 63 (1972): 150–54.

Draper, Joan E. "Chicago: Planning Wacker Drive." In Zeynep Celik, Diane Favro, and Richard Ingersoll, eds., *Streets: Critical Perspectives on Public Space*, 259–76. Berkeley: University of California Press, 1994.

Dreiser, Theodore, *The Titan.* New York: John Lane, 1914.

———. *The Financier.* 1912. Reprint, New York: Signet, 1967.

———. *Sister Carrie.* London: Heinemann, 1901.

Drury, John. *Old Chicago Houses.* New York: Bonanza, 1941.

Duis, Perry R. *The Saloon: Public Drinking in Chicago and Boston, 1880–1920.* Urbana: University of Illinois Press, 1983.

———. *Chicago: Creating New Traditions.* Chicago: Chicago Historical Society, 1976.

Dunne, Edward F. *Illinois: The Heart of the Nation.* 5 vols. Chicago: Lewis, 1933.

Dunne, Edward F. *Dunne: Judge, Mayor, Governor.* Comp. and ed. William L. Sullivan. Chicago: Windemere, 1916.

Ebner, Michael H. *Creating Chicago's North Shore: A Suburban History.* Chicago: University of Chicago Press, 1988.

Einhorn, Robin L. *Property Rules: Political Economy in Chicago, 1833–1872.* Chicago: University of Chicago Press, 1991.

———. "A Taxing Dilemma." *Chicago History* 18 (Fall 1989): 34–51.

Elkin, Stephen L. *City and Regime in the American Republic.* Chicago: University of Chicago Press, 1987.

Elkind, Sarah S. "Building a Better Jungle: Anti-Urban Sentiment, Public Works, and Political Reform in American Cities, 1880–1930." *Journal of Urban History* 24, no. 1 (November 1997): 53–78.

Ely, Richard. "Pullman: A Social Study," *Harper's New Monthly Magazine* 70 (February 1885): 453–66.

———. *Ground Under Our Feet: An Autobiography.* New York: Macmillan, 1938.

Ensslen, Klaus, and Heinz Ickstadt. "German Working-Class Culture in Chicago: Continuity and Change in the Decade from 1900 to 1910." In Hartmut Keil and John B. Jentz, eds., *German Workers in Industrial Chicago, 1850–1910: A Comparative Perspective,* 236–52. DeKalb: Northern Illinois University Press, 1983.

Epstein, Jason. "The Tragical History of New York." *New York Review of Books,* April 9, 1992: 45–51.

Evans, Sara M. "Women's History and Political Theory: Toward a Feminist Approach to Public Life." In Nancy A. Hewitt and Suzanne Lebsock, eds., *Visible Women: New Essays on American Activism,* 119–39. Urbana: University of Illinois Press, 1993.

Faires, Nora. "Occupational Patterns of German-Americans in Nineteenth-Century Cities." In Hartmut Keil and John B. Jentz, eds., *German Workers in Industrial Chicago, 1850–1910: A Comparative Perspective,* 37–51. DeKalb: Northern Illinois University Press, 1983.

Fairfield, John D. *The Mysteries of the Great City: The Politics of Urban Design, 1877–1937.* Columbus: Ohio State University Press, 1993.

Fairlie, John A. "The Street Railway Question in Chicago." *Quarterly Journal of Economics* 21 (1907): 371–404.

Feffer, Andrew. *The Chicago Pragmatists and American Progressivism.* Ithaca: Cornell University Press, 1993.

Fehrenbacher, Don E. *Chicago Giant: A Biography of "Long John" Wentworth.* Madison, Wisc.: American History Research Center, 1957.

Filene, Peter G. "An Obituary for 'The Progressive Movement.'" *American Quarterly* 22 (1970): 20–34.

Fine, Lisa M. *The Souls of the Skyscraper: Female Clerical Workers in Chicago, 1870–1930.* Philadelphia: Temple University Press, 1990.

Fishman, Robert. "The Metropolitan Tradition in American Planning." Paper presented to workshop at the Woodrow Wilson International Center for Scholars Washington, D.C., September 23–24, 1994.

———. *Bourgeois Utopias: The Rise and Fall of Suburbia.* New York: Basic Books, 1987.

Flanagan, Maureen A. *Charter Reform in Chicago.* Carbondale: Southern Illinois University Press, 1987.

———. "Women in the City, Women of the City? Where Do Women Fit in Urban History?" *Journal of Urban History* 23, no. 3 (1997): 251–59.

———. "Gender and Urban Political Reform: The City Club and the Woman's City Club of Chicago in the Progressive Era." *American Historical Review* 95, no. 4 (October 1990): 1032–50.

Flinn, John J. *The Mysterious Disappearance of Helen St. Vincent: A Story of the Vanished City.* Chicago: Geo. K. Hazlitt, n.d.

Florance, Howard. "New York City Today." *American Review of Reviews,* October 1925: 376–79.

Foner, Eric, ed. *The New American History.* Philadelphia: Temple University Press, 1990.

Foreman, Milton J. "Chicago New Charter Movement: Its Relation to Municipal Ownership." *Annals of the American Academy of Political and Social Science,* 31 (1908): 639–48.

Franch, John. "Opposite Sides of the Barricade." *Chicago History* 24, no. 2 (Summer 1995): 38–57.

Frear, Alexander. "The Great Fire of 1871." In Bessie Louise Pierce, comp., *As Others See Chicago: Impressions of Visitors, 1673–1933,* 191–204. Chicago: University of Chicago Press, 1933.

Fredrickson, George M. "The Old New Order." *New York Review of Books,* March 25, 1993: 40–42.

Fuchs, Ester R. *Mayors and Money: Fiscal Policy in New York and Chicago.* Chicago: University of Chicago Press, 1992.

Funchion, Michael F. "Irish Chicago: Church, Homeland, Politics, and Class: The Shaping of an Ethnic Group, 1870–1900." In Melvin G. Holli and Peter d'A. Jones, eds., *Ethnic Chicago,* rev. ed., 4–45. Grand Rapids, Mich.: William B. Eeridmas, 1984.

Giedion, Sigfried. *Space, Time, and Architecture: The Growth of a New Tradition.* Cambridge, Mass.: Harvard University Press, 1941.

Gilbert, James. *Perfect Cities: Chicago's Utopias of 1893.* Chicago: University of Chicago Press, 1991.

Gilfoyle, Timothy J. *The City of Eros: New York City, Prostitution, and the Commercialization of Sex, 1790–1920.* New York: Norton, 1992.

Ginger, Ray. *Altgeld's America: The Lincoln Ideal versus Changing Realities.* 1958. Reprint, New York: Markus Wiener, 1988.

———. *Age of Excess: The United States from 1877 to 1914.* 2d ed. New York: Macmillan, 1975.

Gorn, Elliott J. "Selling Urban Values." *Journal of Urban History* 24, no. 4 (May 1998): 524–33.

Gosnell, Harold F. *Machine Politics: Chicago Model.* 1937. Reprint, New York: AMS, 1969.

Gottfried, Alex. *Boss Cermak of Chicago: A Study of Urban Political Leadership.* Seattle: University of Washington Press, 1962.

Granger, Bill, and Lori Granger. *Lords of the Last Machine: The Story of Politics in Chicago.* New York: Random House, 1987.

Grant, Bruce. *Fight for a City: The Story of the Union League Club of Chicago and Its Times, 1880–1955.* Chicago: Rand McNally, 1955.

Gray, Esther. *Tale of an Amateur Adventuress: The Autobiography of Esther Gray.* Abr. and ed. Elizabeth Kingsbury. Cincinnati: Editor, 1898.

Green, Paul Michael. "Irish Chicago: The Multi-Ethnic Road to Machine Success." In Melvin G. Holli and Peter d'A. Jones, eds., *Ethnic Chicago*, rev. ed.: 412–59. Grand Rapids, Mich.: William B. Eeridmas, 1984.

Green, Paul M[ichael], and Melvin G. Holli, eds. *The Mayors: The Chicago Political Tradition.* Carbondale: Southern Illinois University Press, 1987.

Greer, Scott, ed. *Ethnics, Machines, and the American Urban Future.* Cambridge, Mass.: Harvard University Press, 1982.

Griffith, Ernest. *A History of American City Government: The Conspicuous Failure, 1870–1900.* New York: National Municipal League; Lanham, Md.: University Press of America, 1983.

———. *A History of American City Government: The Progressive Years and their Aftermath, 1900–1920.* New York: National Municipal League; Lanham, Md: University Press of America, 1983.

Grosser, Hugo S. "The Movement for Municipal Ownership in Chicago." *Annals of the American Academy of Political and Social Science*, January 1906: 72–90.

Grossman, James R. *Land of Hope: Chicago, Black Southerners, and the Great Migration.* Chicago: University of Chicago Press, 1989.

Guinther, John. *Direction of Cities.* New York: Viking, 1996.

Gutman, Herbert G. *Work, Culture and Society in Industrializing America: Essays in American Working-Class History.* New York: Knopf, 1976.

Haines, Michael R. "Industrial Work and the Family Life Cycle, 1889–1890." *Research in Economic History* 4 (1979): 289–356.

Hales, Peter B. *Silver Cities: The Photography of American Urbanization, 1839–1915.* Philadelphia: Temple University Press, 1984.

Haller, Mark H. "Urban Vice and Civic Reform: Chicago in the Early Twentieth Century." In Kenneth T. Jackson and Stanley K. Schultz, eds., *Cities in American History*, 290–305. New York: Knopf, 1972.

Hammack, David C. *Power and Society: Greater New York at the Turn of the Century.* New York: Russell Sage Foundation, 1982.

———. "Problems of Power in the Historical Study of Cities, 1800–1960." *American Historical Review* 83, no. 2 (April 1978): 323–49.

Harrison, Carter Henry [Sr.]. *A Race with the Sun.* New York: G. P. Putnam's Sons; Chicago: W. E. Dibble, 1889.

Harrison, Carter H[enry], Jr. *Growing Up with Chicago.* Chicago: Ralph Fletcher Seymour, 1944.

———. *Stormy Years: The Autobiography of Carter H. Harrison, Five Times Mayor of Chicago.* Indianapolis: Bobbs-Merrill, 1935.

Harrison, Elizabeth. "The Fair White City, or, A Story of the Past, Present and Future." *In Story-Land*, 65–77. Chicago: Stigma, 1895.

Hartman, Donald K., ed. *Fairground Fiction: Detective Stories of the World's Columbian Exposition.* Kenmore, N.Y.: Motif, 1992.

Harzig, Christiane. "Chicago's German North Side, 1880–1890: The Structure of a Gilded Age Ethnic Neighborhood." In Hartmut Keil and John B. Jentz, eds., *German Workers in Industrial Chicago, 1850–1910: A Comparative Perspective*, 127–45. DeKalb: Northern Illinois University Press, 1983.

Hatton, Augustus Raymond. *Digest of City Charters Together with Other Statutory and Constitutional Provisions Relating to Cities.* Chicago: Chicago Charter Convention, 1906.

Hawthorne, Julian. *Humors of the Fair.* Chicago: E. A. Weeks, 1893.

Hayner, Don, and Tom McNamee. *Streetwise Chicago: A History of Chicago Street Names.* Chicago: Loyola University Press, 1988.

Hays, Samuel P. *The Response to Industrialism, 1885–1914*, 2d ed. Chicago: University of Chicago Press, 1995.

———. "The Politics of Reform in Municipal Government in the Progressive Era." *Pacific Northwest Quarterly* 55, no. 4 (October 1964): 157–69.

Heilman, Ralph E. "Chicago Traction: A Study of the Efforts of the Public to Secure Good Service." *American Economic Association Quarterly* 9, no. 2 (1908): 313–409.

Heine, Jorge. *The Last Cacique:. Leadership and Politics in a Puerto Rican City.* Pittsburgh: University of Pittsburgh Press, 1993.

Heise, Kenan. *Chaos, Creativity, and Culture: A Sampling of Chicago in the Twentieth Century.* Salt Lake City: Gibbs-Smith, 1998.

Heiss, Christine. "German Radicals in Industrial America: The Lehr-und Wehr-Verein in Gilded Age Chicago." In Hartmut Keil and John B. Jentz, eds., *German Workers in Industrial Chicago, 1850–1910: A Comparative Perspective*, 206–22. DeKalb: Northern Illinois University Press, 1983.

Herrick, Robert. *The Web of Life*. New York: Macmillan, 1900.

Hewitt, Nancy A., and Suzanne Lebsock, eds. *Visible Women: New Essays on American Activism*. Urbana: University of Illinois Press, 1993.

Higgs, Robert. "Cities and Yankee Ingenuity, 1870–1920." In Kenneth T. Jackson and Stanley K. Schultz, eds., *Cities in American History*, 16–22. New York: Knopf, 1972.

Hirsch, Arnold. "The Black Struggle for Integrated Housing in Chicago." In Melvin G. Holli and Peter d'A. Jones, eds., *Ethnic Chicago*, rev. ed., 380–411. Grand Rapids, Mich.: William B. Eeridmas, 1984.

Hirsch, Susan E., and Robert I. Goler, eds. *A City Comes of Age: Chicago in the 1890s*. Chicago: Chicago Historical Society, 1990.

Hoffman, Donald. *The Architecture of John Wellborn Root*. Baltimore: Johns Hopkins University Press, 1973.

Hoffman, Donald, ed. *The Meanings of Architecture: Buildings and Writings by John Wellborn Root*. New York: Horizon, 1967.

Hoffman, Peter M. "The Race Riots." http://cpl.lib.uic.edu/004chicago/disasters/riots_race.html. Accessed December 1, 1999.

Hofstadter, Richard. *The Progressive Historians: Turner, Beard, Parrington*. Chicago: University of Chicago Press, 1979.

———. *The Structure of American History*. Englewood Cliffs, N.J.: Prentice-Hall, 1964.

———. *The Progressive Movement*. Englewood Cliffs, N.J.: Prentice-Hall, 1963.

———. *The Age of Reform: From Bryan to F.D.R.* New York: Knopf, 1955.

Holley, Marietta ["Josiah Allen's Wife"]. *Samantha at the World's Fair*. New York: Funk and Wagnalls, 1893.

Holli, Melvin G. "The Great War Sinks Chicago's German *Kultur*." In Melvin G. Holli and Peter d'A. Jones, eds., *Ethnic Chicago*, rev. ed., 460–512. Grand Rapids, Mich.: William B. Eeridmas, 1984.

———. "Social and Structural Reform: A Critical View of Municipal Government." In Kenneth T. Jackson and Stanley K. Schultz, eds., *Cities in American History*, 393–403. New York: Knopf, 1972.

Holli, Melvin, and Peter d'A Jones, eds. *Ethnic Chicago*, rev. ed. Grand Rapids, Mich.: William B. Eeridmas, 1984.

Holt, Glen E. "The Birth of Chicago: An Examination of Economic Parentage." *Journal of the Illinois State Historical Society* 76 (1983): 82–94.

———. "The Changing Perception of Urban Pathology: An Essay on the Development of Mass Transit in the United States." In Kenneth T. Jackson and Stanley K. Schultz, eds., *Cities in American History*, 324–43. New York: Knopf, 1972.

Holt, Glen E., and Dominic A. Pacyga. *Chicago: A Historical Guide to the Neighborhoods: The Loop and the South Side*. Chicago: Chicago Historical Society, 1979.

Hood, Clifton. *722 Miles: The Building of the Subways and How They Transformed New York.* New York: Simon and Schuster, 1993.

Horowitz, Helen Lefkowitz. *Culture and the City: Cultural Philanthropy in Chicago from the 1880s to 1917.* Lexington: University Press of Kentucky, 1976.

Hotchkiss, Willard E. "Chicago Traction: A Study in Political Evolution." *Annals of the American Academy of Political and Social Science* 28, no. 3 (1906): 27–46.

Hoy, Suellen. "Caring for Chicago's Women and Girls: The Sisters of the Good Shepherd, 1859–1911." *Journal of Urban History* 23, no. 3 (March 1997): 260–94.

Hoyt, Homer. *One Hundred Years of Land Values in Chicago: The Relationship of the Growth of Chicago to the Rise in Its Land Values, 1830–1933.* Chicago: University of Chicago Press, 1933.

Hunter, Robert. *Tenement Conditions in Chicago: Report of the Investigating Committee of the City Homes Association.* Chicago: City Homes Association, 1901.

Hutchinson, William T. *Cyrus Hall McCormick.* 2 vols. New York: Century, 1930–35.

Ickes, Harold. *The Autobiography of a Curmudgeon.* New York: Reynal and Hitchcock, 1943.

Jackson, Kenneth T. *The Crabgrass Frontier: The Suburbanization of America.* Oxford, U.K.: Oxford University Press, 1985.

Jackson, Kenneth T., and Stanley K. Schultz, eds. *Cities in American History.* New York: Knopf, 1972.

Jaher, Frederick Cople. *The Urban Establishment: Upper Strata in Boston, New York, Charleston, Chicago, and Los Angeles.* Urbana: University of Illinois Press, 1982.

James, Edmund J. *The Charters of the City of Chicago*, Part 2: *The City Charters, 1838–1851.* Chicago: University of Chicago Press, 1899.

Jenks, Tudor. *The Century World's Fair Book for Boys and Girls: "Being The Adventures of Harry and Philip with Their Tutor, Mr. Douglass, at the World's Columbian Exposition."* New York: Century, 1893.

Jensen, Richard. *The Winning of the Midwest: Social and Political Conflict, 1888–1896.* Chicago: University of Chicago Press, 1971.

Jentz, John B. "Skilled Workers and Industrialization: Chicago's German Cabinetmakers and Machinists, 1880–1900." In Hartmut Keil and John B. Jentz, eds., *German Workers in Industrial Chicago, 1850–1910: A Comparative Perspective*, 73–85. DeKalb: Northern Illinois University Press, 1983.

Jetter, Helen R. *Trends of Population on the Region of Chicago.* Chicago: University of Chicago Press, 1927.

Johnson, David A. *Planning the Great Metropolis: The 1929 Regional Plan of New York and Its Environs.* New York: E. and F. N. Spon, 1996.

Johnson, Claudius O. *Carter Henry Harrison I: Political Leader*. Chicago: University of Chicago Press, 1928.

Jones, Peter d'A., and Melvin G. Holli. "Introduction." In Melvin G. Holli and Peter d'A. Jones, eds., *Ethnic Chicago*, rev. ed., 1–13. Grand Rapids, Mich.: William B. Eeridmas, 1984.

Kammen, Michael, ed. *The Past Before Us: Contemporary Historical Writing in the United States*. Ithaca: Cornell University Press, 1980.

Kantowicz, Edward R. "Polish Chicago: Survival Through Solidarity." In Melvin G. Holli and Peter d'A. Jones, eds., *Ethnic Chicago*, rev. ed., 214–38. Grand Rapids, Mich.: William B. Eeridmas, 1984.

———. *Polish-American Politics in Chicago, 1888–1940*. Chicago: University of Chicago Press, 1975.

Kaplan, Justin. *Lincoln Steffens: A Biography*. New York: Simon and Schuster, 1974.

Karamanski, Theodore J. "Memory's Landscape." *Chicago History* 26, no. 2 (1997): 54–72.

Karl, Barry D. *Charles E. Merriam and the Study of Politics*. Chicago: University of Chicago Press, 1974.

Katznelson, Ira. *City Trenches: Urban Politics and the Patterning of Class in the United States*. New York: Pantheon, 1981.

Keating, Ann Durkin. *Building Chicago: Suburban Developers and the Creation of a Divided Metropolis*. Columbus: Ohio State University Press, 1988.

Keil, Hartmut. "Chicago's German Working Class in 1900." In Hartmut Keil and John B. Jentz, eds., *German Workers in Industrial Chicago, 1850–1910: A Comparative Perspective*, 19–36. DeKalb: Northern Illinois University Press, 1983.

Keil, Hartmut, and John B. Jentz. "Introduction." In Hartmut Keil and John B. Jentz, eds., *German Workers in Industrial Chicago, 1850–1910: A Comparative Perspective*, 1–18. DeKalb: Northern Illinois University Press, 1983.

Keil, Hartmut, and John B. Jentz, eds. *German Workers in Industrial Chicago, 1850–1910: A Comparative Perspective*. DeKalb: Northern Illinois University Press, 1983.

Kelley, Florence. *Notes of Sixty Years: The Autobiography of Florence Kelley*. Ed. Kathryn Kish Sklar. Chicago: C. H. Kerr, 1986.

———. *First Report of the Factory Inspectors of Illinois on Small-Pox in the Tenement House Sweatshops of Chicago*. Springfield, Ill.: H. W. Rokker, State Printer and Binder, 1894.

Kennedy, Lawrence W. *Planning the City upon a Hill. Boston since 1630*. Amherst: University of Massachusetts Press, 1992.

Kenney, William Howland. *Chicago Jazz: A Cultural History, 1904–1930*. Oxford, U.K.: Oxford University Press, 1993.

Kipling, Rudyard. "How I Struck Chicago, and How Chicago Struck Me: Of Religion, Politics, and Pig-Sticking, and the Incarnation of the City among Shambles." In Bessie Louise Pierce, comp., *As Others See Chicago: Impressions of Visitors, 1673–1933*, 250–61. Chicago: University of Chicago Press, 1933.

Klein, Maury. "The Robber Barons' Bum Rap." *City Journal* 5, no. 1 (1995): 90–100.

Kleppner, Paul. *Continuity and Change in Electoral Politics, 1893–1928*. New York: Greenwood Press, 1987.

———. *Chicago Divided: The Making of a Black Mayor*. DeKalb: Northern Illinois University Press, 1985.

———. *The Third Electoral System, 1853–1892: Parties, Voters, and Political Cultures*. Chapel Hill: University of North Carolina Press, 1979.

Knupfer, Anne Meis. "For Home, Family, and Equality: African American Women's Clubs." *Chicago History* 27, no. 2 (Summer 1998): 5–25.

Kopan, Andrew T. "Greek Survival in Chicago: The Role of Ethnic Education, 1890–1980." In Melvin G. Holli and Peter d'A. Jones, eds., *Ethnic Chicago*, rev. ed., 109–68. Grand Rapids, Mich.: William B. Eeridmas, 1984.

Kotter, John P., and Paul R. Lawrence. *Mayors in Action: Five Approaches to Urban Governance*. New York: Wiley, 1974.

Krambles, George, and Arthur H. Peterson. *CTA at 45: Recollections of the First 45 Years of the Chicago Transit Authority*. Oak Park, Ill.: George Krambles Transit Scholarship Foundation, 1993.

Krausz, Sigmund. *Street Types of Chicago:. Character Studies*. Chicago: Max Stern and Co., 1892.

Kraut, Alan M. *The Huddled Masses: The Immigrant in American Society, 1880–1921*. Arlington Heights, Ill.: Harlan Davidson, 1982.

Kuropas, Myron Bohdon. "Ukrainian Chicago: The Making of a Nationality Group." In Melvin G. Holli and Peter d'A. Jones, eds., *Ethnic Chicago*, rev. ed., 169–213. Grand Rapids, Mich.: William B. Eeridmas, 1984.

Kutler, Stanley I., and Stanley N. Katz, eds. *The Promise of American History: Progress and Prospects*. Baltimore: Johns Hopkins University Press, 1982.

Lakier, Aleksandr Borisovich. *A Russian Looks at America: The Journey of Aleksandr Borisovich Lakier in 1857*. Trans. and ed. Arnold Schrier and Joyce Story. Chicago: University of Chicago Press, 1979.

Lancaster, Clay. *The American Bungalow, 1880–1930*. New York: Abbeville, 1985.

Landau, Sarah Bradford, and Carl W. Condit. *Rise of the New York Skyscraper, 1865–1913*. New Haven: Yale University Press, 1996.

Lasch, Christopher. *The True and Only Heaven: Progress and Its Critics*. New York: Norton, 1991.

Lash-Quinn, Elisabeth. *Black Neighbors: Race and the Limits of Reform in the American Settlement House Movement, 1890–1945.* Chapel Hill: University of North Carolina Press, 1993.

Levine, Bruce Carlan. "Free Soil, Free Labor, and *Freimanner*: German Chicago in the Civil War Era." In Hartmut Keil and John B. Jentz, eds., *German Workers in Industrial Chicago, 1850–1910. A Comparative Perspective,* 163–82. DeKalb: Northern Illinois University Press, 1983.

Lewis, Arnold. "Time is Money." *Chicago History,* 37, no. 1 (Spring 1998): 4–21.

———. *An Early Encounter with Tomorrow: Europeans, Chicago's Loop, and the World's Columbian Exposition.* Urbana: University of Illinois Press, 1997.

Lind, Alan R. *Chicago Surface Lines.* 3d ed. Park Forest, Ill.: Transport History Press, 1979.

Lindsey, Almont. *The Pullman Strike: The Story of a Unique Experiment and of a Great Labor Upheaval.* Chicago: University of Chicago Press, 1942.

Link, Arthur S., and Richard L. McCormick. *Progressivism.* Arlington Heights, Ill.: Harlan Davidson, 1983.

Litt, Edgar. *Beyond Pluralism: Ethnic Politics in America.* Glenview, Ill.: Scott, Foresman, 1970.

Lloyd, Lewis, and Henry J. Smith. *Chicago: The History of Its Reputation.* New York: Harcourt, Brace, 1929.

Longstreet, Stephen. *Chicago, 1860–1919.* New York: David McKay, 1973.

Lovoll, Odd S. *A Century of Urban Life: The Norwegians in Chicago before 1930.* Northfield, Minn.: Norwegian-American Historical Association, 1988.

Low, David. *Lost Chicago.* New York: Wings, 1975.

Lukas, J. Anthony. *Common Ground: A Turbulent Decade in the Lives of Three American Families.* New York: Vintage, 1986.

Lurie, Jonathan. *The Chicago Board of Trade, 1859–1905: The Dynamics of Self-Regulation.* Urbana: University of Illinois Press, 1979.

Lynch, Lawrence L. [Emma Murdock Van Deventer]. *A Blind Lead: Daring and Thrilling Adventures, Clever Detective Work.* Chicago: Alex T. Loyd, 1912.

———. *The Last Stroke.* Chicago: Alex T. Loyd, 1896.

———. *A Dead Man's Stem.* Chicago: Alex T. Loyd, 1893.

———. *Moina, or, Against the Mighty.* Chicago: Alex T. Loyd, 1891.

———. *A Slender Clue.* Chicago: Alex T. Loyd, 1891.

———. *The Lost Witness, or, The Mystery of Leah Paget.* Chicago: Alex T. Loyd, 1890.

———. *The Diamond Coterie.* Chicago: Alex T. Loyd, 1889.

———. *Madeline Payne, the Detective's Daughter.* Chicago: Alex T. Loyd, 1889.

———. *A Mountain Mystery, or, The Outlaws of the Rockies.* Chicago: Alex T. Loyd, 1889.

———. *Dangerous Ground, or, the Rival Detectives.* Chicago: Alex T. Loyd, 1885.

Lynd, Robert, and Helen Lynd. *Middletown in Transition: A Study in Cultural Conflicts*. New York: Harcourt, Brace, 1937.

MacDougall, Elisabeth Blair, ed. *The Architectural Historian in America*. Studies in the History of Art, no. 35. Center for Advanced Study in the Visual Arts Symposium Papers, no 19. Washington, D.C.: National Gallery of Art, 1990.

Mackie, Pauline Bradford. "In Old Vienna." *New Peterson Magazine* 3 (February 1894): 118–21.

Mahoney, Olivia. "Expanding Empire: Chicago and the West." *Chicago History* 26, no. 1 (1997): 4–21.

Makgaigan, Varvara. "Pis'ma iz Ameriki." *Severnyi vestnik* 1893, nos. 5–13 (June 1893–December 1893).

Maltbie, Milo Roy, ed. *The Street Railways of Chicago: Report of the Civic Federation of Chicago*. Chicago: Civic Federation of Chicago, 1901.

Mayer, Harold M., and Richard C. Wade. *Chicago: Growth of a Metropolis*. Chicago: University of Chicago Press, 1969.

Mayfield, Loomis. "Chicago Wasn't Ready for Reform." *Journal of Urban History* 20, no. 4 (August 1994): 564–76.

Mazur, Edward. "Jewish Chicago: From Diversity to Community." In Melvin G. Holli and Peter d'A. Jones, eds., *Ethnic Chicago*, rev. ed., 46–68. Grand Rapids, Mich.: William B. Eeridmas, 1984.

McCaffrey, Lawrence J., Ellen Skerrett, Michael F. Funchion, and Charles Fanning, eds. *The Irish in Chicago*. Urbana: University of Illinois Press, 1987.

McCarthy, Michael P. "Prelude to Armageddon: Charles E. Merriam and the Chicago Mayoral Election of 1911." *Journal of the Illinois State Historical Society* 67, no. 5 (November 1974): 505–18.

McCormick, Cyrus. *The Century of the Reaper*. Boston: Houghton Mifflin, 1931.

McCormick, Richard L. "Public Life in Industrial America, 1877–1917." In Eric Foner, ed., *The New American History*, 93–117. Philadelphia: Temple University Press, 1990.

McDonald, Terrence J. *The Parameters of Urban Fiscal Policy: Socioeconomic Change and Political Culture in San Francisco, 1860–1906*. Berkeley: University of California Press, 1987.

McDonald, Terrence J., and Sally K. Ward, eds. *The Politics of Urban Fiscal Policy*. Beverly Hills: Sage, 1984.

McShane, Clay. "Transforming the Use of Urban Space: A Look at the Revolution in Street Pavements, 1880–1924." *Journal of Urban History* 5, no. 3 (May 1979): 279–307.

Merriam, Charles E. *Scrambled Government: Who Rules What in Chicagoland?* Chicago, 1934.

———. *Chicago: A More Intimate View of Urban Politics*. New York: Macmillan, 1929.

————. *A Report on an Investigation of the Municipal Revenues of Chicago.* Chicago: City Club of Chicago, 1906.

Meyerowitz, Joanne J. *Women Adrift: Independent Wage Earners in Chicago, 1880–1930.* Chicago: University of Chicago Press, 1988.

Miller, Donald L. *City of the Century: The Epic of Chicago and the Making of America.* New York: Simon and Schuster, 1996.

Miller, Donald L., ed. *The Lewis Mumford Reader.* New York: Pantheon, 1986.

Miller, Francesca Falk. *The Sands: The Story of Chicago's Front Yard.* Chicago: Valentine-Newman, 1948.

Miller, Ross. *American Apocalypse: The Great Fire and the Myth of Chicago.* Chicago: University of Chicago Press, 1990.

Miller, Zane. "Bosses, Machines, and the Urban Political Process." In Scott Greer, ed., *Ethnics, Machines, and the American Urban Future,* 51–84. Cambridge, Mass.: Harvard University Press, 1982.

Mills, C. Wright. *The Power Elite.* New York: Oxford University Press, 1956.

————. *White Collar: The American Middle Classes.* New York: Oxford University Press, 1951.

Mittelman, Edward B. "Chicago Labor in Politics, 1877–1896." *Journal of Political Economy* 28 (1920): 407–27.

Moffatt, Bruce G. *The "L": The Development of Chicago's Rapid Transit System, 1888–1932.* Chicago: Central Electric Railfans' Association, 1995.

Mohl, Raymond A. "The Missing Dimension in U.S. Urban History." *Journal of Urban History* 25, no. 1 (1998): 3–21.

Monkkonen, Eric H. *America Becomes Urban: The Development of U.S. Cities and Towns, 1780–1980.* Berkeley: University of California Press, 1988.

Moore, Bernard F. *The Girl from Midway: A Farce Comedy in One Act.* Clyde, Ohio: Ames, 1895.

Mumford, Lewis. "Towards Modern Architecture." In Donald L. Miller, ed., *The Lewis Mumford Reader,* 49–72. New York: Pantheon, 1986.

————. "What Is a City?" In Donald L. Miller, ed., *The Lewis Mumford Reader,* 104–7. New York: Pantheon, 1986.

————. *Sticks and Stones: A Study of American Architecture and Civilization.* New York: Boni and Liveright, 1924.

Neely, Frank T. *Looking Forward: An Imaginary Visit to the World's Fair.* Chicago: F. T. Neely, 1889.

Nelli, Humbert S. *Italians in Chicago, 1880–1930: A Study in Ethnic Mobility.* Oxford, U.K.: Oxford University Press, 1970.

Nelson, Bruce. *Beyond the Martyrs: A Social History of Chicago's Anarchists, 1870–1900.* New Brunswick, N.J.: Rutgers University Press, 1988.

The New Chicago Charter: Why It Should Be Adopted at the Special Election, September 17. Chicago: Civic Federation of Chicago, 1907.

Norton, Samuel Wilber. *Chicago Traction: A History Legislative and Political.* Chicago, 1907.

Nute, Kevin. *Frank Lloyd Wright and Japan: The Role of Traditional Japanese Art and Architecture in the Work of Frank Lloyd Wright.* New York: Van Nostrand Reinhold, 1993.

Oestreicher, Richard [J.]. "Urban Working-Class Political Behavior and Theories of American Electoral Politics, 1870–1940." *Journal of American History* 74, no. 4 (1988): 1257–86.

———. "Industrialization, Class, and Competing Cultural Systems: Detroit Workers, 1875–1900." In Hartmut Keil and John B. Jentz, eds., *German Workers in Industrial Chicago, 1850–1910: A Comparative Perspective,* 52–73. DeKalb: Northern Illinois University Press, 1983.

O'Gorman, James E. *Three American Architects: Richardson, Sullivan, and Wright, 1865–1915.* Chicago: University of Chicago Press, 1991.

O'Neill, William L. *The Progressive Years: America Comes of Age.* New York: Dodd, Mead, 1975.

Ostrogorski, Moisei. *Democracy and the Organization of Political Parties.* New York: Macmillan, 1902.

Painter, Nell Irvin. *Standing at Armageddon: The United States, 1877–1919.* New York: Norton, 1987.

Payne, Elizabeth A. *Reform, Labor, and Feminism: Margaret Dreier Robins and the Women's Trade Union League.* Urbana: University of Illinois Press, 1988.

Payne, Will. *Mr. Salt: A Novel.* Boston: Houghton, Mifflin, 1904.

People of Chicago. Chicago: City of Chicago, 1976.

Peters, Tom F. "The Relative Value of Invention and the History of the Tall Building." In Lynn S. Beedle, ed., *Second Century of the Skyscraper,* 25–32. New York: Van Nostrand Reinhold, 1988.

Peterson, Jacqueline. "The Founding Fathers: The Absorption of French-Indian Chicago, 1816–1837." In Melvin G. Holli and Peter d'A. Jones, eds., *Ethnic Chicago,* rev. ed., 300–37. Grand Rapids, Mich.: William B. Eeridmas, 1984.

Philpott, Thomas Lee. *The Slum and the Ghetto: Immigrants, Blacks, and Reformers in Chicago, 1880–1930.* Belmont, Calif.: Wadsworth, 1991.

———. *The Slum and the Ghetto: Neighborhood Deterioration and Middle-Class Reform, Chicago, 1880–1930.* Oxford, U.K.: Oxford University Press, 1978.

Pierce, Bessie Louise. *A History of Chicago.* Vol. 3: *The Rise of a Modern City, 1871–1893.* Chicago: University of Chicago Press, 1957.

Pierce, Bessie Louise, comp. *As Others See Chicago: Impressions of Visitors, 1673–1933.* Chicago: University of Chicago Press, 1933.

Plan of Chicago. Chicago: Commercial Club of Chicago, 1909.

The Plan of Chicago in 1925. Chicago: Chicago Plan Commission, 1925.

Platt, Harold L. *The Electric City: Energy and the Growth of the Chicago Area, 1880–1930*. Chicago: University of Chicago Press, 1991.

Pliskii, Nikolai. *Podrobnyi putevoditel' na Vsemirnuiu Kolumbovu vystavku v Chikago, 1893ogo goda*. St. Peterburg: Stefanov i Kachka, 1893.

Plumbe, George Edward. *Chicago: Its Natural Advantages as an Industrial and Commercial Center and Market*. Chicago: Civic-Industrial Committee of the Chicago Association of Commerce, 1910.

Pollard, Percival. "The White City's Dream." *Dreams of To-Day*. Chicago: Way and Williams, 1897.

Polsby, Nelson. *Community Power and Political Theory: A Further Look at Problems of Evidence and Inference*, 2d ed. New Haven: Yale University Press, 1980.

Porter, Glenn. *The Rise of Big Business, 1860–1920*, 2d ed. Arlington Heights, Ill.: Harlan Davidson, 1992.

Preliminary Report on Need for New City Charter. Chicago: Civic Federation of Chicago, 1902.

Rakove, Milton L. *Don't Make No Waves, Don't Back No Losers: An Insider's Analysis of the Daley Machine*. Bloomington: Indiana University Press, 1975.

Rathborne, St. George. *The Bachelor of the Midway*. New York: Mascot, 1894.

Reiff, Janice L. "A Modern Lear and His Daughters: Gender in the Model Town of Pullman." *Journal of Urban History* 23, no. 3 (March 1997): 316–41.

"Remembering the Great Chicago Fire." *Chicago History* 25, no. 3 (Fall 1996): 24–39.

Report of Special Committee of the City Council of Chicago on Streetrail Franchises and Operations. Chicago: Chicago City Council, 1898.

Report of the Executive Committee, to Be Submitted to the Convention at Its Next Meeting, December 15, 1902. Chicago: New Charter Convention, 1902.

Reps, John W. *The Making of Urban America: A History of City Planning in the United States*. Princeton: Princeton University Press, 1992.

Resolutions and Communications Received at Meeting Held January 19, 1909. Chicago: City Charter Convention, 1909.

Rex, Frederick. *The Mayors of the City of Chicago from March 4, 1837, to April 13, 1933*. Chicago: Chicago Municipal Reference Library, 1934.

———. *Index to Andreas' History of Chicago*. Chicago: Municipal Reference Library, 1956.

Richardson, Lucius S. *The Civic Federation and Municipal Government*. St. Louis: Civic Federation of St. Louis, 1896.

Ritchie, Alan. "The Philosophy and the Future of the Skyscraper." In Lynn S. Beedle, ed., *Second Century of the Skyscraper*, 3–10. New York: Van Nostrand Reinhold, 1988.

Rodgers, Daniel T. "In Search of Progressivism." *Reviews in American History* 10, no. 4 (December 1982): 113–32.

Root, John Wellborn. "Architects of Chicago." *Inland Architect and News Record*, 16, no. 8 (January 1891): 91–92

———. "A Great Architectural Problem." *Inland Architect and News Record* 15, no. 5 (June 1890): 67–71.

Rusk, David. *Cities without Suburbs.* Washington, D.C.: Woodrow Wilson Center Press, 1993.

Rybczynski, Witold. *City Life: Urban Expectations in a New World.* New York: Scribner, 1995.

Saliga, Pauline A. "Bridging Two Eras." In Pauline A. Saliga, ed., *The Sky's the Limit: A Century of Chicago Skyscrapers*, 17–94. New York: Rizzoli, 1990.

———. "Mid-American Metropolis." In Pauline A. Saliga, ed., *The Sky's the Limit: A Century of Chicago Skyscrapers*, 95–174. New York: Rizzoli, 1990.

———. "Postwar Modernism and Postmodernism." In Pauline A. Saliga, ed., *The Sky's the Limit: A Century of Chicago Skyscrapers*, 175–289. New York: Rizzoli, 1990.

Saliga, Pauline A., ed. *The Sky's the Limit: A Century of Chicago Skyscrapers.* New York: Rizzoli, 1990.

Sawislak, Karen. *Smoldering City: Chicagoans and the Great Fire, 1871–1874.* Chicago: University of Chicago Press, 1995.

Schneider, Dorothee. "For Whom Are All the Good Things in Life? German-American Housewives Discuss Their Budgets." In Hartmut Keil and John B. Jentz, eds., *German Workers in Industrial Chicago, 1850–1910: A Comparative Perspective*, 145–62. DeKalb: Northern Illinois University Press, 1983.

Schneirov, Richard. "Class Conflict, Municipal Politics, and Governmental Reform in Gilded Age Chicago, 1871–1975." In Hartmut Keil and John B. Jentz, eds., *German Workers in Industrial Chicago, 1850–1910: A Comparative Perspective*, 183–205. DeKalb: Northern Illinois University Press, 1983.

———. "Chicago's Great Upheaval of 1877." *Chicago History* 9, no. 1 (Spring 1980): 2–17.

Sekler, Eduard F. "Sigfried Giedion at Harvard University." In Elisabeth Blair MacDougall, ed., *The Architectural Historian in America*, 265–73. Studies in the History of Art, no. 35. Center for Advanced Study in the Visual Arts Symposium Papers, no. 19. Washington, D.C.: National Gallery of Art, 1990.

Sennett, Richard. *Families against the City: Middle Class Homes of Industrial Chicago, 1872–1890.* New York: Vintage, 1970.

Sinclair, Harold. *The Years of Growth, 1861–1893.* New York: Doubleday, Doran, 1940.

Sinclair, Upton. *The Jungle*. New York: Bantam, 1981.

Sixth and Seventh Ward Charter Committee (Republican). *Plan and Purpose*. Chicago: Sixth and Seventh Ward Charter Committee, 1904.

Sklar, Kathryn Kish. *Florence Kelley and the Nation's Work*. 2 vols. New Haven: Yale University Press, 1995.

Skowronek, Stephen. *Building a New American State: The Expansion of National Administrative Capacities, 1877–1920*. Cambridge, U.K.: Cambridge University Press, 1982.

Slayton, Robert A. "Labor and Urban Politics: District 31, Steel Workers Organizing Committee, and the Chicago Machine." *Journal of Urban History* 23, no. 1 (November 1996): 29–65.

———. *Back of the Yards: The Making of Local Democracy*. Chicago: University of Chicago Press, 1986.

Smith, Carl S. *Urban Disorder and the Shape of Belief: The Great Chicago Fire, the Haymarket Bomb, and the Model Town of Pullman*. Chicago: University of Chicago Press, 1995.

———. *Chicago and the American Literary Imagination, 1880–1920*. Chicago: University of Chicago Press, 1984.

Snyder, Robert W. *The Voice of the City:. Vaudeville and Popular Culture in New York*. Oxford: Oxford University Press, 1989.

Spear, Allan H. *Black Chicago: The Making of a Negro Ghetto, 1890–1920*. Chicago: University of Chicago Press, 1967.

Stamper, John W. *Chicago's North Michigan Avenue: Planning and Development, 1900–1930*. Chicago: University of Chicago Press, 1991.

Stead, F. Herbert. "The Civic Life of Chicago." *Review of Reviews* 8 (July 1893): 93–96.

Stead, William Thomas. *If Christ Came to Chicago! A Plea for the Union of All Who Love in the Service of All Who Suffer*. Chicago: Laird and Lee, 1894.

———. "From the Old World to the New, or, A Christmas Story of the World's Fair, 1893." *Review of Reviews*, Christmas 1892.

Steffens, Lincoln. *The Autobiography of Lincoln Steffens*, 2 vols. New York: Harcourt, Brace, and World, 1931.

———. *The Shame of the Cities*. 1904. Reprint, New York: Hill and Wang, 1992.

Stern, Robert A. M., Gregory Gilmartin, and John Massengale. *New York 1900: Metropolitan Architecture and Urbanism, 1890–1915*. New York: Rizzoli, 1983.

Stern, Robert A. M., Thomas Mellins, and David Fishman. *New York 1880: Architecture and Urbanism in the Gilded Age*. New York: Monacelli, 1999.

Stevens, Charles McClellan ["Quondam"]. *The Adventures of Uncle Jeremiah and Family at the Great Fair: Their Observations and Triumphs*. Chicago: Laird and Lee, 1893.

Street, Ada Hilt, and Julian Leonard Street. *Tides*. Garden City, N.Y.: Doubleday, Page, 1926.

Street, Julian [Leonard]. "Chicago's Individuality." In Bessie Louise Pierce, comp., *As Others See Chicago. Impressions of Visitors, 1673–1933*, 441–60. Chicago: University of Chicago Press, 1933.

Stromquist, Shelton. *A Generation of Boomers: The Pattern of Railroad Labor Conflict in Nineteenth-Century America*. Urbana: University of Illinois Press, 1987.

Sugrue, Thomas J. "More than Skin Deep: Redevelopment and the Urban Crisis." *Journal of Urban History* 22, no. 6 (September 1996): 750–59.

Suhrbur, Thomas J. "Ethnicity in the Formation of the Chicago Carpenters Union: 1855–1890." In Hartmut Keil and John B. Jentz, eds., *German Workers in Industrial Chicago, 1850–1910: A Comparative Perspective*, 86–103. DeKalb: Northern Illinois University Press, 1983.

Sunny, Bernard E. *The Proposed Amendment to the Constitution of the State of Illinois and a New Charter for Chicago*. Chicago: Civic Federation of Chicago, 1904.

Sutherland, Douglas. *Fifty Years on the Civic Front: A History of the Civic Federation*. Chicago: Civic Federation of Chicago, 1943.

———. *Federal "Aid."* Chicago: Civic Federation of Chicago, 1921.

Talbot, Allan R. *The Mayor's Game: Richard Lee of New Haven and the Politics of Change*. New York: Praeger, 1970.

Tamarkin, Bob. "Only the Market Knows." *Chicago Times Magazine* 1, no. 2 (November–December 1987): 54–61.

———. *The New Gatsbys: Fortunes and Misfortunes of Commodity Traders*. New York: Morrow, 1985.

Tarr, Joel A. *A Study in Boss Politics: William Lorimer of Chicago*. Urbana: University of Illinois Press, 1971.

Tax Inequalities in Illinois. Chicago: Civic Federation of Chicago, 1911.

Teaford, Jon C. *Cities of the Heartland: The Rise and Fall of the Industrial Midwest*. Bloomington: Indiana University Press, 1993.

———. *The Unheralded Triumph: City Government in America, 1870–1900*. Baltimore: Johns Hopkins University Press, 1984.

———. "Finis for Tweed and Steffans: Rewriting the History of Urban Rule." In Stanley I. Kutler and Stanley N. Katz, eds., *The Promise of American History: Progress and Prospects*, 133–49. Baltimore: Johns Hopkins University Press, 1982.

Thelen, David P. "Urban Politics: Beyond Bosses and Reformers." *Reviews in American History* 7, no. 3 (September 1979): 406–12.

Turner, Frederick Jackson. *The Frontier in American History*. New York: H. Holt, 1920.

Tuttle, William M., Jr. "Contested Neighborhoods and Racial Violence: Chicago in 1919: A Case Study." In Kenneth T. Jackson and Stanley K. Schultz, eds., *Cities in American History*, 232–48. New York: Knopf, 1972.

———. *Race Riot: Chicago in the Red Summer of 1919*. New York: Atheneum, 1970.

Twombly, Robert. *Power and State: A Critique of Twentieth-Century Architecture in the United States*. New York: Hill and Wang, 1996.

United States Department of Commerce. Bureau of the Census. *State and Local Government Special Studies, No. 38*. Washington, D.C.: U.S. Government Printing Office, 1955.

———. *State and Local Government Special Studies, No. 25*. Washington, D.C.: U.S. Government Printing Office, 1948.

———. *Thirteenth Census of the United States*. Washington, D.C.: U.S. Government Printing Office, 1913.

Van Zanten, David. "Chicago in Architectural History." In Elisabeth Blair MacDougall, ed., *The Architectural Historian in America*, 91–99. Studies in the History of Art, no. 35. Center for Advanced Study in the Visual Arts Symposium Papers, no. 19. Washington, D.C.: National Gallery of Art, 1990.

Veblen, Thorstein. *Higher Learning in America: A Memorandum on the Conduct of Universities by Business Men*. New York: B. W. Huebsch, 1918.

———. *The Instinct of Workmanship and the State of the Industrial Arts*. New York: B. W. Huebsch, 1918.

———. *The Theory of the Leisure Class*. 1899. Reprint, New York: Viking Press, 1967.

Veniukov, I. M. "Illinois i Chikago." *Nabliudatel'* 1893, no. 5 (May): 257–72.

Wade, Louise Carroll. *Chicago's Pride: The Stockyards, Packingtown, and Environs in the Nineteenth Century*. Urbana: University of Illinois Press, 1987.

Wade, Richard C. *Chicago: Growth of a Metropolis*. Chicago: University of Chicago Press, 1969.

Ward, A. B. "A Medley of the Midway Plaisance." In *Short Stories from Outing*, 91–114. New York: Outing, 1895.

Warner, Sam Bass, Jr. *Urban Wilderness: A History of the American City*. New York: Harper and Row, 1972.

———. *The Private City: Philadelphia in Three Periods of Its Growth*. Philadelphia: University of Pennsylvania Press, 1968.

———. *Streetcar Suburbs: The Process of Growth in Boston, 1870–1900*. Cambridge, Mass.: Harvard University Press, 1962.

Warren, Arthur. "Phillip D. Armour: His Manner of Life, His Immense Enterprises in Trade and Philanthropy." *McClure's Magazine* 2 (December 1893–May 1894): 260–80.

Weber, Henry P., comp. *An Outline History of Chicago Traction*. Chicago: Chicago Railways Company, 1936.

Wendt, Lloyd, and Herman Kogan. *Bosses in Lusty Chicago: The Story of Bathhouse John and Hinky Dink*. 1943. Reprint, Bloomington: University of Indiana Press, 1967.

Whitaker, Craig. *Architecture and the American Dream*. New York: Clarkson N. Potter, 1996.

Wiebe, Robert H. *The Search for Order, 1877–1920*. New York: Hill and Wang, 1967.

Willie, Lois. *Forever Open, Clear, and Free: The Historic Struggle for Chicago's Lakefront*. Chicago: Henry Regnery, 1972.

Willis, Carol. *Form Follows Finance: Skyscrapers and Skylines in New York and Chicago*. New York: Princeton Architectural Press, 1995.

Wills, Garry. "Sons and Daughters of Chicago." *New York Review of Books*, June 9, 1994, pp. 52–59.

———. "Chicago Underground." *New York Review of Books*, October 21, 1993: 15–22.

Winslow, Helen M. "Met on the Midway." *Frank Leslie's Popular Monthly* 36 (October 1893): 501–4.

Wish, Harvey. "Altgeld and the Progressive Tradition." *American Historical Review* 46, no. 4 (July 1941): 813–31.

Wolfinger, Raymond. *The Politics of Progress*. Englewood Cliffs, N.J.: Prentice-Hall, 1974.

Wood, Edith Elmer. "Martha Ellen at the Chicago Exposition." *Shoulder Straps and Sun Bonnets*, 41–57. New York: Henry Holt, 1901.

Wright, Gwendolyn. *Moralism and the Model Home: Domestic Architecture and Cultural Conflict in Chicago, 1873–1913*. Chicago: University of Chicago Press, 1980.

Wrigley, Julia. *Class, Politics, and Public Schools: Chicago, 1900–1950*. New Brunswick, N.J.: Rutgers University Press, 1982.

Yandell, Enid, Jean Loughborough, and Laura Hayes. *Three Girls in a Flat*. Chicago: Knight, Leonard, 1892.

Znaniecki, Florian, and William I. Thomas. *The Polish Peasant in Europe and America*. 1918–20. Reprint, ed. and abridged by Eli Zaretsky. Urbana: University of Illinois Press, 1984.

Zorbaugh, Harvey Warren. *The Gold Coast and the Slum: A Sociological Study of Chicago's Near North Side*. Chicago: University of Chicago Press, 1929.

Zukowsky, John. "Introduction." In Pauline A. Saliga, ed., *The Sky's the Limit: A Century of Chicago Skyscrapers*, 6–16. New York: Rizzoli, 1990.

Zukowsky, John, ed. *Chicago Architecture, 1872–1922*. Chicago: Art Institute of Chicago, 1987.

Zunz, Olivier. *The Changing Face of Inequality: Urbanization, Industrial Development, and Immigrants in Detroit, 1880–1920*. Chicago: University of Chicago Press, 1982.

———. *Making America Corporate, 1870–1920*. Chicago: University of Chicago Press, 1990.

Dissertations

Becker, Richard Edward. "Edward Dunne: Reform Mayor of Chicago, 1905–1907." Ph.D. diss., University of Chicago. Chicago, 1971.

Belcher, Wyatt Winton. "The Economic Rivalry between St. Louis and Chicago, 1850–1880." Ph.D. diss., Columbia University, 1947.

Bluestone, Daniel M. "Landscape and Culture in Nineteenth-Century Chicago." Ph.D. diss., University of Chicago, 1984.

Branham, Charles. "The Transformation of Black Political Leadership in Chicago, 1864–1942." Ph.D. diss., University of Chicago, 1981.

Bushnell, Charles Joseph. "The Social Problem at the Chicago Stock Yards." Ph.D. diss., University of Chicago, 1902.

Cressey, Paul Frederick. "The Succession of Cultural Groups in the City of Chicago." Ph.D. diss., University of Chicago. Chicago, 1930.

Dostoglu, Sibel Bozdogan. "Towards Professional Legitimacy and Power: An Inquiry into the Struggle, Achievements, and Dilemmas of the Architectural Profession through an Analysis of Chicago, 1871–1909." Ph.D. diss., University of Pennsylvania, 1983.

Errant, James W. "Trade Unionism in the Civil Service of Chicago, 1895 to 1930." Ph.D. diss., University of Chicago, 1939.

Green, Paul Michael. "The Chicago Democratic Party, 1840–1920: From Factionalism to Political Organization." Ph.D. diss., University of Chicago, 1975.

Heilman, Ralph Emerson. "Chicago Traction: A Study of the Efforts of the City to Secure Good Service." Ph.D. diss., Harvard University, 1912.

Homel, Michael Wallace. "Negroes in the Chicago Public Schools, 1910–1941." Ph.D. diss., University of Chicago, 1972.

Keating, Ann Durkin. "Governing the New Metropolis: The Development of Urban and Suburban Governments in Cook County, Illinois, 1831–1902." Ph.D. diss., University of Chicago, 1984.

Lee, Guy A. "History of the Chicago Grain Elevator Industry, 1840–1890." Ph.D. diss., Harvard University, 1938.

Leidenberger, Georg. "Working-Class Progressivism and the Politics of Transportation in Chicago, 1895–1907." Ph.D. diss., University of North Carolina, Chapel Hill, 1995.

Marks, Donald D. "Polishing the Gem of the Prairie: The Evolution of Civic Reform Consciousness in Chicago, 1874–1900." Ph.D. diss., Northwestern University, 1960.

Mayfield, Loomis. "The Reorganization of Urban Politics: The Chicago Growth Machine after World War II." Ph.D. diss., University of Pittsburgh, 1996.

Maynard, David Macrum. "The Operation of the Referendum in Chicago." Ph.D. diss., University of Chicago, 1930.

Mazur, Edward H. "Minyans for a Prairie City: The Politics of Chicago Jewry, 1850–1940." Ph.D. diss., University of Chicago, 1974.

McCarthy, Michael. "Businessmen and Professionals in Municipal Reform: The Chicago Experience, 1887–1920." Ph.D. diss., Northwestern University, 1971.

Moore, Elizabeth A. "Life and Labor: Margaret Dreier Robins and the Women's Trade Union League." Ph.D. diss., University of Illinois, Chicago Circle, 1982.

Murphy, Marjorie. "From Artisans to Semi-Professionals: White Collar Unionism among Chicago Public School Teachers, 1870–1930." Ph.D. diss., University of California, Davis, 1981.

Myers, Howard Barton. "The Policing of Labor Disputes in Chicago: A Case Study." Ph.D. diss., University of Chicago, 1929.

O'Connell, James C. "Technology and Pollution: Chicago's Water Policy, 1833–1930." Ph.D. diss., University of Chicago, 1980.

Pace, Barney. "An Experimental Novel about the Columbian Exposition of 1893: The Fame and Fortune of Jimmie Dawson." Ph.D. diss., University of Michigan, 1982.

Philip, William Booth. "Chicago and the Downstate: A Study of Their Conflicts, 1870–1934." Ph.D. diss., University of Chicago, 1940.

Sawislak, Karen Lynn. "Smoldering City: Class, Ethnicity, and Politics in Chicago at the Time of the Great Fire, 1867–1874." Ph.D. diss., Yale University, 1990.

Schneirov, Richard. "The Knights of Labor in the Chicago Labor Movement and Municipal Politics, 1877–1887." Ph.D. diss., Northern Illinois University, 1984.

Schultz, Rima Lunin. "The Businessman's Role in Western Settlement: The Entrepreneurial Frontier: Chicago, 1833–1872." Ph.D. diss., Boston University, 1985.

Street, Paul Louis. "Working in the Yards: A History of Class Relations in Chicago's Meatpacking Industry, 1886–1943." Ph.D. diss., State University of New York at Binghamton, 1993.

Tingley, Ralph R. "From Carter Harrison II to Fred Busse: A Study of Parties and Personages from 1896 to 1907." Ph.D. diss., University of Chicago, 1950.

Townsend, Andrew Jacke. "The Germans of Chicago." Ph.D. diss., University of Chicago, 1927.

Weber, Robert David. "Rationalizers and Reformers: Chicago Local Transportation in the Nineteenth Century." Ph.D. diss., University of Wisconsin, Madison, 1971.

Yates, Donatta M. "Women in Chicago Industries, 1905–1915: A Study of Working Conditions in Factories, Laundries, and Restaurants." M.A. thesis, University of Chicago, 1948.

Zingler, Leonard M. "Financial History of the Chicago Street Railways." Ph.D. diss., University of Illinois, Urbana, 1931.

MOSCOW AND RUSSIAN CITIES

Newspapers

Moskovskii listok

Books and Articles

Aksakova-Sirves, T. A. "Gimnazicheskie gody." In Iu. Aleksandrov, V. Enisherlov, and D. Ivanov, eds., *Moskovskii al'bom. Vospominaniia o Moskve i moskvichakh XIX–XX vekov*, 214–47. Moscow: Nashe nasledie, 1997.

Alaverdian, Stepan Karapetovich. *Zhilishchnyi vopros v Moskve*. Yerevan: Izdatel'stvo A.N. Armianskoi S.S.R., 1961.

Aleksandrov, Iu. "Gogolevskii bul'var." In A. S. Kiselev et al., eds., *Moskovskii arkhiv. Istoriko-kraevedcheskii al'manakh*, 95–106. Moscow: Moskovskoe gorodskoe ob"edinenie arkhivov, 1996.

Aleksandrov, Iu., V. Enisherlov, and D. Ivanov, eds. *Moskovskii al'bom. Vospominaniia o Moskve i moskvichakh XIX–XX vekov*. Moscow: Nashe nasledie, 1997.

Alston, Patrick L. *Education and the State in Tsarist Russia*. Stanford: Stanford University Press, 1969.

Anan'ich, B[oris] V. "Novyi kurs. 'Narodnoe samoderzhavie' Aleksandra III i Nikolaia II." In B. V. Anan'ich, R. Sh. Ganelin, and V. M. Paneiakh, eds., *Vlast' i reformy. Ot samoderzhavnoi k sovetskoi Rossii*, 371–79. St. Petersburg: Izdatel'stvo Dmitrii Bulanin, 1996.

———. "Predislovie." In B. V. Anan'ich, R. Sh. Ganelin, and V. M. Paneiakh, eds., *Vlast' i reformy. Ot samoderzhavnoi k sovetskoi Rossii*, 3–10. St. Petersburg: Izdatel'stvo Dmitrii Bulanin, 1996.

———. "Rossiia na paroge XX stoletiia. Samoderzhavie Nikolaia II. Reformy S. Iu. Witte." In B. V. Anan'ich, R. Sh. Ganelin, and V. M. Paneiakh, eds., *Vlast' i reformy. Ot samoderzhavnoi k sovetskoi Rossii*, 399–437. St. Petersburg: Izdatel'stvo Dmitrii Bulanin, 1996.

———. *Bankirskie doma v Rossii, 1860–1914gg. Ocherki istorii chastnogo predprinimatel'stva* Leningrad: Nauka, Leningradskoe otdelenie, 1991.

———. "Foreign Loans and Russia's Economic Development, 1864–1914 (The Gold Standard and Railway Construction)." Paper presented at the Tenth International Economic History Congress, Leuven, Belgium, 1990.

———. "Pravovoe polozhenie bankirskikh zavedenii v Rossii (1880-e gody–1914g.)." In S. L. Tikhvinskii, ed., *Sotsial'no-ekonomicheskoe razvitie Rossii. Sbornik statei k 100-letiiu so dnia rozhdeniia Nikolaia Mikhailovicha Druzhinina*, 206–21. Moscow: Nauka, 1986.

———. "The Economic Policy of the Tsarist Government and Enterprise in Russia from the End of the Nineteenth through the Beginning of the Twentieth Century." In Greg Guroff and F. V. Carstensen, eds., *Entrepreneurship in Imperial Russia and the Soviet Union*, 125–39. Princeton: Princeton University Press, 1983.

———. *Rossiia i mezhdunarodnyi kapital, 1897–1914*. Leningrad: Nauka, Leningradskoe otdelenie, 1970.

Anan'ich, B[oris] V., R. Sh. Ganelin, and V. M. Paneiakh, eds. *Vlast' i reformy. Ot samoderzhavnoi k sovetskoi Rossii*. St. Petersburg: Izdatel'stvo Dmitrii Bulanin, 1996.

Anderson, Barbara A. "Who Chose the Cities? Migrants to Moscow and St. Petersburg Cities in the Late Nineteenth Century." In Ronald Demos Lee et al., eds., *Population Patterns in the Past*, 277–96. New York: Academic, 1977.

Andreeva-Bal'mont, E. A. "Deistvo v Briusovskom pereulke." In Iu. Aleksandrov, V. Enisherlov, and D. Ivanov, eds., *Moskovskii al'bom. Vospominaniia o Moskve i moskvichakh XIX–XX vekov*, 53–91. Moscow: Nashe nasledie, 1997.

Allhouse, Robert H., ed. *Photographs for the Tsar: Pioneering Photography of Sergei Mikhailovich Prokudin-Gorskii Commissioned by Tsar Nicholas II*. New York: Dial Press, 1980.

Antsiferov, Nikolai Pavlovich. *"Nepostizhimyi gorod . . ." Dusha Peterburga. Peterburg Dostoevskogo. Peterburg Pushkina*. St. Petersburg: Lenizdat, 1991.

Anweiler, Oskar. *The Soviets: The Russian Workers, Peasants, and Soldiers Councils, 1905–1912*. Trans. Ruth Hein. New York: Pantheon, 1974.

Armstrong, John A. "Socializing for Modernization in a Multiethnic Elite." In Greg Guroff and F. V. Carstensen, eds., *Entrepreneurship in Imperial Russia and the Soviet Union*, 84–103. Princeton: Princeton University Press, 1983.

Arzumanova, O. I., A. G. Kuznetsova, T. N. Makarova, and V. A. Nevskii. *Muzei-zapovednik 'Abramtsevo'*. Moscow: Izobrazitel'noe Iskusstvo, 1988.

Ascher, Abraham. *The Revolution of 1905*. Vol. 1: *Russia in Disarray*. Vol. 2: *Authority Restored*. Stanford: Stanford University Press, 1988–92.

Ashukin, N. S., ed. *Ushedshaia Moskva. Vospominaniia sovremennikov o Moskve vtoroi poloviny XIX veka*. Moscow: Moskovskii rabochii, 1964.

Astrov, Nicholas J. "The Municipal Government and the All-Russian Union of Towns." In Paul G. Gronsky and Nicholas J. Astrov, eds., *The War and the Russian Government*, 129–321. 1929. Reprint, New York: Howard Fartig, 1973.

Astrov, Nikolai Ivanovich. *Vospominiia*. Paris: YMCA Press, 1941.

Babushkin, Ivan. *Recollections of Ivan Vasilyevich Babushkin (1893–1900)*. Moscow: Foreign Languages, 1957.

Bailes, Kendall E. "Reflections on Russian Professions." In Harley D. Balzer, ed., *Russia's Missing Middle Class: The Professions in Russian History*, 39–54. Armonk, N.Y.: M. E. Sharpe, 1996.

Bakhrushin, V. "Opisanie postroeniia khrama Sv. Vasiliia Ispovednika v Moskve za Rogozhskoi zastavoi v Novoi Derevne." In A. S. Kiselev et al., eds., *Moskovskii arkhiv. Istoriko-kraevedcheskii al'manakh*, 131–53. Moscow: Moskovskoe gorodskoe ob"edinenie arkhivov, 1996.

Baltiskii, G. "Vnieshnii vid' Moskvy srediny XIX vieka." *Moskva v' eia proshlom' i nastoiashchem'* 10: 9–76.

Balzer, Harley D. "Conclusion: The Missing Middle Class." In Harley D. Balzer, ed., *Russia's Missing Middle Class: The Professions in Russian History*, 293–320. Armonk, N.Y.: M. E. Sharpe, 1996.

———. "The Engineering Profession in Tsarist Russia." In Harley D. Balzer, ed., *Russia's Missing Middle Class: The Professions in Russian History*, 55–88. Armonk, N.Y.: M. E. Sharpe, 1996.

Balzer, Harley D., ed. *Russia's Missing Middle Class: The Professions in Russian History*. Armonk, N.Y.: M. E. Sharpe, 1996.

Baranov, Evgenii Zakharovich. *Moskovskie legendy: zapisannye Evgeniem Baranovym*. Comp. Vera Bokova. Moscow: Literatura i politika, 1993.

Baranova, S. "Kirpich staroi Moskvy." In A. S. Kiselev et al., eds., *Moskovskii arkhiv. Istoriko-kraevedcheskii al'manakh*, 59–75. Moscow: Moskovskoe gorodskoe ob"edinenie arkhivov, 1996.

Bater, James H. *St. Petersburg: Industrialization and Change*. Montreal: McGill–Queen's University Press, 1976.

Batiushkov, K. N. "Progulka po Moskve." In Iu. Aleksandrov, V. Enisherlov, and D. Ivanov, eds., *Moskovskii al'bom. Vospominaniia o Moskve i moskvichakh XIX–XX vekov*, 20–28. Moscow: Nashe nasledie, 1997.

Beksler, A. "O vozraste Teremka na Nikol'skoi." In A. S. Kiselev et al., eds., *Moskovskii arkhiv. Istoriko-kraevedcheskii al'manakh*, 490–94. Moscow: Moskovskoe gorodskoe ob"edinenie arkhivov, 1996.

Beliaev, I. "Obozrenie Moskvy. Vneshnii vid stolitsy." In A. S. Kiselev et al., eds., *Moskovskii arkhiv. Istoriko-kraevedcheskii al'manakh*, 405–20. Moscow: Moskovskoe gorodskoe ob"edinenie arkhivov, 1996.

Beliaev, S. G. *Banki i finansy Rossii istoriia. Russko-frantsuzskie bankovskie gruppy v periode ekonomicheskogo pod"ema, 1909–1914gg*. Saint Petersburg: AO "eN-Pi," 1995.

Belinskii, V. G. "Peterburg i Moskva." In V. G. Belinskii and N. A. Nekrasov, eds., *Fiziologiia Peterburga*. With commentary by V. A. Nedzvetskii. Moscow: Sovetskaia Rossiia, 1984, pp. 42–72.

Belinskii, V. G., and N. A. Nekrasov, eds. *Fiziologiia Peterburga*. With commentary by V. A. Nedzvetskii. Moscow: Sovetskaia Rossiia, 1984.

Belitskii, Ia. M. *Zabytaia Moskva.* Moscow: Moskovskii rabochii, 1994.

Belitskii, Ia. M., and G. N. Glezer. *Moskva neznakomaia.* Moscow: Stroiizdat, 1993.

Belousov, I. A. "Ushedshaia Moskva." In N. S. Ashukin, ed., *Ushedshaia Moskva. Vospominaniia sovremennikov o Moskve vtoroi poloviny XIX veka,* 298–369. Moscow: Moskovskii rabochii, 1964.

Belyi, Andrei. "Staryi Arbat." In Iu. Aleksandrov, V. Enisherlov, and D. Ivanov, eds., *Moskovskii al'bom. Vospominaniia o Moskve i moskvichakh XIX–XX vekov,* 171–79. Moscow: Nashe nasledie, 1997.

———. *Na rubezhe dvukh stoletii. Vospominaniia.* 1929. Reprint, Moscow: Khudozhestvennaia literatura, 1989.

———. *Moskva.* Moscow, 1926.

Benjamin, Walter. *Moscow Diary.* Ed. Gary Smith. Trans. Richard Sieburth. Cambridge, Mass.: Harvard University Press, 1986.

Berman, Marshall. *All That Is Solid Melts into Air: The Experience of Modernity.* New York: Simon and Schuster, 1985.

Berton, Kathleen. *Moscow: An Architectural History.* London: I. B. Tauris, 1990.

Besancon, Alain. "La Russie et 'l'esprit du capitalisme.'" *Cahiers du monde russe et sovietique* 8, no. 4 (October–December 1967): 509–27.

Bill, Valentine T. *The Forgotten Class: The Russian Bourgeoisie from the Earliest Beginnings to 1900.* New York: Praeger, 1959.

Bittner, Stephen V. "Green Cities and Orderly Streets." *Journal of Urban History* 25, no. 1 (1998): 22–56.

Black, Cyril E. "Russian and Soviet Entrepreneurship in a Comparative Context." In Greg Guroff and F. V. Carstensen, eds., *Entrepreneurship in Imperial Russia and the Soviet Union,* 3–10. Princeton: Princeton University Press, 1983.

Blackwell, William [L]. "The Russian Entrepreneur in the Tsarist Period: An Overview." In Greg Guroff and F. V. Carstensen, eds., *Entrepreneurship in Imperial Russia and the Soviet Union,* 13–26. Princeton: Princeton University Press, 1983.

———. *The Industrialization of Russia: An Historical Perspective.* New York: Thomas Y. Crowell, 1970.

———. *The Beginnings of Russian Industrialization, 1800–1860.* Princeton: Princeton University Press, 1968.

Boborykin, Petr. *Kitai-gorod.* 1883. Reprint, Moscow: Gosudarstvennoe izdatel'stvo khudozhestvennyi literatury, 1957.

Bocharov, N. "Metallicheskoe usoroch'e dopetrovskoi Moskvy." In A. S. Kiselev et al., eds., *Moskovskii arkhiv. Istoriko-kraevedcheskii al'manakh,* 28–40. Moscow: Moskovskoe gorodskoe ob"edinenie arkhivov, 1996.

Bogolepova, I. N. "Finansovyi kapital v zhelesnodorozhnom stroitel'stve Rossii nakanune pervoi mirovoi voiny." *Voprosy istorii* 1979, no. 9: 52–60.

Bogoslovskii, M. M. "Moskva v 1870–1890-kh godakh." In Iu. Aleksandrov, V. Enisherlov, and D. Ivanov, eds., *Moskovskii al'bom. Vospominaniia o Moskve i moskvichakh XIX–XX vekov*, 92–111. Moscow: Nashe nasledie, 1997.

Bokhanov, A. N. *Krupnaia burzhuaziia Rossii*. Moscow, Nauka, 1992.

Boldina, E. G. "Statisticheskii portret Moskvy na 1910 god." In A. S. Kiselev et al., eds., *Moskovskii arkhiv. Istoriko-kraevedcheskii al'manakh*, 162–82. Moscow: Moskovskoe gorodskoe ob"edinenie arkhivov, 1996.

Bondarenko, I. A. "Predislovie." In N. F. Gulianitskii, ed., *Arkhitekturno-gradostroitel'noe razvitie Moskvy. Arkhitekturnoe nasledstvo 42*, 5–7. Moscow: NIITAG, 1997.

Bonnell, Victoria E. *Roots of Rebellion: Workers' Politics and Organizations in St. Petersburg and Moscow, 1900–1914*. Berkeley: University of California Press, 1983.

———. "Radical Politics and Organized Labor in Pre-revolutionary Moscow, 1905–1914." *Journal of Social History* 12, no. 2 (1979): 282–300.

Borisov, I. "Upakovka-delo ser'eznoe." In A. S. Kiselev et al., eds., *Moskovskii arkhiv. Istoriko-kraevedcheskii al'manakh*, 516–25. Moscow: Moskovskoe gorodskoe ob"edinenie arkhivov, 1996.

Borisova, Elena Andreevna. *Russkaia arkhitektura vtoroi poloviny XIX veka*. Moscow: Nauka, 1989.

———. "Breaking with Classicism: Historicism in Nineteenth-Century Russia." In Catherine Cook and Alexander Kudriavtsev, eds., *Uses of Tradition in Russian and Soviet Architecture*, 17–23. Architectural Design Profile no. 68. London: Academy Group, 1987.

Borisova, Elena Andreevna, and Grigorii Iu. Sternin. *Russkii modern*. Moscow: Galart, 1994.

Botkina, Aleksandra Pavlovna. *Pavel Mikhailovich Tret'iakov v zhizni i iskusstve*. Moscow: Izdatel'stvo Tret'iakovskoi Galerei, 1951.

Bouton, John Bell. *Roundabout to Moscow: An Epicurean Journey*. New York: D. Appleton, 1887.

Bovykin, V[alerii] I[vanovich]. "O vzaimootnosheniiakh rossiiskikh bankov s promyshlennost'iu do serediny 90-x godov XIX v." In S. L. Tikhvinskii, ed., *Sotsial'no-ekonomicheskoe razvitie Rossii. Sbornik statei k 100-letiiu so dnia rozhdeniia Nikolaia Mikhailovicha Druzhinina*, 195–206. Moscow: Nauka, 1986.

———. *Zarozhdenie finansovogo kapitala v Rossii*. Moscow: Izdatel'stvo Moskovskogo universiteta, 1967.

Bovykin, V[alerii] I[vanovich], and Iu. A. Petrov. *Kommercheskie banki Rossiiskoi imperii*. Moscow: Perspektiva, 1994.

Bradley, Joseph C. "Merchant Moscow after Hours: Voluntary Associations and Leisure." In James L. West and Iurii A. Petrov, eds., *Merchant Moscow: Images of Russia's Vanished Bourgeoisie*, 133–43. Princeton: Princeton University Press, 1998.

————. "Russia's Cities of Dreadful Delight." *Journal of Urban History* 24, no. 1 (November 1997): 120–29.

————. *Muzhik and Muscovite: Urbanization in Late Imperial Russia*. Berkeley: University of California Press, 1985.

Briusov, Valerii. *Dnevniki, 1891–1910*. Moscow: Izdanie M. i S. Sabashnikovykh, 1927.

————. *Iz moei zhizni. Moia iunost', Pamiati*. Moscow: Izdanie M. i S. Sabashnikovykh, 1927.

Brooks, Jeffrey. *When Russia Learned to Read: Literacy and Popular Culture, 1861–1917*. Princeton: Princeton University Press, 1985.

————. "The Zemstvo and the Education of the People." In Terence Emmons and Wayne S. Vucinich, eds., *The Zemstvo in Russia: An Experiment in Local Self-Government*, 243–78. Cambridge, U.K.: Cambridge University Press, 1982.

Brower, Daniel R. "The Penny Press and Its Readers." In Stephen P. Frank and Mark D. Steinberg, eds., *Cultures in Flux: Lower-Class Values, Practices, and Resistance in Late Imperial Russia*, 147–67. Princeton: Princeton University Press, 1994.

————. *The Russian City between Tradition and Modernity, 1850–1900*. Berkeley: University of California Press, 1990.

Brown, Julie V. "Professionalization and Radicalization: Russian Psychiatrists Respond to 1905." In Harley D. Balzer, ed., *Russia's Missing Middle Class: The Professions in Russian History*, 143–68. Armonk, N.Y.: M. E. Sharpe, 1996.

Brumfield, William Craft. "Aesthetics and Commerce: The Architecture of Merchant Moscow, 1890–1917." In James L. West and Iurii A. Petrov, eds., *Merchant Moscow: Images of Russia's Vanished Bourgeoisie*, 119–31. Princeton: Princeton University Press, 1998.

————. *The Origins of Modernism in Russian Architecture*. Berkeley: University of California Press, 1991.

————. "Architectural Design in Moscow, 1890–1917: Innovation and Retrospection." In William Craft Brumfield, ed., *Reshaping Russian Architecture: Western Technology, Utopian Dreams*, 43–66. Washington, D.C.: Woodrow Wilson Center Press; Cambridge, U.K.: Cambridge University Press, 1990.

————. "Dai bassifondi all'edifico superiore dei Torgovye Rjady: il *design* delle gallerie commerciali di Mosca." *Ricerche di Storia dell'arte* 39 (1990): 7–16.

————. *Reshaping Russian Architecture: Western Technology, Utopian Dreams*. Cambridge, U.K.: Cambridge University Press, 1990.

————. "Russian Perceptions of American Architecture, 1870–1917." In William Craft Brumfield, ed., *Reshaping Russian Architecture: Western Technology, Utopian Dreams*, 43–66. Washington, D.C.: Woodrow Wilson Center Press; Cambridge, U.K.: Cambridge University Press, 1990.

Brumfield, William Craft, and Blair A. Ruble, eds. *Russian Housing in the Modern Age: Design and Social History*. Washington, D.C.: Woodrow

Wilson Center Press; Cambridge, U.K.: Cambridge University Press, 1993.

Brym, Robert J. *The Jews of Moscow, Kiev and Minsk: Identity, Antisemitism, Emigration.* New York: New York University Press, 1994.

Bul'gakov, Mikhail. *The Master and Margarita.* Trans. Diana Burgin and Katherine O'Connor. New York: Vintage, 1996.

Bunin, Ivan. *The Gentleman from San Francisco and Other Stories.* Trans. David Richards and Sophie Lund. New York: Penguin, 1987.

――――. "Okaiannye dni." In Iu. Aleksandrov, V. Enisherlov, and D. Ivanov, eds., *Moskovskii al'bom. Vospominaniia o Moskve i moskvichakh XIX–XX vekov,* 326–38. Moscow: Nashe nasledie, 1997.

Burds, Jeffrey. *Peasant Dreams and Market Politics: Labor Migration and the Russian Village, 1861–1905.* Pittsburgh: University of Pittsburgh Press, 1998.

Burgov, A. "Staro-Preobrazhenskii dvorets." In A. S. Kiselev et al., eds., *Moskovskii arkhiv. Istoriko-kraevedcheskii al'manakh,* 41–58. Moscow: Moskovskoe gorodskoe ob"edinenie arkhivov, 1996.

Buryshkin, Pavel A. *Moskva kupecheskaia.* 1954. Reprint, Moscow: Sovremennik, 1991.

Buseva-Davydova, I. L., M. V. Nashchokina, and M. I. Astaf'eva-Dlugach. *Moskva. Arkhitekturnyi putevoditel'.* Moscow: Stroiizdat, 1997.

Carstensen, Fred V. "Foreign Participation in Russian Economic Life: Notes on British Enterprise, 1865–1914." In Greg Guroff and F. V. Carstensen, eds., *Entrepreneurship in Imperial Russia and the Soviet Union,* 140–58. Princeton: Princeton University Press, 1983.

Chase, William J. *Workers, Society, and the Soviet State: Labor and Life in Moscow, 1918–1929.* Urbana: University of Illinois Press, 1987.

Chernevich, Elena, and Mikhail Anikst, in collaboration with Nina Baburina. *Grafica Russa, 1880–1917.* Florence: Cantini Editore, 1990.

Chernukha, V. G. "Velikie reformy. Popytka predoleniia krizisa i gosudarstvennykh delakh." In B. V. Anan'ich, R. Sh. Ganelin, and V. M. Paneiakh, eds., *Vlast' i reformy. Ot samoderzhavnoi k sovetskoi Rossii,* 283–367. St. Petersburg: Izdatel'stvo Dmitrii Bulanin, 1996.

Chernyaev, V. Iu. "Rossiiskoe samoderzhavie nakanunye revoliutsii. Vnytripoliticheskii kurs V. K. Pleve." In B. V. Anan'ich, R. Sh. Ganelin, and V. M. Paneiakh, eds., *Vlast' i reformy. Ot samoderzhavnoi k sovetskoi Rossii,* 439–54. St. Petersburg: Izdatel'stvo Dmitrii Bulanin, 1996.

Chetverikov, Sergei I. *Bezvozvratno ushedshaia Rossiia. Neskol'ko stranits iz knigi moei zhizni.* Berlin: Moskva-Logos, 192?.

Chvidkovski [Shvidkovskii], Dmitri. "Le monde du 'Zamoskvoretche' dans la culture de Moscou." In Olda Morel et al., eds., *La maison Igoumnov: Residence de l'ambassadeur de France à Moscou,* 33–41, 140–43. Paris: Les amis de la maison Igoumnov, 1993.

Chvidkovski [Shvidkovskii], Dmitri, and J. M. Perouse de Montclos. *Moscou. Patrimoine architectural.* Paris: Flammarion, 1997.

City of Moscow, Statistical Bureau. *Atlas statistique de la ville de Moscou: Explication des diagrammes et des cartogrammes.* Moscow: Typographie Ferd. Neuburger, 1890.

Clark, Katerina. *Petersburg: Crucible of Cultural Revolution.* Cambridge, Mass.: Harvard University Press, 1995.

Clowes, Edith W. "Merchants on Stage and in Life: Theatricality and Public Consciousness." In James L. West and Iurii A. Petrov, eds., *Merchant Moscow: Images of Russia's Vanished Bourgeoisie,* 147–59. Princeton: Princeton University Press, 1998.

Clowes, Edith W., Samuel D. Kassow, and James L. West, eds. *Between Tsar and People: Educated Society and the Quest for Public Identity in Late Imperial Russia.* Princeton: Princeton University Press, 1991.

Colton, Timothy J. *Moscow: Governing the Socialist Metropolis.* Cambridge, Mass.: Harvard University Press, 1995.

Conroy, Mary Schaeffer. "Introduction." In Mary Schaeffer Conroy, ed., *Emerging Democracy in Late Imperial Russia: Case Studies on Local Self-Government (the Zemstvos), State Duma Elections, the Tsarist Government, and the State Council before and during World War One,* 1–29. Niwot: University of Colorado Press, 1998.

Conroy, Mary Schaeffer, ed. *Emerging Democracy in Late Imperial Russia: Case Studies on Local Self-Government (the Zemstvos), State Duma Elections, the Tsarist Government, and the State Council before and during World War One.* Niwot: University of Colorado Press, 1998.

Cook, Catherine, and Alexander Kudriavtsev, eds. *Uses of Tradition in Russian and Soviet Architecture.* Architectural Design Profile no. 68. London: Academy Group, 1987.

Coopersmith, Jonathan. *The Electrification of Russia, 1880–1926.* Ithaca: Cornell University Press, 1992.

Cracraft, James. *The Petrine Revolution in Russian Architecture.* Chicago: University of Chicago Press, 1988.

———. *The Petrine Revolution in Russian Imagery.* Chicago: University of Chicago Press, 1997.

Darlington, Thomas. *Education in Russia.* Special Reports on Educational Subjects. London: Great Britain Education Board, 1909.

Davies, Norman. *Heart of Europe: A Short History of Poland.* New York: Oxford University Press, 1984.

de Custine, A. Marquis. "Rossiia v 1839 godu." In Iu. Aleksandrov, V. Enisherlov, and D. Ivanov, eds., *Moskovskii al'bom. Vospominaniia o Moskve i moskvichakh XIX–XX vekov,* 29–44. Moscow: Nashe nasledie, 1997.

De Magistris, Alessandro. *Mosca 1900–1950: Nascita di una capitale.* Milan: CLUPguide, 1994.

Diodorov, I. A. "'Na semi kholmakh' kati Golitsynoi." In Iu. Aleksandrov, V. Enisherlov, and D. Ivanov, eds., *Moskovskii al'bom. Vospominaniia o Moskve i moskvichakh XIX–XX vekov*, 539–40. Moscow: Nashe nasledie, 1997.

Dudzhinskaia, E. A. "Stroitel'stvo zheleznykh dorog v Rossii v ekonomicheskoi programme slavianofilov." In S. L. Tikhvinskii, ed., *Sotsial'no-ekonomicheskoe razvitie Rossii. Sbornik statei k 100-letiiu so dnia rozhdeniia Nikolaia Mikhailovicha Druzhinina*, 172–83. Moscow: Nauka, 1986.

Dumas, Alexandre. *Adventures in Czarist Russia*. 1860. Reprint, trans. and ed. A. E. Murch. London: Peter Owen, 1960.

Dzhynkovskii, V. "Navodenie v Moskve v 1908 godu." In A. S. Kiselev et al., eds., *Moskovskii arkhiv. Istoriko-kraevedcheskii al'manakh*, 447–54. Moscow: Moskovskoe gorodskoe ob"edinenie arkhivov, 1996.

Eklof, Ben. "Introduction." In Ben Eklof, John Bushnell, and Larissa Zakharova, eds., *Russia's Great Reforms, 1855–1881*, vii–xvi. Bloomington: Indiana University Press, 1994.

———. *Russian Peasant Schools: Officialdom, Village Culture, and Popular Pedagogy, 1861–1914*. Berkeley: University of California Press, 1986.

Eklof, Ben, John Bushnell, and Larissa Zakharova, eds. *Russia's Great Reforms, 1855–1881*. Bloomington: Indiana University Press, 1994.

Emel'ianova, Irina. "Moskva, potapovskii." In Iu. Aleksandrov, V. Enisherlov, and D. Ivanov, eds., *Moskovskii al'bom. Vospominaniia o Moskve i moskvichakh XIX–XX vekov*, 448–59. Moscow: Nashe nasledie, 1997.

Emmons, Terence, and Wayne S. Vucinich, eds. *The Zemstvo in Russia: An Experiment in Local Self-Government*. Cambridge, U.K.: Cambridge University Press, 1982.

Engel, Barbara Alpern. *Between the Fields and the City: Women, Work, and Family in Russia, 1861–1914*. Cambridge, U.K.: Cambridge University Press, 1994.

———. *Mothers and Daughters: Women of the Intelligentsia in Nineteenth-Century Russia*. Cambridge, U.K.: Cambridge University Press, 1983.

Engel, Barbara [Alpern], and Clifford Rosenthal. *Five Sisters: Women against the Tsar*. New York: Knopf, 1975.

Engelstein, Laura. *Moscow, 1905: Working-Class Organization and Political Conflict*. Stanford: Stanford University Press, 1982.

Engman, Max, "'An Imperial Amsterdam'? The St. Petersburg Age in Northern Europe." In Theo Barker and Anthony Sutcliffe, eds., *Megalopolis: The Giant City in History*, 73–85. London: St. Martin's, 1993.

Fitgerald, Penelope. *The Beginning of Spring*. London: William Collins Sons, 1988.

Flynn, James T. "Tuition and Social Class in the Russian Universities: S. S. Uvarov and 'Reaction' in the Russia of Nicholas I." *Slavic Review* 35, no. 2 (1976): 232–48.

Fond Sorosa. *Gumanitarnaia nauka v Rossii; sorovskie laureaty. Istoriia, arkheologiia, kul'turnaia antropologiia i etnografiia.* Moscow: Fond sorosa, 1996.

Frank, Stephen P., and Mark D. Steinberg, eds. *Cultures in Flux: Lower-Class Values, Practices, and Resistance in Late Imperial Russia.* Princeton: Princeton University Press, 1994.

Freeze, Gregory. "The *Soslovie* (Estate) Paradigm and Russian Social History." *American Historical Review* 91, no. 1 (1986): 11–36.

Frieden, Nancy M[andelker]. "The Politics of Zemstvo Medicine." In Terence Emmons and Wayne S. Vucinich, eds., *The Zemstvo in Russia: An Experiment in Local Self-Government*, 315–42. Cambridge, U.K.: Cambridge University Press, 1982.

———. *Russian Physicians in an Era of Reform and Revolution, 1856–1905.* Princeton: Princeton University Press, 1981.

Frierson, Cathy A. *Peasant Icons: Representations of Rural People in Late 19th Century Russia.* Oxford, U.K.: Oxford University Press, 1993.

Galkina, N. G., and M. N. Grigor'eva. *Perepiska P. M. Tret'iakova i V. V. Stasova.* Moscow: Iskusstvo, 1949.

Garniuk, S., A. Kats, and A. Sonichev. "Kusok kommunizma. Moskovskoe metro glazami sovremennikov." In A. S. Kiselev et al., eds., *Moskovskii arkhiv. Istoriko-kraevedcheskii al'manakh*, 343–61. Moscow: Moskovskoe gorodskoe ob"edinenie arkhivov, 1996.

Gatrell, Peter. "The Meaning of the Great Reforms in Russian Economic History." In Ben Eklof, John Bushnell, and Larissa Zakharova, eds., *Russia's Great Reforms, 1855–1881*, 84–101. Bloomington: Indiana University Press, 1994.

Geilikman, T. B. *Istoriia obshchestvennogo dvizheniia Evreev v Pol'she i Rossii.* Moscow: Gosudarstvennoe izdatel'stvo, 1930.

Geinike, N. A., N. S. Elagin, N. A. Efimova, and I. I. Shitts, eds. *Po Moskvie. Progulki po Moskvie i eia khudozhestvennym" i prosvietitel'nym" uchrezhdeniiam".* Moscow: Izdanie M. i S. Sabashnikovykh", 1917.

Ger'e, V. "O Moskovskoi gorodskoi dume." In A. S. Kiselev et al., eds., *Moskovskii arkhiv. Istoriko-kraevedcheskii al'manakh*, 421–38. Moscow: Moskovskoe gorodskoe ob"edinenie arkhivov, 1996.

Gerschenkron, Alexander. *Europe in the Russian Mirror: Four Lectures in Economic History.* Cambridge, U.K.: Cambridge University Press, 1970.

———. *Economic Backwardness in Historical Perspective: A Book of Essays.* Cambridge, Mass.: Harvard University Press, 1962.

Gessen, Iulii I. *Istoriia evreiskago naroda v Rossii.* St. Petersburg: Tipografiia L. Ia. Ganzburga, 1916.

Giliarovskii, V. A. *Sochineniia v 4 tomakh.* Gen ed. V. M. Lobanov; text prep. and notes E. Kiseleva. Moscow: Biblioteka 'Ogonek,' Izd. 'Pravda,' 1967.

Gindin, I. F. *Gosudarstvennyi bank i ekonomicheskaia politika tsarskogo pravitel'stva, 1861–1892 gody.* Moscow: Gosfinizdat, 1960.

———. *Russkie kommercheskie banki. Iz istorii finansovogo kapitala v Rossii.* Moscow: Gosfinizdat, 1948.

———. *Banki i promyshlennost' v Rossii. K voprosu o finansovom kapitale v Rossii.* Moscow: Promizdat, 1927.

Gleason, Abbott. "The Great Reforms and the Historians since Stalin." In Ben Eklof, John Bushnell, and Larissa Zakharova, eds., *Russia's Great Reforms, 1855–1881*, 1–16. Bloomington: Indiana University Press, 1994.

Gleason, William. "Public Health, Politics, and Cities in Late Imperial Russia." *Journal of Urban History* 16, no. 4 (August 1990): 341–65.

Glickman, Rose L. *Russian Factory Women: Workplace and Society, 1880–1914.* Berkeley: University of California Press, 1984.

Gohstand, Robert. "The Shaping of Moscow by Nineteenth-Century Trade." In Michael F. Hamm, ed., *The City in Russian History*, 160–81. Lexington: University Press of Kentucky, 1976.

Gorin, Nikolai. "Russkoe p'ianstvo kak sotsial'no-kul'turnyi fenomen." *Vlast'* 1998, no. 3: 50–57.

Grigor'ev, Apollon. "Moi literaturnye i nravstvennye skital'chestva." In Iu. Aleksandrov, V. Enisherlov, and D. Ivanov, eds., *Moskovskii al'bom. Vospominaniia o Moskve i moskvichakh XIX–XX vekov*, 45–52. Moscow: Nashe nasledie, 1997.

Grigor'eva, M. N., and A. N. Shchekotova, eds., *Pis'ma I. E. Repina. Perepiska s P. M. Tret'iakovym. 1873–1898* Moscow: Iskusstvo, 1946.

Gronsky, Paul G., and Nicholas J. Astrov, eds. *The War and the Russian Government.* 1929. Reprint, New York: Howard Fartig, 1973.

Grove, Henry M. *Moscow.* London: Adam and Charles Black, 1912.

Gulianitskii, N. F., ed. *Arkhitekturno-gradostroitel'noe razvitie Moskvy. Arkhitekturnoe nasledstvo 42.* Moscow: NIITAG, 1997.

Guroff, Greg, and F. V. Carstensen, eds. *Entrepreneurship in Imperial Russia and the Soviet Union.* Princeton: Princeton University Press, 1983.

Haimson, Leopold. "Russian Workers' Political and Social Identities: The Role of Social Representations in the Interaction between Members of the Labor Movement and the Social Democratic Intelligentsia." In Reginald E. Zelnik, ed., *Workers and Intelligentsia in Late Imperial Russia: Realities, Representations, Reflections*, 145–71. Berkeley: University of California International and Area Studies, 1999.

Halsey, Francis W., ed. *Seeing Europe with Famous Authors*, Vol. 10: *Russia, Scandinavia, and the Southeast.* New York: Funk and Wagnalls, 1914.

Hamm, Michael F. *Kiev: A Portrait, 1800–1917.* Princeton: Princeton University Press, 1993.

———. "The Breakdown of Urban Modernization: A Prelude to the Revolutions of 1917." In Michael F. Hamm, ed., *The City in Russian History*, 182–200. Lexington: University Press of Kentucky, 1976.

Hamm, Michael F., ed. *The City in Russian History.* Lexington: University Press of Kentucky, 1976.

Hanchett, Walter. "Tsarist Statutory Regulation of Municipal Government in the Nineteenth Century." In Michael F. Hamm, ed., *The City in Russian History*, 91–114. Lexington: University Press of Kentucky, 1976.

Hans, Nicholas A. *History of Russian Educational Policy (1701–1917).* New York: Russell and Russell, 1964.

Hausmann, Guido. "Akademische Berufsgruppen in Odessa, 1850–1917." In Charles McClelland, Stephan Merl, and Hannes Siegrist, eds., *Professionen im modernen Osteuropa*, 427–63. Berlin: Duncker and Humblot, 1995.

Henriksson, Anders. *The Tsar's Loyal Germans: The Riga German Community: Social Change and the Nationality Question, 1855–1905.* East European Monographs. New York: Columbia University Press, 1983.

Herlihy, Patricia. *Odessa: A History, 1794–1914.* Cambridge, Mass.: Harvard University Press, 1986.

Hildermeier, Manfred. "The Socialist Revolutionary Party of Russia and Workers, 1900–1914." In Reginald E. Zelnik, ed., *Workers and Intelligentsia in Late Imperial Russia: Realities, Representations, Reflections*, 206–27. Berkeley: University of California International and Area Studies, 1999.

Hoffman, David L. *Peasant Metropolis: Social Identities in Moscow, 1929–1941.* Ithaca: Cornell University Press, 1994.

Holmgren, Beth. *Rewriting Capitalism: Literature and the Market in Late Tsarist Russia and the Kingdom of Poland.* Pittsburgh: University of Pittsburgh Press, 1998.

Hutchinson, John F. "Politics and Medical Professionalization after 1905." In Harley D. Balzer, ed., *Russia's Missing Middle Class: The Professions in Russian History*, 89–116. Armonk, N.Y.: M. E. Sharpe, 1996.

———. "Who Killed Cock Robin? An Inquiry into the Death of Zemstvo Medicine." In Susan Gross Solomon and John F. Hutchinson, eds., *Health and Society in Revolutionary Russia*, 3–26. Bloomington: Indiana University Press, 1990.

Iaroslavskii, G. "Gorodskoe samoupravlenie Moskvy." *Moskva v' eia proshlom' i nastoiashchem'* 12: 17–48.

Ignatiev, Paul N., Dmitry M. Odinetz, and Paul J. Novgorodtsev. *Russian Schools and Universities in the World War.* New Haven: Yale University Press, 1929.

Ikonnikov, A. V. "Moskva XX veka: utopii i real'nost'." In N. F. Gulianitskii, ed., *Arkhitekturno-gradostroitel'noe razvitie Moskvy. Arkhitekturnoe nasledstvo 42*, 201–27. Moscow: NIITAG, 1997.

———. *Tysiacha let Russkoi arkhitektury. Razvitie traditsii.* Moscow: Iskusstvo, 1990.

———. *Arkhitektura Moskvy, XX vek.* Moscow: Moskovskii rabochii, 1984.

Il'in, I. "Grammofony v pivnoi." In A. S. Kiselev et al., eds., *Moskovskii arkhiv. Istoriko-kraevedcheskii al'manakh*, 530. Moscow: Moskovskoe gorodskoe ob"edinenie arkhivov, 1996.

Il'in, M. *Moskva. Pamiatniki arkhitektury XVII–pervoi tretii XIX veka.* Moscow: Iskusstvo, 1975.

———. *Moskva. Pamiatniki arkhitektury XIV–XVII vekov.* Moscow: Iskusstvo, 1973.

Institut etnografii AN S.S.S.R., Leningradskaia chast'. *Malye i dispersnye etnicheskie gruppy v Evropeiskoi chasti SSSR.* Moscow: Moskovskii filial Geogr. Ob-va S.S.S.R., 1985.

Ippo, S. B. *Moskva i London". Istoricheskie, obshchestvennyi i ekonomicheskaia ocherki i issledovaniia.* Moscow: Universitetskaia tipografiia, 1888.

Iukhneva, Natalia Vasil'evna. "Etnicheskii sostav gorodskogo naseleniia Rossii v kontse XIXv." In Fond sorosa, *Gumanitarnaia nauka v Rossii; sorovskie laureaty. Istoriia, arkheologiia, kul'turnaia antropologiia i etnografiia,* 399–408. Moscow: Fond sorosa, 1996.

———. "Etnicheskaia territoriia i nekotorye osobennosti rasseleniia evreev-ashkenazov Rossii v kontse XIX v. (Opyt kartograficheskogo analiza dannykh perepisi 1897 g.)." In Institut etnografii AN S.S.S.R.—Leningradskaia chast', *Malye i dispersnye etnicheskie gruppy v Evropeiskoi chasti SSSR,* 56–70. Moscow: Moskovskii filial Geogr. Ob-va SSSR, 1985.

———. *Etnicheskii sostav i etnosotsial'naia struktura naseleniia Peterburga. Vtoraia polovina XIX–nachalo XX veka. Statisticheskii analiz.* Leningrad: Nauka, 1984.

Ivanov, E. P. "Bukinisty, ili knizhniki." In Iu. Aleksandrov, V. Enisherlov, and D. Ivanov, eds., *Moskovskii al'bom. Vospominaniia o Moskve i moskvichakh XIX–XX vekov,* 248–62. Moscow: Nashe nasledie, 1997.

Ivanov, Iu., and O. Masnitsyna. "Kuntsevskii monastyr'." In A. S. Kiselev et al., eds., *Moskovskii arkhiv. Istoriko-kraevedcheskii al'manakh,* 154–60. Moscow: Moskovskoe gorodskoe ob"edinenie arkhivov, 1996.

Ivanov, N. "Moskovskaia tema olega grosse." In Iu. Aleksandrov, V. Enisherlov, and D. Ivanov, eds., *Moskovskii al'bom. Vospominaniia o Moskve i moskvichakh XIX–XX vekov,* 537–38. Moscow: Nashe nasledie, 1997.

Jahn, Hubertus. "Patriots or Proletarians? Russian Workers and the First World War." In Reginald E. Zelnik, ed., *Workers and Intelligentsia in Late Imperial Russia: Realities, Representations, Reflections,* 330–47. Berkeley: University of California International and Area Studies, 1999.

Joffe, Muriel, and Adele Lindenmeyr. "Daughters, Wives, and Partners: Women of the Moscow Merchant Elite." In James L. West and Iurii A. Petrov, eds., *Merchant Moscow: Images of Russia's Vanished Bourgeoisie,* 95–108. Princeton: Princeton University Press, 1998.

Johnson, Robert E. *Peasant and Proletarian: The Working Class of Moscow in the Late Nineteenth Century.* New Brunswick, N.J.: Rutgers University Press, 1979.

Johnson, William H. E. *Russia's Educational Heritage.* Pittsburgh: Carnegie Press, 1950.

Kaganov, Grigorii. *Sankt-Peterburg: obrazy prostranstva.* Moscow: Indrik, 1995.

Kahan, Arcadius. *Studies and Essays on the Soviet and East European Economies.* 2 vols. Ed. Peter B. Brown. Newtonville, Mass.: Oriental Research Partners, 1992, 1994.

———. *Essays in Jewish Social and Economic History.* Ed. Roger Weiss. Chicago: University of Chicago Press, 1986.

———. *The Plow, the Hammer, and the Knout: An Economic History of Eighteenth-Century Russia.* Chicago: University of Chicago Press, 1985.

———. "Notes on Jewish Entrepreneurship in Tsarist Russia." In Greg Guroff and F. V. Carstensen, eds., *Entrepreneurship in Imperial Russia and the Soviet Union,* 104–24. Princeton: Princeton University Press, 1983.

Kalmykov, Sergei V. "Commercial Education and the Cultural Crisis of the Moscow Merchant Elite." In James L. West and Iurii A. Petrov, eds., *Merchant Moscow: Images of Russia's Vanished Bourgeoisie,* 109–16. Princeton: Princeton University Press, 1998.

Karamzin, N. M. "Zapiska o Moskovskikh dostopamiatnostiakh." In Iu. Aleksandrov, V. Enisherlov, and D. Ivanov, eds., *Moskovskii al'bom. Vospominaniia o Moskve i moskvichakh XIX–XX vekov,* 9–19. Moscow: Nashe nasledie, 1997.

Kareev, N. "O Moskve." In A. S. Kiselev et al., eds., *Moskovskii arkhiv. Istoriko-kraevedcheskii al'manakh,* 403–4. Moscow: Moskovskoe gorodskoe ob"edinenie arkhivov, 1996.

Kassow, Samuel. "Professionalism among University Professors." In Harley D. Balzer, ed., *Russia's Missing Middle Class: The Professions in Russian History,* 197–222. Armonk, N.Y.: M. E. Sharpe, 1996.

Kazanskii, E. I. "Muzyka v' Moskvie." *Moskva v' eia proshlom' i nastoiashchem'* 11: 60–90.

Kean, Beverly Whitney. *French Painters, Russian Collectors: The Merchant Patrons of Modern Art in Pre-Revolutionary Russia.* London: Hodder and Stoughton, 1994.

Kelly, Laurence, comp. *Moscow: A Traveler's Companion.* New York: Atheneum, 1984.

Khan-Magomedov, S. O. "Poiskii putei rekonstruktsii i razvitiia planirovochnoi struktury Moskvy v 1918–1932gg." In N. F. Gulianitskii, ed., *Arkhitekturno-gradostroitel'noe razvitie Moskvy. Arkhitekturnoe nasledstvo 42,* 185–200. Moscow: NIITAG, 1997.

Kharkeevich, Iu. "Gorodskie fonari." In A. S. Kiselev et al., eds., *Moskovskii arkhiv. Istoriko-kraevedcheskii al'manakh,* 510–15. Moscow: Moskovskoe gorodskoe ob"edinenie arkhivov, 1996.

Kharkhordin, Oleg, and Theodore P. Gerber. "Russian Directors' Business Ethic: A Study of Industrial Enterprises in St. Petersburg, 1993." *Europe-Asia Studies* 46, no. 7 (November 1994): 1075–107.

Khokhlova, E. "Zemlia nariadna, dushista i tepla." In Iu. Aleksandrov, V. Enisherlov, and D. Ivanov, eds., *Moskovskii al'bom. Vospominaniia o Moskve i moskvichakh XIX–XX vekov*, 534–36. Moscow: Nashe nasledie, 1997.

Kir'ianov, Iurii I. "The Mentality of the Workers of Russia at the Turn of the Twentieth Century." In Reginald E. Zelnik, ed., *Workers and Intelligentsia in Late Imperial Russia: Realities, Representations, Reflections*, 76–101. Berkeley: University of California International and Area Studies, 1999.

Kirichenko, Evgeniia Ivanovna "Arkhitekturno-gradostroitel'noe razvitie Moskvy v seredine XIX–nachale XXvv." In N. F. Gulianitskii, ed., *Arkhitekturno-gradostroitel'noe razvitie Moskvy. Arkhitekturnoe nasledstvo 42*, 144–84. Moscow: NIITAG, 1997.

———. "Tramvai i gradostroitel'noe razvitie Moskvy." In A. S. Kiselev et al., eds., *Moskovskii arkhiv. Istoriko-kraevedcheskii al'manakh*, 204–17. Moscow: Moskovskoe gorodskoe ob"edinenie arkhivov, 1996.

———. "The Historical Museum: A Moscow Design Competition, 1875–1883." In Catherine Cook and Alexander Kudriavtsev, eds., *Uses of Tradition in Russian and Soviet Architecture*, 24–26. Architectural Design Profile no. 68. London: Academy Group, 1987.

———. *Russkaia arkhitektura 1830–1910-kh godov*. Moscow: Iskusstvo, 1982.

———. *Moskva na rubezhe stoletii*. Moscow: Stroiizdat, 1977.

———. *Moskva. Pamiatniki arkhitektury 1830–1910-kh godov*. Moscow: Iskusstvo, 1975.

Kirillov, Vladimir. *Arkhitektura Russkogo Moderna*. Moscow: Nauka, 1979.

Kiselev, A. "O chem eta kniga." In A. S. Kiselev et al., eds., *Moskovskii arkhiv. Istoriko-kraevedcheskii al'manakh*, 7–10. Moscow: Moskovskoe gorodskoe ob"edinenie arkhivov, 1996.

Kiselev, A. S., et al., eds. *Moskovskii arkhiv. Istoriko-kraevedcheskii al'manakh*. Moscow: Moskovskoe gorodskoe ob"edinenie arkhivov, 1996.

Kizevetter, Aleksandr A. *Na rubezhe dvukh stoletii (Vospominaniia 1881–1914)*. Prague: Orbis, 1929.

———. *Miestnoe samoupravlenie v' Rossii. IX–XIX st. Istoricheskii ocherk'*. Moscow: Izd. Moskovskogo universiteta, 1910.

Kleinbort, L. M. *Istoriia bezrabotnitsy v Rossii, 1857–1919*. Moscow, 1925.

———. *Ocherki rabochei intelligentsii*. Vol. 1: *1905–1916*. Petrograd: Nachatki znanii, 1925.

Klimochkina, I. Ia. *Narodnye universitety v Rossii (1905–1917)*. Moscow: Nauka, 1970.

Kniazev, Evgenii. "Vol'nyi universitet." *Vash Vybor* 1995, no. 1: 34–36.

Kocheshkov, G. N. *Rossiiskie zemlevladel'tsy v 1917*. Iaroslavl': Iargospeduniv, 1994.

Koenker, Diane. *Moscow Workers and the 1917 Revolution*. Princeton: Princeton University Press, 1981.

Konechnyi, A. M., and K. A. Kumpan. "Peterburg v zhizni i trudakh N. P. Antsiferova." In Nikolai Pavlovich Antsiferov, ed., *"Nepostizhimyi gorod . . . Dusha Peterburga. Peterburg Dostoevskogo. Peterburga Pushkina*, 5–23. St. Petersburg: Lenizdat, 1991.

Korelin, A. P. "Sotsial'nyi sostav uchastnikov kreditnoi kooperatsii v Rossii v kontse XIX–nachale XXv." In S. L. Tikhvinskii, ed., *Sotsial'no-ekonomicheskoe razvitie Rossii. Sbornik statei k 100-letiiu so dnia rozhdeniia Nikolaia Mikhailovicha Druzhinina*, 221–34. Moscow: Nauka, 1986.

Korovainikov, V., and N. Egorova. "Podzemnaia Moskva: dve tochki zreniia." In A. S. Kiselev et al., eds., *Moskovskii arkhiv. Istoriko-kraevedcheskii al'-manakh*, 318–34. Moscow: Moskovskoe gorodskoe ob"edinenie arkhivov, 1996.

Korovin, Konstantin. "Moi rasskazy." In Iu. Aleksandrov, V. Enisherlov, and D. Ivanov, eds., *Moskovskii al'bom. Vospominaniia o Moskve i moskvichakh XIX–XX vekov*, 351–60. Moscow: Nashe nasledie, 1997.

Kotkin, Stephen. *Magnetic Mountain: Stalinism as a Civilization*. Berkeley: University of California Press, 1995.

Kozlov, V. "Istoriia i sud'ba Moskovskogo arkhiva." In A. S. Kiselev et al., eds., *Moskovskii arkhiv. Istoriko-kraevedcheskii al'manakh*, 238–49. Moscow: Moskovskoe gorodskoe ob"edinenie arkhivov, 1996.

———. "Pamiatnik Tsariu-Osvoboditeliu v Kremle." In A. S. Kiselev et al., eds., *Moskovskii arkhiv. Istoriko-kraevedcheskii al'manakh*, 218–37. Moscow: Moskovskoe gorodskoe ob"edinenie arkhivov, 1996.

Krasheninnikova, A. R. "Vysshee zhenskoe obrazovanie v' Moskvie," *Moskva v' eia proshlom' i nastoiashchem'* 12: 106–20.

Krasnov, Vasilii. "Khodynka." In Iu. Aleksandrov, V. Enisherlov, and D. Ivanov, eds., *Moskovskii al'bom. Vospominaniia o Moskve i moskvichakh XIX–XX vekov*, 141–69. Moscow: Nashe nasledie, 1997.

Kumanev, V. A. *Revoliutsiia i prosveshchenie mass*. Moscow: Nauka, 1973.

Kupovetskii, M. S. "Evreiskoe naselenie Moskvy (xv–xxvv.)." In E. M. Pospelov et al., eds., *Etnicheskie gruppy v gorodakh Evropeiskoi chasti SSSR (formirovanie, rasselenie, dinamika kul'tury)*, 58–71. Moscow: Moskovskii filial Geograficheskogo obshchestva S.S.S.R., 1987.

Kustova, M. "Aromaty moskovskoi stariny." In A. S. Kiselev et al., eds., *Moskovskii arkhiv. Istoriko-kraevedcheskii al'manakh*, 526–29. Moscow: Moskovskoe gorodskoe ob"edinenie arkhivov, 1996.

Kuznetsov, B. "Poslednii vzlet 'imperskogo' stilia." In A. S. Kiselev et al., eds., *Moskovskii arkhiv. Istoriko-kraevedcheskii al'manakh*, 362–71. Moscow: Moskovskoe gorodskoe ob"edinenie arkhivov, 1996.

Kuzovleva, O. "Upravliat' Moskvoi neprosto." In A. S. Kiselev et al., eds., *Moskovskii arkhiv. Istoriko-kraevedcheskii al'manakh*, 183–202. Moscow: Moskovskoe gorodskoe ob"edinenie arkhivov, 1996.

Latur, Alessandra, with the assistance of Antoniny Manina and Andreia Nekrasov. *Moskva, 1890–1991.* Moscow: Iskusstvo, 1997.

Latysheva, Galina, and Mikhail Rabinovich. *Moskva i Moskovskii krai v proshlom.* Moscow: Moskovskii rabochii, 1973.

Laverychev, V. Ia. "Samoderzhavie i krupnaia burzhuaziia posle 1861 g." In S. L. Tikhvinskii, ed., *Sotsial'no-ekonomicheskoe razvitie Rossii. Sbornik statei k 100-letiiu so dnia rozhdeniia Nikolaia Mikhailovicha Druzhinina,* 183–94. Moscow: Nauka, 1986.

———. *Krupnaia burzhuaziia v poreformennoi Rossii, 1861–1900.* Moscow: Mysl', 1974.

———. "Russkie kapitalisty i periodicheskaia pechat' vtoroi poloviny XIX v." *Istoriia SSSR* 1972, no. 1: 26–47.

———. *Tsarism i rabochii vopros v Rossii, 1861–1917.* Moscow: Mysl', 1972.

———. "Moskovskie fabrikanty i sredneaziatskii khlopok." *Vestnik Moskovskogo Universiteta* 9, no. 1 (January–February 1970): 53–72.

———. "Nekotorye osobennosti razvitiia monopolii v Rossii (1900–1914gg.)." *Istoriia SSSR* 1969, no. 3: 80–97.

———. *Po tu storonu barrikad (iz istorii bor'by Moskovskoi burzhuazii s revoliutsii.* Moscow: Mysl', 1967.

———. "K voprosu ob osobennostiakh eksporta tkanei iz Rossii v kontse XIX–nachale XX veka." *Vestnik Moskovskogo universiteta* 9, no. 6 (1965): 58–69.

———. "Moskovskie promyshlenniki v gody pervoi russkoi revoliutsii." *Vestnik Moskovskogo universiteta* 9, no. 3 (1964): 37–53.

———. *Monopolisticheskii kapital v tekstil'noi promyshlennosti Rossii, 1900–1917.* Moscow: Nauka, 1963.

Lekomtsev, M. "Osobniak na Prechistenke." In A. S. Kiselev et al., eds., *Moskovskii arkhiv. Istoriko-kraevedcheskii al'manakh,* 85–94. Moscow: Moskovskoe gorodskoe ob"edinenie arkhivov, 1996.

Levin', Isaak Il'ich. *Aktsionernye kommercheskie banki v Rossii.* Petrograd: R. Bielopol'skii i Ko., 1917.

Levin-Stankevich, Brian L. "The Transfer of Legal Technology and Culture: Law Professionals in Tsarist Russia." In Harley D. Balzer, ed., *Russia's Missing Middle Class: The Professions in Russian History,* 223–50. Armonk, N.Y.: M. E. Sharpe, 1996.

Lewis, Robert A., and Richard H. Rowland. "Urbanization in Russia and the USSR, 1897–1970." In Michael F. Hamm, ed., *The City in Russian History,* 205–21. Lexington: University Press of Kentucky, 1976.

Lieven, Dominic C. B. *Russia's Rulers under the Old Regime.* New Haven: Yale University Press, 1989.

Lindenmeyr, Adele. *Poverty Is Not a Vice: Charity, Society, and the State in Imperial Russia.* Princeton: Princeton University Press, 1996.

———. "The Rise of Voluntary Associations during the Great Reforms: The Case of Charity." In Ben Eklof, John Bushnell, and Larissa Zakharova, eds., *Russia's Great Reforms, 1855–1881*, 264–79. Bloomington: Indiana University Press, 1994.

Linnichenko, I. "Maniia pereimenovaniia." In A. S. Kiselev et al., eds., *Moskovskii arkhiv. Istoriko-kraevedcheskii al'manakh*, 262–70. Moscow: Moskovskoe gorodskoe ob"edinenie arkhivov, 1996.

Luzhkov, Iurii. *My deti tvoi, Moskva.* Moscow: Vagrius, 1996.

———. "Moskva—stolitsa patriarkhal'naia." *Obshchaia gazeta* 1994, no. 26 (July 1–7).

Magid, A. *The Tretyakov Dynasty.* Moscow: Foreign Languages, 1960.

Makarevich, G. V., et al., eds. *Pamiatniki arkhitektury Moskvy: Zamoskvorech'e.* Moscow: Iskusstvo, 1994.

———. *Pamiatniki arkhitektury Moskvy: Belyi gorod.* Moscow: Iskusstvo, 1989.

———. *Pamiatniki arkhitektury Moskvy: Zemlianoi gorod.* Moscow: Iskusstvo, 1989.

Makarevich, G. V., M. V. Posokhin, et al., eds. *Pamiatniki arkhitektury Moskvy: Kreml', Kitai-gorod, tsentral'nye ploshchadi.* Moscow: Iskusstvo, 1982.

Malafeeva, S. "Poltora veka Petrovskogo parka." In A. S. Kiselev et al., eds., *Moskovskii arkhiv. Istoriko-kraevedcheskii al'manakh*, 107–17. Moscow: Moskovskoe gorodskoe ob"edinenie arkhivov, 1996.

Mamontov, V. S. *Vospominaniia o Russkikh khudozhnikakh.* Moscow: Izdatel'stvo Akademii khudozhestv S.S.S.R., 1950.

Mashkov, I. P. *Putevoditel' po Moskve.* Moscow: Moskovskoe arkhitekturnoe obshchestvo, 1913.

McClelland, James C. *Autocrats and Academics: Education, Culture, and Society in Tsarist Russia.* Chicago: University of Chicago Press, 1979.

McDaniel, Timothy. *The Agony of the Russian Idea.* Princeton: Princeton University Press, 1996.

———. *Autocracy, Modernization, and Revolution in Russia and Iran.* Princeton: Princeton University Press, 1991.

———. *Autocracy, Capitalism, and Revolution in Russia.* Berkeley: University of California Press, 1988.

McKay, John P. *Pioneers for Profit Foreign Entrepreneurship and Russian Industrialization, 1885–1913.* Chicago: University of Chicago Press, 1970.

———. *The News under Russia's Old Regime: The Development of a Mass Circulation Press.* Princeton: Princeton University Press, 1991.

McReynolds, Louise. "Urbanism as a Way of Russian Life." *Journal of Urban History* 20, no. 2 (February 1994): 240–51.

Meehan-Waters, Brenda. *Holy Women of Russia: The Lives of Five Orthodox Women Offer Spiritual Guidance for Today.* San Francisco: Harper, 1993.

Mendeleev, Dmitrii. "Introduction." *The Industries of Russia*, Vols. 1–2:

Manufactures and Trade. Trans. John M. Crawford. Chicago: World Columbian Exposition, 1893.

Menzbir, M. "Moskovskii universitet v noiabre 1917 goda." In A. S. Kiselev et al., eds., *Moskovskii arkhiv. Istoriko-kraevedcheskii al'manakh*, 485–88. Moscow: Moskovskoe gorodskoe ob"edinenie arkhivov, 1996.

Mikhailovskii, A. "Munitsipal'naia Moskva." In N. A. Geinike, N. S. Elagin, N. A. Efimova, and I. I. Shitts, eds., *Po Moskvie. Progulki po Moskvie i eia khudozhestvennym" i prosvietitel'nym" uchrezhdeniiam"*, 121–58. Moscow: Izdanie M. i S. Sabashnikovykh", 1917.

Miliukov, Paul. *Political Memoirs, 1905–1917*. Ed. Arthur P. Mendel; trans. Carl Goldberg. Ann Arbor: University of Michigan Press, 1967.

Mironov, Boris. *Russkii gorod v 1740–1860-e gody: demograficheskoe, sotsial'-noe, i ekonomicheskoe razvitie*. Leningrad: Nauka-Leningradskoe otdelenie, 1990.

Moleva, N. M. *Moskvy ozhivshie predaniia*. Moscow: Pedagogika, 1997.

Molokova, Tat'iana Alekseevna, and Vladimir Pavlovich Frolov. *Istoriia Moskvy v pamiatnikakh kultury k 850-letiiu stolitsy*. Moscow: Moskovskii litsei, 1997.

Monas, Sidney. "Petersburg and Moscow as Cultural Symbols." In Theophanis George Stavrou, ed., *Art and Architecture in Nineteenth-Century Russia*, 26–39. Bloomington: Indiana University Press, 1983.

Morel, Olda, et al. *La maison Igoumnov: Residence de l'ambassadeur de France à Moscou*. Paris: Les amis de la maison Igoumnov, 1993.

Morozov, B. "Nakhodki v arkhivakh moskvichei XVII veka." In A. S. Kiselev et al., eds., *Moskovskii arkhiv. Istoriko-kraevedcheskii al'manakh*, 76–84. Moscow: Moskovskoe gorodskoe ob"edinenie arkhivov, 1996.

Morozova, M. K. "Moi vospominaniia." In Iu. Aleksandrov, V. Enisherlov, and D. Ivanov, eds., *Moskovskii al'bom. Vospominaniia o Moskve i moskvichakh XIX–XX vekov*, 180–213. Moscow: Nashe nasledie, 1997.

Murrell, Kathleen Berton. *Moscow Art Nouveau*. London: Philip Wilson, 1997.

Naidenov', Nikolai A. *Vospominaniia o vidennom, slyshannom i isputannom. 1903–5*. Reprint, Newtonville, Mass.: Oriental Research Partners, 1976.

Nardova, Valeriia A. "Municipal Self-Government after the 1870 Reform." Trans. Lori A. Citti. In Ben Eklof, John Bushnell, and Larissa Zakharova, eds., *Russia's Great Reforms, 1855–1881*, 181–96. Bloomington: Indiana University Press, 1994.

———. *Samoderzhavie i gorodskie dumy v Rossii v kontse XIX–nachale XX veka*. St. Petersburg: Nauka, 1994.

———. *Gorodskoe samoupravlenie v Rossii v 60-kh–nachale 90-kh godov XIX vekov: Pravitel'stvennaia politika*. Leningrad: Nauka Leningradskoe otdelenie, 1984.

Nemirovich-Danchenko, Vasilii I. *Gorodskoi golova: roman'*. St. Petersburg: Izd. P. P. Soikina, 1904.

Nemirovitch-Dantchenko, Vladimir. *My Life in the Russian Theatre*. Trans. John Cournos. Boston: Little, Brown, 1936.

Nenarokomova, I. S. *Pavel Tret'iakov i ego galereia*. Moscow: Galart, 1994.

Neuberger, Joan. "When the Word Was the Deed: Workers vs. Employers before the Justices of the Peace." In Reginald E. Zelnik, ed., *Workers and Intelligentsia in Late Imperial Russia: Realities, Representations, Reflections*, 292–308. Berkeley: University of California International and Area Studies, 1999.

———. *Hooliganism: Crime, Culture, and Power in St. Petersburg, 1900–1914*. Berkeley: University of California Press, 1993.

Neumaier, Diane. "A Note on Photography in Russia." In James L. West and Iurii A. Petrov, eds., *Merchant Moscow: Images of Russia's Vanished Bourgeoisie*, 19–24. Princeton: Princeton University Press, 1998.

Nikfontov, Aleksandr Sergeevich. *Moskva vo vtoroi polovine XIX stoletiia. Stenogramma publichnoi lektsii, prochitannoi 26 marta 1947 goda v lektsionnom zale v Moskve*. Moscow: Izdatel'stvo "Pravda," 1947.

Nikolaeva, T. "Velosipedy na ulitsakh Moskvy." In A. S. Kiselev et al., eds., *Moskovskii arkhiv. Istoriko-kraevedcheskii al'manakh*, 507–9. Moscow: Moskovskoe gorodskoe ob"edinenie arkhivov, 1996.

Nikol'skaia, T. "Moskovskie mostovye." In A. S. Kiselev et al., eds., *Moskovskii arkhiv. Istoriko-kraevedcheskii al'manakh*, 498–502. Moscow: Moskovskoe gorodskoe ob"edinenie arkhivov, 1996.

———. "Samodvizhyshchiesia ekipazhi." In A. S. Kiselev et al., eds., *Moskovskii arkhiv. Istoriko-kraevedcheskii al'manakh*, 503–6. Moscow: Moskovskoe gorodskoe ob"edinenie arkhivov, 1996.

Norman, Geraldine. *The Hermitage: The Biography of a Great Museum*. New York: Fromm International, 1998.

Novikov, Mikhail Mikhailovich. *Ot Moskvy do N'iu-Iorka. Moia zhizn' v nauke i politike*. New York: Chekhov Press, 1952.

Odintsov, Aleksandr, ed. *Moskovskaia gorodskaia duma*. Moscow: Izdanie Aleksandra Odintsova, 1897.

Okynev, N. P. "Dnevnik Moskvicha." In Iu. Aleksandrov, V. Enisherlov, and D. Ivanov, eds., *Moskovskii al'bom. Vospominaniia o Moskve i moskvichakh XIX–XX vekov*, 289–99. Moscow: Nashe nasledie, 1997.

Orlovsky, Daniel T. "Professionalism in the Ministerial Bureaucracy on the Eve of the February Revolution of 1917." In Harley D. Balzer, ed., *Russia's Missing Middle Class: The Professions in Russian History*, 267–92. Armonk, N.Y.: M. E. Sharpe, 1996.

Osinov, Valerii. "Reka-kormilitsa." *Byloe* 1998, no. 2: 8–9.

Osorgin, M. A. "Knizhnaia lavka pisatelei." In Iu. Aleksandrov, V. Enisherlov, and D. Ivanov, eds., *Moskovskii al'bom. Vospominaniia o Moskve i moskvichakh XIX–XX vekov*, 339–50. Moscow: Nashe nasledie, 1997.

Ostroumov, S. S. *Prestupnost' i ee prichiny v dorevoliutsionnoi Rossii*. Moscow: Izdatel'stvo Moskovskogo universiteta, 1980.

Owen, Thomas C. "Doing Business in Merchant Moscow." In James L. West and Iurii A. Petrov, eds., *Merchant Moscow: Images of Russia's Vanished Bourgeoisie*, 29–36. Princeton: Princeton University Press, 1998.

———. *Russian Corporate Capitalism from Peter the Great to Perestroika*. Oxford, U.K.: Oxford University Press, 1995.

———. *The Corporation under Russian Law, 1800–1917: A Study in Tsarist Economic Policy*. Cambridge, U.K.: Cambridge University Press, 1991.

———. "Entrepreneurship and the Structure of Enterprise in Russia, 1800–1880." In Greg Guroff and F. V. Carstensen, eds., *Entrepreneurship in Imperial Russia and the Soviet Union*, 59–83. Princeton: Princeton University Press, 1983.

———. *Capitalism and Politics in Russia: A Social History of the Moscow Merchants, 1855–1905*. Cambridge, U.K.: Cambridge University Press, 1981.

Pasternak, A. L. "Ploshchad' Khrama Khrista spasitelia." In Iu. Aleksandrov, V. Enisherlov, and D. Ivanov, eds., *Moskovskii al'bom. Vospominaniia o Moskve i moskvichakh XIX–XX vekov*, 413–32. Moscow: Nashe nasledie, 1997.

Pearl, Deborah L. "Narodnaia Volia and the Worker." In Reginald E. Zelnik, ed., *Workers and Intelligentsia in Late Imperial Russia: Realities, Representations, Reflections*, 55–75. Berkeley: University of California International and Area Studies, 1999.

Pennar, Karen. "Daily Life among the Morozovs." In James L. West and Iurii A. Petrov, eds., *Merchant Moscow: Images of Russia's Vanished Bourgeoisie*, 73–81. Princeton: Princeton University Press, 1998.

Petrov, Feodor A. "Crowning the Edifice: The Zemstvo, Local Self-Government, and the Constitutional Movement, 1864–1881." Trans. Robin Bisha. In Ben Eklof, John Bushnell, and Larissa Zakharova, eds., *Russia's Great Reforms, 1855–1881*, 197–213. Bloomington: Indiana University Press, 1994.

Petrov, Iurii A. "'Moscow City': Financial Citadel of Merchant Moscow." In James L. West and Iurii A. Petrov, eds., *Merchant Moscow: Images of Russia's Vanished Bourgeoisie*, 45–50. Princeton: Princeton University Press, 1998.

———. *Dinastiia Riabushinskikh*. Moscow: Russkaia kniga, 1997.

———. "Kartel'noe soglashenie rossiiskikh bankov." *Voprosy istorii* 1986, no. 6: 173–77.

Petrov, Iu[rii]. A., and S. V. Kalmykov. *Sberegatel'noe delo v Rossii. Vekhi istorii*. Moscow: K.I.T., 1995.

Pisar'kova, Liubov' Fedorovna. "Gorodskie golovy Moskvy (1863–1917gg.)." *Otechestvennaia istoriia* 1997, no. 2: 3–19.

Polianskii, N. N. "Moskovskii al'bom." In Iu. Aleksandrov, V. Enisherlov, and D. Ivanov, eds., *Moskovskii al'bom. Vospominaniia o Moskve i moskvichakh XIX–XX vekov*, 263–71. Moscow: Nashe nasledie, 1997.

Polunin, Vladimir. *Three Generations: Family Life in Russia, 1845–1902.* Trans. A. F. Birch-Jones. London: Leonard Hill, 1957.

Portal, R. "Industriels moscovites: le secteur cotonnier (1861–1914)." *Cahiers du monde Russe et Sovietique* 4, nos. 1–2 (January–June 1963): 5–46.

Porter, Thomas, and William Gleason. "The Zemstvo and the Transformation of Russian Society." In Mary Schaeffer Conroy, ed., *Emerging Democracy in Late Imperial Russia: Case Studies on Local Self-Government (the Zemstvos), State Duma Elections, the Tsarist Government, and the State Council before and during World War One,* 60–87. Niwot: University of Colorado Press, 1998.

———. "The Democratization of the Zemstvo During the First World War." In Mary Schaeffer Conroy, ed., *Emerging Democracy in Late Imperial Russia: Case Studies on Local Self-Government (the Zemstvos), State Duma Elections, the Tsarist Government, and the State Council before and during World War One,* 228–42. Niwot: University of Colorado Press, 1998.

Pospelov, E. M., et al., eds. *Etnicheskie gruppy v gorodakh Evropeiskoi chasti SSSR (formirovanie, rasselenie, dinamika kul'tury).* Moscow: Moskovskii filial Geograficheskogo obshchestva S.S.S.R., 1987.

Potkina, Irina V. "Moscow's Commercial Mosaic." In James L. West and Iurii A. Petrov, eds., *Merchant Moscow: Images of Russia's Vanished Bourgeoisie,* 37–44. Princeton: Princeton University Press, 1998.

Potolov, Sergei I. "Petersburg Workers and the Intelligentsia on the Eve of the Revolution of 1905–7: The Assembly of Russian Factory and Mill Workers of the City of St. Petersburg." In Reginald E. Zelnik, ed., *Workers and Intelligentsia in Late Imperial Russia: Realities, Representations, Reflections,* 102–15. Berkeley: University of California International and Area Studies, 1999.

Potolov, S[ergei] I., et al., eds. *Rabochie i intelligentsii Rossii v epokhu reform i revoliutsii, 1861–fevral' 1917 g.* St. Peterbsurg: St. Peterburgskii filial Instituta rossiiskoi istorii R.A.N., 1997.

Primachenko, Pavel. "Napoleon knizhnogo delo," *Byloe* 1998, no. 2: 10.

Provorikhina, A. S. "Moskovskoe staroobriadchestvo." *Moskva v' eia proshlom' i nastoiashchem'* 12: 49–75.

Pyliaev, M. I. *Staraia Moskva.* 1891. Reprint, Moscow: Svarog, 1995.

———. *Stari Peterburg. Rasskazy iz byloi zhizni stolitsy.* St. Petersburg: Izdatel'stvo A. S. Suvorina, 1887.

Raeff, Marc. *Political Ideas and Institutions in Imperial Russia.* Boulder: Westview, 1994.

———. *Understanding Imperial Russia: State and Society in the Old Regime.* Trans. Arthur Goldhammer. New York: Columbia University Press, 1984.

———. "The Bureaucratic Phenomena of Imperial Russia, 1700–1905." *American Historical Review* 84, no. 2 (April 1979): 399–411.

Ramer, Samuel C. "Professionalism and Politics: The Russian Feldsher Movement, 1891–1918." In Harley D. Balzer, ed., *Russia's Missing Middle Class: The Professions in Russian History*, 117–42. Armonk, N.Y.: M. E. Sharpe, 1996.

———. "The Zemstvo and Public Health." In Terence Emmons and Wayne S. Vucinich, eds., *The Zemstvo in Russia: An Experiment in Local Self-Government*, 279–314. Cambridge, U.K.: Cambridge University Press, 1982.

Rappoport, A. S. *Home Life in Russia*. New York: Macmillan, 1913.

Rashin, Adol'f Grigor'evich. *Naselenie Rossii za 100 let (1811–1913gg). Statisticheskie ocherki*. Moscow: Gosstatizdat, 1956.

Rawson, Don. *Russian Rightists and the Revolution of 1905*. Cambridge, U.K.: Cambridge University Press, 1995.

Resin, V. "K chitateliu." In A. S. Kiselev et al., eds., *Moskovskii arkhiv. Istoriko-kraevedcheskii al'manakh*, 5–6. Moscow: Moskovskoe gorodskoe ob"edinenie arkhivov, 1996.

Rieber, Alfred J. "Interest-Group Politics in the Era of the Great Reforms." In Ben Eklof, John Bushnell, and Larissa Zakharova, eds., *Russia's Great Reforms, 1855–1881*, 58–83. Bloomington: Indiana University Press, 1994.

———. *Merchants and Entrepreneurs in Imperial Russia*. Chapel Hill: University of North Carolina Press, 1982.

Robbins, Richard G., Jr. "The Limits of Professionalization: Russian Governors at the Beginning of the Twentieth Century." In Harley D. Balzer, ed., *Russia's Missing Middle Class: The Professions in Russian History*, 251–66. Armonk, N.Y.: M. E. Sharpe, 1996.

———. *The Tsar's Viceroys: Russian Provincial Governors in the Last Years of the Empire*. Ithaca: Cornell University Press, 1987.

Robson, Roy R. *Old Believers in Modern Russia*. DeKalb: Northern Illinois University Press, 1995.

Rogatko, Sergei. "Botkiny." *Byloe* 1998, no. 2: 7.

Rogger, Hans. *Jewish Policies and Right-Wing Politics in Imperial Russia*. Berkeley: University of California Press, 1986.

———. *Russia in the Age of Modernisation and Revolution, 1881–1917*. London: Longman, 1983.

Romaniuk, Sergei. *Iz Istorii Moskovskikh pereulkov*. Moscow: Moskovskii rabochii, 1988.

Roosa, Ruth AmEnde. *Russian Industrialists in an Era of Revolution: The Association of Industry and Trade, 1906–1917*. Ed. Thomas C. Owen. Armonk, N.Y.: M. E. Sharpe, 1997.

———. "Russian Industrialists during World War I: The Internationalization of Economics and Politics." In Greg Guroff and F. V. Carstensen, eds., *Entrepreneurship in Imperial Russia and the Soviet Union*, 159–87. Princeton: Princeton University Press, 1983.

Roosevelt, Priscilla R. *Life on the Russian Country Estate: A Social and Cultural History.* New Haven: Yale University Press, 1995.

Rosenberg, William G. "Representing Workers and the Liberal Narrative of Modernity." In Reginald E. Zelnik, ed., *Workers and Intelligentsia in Late Imperial Russia: Realities, Representations, Reflections,* 228–59. Berkeley: University of California International and Area Studies, 1999.

Rossinskaia, E., and Iu. Chichgagova. "Arkhitekturnaia sem'ia Chichagovykh." In A. S. Kiselev et al., eds., *Moskovskii arkhiv. Istoriko-kraevedcheskii al'manakh,* 118–30. Moscow: Moskovskoe gorodskoe ob"edinenie arkhivov, 1996.

Rowland, Richard H. "Urban In-Migration in Late Nineteenth-Century Russia." In Michael F. Hamm, ed., *The City in Russian History,* 115–24. Lexington: University Press of Kentucky, 1976.

Ruane, Christine. "Caftan to Business Suit: The Semiotics of Russian Merchant Dress." In James L. West and Iurii A. Petrov, eds., *Merchant Moscow: Images of Russia's Vanished Bourgeoisie,* 53–60. Princeton: Princeton University Press, 1998.

———. *Gender, Class, and the Professionalization of Russian City Teachers, 1860–1914.* Pittsburgh: University of Pittsburgh Press, 1994.

Ruble, Blair A. *Money Sings: The Politics of Urban Space in Post-Soviet Yaroslavl.* Washington, D.C.: Woodrow Wilson Center Press, 1995; Cambridge, U.K.: Cambridge University Press.

———. *Leningrad: Shaping a Soviet City.* Berkeley: University of California Press, 1990.

Ruckman, Jo Ann. *The Moscow Business Elite: A Social and Cultural Portrait of Two Generations, 1840–1905.* DeKalb: Northern Illinois University Press, 1984.

Russell, John. "The Twilight of the Russian Bourgeoisie." *New York Times,* May 19, 1991: H35-H36.

Ruud, Charles A. *Russian Entrepreneur: Publisher Ivan Sytin of Moscow, 1851–1934.* Montreal: McGill–Queen's University Press, 1990.

Ryndzhinskii, P. G. "K opredeleniiu razmerov agrarnogo perenaseleniia v Rossii na rubezhe XIX–XXv." In S. L. Tikhvinskii, ed., *Sotsial'no-ekonomicheskoe razvitie Rossii. Sbornik statei k 100-letiiu so dnia rozhdeniia Nikolaia Mikhailovicha Druzhinina,* 155–72. Moscow: Nauka, 1986.

Savarenskaia, T. F., et al. *Arkhitekturnye ansambli Moskvy XV–nachala XX vekov. Printsipy khudozhestvennogo edinstva.* Moscow: Stroiizdat, 1997.

Scherrer, Jutta. "The Relationship between the Intelligentsia and Workers: The Case of the Party Schools in Capri and Bologna." In Reginald E. Zelnik, ed., *Workers and Intelligentsia in Late Imperial Russia: Realities, Representations, Reflections,* 172–85. Berkeley: University of California International and Area Studies, 1999.

Schmidt, Albert J. "Westernization as Consumption: Estate Building in the Moscow Region during the Eighteenth Century." *Proceedings of the American Philosophical Society* 139, no. 4 (1995): 380–419.

———. *The Architecture and Planning of Classical Moscow: A Cultural History.* Philadelphia: American Philosophical Society Press, 1989.

Schwarz, Solomon M. *The Jews in the Soviet Union.* Syracuse: Syracuse University Press, 1951.

Semler, Helen Boldyreff. *Discovering Moscow.* New York: St. Martin's, 1989.

Seregny, Scott J. "Professional Activism and Association among Russian Teachers, 1864–1905." In Harley D. Balzer, ed., *Russia's Missing Middle Class: The Professions in Russian History*, 169–96. Armonk, N.Y.: M. E. Sharpe, 1996.

Shakhanov, A. "Kniaz' Iurii Dolgorukii i iubilei 1947 goda." In A. S. Kiselev et al., eds., *Moskovskii arkhiv. Istoriko-kraevedcheskii al'manakh*, 335–42. Moscow: Moskovskoe gorodskoe ob"edinenie arkhivov, 1996.

———. "Arkhitektura Moskvy." *Moskva v' eia proshlom' i nastoiashchem'* 11: 117–25.

Shamurin', Iu.. I. "Khudozhestvennaia zhizn' Moskvy v' XIX vek"." *Moskva v' eia proshlom' i nastoiashchem'* 11: 91–116.

Shastillo, Mikhail K. "Peasant Entrepreneurs and Worker Peasants: Labor Relations in Merchant Moscow." In James L. West and Iurii A. Petrov, eds., *Merchant Moscow: Images of Russia's Vanished Bourgeoisie*, 85–93. Princeton: Princeton University Press, 1998.

Shchepkin', M. P. *Obshchestvennoe khoziaistvo goroda Moskvy v 1863–1887 godakh. Istoriko-statisticheskoe opisanie.* Moscow: Moskovskaia gorodskaia tipografiia, 1890.

Shipov", Dimitrii Nikolaevich. *Vospominaniia i dumy o perezhitom".* Moscow: Pechatnaia S. P. Iakovleva, 1918.

Shmidt, S. O., et al., eds. *Moskva entsiklopediia.* Moscow: Nauchnoe izdatel'stvo 'Bol'shaia Rossiiskaia entsiklopediia,' 1997.

Shokhin, L. "Neskol'ko shtrikhov iz istorii Moskvy v perepiske grada S. D. Sheremeteva." In A. S. Kiselev et al., eds., *Moskovskii arkhiv. Istoriko-kraevedcheskii al'manakh*, 439–40. Moscow: Moskovskoe gorodskoe ob"edinenie arkhivov, 1996.

Shukhova, Elena. "Doma Deshevykh kvartir." *Byloe* 1998, no. 2: 12.

Shul'gin, V. V. "Donskoi monastyr'." In Iu. Aleksandrov, V. Enisherlov, and D. Ivanov, eds., *Moskovskii al'bom. Vospominaniia o Moskve i moskvichakh XIX–XX vekov*, 371–78. Moscow: Nashe nasledie, 1997.

Shvidkovskii, Dmitrii. "Pamiat' Moskvy." In Iu. Aleksandrov, V. Enisherlov, and D. Ivanov, eds., *Moskovskii al'bom. Vospominaniia o Moskve i moskvichakh XIX–XX vekov*, 5–8. Moscow: Nashe nasledie, 1997.

Shvidkovskii, Dmitrii, and Ekaterina Shorban. *Moskovskie osobniaki.* Moscow: Panas-aero, 1997.

Shvidkovskii, Dmitrii. *Also see* Chvidkovski, Dmitrii.

Skorniakova, Natal'ia. *Staraia Moskva. Graviury i litografii xvi–xix vekov iz sobraniia gosudarstvennogo istoricheskogo muzeia.* Moscow: Galart, 1996.

Slutskii, S. "Na ulitsakh Moskvy." In A. S. Kiselev et al., eds., *Moskovskii arkhiv. Istoriko-kraevedcheskii al'manakh,* 441–46. Moscow: Moskovskoe gorodskoe ob"edinenie arkhivov, 1996.

Smeliansky, Anatoly. *Is Comrade Bulgakov Dead? Mikhail Bulgakov at the Moscow Art Theatre.* Trans. Arch Tait. New York: Routledge, 1993.

Smirnov, Dmitrii Nikolaevich. *Nizhegorodskaia starina.* Nizhnii Novgorod: Nizhegorodskaia iarmarka, 1995.

Smith, S. A. "Workers, the Intelligentsia, and Social Democracy in St. Petersburg, 1895–1917." In Reginald E. Zelnik, ed., *Workers and Intelligentsia in Late Imperial Russia: Realities, Representations, Reflections,* 186–205. Berkeley: University of California International and Area Studies, 1999.

Solomon, Susan Gross, and John F. Hutchinson. "Introduction." In Susan Gross Solomon and John F. Hutchinson, eds., *Health and Society in Revolutionary Russia,* ix–xiv. Bloomington: Indiana University Press, 1990.

Solomon, Susan Gross, and John F. Hutchinson, eds. *Health and Society in Revolutionary Russia.* Bloomington: Indiana University Press, 1990.

Stanislavskii[-Alekseev], Konstantin Sergeevich. *My Life in Art.* Moscow: Foreign Languages, 1958.

Starr, S. Frederick. *Decentralization and Self-Government in Russia, 1830–1870.* Princeton: Princeton University Press, 1972.

Stavrou, Theophanis George, ed. *Art and Architecture in Nineteenth-Century Russia.* Bloomington: Indiana University Press, 1983.

Steinberg, Mark D. "The Injured and Insurgent Self: The Moral Imagination of Russia's Lower-Class Writers." In Reginald E. Zelnik, ed., *Workers and Intelligentsia in Late Imperial Russia: Realities, Representations, Reflections,* 309–29. Berkeley: University of California International and Area Studies, 1999.

Steinberg, Mark D., and Stephen P. Frank. "Introduction." In Stephen P. Frank and Mark D. Steinberg, eds., *Cultures in Flux: Lower-Class Values, Practices, and Resistance in Late Imperial Russia,* 1–10. Princeton: Princeton University Press, 1994.

Stenograficheskie otchety o sobraniiakh" Moskovskoi gorodskoi dumy. Moscow: Gorodskaia duma, 1889–1908.

Stites, Richard. *The Women's Liberation Movement in Russia: Feminism, Nihilism, and Bolshevism, 1860–1930.* Princeton: Princeton University Press, 1978.

Strekalov, A. "Ikony na zdanii Verkhnikh torgodykh riadov." In A. S. Kiselev et al., eds., *Moskovskii arkhiv. Istoriko-kraevedcheskii al'manakh,* 495–97. Moscow: Moskovskoe gorodskoe ob"edinenie arkhivov, 1996.

Suny, Ronald Grigor. "Toward a Social History of the October Revolution." *American Historical Review* 88, no. 1 (February 1983): 31–52.

Surh, Gerald D. "The Petersburg Workers' Organization and the Politics of 'Economism,' 1900–1903." In Reginald E. Zelnik, ed., *Workers and Intelligentsia in Late Imperial Russia: Realities, Representations, Reflections*, 116–44. Berkeley: University of California International and Area Studies, 1999.

Swift, E. Anthony. "Workers' Theater and 'Proletarian Culture' in Prerevolutionary Russia, 1905–17." In Reginald E. Zelnik, ed., *Workers and Intelligentsia in Late Imperial Russia: Realities, Representations, Reflections*, 260–91. Berkeley: University of California International and Area Studies, 1999.

Sytin, Petr Vasil'evich. *Istoriia planirovki i zastroiki Moskvy*. Vol 3, *Pozhar Moskvy v 1812 godu i stroitel'stvo goroda v techenie 50 let: 1812–1862*. Moscow: Moskovskii rabochii, 1972.

———. *Iz istorii moskovskikh ulits (ocherki)*. 3d ed. Moscow: Moskovskii rabochii, 1958.

———. *Kommunal'noe khoziaistvo. Blagoustroistvo Moskvy v sravnenii s blagoustroistvom drugikh bol'shikh gorodov*. Moscow: Novaia Moskva, 1926.

Taranov, E. "Gorod kommunizma (idei liderov 50–60-x godov i ikh voploshchenie)." In A. S. Kiselev et al., eds., *Moskovskii arkhiv. Istoriko-kraevedcheskii al'manakh*, 372–90. Moscow: Moskovskoe gorodskoe ob"edinenie arkhivov, 1996.

Taranovski, Theodore, ed. and trans. *Reform in Modern Russian History: Progress or Cycle?* Cambridge, U.K.: Cambridge University Press; Washington, D.C: Woodrow Wilson Center Press, 1995.

Thurston, Robert W. *Liberal City, Conservative State: Moscow and Russia's Urban Crisis, 1906–1914*. Oxford, U.K.: Oxford University Press, 1987.

Tikhomirov, M. "Detskie gody. Moskva i Podmoskov'e." In A. S. Kiselev et al., eds., *Moskovskii arkhiv. Istoriko-kraevedcheskii al'manakh*, 455–84. Moscow: Moskovskoe gorodskoe ob"edinenie arkhivov, 1996.

Tikhvinskii, S. I. ed., *Sotsial'no-ekonomicheskoe razvitie Rossii. Sbornik statei k 100-letiiu so dnia rozhdeniia Nikolaia Mikhailovicha Druzhinina*. Moscow: Nauka, 1986.

Tolstoi, Ivan Ivanovich. *Dnevnik, 1906–1916*. St. Petersburg: Fond regional'nogo razvitiia Sankt-Peterburga/Evropeiskii dom/Evropeiskii universitet v Sankt-Peterburge, 1997.

Tolstoy, Leo. *Anna Karenina*. 1877. Reprint, trans. Louise and Aylmer Maude, Oxford, U.K.: Oxford University Press, 1980.

Tomskii, N. V. *Obraz tvoi, Moskva*. Moscow: Moskovskii rabochii, 1982.

Topchiian, Ia. A., et al., eds. *Atlas: Pamiatniki arkhitektury Moskvy*. Moscow: Federal'naia sluzhba geodezii i kartografii Rossii, 1996.

Troyat, Henri. *Daily Life in Russia under the Last Tsar.* Trans. Malcolm Barnes. Stanford: Stanford University Press, 1979.

Trubetskaia, E. V. "Palaty na prechistenke." In Iu. Aleksandrov, V. Enisherlov, and D. Ivanov, eds., *Moskovskii al'bom. Vospominaniia o Moskve i moskvichakh XIX–XX vekov*, 460–82. Moscow: Nashe nasledie, 1997.

Tsvetaeva, Marina. "Dom u starogo pimena." In Iu. Aleksandrov, V. Enisherlov, and D. Ivanov, eds., *Moskovskii al'bom. Vospominaniia o Moskve i moskvichakh XIX–XX vekov*, 379–412. Moscow: Nashe nasledie, 1997.

Ulianova, Galina. *Blagotvoritel'nost' Moskovskikh predprinimatelei 1860–1914 gg. Moscow:* Izdatel'stvo ob"edineniia "Moskoarkhiv," 1999.

———. "Old Believers and New Entrepreneurs: Religious Belief and Ritual in Merchant Moscow." In James L. West and Iurii A. Petrov, eds., *Merchant Moscow: Images of Russia's Vanished Bourgeoisie*, 61–71. Princeton: Princeton University Press, 1998.

———. "Pages of History: Private Donations in the Municipal Funding of Moscow Charity Institutions at the Beginning of the Twentieth Century." *World Learning Forum: NGO Law in Brief* 1 (Winter 1995): 9–10.

Urusova, S. S. "Gody voiny." In Iu. Aleksandrov, V. Enisherlov, and D. Ivanov, eds., *Moskovskii al'bom. Vospominaniia o Moskve i moskvichakh XIX–XX vekov*, 433–47. Moscow: Nashe nasledie, 1997.

Valkenier, Elizabeth Kridl. "Book Review: *Merchant Moscow: Images of Russia's Vanished Bourgeoisie*, edited by James L. West and Iurii A. Petrov." *Harriman Review* 10, no. 4 (August 1998): 38–40.

Varentsov, N. A. "Khludovy." In Iu. Aleksandrov, V. Enisherlov, and D. Ivanov, eds., *Moskovskii al'bom. Vospominaniia o Moskve i moskvichakh XIX–XX vekov*, 112–40. Moscow: Nashe nasledie, 1997.

Vashchilo, N., I. Rabotkevich, and S. Slepukhina. "Ploshchad' prosveshcheniia." In A. S. Kiselev et al., eds., *Moskovskii arkhiv. Istoriko-kraevedcheskii al'manakh*, 250–61. Moscow: Moskovskoe gorodskoe ob"edinenie arkhivov, 1996.

Vasil'chikov, I. S. "To, chto mne vospomnilos'." In Iu. Aleksandrov, V. Enisherlov, and D. Ivanov, eds., *Moskovskii al'bom. Vospominaniia o Moskve i moskvichakh XIX–XX vekov*, 314–25. Moscow: Nashe nasledie, 1997.

Vasil'chikova, L. I. "Mimoletnoe." In Iu. Aleksandrov, V. Enisherlov, and D. Ivanov, eds., *Moskovskii al'bom. Vospominaniia o Moskve i moskvichakh XIX–XX vekov*, 301–13. Moscow: Nashe nasledie, 1997.

Vasilich', G. "Ulitsy i liudi sovremennoi Moskvy." *Moskva v' eia proshlom' i nastoiashchem'* 12: 3–16.

———. "Moskva, 1850–1910g." *Moskva v' eia proshlom' i nastoiashchem'* 11: 2–38.

Vendina, Ol'ga, ed. "Moskau: Eine Stadt verandert ihr Gesicht." *Berichte des Bundesinstituts fur ostwissenschaftliche und internationale Studien* 43 (1994).

Vertinskii, Aleksandr. "Ia artist." In Iu. Aleksandrov, V. Enisherlov, and D. Ivanov, eds., *Moskovskii al'bom. Vospominaniia o Moskve i moskvichakh XIX–XX vekov*, 272–88. Moscow: Nashe nasledie, 1997.

Vinogradov, N. "Stolitsa v 1918 godu. Iz dnevnikov. Publikatsiia V. Tentiukova." In A. S. Kiselev et al., eds., *Moskovskii arkhiv. Istoriko-kraevedcheskii al'manakh*, 272–317. Moscow: Moskovskoe gorodskoe ob"edinenie arkhivov, 1996.

Vodarsky, Ia. E. "The Impact of Moscow on the Development of Russia." In Theo Barker and Anthony Sutcliffe, eds. *Megalopolis: The Giant City in History*, 86–95. London: St. Martin's, 1993.

Voldina, E. "Narodnye proetky pamiatnika grafu L. N. Tolstomu." In A. S. Kiselev et al., eds., *Moskovskii arkhiv. Istoriko-kraevedcheskii al'manakh*, 530–37. Moscow: Moskovskoe gorodskoe ob"edinenie arkhivov, 1996.

Volkov, Solomon. *St. Petersburg: A Cultural History*. Trans. Antonina W. Bouis. New York: Free Press, 1995.

von Laue, Theodore H. *Why Lenin? Why Stalin? A Reappraisal of the Russian Revolution, 1900–1930*. Philadelphia: J. B. Lippincott, 1964.

———. *Sergei Witte and the Industrialization of Russia*. New York: Columbia University Press, 1963.

Vydro, M. Ia. *Naselenie Moskvy (po materialam perepisei naseleniia, 1871–1970gg.)* Moscow: Statistika, 1976.

Walicki, Andrzej. *The Slavophile Controversy: History of a Conservative Utopia in Nineteenth-Century Russian Thought*. Trans. Hilda Andrews-Ruiecka. Oxford, U.K.: Oxford University Press, 1975.

Wallace, D. Mackenzie. *Russia*. London: Cassell Petter and Galpin, 1877.

West, James L. "The Fate of Merchant Moscow." In James L. West and Iurii A. Petrov, eds., *Merchant Moscow: Images of Russia's Vanished Bourgeoisie*, 173–78. Princeton: Princeton University Press, 1998.

———. "Merchant Moscow in Historical Context." In James L. West and Iurii A. Petrov, eds., *Merchant Moscow: Images of Russia's Vanished Bourgeoisie*, 3–12. Princeton: Princeton University Press, 1998.

———. "A Note on Old Belief." In James L. West and Iurii A. Petrov, eds., *Merchant Moscow: Images of Russia's Vanished Bourgeoisie*, 13–18. Princeton: Princeton University Press, 1998.

———. "Visions of Russia's Entrepreneurial Future: Pavel Riabushinsky's Utopian Capitalism." In James L. West and Iurii A. Petrov, eds., *Merchant Moscow: Images of Russia's Vanished Bourgeoisie*, 161–70. Princeton: Princeton University Press, 1998.

———. "The Riabushinsky Circle: *Burzhuaziia* and *Obshchestvennost'* in Late Imperial Russia." In Edith W. Clowes, Samuel D. Kassow, and James L. West, eds., *Between Tsar and People: Educated Society and the Quest for Public Identity in Late Imperial Russia*, 41–56. Princeton: Princeton University Press, 1991.

West, James L., and Iurii A. Petrov, eds. *Merchant Moscow: Images of Russia's Vanished Bourgeoisie.* Princeton: Princeton University Press, 1998.

Wieczynski, Joseph L., ed. *The Modern Encyclopedia of Russian and Soviet History.* 61 vols. Gulf Breeze, Fla.: Academic International, 1976–97.

Williams, Robert C. *The Other Bolsheviks: Lenin and His Critics, 1904–1914.* Bloomington: Indiana University Press, 1986.

Wirtschafter, Elise Kimerling. *Social Identity in Imperial Russia.* DeKalb: Northern Illinois University Press, 1997.

Wolff, David. *To the Harbin Station: The Liberal Alternative in Russian Manchuria, 1898–1914.* Stanford: Stanford University Press, 1999.

Wortman, Richard S. *Scenarios of Power. Myth and Ceremony in Russian Monarchy.* Vol.1, *From Peter the Great to the Death of Nicholas I.* Princeton: Princeton University Press, 1995.

———. "Moscow and Petersburg: The Problem of Political Center in Tsarist Russia, 1881–1914." In Sean Wilentz, ed., *Rites of Power: Symbolism, Ritual, and Politics since the Middle Ages,* 244–74. Philadelphia: University of Pennsylvania Press, 1985.

Zabielin, I[van]. "Vospominaniia o zhizni." In A. S. Kiselev et al., eds., *Moskovskii arkhiv. Istoriko-kraevedcheskii al'manakh,* 392–402. Moscow: Moskovskoe gorodskoe ob"edinenie arkhivov, 1996.

———. *Istoriia goroda Moskvy.* Moscow: I. N. Kushnerev", 1905.

Zaitsev, Boris. "Ulitsa sv. Nikolaia." In Iu. Aleksandrov, V. Enisherlov, and D. Ivanov, eds., *Moskovskii al'bom. Vospominaniia o Moskve i moskvichakh XIXBXX vekov,* 361–70. Moscow: Nashe nasledie, 1997.

Zakharova, Larissa. "Autocracy and the Reforms of 1861–1874 in Russia: Choosing Paths of Development." Trans. Daniel Field. In Ben Eklof, John Bushnell, and Larissa Zakharova, eds., *Russia's Great Reforms, 1855–1881,* 19–39. Bloomington: Indiana University Press, 1994.

Zaklinskii, P. A., V. S. Zaporozets, R. A. Liubimtsev, and I. P. Maksimenko. *Moskva na rubezhe XIX–XX vekov. Pochtovaia otkrytka.* Moscow: Muzei istorii goroda Moskvy, 1997.

Zamiatin, A. N., and D. N. Zamiatin. *Khrestomatiia po geografii Rossii: Obraz strany: Russkie stolitsy. Moskva i Peterburg.* Moscow: MIROS, 1993.

Zamiatin, Evgenii. *A Soviet Heretic: Essays by Yevgeny Zamyatin.* Ed. and trans. Mirra Ginsburg. Evanston: Northwestern University Press, 1992.

Zelnik, Reginald E. "Workers and Intelligentsia in the 1870s: The Politics of Sociability." In Reginald E. Zelnik, ed., *Workers and Intelligentsia in Late Imperial Russia: Realities, Representations, Reflections,* 16–54. Berkeley: University of California International and Area Studies, 1999.

Zelnik, Reginald E., ed. *Workers and Intelligentsia in Late Imperial Russia: Realities, Representations, Reflections.* Berkeley: University of California International and Area Studies, 1999.

Zhamurina, Z. I. "Moskovskie teatry v' XIX viekie." *Moskva v' eia proshlom' i nastoiashchem'* 11: 29–59.

Zheludkov, D., and O. Trubnikova. "Dereviannoe chudo v Kolomenskom." In A. S. Kiselev et al., eds., *Moskovskii arkhiv. Istoriko-kraevedcheskii al'manakh*, 12–27. Moscow: Moskovskoe gorodskoe ob"edinenie arkhivov, 1996.

Ziloti, V. P. *V dome Tret'iakova*. New York: Chekhov Press, 1954.

Dissertations

Balzer, Harley David. "Educating Engineers: Economic Politics and Technical Training in Tsarist Russia." Ph.D. diss., University of Pennsylvania, 1980.

Beliajeff, Anthony Serge. "The Rise of the Old Orthodox Merchants of Moscow, 1771–1894." Ph.D. diss., Syracuse University, 1975.

Bronson, Susan. "Enlightening the Urban Poor: Adult Education in Late Imperial Russia, 1859–1914." Ph.D. diss., University of Michigan. 1995.

Brooks, Jeffrey Peter. "Liberalism, Literature, and the Idea of Culture: Russia, 1905–1914." Ph.D. diss., Stanford University, 1972.

Cohen, Aaron Joseph. "Making Modern Art National: Mass Mobilization, Public Culture, and Art in Russia during the First World War." Ph.D. diss., Johns Hopkins University, 1998.

Gately, Michael Owen. "The Development of the Russian Cotton Textile Industry in the Pre-Revolutionary Years, 1861–1913." Ph.D. diss., University of Kansas, 1968.

Grover, Stuart Ralph. "Savva Mamontov and the Mamontov Circle, 1870–1905: Art Patronage and the Rise of Nationalism in Russian Art." Ph.D. diss., University of Wisconsin, Madison, 1971.

Hanchett, Walter S. "Moscow in the Late Nineteenth Century: A Study in Municipal Self-Government." Ph.D. diss., University of Chicago. 1964.

Roosa, Ruth AmEnde. "The Association of Industry and Trade, 1906–1914: An Examination of the Economic Views of Organized Industrialists in Prerevolutionary Russia." Ph.D. diss., Columbia University, 1967.

Slusser, Robert Melville. "The Moscow Soviet of Workers' Deputies of 1905: Origins, Structures, and Policies." Ph.D. diss., Columbia University, 1963.

Thurston, Robert William. "Urban Problems and Local Government in Late Imperial Russia: Moscow, 1906–1914." Ph.D. diss., University of Michigan, 1980.

Ulianova, Galina Nikolaevna. "Blagotvoritel'nost' Moskovskikh predprinimatelei, 1860-e–1914g." Dissertatsiia na soiskanie uchenoi stepeni kandidata istoricheskikh nauk, Rossiiskaia Akademiia Nauk, 1995.

West, James Lawrence. "The Moscow Progressists: Russian Industrialists in Liberal Politics, 1905–1914." Ph.D. diss., Princeton University, 1974.

OSAKA AND JAPANESE CITIES

Newspapers

Japan Weekly Chronicle (Kobe)

Books and Articles

Akita, George. *Foundations of Constitutional Government in Modern Japan, 1868–1900.* Cambridge, Mass.: Harvard University Press, 1967.

Akizuki, Kengo. "Institutionalizing the Local System: The Ministry of Home Affairs and Intergovernmental Relations in Japan." In Hyung-ki Kim, Michio Muramatsu, T. J. Pempel, and Kozo Yamamura, eds., *The Japanese Civil Service and Economic Development*, 337–66. Oxford, U.K.: Clarendon, 1995.

Alletzhauser, Al. *The House of Nomura: The Inside Story of the World's Most Powerful Company.* London: Bloomsbury, 1990.

Allinson, Gary. *Japanese Urbanism: Industry and Politics in Kariya, 1872–1972.* Berkeley: University of California Press, 1975.

Altman, Albert. "The Press." In Marius Jansen and Gilbert Rozman, eds., *Japan in Transition: From Tokugawa to Meiji*, 231–47. Princeton: Princeton University Press, 1986.

Aqua, Ronald. "Mayoral Leadership in Japan: What's in a Sewer Pipe?" In Terry Edward MacDougall, ed., *Political Leadership in Contemporary Japan*, 115–26. Ann Arbor: Center for Japanese Studies, University of Michigan, 1982.

Austin, Gareth, and Kaoru Sugihara. "Local Suppliers of Credit in the Third World, 1750–1960: Introduction." In Gareth Austin and Kaoru Sugihara, eds., *Local Suppliers of Credit in the Third World, 1750–1960*, 1–25. New York: St. Martin's, 1993.

Austin, Gareth, and Kaoru Sugihara, eds. *Local Suppliers of Credit in the Third World, 1750–1960.* New York: St. Martin's, 1993.

Baxter, James C. *The Meiji Unification through the Lens of Ishikawa Prefecture.* Cambridge, Mass.: Harvard University Press, 1994.

Beard, Charles A. *The Administration and Politics of Tokyo: A Survey and Opinions.* New York: Macmillan, 1923.

Bernstein, Gail Lee. *Japanese Marxist: A Portrait of Kawakami Hajime, 1879–1946.* Cambridge, Mass.: Harvard University Press, 1976.

Bernstein, Gail Lee, ed. *Recreating Japanese Women, 1600–1945.* Berkeley: University of California Press, 1991.

Bestor, Theodore C. *Neighborhood Tokyo.* Stanford: Stanford University Press, 1989.

Bognar, Botond. *The Japan Guide.* New York: Princeton Architectural Press, 1995.

Bolitho, Harold. "Sumo and Popular Culture: The Tokugawa Period." In Gavan McCormack and Yoshio Sugimoto, eds., *The Japanese Trajectory: Modernization and Beyond*, 17–32. Cambridge, U.K.: Cambridge University Press, 1988.

Bowen, Roger W. *Rebellion and Democracy in Meiji Japan: A Study of Commoners in the Popular Rights Movement.* Berkeley: University of California Press, 1980.

Chambliss, William Jones. *Chiaraijima Village: Land Tenure, Taxation, and Local Trade, 1818–1884.* Tucson: University of Arizona Press, 1965.

Chubachi, Masayoshi, and Koji Taira. "Poverty in Modern Japan: Perceptions and Realities." In Hugh Patrick, ed., with the assistance of Larry Meissner, *Japanese Industrialization and Its Social Consequences*, 391–437. Berkeley: University of California Press, 1976.

The City of Osaka: Its Government and Administration. Osaka: Osaka Shiyakusho (municipal office), 1953.

Colcutt, Martin. "Buddhism: The Threat of Eradication." In Marius Jansen and Gilbert Rozman, eds., *Japan in Transition: From Tokugawa to Meiji*, 143–67. Princeton: Princeton University Press, 1986.

Cole, Robert E., and Ken'ichi Tominaga. "Japan's Changing Occupational Structure and Its Significance." In Hugh Patrick, ed., with the assistance of Larry Meissner, *Japanese Industrialization and Its Social Consequences*, 53–95. Berkeley: University of California Press, 1976.

Cost of Living among Laborers in Osaka. Osaka: Municipal Bureau of Labor Research, 1921.

Craig, Albert M. "The Central Government." In Marius Jansen and Gilbert Rozman, eds., *Japan in Transition: From Tokugawa to Meiji*, 36–67. Princeton: Princeton University Press, 1986.

Craig, Albert [M.], ed. *Japan: A Comparative View.* Princeton: Princeton University Press, 1979.

Crawcour, E. Sydney. "The Tokugawa Heritage." In William W. Lockwood, ed., *The State and Economic Enterprise in Japan: Essays in the Political Economy of Growth*, 17–44. Princeton: Princeton University Press, 1965.

Davis, Sandra T. W. *Intellectual Change and Political Development in Early Modern Japan: Ono Azusa, a Case Study.* Rutherford, N.J.: Fairleigh Dickinson University Press, 1980.

De Vos, George, Lizabeth Hauswald, and Orin Borders. "Cultural Differences in Family Socialization: A Psychocultural Comparison of Chinese and Japanese." In Albert Craig, ed., *Japan: A Comparative View*, 214–74. Princeton: Princeton University Press, 1979.

De Vos, George, and Hiroshi Wagatsuma, eds. *Japan's Invisible Race: Caste in Culture and Personality.* Berkeley: University of California Press, 1966.

Doi, Takeo. "Uchimura Kanzo: Japanese Christianity in Comparative Perspective." In Albert Craig, ed., *Japan: A Comparative View*, 182–213. Princeton: Princeton University Press, 1979.

Dore, R. P. "Industrial Relations in Japan and Elsewhere." In Albert Craig, ed., *Japan: A Comparative View*, 324–70. Princeton: Princeton University Press, 1979.

———. "The Modernizer as a Special Case: Japanese Factory Legislation, 1882–1911." *Comparative Studies in Society and History* 11, no. 4 (October 1969): 433–50.

Duus, Peter. *Party Rivalry and Political Change in Taisho Japan.* Cambridge, Mass.: Harvard University Press, 1968.

Finn, Dallas. *Meiji Revisited: The Sites of Victorian Japan.* New York: Weatherhill, 1995.

Fogel, Joshua A. *Politics and Sinology: The Case of Naito Konan (1866–1934).* Cambridge, Mass.: Harvard University Press, 1984.

Fraser, Andrew. "The House of Peers (1890–1905): Structure, Groups, and Role." In Andrew Fraser, R. H. P. Mason, and Philip Mitchell, *Japan's Early Parliaments, 1890–1905: Structure, Issues, and Trends*, 8–36. London: Routledge, 1995.

———. "Land Tax Increase: The Debates of December 1898." In Andrew Fraser, R. H. P. Mason, and Philip Mitchell. *Japan's Early Parliaments, 1890–1905: Structure, Issues, and Trends*, 37–66. London: Routledge, 1995.

———. "Local Administration: The Example of Awa-Tokushima." In Marius B. Jansen and Gilbert Rozman, eds., *Japan in Transition: From Tokugawa to Meiji*, 111–31. Princeton: Princeton University Press, 1986.

Fraser, Andrew, R. H. P. Mason, and Philip Mitchell, *Japan's Early Parliaments, 1890–1905: Structure, Issues, and Trends.* London: Routledge, 1995.

Fruin, W. Mark. *Kikkoman: Company, Clan, and Community.* Cambridge, Mass.: Harvard University Press, 1983.

Gleason, Alan H. "Economic Growth and Consumption in Japan." In William W. Lockwood, ed., *The State and Economic Enterprise in Japan: Essays in the Political Economy of Growth*, 391–444. Princeton: Princeton University Press, 1965.

Gordon, Andrew. *The Evolution of Labor Relations in Japan: Heavy Industry, 1853–1955.* Cambridge, Mass.: Harvard University Press, 1985.

Great Osaka: A Glimpse of the Industrial City. Osaka: Osaka Shiyakusho (municipal office), 1925.

A Guide to Osaka. Osaka: Osaka Hotel Company, 1913.

Hanes, Jeffrey E. "From Megalopolis to Megaroporisu." *Journal of Urban History* 19, no. 2 (February 1993): 56–94.

Hanley, Susan B. "The Material Culture: Stability in Transition." In Marius Jansen and Gilbert Rozman, eds., *Japan in Transition: From Tokugawa to Meiji*, 447–69. Princeton: Princeton University Press, 1986.

Hastings, Sally Ann. *Neighborhood and Nation in Tokyo, 1905–1937.* Pittsburgh: University of Pittsburgh Press, 1995.

Hauser, William B. "Osaka Castle and Tokugawa Authority in Western Japan." In Jeffrey P. Mass and William B. Hauser, eds., *The Bakufu in Japanese History*, 153–72. Stanford: Stanford University Press, 1985.

———. "Osaka: A Commercial City in Tokugawa Japan." *Urbanism Past and Present* 5 (Winter 1977–78): 23–36.

———. *Economic Institutional Change in Tokugawa Japan: Osaka and the Kinai Cotton Trade.* Cambridge, U.K.: Cambridge University Press, 1974.

Havens, Thomas R. H. *Farm and Nation in Modern Japan: Agrarian Nationalism, 1870–1940.* Princeton: Princeton University Press, 1974.

Hayami, Akira. "Population Changes." In Marius Jansen and Gilbert Rozman, eds., *Japan in Transition: From Tokugawa to Meiji*, 280–317. Princeton: Princeton University Press, 1986.

Hazama, Hiroshi. "Historical Changes in the Life Style of Industrial Workers." In Hugh Patrick, ed., with the assistance of Larry Meissner, *Japanese Industrialization and Its Social Consequences*, 21–51. Berkeley: University of California Press, 1976.

Hirschmeier, Johannes. "Shibusawa Eiichi: Industrial Pioneer." In William W. Lockwood, ed., *The State and Economic Enterprise in Japan: Essays in the Political Economy of Growth*, 209–47. Princeton: Princeton University Press, 1965.

———. *The Origins of Entrepreneurship in Meiji Japan.* Cambridge, Mass.: Harvard University Press, 1964.

Horie, Yasuzo. "Modern Entrepreneurship in Meiji Japan." In William W. Lockwood, ed., *The State and Economic Enterprise in Japan: Essays in the Political Economy of Growth*, 183–208. Princeton: Princeton University Press, 1965.

Hotta, Akio. "Shushi jijo to Shichosa no Kensetu." In Shinshu Osakashishi Hensei Iinkai, *Shinshu Osakashishi* 6, chp. 1, sec. 1, sub. 3: 19–33. Osaka: Osaka City Government, 1994.

Howell, David L. *Capitalism from Within: Economy, Society, and the State in a Japanese Fishery.* Berkeley: University of California Press, 1995.

Ichihara, M. *The Official Guide-Book to Kyoto and the Allied Prefecture.* Kyoto: Meishinsha, 1895.

Ike, Nobutaka. *The Beginnings of Political Democracy in Japan.* Baltimore: Johns Hopkins University Press, 1950.

Inoue, Hiroshi. "*Rakugo, Manzai* and *Kigeki*: The Arts of Laughter." *Japan Foundation Newsletter* 23, no. 4 (January 1996): 1–4, 15.

Jansen, Marius B. "The Ruling Class." In Marius Jansen and Gilbert Rozman, eds., *Japan in Transition: From Tokugawa to Meiji*, 68–90. Princeton: Princeton University Press, 1986.

———. "On Foreign Borrowing." In Albert Craig, ed., *Japan: A Comparative View*, 18–48. Princeton: Princeton University Press, 1979.

Jansen, Marius [B.], and Gilbert Rozman, eds. *Japan in Transition: From Tokugawa to Meiji*. Princeton: Princeton University Press, 1986.

Katayama Sen. *Vospominaniia*. Moscow: Nauka, 1964.

————. "K 15-letiiu risovykh buntov 1918 goda v Iaponii." *Kommunisticheskii internatsional* 1933, nos. 26–27: 11–18. Reprinted in Sen Katayama, *Sen Katayama. Stat'i i memuary (k stoletiiu so dnia rozhdeniia)*, 121–39. Moscow: Izd. vostochnoi literatury, 1959.

————. *Sen Katayama. Stat'i i memuary (k stoletiiu so dnia rozhdeniia)*. Moscow: Izd. vostochnoi literatury, 1959.

————. *The Labor Movement in Japan*. Chicago: Charles H. Kerr, 1918.

Kerr, Alex. *Lost Japan*. Oakland, Calif.: Lonely Planet, 1996.

Kim, Hyung-ki, Michio Muramatsu, T. J. Pempel, and Kozo Yamamura, eds. *The Japanese Civil Service and Economic Development*. Oxford, U.K.: Clarendon, 1995.

Kinzley, W. Dean. "Japan's Discovery of Poverty: Changing Views of Poverty and Social Welfare in the Nineteenth Century." *Journal of Asian History* 22, no. 1 (1988): 1–24.

Kodama, Toru. "The Experimentation of the Garden City in Japan." *Kikan Keizai Kenkyu* (Quarterly Journal of Economic Studies of the Institute for Economic Research at Osaka City University) 16, no. 1 (1993): 47–70.

Kublin, Hyman. *Asian Revolutionary: The Life of Sen Katayama*. Princeton: Princeton University Press, 1964.

Landes, David S. "Japan and Europe: Contrasts in Industrialization." In William W. Lockwood, ed., *The State and Economic Enterprise in Japan: Essays in the Political Economy of Growth*, 93–182. Princeton: Princeton University Press, 1965.

Lanman, Charles. *Leading Men of Japan with an Historical Summary of the Empire*. Boston: D. Lothrop, 1883.

Lewis, Michael. *Rioters and Citizens: Mass Protest in Imperial Japan*. Berkeley: University of California Press, 1990.

Lebra, Joyce. *Okuma Shigenobu: Statesman of Meiji Japan*. Canberra: Australian National University Press, 1973.

Lockwood, William W. "Prospectus and Summary." In William W. Lockwood, ed., *The State and Economic Enterprise in Japan: Essays in the Political Economy of Growth*, 3–14. Princeton: Princeton University Press, 1965.

Lockwood, William W., ed. *The State and Economic Enterprise in Japan: Essays in the Political Economy of Growth*. Princeton: Princeton University Press, 1965.

MacDougall, Terry Edward, ed. *Political Leadership in Contemporary Japan*. Ann Arbor: Center for Japanese Studies, University of Michigan, 1982.

Mason, R. H. P. "The Debate on Poor Relief, 1890." In Andrew Fraser, R. H. P. Mason, and Philip Mitchell, *Japan's Early Parliaments, 1890–1905: Structure, Issues, and Trends*, 67–90. London: Routledge, 1995.

Mass, Jeffrey P., and William B. Hauser, eds. *The Bakufu in Japanese History.* Stanford: Stanford University Press, 1985.

McClain, James L., John M. Merriman, and Kaoru Ugawa, eds. *Edo and Paris: Urban Life and the State in the Early Modern Era.* Ithaca: Cornell University Press, 1994.

McCormack, Gavan, and Yoshio Sugimoto, eds. *The Japanese Trajectory: Modernization and Beyond.* Cambridge, U.K.: Cambridge University Press, 1988.

McLaren, Walter Wallace. *A Political History of Japan During the Meiji Era, 1867–1912.* New York: Scribner's, 1916.

Menpes, Mortimer. *Japan: A Record in Colour.* London: Adam and Charles Black, 1905.

Mima, Yuzo. "Meiji Koki Osaka no Kogyo." In Shinshu Osakashishi Hensei Iinkai, *Shinshu Osakashishi* 7, chp. 2, sec. 2, sub. 1: 234–46. Osaka: Osaka City Government, 1994.

Minami, Ryoshin. "The Introduction of Electric Power and Its Impact on the Manufacturing Industries: With Special Reference to Smaller Scale Plants." In Hugh Patrick, ed., with the assistance of Larry Meissner, *Japanese Industrialization and Its Social Consequences*, 299–325. Berkeley: University of California Press, 1976.

Mitchell, Philip. "The Japanese Commercial Code of 1890 and Its Reception in the First Two Sessions of the Imperial Diet, 1890–1." In Andrew Fraser, R. H. P. Mason, and Philip Mitchell, *Japan's Early Parliaments, 1890–1905: Structure, Issues, and Trends*, 196–235. London: Routledge, 1995.

Mizuta, Hiroshi. "Historical Introduction." In Chuhei Sugiyama and Hiroshi Mizuta, eds., *Enlightenment and Beyond: Political Economy Comes to Japan*, 3–33. Tokyo: University of Tokyo Press, 1988.

Molony, Barbara. "Activism among Women in the Taisho Cotton Textile Industry." In Gail Lee Bernstein, ed., *Recreating Japanese Women, 1600–1945*, 217–38. Berkeley: University of California Press, 1991.

Muramatsu, Michio. *Local Power in the Japanese State.* Trans. Betsey Scheiner and James White. Berkeley: University of California Press, 1988.

Najita, Tetsuo. *Visions of Virtue in Tokugawa Japan: The Kaitokydo Merchant Academy of Osaka.* Chicago: University of Chicago Press, 1987.

———. *Hara Kei and the Politics of Compromise, 1905–1915.* Cambridge, Mass.: Harvard University Press, 1967.

Najita, Tetsuo, and J. Victor Koschmann, eds. *Conflict in Modern Japanese History: The Neglected Tradition.* Princeton: Princeton University Press, 1982.

Nakao, Toshimitsu. "Dai-gokai Naikoku Kangyo Hakurankai to Shisei." In Shinshu Osakashishi Hensei Iinkai, *Shinshu Osakashishi* 6, chp. 1, sec. 2, sub. 1: 34–38. Osaka: Osaka City Government, 1994.

————. "Senso to Gyozaisei." In Shinshu Osakashishi Hensei Iinkai, *Shinshu Osakashishi* 6, chp. 1, sec. 2, sub. 2: 48–63. Osaka: Osaka City Government, 1994.

Nishikawa, Shunsaku. "Grain Consumption: The Case of Choshu." In Marius Jansen and Gilbert Rozman, eds., *Japan in Transition: From Tokugawa to Meiji*, 421–46. Princeton: Princeton University Press, 1986.

Noguchi, Takehiko. "Love and Death in the Early Modern Novel: America and Japan." In Albert Craig, ed., *Japan: A Comparative View*, 160–81. Princeton: Princeton University Press, 1979.

Nolte, Sharon H., and Sally Ann Hastings. "The Meiji State's Policy toward Women, 1890–1910." In Gail Lee Bernstein, ed., *Recreating Japanese Women 1600–1945*, 165–68. Berkeley: University of California Press, 1991.

Norman, E. Herbert. *Japan: Emergence as a Modern State: Political and Economic Problems of the Meiji Period*. New York: Institute of Pacific Relations, 1940.

Notehelfer, F. G. *Japan Through American Eyes: The Journal of Francis Hall, Kanagawa and Yokohama, 1859–1866*. Princeton: Princeton University Press, 1992.

————. *American Samurai: Captain L. L. Janes and Japan*. Princeton: Princeton University Press, 1985.

————. *Kotoku Shusui: Portrait of a Japanese Radical*. Cambridge, U.K.: Cambridge University Press, 1971.

Oda, Sakunosuke. *Stories of Osaka Life*. Trans. Burton Watson. New York: Columbia University Press, 1990.

Ohkawa, Kazushi, and Henry Rosovsky. "A Century of Japanese Economic Growth." In William W. Lockwood, ed., *The State and Economic Enterprise in Japan. Essays in the Political Economy of Growth*, 47–92. Princeton: Princeton University Press, 1965.

Oshima, Harry T. "Meiji Fiscal Policy and Economic Progress." In William W. Lockwood, ed., *The State and Economic Enterprise in Japan: Essays in the Political Economy of Growth*, 353–89. Princeton: Princeton University Press, 1965.

An Outline of Municipal Administration of the City of Osaka. Osaka: Osaka Shiyakusho (municipal office), 1930.

Patrick, Hugh. "An Introductory Overview." In Hugh Patrick, ed., with the assistance of Larry Meissner, *Japanese Industrialization and Its Social Consequences*, 1–17. Berkeley: University of California Press, 1976.

Patrick, Hugh, ed., with the assistance of Larry Meissner. *Japanese Industrialization and Its Social Consequences*. Berkeley: University of California Press, 1976.

Pelzel, John C. "Factory Life in Japan and China Today." In Albert Craig, ed., *Japan: A Comparative View*, 371–431. Princeton: Princeton University Press, 1979.

Pempel, T. J., and Michio Muramatsu. "The Japanese Bureaucracy and Economic Development: Structuring a Proactive Civil Service." In Hyungki Kim, Michio Muramatsu, T. J. Pempel, and Kozo Yamamura, eds., *The Japanese Civil Service and Economic Development*, 19–76. Oxford, U.K.: Clarendon, 1995.

Present-day Osaka. Osaka: Osaka Shiyakusho (municipal office), 1915.

Price, John. "A History of the Outcaste: Untouchability in Japan." In George De Vos and Hiroshi Wagatsuma, eds., *Japan's Invisible Race: Caste in Culture and Personality*, 6–30. Berkeley: University of California Press, 1966.

Pyle Kenneth B. *The Making of Modern Japan*. Lexington, Mass: D. C. Heath, 1978.

———. "Advantages of Fellowship: German Economics and Japanese Bureaucrats, 1890–1925." *Journal of Japanese Studies* 1, no. 1 (Autumn 1974): 51–65.

———. "The Technology of Japanese Nationalism: The Local Improvement Movement, 1900–1918." *Journal of Asian Studies* 33, no. 1 (November 1973): 127–64.

———. *The New Generation in Meiji Japan: Problems of Cultural Identity, 1885–1895*. Stanford: Stanford University Press, 1969.

Rosovsky, Henry. *Capital Formation in Japan, 1868–1940*. Glencoe, Ill.: Free Press, 1961.

Rozman, Gilbert. "Castle Towns in Transition." In Marius Jansen and Gilbert Rozman, eds., *Japan in Transition: From Tokugawa to Meiji*, 318–46. Princeton: Princeton University Press, 1986.

Rubinger, Richard. "Education: From One Room to One System." In Marius Jansen and Gilbert Rozman, eds., *Japan in Transition: From Tokugawa to Meiji*, 195–230. Princeton: Princeton University Press, 1986.

Saito, Osamu. "Bringing the Covert Structure of the Past to Light." *Journal of Economic History* 49, no. 4 (1989): 992–99.

———. "The Rural Economy: Commercial Agriculture, By-employment, and Wage Work." In Marius Jansen and Gilbert Rozman, eds., *Japan in Transition: From Tokugawa to Meiji*, 400–20. Princeton: Princeton University Press, 1986.

Sato, Seizaburo. "Response to the West: The Korean and Japanese Patterns." In Albert Craig, ed., *Japan: A Comparative View*, 105–29. Princeton: Princeton University Press, 1979.

Sawada, Michiko. *Tokyo Life, New York Dreams: Urban Japanese Visions of America, 1890–1924*. Berkeley: University of California Press, 1996.

Saxonhouse, Gary R. "Productivity Change and Labor Absorption in Japanese Cotton Spinning, 1891–1935." *Quarterly Journal of Economics* 16, no. 2 (May 1977): 195–219.

———. "Country Girls and Communication among Competitors in the Japanese Cotton-Spinning Industry." In Hugh Patrick, ed., with the assistance of

Larry Meissner, *Japanese Industrialization and Its Social Consequences*, 97–125. Berkeley: University of California Press, 1976.

Schaede, Ulrike. *Geldpolitik in Japan, 1950–1985.* Marburg: Forderverein Marburger Japan-Reihe, 1989.

Scheiner, Irwin. *Christian Converts and Social Protest in Meiji Japan.* Berkeley: University of California Press, 1970.

Schwaab, Dean J. *Osaka Prints.* New York: Rizzoli, 1989.

Scidmore, Eliza Ruhamah. *Jinrikisha Days in Japan.* New York: Harper, 1891.

Seidensticker, Edward. *Low City, High City: Tokyo from Edo to the Earthquake: How the Shogun's Ancient Capital Became a Great Modern City, 1867–1923.* New York: Knopf, 1983.

———. *Kafu the Scribbler: The Life and Writings of Nagai Kafu, 1879–1959.* Stanford: Stanford University Press, 1965.

Shaw, Glenn. *Osaka Sketches.* Tokyo: Hokuseido, 1929.

Shibamura Atsuki. "Dai-Osaka no Kensetsu." In Shinshu Osakashishi Hensei Iinkai, *Shinshu Osakashishi* 7, chp. 1, sec. 1, sub. 1: 3–25. Osaka: Osaka City Government, 1994.

———. "Gyozaisei no Kozo Henka." In Shinshu Osakashishi Hensei Iinkai, *Shinshu Osakashishi* 6, chp. 1, sec. 5, sub. 1: 120–34. Osaka: Osaka City Government, 1994.

———. "Zaisei Kiki no Sinko to Osakashi Zaisei." In Shinshu Osakashishi Hensei Iinkai, *Shinshu Osakashishi* 7, chp. 1, sec. 1, sub. 2: 25–44. Osaka: Osaka City Government, 1994.

Shinshu Osakashishi Hensei Iinkai. *Shinshu Osakashishi.* Vols. 6 and 7. Osaka: Osaka City Government, 1994.

Shiraishi Bon. "Merchants of Osaka." *Japan Quarterly* 5 (1958): 169–77.

Silberman, Bernard [S]. "The Structure of Bureaucratic Rationality and Economic Development in Japan." In Hyung-ki Kim, Michio Muramatsu, T. J. Pempel, and Kozo Yamamura, eds., *The Japanese Civil Service and Economic Development*, 135–73. Oxford, U.K.: Clarendon, 1995.

———. *Ministers of Modernization: Elite Mobility in the Meiji Restoration, 1868–1873.* Tucson: University of Arizona Press, 1964.

Smith, Henry D., II. "The Edo-Tokyo Transition: In Search of Common Ground." In Marius Jansen and Gilbert Rozman, eds., *Japan in Transition: From Tokugawa to Meiji*, 347–75. Princeton: Princeton University Press, 1986.

———. "Tokyo and London; Comparative Conceptions of the City." In Albert Craig, ed., *Japan: A Comparative View*, 49–103. Princeton: Princeton University Press, 1979.

———. "Tokyo as an Idea: An Exploration of Japanese Urban Thought until 1945." *Journal of Japanese Studies* 4, no. 1 (Winter 1978): 45–80.

Smith, Thomas C. *Native Sources of Japanese Industrialization, 1750–1920.* Berkeley: University of California Press, 1988.

———. "The Right to Benevolence: Dignity and Japanese Workers, 1890–1920." *Comparative Studies in Society and History* 26, no. 4 (October 1984): 587–612.

———. "Premodern Economic Growth: Japan and the West." *Past & Present* 60 (1973): 127–60.

———. *The Agrarian Origins of Modern Japan.* New York: Atheneum, 1966.

———. "Japan's Aristocratic Revolution." *Yale Review* 50 (Spring 1961): 370–83.

———. *Political Change and Industrial Development in Japan: Government Enterprise, 1868–1880.* Stanford: Stanford University Press, 1955.

The Souvenir Guide to Osaka and the Fifth National Industrial Exhibition. Osaka: Hakurankai Kyosankai [municipal office], 1903.

Sugihara Shiro. "Economists in Government: Okubo Toshimichi, the 'Bismarck of Japan', and His Times." In Chuhei Sugiyama and Hiroshi Mizuta, eds., *Enlightenment and Beyond: Political Economy Comes to Japan,* 211–21. Tokyo: University of Tokyo Press, 1988.

———. "Economists in Journalism: Liberalism, Nationalism, and Their Variants." In Chuhei Sugiyama and Hiroshi Mizuta, eds., *Enlightenment and Beyond: Political Economy Comes to Japan,* 237–53. Tokyo: University of Tokyo Press, 1988.

Sugihara Shiro and Nishizawa Tamotsu. "In the 'Commercial Metropolis' Osaka: Schools of Commerce and Law." In Chuhei Sugiyama and Hiroshi Mizuta, eds., *Enlightenment and Beyond: Political Economy Comes to Japan,* 189–207. Tokyo: University of Tokyo Press, 1988.

Sugiyama, Chuhei, and Hiroshi Mizuta, eds. *Enlightenment and Beyond: Political Economy Comes to Japan.* Tokyo: University of Tokyo Press, 1988.

Suzuki, Hiroyuki, and Toharu Hatsuda. *Urban Architecture in Taisho: A Visual Anthology.* Tokyo: Kashiwa-shobo, 1992.

Tada Michitaro. "Osaka Popular Culture: A Down-to-Earth Appraisal." In Gavan McCormack and Yoshio Sugimoto, eds., *The Japanese Trajectory: Modernization and Beyond,* 33–53. Cambridge, U.K.: Cambridge University Press, 1988.

Taira, Koji. "Urban Poverty, Ragpickers, and the 'Ants' Villa' in Tokyo." *Economic Development and Cultural Change* 17, no. 2 (January 1969): 155–77.

Tamaki, Norio. "Economists in Parliament: The Fall of Bimetallism in Japan." In Chuhei Sugiyama and Hiroshi Mizuta, eds., *Enlightenment and Beyond: Political Economy Comes to Japan,* 223–36. Tokyo: University of Tokyo Press, 1988.

Tanaka, Stefan. *Japan's Orient: Rendering Pasts into History.* Berkeley: University of California Press, 1993.

Tanizaki, Junichiro. *Quicksand.* Trans. Howard Hibbett. New York: Vintage, 1993.

———. *The Reed Cutter and Captain Shigemoto's Mother.* Trans. Anthony H. Chambers. New York: Vintage, 1993.

———. *The Makioka Sisters.* Trans. Edward G. Seidensticker. New York: Wideview/Perigee, 1981.

Toby, Ronald P. "Changing Credit: From Village Moneylender to Rural Banker in Protoindustrial Japan." In Gareth Austin and Kaoru Sugihara, eds., *Local Suppliers of Credit in the Third World, 1750–1960,* 55–90. New York: St. Martin's, 1993.

———. "Both a Borrower and a Lender Be: From Village Moneylender to Rural Banker in the Tempo Era." *Monumenta Nipponica* 46, no. 4 (Winter 1991): 483–512.

———. *State and Diplomacy in Early Modern Japan: Asia in the Development of the Tokugawa Bakufu.* Princeton: Princeton University Press, 1984.

Topekha, R. "Put revoliutsionera." In Sen Katayama, *Sen Katayama. Stat'i i memuary (k stoletiiu so dnia rozhdeniia),* 3–24. Moscow: Izd. vostochnoi literatury, 1959.

Totten, George O., and Hiroshi Wagatsuma. "Emancipation: Growth and Transformation of a Political Movement." In George De Vos and Hiroshi Wagatsuma, eds., *Japan's Invisible Race: Caste in Culture and Personality,* 33–68. Berkeley: University of California Press, 1966.

Tsurumi, E. Patricia. *Factory Girls: Women in the Thread Mills of Meiji Japan.* Princeton: Princeton University Press, 1990.

Umegaki, Michio. *After the Restoration: The Beginning of Japan's Modern State.* New York: New York University Press, 1988.

———. "From Domain to Prefecture." In Marius Jansen and Gilbert Rozman, eds., *Japan in Transition: From Tokugawa to Meiji,* 91–110. Princeton: Princeton University Press, 1986.

Uno, Kathleen. "Laboring Classes in Urban Japan." *Journal of Urban History* 24, no. 4 (May 1988): 507–9.

Vandercammen, Jan. "The Osaka Foreign Settlement: A Study of the Osaka Municipal Council Based upon the Minutes of the Council Meetings, 1869–1899." Osaka, 1996.

Veblen, Thorstein. "The Opportunity of Japan." *Journal of Race Development* 6 (July 1915). Reprinted in Thorstein Veblen, *Essays in Our Changing Order.* Ed. Leon Ardzrooni. New York: Augustus M. Kelley, 1964.

Vogel, Ezra. "Nation-Building in Modern East Asia: Early Meiji (1868–1890) and Mao's China (1949–1971)." In Albert Craig, ed., *Japan: A Comparative View,* 130–58. Princeton: Princeton University Press, 1979.

Wagatsuma, Hiroshi. "Postwar Political Militance." In George De Vos and Hiroshi Wagatsuma, eds., *Japan's Invisible Race: Caste in Culture and Personality,* 112–28. Berkeley: University of California Press, 1966.

Waters, Neil L. *Japan's Local Pragmatists: The Transition from Bakumatsu to Meiji in the Kawasaki Region.* Cambridge, Mass.: Harvard University Press, 1983.

Weiner, Michael. *The Origins of the Korean Community in Japan, 1910–1923.* Atlantic Highlands, N.J.: Humanities Press International, 1989.

White, Oswald. *Report on Japanese Labor.* London: His Majesty's Stationery Office, 1920.

Williams, W. W. "Osaka: 25 Fascinating Facts." In *Hemispheres* (United Airlines' in-flight magazine), October 1994: 27–28.

Wray, William D. "Shipping: From Sail to Steam." In Marius Jansen and Gilbert Rozman, eds., *Japan in Transition: From Tokugawa to Meiji,* 248–71. Princeton: Princeton University Press, 1986.

Yamamura, Kozo. "The Role of Government in Japan's 'Catch-Up' Industrialization: A New Institutionalist Perspective." In Hyung-ki Kim, Michio Muramatsu, T. J. Pempel, and Kozo Yamamura, eds., *The Japanese Civil Service and Economic Development,* 102–32. Oxford, U.K.: Clarendon, 1995.

———. "The Meiji Land Tax Reform and Its Effects." In Marius Jansen and Gilbert Rozman, eds., *Japan in Transition: From Tokugawa to Meiji,* 382–99. Princeton: Princeton University Press, 1986.

———. "Pre-Industrial Landholding Patterns in Japan and England." In Albert Craig, ed., *Japan: A Comparative View,* 276–323. Princeton: Princeton University Press, 1979.

———. *A Study of Samurai Income and Entrepreneurship: Quantitative Analyses of Economic and Social Aspects of the Samurai in Tokugawa and Meiji Japan.* Cambridge, Mass.: Harvard University Press, 1974.

Yazaki, Takeo. *Social Change and the City in Japan: From Earliest Times through the Industrial Revolution.* Tokyo: Japan Publications, 1968.

———. *The Japanese City: A Sociological Analysis.* Rutland, Vt.: Japan Publications, 1963.

Young, A. Morgan. *Japan in Recent Times, 1912–1926.* New York: William Morrow, 1929.

Dissertations

Hanashiro, Roy Seijun. "The Establishment of the Japanese Imperial Mint and the Role of Hired Foreigners, 1868–1875." Ph.D. diss., University of Hawaii, 1988.

Hanes, Jeffrey Eldon. "Seki Hajime and the Making of Modern Osaka." Ph.D. diss., University of California, Berkeley, 1988.

Hayase, Yukiko. "The Career of Goto Shimpei: Japan's Statesman of Research, 1857–1929." Ph.D. diss., Florida State University, 1974.

MacDougall, Terry Edward. "Political Opposition and Local Governance in Japan: The Significance of Emerging Progressive Local Leadership." Ph.D. diss., Yale University, 1975.

Saxonhouse, Gary. "Productivity Change and Japanese Cotton Spinning, 1891–1935." Ph.D. diss., Yale University, 1971.

Waters, Neil LeRoy. "A Political History of the Kawasaki Region: 1860–1890." Ph.D. diss., University of Hawaii, Honolulu, 1979.

Archival Records

National Archives and Records Administration, Department of State General Records. Class 8 [Internal Affairs of States], Country 94 [Japan], Areas 00 [Political Affairs], 40 [Social Matters], 50 [Economic Matters], 1910–1929.

Index

451

Other books in the series (*continued from page iii*)